Charles River

Ferry to Charles Town

Bartons Point

Copper Works

Rope Walk

Rope Walk

Lee's Ship Yard

Eb N. Mill Damm

N. Water Mill

Gees Ship Yd

Hudsons Point

Hunt & White's Ship Yd

Mill Pond.

Bowling Green

Ferry Way

Burying Place

Bakers

Rucks W.

Water Mill

Salem Street

North Street

Boroughs Ship Y.

Back Street

10

Middle Street

Hanover

Union

Fifth Street

Lee's Ship Yd

Ship Street

Lynn Street

Thorntons Ship Yard

N. Battery

Cornhill

Wallworths Wharfe

Old Wharfe

Clarks Wharfe

Burroughs W.

Green & Greenwood Ship Yd & Wharfe

Bedlington W.

Clarks Ship Yd

Scarlets Wharfe.

King Street

ools Wharf

Oliver's Dock

Farmers W.

Tools Wharf

LONG WHARFE

Old Wharfe

HARBOUR

Greenleaf's Yd

Long Wharf

Wings sh Yd

Oliver's Wharfe

Gates Sh Yd

Old Wharfe

Fort Hill

S. Battery.

Hubbards W.

Grays W.

ng. Boston N E. 1722. Sold by Cap.t John Bonner and Will.m Price against ÿ Town House where may be had all Sorts of Prints Mapps &c.

Benjamin Franklin

Arthur Bernon Tourtellot

AUTHOR:

The Presidents on the Presidency
Bibliography of the Battles of Lexington and Concord
William Diamond's Drum—The Beginning of the
War of the American Revolution
An Anatomy of American Politics
Woodrow Wilson Today
The Charles (Rivers of America Series)
The History and Romance of the Horse
Be Loved No More

EDITOR:

Toward the Well-being of Mankind
A Contribution to the Heritage of Every American
Life's Picture History of World War II

Benjamin Franklin

THE SHAPING OF GENIUS
THE BOSTON YEARS

Arthur Bernon Tourtellot

DOUBLEDAY & COMPANY, INC.
GARDEN CITY, NEW YORK
1977

Library of Congress Cataloging in Publication Data

Tourtellot, Arthur Bernon.
Benjamin Franklin: the shaping of genius, 1706–1723.

Bibliography: p. 441
Includes index.
1. Franklin, Benjamin, 1706–1790.   2. Statesmen—
United States—Biography.
E302.6.F8T7   973.3'092'4[B]
ISBN 0-385-03230-7
Library of Congress Catalog Card Number 76–12054

FOR

WALTER MUIR WHITEHILL

Affectionate and Witty Student of Boston
Knowing and Urbane Citizen of the World

Κουρίζων νίκησεν ἀειδομενους ἐλα
τῆρας, γηραλέος δέ νέουσ δεῖξεν
ἀφαυροτέρους.

While yet a youth he overcame the
celebrated drivers, and in his old
age he showed that the young were
his inferiors.
—Inscription to Constantinus

Contents

Preface

Acknowledgment is gratefully made to the President and Fellows of Harvard College for permission to publish Chapter IX, which originally appeared, slightly altered, under the title "The Early Reading of Benjamin Franklin," in the *Harvard Library Bulletin*, XXIII, No. 1 (January 1975). I am also indebted to Edwin E. Williams, editor of the *Bulletin*, and to Rene Kuhn Bryant, its associate editor, for their most helpful suggestions and editings.

Over the decade during which this book was written, I have been most generously aided by the community of scholars and archivists, both in the United Kingdom and in the United States, whose fields of expertise have touched in one way or another on the long life and varied achievements of Franklin, his heritage, and his times. I had occasion to remark, in the *American Historical Review*, LXXIX, No. 4, on "how thoroughly and how longingly Franklin was an Englishman . . ."; he was, of course, not only the product of a wholly English heritage but was born, a subject of Queen Anne, in what was still an English town, albeit a distant one. And during his years in Boston, there was a continuity of experience and, to a considerable extent, of values between old England and New England, with, in a general social sense, more in common between the two when Franklin left Boston in 1723 than when he was born there in 1706. Moreover, except for some abrasive episodes in Whitehall, the English treated Franklin as their countryman, honoring and befriending him. In exploring the English background of the Franklins, I found this high regard, even affection, for Benjamin Franklin still evident, and I am very deeply obligated to many in the United Kingdom who gave generously of their time and their knowledge to aid me in piecing together the English histories of the Franklin and Folger families. Among them were the Rector of Ecton and Warden of Ecton House, the Reverend Thory R. Bonsey, incumbent of the Church of St. Mary Magdalen, with which the Franklins were associated for generations; Lord Saye and Sele and Mr. Jeremy S. W. Gibson, President and Secretary respectively, of the Banbury Historical Society, Oxfordshire, where Franklin's father lived briefly before leaving

England for Boston; Mr. W. O. Hassall, Secretary of the Oxfordshire Record Society; Mr. H. M. Walton Archivist of the Oxfordshire County Record Office; Mr. P. I. King, Chief Archivist of the Northamptonshire Record Office at Delapre Abbey; Mr. D. M. Gibbons, of Norwich, Norfolk, whence Franklin's mother's family emigrated to Nantucket; Miss J. M. Kennedy, Archivist of the Norfolk and Norwich Record Office; Mr. David Hinton, of the Ashmolean Museum, Oxford; Mr. Robert Shackleton, Director, and Mr. R. W. Hunt, Keeper of Western Manuscripts, the Bodleian Library, Oxford; Mr. A. W. Pain, Borough Librarian and Keeper of the Museum at Banbury; Professor J. H. Plumb, Christ's College, Cambridge; Sir William Hodge, Vice-president and Secretary of the Royal Society; Nancy and Trevor Russell-Cobb, of London, to whose friendship I owe counsel on pictorial sources and the long-forgotten monograph on Ecton's history by John Cole; Mr. J. R. Ede, Keeper of Public Records, London; and Mr. T. C. Skeat, Keeper of Manuscripts, the British Museum. Mr. Christopher Trayne Tourtellot, the University of Aberdeen, aided greatly in tracking down Franklin's frequently elliptical Latin passages.

In the United States, many individuals and institutions were most helpful: Mr. Marcus A. McCorison, Director and Librarian, and Mr. William L. Joyce, Curator of Manuscripts, the American Antiquarian Society; Professor Douglas W. Bryant, University Librarian, Professor William H. Bond, Director of the Houghton Library, and Mr. Rodney Dennis, its Curator of Manuscripts, at Harvard University; Mr. Stephen T. Riley, Director, the Massachusetts Historical Society; Mr. Brooke Hindle, Director, the Museum of Science and Industry, the Smithsonian Institution; Professor G. B. Warden, Harvard University, formerly an editor of *The Papers of Benjamin Franklin*; Mr. Kenneth C. Cramer, Archivist, the Dartmouth College Libraries; Mr. Walter Muir Whitehill, Director and Librarian Emeritus, the Boston Athenaeum; Miss Ruth Easterbrook Thomas, of Boston; Mr. Jonathan B. Tourtellot, of Washington; and Dr. James J. Hesslin, Director, New-York Historical Society.

I am also indebted to many of that generous breed of old friends who bear patiently with the sometimes obsessive concern of authors of works, prolonged in the writing, with problems that arise and who contribute to their resolution by their forbearance. Among those in England, I feel particularly obliged to Mr. Alan Campbell-Johnson, Mr. Charles Collingwood, Mr. Timothy Eckersley, Mr. Alexander Eliot, Mr. H. Maurice Lancaster, Mr. Archibald Gracie Ogden, Miss Tina Packer, and Miss Terry Rice; and, in America, to Mr. Thomas Boylston Adams, President of the Massachusetts Historical Society, and his son, Mr. Henry Adams, both of whom had some provocative thoughts on the nature of genius, in each case somewhat more stringent than either those of their great forebear, John Adams, who applied the term to Franklin, or my own; Mr. J. Russell Wiggins, President of the American Antiquarian Society, a rare and happy combination of journalist and scholar; Mr. Orville Prescott, formerly of *The New York Times*, blessed with the same gifts; Mr. Joseph J. Thorndike, Jr., Editorial Director of *American Heritage*, and Mr. Oliver Jensen, its Editor; Mr. L. H. Butterfield and Mr. Wendell D. Garrett, formerly Editor and Associate Editor respectively of *The Adams Papers*; Miss Nancy Lane, formerly Managing Editor of the *American Historical Review*; Miss Josephine Lyons; Mr. J. Alfred Dinsmore; Mr. James T. Flexner; Mr. Richard C. Hottelet; and in British Columbia, Professor Sydney Jackman, of the University of Victoria.

In acquiring copies of documents, scarce printed works, and illustrations, the professional skill of Miss Helen M. Brown was of very great help. Mrs. Nellie Nelson and, for the major part of the book, Mrs. Judy Stabile were meticulous and most attentive in the preparation of the manuscript. Mr. Kenneth McCormick, long my editor and my friend, went far beyond any professional calls upon his time and interest to give warmly and wisely of his counsel and encouragement. Finally, the book owes its completion, in great measure, to my introduction, by an old friend—my wife, Elizabeth Davis Tourtellot—to the enchanting island, described by Homer as "a land called Crete in the midst of the wine-dark sea, a fair land and a rich . . ." where most of the book was written, and to her bearing with serenity and grace my preoccupation with the work in Westport, where the rest of it was written and all of it envisioned.

A.B.T.

Aghios Nicolaos, Crete
Westport, Connecticut
1965–75

INTRODUCTION

Franklin and the Nature of Genius

Genius, both in nature and in definition, has proven one of the most elusive concepts improvised by man in his long effort to account for the rare rise in his midst of men and women of such transcendent gifts of original insight and striking achievement as to make them otherwise inexplicable. The term has sometimes been used with the utmost economy and almost mystic restraint, reserved for only those—perhaps as few as one or two in a given age, as, for example, Shakespeare among Elizabethans—who towered so high and so luminously above both their contemporaries and those who went before as to be larger than human: demigods, no amount of the probing of whose lives could identify the forces, hereditary, environmental, or individual, that influenced their development and fruition. At the opposite extreme, the word, in latter times particularly, has been used so bounteously as to defy definition, lumping together, indiscriminately such qualities as talent, application, innovativeness, and merely exceptional competence within guidelines already established. Genius, according to the more disciplined criteria, breaks through guidelines, leaps over and beyond them, and then creates its own.

The use of the word in this sense of the fifth definition in the Oxford English Dictionary—"native intellectual power of an exalted type," and "instinctive and extraordinary capacity for imaginative creation, original thought, invention, or discovery"—was a product of Benjamin Franklin's time, an innovation of the eighteenth century and of the English, though it had its root in one of the simplest and most seminal words in any language, the Latin *genere*, to beget, to bring into being. It was not in common enough usage for Dr. Johnson to give it as even a subsidiary definition in his dictionary, published in 1755, though he himself used it, with characteristic Johnsonian thunder, as early as 1750, in the third *Rambler*: "There is a certain race of men that either imagine it their duty or make it their amusement to hinder the reception of every work of learning or of genius. . . ." A decade or more earlier, the term had been used by two members of the Scriblerus Club, Swift ("When a true genius appears in the world, you may know him by this sign, that the dunces are all in confederacy against him.") and Pope (". . . One whose fires/True Genius kindles . . ."), and in fiction by Fielding in *Tom Jones*, making a significant distinction: "By the wonderful force of genius only, without the least assistance of learning. . . ." Even earlier, in 1711, Addison devoted an entire *Spectator* (No. 160) to a consideration of genius, though he limited his concern to men of letters, ". . . who by the mere strength of natural Parts, and without any Assistance of Art [i.e. artfulness] or Learning, have produced Works that were the Delight of Their own Times and the Wonder of Posterity," and he deprecated genius in other arts and the sciences on the grounds that it "takes a kind of Tincture from them, and falls unavoidably into Imitation."

Did Benjamin Franklin qualify? John Adams, who was not among his warmest personal admirers and was sorely tried, when he was one of the American peace commissioners in Paris, by the sage's easy way with women, his love of comfort, and his reluctance to offend, thought so, and may have been, in the *Boston Patriot*, May 15, 1811, the first to apply the word *genius* to Franklin—and with a sweeping totality, albeit in a grudging context: "Franklin had a great genius, original, sagacious, and inventive, capable of discoveries in science no less than of improvements in the fine arts and the mechanic arts. He had a vast imagination, equal to the comprehension of the greatest objects, and capable of a steady and cool comprehension of them."

As used by Adams and by other writers of Franklin's time, "genius" was a literary term, not a scientific one, and a subjective term, not a psychometric one. It still is. Some faltering attempts have been made to measure "potential genius" in children by fixing arbitrarily-arrived-at intelligence quotient scores that have varied from qualifying one in two hundred and fifty to qualifying one in two hundred thousand. But "potential genius" is a misleading phrase. Genius is never potential; it is always actual, only its achievement is potential, and its realization is inevitable because of its inherent compulsiveness. Though it may long go unrecognized, it can be neither smothered nor aborted. The geneticists have been no more helpful, nor successful, in their quest for a biological explanation of the phenomenon of genius. The pioneer and, in some respects, one of the ablest among them was a grandson of Erasmus Darwin and a cousin of Charles Darwin, Sir Francis Galton, whose work *Hereditary Genius, an Inquiry into Its Laws and Consequences* was first published in 1869. Galton never arrived at a definition of genius or even at a descriptive statement of what he was talking about when he put the word so prominently in his title. He used the term interchangeably throughout his text with "high ability," including that "of certain classes of Oarsmen and Wrestlers," and set forth the astonishing proposition that "high reputation is a pretty accurate test of high ability." But it made no difference in the end, except to emphasize the elusive nature of genius, because Sir Francis abandoned the term altogether, claiming "a studious abstinence throughout the work from speaking of genius as a special quality"; he concluded that his title "seems apt to mislead, and if it could be altered now, it should appear as *Hereditary Ability.*"

William James came closer to the mark, in *The Principles of Psychology*, with the lean but perspicacious simplification, "Genius, in truth, means little more than the faculty of perceiving in an unhabitual way." And Woodrow Wilson, a better man of letters than he has yet been estimated, once identified genius as one with a mind "whose vision swept many an horizon which those about him dreamed not of, that mind that comprehended what it had never seen, and understood the language of affairs with the ready ease of one to the manner born—or that nature which seemed in its varied richness to be the familiar of men of every way of life." The words were written of Lincoln, but despite the vast differences in temperament and concerns between the two men, they could equally be applied to Franklin, and so could Wilson's more general observation, somewhat supernal in its language, perhaps, but essential in its truth: "Nature pays no tribute to aristocracy, subscribes to no creed or caste, renders fealty to no monarch or master of any name or kind. Genius is no snob. It does not run after titles or seek by preference the high circles of society. It affects humble company as well as great. It pays no special tribute to universities or learned societies or conventional standards of greatness, but serenely chooses its own comrades, its own haunts, its own cradle even, and its own life of adventure and training."

The genius of Franklin is no more susceptible of explanation than that of anyone else. But it is a phenomenon that can be probed—one hopes with some point and significance—by way of both the heritage that lay behind it and the early surroundings of places, personalities, and events that helped shape its articulation and influence its achievement. The result may be little more than an exposition of the infinite variety from which genius springs, and of the infinitely varied expression it takes, and only fragmentarily, if at all, an elucidation of its fundamental nature. But there is an evocative passage in John Adams's diaries, reporting his visit to Shakespeare's birthplace, that explains at least the compulsion to know more. Of Stratford-on-Avon, Adams wrote, "three Doors from the Inn, is the House where he was born, as small and mean, as you can conceive. They shew Us an old Wooden Chair in the Chimney Corner, where He sat. We cutt off a Chip according to the Custom. A Mulberry Tree that he planted has been cutt down, and is carefully preserved for Sale. The House where he died has been taken down and the Spot is now only Yard or Garden. The Curse upon him who should remove his Bones, which is written on his Grave Stone, alludes to a Pile of some Thousands of human

Bones, which lie exposed in that Church. There is nothing preserved of this great Genius which is worth knowing—nothing which might inform Us what Education, what Company, what Accident turned his Mind to Letters and the Drama."

Eighteenth-century Boston suffered from no such taciturnity as did sixteenth-century Stratford, nor did Franklin from the autobiographic reticence of Shakespeare. Yet, much as we know or can learn of Franklin, "what Education, what Company, what Accident turned his Mind," we only cut chips off what remains to be known—as Adams did off Shakespeare's corner chair—of the sturdy heritage and prodigious youth of the first genius born in the New World.

PART ONE

The New Home
and the Old

The lines are fallen unto me in pleasant places; yea,
I have a goodly heritage.
—The Book of Psalms, ca. 980 B.C.

... in a word, our home is nowhere but in the
heavens; in that house not made with hands, whose
maker and builder is God.
—*Reasons and Considerations*
Touching the Lawfulness of
Removing out of England
into the Parts of America,
Robert Cushman, A.D. 1622

Boston's Tithe from Josiah

> I long much to see again my native place and
> lay my bones there.
>
> —Benjamin Franklin[1]

Josiah Franklin, the tallow chandler of Milk Street, took the infant on the
very day of its birth from the little house across the narrow roadway to the
somber cedar meetinghouse of the Third Church, called the South
Church because, when it was founded in 1669, it was the southernmost of
the three churches on the Shawmut peninsula that the English had
renamed Boston. There, out of his mother's womb for less than a single
rising and setting of the sun, the tiny child was taken, on this bleak January Sunday of 1706, into the hands of the Reverend Samuel Willard, the
aging and ailing pastor, who also acted as president of Harvard College,
and was sprinkled with icy water "in the name of the Father, and of the
Son, and of the Holy Ghost"—an occasion which was, according to the
Third Church's Confession of Faith, "a sign and seal of the convenant of
grace, of his ingrafting into Christ, of regeneration of sins, and of his giving up unto God through Jesus Christ, to walk in newness of life. . . ."[2]

To Josiah Franklin, at forty-eight not young to be adding to his family
and yet, with almost half his life still before him, not old for his years, the
birth of this sturdy son was an event which was far from unfamiliar. He
had been a father since he was twenty-one. His first wife, Anne Child, had
borne him seven children, though the last two, both sons, had died in a
matter of days, the young mother not surviving the second of them. And
seven times, too, his mature and hearty second wife, Abiah Folger, had
borne him children, in all cases safely and with her enormous vitality undiminished. But birth, like death, is familiar only in the abstract; in the
particular, it is always strange, always new, always unique. Sitting in the
gaunt, drafty labyrinth of the Third Church's square-backed pews, Josiah

---

[1] To Samuel Mather, May 12, 1784, in A. H. Smyth, ed., *The Writings of Benjamin
Franklin* (New York, 1907), IX, 209.
[2] *The Confession of Faith and Form of Covenant of the Old South [Third] Church
in Boston, Massachusetts* (Boston, 1855), 63.

Franklin regarded the birth of this baby as even more significant than the births of his fourteen other children had been. For this was his tenth son —"the tithe of his sons"—and he proposed to devote the child "to the service of the church."[3]

The church was, with his family and his trade, the center of life for Josiah Franklin, and it touched closely upon every aspect of his life. Tradesmen worked six days a week, long days—as many as twelve and fourteen hours—to sustain a livelihood. Twice on Sundays they went to their meetinghouses to listen to lengthy sermons, and on Thursdays to hear lectures often even longer. Such public events as elections and musters were also occasions for sermons; fast days—with day-long praying and sermonizing—were called whenever God, concentrating all His attention on the town of Boston, visited the Heavenly City with severe storms, raging epidemics, or other disasters that showed His dissatisfaction with how the elect were managing affairs. And if everything turned out all right, as it always did eventually, a day of thanksgiving was called with no less demanding duties imposed upon the brethren. But such ecclesiastical marathons were in the blood of the Puritans, and no one was known to object to religious services on the grounds of their length. When the Calvinists of England gathered in the Westminster Assembly, from 1643 to 1649, to purge the Church of England of its liturgical graces and themselves of their sins, one of its members wrote admiringly of an exercise that endured for at least eight hours: "After Dr. Twisse had begun with a brief prayer, Mr. Marshall prayed large two hours, most divinely, confessing the sins of the members of the assembly, in a wonderful, pathetick, and prudent way. After, Mr. Arrowsmith preached an hour, then a psalm; thereafter, Mr. Vines prayed near two hours, and Mr. Palmer preached an hour, and Mr. Seaman prayed near two hours, then a psalm; after, Mr. Henderson brought them to a sweet conference of the heat confessed in the assembly, and often seen faults to be remedied, and the conveniency to preach against all sects, especially Anabaptists and Antinomians. Dr. Twisse closed with a short prayer and blessing."[4]

As familiar with the Third Church's plain interior, from the endless hours spent there, as with that of his own house, Josiah Franklin saw the church as both the basis and the object of his life—a cornerstone of the new Jerusalem that was Boston, as Boston was the cornerstone of the Bible Commonwealth, now, in 1707, approaching the end of its first century and the beginning of its decline.

* * *

The men of Britain who, in the seventeenth century, set out to launch the Bible Commonwealth were strong-willed activists—essentially middle-class, but embracing the whole range of that class, which from the first

---

[3] Benjamin Franklin, *Autobiography*, ed. Leonard W. Labaree *et al.* (New Haven, 1964), 52 (hereafter cited as *Autobiography*).
[4] Robert Baillie, *Letters and Journals, 1637–62* (Glasgow, 1841–42), II, 18.

Elizabeth's time had both stretched upward and reached downward, so that England was already becoming predominantly a middle-class country by the time Boston was settled in 1630.[5] In the higher reaches, the nobility was beginning to lapse into a ceremonial anachronism; and in the lower, the peasantry was shrinking as some rural youth moved into the cities, into the trades, and even, in a few cases, into the universities and those who stayed home acquired acreage of their own and joined the yeomanry. No rejected outcasts of this mobile society, those who challenged the Church of England were among the ablest of Englishmen, led by some of the most learned of churchmen and strengthened by many of the most vigorous of laymen. Men of fibrous character as well as of strong purpose, they saw that purpose, in embarking upon those perilous, interminable voyages across the Atlantic, as less to escape the old than to build anew. For the imperative of the Puritans was a constructive one—not to destroy or even to evade, but to strive, endlessly and pervadingly, to fulfill their vision of the perfect society. For it, they were willing to endure the ordeal of the physical wilderness that they equated with man's spiritual desolation and to face the challenge of the unknown. In all this, there was no room for the lonely repose of the ascetic, the inert acceptance of the mystic, or the ultimate passivity of the martyr. Physically, the challenge was exacting, requiring strength, action, perseverance. And intellectually, it resisted—in fact, flatly rejected—relegating responsibility for theological inquiry to the chancel, restricted to the ordained, or to the cloister, restricted to the recluse; instead, it put the matter firmly in the library, the study, and the meetinghouses, in which church members met as equals.

Nor did building the new Zion stop at requiring physical and intellectual vitality; it commanded a zest of temperament that rendered celibacy, for example, a preposterous proposition for clergy and laity alike and abstinence from strong drink no less improbable. Shortly after his first marriage, Cotton Mather, in 1686, was moved to preach on the subject "Divine Delights,"[6] and twice bereaved of wives, he in both instances acquired new consorts within a matter of months. Wives were considered necessary to the godly life, and liquor was considered a desirable adjunct. Josiah Franklin's friend and contemporary at the South Church, Judge Samuel Sewall, one of the staunchest Puritans of them all, thought an appropriate feature of a "private Fast" in his house, to which he invited the ministers of all three of Boston's churches, all of whom accepted, was the distribution of "Biskets, and Beer, Cider, Wine."[7] And when the Rever-

[5] The process, however, was not constant. In the reign of Charles II a succession of economic measures led to a polarization of English society, as between a landowning ruling class and a mass of nonlanded wage earners, some elements of which survived beyond the Industrial Revolution.

[6] *Diary of Cotton Mather*, Massachusetts Historical Society, *Collections*, 7th Ser., VII, 127.

[7] *Diary of Samuel Sewall*, Massachusetts Historical Society, *Collections*, 5th Ser., V (May 22, 1685).

end Peter Thacher was ordained to the ministry, he assigned priority, in his diary, to the requisites of the occasion in what appeared to be declining order of importance: beer, beef, and preparatory study.[8]

The Puritan society was a hearty society that could never have flourished without a strong content of feeling and ardor. Though the processes and methods of Puritanism were primarily intellectual, certainly the commitment and often the rhetoric were emotional. Josiah Franklin's contemporary (they were five years apart in age), Cotton Mather, the ultimate Puritan, was for his time an intellectual giant—the author of 450 books, a fellow of the Royal Society, and of a mind that was at home equally with the classics and with the sciences. He had the largest library, institutional or personal, in the colonies, some three thousand volumes, and took pride in his ability to write in seven languages. But he was a man, also, who could abandon himself to childish tantrums and lose himself in paroxysms alternatingly of despair and of ecstasy, probably pathological in their intensity. The repeated testimony in his diary that he spent nearly as much time "prostrate in the Dust"[9] on his study floor as he did at his writing table accounts for titles in his immense bibliography as remote from the cerebral tone of the best of his work as *Little Flocks Guarded against Grievous Wolves*, the wolves being Quakers, and *The Right Way to Shake off a Viper*,[10] the viper being gossip, one of Mather's own favorite activities and one, therefore, to which he was peculiarly sensitive when he was the object rather than the agent of its propagation.

The same deep emotional commitment in which Puritanism involved its adherents as individuals led, on the community-wide level, to the fanaticism which, although a sporadic rather than a consistent characteristic of the Puritan experiment, was to become in legend its chief and often its sole identifying mark and which did, in fact, account for almost all of its cruelty—though its intolerance was largely a matter of conviction rather than of feeling. And yet, fervid as it was and often causing no end of trouble to the elect as well as to their victims, emotion seldom triumphed over intellect, because in the end the Puritans distrusted emotion as much in themselves as in others and, on the other hand, had an ultimate trust in the human mind that has characterized few religio-social experiments before or since. So it was that Samuel Sewall, one of the judges who sent the Salem nineteen to their deaths for witchcraft in 1692, "stood up at meeting" in the South Church five years after the brutal event and heard the confession he had written, taking "the Blame and shame of it,"[11] read by the pastor, Dr. Willard, before the assembled congregation.

[8] Hamilton Andrews Hill, *History of the Old South Church* (Boston, 1890), I, 276n.
[9] Mather, *Diary*, VIII, 83.
[10] Boston, 1691, and London, 1711, respectively. The most complete Mather bibliography is in John Langdon Sibley, *Biographical Sketches of Graduates of Harvard University* (Cambridge, 1873–   ), III, 42–158.
[11] Sewall, *Diary*, I, 445.

Josiah Franklin had been in Boston seventeen years when the judge made his memorable confession of guilt—by far the most dramatic event in the Third Church's history, which then spanned nearly half the life of the town itself. During the time, while Puritanism's chief instrument was the human mind and much of its fiber was emotional zeal, it was never able to shed altogether the symbols by which, as much as by their purposes, all institutions live—however repugnant Puritanism may have judged most symbols of the Church of England. Of those that it retained, none was so significant, so essential to its doctrine of the elect, as the most ancient of all—baptism.

* * *

The primal ceremony that Josiah Franklin was witnessing was—insofar as the firm, cerebral doctrine of the Puritans permitted the acknowledgment of any mysteries—the initiation of this, the tithe of his sons, into the basic and sole mystery of Puritan life and thought: that, in his infinite wisdom, God had chosen the elect—those destined for eternal salvation—before a day of their lives had been lived and that, since no one knew whether he was among those chosen, all believers must so live as wholly to vindicate God's mercy, if they were among the elect; fully to understand his all-knowing purpose, whether they were or not; and, through learning rather than through ignorance, bravely to accept his wisdom, if they were not.

Its distant origins lost among the pagan cults of primitive times, the baptismal rite linked the Puritans of Massachusetts with the long line of the aspiring who, from the beginning, sought to read incorporeal meaning into the necessary alliance between man and the water from which he sprang—the perpetual, pervasive insistence that, essential as the element was to his physical survival, it must be no less essential to deeper aspects of his awarenesses and of his spiritual being. From Judaism's purification of proselytes by ritualistic cleansings, the concept was brought to Christianity at the very dawn of the Christian Church—and even before, when a Judean priest's ascetic son, the migrant preacher John, who was to become known as "the Baptist," baptized the multitudes, among them the young teacher Jesus of Nazareth, in the river Jordan.[12]

To Josiah Franklin and his six thousand contemporaries building the New Jerusalem in the town of Boston, baptism was the first of the only two sacraments recognized in Puritan theology, the second being the Lord's Supper; and though the stern intellectualism of Puritanism attributed no mystical presence and no intrinsic powers to either of the

[12] The origins of the Christian rite of baptism are provocatively discussed, with differing emphases, in H. G. Marsh, *The Origin and Significance of the New Testament Baptism* (Manchester, 1941) and in R. E. O. White, *The Biblical Doctrine of Initiation* (London, 1960). The latter title has a thoughtful exposition of proselyte baptism in the context of the Hebrew conception of the covenant. The sources on the Johannine rite are, of course, the Gospels: Matthew 3, Mark 1, and Luke 3.

sacraments—as opposed, in Calvin's reproachful words, to Catholicism's "representing the sacraments as the cause of justification"[13]—all "children of the covenant" (which was to say all the Puritan faithful) were duty-bound to present their infant young for baptism, as a sign that their sons and daughters were born into the covenant "whereby," said Richard Mather, "the Lord takes them to be his."[14]

The importance of infant baptism in the Puritan state was sufficient for it to be the subject of legislative action. In 1644 the Great and General Court, the Massachusetts Bay Colony's legislature, ordered "that if any person or persons within this jurisdiction shall either openly condemn or oppose the baptism of infants, or go about secretly to seduce others from the approbation or use thereof, or shall purposely depart the congregation at the administration of that ordinance . . . every such person or persons shall be sentenced to banishment."[15] That same year a young father, on being brought into court for refusing to have his child baptized, "was sentenced to be whipped."[16] And a decade later, the first president, the chief architect, and a generous benefactor of Harvard College, the Reverend Henry Dunster, for having borne "public testimony, in the church at Cambridge, against the administration of baptism to any infant whatsoever,"[17] was indicted by the grand jury, convicted, sentenced to public admonition, and put under bonds for good behavior. He was furthermore compelled to resign the presidency of Harvard, and ordered at the outset of a long winter (although the General Court later relented and let him stay until March) forthwith to leave, with his wife and young children, the president's house, which he had built at his own expense for the college.

This rigid view of the necessity for infant baptism had its roots in a need as much practical perhaps as spiritual: the continuity of the social experiment that had led this determined people from the settled comfort of England to the raw wilderness that was New England—an experiment both inspired and exacted, in their conviction, by the covenant through which they lived in obedience to God and in common cause with one another.

Josiah Franklin, like all Puritans, saw the covenant as the central fact of life—the binding though voluntary compact between God and man that was the latter's only hope of salvation for his individual life, the only model for his ecclesiastical life, and the only incentive for his societal life. "It has pleased the great God to enter into a treaty and covenant of

[13] Perry Miller, *The New England Mind, Colony to Province* (New York, 1939), 83.
[14] Ibid., 11.
[15] *The Book on the General Lawes and Libertyes* (Cambridge, 1648), 2.
[16] Thomas Hutchinson, *The History of the Colony and Province of Massachusetts Bay*, 2nd ed. (London, 1768), I, 208n.
[17] Cotton Mather, *Magnalia Christi Americana* (Hartford, 1820), IV, 10. There are appreciative accounts of Dunster's very effective presidency in Josiah Quincy, *The History of Harvard University* (Cambridge, 1840), 14–22, and in Samuel Eliot Morison, *Three Centuries of Harvard* (Cambridge, 1942), 10–19.

agreement with us his poor creatures, the articles of which agreement are here comprised," wrote Richard Sibbes. "God, for His part undertakes to convey all that concerns our happiness, upon our receiving of them, by believing on Him."[18] The nature of the compact, whatever its purpose, was —like its terminology—political rather than spiritual, practical rather than mystical, intellectual rather than emotional. Had the doctrine been contrived by any but followers of John Calvin, it would have seemed a coldly arrogant affront to an all-powerful God, for in effect it put man and God on equal footing and executed a bargain between them, which, though heavily dependent upon the Old Testament prophets for its authority, was nevertheless couched as much in the idiom of the market as in the language of the Scriptures. As a matter of fact, the Puritan clergy frequently felt it necessary to remind their flocks that the covenant with God was not different in kind from any other agreement: "We must not make God's Covenant with man so far to differ from Covenants between man and man, as to make it no Covenant at all."[19] And because it was an agreement between equals, it was a compact that demanded of each party as much as it gave. If the elect had great privileges, therefore, they also had great duties. The recognition, definition, and pursuit of those duties constituted the substance of Puritan religious, intellectual, social, and political life, demanding total commitment to God's purpose; vast learning in the whole range of human experience, in order to determine that purpose; and both iron discipline in all private matters and unrelenting diligence in public responsibilities, in order to fulfill it.

The grand objective of those duties—as indeed of all life—was to realize here on earth the Heavenly City envisioned by the prophets, all the necessary directives for which were implicit in the Scriptures. It was the mission of John Winthrop and his six hundred countrymen, in coming to the New World in 1630, fully three quarters of a century before Josiah Franklin ushered his tenth son into the communion of the saints, to establish that holy community in the town of Boston—an experiment in constructing the perfect society which the age and indestructibility of British institutions rendered virtually impossible in England.

To this physically, intellectually, and emotionally vigorous experiment of the Bible Commonwealth, Josiah Franklin, offering his infant son to its furtherance, brought traits and a heritage as if shaped from the beginning for participation in the lofty venture.

[18] Miller, *New England Mind*, 377.
[19] Thomas Blake, *Vindiciae Foederis* (London, 1653), 3.

II

The Franklin Heritage

> Let our Fathers and Grandfathers be valued
> for *their* Goodness, ourselves for our own.
> —Benjamin Franklin[1]

Josiah Franklin was born on the day before Christmas Eve, 1657, in the little village of Ecton that lies sixty-six miles northwest of London amid the gentle hills of Northamptonshire. Franklins had been associated with the village from at least as early as 1561,[2] when one Margerye Francklyne, probably the sister of Josiah's great-grandfather, Thomas Franckline, was married to John Walsh in the ironstone parish church, strangely stately in its rural surroundings, of St. Mary Magdalen. There fourteen Franklin infants were baptized between 1563 and 1677, including Josiah, in 1657; his father, the second Thomas, in 1598; and his grandfather, Henry, in 1573.

Of the parentage of the first Thomas, family hearsay had it that his father was an attorney who lived in Houghton, a village immediately southeast of Northampton, and who had a considerable income from lands. This being in early Tudor Times, the issue of enclosure arose—the practice of landed gentry's enclosing their fields for their own year-round use, thus depriving the community of what previously had always been, in the period between the harvest and the next planting, common pasture lands. This struck the Franklin forebear as unjust to the poorer inhabitants, however beneficial to the landowners; and he "stood in deffence of the poor inhabitants and soe spent his Estate. . . ."[3]

---

[1] *Poor Richard*, 1739 (July), in *The Papers of Benjamin Franklin* (New Haven, 1959–), II, 223 (hereafter cited as *Papers*).

[2] In the *Autobiography* (Yale edition, 1964, 45) Benjamin Franklin stated that the family had at the time of his writing, 1771, "lived in the same Village, Ecton in Northamptonshire, for 300 Years." But in a letter written thirteen years earlier, on July 31, 1758, to his cousin, Mary Franklin Fisher, he said the family were in Ecton "near 200 Years, as early as the Register begins." —*Papers*, VIII, 117.

[3] This account is based on a manuscript in the Yale University Library. It is by Benjamin Franklin the Elder (1650–1727), entitled "A short account of the Family of Thomas Franklin/of Ecton in Northamptonshire." It was written in 1717, when its author was living in Boston, an aging man depending upon his recollections. He refers to this progenitor as his father's grandfather but it had to be a great-grandfather; the term "grandfather," however, was at the time often used to refer to any ancestor prior to

The more remote origins of the Franklins are lost in history, but history as written record was very young when the first Thomas Franckline wandered about the midlands of England seeking his fortune during, in Josiah Franklin's words, "the popish times"[4] of Queen Mary. Nor were recorded sources for history opulent. Land records existed, with some extensive exceptions, from the great survey of William the Conqueror, in 1086, called the Domesday Book, registering past and contemporary ownerships of the lands of England; but titles to land were limited almost entirely to the lords of the manor and a handful of gentry, and lists of tenants were casual and sketchy in the extreme. Beginning in the twelfth century, records of lands granted to ecclesiastical entities were assembled into cartularies, culminating in the *Valor Ecclesiasticus*, of 1535; but they were coldly institutional in character, though implicit in every entry were the seeds of the strife that under the House of Tudor separated the Church of England from Rome, when Henry VIII pronounced himself "on earth Supreme Head of the Church of England" and made his crafty and enigmatic lieutenant, Thomas Cromwell, his vicar-general. Parish registers, in all those mute centuries when the parish and the village were identical, were not introduced until that same Cromwell ordered them to be kept, in 1538; but the clergy and their bishops, cold to a favored layman of the King, who was appointed to deprive the Church of its holdings and bring it into total subjection to the monarch, generally refused to comply with the order. Even after the regency acting for Edward VI, in the first year of the boy king's reign, 1547, commanded obedience, few registers were kept. It was not until a canon was adopted under James I, at the beginning of his reign in 1603, that parish clergy consistently complied with the order to keep the registers and to fill in back entries "from the law's first taking place" or at least from 1558.[5] It was thus no coincidence that the parish registers of Ecton and of its neighboring village, Earl's Barton (where the first recorded Franklin—the first Thomas—was married to Margerie Meadows in 1560) began in 1559 and 1558 respectively.

Before parish registers were kept, only surnames were left through which to trace the emergence of English families from the thousand-years-

---

one's father. In any case, Benjamin Franklin the Elder's account is wholly plausible on historical grounds, since this first Franklin, who was called in the manuscript "Henery," would have been flourishing during the period 1520–60 when there was, in fact, considerable turmoil in Northamptonshire over enclosure. And it is suggestible on genealogical grounds, since the first Thomas Franckline, presumably son of the foregoing, named one of his four sons Henry. The manuscript account of the family is in error on some specific dates, but its general characterizations seem completely tenable and to accord with the facts so far as they can be determined. Benjamin Franklin the Elder wrote other occasional papers of a genealogical or biographical nature, which in general support his reliability.

4 Josiah Franklin to Benjamin Franklin, May 26, 1739, in *Papers*, II, 230.

5 George T. Baker, *The History and Antiquities of the County Northamptonshire*, cited in John Cole, *The History and Antiquities of Ecton* (Scarborough and London, 1825), 12n. The Cole title has valuable material but several chronological errors.

old fusion of Angles, Frisians, Jutes, Saxons, and Normans that achieved the most persistent and permeating acculturation in the Christian era. And it was upon his surname that Josiah Franklin relied to speculate about his family's origin. Until the Conquest in 1066, however, surnames were relatively scarce in England (though they were known in ancient societies—"Judas surnamed Iscariot"); but the Normans brought with them a taste for surnames (commonly derived from places, as in "Jean de Lacy"), and when the Domesday Book was compiled, it required surnames to differentiate landowners bearing the same given names, and also served as the first record of those who had already adopted them.

Surnames were most commonly formed from places of residence, family relationships, diminutives of given names, plain objects, animals, personal characteristics, occupations, and tools relating to them. At first, place names were assumed largely by landowners; hence those with place surnames generally came from higher economic classes, and names like Gloucester and Lancaster were very early associated with ruling families. Later, however, tenants and residents also assumed place names, sometimes merely descriptive of the place, like Hill or Brooks. Paternal relationships (used since biblical times to identify individuals, as in "James the son of Zebedee") became commonplace as surnames simply by adding "son" to the first name (Johnson) or merely the letter "s" (Johns, corrupted to Jones). Diminutives, and derivatives of diminutives, of given names were no less widespread, as Dicks or Dix and Dickson or Dixon. Ordinary animals and objects furnished many of the monosyllabic names— Hawk, for example, and Flint. Personal characteristics—Black or White, for complexion; Long or Short, for stature; Wise or Merriman, for temperament—were widely adopted, having already often been bestowed for clearer identification (Richard the Lion-Hearted). But because not all men had outstanding characteristics or landownership or known family associations (up into the eighteenth century, orphans left at St. Clement's Church, a popular depository for the purpose in London, were surnamed Clements), occupations furnished by far the greatest number of surnames. And so Smith, being the most general trade and carried on alike in city and country, became the commonest of all, followed by such universal pursuits as Farmer, Wheeler, Cooper, Taylor, and Weaver or Webster and, among things identified with occupations, Spear for soldiers, Wood for carpenters, Stone for masons, Ferry for pilots, and Bacon for butchers.

The surname Franklin was variously spelled Franckline, Francklyne, Francklin, and Francklyn in the Ecton parish register, with the permanent spelling first appearing, though without consistency immediately thereafter, in 1646. The root of the name, "Frank," is as old as any word in the Celtic tongue. It was used in Old French, Medieval Latin, Old High German, Old Saxon, and Old Norse as well as in Old English—a remarkably ubiquitous word, which, in pushing its way into new languages and new centuries as they came along, never importantly deviated from its original meaning. To the Franklins, however, seeking a clue in their surname to family origins, it could conceivably confuse as much as it could clarify, for the word "frank" fitted four of the six categories of common sources for surnames. Originally, the word was an adjective meaning "free," from which simple base it roamed through half a dozen associated meanings: lusty, free of restraint; profane, free of restriction; profuse, free of limitations; unadulterated, free of foreign substances; unmistakable, free of error; and with regard to seals or mail, free of cost. Consequently, as far as characteristics go, the surname Franklin could have had any one of eight adjectival meanings as its origin. The common noun "frank" had occupational connotations. In Old Saxon, the word meant a spear and, in Old English, javelin, and so as a surname, it could have originally meant a soldier. As a proper noun, Frank was used to identify those who came from a particular place—the Germanic tribes which settled along the Rhine and later, during the Crusades, the area embracing most of western Europe and especially what was to become France. It was also a diminutive of the given name Francis, and its use as such in some localities exceeded that of its progenitor. Finally, as a verb, frank meant to join wood, as in window sashes, and could thus have indicated one who was by trade a joiner.

About these possibilities of his surname's origin, Josiah Franklin speculated from time to time, less with any sense of gravity or purpose than with the kind of self-occupation that in those quiet days was half mental exercise and half amusement. "Some think we are of a French extract, what was formerly called Franks," Josiah reflected; "some of a free line—a line free from that vassalage which was common to subjects in days of old; some from a bird of long red legs."[6] Though the ornithological reference is elusive, the other two speculations were, in a day still decades away from the first dictionary in the language, remarkably accurate. The second was right, for not only did the Franklin name derive from the Middle English word *frankelein*, a freeman; but by the fourteenth century, "franklin," in its lasting form, had itself become a common noun of that meaning, occurring in the verse of Chaucer and, in Elizabethan times, that of Spenser, in both instances stressing freedom.

* * *

A bent toward freedom was inherent in the English character since the distant day when the barons on the meadow of Runnymede forced from the unwilling King John concessions that began the island's long, slow liberation from the rigid strictures of feudalism. From its earliest history, the Franklin family shared, if without grandeur, with some persistence in that character. The first recorded Franklin—the Thomas Franckline who married Margerie Meadows at Earl's Barton in 1560—was born, probably in the late 1530s, during the long and tyrannical reign of Henry VIII. Yet though England had never known more repressive days, as the King's vice-

[6] Josiah Franklin, in *Papers*, II, 230.

regent, Thomas Cromwell, ruthlessly suspended or ignored the age-old liberties of Englishmen, the realm emerged from the thirty-eight-year ordeal with its subjects prizing rather more than less those liberties which Henry and his determined suffragan had trampled underfoot. And when the barbarous events of Mary's brief reign made it apparent to all England that the return to Rome was to be no less vengeful than the departure, a widespread and enduring resistance to religious as well as to political arbitrary power arose and was expressed in the willingness of hundreds to burn at the stake and hundreds of others to endure exile rather than submit to despotism. As the persecution persisted into the sixth and final year of Mary's bitter, abortive rule, a spirit of Protestantism among the mass of people was fired as consummately as were the bodies of the martyrs.

Though the drama of these conflicts and their resolution was enacted in high places, the effects of them filtered down to the provinces, becoming benignly simplified in the process. In the household of Thomas Franckline's youth, during Mary's reign, when the English Bible was forbidden to be read, the opened book was kept tied with cloth tapes to the underside of the seat of a jointed stool. It was turned upward for family reading, with good Protestant orthodoxy; and some small Franklin was stationed at the door to alert the family whenever an ecclesiastical spy came into sight, in which case the top of the stool was restored to its original position and the Scriptures hidden from sight. "This obscure Family of ours," Benjamin Franklin wrote proudly, passing on from his father and uncle the narrative of this episode to his son, two centuries later, "was early in the Reformation, and cont'd Protestants thro' the Reign of Queen Mary, when they were sometimes in Danger of Trouble on Account of their Zeal against Popery."[7]

Generally, however, Northamptonshire was not distinguished for the fervor of its resistance to Mary's policies. The clergy of the Diocese of Peterborough, see of the county, were ejected for anti-Roman views in only half the proportion of those in the rest of England, due to a flexible theology, a strong sense of survival, or an inspired combination of both. Nevertheless, among the inhabitants there remained a stubborn instinct for Protestant rather than Catholic discipline and practices; and to them the Bishop of Rome seemed an increasingly alien figure and certainly an implausibly remote one to govern the religious lives of Englishmen. And the sole fatal victim of Marian revenge in Northamptonshire, as the Archbishop of Canterbury and close to three hundred others went to their deaths elsewhere, was not a clerical luminary, but a Syresham shoemaker, named John Kurde, who was charged with flatly denying the Roman doctrine of transubstantiation, i.e., that the bread and wine of the communion actually became upon consecration the body and blood of Christ. After a year's imprisonment and resisting the entreaties to recant from the vicar of St. Giles in Northampton, Kurde was brought before an ecclesi-

[7] *Autobiography,* 50.

astical court, summarily condemned to death, and, on the last day of summer in 1557, was burned at the stake outside the city's north gate.

When Elizabeth, daughter of Anne Boleyn and reared a Protestant, acceded to the throne the following year, her natural wisdom and insights, bolstered by shrewd advisers, precluded any such immediate violent redress as had blotted the reign of her half-sister, though in later years they were no match for her stubborn support of the oppressive measures of Archbishop John Whitgift. At the outset of her reign, however, clergy of unrelenting Roman persuasions were merely, at a very gradual pace spread over four years, relieved of their incumbencies, beginning in Northamptonshire with the Bishop of Peterborough and its dean, who had been one of Queen Mary's privy councilors, and ending with the Rector of Desborough, the same who had two years earlier officiated at the marriage of Thomas Franckline.

These matters were of far more than casual interest to the townsmen, villagers, and farmers of the shire. The center of life for them, aside from the long hours of labor to sustain their simple material existence, was the parish church. For young Thomas and Margerie Franckline, who settled in Ecton after their marriage, the church was St. Mary Magdalen's which had stood for over four hundred years, since the 1100s, on a slope rising mildly to the east above the village street. The structure, probably originally only a tiny family chapel, was added to over the centuries until in the 1560s its seventy-eight-foot tower soared over the surrounding cottages and was visible, long before the village itself could be seen, to travelers along the great northern turnpike, joining London and Edinburgh. Most of the villagers in their infancy had been baptized at the church's ancient Saxon font,[8] had been married at its altar, and had at the end been borne through its thirteenth-century doorways to their graves in the churchyard. Below, the village street climbed from the river Nene, up through the village's two thousand acres, to the turnpike, from which travelers turned now and then down into Ecton to feed or shoe their horses.

According to the Domesday Book, in which it was called Echentone, the village was an old one. Inhabited and having two mills for grinding flour by 1086, it was probably first settled before Edward the Confessor's time. Three manors, over the years, were established in Ecton—parts of the overlordship of the Duchy of Lancaster—which was largely a farming area consisting of lovely meadows veined by pleasant brooks separating the village from its neighbors, great shady trees, small wheat fields, and occasional gardens of beans and root vegetables. On the south, it was bordered by the river Nene, flowing northeasterly to The Wash of the North Sea and from time to time flooding the meadows along its banks.

[8] R. M. Serjeantson and W. R. D. Adkins, eds., *The Victorian History of the County of Northampton*, (London, 1902–37), II, 126, state, "The font, which has a circular bowl, was in use in 1825 as a horse-trough at a neighboring farm, and its carved ornamentation has suffered but it is apparently not earlier than the 14th century." The font, now restored and returned to use, is clearly Saxon.

Time mellowed but did not afflict Ecton. It remained a village, though as the seventeenth century approached there were a few more houses along the village street, a few more parishioners in the pews of St. Mary Magdalen's, a few more stones in the churchyard. Thomas Franckline earned his living as a smith—a trade he chose because, after his first choice of an employer, a tailor, proved to keep a "stingy house," the smith to whom he apprenticed himself served "a good toast and beer."[9] He and Margerie Franckline had, in 1563, a son, whom they named Robeart. Two years later they had a daughter whom they took to St. Mary Magdalen's to be christened Jane, but scarcely a week had gone by before the child was carried up the slope again to the churchyard to be buried. Then, at three-year intervals from 1567 to 1573, three more sons were born, and christened, John, James, and Henry—all of them surviving.

In 1574 Franklin entries disappear from the Ecton parish register, not to reappear for twenty-two years; but for seven of those years, the parish register itself disappeared, never to be found again if it had been kept for that period in the first place. In 1595 the name of Thomas's youngest son, Henry, the grandfather of Josiah, reappeared in the registers (which resumed in 1591 and are extant) when he was married at twenty-two to Agnes Joanes, who was the same age. To them a son, named Thomas for the first Franklin, was born sixteen months later; but in the middle of the summer of 1598, while his mother was pregnant with her second child, the little Thomas died. The brother he never saw, born two months later, was also called Thomas in his memory.

Henry Franklin, like his father, became a smith in the village of Ecton; but again in the parish register of Ecton the family name disappeared— this time for the space of thirty years, until 1631 when Henry was buried. He was not, however, away from Ecton all that time, though he certainly was away part of it. For a year and a day, according to his grandson, Josiah, he was in prison "on suspicion of his being the author of some poetry that touched the character of some great man."[10] The culpable poetry has not survived, but an irresistible inclination for versification, if a limited talent for it, ran through at least three generations of Franklins, and Henry Franklin was an enterprising man. He was soon restored to freedom and respectability, however, for in November 1620 he bought some land in Ecton, and eighteen months later bought a house, a barn, and a close to go with it. But in the deed he was described as "of Desborough," some twelve miles north of Ecton, to which Henry Franklin may have found it prudent to move after his imprisonment or where he may have committed the alleged offense in the first place. In any case, in 1630, he was named a constable in Ecton—an office not bestowed lightly. In seventeenth-century villages in England, the constable was answerable not to the sheriff but to the local jurist, whose orders he carried out and to whom he presented any

[9] Josiah Franklin, in *Papers*, II, 230.
[10] Ibid.

offenders he may have arrested as he went about his duty of keeping the King's peace. But he had also many other civil duties, among them aiding in the administering of help to the poor, finding laborers during the harvest, and seeing to it that none of the regulations regarding food prices were violated in the market. The importance of the office of constable and the trust it signified on behalf of the holder's fellow villagers testify to the fact that the Franklins, in Henry's generation, had acquired recognition in the village and, whatever Henry's lyrical venture, its full confidence.[11] In October 1631 Henry Franklin was described in the parish register on his burial as "Husbandman," indicating that, like most village tradesmen who owned land, he had farmed his thirty acres as well as practiced his trade. He left both to his son and only living offspring, Thomas Franklin 2nd, the father of Josiah.

Thomas Franklin 2nd was thirty-three when his father died, and single. His exceptionally long bachelorhood, which was to last five years longer, was attributed by his grandson, Benjamin, to his having fallen in love with a very young girl, Jane White, who was the child of neighbors and for whom he waited until she grew up into, in the words of her sons, "a tall, fair comly person." They were married in 1636, and she bore him nine children, all but one of whom were sons. Of the eight sons, two—twins— died in infancy and two others as relatively young men; but four grew to adulthood, and their lives were to affect one another's significantly. The four were born over a twenty-year space, the oldest son, Thomas Franklin 3rd, in 1637, and the youngest, Josiah, in 1657; between them were John, born in 1643, and Benjamin (who came to be known as "the Elder," in order to distinguish him from his noted nephew), born in 1650. Together they constituted the first generation of Franklins to be caught up sufficiently in the forces of history as themselves to become an indirect influence upon it.

A considerable factor in bringing this about was the family heritage of this fourth generation of recorded Franklins—Josiah's generation. Both their father and grandfather were at home with letters, showing considerable evidence not only of being steady readers but also of a willingness, even an eagerness, to try their hands at writing. They were also gregarious men, not inclined to withdrawal, partly because of the essentially social nature of the English village and partly because of a personality trait of sociality in the family that was to continue dominant for at least two generations into the future. Josiah's father, Thomas 2nd, was, according to

[11] The reconstruction of Henry Franklin's life draws in part upon unpublished notes which Mr. P. I. King, County Archivist at the Northamptonshire Record Office, Delapre Abbey, Northampton, compiled and permitted the present writer to examine. They tend to dispute the long-held belief, first asserted by Benjamin Franklin (*Autobiography*), that there was an ancestral establishment of the family in Ecton for three hundred years before 1771. Josiah Franklin was nearer the facts on this question in his letter to Benjamin of May 26, 1739, but erred in stating that his grandfather, Henry, "had only one son and one daughter." The Ecton parish register lists two sons, the older dying in childhood.

Josiah's brother, Benjamin Franklin the Elder, a cheerful man, pleasant in his conversation and just in his dealings. He was, like many of the Franklins, of an inventive turn and, when he was young, contrived a clock which was still working in his later years. He was—also like many of the Franklins—infinitely versatile in his interests and aptitudes. In English villages the blacksmith was a generalist who turned what skills he had to all projects that were brought to him, but Benjamin the Elder reported that his father "also practiced for diversion the trade of a Turner [i.e., he made furniture legs and balusters by using a lathe to turn the wood], a gunsmith, a surgeion, a scrivener [who wrote legal documents], and wrote as pretty a hand as ever I saw. He was a historian and had some skill in Astronomy and chymistry which made him acceptable company to Mr. John Palmer, the Arch-Deacon of Northampton."

Thomas Franklin 2nd also was the physical prototype of his sons and grandsons. He was of dark complexion, of agreeable facial expression, inclined to be corpulent, quite bald—a condition he neturalized by constantly wearing a cap. Although he was warm and friendly to men of all opinions, religion played a significant but not deeply emotional role in his life, and it took on such major characteristics of Protestantism, which was still morphologically in its extreme youth, as constant repairing to the Scriptures and an addiction to extemporary praying. Hence, the importance of the open Bible taped to the stool's underside that forever remained such a firm symbol in the minds of Benjamin Franklin the Elder and his younger brother, Josiah. Hence, too, inscribed high on the parlor walls of the Franklin house on the village street of Ecton in letters so large that the words ran around all four walls, two verses from the Gospel According to St. John. Characteristically of the Franklins, they were among the more joyful words of the New Testament: "God soe loved the world yt He gave his onley begotten Son that whosoever beleeveth in Him should not perish but have everlasting life. For God sent not his son into this world to condemn the world but that the world through him might be saved." And Benjamin the Elder, as a boy, used to write down in his commonplace book, passages from the Psalms and the New Testament that his father frequently quoted in family prayers.

His mother, Jane White Franklin, was also a powerful influence in the lives of her children and an influence, too, in the life of Ecton. "Exact in her Morals," her son Benjamin the Elder succinctly described her, "and as she was Religiously Educated so also Religiously inclined." Putting into local practice an integral feature of Puritan discipline, though she never left the Church of England, she regularly convened the women of Ecton in two-hour meetings on Thursdays for the purpose of discussing the previous Sunday's sermon, singing the Psalms, and joining together in prayers. When the youngest of her children, Josiah, was still an infant, Jane Franklin became ill with tuberculosis, lingered for some years, and died when he was five. But Benjamin the Elder, in his sixties, still recalled her singing the Fourth Psalm "in the old metre for we then knew no other," and her earnest expostulating to her neighbors on the prophets.

As close to a family chronicler as the family produced, Benjamin the Elder also left, in his commonplace book, touching testimony of the tranquillity of the village and its surrounding countryside and of the part that it played in the life of a boy. It is all in verses, indifferent at best so far as technical grace is concerned, but not without occasional pleasant phrases —a primitive in words, quietly evocative, since he was fifty-two and in London when he wrote them, of a far-off childhood in an age when the near world outside the cottage door was the whole world:

> This is the Church Whose preacher I did fear
> These are the Bells I did Delight to Hear
> This is the Yard Where I did often play
> And this the Ile [aisle in St. Mary Magdalen's] I katechise did say
> Here Lyes the Dust I did so often Dread
> There live'd the Baker that did make the bread
> But Where's the Boyes that Higher did me Lead
> Here stands the stones that did my Haste Retard
> There Lyes the Mother I did Disregard
> That is the street Which I could nere Abide
> And these the Grounds I play'd at Seek and Hide
> This is the pond Whereon I caught a fall
> And that the barn Whereon I play'd at ball
> There Runs the River Where I oft did Fish
> And Either had good sport or did it Wish
> And these the Long broad pleasant Meadows Where
> Noe bouling-Green more Even can Appear
> On the fair Leyes [leas] Ecton's fair Daughters Dance't
> When Charming Martyn his high strain's advanc't
> Here Nappy Ale was sould brew'd by a Friend
> Here in Excess I first of all offend
> And He that Wrote this, here does make an end.[12]

Another of the factors accounting for the emergence from total obscurity of the Franklins was an entirely local personal influence—an enlightened and concerned man, the Venerable John Palmer, Rector of the Ecton parish for thirty-eight years and for fourteen of them also the Archdeacon of Northampton. Palmer came to St. Mary Magdalen's in 1641, when young Thomas Franklin 3rd, oldest of Josiah's siblings, was only four years old and before the others were born. A young man of twenty-nine, Palmer was a linguist of some reputation, the author of several books, and an educator by taste and instinct, who, attracted by their native brightness, took Thomas Franklin and his brothers under his wing

[12] Benjamin Franklin the Elder's commonplace book is in the collections of the American Antiquarian Society, Worcester, Massachusetts. Excerpts were published in *Historical Magazine*, III, 9–12, 50–51, 86–87 (January, February, and March 1859), in Colonial Society of Massachusetts, *Publications*, X (1907), 190–225, and in *Papers*, I, passim.

and educated them. Like most oldest sons of the time, Thomas learned his father's trade and became a smith. He was, however, endowed with a capacity for learning, which he rapidly developed under John Palmer's guidance, and though he was too practical to give up the smithy or the farm, he was also sufficiently practical to turn, in due time, his learning to a profit, thus exemplifying a persistent Puritan genius.

Thomas Franklin 3rd became a kind of country solicitor, drafting contracts, collecting tithes and rentals from the glebe lands for the rector, witnessing wills (including the rector's), and busying himself on a variety of public service projects. He succeeded in getting, by soliciting the villages and the inhabitants of the surrounding countryside, a set of chimes for St. Mary Magdalen's, which played the Fourth Psalm, of which his mother had been so fond—"Hear me when I call . . ."—appropriately enough at four, six, eight, and twelve o'clock on Sundays and, at the same hours on weekdays, with somewhat less immediacy, "Britons Strike Home." Aside from the functionalism of the chosen selections, the chimes served another practical purpose: telling the time, since when a clock was installed in the church tower sixty years earlier no provision had been made for dial plates. Musically inclined, Thomas Franklin 3rd constructed an organ upon which he used to play for his amusement. He also devised a scheme to stop the river Nene's seasonal floodings of the meadows bordering its banks, which seems to have worked effectively. And he kept a school, which he sold to a neighbor when his solicitor work began to occupy most of his time. Dark and, unlike most Franklins, thin, he was, on first sight, of forbidding appearance and of quick temper, but he cooled off fast and rapidly became fair and reasonable. Altogether he was a solid, responsible, and respected yeoman.

A lively, versatile man, Thomas Franklin 3rd together with his father, with John Palmer, and with his brothers John and Benjamin, were the major influences on the early life of Josiah Franklin. A tradition of wide reading, already well established in the family, was encouraged by Palmer and nurtured by the natural inclination of both Thomas and Benjamin, so that Josiah himself, as he grew up in Ecton, became well instructed, accustomed to reading and study, and independent in his thinking—a breed of Englishman sprung from two generations of the age of Elizabeth, exposed to religious dissent and occasionally to political rebellion and not given to servility, economically, politically, intellectually, or spiritually. Such basic values and outlooks, coupled with the environment, the times, and the homely events and accidents that guide the direction of most men's lives, were the governing factors that determined not only which subjects of the crown but which members of individual families, during the reigns of Elizabeth's three immediate successors, were to remain in England and which ones were to leave their ancient home for the arduous venture across the sea.

III

The Puritan Heritage

> History will also afford frequent Opportunities
> of showing . . . the Advantage of a Religious
> Character among private Persons. . . .
> —Benjamin Franklin[1]

The environment of the Northamptonshire in which Josiah Franklin grew up and came to manhood and the events that took place within the county during the century that formed him—particularly in the near shire town of Northampton—conduced to his eventually joining the dissenters at home and then throwing in his lot with those who migrated overseas. "The Family continu'd all of the Church of England till about the End of Charles the 2ds Reign," the younger Benjamin Franklin was to write, "when some of the Ministers that had been outed [*sic*] for Nonconformity, holding Conventicles in Northamptonshire, Benjamin and Josiah adher'd to them, and so continu'd all their Lives."[2] Had Benjamin the Elder and Josiah in their early adulthood not left Ecton and Northamptonshire for Banbury, a hotbed of Puritanism in Oxfordshire, quite possibly they would never have left the Church of England. Yet Northamptonshire, by this time, already had a strong Calvinist inclination that made the drift of the young men to Puritanism not only easy but, given the move to Banbury, perhaps inevitable. For no sooner had Elizabeth and her ministers finally resolved the problem of adherents to Rome than those at the opposite extreme, intent upon purging the Church of England of any remaining symbols of Romanism, began to organize to press their case, to codify it and to put their codification into practice; and that English aptitude for moderation upon which Elizabeth had so much depended, and which her regime did so much to nourish, was once again in danger of subordination by extremists. Nowhere was this more apparent —nor earlier—than in Northamptonshire.

When the Anglican clergy who had been in exile on the Continent, largely in Switzerland, during the implacable reign of Mary, returned after Elizabeth's accession, they brought with them an impressive knowledge of

---

1 "Proposals Relating to the Education of Youth," 1749, in *Papers*, III, 314.
2 *Autobiography*, 50.

all the purifications that the French reformer, Jean Cauvin, had urged upon the Church of Rome long before he became the patron saint, as John Calvin, of the Puritan outcasts. More vigorous episcopates in some dioceses managed to induce the returned exiles to contain their enthusiasm for Calvinism; but in Northampton's diocese, Peterborough, Bishop Edmund Scambler, having spent Mary's reign ministering to a Protestant congregation secretly in London, took a latitudinarian view of the persuasions of the returning exiles and gave his consent to an astonishing set of rules adopted by the clergy of Northampton at a meeting held, in June of 1571, at All Saints' Church, for the conduct of religious affairs in their parishes. The result of this conclave was a document, remarkably self-possessed for its boldness, which defied some of the most venerable of Anglican liturgical practices casually and without bothering to present either apology or rationale. Among "the orders and dealings . . . established and sett up, by the consent of the Bysshop of Peterborough" were the institution of such physical changes to emphasize congregational worship as moving the choir, the organ, and even the altar from chancel and sanctuary down "into the bodie of the church amongst the people"; the establishment of lectures on the Scriptures on Tuesdays and Thursdays—transplanted and continued as a firm practice in New England for two centuries afterward; specific emphasis on the predominance of the sermon over the liturgy; the establishment of courts joining ecclesiastical with civil authority to deal with such offenses as "notorious blasphemy, whoredome, drunkenness, raylinge against religyon, or the preachers thereof, skowdes, rybaulds, and such lyke"; the restriction of bell-ringing, particularly at funerals; and, perhaps most extraordinary in view of the episcopal consent, the introduction of "A porçon of Calvyns Catechisme" for the instruction and examining of the young.[3] That these strictures were actually put into practice was convincingly evidenced sixty-six years later, when Archbishop Laud—determined to check Puritanism—appointed a commission to inspect the churches and it found the stalls taken out of the chancel of All Saints', the altar moved to the nave, and a cross taken down from its place over the altar and replaced with the coat of arms of the city of Northampton, "as if it were towne's church and not Christ's."

Aiding and abetting the clergy, a prominent layman in the adjacent shire of Buckingham, Peter Wentworth, a leader in Parliament and nephew by marriage of Sir Philip Sidney, took to inviting his Northamptonshire neighbors to his house to partake of communion according to the nonsacerdotal practices of the Puritans. And as early as 1587, although Bishop Scambler had been translated to Norwich and a more disciplined churchman named to replace him, the clergy of Northamptonshire divided themselves into presbyteries, or classes, and voluntarily submitted

[3] The complete documents are in the Domestic State Papers, *Cal. S. P. Dom. Eliz.* lxxviii, 38, at the Public Record Office in London.

themselves to these bodies' orders and decrees, one of the first of them prohibiting use of the sign of the cross in baptism. But when the leader of the insurgent clergy, the curate of St. Peter's in Northampton, who presided over one of the presbyteries, was cited on eight charges of violating his ordination commitments and flatly refused to put in an appearance, he was summarily sent to prison, and many of his nonconforming colleagues were suspended from their livings.

After the death of Elizabeth, the last of the Tudors, and the accession of the first of the Stuarts, James I, who had been reared uneasily in the Presbyterianism of Scotland, Northamptonshire's two knights, Sir Valentine Knightley and Sir Edward Montague, took advantage of the change in the monarchy to present a petition that the suspension of the nonconforming clergy of their county be lifted. However, James had no intention of weakening the crown by weakening the Established Church, and not only was the Knights' petition rejected but they themselves were strongly rebuked for their pains. Yet during the twenty-two-year reign of James, which, far from befriending the Puritan cause, saw the extension of a royally appointed espiscopacy to the Church of Scotland, Northamptonshire continued in what was by then a relaxed tradition of Puritanism that carried well into the reign of Charles I, when the wardens of All Saints' were excommunicated in 1637 by Archbishop Laud for taking their time about restoring the communion rail and the altar to their original places in the chancel. (After this was finally accomplished, the rail was broken up within six months and the altar was back in the nave again.) The Long Parliament, as Charles's reign went tottering toward its end and he toward the scaffold and as the kingdom drifted into Civil War, favored the Puritans' position, but neither speedily nor substantially enough to please Northamptonshire. There the lay leadership convened to petition Commons for immediately relieving the bishops of their votes in the House of Lords. And Northamptonshire became the first county in England to establish a committee to handle clerical affairs independently of the episcopate—a committee that was functioning two years before the episcopacy was abolished altogether in 1643 as a result of the Cromwellian revolution.

But when the final repudiation of Anglican traditions and practices was achieved with the banning of the Book of Common Prayer and the official institution of presbyteries to govern the church, Northamptonshire—as though its mission had been fulfilled—lost all interest in religious pioneering. Probably the independent temperament of the shire could accommodate itself no more to the discipline of the lord brethren than to the edicts of the lord bishops; possibly, however, in ecclesiastical affairs at least, the shire was determined to be opposed to any order as long as it was the existing order. And when, after the Protectorate fell, the monarchy was restored with Charles II, the laity of Northamptonshire was in the vanguard of those demanding the restoration of bishops.

With the knowledgeable Archdeacon of Northampton as its rector from the reign of Charles I, through the Protectorate and well into Charles II's reign, Ecton refrained from any wide doctrinal swings, the little parish going on serenely under John Palmer's skilled and diplomatic guidance until his death in 1679 and then for another generation during the successive incumbencies of his two sons. Something of this theological serenity was communicated to all the Franklins, except Benjamin the Elder and Josiah; and even they, at the height of their Puritanism, were distinguished more for steadfast devotion than for fiery fervor. As for the others, their father Thomas 2nd was, according to Benjamin the Elder, "a lover of good men of all denominations He was most inclined to the presbyterian Government [i.e., of the church] and discipline, but when Charles 2nd return'd he went to church [i.e., Church of England] alsoe for peace and order sake." Thomas 3rd, who built an estate of two thousand pounds largely through the patronage of the Archdeacon and of the Lord of Ecton Manor, Thomas Catesby, was, his brother noted, "Highly for the Church of Eng. yet wanted a cordial love for its Ministers and toward his end [not until 1702, after both the Archdeacon and Catesby had long been dead] had almost turned dissenter." As for the other brothers, Samuel, who went to Southwark in London to become a silk weaver, remained, for his brief life of twenty-three years, in the Church of England. John, though he was the first of the brothers to go to Branford, had too harried a personal life there to become involved in religious dissent. And of Joseph, who became a builder in Suffolk, Benjamin the Elder reported, "his judgment was for the Church of England, but his wife was otherwise inclined."

The course that eventually led Benjamin the Elder and Josiah to Banbury, and to Puritanism, was first followed by John, their older brother, and the inducement was economic. Villages of the size of Ecton, with only three or four hundred people, were far too small to support any but the oldest sons as new generations came along, and younger sons customarily set out on their own to learn trades elsewhere and then find places to practice them. This was the path taken by all the younger Franklins, and John accordingly went to London and there, in the Thomas Street establishment of a Mr. Glover, he learned to be a cloth dyer. Benjamin the Elder soon followed him there and became an apprentice to a skein silk dyer named Pratt for five years and, for two more, to another named Paine. With many duties, few rights, and no pay, the long, lean apprenticeships often in strange surroundings were lonely and grim periods, especially to boys from rural villages where they were related to many and known by name to all. For Benjamin the Elder those days were made far more bearable by the proximity of his brother John, seven years his senior, who, he recalled, "was as a father to me and helped me thro' my troubles with Mr. Pratt to whom I served five years of my time. He was of a very pleasant conversation, could sute himself to any company, and did when he pleased insinuate himself into the good opinion of persons of all Qualities and conditions. . . .[4]

The close ties bred in the little village of Ecton among the Franklins persisted long after the sons of Thomas Franklin had, of necessity, drifted away to London and to other towns in order to establish their livelihoods, and were to persist long years afterward when they and their children were separated by the Atlantic. Benjamin the Elder recalled that when John was young, he and an older brother, Samuel, "the most comely person in the family . . . loved one the other Entirely, insomuch that when one had done a fault the other would plead and procure his pardon before he came in sight."[5] And when John, after some years in London, concluded that the city was not conducive to his health, and accordingly settled at Banbury not more than twenty-seven miles from Ecton just over the Northamptonshire line in Oxfordshire, where he had kinsmen on his mother's side, to open a dyeing establishment, his young sister, Hannah, came from Ecton to keep house for him. And then his youngest brother, Josiah, went to Banbury to live with him, too, to learn the trade of dyer.

The choice of a trade was easily the most momentous decision that a young man made in his life; and such other choices as a permanent residence and a wife were in all cases influenced and in many cases determined by it. Moreover, in a land increasingly dependent economically upon mercantilism, with no possible way for village farms to provide livings for from three to seven or more sons in a family, apprenticeships were prized as a certification to the right to make a living—so prized that, in Queen Elizabeth's reign, they were limited to forty-shilling freeholders; and, as late as 1621, effectively restricting access to apprenticeships, an Act of Parliament prohibited those without property from moving to towns or cities, and migrant children were "bound" to serve apprenticeships in such remote places as Barbados and Virginia. And though the act ceased to be enforced during the Protectorate, the value it attached to apprenticeships persisted, the trades becoming a powerful political and a persistent economic force, with entry into them jealously guarded and the seven-year duration of apprenticeships continuing in effect until the early nineteenth century. Consequently, members of a family helped one another find apprenticeships; and specific trades as a result tended to run in families. Thus, of the five boys, excepting the eldest who inherited his father's trade, in Josiah Franklin's generation, three—John, Benjamin the Elder, and Josiah—became dyers, a trade that prospered in the good times of Charles II's reign because of the flourishing cloth industry and because of

---

[4] Ibid.
[5] Benjamin Franklin the Elder (1650–1727), "A short account of the Family of Thomas Franklin of Ecton in Northamptonshire." MS in Yale University Library.

the delight taken in colorful dress during the Restoration as relief from the drabness of Cromwell's rule.

* * *

The exact date of Josiah Franklin's beginning his apprenticeship under his brother, John, at Banbury, is not known, but it is unlikely to have been earlier than 1666, when Josiah was eight, or later than 1672, when he was fourteen. In 1665 his sixty-seven-year-old father was urged to rent the family property in Ecton by his oldest son, Thomas Franklin 3rd, who, prospering as a tobacconist and the proprietor-master of a day school, invited his father to come and live with him. The experiment failed, however, largely due to Thomas's "temper being passionate," said Benjamin the Elder. And so the father went to Banbury to live with John. He may have taken his youngest son, Josiah, with him, in which case Josiah probably started his apprenticeship about 1666. He would have been young to enter the textile trade, but not impossibly so, for there are records of children as young as four being set to work winding yarn on quills and then, at about seven, beginning their apprenticeships. But the more common thing was for a boy to become apprenticed somewhere between twelve and fourteen. Had this been the case with young Josiah, the probability is that he stayed in Ecton with his brother, at whose school he may have studied. In later years, however, Josiah recalled that he "lived with" his brother John, who had "purchased a house by the mill" in Banbury, for eleven years.[6] If Josiah lived with John until his marriage (no later than 1677), he was nine when he went there. If he lived with John after his marriage until his departure for America in 1683—a less likely possibility—he would have been fourteen.

In any case, though his master was his brother, Josiah was bound by the same severe articles that governed all apprenticeships: He would be taught the craft of dyeing (a complicated one because it involved not only the dyeing of threads, woven cloth, and garments but also the intricate concocting of the dyestuffs), and he would be provided with food, lodging, and laundering. He, on his side, committed himself wholly, day, night, weekends, to his master's service, specifically agreeing to patronize no taverns, reveal no secrets, buy or sell nothing, do no gambling, contract no marriage agreement, and never absent himself, but on the other hand to follow all orders of his master promptly, cheerfully, and without question. For seven years, in short, he bartered his freedom for his training.

Under conditions of such severity, Josiah was fortunate that his master was his brother, not only because of the strong fraternal sense among the Franklin brothers that lasted all their lives but also because John Franklin was by nature an agreeable man. Moreover, not only was Josiah's sister running John's household, but his father had moved to Banbury, too, hav-

⁶ MS letter, Josiah Franklin to Captain Benjamin Franklin, Blenheim, England (January 11, 1743/4), in Boston Public Library.

ing turned over his smithy and farm to his oldest son a few years after his
first wife's death in 1662. Thus, the boy Josiah, last and youngest of a family unit formed thirty years earlier, was still to grow to manhood under the
influence of his Ecton family.

But Banbury was not Ecton, and that was to make an enormous
difference. In the first place, compared to the tiny village of Ecton, which
the busy kingdom of the Stuarts passed by on the great road from London
to Edinburgh, Banbury was a bustling market town, a crossroads where
Oxfordshire and Northamptonshire came together, five times the size of
Ecton and doubling in size between the reigns of Elizabeth and Charles
II. As Ecton was silent and unknown, so Banbury became legendary and
renowned far beyond either its size or its real significance. For centuries
the cakes and buns of Banbury were noted, and one of the earliest imports
of New England in the 1630s were Banbury cakes, which somehow survived the weeks-long voyage and became as well known in the New World
as the Old. And every child of English origin knew the nursery rhyme that
had him riding "a cockhorse to Banbury Cross"—crosses denoting the
market places in medieval market towns. The same cross also symbolized
Banbury's early and fervid embracement of Puritanism. Sixty years before
the Franklins arrived there, and while Elizabeth still lived with her triumph of re-establishing the Church of England to the satisfaction of a reassuring majority of her subjects, "The inhabitants of Banbury being far
gone in Puritanism," wrote the Reverend Anthony Rivers, in January
1601, to a clerical colleague, "in a furious zeal tumultuously assailed the
Cross that stood in their Market Place and so defaced it that they scarcely
left one stone upon another.[7]

But early as it was in the struggle of English Puritanism to reform first a
church and then a society, Banbury had been in the battle even earlier. As
far back as 1588, its representative in the House of Commons, Anthony
Cope, of Hanwell Castle, had the conviction and the daring to introduce
a new Book of Common Prayer to replace the second book of 1552, which
had been kept alive, during Queen Mary's revival of the Latin rite, by the
clergy exiled on the Continent, and which was restored to use throughout
the kingdom by the Act of Uniformity of 1559 shortly after Elizabeth's
succession. Elizabeth promptly suppressed Cope's liturgical effort, the general intent of which was to purify the service of Holy Communion from
such Roman survivals as rubrics that tolerated ornamentation of altars and
rhetorical references to the presence of the body and blood of Christ in
the bread and wine. Anthony Cope—whose surname, in view of his persuasions about ritualistic vestments, must have been a source as much of
delight to his ecclesiastical foes as of distress to himself—was hailed before
the Privy Council and committed to the Tower of London. But within a
year, Elizabeth released him and in 1596 knighted him; and as Sir An-

[7] To the Reverend Henry Garnet, cited in William Potts, *A History of Banbury*
(Banbury, 1958), 121.

thony, he became patron and host to clergy ejected from their livings because of their dissent from Church of England practices. He also touched off riots in Banbury—but won his point in the end—by attacking the Maypole, which was anathema to the Puritans from their beginnings because it represented the taint not only of medievalism and its corrupt ecclesiasticism but also of paganism, with its abandonment of reason; and the Maypole disappeared in Banbury in 1589, the year that Cope was released from the Tower.[8]

Sir Anthony also conducted fiery and successful campaigns in Banbury against May games, morris dances, and Whitsun ales; and by the time he was knighted, he had led, through the influence of his patronage as well as the force of his personality, his home parish of Hanwell and the neighboring Banbury parish well forward into the vanguard of Puritanism. In 1590 the Reverend Thomas Brasbridge, a native of Banbury and its vicar since 1581, resigned his office on grounds of conscientious objections to Church of England practices. In a gesture of open defiance of the episcopal establishment, the townspeople continued to support him until his death twelve years later.

At Hanwell, the site of Cope's castle outside Banbury, the rector was the Reverend John Dod, a friend and one of the literary executors of Thomas Cartwright, the reformer who was expelled from Cambridge, as a professor and university preacher, for advocating that the Scriptures called for the government of the church by ministers rather than by bishops and that their ministers should be chosen by the people in their individual parishes. Politically this was essentially an egalitarian proposal—and Puritanism remained an egalitarian movement—because it presupposed an equal voice among the members of a parish in choosing their clergy and an equal voice among the clergy in running the church as a whole body of Christians. This essential doctrine of Puritan practice, however, was full of dangers not only to the episcopacy, which would have been first rendered impotent and then abandoned, but also to the monarchy and to the state, for Puritanism conceived the state as subservient to the church and not, as Elizabeth and her father had constructed it, as the church's master. For this principle, Cartwright, the chief articulator of Elizabethan Puritanism, never gave up the fight, though deprived of his pulpit and once imprisoned for two years.

When Cartwright died in 1603, John Dod was among the foremost to continue the battle, and for his zeal was suspended from his Hanwell parish by the Bishop of Oxford before a year had passed—a measure which

---

[8] Maypoles threatened also to contaminate the New Jerusalem. At Mount Wollaston, Massachusetts, in 1628, Thomas Morton was a sore trial to William Bradford, governor of the Plymouth Colony, because he "set up a May-pole, drinking and dancing aboute it many days together . . ." until John Endicott, visiting the recalcitrant settlement "caused yt May-polle to be cutt downe, and rebuked them for their profannes, and admonished them to looke ther should be better walking. . . ."—William Bradford, *History of Plimouth Colony* (Boston, 1899), 285–86.

failed to make its point, Dod observing on a similar occasion "That the removing of a minister was like the draining of a fish pond: the good fish will follow the water, but eels, and other baggage fish will stick in the mud."[9] A man of ubiquitous wit, solid learning, cheerful adaptability, and great personal magnetism, Dod immediately won over his successor at Hanwell, Robert Harris, with such thoroughness that the latter rose sufficiently high in the regard of the Puritans to become master of Trinity College, at Oxford, under the sponsorship of Cromwell during the Protectorate. In his twenty years at Hanwell, Dod was the steady object of admiration from Sir Anthony Cope, who saw to it that, barred from the pulpit, Dod "lectured" in Banbury for the next twenty years. Stimulated rather than depressed by his "silencing," Dod poured forth a series of books and utterances that made him the most widely read preacher of his generation, becoming known as Decalogue Dod for his pithy and aphoristic exposition of the Ten Commandments, which went through nineteen editions and which, with characteristic Puritan acumen, he rapidly followed up with similar expositions of the Lord's Prayer and the Proverbs—all of them bursting with what became known to his colleagues and followers as "Mr. Dod's Sayings." Said his successor at Hanwell, "If all his Apopthegmes were collected, they would exceed all that Plutarch in Greek or others in Latin since have published."[10] Such sententiousness remained a characteristic of Puritanism on both sides of the Atlantic, several of the Franklins practicing it with zest if not always with grace for nearly two centuries.

The contagion of clerical dissent at Banbury kept the parish constantly exposed to Puritan thought both from the lecturers outside the church and from incumbent clergy within who openly preached Puritan principles, stopping just short of urging the expulsion of their bishops. Among these "mild" Calvinists was William Whateley, vicar of Banbury for the three decades preceding the beginning of the parliamentary phase of the Puritan Revolution. His voice was so powerful that he was widely known as the "Roaring Bay of Banbury" and "A Son of Thunder." Banbury, of which his father was mayor, was his home city; and he had actually been a dissenting lecturer there for six years before becoming vicar, revealing where not only his sympathies but also those of the mayor lay.

Succeeding in 1648 to the volatile vicariate of Banbury and destined to be an influence of determining force in the lives of the Franklins was a man of extraordinary character and intellect, Samuel Wells, a native of Oxford. There he received his baccalaureate from New College and his master's degree from Magdalen, and then taught school for two years before his ordination. During the revolution, he was the chaplain of the Earl

---

[9] The comment was reported to have been made when John Cotton was forced to flee the charge of St. Botolph's in Boston, Lincolnshire, in 1633 and is reported in his great-grandson, Cotton Mather, *Magnalia Christi Americana* (Boston, 1820), I, 241.

[10] William Durham, *The life and death of that judicious divine, and accomplish'd preacher, Robert Harris, D.D.* (London, 1660), 57.

of Essex, who commanded the parliamentary forces, and in 1647 became the rector of a remote and comfortable parish in Berkshire, where he ministered to no more than twenty contented families. At heart a teacher, Wells found that a single year of pastoral repose was enough for him, and he went to the larger, poorer, more restless parish at Banbury, where there was a greater appetite for his teaching.

Little more than a year after his induction at Banbury, Wells organized a group of the clergy of Oxfordshire and Northamptonshire to petition the Parliament against its resolve to try Charles I for high treason, which, he fully understood, meant trying the King for his life. Charles was brought before the special tribunal in Westminster on January 20, 1649. On January 21 Wells had the signatures of nineteen clergymen on his petition. On the twenty-fifth he and a colleague, John Bagley of Fringford, were in London and presented the petition to Sir Thomas Fairfax, who had defeated Charles at Naseby, the last and decisive battle of the war, and who was appointed to preside over the parliamentary commission to try the King. Deeply troubled at the finality of regicide (he would have approved deposition), Fairfax had also been importuned in letters from the heir apparent and the Queen to save the King. And when his name as first judge was called at the opening of the trial, Fairfax did not answer, his wife calling out from the gallery in Westminster that he had too much sense to attend the session. The other commissioners, nevertheless, proceeded with the summary trial, and the foregone sentence of execution of "the capital and grand author of our troubles"—Charles Stuart, King of England—was pronounced on January 27, and carried out three days later, in the street outside the banqueting house of Whitehall Palace, "by the severing of his head from his body." With thousands of other troubled Englishmen—Puritans as well as Royalists—Wells departed London, stunned and saddened by "the most execrable murder that was ever committed since that of our blessed Savior."[11]

During the days of the Protectorate, from 1649 until 1660, Samuel Wells presided over the spiritual and, to a great extent, the intellectual lives of the people of Banbury, and continued for two years into the period of the Restoration. In 1662, after Charles II was restored to the throne and the English bishops to their sees, he was ejected from his parish, along with two thousand other nonconforming clergymen in other communities; but he continued to live in Banbury with his wife and twelve children and to lecture members of his former congregation at conventicles (secret meetings), until any such meetings exceeding five participants were forbidden by the Conventicle Act of 1664. In 1665, when the hold of the nonconforming clergy upon their followers showed no signs of

[11] Although the characterization is in Lord Clarendon's highly partisan *True Historical Narrative of the Rebellion and Civil Wars in England* (London, 1702–4), it expressed also the haunting sense of remorse that many of the Puritan-Parliamentarians, like Wells, had of the event.

weakening, the Five-Mile Act was passed, requiring all nonconforming clergy either to swear loyalty to the doctrine and practices of the Church of England or to stay at least five miles away from any incorporated towns or from any parish to which they had once ministered. Wells accordingly moved, with his swarm of children, to Deddington, barely in excess of five miles from Banbury, and from there deluged his ex-parishioners in Banbury with letters telling them exactly what he would have told them had he been allowed to stay in their midst. For seven years while resident five miles distant, Wells continued to be a dominant influence on the people, particularly the young, of Banbury, and as soon as "the iniquity of the times would permit, he return'd to Banbury and there purchased a pleasant dwelling and there continued till his death."[12]

* * *

Banbury had been under the influence of Samuel Wells for at least fifteen years when the first of the Franklin brothers, John, arrived there, and for a score or more by the time Josiah, the youngest, got there in the early 1670s. The appeal of Wells to the Franklins and their contemporaries among the Banbury yeomanry, as of the Puritan clergy all over England throughout the reigns of Elizabeth and the Stuarts, was largely to their minds rather than to their emotions—hence, the emergence of the Bible and the sermon as the chief elements in Puritan worship and the reservations about music and the liturgy.

The heart of the Puritan movement was the reading of the Bible—not just on ecclesiastical occasions but constantly, lingeringly, and intensively, not primarily alone but in the company of others, and not only for absorption but for discussion. Though not above entertaining suspicion, the Puritans had contempt for ignorance; and an ignorant believer to them was no believer at all. Puritanism was a peculiarly social movement in an intellectual sense, for it made exposition and discussion an integral part of religious experience; and knowledge and understanding of the Bible were as important as acceptance of it, as Josiah Franklin's mother's Thursday meetings in her Ecton parlor demonstrated years earlier when Ecton experienced gentle stirrings of the movement. No body of Christians ever took more eagerly to the assurance of Christ, "For where two or three are gathered together in my name, there am I in the midst of them," than did the Puritans, and the need to discuss the Bible furnished an excellent and perpetual reason to meet together.

There was still, too, even as late as Josiah Franklin's apprentice days in Banbury in the 1670s, an atmosphere of discovery about the Bible among the English laity. It was little more than two hundred years since Gutenberg first printed the Psalter and not much longer since John Wycliffe, the Yorkshire-born theologian, supervised a monumental translation of the Bible into English—not the first in the language but the first in an idiom

---

[12] Benjamin Franklin the Elder to the Reverend Edmund Calamy, May 7, 1705. MS in Yale University Library.

that, if literal, nevertheless carried strength and clarity of meaning to nonscholars. A religious, political, and intellectual independent, and as resolute in his independence as the sturdy North Country in which he was born in 1320, John Wycliffe anticipated the Puritan movement, by almost three centuries, in many particulars—the doctrine of predestined salvation, rejection of clerical celibacy, skepticism of papal authority, and repudiation of the doctrine of the corporal presence of Christ in the Eucharist—but in none more clearly than in his insistence that both the learned and the laity repair directly to the Bible, and not to the priests or scholars, as the sole source of Christian belief. His translation of the Bible, based on the Vulgate, the Latin version that had been used in the Roman Church from as early as the sixth century, initiated a trend that was eventually to liberate the unlearned from a gospel that reached them only after it was distilled by the clergy and the communities of scholars under their control. Supervising a small band of old friends and sympathetic colleagues, Wycliffe finished the translation not long before his death in 1384.

Yet, though Wycliffe's life and work had a fairly immediate if only germinal effect on the birth of the Reformation on the Continent and a more subtle effect upon its intellectual precursors in England, no text of the Bible fell into the hands of the English laity generally until a century or more later, for lack as much of a plausible method of reproducing it as of ecclesiastical approval. Nearly sixty years passed after Wycliffe's translation before Gutenberg brought his varied skills to bear upon the contrivance of movable type; there was, until then, only block printing for crude pictures, cloth designs, and the briefest, most skeletal texts, more extensive documents still being laboriously copied by hand in the scriptoria of the monasteries.

No social or physical force so accelerated the reformist movement as the introduction of movable type and its unprecedented impact upon human communications and the dissemination of knowledge and ideas. Nor were its implications lost upon the English hierarchy. By the time William Caxton set up the first printing press in the realm at Westminster in 1476 and the possibility arose that any man capable of reading could have direct access to the ultimate root of all dogma, both the hierarchy and the civil authority dependent upon its support became gravely concerned with the free and broadened discussion among laymen as well as clergy such access would bring about. And the concern was well justified, for the end of total ecclesiastical authority was inevitable once men could interpret the great words for themselves, and the power of the civil authority in league with the church was bound, too, to be eclipsed. By the 1520s, William Warham, Archbishop of Canterbury, and his successor as Lord Chancellor, Thomas Cardinal Wolsey, the Archbishop of York, were desperately seeking methods to control the distribution of any religious literature —a step with which their monarch, Henry VIII, and his ministers wholly agreed. For it was clear to them even then, as a knowing Puritan lawyer was to observe a century later, "When we are treating of worldly affairs, we ought to be very tender how we seek to reconcile that to God's law which we cannot reconcile to men's equity: or how we make God the author of that constitution which man reaps inconvenience from."[13]

Aware, moreover, of the stimulating effect that Wycliffe's writings had had upon the rise of continental Protestantism, the English establishment had little intention of allowing distribution of biblical texts or the commentaries on them that would inevitably follow. Every form of suppression was tried—censorship, licensing, ecclesiastical trials, capricious charges of heresy, and the policing and harassing of the booksellers, one of whom was summoned to explain himself for printing, of all things, a sermon *against* heretical books by John Fisher, the Bishop of Rochester, who completed the irony by joining the poor printer's accusers.

But the profound revolution that the printed word had already launched on the Continent through the spread of knowledge and ideas was no more to be stopped on the shores of the English Channel than was the wind. Transcending geographical and political boundaries, the revolution in communications was a broad human movement, centered for the time on theology, because when Gutenberg's achievement let loose a flood of information, inquiry, and speculation, the central fact of life most to be illumined was the ancient, guarded intimacy between man and his God. From time immemorial, the masses of men had simply believed what they were told. When they occurred at all, speculations were for the few learned, and schisms were for the even fewer esoteric, of whom the mass of Christendom never heard, much less had any understanding. And now, as medievalism sank deeper into the past while the fifteenth century approached its close, the printers were changing all that; knowledge and questioning were beginning to stir men's minds and to shape their beliefs.

Had England not already become a maritime nation, the bishops and civil ministers may have staved off a little longer the incursion that the printed word made upon their institutions. But English ships brought back from their journeyings to continental ports more than their cargoes. With them also came new ideas in the minds of their crews—ideas already well planted in the minds of many of their continental peers, seeded in part by John Wycliffe. The first suspicions in England that the Roman Church might have slipped into error thus drifted circuitously, over a period of a century and a half, from the Lutterworth rectory of Wycliffe in Leicestershire, through the towns and villages of Europe, back to the ports of Britain. But the heresies of Martin Luther began to flow into the island kingdom in more portable form than sailors' minds when books of his writings made their way from hand to hand throughout the country, despite a statute of Richard III's time, which had been enacted in 1484—eight years after Caxton's press was set up, convenient to government control at Westminster should the need arise—and severely restricted

[13] Henry Parker, *Jus Populi* (London, 1644), 57.

the sale of books from overseas. Though the original intent of the 1484 statute was not so much to discourage the reading of foreign books as it was to encourage, by trade protection, the printers at home, during the sixteenth century a whole complex of regulations was constructed by the Tudors to control printing, in response to increased criticism of church and state. Outright censorship and bannings, however, remained primarily an ecclesiastical matter.

In 1524 William Tyndale's magnificent translation of the New Testament was prepared for the press as he lived in exile in Germany and, printed a year later in Worms, was smuggled into England, causing perhaps more consternation in high places than any publication, not excepting Martin Luther's own recalcitrant tracts, since the brief history of the press began. Cuthbert Tunstall, the Bishop of London, whom Tyndale had sought as a patron but from whose see he was now a refugee, ordered his four archdeacons to round up and call in all the copies in their jurisdictions; and William Warham, the Archbishop of Canterbury, went him one better by dispatching agents to the Continent in an attempt to get copies at their source and there destroy them. Despite their efforts, however, copies continued to circulate all over England; and as it became a primary instrument of Lutheranism on the Continent, the translation became also the principal vehicle of Puritanism in England. Seamen continued to bring copies home from continental ports[14]; secret societies of merchants were formed to obtain copies of the work for their private use; Robert Barnes, the Augustinian prior in Cambridge, appointed himself a promoter of the forbidden book among leading laymen, who then in turn converted the young clergy of their home parishes to its use. The young clergy, in turn, introduced the reading of it to the families in their cures, as certainly the Franklins at Ecton had been exposed to it, probably during the incumbency of Thomas Saunders, who went there from the priory of Chacombe near Oxford. In addition to being a superb translation, Tyndale's work contained, however, prefaces, prologues, and marginalia of his own origin that cast doubt upon the authority of priests and princes over that of the Scriptures. Clearly, as determined and calculating a monarch as Henry VIII could not depend upon inefficient churchmen to handle the matter.

Henry moved with his characteristically self-serving instinct to contrive a plot. In order to demonstrate to the Church at Rome how necessary he was to the defense of the faith in England, he waited until the ineffective restraints of the bishop had failed, and copies of Tyndale were all over England, before ordering that "no person or persons do from henceforth presume to bring into this realm, or do sell, receive, take, or detain any book or work, printed or written, which is made, or hereafter shall be

---

[14] A. G. Dickens, *Lollards and Protestants in the Diocese of York* (Oxford, 1959), 24–27, cites diocesan records of Lincoln probing into the Protestant leanings of some Hull mariners, one of whom had with him a copy of Tyndale's translation.

made against the faith catholic, or against the holy decrees, laws and ordinances of holy church, or in reproach, rebuke, or slander of the king, his honorable council, or his lords spiritual or temporal. . . ."[15] Thus, Henry not only appeared as an indispensable stronghold of "the faith catholic" but in the same document managed to equate the King and his honorable council with the faith even as he was already planning divorce, in defiance of that faith, from his aging consort, Catherine of Aragon. In the process, he was defending, too, the civil establishment from the threat of individualism implicit in every man's reading the Bible for himself. To consolidate both his indispensability to Rome and his authority at home, and with the projected divorce still to try both sorely, he had to make his edict more than an eloquent gesture. Accordingly, in a few short months, at least four men were burned at the stake for selling the Tynsdale translations; and during the next six years, other offenders were meted out the same fate until, his divorce effected at the cost of a break with Rome, Henry suffered a reversal of his convictions about the sanctity of the Scriptures against translations into English. He found, to his enormous satisfaction, that the translation offered no evidence at all that the Pope, as Bishop of Rome, should rule all Christendom. Thereafter, he not only permitted the Tyndale translation to be circulated freely in his kingdom for the first time but also authorized the first printing in England of any edition of the Bible and the preparation of a complete English text to supersede Tyndale's partial translation.

The selection of the text, resting with Thomas Cromwell, the vicar-general, permitted little latitude, and there was probably no alternative to turning to a former student of Robert Barnes at Cambridge, an Augustinian friar, Miles Coverdale, who, while in exile for his reformist views, had produced a translation based partly on Tyndale and partly upon existing translations into other languages. Despite its multiple derivation, the translation had literary merit of a high order, for Coverdale was a craftsman of considerable scholarship and sophistication; he also prudently omitted the obiter dicta that had emblazoned the margins of Wycliffe and Tyndale. After his Bible, "Set Foorth with the Kynges most gracious licence," was printed at Southwark by James Nicholson in 1535, it proved so successful that the edition was sold out, and two revised editions were printed in the next two years. A competitive version translated by John Rogers, an English chaplain in Antwerp, was also published in the 1530s, under license of Thomas Cromwell, by a London grocer turned printer named Richard Grafton, who asked the vicar-general to require every cleric to buy a copy and every abbot to buy six. Cromwell went further and issued, on the King's authority, orders for every parish priest in England to provide an English Bible for the laity to read and every bishop to make certain that a date was fixed for this to be accomplished. Thus, in

15 *Proclamation for resisting and withstanding of most damnable Heresies* (London, 1529), in Society of Antiquaries, Burlington House, London.

no more than a decade, did the Church of England, under Henry's shifting edicts, come full circle on the far from trivial matter of his subjects'
reading the Bible.

The driving mind of Cromwell, however, was not satisfied with either of
the English versions available to his countrymen, and in 1538 he assigned
Coverdale to produce a revised text, and Grafton to print it, financing
with his personal funds the cost of the venture and supervising the entire
project. The work, after some vicissitudes due to Cromwell's insistence
that Grafton do the printing in Paris, because "printing is finer there than
elsewhere,"[16] was published in 1539; and no doubt aided by some strategic prodding of the clergy by the vicar-general and certainly by his insistence, against the advice of the King's printer, that its price be kept
down to ten shillings, it was an immediate success, becoming known in its
time and to history as the "Great Bible." In 1540 a second edition was
published, this time with a noble and eloquent preface by Thomas
Cranmer, the Archbishop of Canterbury.

Cromwell realized his bold dream of a great English Bible only too well
for the taste of his scheming sovereign. No sooner was the second edition
of the Great Bible published than Henry, by then safely divorced, separated from Rome, and wholly in charge of the English Church, concluded
that Cromwell was guilty of allowing a spirit of Protestantism to infiltrate
the translation—a spirit he saw as a threat to his own authority as
defender of the faith and temporal head of the Church of England. Accordingly in July 1540—just three months after he had been granted the
soaring title "Lord Great Chamberlain"—Thomas Cromwell was summarily beheaded, without trial, for this and other "heretical" and "traitorous"
offenses.

Two years later, again taking the Church of England full circle—this
time in much less than a decade—the King induced Parliament to ban
reading the Bible in church and by the common people, though the nobility could read it to their children and merchants and gentlewomen to
themselves. There were, however, thousands of copies of the Great Bible
all over the island, and there was no way on earth to recall or destroy
them. Apprentices and journeymen hid copies under their mattresses;
shepherds tucked them in their clothing; a London tailor read aloud from
a copy in the very seat of the Bishop of London, St. Paul's on Ludgate
Hill. And long after the death of Henry in 1547, through the brief six-year
reign of his son, the boy Edward VI, and the briefer reign of his first
daughter, Mary, and into the reign of Elizabeth, the Great Bible was to be
the most widely owned book in the kingdom. It was this version that the
Franklins, in Ecton, defending its use no less than its possession, kept so
guardedly taped to the underside of a stool during the years that the determinedly Catholic Mary forbade its use.

[16] A. W. Pollard, *Records of the English Bible, 1525–1611* (London, 1911), 249f.

Not until the first Elizabeth had been on the throne for two years was it superseded, in 1560, by the Geneva Bible, with a preface by John Calvin and the reference to the garments of Adam and Eve that won it the sobriquet "Breeches Bible." The Geneva Bible was produced in that city by the little band of exiles that followed John Knox there. Accordingly, it was distinguished by marginalia that made no disguise of their compilers' attitudes about the Established Church, its doctrines, and its practices. But it was enormously popular both within the churches of England and in the households of churchmen and dissenters alike; and although the bishops, disturbed by its dissenting bias, produced a version of their own, less offensive to the episcopate, which was introduced into the churches, the Geneva Bible's popularity remained undiminished until the masterpiece of the language, the Authorized Version, appeared in 1611, in the ninth year of the reign of James I, whose name it came to bear.

Probably the most remarkable single work in the English language, the King James Version was the lineal descendant of the Great Bible of 1539 and the heir through it to the vast literary gifts of Thomas Cranmer. Though authorized by the Church of England, the mighty project of the new translation was first proposed, in 1604, by the Puritan president of Corpus Christi College, John Reynolds—the happy and lasting, if wholly unanticipated, result of a conference held for the purpose of resolving religious differences at Hampton Court, which turned out in all other respects to widen rather than narrow the gap dividing the church between its defenders and its dissidents. The King himself ruled that there would be no marginalia to advance the views of either side. Fifty-four translators —some Puritan in their views and some traditionalists—were engaged, divided into companies of nine each, with two companies at Cambridge, two at Oxford, and two at Westminster. For two years they labored and then submitted their draft to be revised during the succeeding nine months by a group of six editors, two from each of the centers of study.

The King James Version, in over three and a half centuries still unopposed for its power and depth and grace, became the cornerstone not only of English-speaking Christendom but also of the English language and literature. A proud possession of virtually every literate family in the realm, it was instructor in theology, exemplifier in letters, and arbitrator in human relations. Perhaps among no people in so short a time did the total influence of a single book become so pervasive and so deep. And of no generations was this so true as of those, born in the late years of Elizabeth's reign and the early years of the Stuarts', who under the compulsion of the Bible eventually set out to establish a new church, a new society, and a new order of things, to which, in the characterization visited upon it by history, the Bible gave its very name in "the Bible Commonwealth." For the realization of this heavenly state, Englishmen sailed to the New World—among them, in 1683, the young cloth dyer—Josiah Franklin.

PART TWO

The Heavenly City of Josiah Franklin

And I saw a new heaven and a new earth: for the first heaven and the first earth were passed away; and there was no more sea. And I John saw the holy city, new Jerusalem, coming down from God out of heaven. . . . And there shall in no wise enter into it any thing that defileth, neither whatsoever worketh abomination, or maketh a lie: but they which are written in the Lamb's book of life.
>   —The Revelation of John, A.D. ca. 81–96

If these be they, how is it that I find
   In stead of holiness Carnality,
In stead of heavenly frames an Earthly mind,
   For burning zeal luke-warm Indifferency,
For flaming love, key-cold Dead-heartedness,
   For temperance (in meat, and drinke, and clothes) excess?
>   —God's Controversy with New-England,
>   Michael Wigglesworth, A.D. 1662

IV

The Migration

> Doct[rine] to be prea[che]d . . . That Virtu-
> ous Men ought to league together to
> strengthen the Interest of Virtue in the
> World; and so strengthen themselves in Vir-
> tue.
>
> —Benjamin Franklin[1]

The Bible Commonwealth in New England was, in its origin and in its first compulsions, a social and intellectual experiment in constructing a state whose central purpose was to permit and inspire its inhabitants to live in accord with its version of the Christian imperative. The events of the half century since its inception in 1630, however, had clouded its vision and diluted its purpose. Though this was, on the whole, a subtle process, it was, in one respect, inevitable. The state's vision and purpose came inevitably to embrace the material, in addition to the spiritual, interests of its citizens; and it began to attract to its shores many who were stirred no less by economic than by religious aspirations. But if both religious and economic interests could be advanced in one step, so much the better, for it fully accorded with Puritan orthodoxy. Such was undoubtedly the motive of Josiah Franklin in his decision to migrate to Boston.

Writing his autobiography at Twyford in England, in 1771, Benjamin Franklin ascribed the migration of his father, Josiah, to New England to political harassment still visited, although in limited measure, upon the dissenters as late as 1683[2]: "The Conventicles having been forbidden by Law, and frequently disturbed, induced some considerable men of his Acquaintance to remove to that Country, and he was prevailed with to accompany them thither, where they expected to enjoy their Mode of Religion, with Freedom." Actually, though Cotton Mather wrote in December of that year, ". . . persecutions of the Dissenters do increase in England and to a marvellous height, and many persons of all ranks are

---

[1] Untitled paper, ca. 1731, in *Papers*, I, 213.

[2] *The Autobiography* fixes the date as "about 1682." Josiah Franklin left England in the summer of 1683.

forced to fly,"[3] there was no acute general persecution of dissenters in 1683. Conventicles had been banned by the Conventicle Act of 1664, forbidding any nonconformist religious meeting by more than five people except in private homes, but Charles II's Declaration of Indulgence of March 1672 so freed dissenters from such restrictions that, even though Parliament repudiated the declaration the following year, they seldom again went into hiding. And Banbury's dissenting cleric, Samuel Wells, was, at the time of his death in 1678, on terms of congenial intimacy with the incumbent who succeeded him in the parish of the Established Church.

Josiah Franklin, from all the indications of his later life, appears to have been a man of solid conviction and thorough integrity. But he was not at all fanatical in his nonconformity with the church of his forebears, and there is little likelihood that, had he been in a more settled period of his life, he would have left England. He had, after all, lived for eleven years in the household of his brother, John, who never left the Church of England, and with his father, who also remained a communicant to the end of his life.

Certainly the Franklins were not a breed likely to be so fired with religious zeal as to make it the sole determining factor in governing major decisions in their lives. As a matter of fact, all evidence suggests that it was a spirit of independence, coupled with a kind of intellectual liveliness and earthy practicality, rather than controlling doctrinal persuasions, that led the only two Franklins, Benjamin the Elder and Josiah, who became Puritans, to follow that course. And in Samuel Wells, they had a mentor not given to fanaticism in his views, as his effort to save the life of Puritanism's archfoe, Charles I, nobly demonstrated.

As for John Franklin, who had a considerable influence on both his younger brothers, having guided Benjamin the Elder through his lonely apprenticeship in London and having taken Josiah as his own apprentice in Banbury, his early adulthood was too occupied with terrestrial problems to allow much time for the spiritual. Although he succeeded in establishing himself in the dyeing trade, John Franklin had much more difficulty in his efforts to find a wife—an acquisition almost as economically essential as a good trade. Nearly forty years old when he finally succeeded, John seemed usually to have balked whenever his relationship with a woman approached the marrying stage. As a suitor, he would set out to win the affections of a likely matrimonial prospect and then, after he had done so, would drop her abruptly in a dispute over some trifle. One of his friends in Banbury, "reproving him for courting and, for such little causes, leaving soe many whose Affections he had gained, told him that it would return upon him, that he would be met with and take up with the Worst at last and indeed soe he did, according to his own confession. . . ." The "Worst" with whom he took up, and whom he married,

[3] MS letter to John Cotton, December 20, 1683, in American Antiquarian Society.

probably in 1682, was Ann Jeffs, from a village in Warwickshire.[4] She brought him a dowry of handsome dimensions for the times, £250, and produced a son and two daughters. The great failing of Ann, whom John said in all other respects he adored, was that she "proved neither capable nor careful" in assisting him in his business (which, like most tradesmen, other than those in the building and extracting trades, he carried on adjacent to his home), or in the financial management of his household—but he said that it was probably just as well, for otherwise he may have valued her too highly.

Josiah meanwhile had completed his apprenticeship in John's Banbury establishment and had gone back to Ecton to find Anne, the daughter of Robert Child, as his young bride, and brought her back to Banbury to marry, probably in 1676–77, when he was nineteen. The young couple had a daughter, Elizabeth, born in March 1678, at Ecton; and three years later in 1681 a boy, Samuel, was born in Banbury. By the time his older brother and former master had finally found and married Ann Jeffs, then, Josiah had already been married for at least five years and was supporting a wife and his first two children. It is very likely that during this time, his apprenticeship over, he worked for John as a paid employee. By 1683 the situation clearly was causing economic strain, with John's business, prosperous as it may have been or in the midst of one of the depressions that periodically afflicted the textile industry, stretched to support too many people: John and his wife and a child due in September; and Josiah with his wife and two children, with a third born in May 1683. Old Thomas Franklin, their father, had died in John's house at Banbury on March 21, 1662, at the age of eighty-four; but even with him gone, the business would be supporting eight people before 1683 ended. Clearly, it was indicated that, to support his young family, Josiah would have to find a place other than Banbury in which to pursue his trade. His brother, Benjamin the Elder, recalled, ". . . things not succeeding there according to his [Josiah's] mind, with the leave of his friends and father he went to New England in the year 1683. . . ."

Benjamin the Elder's words suggested that economic prudence at least as much as religious conviction accounted for Josiah's decision to leave England for Boston. The economic situation bears him out. Although the Cromwell revolution had released the death grip in which the monarchy had held the English economy and the Restoration in turn had promoted a degree of stability, the final transition of England from an agrarian to a predominantly mercantile-industrial society had not yet been fully

[4] Benjamin Franklin the Elder (1650–1727), "A Short Account of the Family of Thomas Franklin of Ecton in Northamptonshire." The manuscript identified the Warwickshire home of Ann Jeffs as "Marson," but there is no such village in Warwickshire. *Papers*, I, li, refers to it as "Marston." But it was almost certainly Marton, which lay seventeen miles north of Banbury on the road to Coventry. John Franklin did not long survive his marriage, dying in Banbury in 1691 at forty-eight, after lancing a boil in his crotch without medical help and thereby causing a gangrenous infection.

achieved. The Statute of Apprentices of 1563, for example, was in effect throughout the seventeenth century and, in some respects, into the eighteenth, including its provision for compulsory service in husbandry by all not exempt because of independent means or service in certain specified occupations; and two years after the Restoration, Parliament passed an act prohibiting weavers in East Anglia from working at their looms from mid-August until mid-September, when they were expected to work bringing in the harvest.[5]

Nor had the artisan—still working for the most part, except for the extracting industries such as coal and iron, in his own home—yet arrived at a level of living that fully compensated for his giving up the life on the land that had assured him of food, fuel, and lodging of sorts, even if little more. Hence, though he was somewhat ahead of his farmer-forebears in pence and shillings, he was still far from out of economic peonage. In the decade that Josiah Franklin left Banbury for Boston, there were an estimated 1,348,586 households in England and Wales with a total income of £44,886,020. Three per cent of the families received about 30 per cent of the total income, while at the other end of the scale nearly 60 per cent received less than 20 per cent of total family income—which meant that more than half of the people of England under the last of the Stuarts were living on the brink of poverty.[6] Even with diets limited to bread, cheese, and beer (which alone took two thirds of a working family's income), the annual cost of living exceeded wages paid. In 1683 the minimal cost of living was estimated by Chief Justice Sir Matthew Hale as twenty-six pounds a year—when the annual income of eight out of thirteen English households was less than twenty pounds.[7] The result of this difference was that the great majority of English families in the seventeenth century lived out their lives in a manner so sparse as, physically, to mean little more than mere survival. After spending two thirds of its income on food, the average family paid another fifth of it—about five pounds—for fuel, rent, and clothes. This left one pound for everything else, such as soap and candles, which were regarded less as necessities than luxuries. Skilled artisans, such as the Franklins were, did somewhat better than these figures, which represent the income of unskilled workers, but only to the degree that they could afford an occasionally more varied diet, pay a slightly higher rent, and use soap and candles with less punishing frugality. On the other hand, the tradesman was subject to the vagaries of an economic system in which he had no voice; and the seasonal character of many of its elements frequently left him in eager pursuit of work as a farm hand for minimal wages that provided only bare sustenance.

[5] *Statutes*, V, 373 (1662).
[6] These statistics were compiled for 1688 by Gregory King, a statistician, who, after making some sampling surveys, estimated the number of families in each socioeconomic category, the number of individuals in each category, and the yearly income. In appendix to Sir George Clark, *The Wealth of England from 1496 to 1760* (London, 1946).
[7] Sir Matthew Hale, *Discourse Touching Provision for the Poor* (London, 1683), 6.

The amount of toil that went into the eking out of this scant existence was prodigious. The normal working day was twelve hours, but few independent artisans could limit themselves to that in periods when work was plentiful. Domestic artisans were wholly dependent upon entrepreneurs who acquired the raw material and from whom one craftsman after another, working in their own cottages, picked it up to process it. The finished product was then returned to the entrepreneur, who sold it. In the textile industry, always subject to depressed interludes because of rises in imports or drops in domestic consumption, the home artificers made the most of prosperous periods, seeking to earn enough to weather any barren spell. A vade mecum written, in 1675, for the spiritual guidance of those in the weaver's trade or contemplating it, observed ". . . many a poor weaver sits at his loom from four in the morning till eight, nine, ten at night, but to get seven, eight or ten shillings a week for a livelihood"[8] —a total of from sixteen to eighteen hours out of every twenty-four, which would seem to leave little time for any response to spiritual guidance short of total resignation. If the artisan worked on his employer's premises, he was little better off than those who labored at home. The Statute of Apprentices of 1563—for two centuries the controlling legislation on labor— required ". . . all artificers and labourers . . . betwixt the middle of the months of March and September be and continue at work at or before 5 of the clock in the morning and continue at work and not depart until betwixt 7 and 8 of the clock at night . . . and between the middle of September and the middle of March shall be and continue from the spring of the day in the morning until the night of the same day, except it be in time afore appointed for breakfast and dinner. . . ."[9]

For the English artisan, then, in the days of Josiah Franklin, the business of earning a sparse living was incessant drudgery day after day, except for Sundays and the second Tuesday of every month, which the Puritans during Cromwell's regime, for all their austerity, declared an inviolate day of "recreation and relaxation."[10] And as the seventeenth century approached its last decade, that living was almost as uncertain as it was sparse—particularly for those, like the Franklins, who worked in the textile trades. For over half a century following the first ten years of Charles II's reign, the textile industry was in a state of recurring depressions.

Woolens were, of course, the great native industry from medieval times, but foreign manufacturers by the 1680s were cutting down England's exports and, in the case of Spain, for example, were even shipping cloth to England to be sold at lower prices than the domestic product. Flax, despite laws introduced by the Tudors requiring landowners to devote specific amounts of acreage to its growth in England, was raised cheaper and in greater amounts on the Continent. The cotton and silk industries

[8] *The Weaver's Pocket-Book or Weaving Spiritualized* (London, 1675), 84.
[9] *Statutes*, IV, Pt. i, 416.
[10] *Acts and Ordinances of the Interregnum* (London, 1647), I, 954.

were, of course, dependent upon Europe and Asia for their raw materials, and it speaks well for the genius of British mercantilism that, in spite of this dependence, England gained a commanding position in the manufacture of both fabrics. Nevertheless, though the English were superior in the manufacturing of cloth, they were inferior to the Low Countries and France in the finishing of it, and for decades a major dispute in Commons centered on whether the export of cloth "undyed or undressed" from England should be permitted, lest English finishers find their occupations disappearing. Licenses to export and prohibitions against it alternated unpredictably throughout the years of the Stuarts; and as the number of dyers in England increased, their prospects of steady employment became unpredictable. At the same time, the rigid provisions of the Statutes of Apprentices and of Artificers of 1563 were still in effect, making it impossible for men to shift from one trade to another and leaving the unemployed with only seasonal employment as farm laborers, occupying, at three and a half pounds a year, the lowest rung in the economic ladder.

To Josiah Franklin, a young man of twenty-five with a wife and three small children, the prospects for a dyer of cloth were at best cloudy. And so, "things not succeeding there according to his mind," he took his young family and left England, which, in the long life ahead of him, he was never to see again, for the town of Boston, three thousand miles of ocean and eight to twelve weeks of rough voyaging away. The family set sail from London, in the words of Benjamin the Elder, "at that time when the Noble Lord Russell was murdered." Lord Russell, an advocate of religious freedom convicted, on what was fully known to be fake testimony, of complicity in the anti-Catholic Rye House Plot to murder Charles II and his brother, the Duke of York (later, as James II, to become the third and last deposed monarch of England), was beheaded at Lincoln's Inn Fields on July 21, 1683. And so it was in midsummer of that year when the Franklins left for Boston.

* * *

The westward crossing of the Atlantic in 1683 was a long voyage. Nearly two centuries had passed since 1497, when the mariner Giovanni Caboto, having sailed for the first time the northern route from England to America, planted the flag of his native Venice and (as John Cabot, under the patronage of Henry VIII) the banner of St. George, on the bleak North American coast somewhere between Cape Breton and Labrador; with a crew of eighteen it had taken him seven and a half weeks to make the nineteen-hundred-mile voyage from Bristol. In 1602 Bartholomew Gosnold, the first mariner to sail a direct course from England to New England, took seven weeks and two days for the much longer voyage from Falmouth in Cornwall to Hampton, New Hampshire. In the later seventeenth century, it took at least as long; and, with larger, more cumbersome vessels manned by crews of over fifty and carrying a score or more pieces of heavy ordnance, it often took longer. The *Mayflower*, with 102 passengers and crew aboard, took nearly ten weeks in the autumn of 1620. The *Arabella*, bearing John Winthrop and the first permanent settlers of Boston, took over nine weeks in the passage from Southampton in the spring of 1630. Fifty-three years later, sailing early in August and not arriving in Boston until sometime in October, the ship carrying the young Franklin family took at least as long.

Oceanic sailing vessels, virtually unchanged since the age of the Tudor explorers, were still in 1683 stubby, high-pooped leviathans. In defiance of every principle of dynamics, these three-masted, bark-rigged ships pushed rather than sliced their path through mountainous seas. Even such small advances as the jib sail at the bowsprit and the steering wheel, replacing the ancient whipstaff aft, were years away. The lumbering frigates, when they were not squatting becalmed, bobbed and plodded their way at a pace ranging in average speeds of from thirty-five to fifty-five miles a day, or about two knots.

The seemingly interminable duration of the voyage was matched by its discomfort. On the high seas, the barks of the seventeenth century did not sail serenely. Heaving and rolling, they plunged deep into the troughs between waves that broke around them and then rose dizzily on their crests only to crash again. Decks were constantly awash, often sweeping desperately needed cattle into the sea. Meanwhile, the winds howled and rang for days on end in the ship's shrouds. The combination of boisterous winds and violent motion made sleep in the crowded quarters at best sporadic and, at worst, impossible. Seasickness, of course, was common—particularly during the first weeks out, and both cures and sympathy were in short supply. Accidents, to seamen aloft in the rigging during tempests and to unwary passengers on deck, were frequent. Deaths at sea, especially among little children, were ordinary, with almost every vessel reporting on arrival one or two such instances and sometimes a score or more.

Every functional aspect of daily living—sleeping, sanitation, ventilation, exercise, eating—was in one way or another severely reduced to a level of captive survival. Bathing was impossible. Drinking water, dependent on rainstorms for replenishment, was at a premium. During storms, passengers could remain on deck and be drenched or crowd in the musty cabin below for hour after hour of near suffocation. When illness occurred, as it did inevitably, there was no space to isolate the stricken, and the slightest contagion ran through the whole complement of passengers and crew. And through it all, the diet was almost punitive in nature and as monotonous as it was dreary: salt pork, salt beef, and salt cod; hard bicuits and rancid butter (if any at all); coarse oatmeal and dried peas; beer and cider. The total abstinence from fresh fruits and vegetables for periods of up to three months bore its toll in scurvy and other vitamin-deficiency disorders.

The unhappy voyages more often than not ended with vessels limping into port, their passengers bruised, exhausted, and malnourished. For the Franklins, with two very young children and a babe in arms, the ordeal must have been particularly trying. But they had youth on their side, Josiah being only twenty-five, and they had also the zest of a new land and a new life directly ahead of them. And on the October day when their ship put into Boston Harbor, after all those weary days and weeks at sea, it must have seemed, for all its forlornness as contrasted to the busy ports of England, inviting and welcome.

At first sight from sea, however, the Outer Harbor of Boston was more formidable than hospitable. Great rocks off Marblehead and Nahant lay to the starboard. Larboard, the channel into the Inner Harbor, afforded only narrow and perilous passage between the hills of Point Allerton on the mainland and the jagged rocks of a cluster of barren islands named for Elder Brewster, in 1621, by Myles Standish and nine friends, who ventured up the coast from Plymouth with three Indians as guides to find out what was there. In 1683 the islands of the Outer Harbor were still uninhabited, either too rocky for vegetation or heavily wooded. As a ship passed westward toward the Inner Harbor, the islands became more numerous, and signs of human habitation appeared—pastures with cattle and sheep grazing, farm lands and orchards that provided the hilly peninsular town of Boston with its food supply, gallows from which pirates were hanged, fishing weirs, sawyers' sheds, and occasionally wrecked shallops that did not make it through the devious passages among the islands. The names of the islands were revealing of either their use or their shape: Sheep's Island, Apple, Hog, Hangman's, Graves, Long Island, Pigg, Deer, Green, Bird, Calf, Nut. Dominating them all as the Inner Harbor was approached was Castle Island, so named because, even before a fortification was built there in 1634, it stood so high and impregnable as to resemble a natural buttress against any unfriendly vessels bent on reaching the town of Boston two and a half miles beyond. In 1683 the fourth in a succession of castlelike forts was perched atop the island, its twenty-three mounted guns affording a full sweep of the channel while seven others stabbed out directly into a ship's course from a battery below.

Once beyond Castle Island, the arriving vessel was in the Inner Harbor. To the south were the broad flats, flooded at high tide, of Dorchester at the bay of Roxbury and to the north, the Charles River, whose wide mouth had deceived Captain John Smith in 1614 into thinking that the river "doth pearce many daies journeis the intralles of that Countrey."[11] Between them there jutted out into the harbor the fistlike peninsula called by the Indians "Shawmut"—the place of living fountains—because of its many fresh-water springs, which accounted for John Winthrop's party settling there in 1630. The natural surroundings of Boston never failed to impress early travelers: the broad expanses of water virtually making the town an island save for a thin neck of land to the west; the scores of islands dotting the Outer and Inner harbors; the marshes stretching out

[11] Edward Arber and A. G. Bradley, eds., *Travels and Works of Captain John Smith* (Edinburgh, 1910), 100.

behind the town; and three great hills, on the highest of which stood a
gaunt column from which a fire pot was suspended for use as a beacon,
dominating lesser hills, one with a fort, another with a windmill, which
crowded the little town right down to the edge of the sea. To the voyagers
aboard the ship carrying the Franklin family, the prospect of the town was
much as it was to an observant traveler, William Wood, who first saw it
four years after its settlement:

> [Its] situation is very pleasant, being a *Peninsula,* hem'd in on the South-
> side with the Bay of *Roxberry,* on the North-side with *Charles-river,* the
> Marshes on the back-side, being not halfe a quarter of a mile over, so that
> a little fencing will secure their Cattle from the Woolves. Their greatest
> wants be Wood, and Medow-ground, which never were in that place; being
> constrayned to fetch their building-timber, and fire-wood from the Ilands
> in Boates, and their Hay in Loyters: It being a necke and bare of wood:
> they are not troubled with three great annoyances, of Woolves, Rattle-
> snakes, and Musketoes. These that live here upon their Cattle, must be
> constrayned to take Farmes in the Countrey, or else they cannot subsist;
> the place being too small to containe many, and fittest for such as can
> Trade into *England,* for such commodities as the Countrey wants, being
> the chiefe place for shipping and merchandize.
>   This *necke of land* is not above foure miles in compasse, in forme al-
> most square, having on the South-side at one corner, a great broad hill,
> whereon is planted a Fort, which can command any ship as shee sayles
> into any Harbour within the still Bay. On the North side is another Hill,
> equall in bignesse, whereon stands a Winde-mill. From the top of this
> Mountaine a man may over-looke all the Ilands which lie before the Bay,
> and discry such ships as are upon the Sea-coast.[12]

Since Wood's visit, the town had erected the beacon atop the highest of
the three hills called Trimountain—later abbreviated to Tremont. The
central hill, rising to a height of 138 feet, had been called Sentry Hill from
the beginning of the settlement, but in 1634 the beacon was installed so
that the sentry on duty could light it and warn the countryside should any
dangers arise. Protruding from the peculiarly flat top of the hill, the beacon was a tall, unsightly pole of sixty-five feet, with crosspieces serving as
foot rungs and a black iron pot full of oil suspended from a spar. Visible
for miles around from sea and land, it bore grim resemblance to a gallows.
On a lower hill to the north, which rose fifty feet above the water, the oldest of the town's three or four windmills stood, its commanding position
giving it the advantage of any winds. And to the southeast of Trimountain, close to the point where incoming ships approached the Town Dock,
stood Fort Hill, on the waterside abrupt and rugged for its eighty feet of
height and on the shoreside rising gently and gradually; and on its broad
summit stood a stockade which guarded the Inner Harbor. Between
Windmill Hill and Fort Hill and cowering below the brooding heights of

---

[12] *New England Prospects* (London, 1634), quoted in Nathaniel B. Shurtleff, A
Topographical and Historical Description of Boston (Boston, 1871), 40–41.

Tremont was the town of Boston, nestled like a miniature village along the edge of the sea—the steeples of its four churches, the cupolas of its two public buildings, a Town House and a Province House, and the chimneys of its 750 houses standing out above streets that even in the town's infancy had become crowded with structures because of the limited space. A Huguenot refugee, coming to Boston at the same time of the year as the Franklins did (though four years later, in October 1687), wrote a description of the town as approached by sea for the guidance of fellow migrants from France:

> We sighted Cape Coot [Cod], which is twenty Leagues from Boston towards the South, and on the Morrow we arrived at Boston, after having fallen in with a Number of very pretty Islands that lie in Front of Boston, most of them cultivated and inhabited by Peasants, which form a very fine View. Boston is situated at the Head of a Bay possibly three or four Leagues [nine or twelve miles] in Circumference, shut in by the Islands of which I have told you. Whatever may be the Weather, Vessels lie there in Safety. The town is built on the Slope of a little Hill, and is as large as La Rochelle. The Town and the Land outside are not more than three Miles in Circuit, for it is almost an Island; it would only be necessary to cut through a Width of three hundred Paces, all Sand, which in less than twice twenty-four Hours would make Boston an Island washed on all Sides by the Sea. The Town is almost wholly built of wooden Houses; but since there have been some ravages by Fire, building of Wood is no longer allowed. . . .[13]

The natural beauty of the surroundings of this young town, little more than half a century old and of less than six thousand souls, set so close to the sea as to seem almost a part of it, was striking: the blue harbor, dotted by green islands punctuated here and there by the mottled rocks; the golden grasses of the marshes all around; the tall hills behind the town and the gentler hills on each side; and the village itself—the steeples, the chimneys, and the few cupolas—catching the shifting sunlight as it rose over the water and set behind the marshes. And of all the times of the year, all this was at its fairest in October, when the sky and water were radiant in the clear air, the many hues of autumn were beginning to emblazon the hills, and the climate was both gentle and bracing.

* * *

The brightness of the economic outlook for the Franklin family may have seemed to them to match that of their new surroundings. Their passage had cost them, at the rates then current, from eight to ten pounds for the two adults and whatever they may have bargained for with the ship's master for the three children—perhaps four or five pounds additional. This bold investment of up to fifteen pounds would have represented the

---

[13] Anonymous MS in the Library of Geneva, quoted in Shurtleff, *Description of Boston*, 47ff.

total earnings of an artisan for a period of six months or more.[14] When weighed against the economic prospects of New England, however, the speculation was far from hazardous. The comparative brightness of those prospects was, by 1683, well known in old England, and unquestionably word of this had reached the Franklins in Banbury. Extravagantly as they may have been reported in the accounts of some travelers, there was a steady stream of informative, reasonably realistic accounts comparable to that written by the Huguenot settler to aid his fellow refugees, whom he would have had no purpose in attempting to deceive.

There were three basic factors that were of controlling significance to a migrant who would have to earn a living on his arrival: the demand for labor, skilled and unskilled; wages; and the cost of materials, including food. On all three counts, the outlook for the arriving Franklins was wholly reassuring, if the Huguenot's report can be believed, though it was addressed largely to people of some means: "You can bring with you hired Help in any Vocation whatever; there is an absolute Need for them to till the Land. You may also own Negroes and Negresses; there is not a House in Boston, however small may be its Means, that has not one or two. There are those that have five or six, and all make a good Living. You employ Savages to work your Fields, in Consideration of one Shilling and a half a Day and Board, which is eighteen pence; it being always understood that you must provide them with Beasts or Utensils for Labor."[15] Since unskilled labor in England at the time, working the fields, earned fourteen pence a day,[16] as compared to the New Englander's thirty-six pence, including board, the earning power of labor was considerably enhanced.

In the case of most of the necessities of life more could be bought in New England with the money earned—which meant a generally higher standard of living. "Pasturage abounds here," the Huguenot pamphleteer wrote. "You can raise every kind of Cattle, which thrive well. An Ox costs from twelve to fifteen Crowns; a Cow, eight to ten; Horses from ten to fifty Crowns, and in Plenty. There are even wild ones in the Woods, which are yours if you can catch them. Foals are sometimes caught. Beef costs two Pence the Pound; Mutton, two Pence; Pork from two to three Pence, according to the Season; Flour fourteen Shillings the one hundred and twelve Pound, all bolted; Fish is very cheap, and Vegetables also; Cabbage, Turnips, Onions and Carrots abound here. Moreover, there are Quantities of Nuts, Chestnuts, and Hazelnuts wild. These Nuts are small but of wonderful Flavor. I have been told that there are other Sorts which we shall see in the Season. I am assured that the Woods are full of Strawberries in their Season. I have seen Quantities of wild Grapevine, and eaten grapes of very good Flavor, kept by one of my Friends. There is no

---

[14] In 1689 the cost of a single adult passage was five pounds, as recorded in the financial records of King's Chapel, Henry Wilder Foote, *Annals of King's Chapel* (Boston, 1882), I, 110.

[15] Shurtleff, *Description of Boston*, 48.

[16] E. Lipson, *The Economic History of England*, 3rd ed. (London, 1943), II, 388.

doubt that the Vine will do very well; there is some little planted in the Country, which has grown.

"The Rivers are full of Fish, and we have so great a Quantity of Sea and River Fish that no account is made of them."[17]

To make the most of this economic Elysium, Josiah Franklin had to establish himself as soon as possible in a trade. He found that in an essentially frontier society, the most pressing demand was not for dyers—particularly silk dyers. The basis of the economy in frontier societies necessarily was the exporting of raw materials, if they could be spared, and not their importing, and the importing of finished materials, if they were essential, rather than their exporting. Silk was not essential. It was costly to import, either as thread or as finished cloth. As for exporting finished cloth, if the competing countries of Europe had found the product of England inferior to their own, it was unlikely that an English colonial outpost across the sea would do better. So little dyeing, in fact, went on in the colonies during the last quarter of the seventeenth century that virtually all dyewoods were declared "enumerated commodities"—that is, they were to be exported to British ports overseas. Moreover, in Massachusetts, the use of silk as apparel, dyed or undyed, was forbidden all those below the highest rank or income: ". . . that men or women of meane condition should take uppon them the garbe of gentlemen by wearinge gold or silk lace, or buttons, or poynts, at their knees, or to walke in great boots, or women of the same ranke to wear silke or taffeta hoods, or scarfs, which though allowable to persons of greater estates or more liberal education, yet we cannot but judge them intolerable in persons of such like condition."[18] Aside from this blunt discouragement of the general wearing of silk, the price of the cloth ruled it out for all but a handful of the richest. In the New England of the 1680s, it cost but nine shillings to make a broadcloth coat for a man, while it cost over three times that amount, a pound and eight shillings, for "makeing a silk laced Gowne for Mrs."[19]

Josiah Franklin was far too shrewd to attempt to establish himself in a trade that had neither the unqualified approval of the governing nor the broad patronage of the governed. But in Massachusetts—unlike England—there was no law against moving from one trade to another. Accordingly, he moved to one that dealt in basic needs and one also that, unlike dyeing with its intricate chemistry, was uncomplicated to master. He became a tallow chandler.

Tallow was the essential ingredient in soap and candles, the use of neither of which was forbidden those "of meane condition." The market, therefore, was unlimited and would grow with the population. Oddly enough, too, it was not an overcrowded trade. For most of the first fifty

[17] Shurtleff, *Description of Boston*, 49.
[18] General Laws of The Massachusetts Colony.
[19] MS accounting, "Mr. Jonathan Corwin Debtor to William Sweatland," in American Antiquarian Society.

years of the settlements of New England, tallow was in extremely short supply, because cattle were limited and slaughtered only sparingly. As late as 1676, seven years before the arrival of Josiah Franklin, when 129 "Handycraftsmen" of Boston petitioned the General Court to protect them from the competition of newcomers' opening shops in their trades, there was not a single soap or candle maker among them. And of forty-one occupations listed for property owners in *The Book of Possessions*, the first roster of Boston property owners compiled in the mid-1600s, and for members of the First Church, there was but one mention of a tallow chandler as compared to twelve shoemakers, eleven tailors, three brewers, and two vintners.[20] The making of soap was, during those early years, an annual domestic task, usually undertaken by housewives in the autumn and using the entire year's accumulation of refuse grease to make enough soap to last the next year. The operation was a dreary business, involving making lye from pouring water over barrels containing six bushels of fireplace ashes until the lye seeped through outlets, and then boiling the lye with the grease in a great kettle. It took all day, and the result was an unappealing jellylike mass that was doled out by the cupful over the year for household washes that were limited to monthly or bimonthly occasions in order to make the most of each use of the precious soap. As for candles, they too were either made at home, usually from the vegetable fat of the bayberry bush, or dispensed with altogether and replaced by torches made of candlewood, a euphemism for the fat, tar-drenched pitch pine that abounded along the New England coast. When candles were made at home, the work was laborious, requiring constant attention and producing as a result of a long day's work no more than a few scores of candles.

By the time Josiah Franklin arrived in Boston, however, some of the burdens of a frontier life were beginning to be lightened significantly. Cattle, for example, were no longer a rarity, with the results that such by-products as leather and tallow became less scarce, and although the greatest part of daily life was monotonous travail for many, some amenities were emerging in the lives of most and, in the case of the growing number of affluent, some luxuries as well. The latter included candles, which were sold largely to public buildings and to a few of the richer inhabitants. And tallow generally was gradually becoming a product to be bought to supplement that supplied by kitchen leavings. It is quite probable that Josiah Franklin made and sold some soap at the outset of his Boston establishment, but his primary business was a dealer in tallow, buying fat from slaughterhouses and reducing it to usable forms for the town's households, and secondarily making and selling candles.

Having settled on a trade, Josiah Franklin needed to find a building in which to practice it and to house his family. He found one in the heart of

---

[20] *The Book of Possessions of the Inhabitants of the Town of Boston*, an inventory of real estate owned by the inhabitants, was authorized by the General Court in 1634 but appears to have been compiled much later, sometime between 1646 and 1652.

the town, across Fort Street from the cedar meetinghouse of the Third (South) Church and just a few yards from the High Street (now Washington Street[21]), the main thoroughfare of the town dominated by Peter Sergeant's handsome three-story brick house that faced down Fort Street toward the sea. Fort Street (now Milk Street) ran vaguely west to east and extended but a short distance until it passed over a creek. On the north side of the street, at the corner of the High Street was the somber, brooding presence of the meetinghouse, pleasantly set on what had been Governor Winthrop's green and the site of his house. Behind the church, down as far as the creek, were only three houses, sufficiently impressive to be referred to as mansions and set spaciously on grounds that stretched through to the next street to the north. But on the south side of Fort Street, with roughly the same amount of frontage, were crowded nine houses, most of them small and originally built and occupied by artisans. The westernmost of these properties, running from the corner of the High-Street directly opposite the meetinghouse, belonged, in 1783, to Nathaniel Reynolds, who had inherited it from his father, Robert, a shoemaker. *The Book of Possessions* listed the Reynolds house as being on the corner, and the house immediately east of it as belonging to John Stevenson, also a shoemaker. The latter was a tiny house, situated on a plot only about thirty feet wide, and was apparently later acquired by Robert Reynolds some time subsequent to 1646, when the house twice changed owners.[22] Nathaniel Reynolds, in addition to following his father's trade of shoemaker, was the town's inspector of leather, a constable, and a lieutenant in the militia. He also owned other real estate in Boston and seems from the frequency of transactions recorded in the register of deeds to have been something of a property speculator. In November 1683, a month after Josiah Franklin arrived, Reynolds mortgaged the Fort Street house, then occupied by young Robert Breck, an old South member, and his family. Shortly afterward, Reynolds left Boston for Rhode Island, and Breck left the Fort Street house, probably for less humble quarters. And Josiah and Ann Franklin, with their three children, moved in, unquestionably greatly satisfied, after the uncertain years at Banbury and the long ocean voyage, to have at last a home.

The house was a small peaked-roof frame building of two and a half stories, the side of it, twenty feet across, facing the street and its front, even less in length, opening on a narrow alley. The ground floor was one room—a combined dining and living area—with two windows looking out

[21] The nomenclature of the High Street changed with the political status of Boston: It became Marlborough Street in 1708, in honor of the duke, and Washington Street in 1789, in honor of the general. Fort Street had become Milk Street by 1708, probably after Milk Street, London.

[22] Justin Winsor, ed., *The Memorial History of Boston*, II, xxix, states, regarding John Stevenson, "His widow married William Blackstone, and the lot passed in 1646 to Abraham Page; and then, same year, to John Hansett of Roxbury; but the spot got its chief glory sixty years later when Benjamin Franklin was born here." Stevenson's widow did not marry Blackstone until 1659.

onto the street and another window and a door onto the alley, and an enormous fireplace used for both cooking and heating and apparently also, at least in the earliest days of the Franklins there, for processing the tallow. There was also on the ground floor a closet and an entryway, with a flight of stairs leading up to the second floor and another flight to the basement. At the rear, in a drawing of the house done years later after its Franklin associations had conferred fame on it, there appears a shed-roofed single-story addition; but it was a rather ramshackle affair and looks as if it were attached—possibly as a wood shed, storage pantry, or kitchen —much later. The second story of the house, which protruded a few inches out from the first, consisted also of but one room; and the third floor was merely an unfinished attic with a window at each end. There was a cellar, with a bulkhead door opening onto the street. Only the streetside of the house was clapboarded, the other walls being covered, like the roof, with rough-hewn shingles.[23] Modest as it was, the little house presented a cozy, pleasant aspect. Its windows were large for its size and offered agreeable vistas of the churchyard across the street, the busy corner of the High Street with Sergeant's great cupola-topped house looking down on it, and, all around, its counterparts of shingle and clapboard, bustling with children, home-operated crafts and shops, and small gardens.

For a man of Josiah Franklin's sturdiness and self-sufficiency, moreover, it was a manageable establishment. And with his peers all along Fort Street and along the street behind him, he would be sharing in a common quest, making his own way in the new land and getting into league with his God, his conscience, and his fellow man. To aid him in all this, there stood across the street the South Church, youngest of the Congregational churches in Boston and the most liberal—the first chink in the iron armor of the John Cotton/Increase Mather/Cotton Mather Puritan heirarchy, which had, for fifty years, constituted an ecclesiastical, intellectual, and social dictatorship more absolute in Boston than the political dictatorship of Oliver Cromwell ever aspired to be in England.

---

[23] The description is based on Shurtleff, *Description of Boston*, 615ff., which has some inconsistencies and the perils of the memory of an old gentleman known to Shurtleff as having been born in the house not long before its destruction by fire in 1810. Moreover, the house was rebuilt at least once, for Judge Sewall reported that the house was burned in 1690 (*Diary*, I, 330).

V

Compromise in Zion

> . . . I think vital Religion has always suffer'd when Orthodoxy is more regarded than Virtue.
>
> —Benjamin Franklin[1]

The South Church, where Josiah Franklin "owned the covenant" on September 27, 1865, two years after his arrival in Boston, came into being, not in fulfillment of the Puritan quest for the Heavenly City, but as the product of a bitter dispute that both reflected and, to an extent, advanced the inevitable collapse of a utopian vision that, for all its stern intellectualizing in a community devoted to learning, was dependent for its survival upon the wistful political fantasy that a band of pious men could declare themselves the elect of God and persuade all others to abide by their judgments. The Puritans in their American experiment sought, in all earnestness, to establish in the New England wilderness, in isolated remoteness from the ceremonial hegemony of an episcopacy and the inevitable ambivalence of a state-subservient church, a religious order rooted only in the Scriptures and dedicated not partly to the aggrandizement of the state but solely to the glorification of God. But the institutions they created to bring this about were essentially, probably necessarily, political—beginning with the concept of the covenant itself.

The implement by which the elect were to bring about God's kingdom on earth was, of course, the church. But the church was to be self-governing, which is to say by its own members, and the "form" by which this was to be achieved was the covenant—the agreement under which those of the congregation "submitted to the watch of the Church" by owning the covenant to be a true exposition of the relationship that existed among God, who was a kind of party of the first part, the church, which was a party of the second part, and the individual who, for all practical purposes, made the second party his exclusive agent for all dealings with the first party. The whole authority of the church derived from this consent of the individual to subject himself to the church's discipline. Neither

[1] Draft letter to his parents, April 13, 1738, in *Papers*, II, 202.

his pastor nor his brethren had any mystical, divinely inspired or historic authority over him unless he owned the covenant and thereby voluntarily submitted himself to their authority. This keystone of the Puritan version of ecclesiasticism was less the product of any direct democratic impulse than an explicit reaction against the externally imposed authority of the crown-appointed bishops in the Church of England and their claims to the apostolic succession as the source of their authority. The priesthood of the Puritans, mutually ordained as it was, and their lay leadership—the elders and deacons—never meant the covenant to be an avenue either to individual self-determinism or to popular sovereignty. The theory of the church covenant, which was no part of Puritanism in England (though the general covenant between God and man ingrained in Hebraic and Christian literature was the subject of new emphasis in Calvinist homiletics everywhere) was the product primarily of New England Puritanism— an expedient that provided for conferring upon the churches authority that they could not otherwise claim without encountering an indefensible contradiction of the very grounds on which they had repudiated the authority of the Anglican bishops. But those who subscribed to the covenants of the New England churches did not by that act assume a voice in the government of their churches; they simply attested their consent to be governed—a concept in the exegesis of democracy as old in English politics as Magna Carta.

This limited vision of democracy was implicit in the Puritan proposition from the beginning of its American development. John Cotton, for thirty years teacher of the First Church in Boston and a close friend of John Winthrop, the first governor of the colony, was driven, in 1636, to putting it rather more starkly than most of his colleagues in the colony's clerical or civil life, when his friend, the First Viscount Saye and Sele, pressed him on the curious matter of only church members' being allowed to vote or to hold public office. After being publicly accused by the Lord Chancellor, the Earl of Clarendon, of being "the oracle of all those who were called Puritans in the worst sense," the viscount had written Cotton suggesting that he had been giving some thought to migrating to Boston but expressing some reservations about the severely restricted franchise. John Cotton made no evasions in his reply, effectively altering the viscount's intentions: "Democracy, I do not conceyve that ever God did ordeyne as a fitt government eyther for church or commonwealth. If the people be governors, who shall be governed?"[2] But Cotton was a man of considerable insight into political systems and of considerable agility in Congregational apologetics, and he unquestionably knew that, in his private letter to the viscount, he was vastly oversimplifying a drift toward self-rule in the Western world with which the premises of Puritanism were as essentially

[2] John Cotton to Lord Saye and Sele. The comment has been much quoted, but for its full context, see Thomas Hutchinson, *History of Massachusetts Bay*, 3rd ed. (Salem, 1795), I, 437.

in conflict as they were with the Church of England. The overriding premise of Puritanism was pessimistic—that the dismal fate of man was sealed. That of democracy was optimistic—full of confidence in humankind's capacity to shape its own destiny.

Despite all this, there were deep in the Puritan awareness—so deep as to constitute a determining part of the Puritan character—democratic ingredients that were bound to surface and ultimately undo the wilderness Zion as the haven of religious elitists. As generic characteristics of the Puritans, these forces may have had their origin in the cartilaginous doctrine of Calvinism, but they owed their development to the wilderness surroundings that rendered them less virtues than requisites: ". . . we are brought out of a fat land into a wilderness," wrote Peter Bulkeley, the first teacher of the Church at Concord, "and here we met with necessities."[3] For the wilderness experience was a basic element in the Puritans' venture, not alone because only in the wilderness would they be safely distant from the intrusion of extraneous liturgies and corrupt institutions, but also because survival there was in itself a test of their determination to bring about God's kingdom on earth and, in the process, to prove themselves worthy of the place reserved for the chosen in the eternal realm above; and they saw their ordeal as a counterpart of the ordeal of Christ in the wilderness on the eve of the crucifixion. And so basic traits essential to participants in a workable democratic process began to inhere in the builders of the wilderness Zion, as much forced upon them by their surroundings as inspired in them by their convictions. These were self-reliance; a respect for the individual; a sense of duty, of accountability, and of responsibility; the recognition of the need to know; and, finally, a groping toward egalitarianism—not absolute but to the extent that every man had the right as well as the responsibility to make up his own mind and pay the penalty if he turned out to be wrong, very much as Josiah Franklin's father, in Ecton, was determined to read the Bible for himself and make up his own mind as to its meaning. And even though the dynamics of Puritanism and democracy had little in common, these common traits moved the former, for all its rigidity and tenacity, inexorably toward the latter.

The first traumatic evidences of this appeared in 1662, when the firm grip of the elect on the government of both the churches and the commonwealth was severely shakened. There were two basic assumptions involved. One was that every congregation was capable of being its sole master, even the pastor having to become a member of that congregation before he could be called to its pastorate. A parallel assumption was that the commonwealth, since it existed for the sake of the church rather than as an equal entity, should be governed by the same people who governed the churches. "It is better that the commonwealth be fashioned to the set-

---

[3] Peter Bulkeley, *The Gospel Covenant* (London, 1646), 143.

ting forth of Gods house, which is his church: than to accomodate the church frame to the civill state," John Cotton told Lord Saye and Sele.[4] And those who did the fashioning were the members of the churches.

Membership in a church was a difficult and for many, even of the pious, an impossible thing to achieve. It involved the presentation of evidence satisfactory to the church's leadership, that the supplicant had experienced a "conversion"—a kind of new birth in his maturity, a divine revelation visited upon him of his unworthiness and at the same time of his being among those singled out from all the unworthy sinners since Adam for salvation. This central episode in the life of a church member was, in his mind, no vague occurrence. The elect, the "visible saints," could remember all their lives the very day and hour of it. Their public testimony of it was soaring, fearful, at once agonized and jubilant but always awe-stricken and astonished, even though their whole lives had been directed to this momentous event. The core, as it was, of the whole Puritan experience and, what is more, of the whole Puritan assertion, it was also, paradoxically, the epitome of such non-Puritan qualities as subjectivity and anti-intellectualism. Nevertheless, it was the key both to the individual Puritan's personal fulfillment and to the perpetuation of the Puritan community, the Heavenly City; for only the children of the converted could be baptized and they, in their turn, would become converted, thus forever renewing and reinvigorating the churches. The difficulty was that, after the zeal of the first generation was spent and counterclaims to constant preoccupation with salvation were made on the attention of succeeding generations, there were not enough conversions and, therefore, not enough visible saints to provide new manna for baptism. The ageless capacity of men to adapt their religions to changing realities came to the rescue.

Although every church theoretically was its own master, the problem was first of all seen as besetting the whole Bible state and, therefore, had to be attacked colony-wide. For a decade and a half, from 1647 to 1662, the clergy mulled over the situation futilely. Finally, the Great and General Court ordered the churches to hold a synod and to come up with a solution. The synod came up with a recommendation that those eligible for baptism be expanded to include, in addition to the issue of the converted or full members of the churches, the children of those who showed no such evidence of grace but who had been themselves baptized and were not "scandalous in life and solemnly owning the Covenant." This doctrine, which came to be known as the Half-Way Covenant, creating a company of halfway members, was anathema to many of the elect, although the majority seemed to go along with it. But the critics, though smaller in number, were among the most powerful Puritan voices, with extremely close ties, familial or intellectual, with the founding fathers. Al-

[4] Hutchinston, *History of Massachusetts Bay*.

though Richard Mather, minister since its founding in 1636 of the church in Dorchester, originally contrived the halfway theory, his son and colleague, Increase, bitterly opposed it (years later he changed his mind when his pragmatism got the better of his theology); Increase's brother, Eleazar, minister of the church in Northampton, also opposed it; John Mayo, the pastor of Boston's influential Second Church, whom Increase Mather was to succeed, was against it; Charles Chauncy, the second president of Harvard, was not only against it but constituted himself a steering committee to mobilize further opposition; and John Davenport, founder of the New Haven colony and one of the most influential ministers in New England, was severely opposed to it. In characteristic Puritan fashion, the opponents of the Half-Way Covenant took to the lectern and the printing press with their differences, and the rhetoric flew far and wide. The two younger Mathers, with John Mayo and Charles Chauncy, published a tract based on the brief they had prepared for the General Court and, equally in Puritan fashion, did not spare their misguided brethren the most lashing language, referring to the enlargement of the right to baptism as "that practice that exposeth the blood of Christ to contempt, and baptism to profanation, the Church to pollution and the Commonwealth to confusion . . ."[5] and President Chauncy laid the whole disaster to incompetent lay delegates to the synod among the messengers from the thirty-four churches involved: "Divers of the Messengers being no Logitians, and so unable to answer Syllogismes, and discern Ambiguities, were overborn."[6] As for John Davenport, he was forever distressed at the perversity of the majority who favored the Half-Way Covenant; he wrote angrily to the son of Governor Winthrop, "God will soone take away the most godly and judicious leaders from so unthanckful and unworthy people, and leave them to be mislead by superficial verbalists."[7]

The verbal deluge reached unbelievable proportions and continued for years. Tract after tract appeared in endless succession, most of them verbose straining at gnats. The covenant, baptism, the intellectual status of the clergy, the dignity of the churches—all, pillars of Puritanism—were drastically diminished, as the obvious stratagem of the Half-Way Covenant to keep the supply of visible saints constant assumed the dimensions of a theological debate fraught less with conviction than with politics. Certainly, the claims of Puritanism to an intellectual, reasoned approach to the godly life came close to being reduced to an absurdity, as learned men argued fiercely the dire consequences of admitting the wrong newborn infants to the company of those eligible for salvation. And there arose a permeating awareness that the rhetoric was exhausting itself as

[5] "The Judgement of the Dissenting Brethren of the Synod," 29, in David Pulsifer, comp., *Papers Relating to the Synod of 1662*, Dexter Collection, Yale University.

[6] Charles Chauncy, *Anti-Synodalia Scripta Americana* (London, 1662), 5.

[7] Letter to John Winthrop, Jr., June 14, 1666, in I. B. Calder, ed., *The Letters of John Davenport: Puritan Divine* (New Haven, 1937), 264.

well as its victims and that the whole dispute would resolve itself on a political level.

*   *   *

The structure of the purified church in New England was essentially political. For all the authority, spiritual and temporal, that the Puritan priests read into their ministries, the ultimate power rested in their congregations. It was they who bestowed upon their pastors and teachers whatever authority they had or claimed to have. It was they who "called" them to their posts. It was they who constituted the corpus of the visible saints. And in their eagerness to be rid of bishops, the Puritan clergy rid themselves also of any appeal to earthly powers higher than their congregations —which left their own authority in fragile state indeed; for Congregationalism was constituted of self-governing political units, and political units are bound sooner or later to act politically. The Half-Way Covenant had severely and irreparably split the theological foundation of the Puritan church; it remained for the latter's political structure to be so shaken that it, too, would never be fully restored.

The arena for the dispute was, unseemly enough, Boston's First Church —the mother church of Puritanism, the church of John Cotton, chief articulator of the Puritan faith, and for twenty years the only church in Boston. Jealous of their elitism, not only as among the elect of God but as members of His primary outpost in the wilderness Zion, the majority of the members of the First Church had taken a very gloomy view of the Half-Way Covenant. Only the moderating force of John Wilson, their pastor from the church's founding, and of Cotton's successor as their teacher, John Norton, had stopped them from precipitating a crisis. Although most of their brethren in the other churches accepted the extension of baptism as inevitable, the First Church members resisted outright acceptance of the Half-Way Covenant; they were persuaded, however, by their ministers into at least a tentative tolerance of the new order. But Wilson died, after thirty-seven years at the First Church, in 1667, when indignation over the Half-Way Covenant was still fervid among his parishioners, and Norton had preceded him to the grave by four years, leaving the disgruntled church without either pastor or teacher.[8] Wilson's death occurred in August 1667, and for nearly a year and a half the First Church was without any clergy, as the members wrangled over the calling of the aged irreconcilable John Davenport from his pastorate at New Haven. Davenport's determined and consistent position against the Half-Way Covenant commended him highly to the First Church majority and equally condemned him to the liberal minority, who saw the death of the church in the resistance to the new doctrine.

[8] The ministers of the Puritan churches were first called "teachers" due to the emphasis on preaching over other pastoral functions. Wilson was made teacher at the First Church, in 1630, and became pastor in 1632. Norton joined him as teacher in 1633, the two leading the congregation as a team until Norton's death in 1663. He was not replaced during the remainder of Wilson's pastorate.

As for Davenport, who would be leaving his life work in New Haven, he was prepared, even eager, to do so. He considered his labors there ruined when the General Court of Connecticut at Hartford had voted, much against his will and his advocacy to the contrary, to unite his precious colony of New Haven, which he had founded in order to bring about "a yet stricter conformity to the *word of God*, in settling all matters, both *civil* and *sacred*, than he had yet seen exemplified in any other part of the world,"[9] with what he regarded as the less godly colony of Connecticut. But as congregations alone could call a pastor, they alone could release him, and Davenport's congregation refused to let him leave to accept the Boston call, particularly since the call, far from being unanimous, was stirring up in the First Church a controversy between the pro- and anti-Half-Way Covenanters that was to become more bitter in the political phase of the conflict than it had been in the doctrinal. In any case, in a stately, righteous, and circuitous letter to the Boston church, the New Haven congregation ended up by flatly refusing to let their pastor go—an extremely rare and not altogether charitable move—even though he had already sent assurances "of my strong inclynation to obey this call."[10] The New Haven congregation's letter to its Boston brethren was composed and signed by Davenport's clerical colleague, Nicholas Street, who reported that "with due Reverence to our Pastours Judgement, we can not but let you understand, that the Brethren have unanimously declared themselves to be of a different aprehention in this matter, we are also the less forward for to attend your motion (from what yourselves express) that the call of the church were not so unanimous as were to be desired, fearefull we are what his tender spirit now in his old age may meet with all on that account and what may be the sad consequence of trouble that may arise in a church divided about his call both to him and to yourselves. . . ."[11]

The New Haven letter turned out to be more distinguished for its prophecy than for its syntax. There was indeed a "sad consequence of trouble," due not only to the dissent of those First Church members who did not agree to the calling of John Davenport, but also to the concealment by the elders of the fact that Davenport's own congregation clearly and forcefully declined to dismiss him and to their reading to the congregation a forged version of a longer, second letter from the New Haven church that deleted all passages that once again clearly expressed its members' refusal to dismiss their pastor. Despite the protests of the First Church dissenters and his own congregation's dissent, Davenport accepted the call and was installed at the age of seventy-one as pastor of the First Church on December 9, 1668. At the same time, a thirty-six-year-old Oxonian, James Allen, a man of wealth and of stubbornly conservative convictions who had been ejected from his English parish in the Established

9 Mather, *Magnalia Christi Americana*, I, 325.
10 Hill, *Old South Church*, I, 18.
11 Ibid., 20.

Church by the Act of Uniformity of 1662, was installed as his teacher-colleague.

During all this display of deception and persistence, the dissenting minority of the First Church, conceding that their views would never get a fair hearing much less any consideration within the church, decided to ask for their dismissal from the congregation so that they could start a new church unafflicted with the obsolescent but determined conservatism of the ancient John Davenport, as he used the prestigious First Church as a platform from which to sound the last gasps of a theocracy that had seen its day. The twenty-eight dissenters were denied the right to withdraw. But they were among the most enlightened, well-established, and respected figures of Boston, with impressive family associations, and were not easily cowed. Among them were John Alden, the son of John Alden and Priscilla Mullins; Edward Raynsford, the brother of Lord Chief Justice Richard Raynsford and one of Winthrop's original settling company; Thomas Brattle, a wealthy merchant and father of the treasurer of Harvard College; Jacob Eliot, nephew of the "Apostle to the Indians," John Eliot, and son of a ruling elder of the First Church. The rest were eminent merchants, holders of high civil posts, and representatives of families who had had prominent associations with the First Church from its beginnings. Having no intention of remaining captives of the droning anachronisms of Davenport, they pressed their case through appeals to the other churches and their clergy, to the governor and his Council, and to the colony's legislature, the Great and General Court. All asserted the right of the dissenters to grants of formal dismissal from the First Church, without prejudice and freeing them to associate themselves with other congregations or a new one of their own. "Seventeen ministers bore a public testimony against the proceedings of the three elders[12] of The First Church in Boston, viz. against Mr. Davenport for leaving his church at New-Haven, contrary to his professed principles, and against all of them for communicating parcels [i.e., parts] only of letters from the church of New-Haven to the church in Boston, by which artifice the church was deceived, and made to believe the church of New-Haven consented to his dismission, when, if the whole had been read it would have appeared they did not. . . . There does not seem to have been that fairness and simplicity in their proceedings which the gospel requires."[13]

In the face of such vigorous support from the clerical community itself, the First Church could no longer restrain its dissenting members from going across the Charles River to Charlestown and starting a new congregation, which had the approval of seven magistrates and the endorsement of the clergy and lay elders of five other Massachusetts churches. But then the two houses of the Great and General Court fell into a dispute over

[12] The reference is to the Reverend John Davenport; to his colleague, the Reverend James Allen; and to the lay ruling elder, James Penn, a powerful Boston landowner, who had served in such posts as town overseer, selectman, and treasurer.
[13] Hutchinson, *History of Massachusetts Bay*, 3rd ed., I, 248.

granting permission for the founding and building of a church by the new congregation in Boston, with the upper house comprised of the magistrates favoring it, and the more conservative lower house made up of the deputies opposing it. The matter became the major issue in the election of 1670, when a majority of the deputies were defeated. The new house of deputies promptly approved the proposed church, adding for good measure that in so doing "we do adhere to the primitive ends of our coming hither, retaining the sober principles of the Congregational way, and the practice of our churches in their present and most athletic constitutions."[14]

And so the Third Church of Boston came into being, and the cedar meetinghouse was built on land, given ironically enough by the widow of the First Church's Rev. John Norton, on the south side of the High Street but a quarter of a mile south, down Cornhill, from the First Church; and it came to be known as the South Church. It called to its pastorate a fifty-year-old physician, Thomas Thacher, the author of the first medical tract to be published in the colonies, who had come to Boston to practice medicine in 1664, previous to which he had been for twenty years the minister of Weymouth, a village south of Boston. Thacher was, due possibly to his work as a physician, of a far gentler and more humane temperament than the original breed of Puritan clerics. His pastorate was brief, lasting only eight years, but it served to be a lasting influence in relaxing the rubrics of New England Calvinism.

The drift of the South Church toward the liberation of Congregationalism from its more stringent founding practices, with repercussions that were to be lasting and permeating, culminated in a resolution adopted by the congregation in February 1678, nine months before Thacher died of a fever contracted at the bedside of a sick parishioner. The resolution, in the composition of which Thacher unquestionably had a hand if he was not the sole author of it, repudiated the cardinal requirement of church membership specified in the Cambridge *Platform of Church Discipline*, written largely by John Cotton and adopted by the churches of the colony and approved by the Great and General Court in 1648. The platform set forth that a public profession of his faith be made by every candidate for membership before the congregation ". . . in such sort as may satisfie 'rational charity' . . ." and "In case any, thro' excessive fear or other infirmity, be unable to make their personal relation of their spiritual estate in publick, it is sufficient that the elders . . . make relation thereof in publick before the church. . . ."[15] The South Church resolution declared, ". . . in case any that desire fellowship with the Church, through scruple of Conscience shall bee unwilling to consent that his

---

[14] Nathaniel B. Shurtleff, ed., *Records of the Governor and Company of the Massachusetts Bay* (Boston, 1854), IV, ii, 495.

[15] The text of the Cambridge platform is in Mather, *Magnalia Christi Americana*, II, 211–36.

Relation shall be read before the Church . . . shall be received as if it had bin made before the Church . . ."[16] providing only that it was given privately to the elders of the church, who were at the time Thacher and Edward Raynsford. Had this simple measure been adopted by Congregationalism sixteen years earlier, the New Jerusalem may have been spared the ordeal occasioned by the strained device of the Half-Way Covenant and the enervating controversy that followed it.

Thacher further advanced the South Church toward new standards of openness by his choice of a younger colleague, who was very soon to succeed him, Samuel Willard. One of the ten members of the Harvard College class of 1659, Willard was pastor of the church at Groton from 1664 to 1676, when his pastorate was abruptly terminated, his meetinghouse destroyed and his congregation murdered or dispersed by a raid of four hundred Indians who leveled the village. Willard, then thirty-six years old, brought his wife and four children to Boston where he became a member of the South Church and was invited by Thacher to preach from time to time. On the last day of March 1678, he was installed as Thacher's colleague, and after Thacher's death in October that year he became pastor of the church.

Samuel Willard soon showed himself to be an independent and, assuming the intrinsic narrowness of the Puritan outlook, a latitudinarian mind, but he was wholly realistic about the nature of the Puritan state. He was quick and explicit to deny that the experiment of the wilderness Zion had anything to do with tolerance or freedom of religion; and, in his denial, he summarized with a succinctness wholly uncharacteristic of Puritan literature the primary intention—the *animus*—of Puritanism: The Anabaptists "are mistaken in the design of our first Planters, whose business was not Toleration: but were professed Enemies of it, and could leave the World professing they *died no Libertines*. Their business was to settle, and (as much as in them lay) secure Religion to Posterity according to that way which they believed was of God."[17] At the same time, Willard insisted, not just in theory but in practice, on opening the doors of the church to the many rather than to the few: "We have in Boston," Edward Randolph, deputy collector of His Majesty's customs in New England, wrote to the Bishop of London, "one Mr. Willard, a minister . . . he is a moderate man and baptiseth those who are refused by the other churches, for which he is hated."[18]

* * *

That the South Church was a flourishing institution, well into its second decade and into the fifth year of the ministry of Samuel Willard when Josiah Franklin arrived in Boston was, in a manner of speaking,

[16] Hill, *Old South Church*, I, 229.
[17] Samuel Willard, *Ne Sutor ultra Crepidam* (Boston, 1681), quoted in Sibley, *Biographical Sketches*, II, 17.
[18] Ibid.

providential. It was unquestionably due to the accident of propinquity that Josiah became associated with the youthful congregation across the street rather than with the aging First Church a five-minute walk up Cornhill or with the stolid church of the Mathers a mile to the north. But it could not have been a happier accident. Samuel Willard had as much in common with Banbury's Samuel Wells, who was, up until Franklin's removal to Boston, the most direct and determining influence on his religious life, as it was possible for one in the Heavenly City to have with one still immersed in the profane world of an England that had pressed its own terms upon God rather than having yielded all to His terms. Moreover, the South Church had a membership considerably above the average in learning, and Josiah Franklin was to be thrown in with some of the most informed and energetic minds in the colony, not just occasionally but constantly in the endless succession of services, lectures, and meetings that characterized the religious and social life of the visible saints—men like the governor and patriarch of the colony, Simon Bradstreet, widower of the colony's first poet, a skilled diplomat, and a conciliator between the colony and the crown, and Samuel Sewall, gregarious and conscionable, onetime fellow and tutor at Harvard, manager of the colony's printing press, major of militia, deputy to the Great and General Court, judge of the Superior Court, and so indefatigable a diarist that he was to become, with Cotton Mather, the primary source on over fifty years of the life of the colony.

As for Josiah Franklin, his gifts of character and of intelligence must very early have commended him to his brethren in the South Church. By the time of his arrival in 1683, the town of Boston was often afflicted with the problem of idlers who had somehow gotten it in their heads that the New World afforded them an opportunity to prosper without toil that the Old World did not. Nothing could have been further from the truth. There were opportunities in the colonies that no longer existed at home, to be sure, and there were economic advantages; but all these required resolution and diligence if the most were to be made of them, and the records of the colony are replete with the sad fate of wistful, uninformed, or merely indolent adventurers, who became public charges or restless drifters. As early as 1662, an almshouse was built to provide food and shelter for the indigent, and private charitable funds had been established five years before, when twenty-seven Scots then resident in Boston, with characteristic prudence, contributed money to serve as a source of "releefe of our selves or any other for which wee may see cause."[19] And at a town meeting just two months before Josiah Franklin arrived, distressed cognizance was taken of "persons & Families yt misspend their time, in idlenesse & tipplinge with great neglect of their callings and suffer ye chil-

[19] Records of the Scot's Charitable Society of Boston, MS, 27.

dren shamefully to spend their time in ye streetes."[20] In a lecture, as the century drew toward its close, Cotton Mather, always on the alert for signs of decadence in "the chief town of New-England and of the English America," castigated both the idle and those whose misguided charity relieved them: "*Idleness*, alas! *idleness* increases in the town exceedingly; idleness, of which there never came any goodness! idleness, which is a 'reproach to any people.' *We* work hard all summer, and the *drones* count themselves wronged if they have it not in the winter divided among them. The *poor* that *can't* work, are objects for your liberality. But the poor that *can* work and *won't*, the best liberality to them is to *make* them. I beseech you, sirs, find out a method quickly, that the idle persons in the town may earn their bread; it were the best piece of charity that could be shown unto them, and equity unto us all."[21] In such a context, the conduct of Josiah Franklin, an industrious dyer, arriving with no important connections in Boston and finding no need for his trade, was impressive to his townsmen—for he had immediately learned a new trade and supported his family by applying himself to it diligently and without complaint.

As Josiah made his way stolidly forward in a trade that was exceptionally grueling even in an age when all physical toil was demanding and oppressive, he bore himself with good humor, with consideration in his relationships with others, and with a soundness of judgment that gained the notice and respect of his townsmen. He was successively chosen as a tithingman, a clerk of the market, and a constable.[22] All of these functions, none of which was popular, required a strong sense of duty and resolution tempered by tact. Franklin was chosen for his post as tithingman by the selectmen, who had been ordered in 1677 by the General Court "to chuse sundry persons, by the name of tithingmen, to inspect the disorders in and by publick and private houses of entertainment, and prophanation of ye Lord's day, and by the County Courts to bee impowered to prevent, and in their capacity to reforme the same."[23] The duties of tithingmen, though in smaller communities limited to policing behavior with regard to the church, such as enforcing attendance at Sunday services and weekday lectures and preventing napping or inattention once attenders were in the meetinghouse, extended in Boston to such social monitoring as rounding up idlers and delivering them to the magistrate and seeking out and bringing to account those guilty of such other victimless offenses as excessive drinking or profanity.

[20] *Report of the Record Commissioners of the City of Boston* (Boston, 1876–1909), VII, 157.

[21] Cotton Mather, *The Bostonian Ebenezer. Some Historical Remarks on the State of Boston*, in *Magnalia Christi Americana*, I, 90ff.

[22] Cf. Robert F. Seybolt, *The Town Officials of Colonial Boston* (Cambridge, 1939), 95, 100, 105.

[23] *Acts and Resolves, Public and Private, of the Province of Massachusetts Bay*, cited in Samuel J. Drake, *The History and Antiquities of Boston* (Boston, 1856), 428.

Since among these offenses forbidden by law was the wearing of garb too elaborate or extravagant for one's means, like brightly colored silks and intricate laces, it was well for Josiah Franklin that he had abandoned his former trade. The duties of a tithingman, who derived his title in English law from his responsibility for keeping an eye on ten households, were somehow more appropriate to one whose occupation concerned cleanliness and light—a soapmaker and candlemaker, for example—than one whose trade was directed solely to fine raiment—for example, a dyer. To execute his duties without incurring the disdain of his neighbors, as he filled the role of what was essentially a town snoop and an informer, required a sensitivity and a sense of fairness that could breed respect rather than resentment. This Josiah Franklin managed, through repeated terms as a tithingman. Far from being avoided as a result of his service in the post, he was sought out by his neighbors and by prominent townsmen for his advice. ". . . I remember well his being frequently visited by leading People, who consulted him for his Opinion in Affairs of the Town or of the Church he belong'd to and show'd a good deal of Respect for his Judgment and Advice,"[24] his son was to recall years later.

The post of constable was actually an extension of that of tithingman but conferred powers of arrest and surveillance in the cases of a much broader range of offenses. Obviously only highly responsible men could be appointed to the post, but often they were just the men who were most reluctant to risk their standing with their neighbors. As a result of so many refusals to serve as constable, fines of such huge dimensions were authorized and imposed for refusing that only the wealthy could avoid duty by paying the fine. Sometimes more severe punishments were administered, as one New Englander discovered when, having refused the post, he was served with a warrant and "he sd. he car'd not a fart . . . for all their warrants." He was seized by the authorities and "whipt till his back be bloody."[25] Despite the fines, of seventeen appointed the year before Franklin served, six refused, one was excused, and three more were replaced after two months' service. The post of constable, however, was becoming more important as the moral force of the first generation of Puritans and their children was spent and newer arrivals, without the same zealous commitment to building the Heavenly City, began to outnumber the original elect, whose own descendants were, in fact, described as being in many cases "the most profligate and debauched wretches in the world."[26] After toiling all day to support their families, the constables spent the precious few hours they may have eked out for their own leisure in patrolling the town to combat what the Reverend Samuel Torrey, successor to Thomas Thacher at Weymouth, had characterized in 1674 as

[24] *Autobiography*, 55.
[25] H. M. Chapin, *Documentary History of Rhode Island* (Providence, 1919), II, 142.
[26] John Dunton, *Letters from New England* (Boston, 1867), 66.

"a spirit of profaneness, a spirit of pride, a spirit of worldliness, a spirit of sensuality, a spirit of gainsaying and rebellion, a spirit of libertinism, a spirit of carnality."[27] What made life busy and also sprightly for the constable was the great number of offenders to be apprehended due to the virtually inexhaustible supply of offenses in the Puritan code of Boston, which may have been reasonably enforceable in the town of 1640, with a population of twelve hundred, but became increasingly difficult as the population rose to five thousand by 1680 and by the end of the century reached ten thousand. In addition to the mathematics of the situation (there were only eleven constables, with the aid of nine tithingmen, during the year of Franklin's first term, policing the morals of ten thousand), there was a sharp rise in public tolerance of relaxed conduct. The state of morals in the Bible Commonwealth of the late 1690s was joyously reported by an English visitor, the satirist Edward Ward. Of the progeny of the visible saints and those that settled after them, he wrote:

> Rum, alias Kill Devil, is as much ador'd by the American English, as a dram of Brandy is by an old Billingsgate. Tis held as the Comforter of their Souls, the Preserver of their Bodys, the Remover of their Cares, and Promoter of their Mirth; and is a Soveraign Remedy against Grumblings of the Guts, a Kibe heel [sore heel], or a Wounded Conscience, which are three Epidemical Distempers that afflict the Country. . . .
>
> Notwithstanding their Sanctity, they are very Prophane in their common Dialect. They can neither drive a Bargain, nor make a Jest, without a Text of Scripture at the end on't. . . .
>
> Their Lecture-Days are call'd by some amongst them, Whore Fair, from the Levity and Wanton Frollicks of the Young People, who when their Devotion's over, have recourse to the Ordinaries, where they plentifully wash away the remembrance of their Old Sins, and drink down the fear of a Fine, or the dread of a Whipping-post. Then Up-tails-all and the Devil's as busy under the Petticoat, as a Juggler at a Fair, or a Whore at a Carnival.
>
> Husking of Indian-Corn, is as good sport for the Amorous Wag-tailies in New-England, as Maying amongst us is for our forward Youths and Wenches. For 'tis observ'd, there are more Bastards got in that Season, than in all the Year beside; which occasions some of the looser Saints to call it Rutting Time.[28]

These observations, merrily expressed as they were by a visiting Englishman, were confirmed, albeit in more concerned language, rather than denied by the resident custodians of faith and morals in the town. In 1698—the same year of which Ward was writing—Cotton Mather, permitting himself a pun, lectured his townsmen: "But beware, I beseech you, of those provoking evils that may expose us to a plague, exceeding all that are in the catalogue of the twenty-eighth of Deuteronomy. Let me go

---

[27] Samuel Torrey, *An Exhortation unto Reformation* (Boston, 1674), 8.

[28] Anonymous, attributed to Edward Ward, *A Trip to New-England with a Character of the Country and People* (London, 1699), 10–11.

on to say, What! shall there be any bawdy-houses in such a time as this! . . . And, Oh! that the drinking-houses in the town might once come under a laudable *regulation*. The town has an enormous number of them. For you that are the town-dwellers, to be oft or long in your visits of the *ordinary*, 'twill certainly expose you to mischiefs more than ordinary."[29]

Judge Sewall's diary was more specific. On Friday, September 3, 1686, he wrote: "Mr. Shrimpton, Capt. Lidget and others come in a coach from Roxbury about 9, aclock or past, singing as they come, being inflamed with Drink: At Justice Morgan's they stop and drink Healths, curse, swear, talk profanely and baudily to the great disturbance of the Town and grief of good people. Such high-handed wickedness has hardly been heard of before in Boston."[30] The same year the judge noted cryptically that Boston's ministers had felt obliged to issue a second warning against "Profane and Promiscuous Dancing" and also that, taking personal action on the morals front, he himself did "send for Edw. Cowel and blame him for his ill carriage [apparently exploring the anatomy of the bride] at Richd. White's Wedding, Dec. 10. He denys the fact, and saith he came not nigh her [i.e., the bride] and stooped down only to take up his Hat taken off in the Crowd."[31] The judge also noted as a "most awfull Instance" the discharge of the Reverend John Cotton, Jr., son of the arch-Puritan, from his Plymouth pastorate "for his Notorious Breaches of the Seventh Comandmt . . ."[32] but made no reference to the fact that the same man had been "excommunicated from the church of which his father had been minister, but upon penitential acknowledgement was restored the next month."[33] Judge Sewall, who seemed destined to be distressed by clerical ventures in adultery, had already participated in a council of churches that had recommended the suspension of the Reverend Thomas Chiever for "Shamefull and abominable Violations of the Seventh Comandment."[34]

* * *

As, in manners and morals, the Boston to which Josiah Franklin migrated, and in which he was to make his way and his children were to shape their lives, was beginning, toward the end of the seventeenth century, to partake more of the nature of Charles II's London than of Governor Winthrop's Heavenly City, the ecclesiastical fabric of Boston was also weakening, and the Puritan procurators seemed powerless to stop the trend, importune as they did to the Almighty and to their brethren— neither seeming to be overly attentive—in mountingly vituperative lan-

[29] Mather, *Magnalia Christi Americana*, I, 100.
[30] Sewall, *Diary*, V, 150–51.
[31] Ibid., I, 122–23.
[32] Ibid., 460.
[33] Sibley, *Biographical Sketches*, I, 496–97.
[34] Sewall, *Diary*, I, 21.

guage. And there perished, with the authority of their words, the authority, too, of the laws they inspired and the punishments they meted out.

As the priests of Puritanism, from John Cotton, the principal architect of the Heavenly City, to Cotton Mather, its chief preservator, understood from the beginning, any spirit of tolerance would be its downfall. "If there be power given to speak great things," Cotton had warned not long before his death in 1652, "then look for great blasphemies, look for a licentious abuse of it."[35] And although the politics of his time forced Cotton Mather into a less stolid stance than his grandfather's, he spent many an hour in sounding alarms about the excesses to which tolerance gave rise. The legal code had also given specific expression to the hazards of unorthodoxy and teemed with such phrases as "damnable heresies" and such punishments as "every such person continuing obstinate therein, after due meanes of Conviction, shall be sentenced to Banishment."[36]

One of the earliest and most "damnable heresies" of all to the early Puritans had been that advanced by the Baptists, or Anabaptists—damnable because of their opposition to infant baptism, an essential of the Heavenly City, since infant baptism, far from merely symbolizing Christians, was held actually to create Christians by the very act of baptism. Just as bad were the Quakers, whose meek and serene belief in the perfectibility of man flew starkly and irreconcilably into the face of the Puritans' fond but agitated preoccupation with man's inherent evil. Worse than either Baptists or Quakers were such general skeptics as Roger Williams and Anne Hutchinson, who seemed at times to be against any and all aspects of both civil and religious authority and, showing no qualms about it, were banished, in Winthrop's words, like lepers. Banishment into the bleak wilderness could, of course, be tantamount to a death sentence (though in the depth of winter a stay of execution, as in the case of Anne Hutchinson, was sometimes granted); and if the banished returned, there were statutory provisions to carry out a graduated series of punishments designed to discourage such returnings, for it must be remembered that, to the Puritans, punishment was not vindictive but to protect the community of the living saints from lethal contamination, such as the Quakers' doctrine that man should be free alike from the clerics, the scholars, and the magistrates: on the first return from banishment, the severing of one ear; on the second, the other ear; on the third, the boring through of he tongue with a hot iron. All these mutilations failing, however, the death penalty for returning Quakers was enacted in 1658, and within a year William Robinson, a former London merchant, and Marmaduke Stevenson, formerly of Yorkshire, who had returned from banishment, were hanged from a limb of the "Great Tree" on Boston Common. Mary Dyer

[35] John Cotton, *An Exposition upon the 13th Chapter of the Revelation* (London, 1656), 72.
[36] *Book of the General Lawes and Libertyes Concerning the Inhabitants of the Massachusets* (Cambridge, 1662), 154.

was hanged the next year and William Leddra the year after that, even as there was en route from England an order from Charles II peremptorily commanding that all punishment of Quakers cease, throwing in, for good measure, another command that the franchise no longer be restricted to church members. Shortly after, in 1662, the King dispatched another letter renewing the charter of the colony but in the process ordering that no one should be denied worship according to the forms of the Book of Common Prayer of the Church of England. By the 1660s, then, the foundations of the Bible Commonwealth were virtually shattered when relative freedom of religion became a condition of the renewed charter; and the long process of dissolving the identity of the Puritan church and the Puritan state began.

In 1679 the dreaded Baptists, with their outspoken rejection of infant baptism, built their own church; and even though at first under an order of the Great and General Court of March 8, 1680, its doors were nailed closed and a notice posted forbidding its use, the authorities' fears of angering the crown by willful disobedience of Charles II's letter of July 24, 1679, requiring tolerance of all forms of Protestant worship, led them to remove the nails and notice shortly and to leave the Baptists in relative peace except for periodic tirades on the error of their ways. As for the Quakers, held in even greater contempt because of the anti-institutional, anticlerical subjective quality of their doctrine through their quiet persistence in the face of banishments, whippings, mutilations, and hangings, and through the sheer strength of their increasing numbers, they prevailed against all persecution and were meeting openly by 1677, when the authorities finally decided that, except for discriminatory laws denying them all civil rights, they too should be left alone to pay a higher price for their heresies.

For all their offenses, however, both the Baptists and the Quakers had something in common with the Congregational establishment: They were dissenters from much of the doctrine and most of the practices of the Church of England, from whose abhorrent ways the colony was still free, years after the death of Charles II, despite his Edict of 1662 insisting on the rights of Englishmen anywhere in his realm to worship, if they chose, according to the offices of the Book of Common Prayer. The throne being separated from the colony by over three thousand miles of turbulent seas, the colony ignored the royal directive. Not a notably zealous breed, Anglican churchmen resident in Boston in 1679 sent a lukewarm petition to the King "that a Church might be allowed them for the exercise of religion according to the Church of England."[37] There is no evidence that the churchmen were sufficiently distressed by their religious impoverishment to do much more to relieve their plight until two external incentives of considerable dimensions were visited upon them. The first of these was the proclivity of Edward Randolph, the principal agent of the crown in

[37] Cited in Foote, *Annals of King's Chapel*, I, 36.

Boston in his role as collector of customs, to meddle in all aspects of colonial life and serve as informer to the King—a practice that he had followed for two years prior to his appointment when he was a royal messenger conveying orders from London to Boston. Randolph saw an active Church of England parish in Boston as a necessary prop to the authority of the King, which for years had been virtually ignored, in the colony. And in 1682 he wrote the Bishop of London, urging "that some able ministers might be appoynted to performe the officies of the church with us," and adding the amazing suggestion that "no marriages hereafter shall be allowed lawfull but such as are made by the ministers of the Church of England"[38]—amazing, and intended to rebuke the Puritans as well as to help support the Anglican clergy, because Randolph knew very well that even the Puritan clergy were forbidden to perform marriage ceremonies, that duty being specifically reserved by law to the magistrates. Thus, Randolph appointed himself as a kind of missionary in reverse, and in a succession of documents urged, in addition to the Bishop of London, whose see embraced the colonies, the Archbishop of Canterbury to send episcopally ordained clergy to Massachusetts. As a result of Randolph's tenacity, there arrived in 1686 the first Anglican clergyman in New England free to conduct worship according to the liturgy of the Book of Common Prayer since the arrival of Boston's solitary first settler, the Reverend William Blackstone, who had come to Boston in 1623 because, he said, he couldn't stand the lord bishops, and left it in 1634, because he found the lord brethren who had arrived in 1630 no more bearable. The new arrival was a young Oxonian, Robert Ratcliffe. Use of any one of three meetinghouses having been denied the young cleric for his service, "he preach'd in the Town-house, and read Common-Prayer in his Surplice, which was so great a Novelty to the Bostonians that he had a very large Audience. . . ."[39]

The second incentive to the establishment of an Anglican church was the arrival of Sir Edmund Andros appointed in 1686 by Charles's successor, James II, as the first royal governor of the newly created "Dominion of New England," just five months after Ratcliffe began his ministry. Andros arrived on Monday, December 20, 1686, and forthwith demonstrated his loyalty to the Church of England by attending Anglican services in the library of the Town House on the following Saturday, Christmas Day, a festival of which the Puritans had forbidden any observance at all. Andros, a royalist to the core, as a boy a page in the royal household and an intimate of James II when Duke of York, bore the barren indignity of worshiping in a public hall for three months; but as Easter approached in 1687, he inspected the three meetinghouses and then on Wednesday of Holy Week sent Randolph around to demand the keys to the South

[38] Thomas Hutchinson, *A Collection of Original Papers Relative to the History of the Colony of Massachusetts Bay*, (London, 1769), II, 271.
[39] Dunton, *Letters from New England*, 187.

Church in order that the Anglicians could hold services there on Good Friday—a day all recognition of which was banned by the Puritans as Papist. The keys were refused, and Judge Sewall went to the governor to tell him why and "show that the Land and the House is ours, and that we can't consent to part with it to such use. . . ."[40] When Friday came, however, the governor, with his retinue, went to the meetinghouse and convinced the sexton that he should not only open the doors to them but also ring the bell to summon Anglican worshipers, thus outraging the Puritan clergy and their faithful by conducting a Church of England service within the walls of a citadel of dissent. The edifice not collapsing, the governor and his fellow churchmen went back again two days later on Easter, observed only as another Sabbath by the Puritans, and held a communion service at eleven in the morning, telling the South Church members that they could have their premises at one-thirty; but the Anglican squatters, Judge Sewall recorded grievedly, "broke off past two because of the Sacrament and Mr. [Robert] Clark's long Sermon; now we were apointed to come ½ hour past one, so 'twas a sad sight to see how full the Street was with people gazing and moving to and fro because had not entrance into the House."[41] For a year the members of the South Church and the intruding Anglicans bickered over who should occupy the building and at what hours, when finally in the spring of 1688, the building of an Anglican church was ordered by the governor, who, when Judge Sewall flatly refused to sell him any of John Cotton's former land, started the construction of King's Chapel on a corner of the sparsely occupied common burial plot. Before it was finished, James II was deposed from the throne of Britain, an event that the Bostonians seized upon to arrest Andros, as James's deputy, imprison him, and finally, on orders from London nine months later, send him back to England. Most of Andros's retinue left with him. The Puritans were elated. "Surely they are such *Harsh fruits* of which we have had a Taste, and may still be seen in the *Faction* there, who wear the Name of the *Church of England*, that there is no great fear of many *New-Englanders* to be *united to their Assembly*. Alas, poor souls! many of them upon the Rising *Light* of Sir *Edmund's* glory did in a Huff run thereto; and now upon his Setting they are left in the Dark how to get fairly off without damage to their Reputation."[42] But the jubilant epitaph was premature, and the accession of William of Orange and Mary, far from bringing reversal of the crown's intention to assure freedom to worship according to the Book of Common Prayer in the colony, strengthened it, for there was strong Stuart blood in the new monarchs, both of them being grandchildren of Charles I. In any case, the young Church of England cleric, Robert Ratcliffe, stayed on after the departure of Andros until King's Chapel was finished and Samuel Myles, of the Har-

[40] Sewall, *Diary*, I, 171.
[41] Ibid., 172.
[42] *Andros Tracts* (Boston, 1868), II, 68.

vard class of 1684, was chosen to succeed him in the capacity of a lay reader until he could get to England to be ordained.

Although King's Chapel was at first threatened with mob action and its rector openly insulted both in the pulpits and in the streets, its establishment gradually came to have a far more profound and more lasting effect upon the temper and the direction of the town than any other ecclesiastical divergence from Puritan orthodoxy. Its establishment, for one thing, was generally coeval with the institution of royal governors, and there was conferred on it from its beginning, as a result, the status of officialdom, with representatives of the crown in Boston regular attendants. Moreover, as Harvard College slipped from the grasp of the Mathers, many of its students were less attracted by Puritan rhetoric than by traditional values and found the graceful Elizabethan language of the liturgy more congenial than the stormy interminable scoldings of the Calvinists, despite Increase Mather's characterization of the Anglican responses as "those broken responds and shreds of Prayer which the Priests and People toss between them like Tennis Balls."[43] The generally high standing of the communicants, so far as authority, wealth, and education went, began to give them a subtle influence on the quality of Boston life, loosening it, restoring some qualities of contrast and delight, easing the heaviness and bleakness of the Calvinist dogma. For the first time, Christmas was celebrated and Easter observed, and the organ given King's Chapel was the first in Boston. Poetry and music, grace and felicity, broader awarenesses and lighter references entered into the dialogue and behavior of life.

All this represented no institutional influence of King's Chapel at all; it had none. It was rather the result of the trickling into the Boston community of a sprinkling of articulate, well-placed individuals who by their views and ways of life demonstrated alternatives to the grim Puritan view and the stern Puritan way that, despite predictions to the contrary, did not bring any lethal retribution. Even Judge Sewall was pleased when, as he was about to sail for England, Robert Ratcliffe stopped him in the street. "He pray'd God Almighty to bless me, and said [he] must wait upon me."[44] And the judge was distressed when Gabriel Bernon, a prominent Anglican layman, nearly missed seeing him in the street: "As I came from Charlestown Lecture I met Mr. Bernon in Sudbury Street; he turn'd from me and would not have seen me; but I spake to him."[45] The second and third generations of Boston settlers were to be particularly influenced by the liberalizing effect that the Church of England had on the town's life. Lacking the intenseness of conviction of the founding fathers, they were hospitable to new ideas, new points of view, and new approaches. The social mix, by the time Josiah Franklin arrived in 1683, had been for

[43] *A Brief Discourse Concerning the unlawfulness of the Common Prayer Worship . . . By a Reverend and Learned Divine* (Boston, 1869), cited in Foote, *Annals of King's Chapel,* I, 96.
[44] Sewall, *Diary,* I, 233.
[45] Ibid., II, 262.

over half a century drearily homogeneous; and the younger and newer Bostonians sought out those who were different in their outlooks and values, and an increasing number of the older tolerated them. Intellectual life was to a great extent stagnating, largely because it had lacked for so long the stimulation of criticism, of dissent, and of contrast. With the grip of the theocracy, real as it still was, nevertheless relaxed, all this began to change, and an extra-Puritanic aspect of the culture began to emerge.

The open organization and, with surprising swiftness, the open acceptance by the Puritan clergy of other communions was also the beginning of the end of the monolithic authority of the Bible Commonwealth as envisioned and defended by John Cotton at its inception. The end was accelerated and sealed by a shattering event far from new in the annals of Christendom and far from either the greatest of its kind in dimensions or the broadest in reach: the ordeal that occurred in Salem village, in 1692, as mass hysteria resulted from the charges of some adolescent girls, whose symptoms were more pathological than demonological, that they were bewitched.

By no means a Puritan phenomenon, the delusion of witchcraft had appeared far less frequently in the Massachusetts Bay Colony than it had in Britain or on the European continent. As old as the concept of a personalized devil and inevitably an intrinsic element of it, deep convictions of the reality of witches antedated Christian societies (as, for example, in the primitive tribes of Africa), but the idea was formalized in the Christian Church during the first year of the papacy of Innocent VIII in 1484. Three years later two German Dominicans of the Roman Church, Henry Kramer and James Sprenger, codified the symptoms and evidences of witchcraft in a treatise which, as *Malleus Maleficarum*, became the principal compendium of the superstition, obtaining for its authors the awesome posts of inquisitors for all northern Germany. In England the literature of the early church, including the Venerable Bede's history, completed in 731, contained references to witchcraft, which continued to be regarded as a recurring risk in the Christian community for the next millennium. A commonplace feature of Elizabethan drama, witchcraft appeared in historic and philosophic works over and over again, even into the Enlightenment. An observer of the Stuarts' England, James Howell, a Member of Parliament in Charles I's reign and "historiographer royal" in Charles II's, who spent eight years in the Fleet prison during the Cromwell interregnum writing a series of expository essays, reported in 1647, "Within the compass of two years, near upon three hundred witches were arraigned, and the major part of them executed, in Essex and Suffolk only. Scotland swarms with them more and more, and persons of good quality are executed daily."[46] A definitive guidebook for justices of the peace and grand juries in England from 1619 until the 1750s gave minute directions for

---

[46] James Howell, *Epistolae Ho-Elianae* (London, 1673), 427, cited in Winsor, *Memorial History*, II, 132.

identifying witches by "marks upon their body, sometimes like a blue or red spot, like a flea-biting, sometimes the flesh sunk in and hollow. . . ."[47] So thoroughly entrenched was the English belief in witchcraft that as profound a thinker as John Locke gave it specific credence in *An Essay Concerning Human Understanding;* and as late as 1765, as brilliant and lucid an intellect as the jurist Sir William Blackstone, in his great *Commentaries,* could caution, "To deny the possibility, nay, actual existence of witchcraft and sorcery is at once flatly to contradict the revealed word of God . . . and the thing itself is a truth to which every nation in the world hath in its turn borne testimony. . . ."[48] So prevalent was the fear of witches in the sixteenth and seventeenth centuries that 30,000 accused witches were executed in Britain, by hanging in England and by burning in Scotland; 75,000 in France; and 100,000 in Germany.[49] In contrast, only 32 executions for witchcraft occurred in the New England colonies altogether, and only 4 in Boston itself.

What made the Salem trials conspicuous was that a total of twenty people were put to death in five months—almost twice as many as in all New England during the previous seventy-two years of its history. But the indictments and trials were not entered into lightly nor nearly as automatically as in England, where Matthew Hopkins, the professional "witch-finder-general," wandered at will over the English countryside seeking out suspects and subjecting them to incredibly offensive physical examinations and ordeals. English jurisprudence subjected his victims to summary trials, which amounted to little more than sentencing sessions, and then Hopkins moved on to another village. In Massachusetts the Salem accusations, spontaneously made by the distraught children, were, in comparison the object of searching inquiry and cautious procedures and caused the most anguished distress. Sir William Phips, the first royal governor of Massachusetts under a new charter negotiated by Increase Mather, had just arrived on his assignment. A practical, hardheaded native of Maine who had achieved riches and a knighthood by salvaging sunken Spanish treasure ships and was almost totally unqualified for statesmanship, he was mystified by all the cant he heard about the Salem witches and helpless as to what to do about it. Probably acting on the counsel of Increase Mather, who had engineered his appointment, he turned the whole matter over to a "Special Commission of Oyer and Terminer," an ad hoc trial court consisting of nine civil magistrates, empowering them to try the accused. The commission moved slowly, trying and convicting only one of more than a hundred suspects during its first month and coming to a dead stop after the single conviction. The governor, a ship's carpenter by trade and wholly

---

[47] Michael Dalton, *Country Justice, containing the Practice, Duty, and Power of Justices of the Peace* (London, 1727), 514.

[48] William Blackstone, *Commentaries on the Laws of England,* 4 vols. (London, 1765–69), IV, 61.

[49] The figures are from William F. Poole, "Witchcraft in Boston," in Winsor, *Memorial History,* II, 131ff.

unjudicial by nature, was baffled by his especially appointed trial body, because, following Cotton Mather's advice, it refused to try those indicted by the magistrates on "spectral evidence"—i.e., evidence that consisted of testimony by alleged victims bearing witness solely against the specters of accused individuals rather than against the individuals themselves in the bewitchment process—despite some popular clamor to get along with the trials anyhow. More interested in the earthier matter of the frontier clashes with the Indians, Phips then dumped the problem into the lap of the Boston Congregational clergy, who filed a report, written by Cotton Mather, repudiating the validity of spectral evidence: "Presumptions whereupon persons may be committed, and, much more, convictions whereupon persons may be condemned as guilty of witchcrafts, ought certainly to be more considerable than barely the accused persons being represented by a spectre unto the afflicted." At the same time, the ministers urged, "The speedy and vigorous prosecution of such as have rendered themselves obnoxious, according to the direction given in the Laws of God and the wholesome statutes of the English nation for the detection of witchcraft."[50] Although the "wholesome statutes," as enforced by Michael Dalton's primitive rubrics, were no better than spectral evidence, the trial judges saw fit to reject the clerical advice and proceed on the flimsiest delusory evidence. Five women were convicted by July 19, when they were all hanged. By August 19, another five people—four men and one woman—were convicted and on that date hanged on the grim summit of Salem's Gallows Hill. Eight more—seven women and a man—followed on September 22; seven others convicted in the same session escaped the gallows, five by confessing (an act considered as evidence of regeneration), one by pleading pregnancy, and one by being slipped out of the prison by friends. Before October was gone, two more were hanged, and another, Giles Corey, was pressed to death for refusing to plead to his indictment—not, according to English law, as punishment but in a futile effort to force a plea from him by torture.

Though centered in Salem, the witchcraft delusion wholly preoccupied Boston all through the torturesome summer of 1692. Through his associations at the South Church, Josiah Franklin was undoubtedly more keenly aware of the phobia than most Boston artisans. Three of the nine judges were South Church members: William Stoughton, a rich and powerful magistrate and the most ruthless of the trial commission; Samuel Sewall, merchant and a member of the Governor's Council, who befriended Josiah Franklin at the South Church and was one of the most troubled of the judges; and Wait Still Winthrop, great-grandson of the Massachusetts Bay Colony's founder, a justice and representative to the Great and General Court but fonder of his military title, Major General. Two of those accused were also contemporary members of the South Church with

[50] The report is in David Levin, ed., *What Happened in Salem?* (New York, 1960), 111.

Franklin. One, the oldest son of the Plymouth Pilgrim, was John Alden, Jr., a founder of the South Church and by now a venerable shipmaster; Alden defied his accusers, some wenches who claimed that he was pinching them in Salem while he was in Boston, attempted unsuccessfully to reason with his judges, most of whom knew him personally, was deposited in a Boston jail to await trial, and had the good sense, with the aid of a Boston clergyman, to escape and stay away until the madness had passed. The other South Church member accused of wizardry was a distinguished merchant, Hezekiah Usher, Jr., who had married, unhappily as it turned out, the widow of the ill-fated President Leonard Hoar of Harvard; detained under guard at a private house rather than in jail, in deference to his high standing in the community, he, too, had his case dismissed as hundreds of others accused were released from custody or surveillance at the mania's end.

The sad dementia came to an end almost as swiftly as it erupted. Conscionable men—largely the clergy of Boston—were acutely stricken with the enormity of the killing of a score of men and women, including a Maine minister who had not been near Salem for nine years. On October 3, ten days after the September 22 executions, Increase Mather read to a group of ministers the manuscript of a strong and biting indictment of the court's dependence upon spectral evidence, reducing its methods to an absurdity: "We ought not to practice witchcraft in order to discover witches." The manuscript, bearing the revealing title "Cases of Conscience Concerning Evil Spirits Personating Men," was immediately distributed by Mather and was published shortly thereafter but not until, with his taste for political maneuvering, he had persuaded fourteen other ministers—his son, Cotton, being a conspicuous exception—to sign the preface and, with the total inability of the Mathers ever to concede Puritan error, had included a craven postscript suggesting the preposterous thesis that the court he was obviously denouncing had thus far not relied solely on the evidence he was condemning.[51]

No such mealymouthed afterword was attached to a letter, published just five days after Mather read his paper, by an eminent layman of the South Church, Thomas Brattle, a young and rich merchant, one of the most learned of Harvard's alumni, a brilliant mathematician, and correspondent of Sir Isaac Newton. Although at thirty-four Brattle did not have the political weight of the elder Mather, he had a far more sophisticated intellect, greater independence of mind, and a much more lucid prose style. He did share with Mather and with the whole community of Puritan tractarians, however, a passion for long and pointed titles that tended to telescope the messages of entire compositions. Devastatingly called "Letter, giving a Full and Candid Account of the Delusion called Witchcraft, which prevailed in New England, and of the Judicial Trials and Executions at Salem, in the County of Essex, of that Pretended

---

[51] *Cases of Conscience* was published by Benjamin Harris in Boston in 1693.

Crime, in 1692," and widely circulated in manuscript form, it brought a luminous ray of justice and humanity to a somber society bereft in large measure of both. Referring to the witchcraft episode as a "malignant" epidemic and the trials as "the processes of judicial blindness," Brattle's straightforward prose, unencumbered by any weight of dogma or apologetics, marched to the heart of the matter in a procession of utterances of towering sanity in what had become a morass of malevolence, deception, suspicion, and contradictions: "Salem superstition and sorcery . . . is not fit to be named in a land of such light as New England is." And broadening the historical implications of the murky concept of spectral evidence: "Liberty was evermore accounted the great privilege of an Englishman; but certainly, if the devil will be heard against us, and his testimony taken, to the seizing and apprehending of us, our liberty vanishes, and we are fools if we boast of our liberty." Finally, with prophetic insight into the durability of the aberrant: "I am afraid that ages will not wear off that reproach and those stains which those things will leave behind them upon our land."[52]

Brattle's pastor, Dr. Willard, also took to the pen to excoriate the methods by which the accused had been indicted, tried, and condemned. As a young minister in Groton, Willard had had an experience with a sixteen-year-old parishioner, Elizabeth Knapp, who first suffered physical fits, probably epileptic, and was later visited with hallucinations and the delusion that a neighboring woman had bewitched her. Willard brought the woman to the stricken girl and got them to talk and pray together, which put an end to the allegation as it did to a similar episode a few weeks later. But during the hysteria besetting the colony in 1692, the voice of Willard was unheeded; ". . . had his notions and proposals been hearkened to, and followed, when these troubles were in their birth, in an ordinary way," wrote Thomas Brattle, "they would never have grown unto that height which now they have."[53] But Willard had not yet achieved the influence he was to have a few years hence, and it was not until the twenty lives were so brutally sacrificed on the gallows that the conscience-stricken heeded his words as they appeared in a sixteen-page dialogue between the voice of Boston (reason) and the voice of Salem (panic). Willard's dramatic device had validity insofar as the clergy of Salem and its vicinity clung relentlessly to spectral evidence while the Boston ministers had opposed it, however softly at the outset, and had disputed the magistrate's admission of it into the trials. Willard, realizing that his dialogue implicitly was highly critical of the three judges, who were his parishioners and friends, and in order to avoid personality conflicts regarding views he thought should be appraised on their merit, published it

---

[52] The Brattle letter (October 8, 1692) is in Massachusetts Historical Society *Collections*, 5th Ser., V (1798), 77.
[53] Ibid.

anonymously. He also kept it moderate in tone and analytical in content with the weight of the argument clearly on the side of Boston.

Witchcraft in New England would have at this point accomplished its historic effect upon the monolithic authority of Puritanism and slipped into history as a tragic aberration defiant of the main current of the Bible Commonwealth rather than consonant with it, had it not been for the monumental ego of Cotton Mather and his congenital insistence upon playing the most conspicuous role in any controversy. After Phips, partly in response to restive messages from London but largely in response to the clear turn in public opinion inspired by the Boston clergy, had suspended the sentences of (and later pardoned) all the remaining convicted and dismissed his special court and after the writings of his father, Increase, of Thomas Brattle, and of Samuel Willard had restored sanity, the contradictory spirit of Cotton Mather was moved to write an incredibly unctuous book praising the judges, castigating the accused, and wholly condoning the evidentiary methods used to convict and hang them. An utterly merciless work, it was patent in its dishonesty and pathetic in its hypocrisy, coming as it did from the least admirable side of a man who was capable at a far riskier time—i.e., at the outset of the trials—of taking a stand against spectral evidence, of opposing such severe punishment, and of offering to take the alleged victims of witchcraft into his own house to cure them instead of sending them to the courtroom to make their accusations. Only twenty-nine years old, Cotton Mather had already published forty-three books, was firmly and prestigiously settled as his father's colleague at the Second Church, and was in an obvious position to become a major influence in both the ecclesiastical and the public affairs of the colony. He was also equipped with a brilliant mind, enormous erudition, and family associations that gave him access to the most powerful forces in New England life. Yet he seemed to require at every turn confirmation of his own singular importance and was at his most mischievous when engaged in efforts that had no other purpose than to confirm it. His book, *The Wonders of the Invisible World*, embarrassed his father, who was forced to write an unconvincing public notice that his son's book was not inconsistent with his own (which it clearly was, as for that matter was the latter's own postscript to that book); its sycophant praise of the incompetent Governor Phips secured the legend on the title page, "Published by the Special Command of his Excellency the Governour"; and it won the public "appropation" of the chief judge, William Stoughton, the most irreconcilable of the judges.

In extenuation of the overt duplicity that his writings on the Salem witchcrafts represented, Cotton Mather showed repeated evidence of a pathological capacity for self-deception, putting his own exceptional intellect to shame in the process. On October 20, 1692, while his father's book was in the press, he could write, in an extraordinary letter to his uncle, John Cotton, Jr., minister of the church in Plymouth:

There are fourteen worthy ministers that have newly set their hands unto a book now in the press, containing *Cases of Conscience* about witchcrafts. I did, in *my* conscience, think that as the humors of this people now run, such a discourse going alone would not only enable our witch-advocates very learnedly to cavil and nibble at the late proceedings against the witches, considered in parcels, while things as they lay in bulk, with their whole dependences, were not exposed; but also everlastingly stifle any further proceedings of justice, and more than so, produce a public and open contest with the judges, who would (tho' beyond the intention of the worthy author and subscribers) find themselves brought unto the bar before the rashest *Mobile* [i.e., mob]. . . .

With what sinful and raging asperity I have been since treated, I had rather forget than relate.[54]

Only an overwhelming sense of his own rectitude could account for this twenty-nine-year-old hierophant's putting his judgment above that of a father whose wisdom and piety he professed to revere and his dismissing his Christian brethren, whose approval he was constantly seeking, as a mere mob. And only a strangely contorted, however gifted, mind could justify —indeed, glorify—the miscarriage of justice in the name of justice.

In any case, the strange publication of *The Wonders of the Invisible World* was to leave a blight on the influence of the Mathers from which it was never fully to recover, condemning Cotton Mather—unjustly and on no grounds other than his own uncontrollable and misguided opportunism in writing a fatuous book—to an ineradicable reputation as the high priest of witchhunters and plunging into obscurity his father's redeeming role in the most tragic chapter in the gaunt history of the wilderness Zion.

* * *

No one in Boston was untouched by all this. Religion was the center of life, not peripheral to it. For two thirds of a century, the church was at the heart of the total life experience, not an adjunct to it. And through the growth of the little settlement numbering seven hundred at its founding in 1630 to the bustling seaport and provincial capital of seven thousand in the 1690s, the clergy had been the ultimate source of wisdom—not just on matters of faith or even of morals—but on politics, on science, and on societal and individual relationships. And second to them, as the public affairs of the town became more intricate and its social mix more complex, were the magistrates—civil officers, appointed rather than elected, whose authority was wide-ranging, who represented the best instructed and the most accomplished of the lay community, and who, though few were lawyers, constituted the entire judicial system. Now, in the last decade of the founding century of the New Jerusalem, just as the Half-Way Covenant had left an irreparable cleft in the fabric of the church, the dispute between the clergy and the magistrates and even *among* the clergy (for the ministers north of Boston tended to share the severe view of the magis-

[54] Kenneth Silverman, ed., *Selected Letters of Cotton Mather* (Baton Rouge, 1971), 45–46.

trates) and the seesawing in the writings of two such eminent figures as the Mathers on such a grave issue as taking human life so shook the structure of the Bible Commonwealth—even though there was little immediate evidence of any instutitional weakening—that skepticism as to not only the infallibility but also the certitude of the Puritan establishment became irrepressible.

To the pragmatic eye of Josiah Franklin, by then in the thirty-sixth year of his life and in the tenth of his residence in Boston, an established tradesman, a full participant in the South Church, and a man, though devout in his religious duties, neither a fanatic nor primarily spiritual in his emphases or outlook, the witchcraft episode could not have helped revealing inherent weaknesses in the totalitarian element in the Puritan proposition. This awareness must have been keenly and memorably sharpened on a Sunday morning in January 1697, forty months after the last convicted witches were hanged, when Franklin and the rest of the South Church congregation were astonished to see Judge Sewall, instead of taking his customary pew, stop at the mourner's bench and there take his place among those who were to confess their sins publicly. As Dr. Willard moved down the aisle toward the pulpit, the judge handed him a slip of paper. While Sewall stood, his head bowed in contrition, the pastor read to the congregation Sewall's acknowledgment that ". . . being sensible, that as to the Guilt contracted upon the opening of the late Commission of Oyer and Terminer at Salem . . . he, upon many accounts, more concerned than any that he knows of, Desires to take the Blame and shame of it, Asking pardon of men, And especially desiring prayers that God, who has an Unlimited Authority, would pardon that sin. . . ."[55] The next day, Cotton Mather, not given to declaring his limitations in public, was seized with one of his periodic fits of despair in the privacy of his study: "Being afflicted last Night, with discouraging Thoughts as if unavoidable *Marks*, of the *Divine Displeasure*, must overtake my *Family*, for not appearing with *Vigor* enough to stop the proceedings of the Judges, when the Inextricable Storm from the *Invisible World* assaulted the *Country*, I did this morning, in prayer with my *Family*, putt my Family into the Merciful Hands of the Lord."[56]

[55] Sewall, *Diary*, I, 445.
[56] Mather, *Diary*, I, 216.

VI

Mark for Sorrow...
Mark for Pleasure

> He that raises a large Family does, indeed,
> while he lives to observe, *stand*, as Watts says,
> a broader Mark for Sorrow; but then he stands
> a broader Mark for Pleasure too.
>
> —Benjamin Franklin[1]

As the Boston of Cotton Mather moved through the close of the century
that had seen its birth and into the beginning of another which was to see
the heavenly vision of its high purpose harbored by Mather's grandfathers, John Cotton and Richard Mather, fade and then all but vanish; as
the town grew from a quiet wilderness outpost to a boisterous, busy
seaport; and as the processes of history imposed upon it a new and more
worldly destiny, Josiah Franklin and his contemporaries were siring the
new generation—the first wholly of the eighteenth century in their outlook and their experience. Children of the Puritans, they were never to
lose the qualities of character and perception that distinguished their fathers and grandfathers. But they were, with few exceptions, to see the
world and their own role in it in less narrow dimensions and far less isolated fulfillment. The architects of the New Jerusalem were, one by one,
disappearing into the tombs and graves of the three "burying grounds," at
Copp's Hill in the North End, near Cotton Mather's Second Church, at
the southeast corner of the Common, and next to the Grammar School,
nearer the South Church and the cottage of the Franklins. Meanwhile,
their children and grandchildren were reproducing their kind with an intensity that seemed to be increasing in proportion to the decline in the intensity of their religious devotion, for large families were a commonplace
in Boston.

[1] To Jonathan Shipley, Bishop of St. Asaph, February 24, 1786, in Smyth, *Writings
of Benjamin Franklin*, IX, 490.

Josiah Franklin's brood—eventually of seventeen—was far from an exception; nor was the span of their births, which covered a period of thirty-four years, from Josiah's twenty-second year when he first became a father in Ecton to his fifty-sixth when his last child was born in Boston. Of the 246 men who were graduated from Harvard College in the classes of 1659 through 1699, fifteen among them had a total of 123 children, most prolific being the Franklins' pastor, Dr. Willard, who had twenty children by two wives—a record approached but not equaled by Adam Winthrop, with eighteen, all of them, however, by one wife. Increase Mather had ten children, and Cotton, his son, had fifteen. The Reverend John Sherman, a product of Emanuel College, Cambridge, who came to Boston in 1634 and became a fellow of Harvard College, had twenty-six children—an achievement greatly admired by Cotton Mather, inducting him to digress from his life of Sherman in *Magnalia Christi Americana* to pay tribute to the fecund of his time, including ". . . a married couple who in one wedlock were parents to *fifty-three* children, at thirty-five births brought into the world: somewhat short of that, but not short of wonder, is a late instance on one mother that has brought forth no less than thirty-nine children," and Sir William Phips, the bumbling governor sponsored by the Mathers, he reminded his readers, was one of twenty-six children.[2] A document of 1675 indicates that the average New England household numbered somewhat more than nine persons.[3]

The reasons behind large families—in addition to the fact that the Puritans were a hardy breed, robust in their eating, vigorous in their drinking, and lusty in their sexual activity—were largely economic and actuarial. Children were an economic necessity to the artisan or tradesman. Boys were able to work in their fathers' shops at a relatively early age, doing simple but time-consuming chores that would otherwise add yet more hours to the already interminable hours of toil that most craftsmen had to spend six days of the week to make a living. And a succession of sons was sought to provide a renewable source of labor over a whole span of years —thirty or forty—and not merely during the father's early married years. As the older sons departed for apprenticeships elsewhere, their younger brothers would fill their places, sweeping the floors, making deliveries, helping in any way that their strength or competence permitted. Girls, too, were essential to the smooth running of homes where everything was done by hand—from the making of cloth to the plucking of poultry. The number of hours of labor that went into the operation of a household of the most modest dimensions and pretensions was prodigious—to keep it warm and clean and to feed and clothe its inhabitants. Here, too, a succession of daughters was needed to provide adequate aid to tragically overworked mothers who were pregnant in many cases for

[2] Mather, *Magnalia Christi Americana*, I, 517.
[3] *New England Historical and Genealogical Register*, XXXIX, 83.

three quarters of their fertile years and whose daughters seldom stayed single to help them very long in a society where men could not easily exist without wives.

Constantly threatening the numerous progeny desired by most colonial families was the ever-present prospect of the early and sudden and, not uncommonly, mass deaths of infants and children. Child mortality was extraordinarily high, and much of the time of many who had themselves grown to adulthood and married was spent in small, sad processions to the burying grounds to inter their children. Childhood diseases of the most lethal sort—smallpox, scarlet fever, diphtheria, cholera—afflicted virtually every family to one extent or another. Nonepidemic diseases such as pneumonia took their toll among the children, too. Thirteen of Cotton Mather's fifteen children died in childhood, three of them within four days of one another. Only six of Adam Winthrop's flock of eighteen survived childhood. On Christmas Day, 1696, with "A very great snow . . . on the Ground" from two days earlier, Judge Sewall buried his little daughter Sarah, the sixth of his fourteen children to die, and went and sat in the family tomb in the south burying ground, contemplating the coffins of his departed family. " 'Twas an awfull yet pleasing Treat," he wrote. "Having said, the Lord knows who shall be brought hether next, I came away."[4] Five months later, the judge was back again, the one "brought hether next" being a still-born son. Sewall, who had so much love of life and courted three women successfully, with stately persistence and ceremonial gifts of almonds and books, and one unsuccessfully, because marriage would mean her giving up the lectures of her favorite preacher, seemed almost intrigued by death. He took a deep and usually contented interest in the corpses of the two wives, eleven children, and as many grandchildren whom he had trudged into the burying ground to deposit in the crowded Sewall tomb. Of his spinster daughter, Hannah: "When I came home I found my Daughter laid out. She expired half an hour past Ten. Her pleasant Countenance was very Refreshing to me." And of his grandson, John Sewall, who died three days later: "Matthew brings him in his coffin to my house in the night, and is set in the best Room; a goodly Corpse."[5] Yet the judge's homely, even companionable attitude toward death was not merely morbid; it was the only way to handle the unbearable intrusion, with relentless frequency, of death upon one's young.

The children of Boston were taught at the earliest age of comprehension not only to accept but to expect to die before they grew up. *The New-England Primer*, first published in 1683, the year that Josiah Franklin arrived in Boston, contained these fatalistic lines for its young readers:

> I in the Burying Place may see
> Graves Shorter there than I;

[4] Sewall, *Diary*, I, 443–44.
[5] Ibid., III, 341–42.

From Death's Arrest no Age is free,
Young Children too may die;
My God, may such an awful Sight,
Awakening be to me!
Oh! that by early Grace I might
For Death prepared be.[6]

Josiah Franklin and his wife Anne, for the first ten years of their marriage, were spared the anguish of burying a child. The two daughters, Elizabeth and Hannah, and the son, Samuel, who had accompanied them from England all lived to maturity. There followed in Boston the birth of another son, named Josiah for his father, in 1685, and another daughter, called Anne for her mother, in 1687, both of whom also survived into adulthood. And by five years after the Franklins' arrival, the little house in Milk Street had resident in it, in addition to the youthful parents, five healthy children. But the sixth child and third son, born in 1688 and named Joseph, died after five short days of life; and another son, also named Joseph for his dead brother, born a year and a half later, lived only fifteen days, surviving his mother by scarcely a week. So death, which had somehow avoided the little family, struck three times within eighteen months, and a phase of the life of Josiah Franklin was over as he made his way with a few friends of the South Church up School Street to the burying ground during the hot days of July 1689, to bury first his wife, three thousand miles away from her birthplace in Ecton, and then his seventh child, not three thousand feet from his birthplace in Milk Street.

Although death can never be institutionalized, rendered impersonal, by doctrine or custom—it is final and absolute and almost always, to one degree or another, forever changes the lives of some of the living—Puritan convictions and the relentless facts of life combined to condition the attitudes of men and women toward death, even of the young. It was literally an everyday occurrence, in a small community of large and interrelated families, for almost everyone to have traffic with death. His membership in the South Church, the busy little tallow shop, with its limited competition, which unquestionably dealt with at least a third of the seven hundred households in the town in the personal direct way common to artisans and their patrons, and the compact neighborhood in which he lived—all these would have kept the awareness of Josiah Franklin touched by death over and over again, but without a heavy morbidness. Funerals were, in fact, social occasions of considerable importance. Rings, scarves, and gloves were given by the dozens to friends of the deceased, sent around to their homes by way of special invitations to the funerals, and postfuneral repasts were rich with strong drink and foods of exceptional fineness that would on lesser occasions have been an indulgence. Men of

[6] *The New-England Primer or Milk for Babes* was first printed in 1683 but appeared in scores of editions for a century and a half, until 1830 when it ceased to be used.

prominence took pride in the number of scarves or rings that they accrued, sometimes numbering into the hundreds, as total costs for laying away the dead sometimes amounted in expenditures to a half or more of a man's estate. Nor were such expenses limited to the rich or prosperous. The Mathers' church undertook to pay the funeral expenses of Michael Powell, an ancient, impoverished parishioner, and the bill for expenses is revealing: a total of twelve shillings, little more than half a pound, was spent for the grave and coffin together, while "five pounds, fifteen shillings were spent for gloves; three pounds, seventeen shillings for wine."[7] Judge Sewall spent, quite happily, a major part of his time attending funerals, and he lingered fondly over the details in his diary, which at times seems more preoccupied with death than with life. Within two weeks in the fall of 1963, he recorded his attendance at the funerals of his own infant daughter, two sons of Adam Winthrop, and Cotton Mather's daughter, Mary. Frequently, Sewall would use funerals that he attended to make appraisals both of the living attending the event and of the deceased who occasioned it:

> June 1, 1697. I goe to the Funeral of my Tutor, Mr. Thomas Graves [a preacher, magistrate, and physician, who was a tutor at Harvard when Sewall was a student]; accompanied Col. Pynchon, Mr. Cook, Addington, Sergeant, Saffin. Bearers were, Capt. Byfield, Mr. Leverett; Capt. Sprague, Capt. Haṁond; Mr. James Oliver, Mr. Simon Bradstreet. Charlestown Gent. had gloves; Mr. Danforth had none that I observ'd. Mr. Morton is very short-breath, sat upon a Tomb in the burying-place, and said, for ought he knew he should be next. Mr. Willard, Pierpont, N.H., Mr. Brattle, and Mr. Angier, Mr. Wadsworth there. Mr. Graves was a godly, learned Man, a good Tutor, and solid preacher: His obstinate adherence to some superstitious conceipts of the Coṁon-Prayerbook, bred himself and others a great deal of Trouble: yet I think he kept to the Church at Charlestown as to his most constant attendance; especially on the Lord's Day. Has left one son by Mr. Stedman's daughter.
>
> My Tutors are gon; the Lord help me to do worthily while I stay here; and be in a readiness to follow after.[8]

The judge not only recorded the scores of funerals he attended every year, but kept in his commonplace book a careful and systematic inventory of the scarves, gloves, rings, and escutcheons that he received as a mourner. In one period of sixty-three weeks, he entered no fewer than eighty-three items, including thirty-five pairs of gloves, thirty scarves, eleven rings, and seven escutcheons.[9] As he himself moved toward the family tomb in other than a visiting capacity, he expressed regret that, as one ages, there are fewer contemporaries left to help inter him. After at-

[7] John Nicholls Booth, *The Second Church in Boston* (Boston, n.d.), 3.
[8] Sewall, *Diary*, I, 454.
[9] Ibid., II, 10.

tending the funeral of his classmate, Edward Taylor, he wrote: "Now I can go to no more Funerals of my Class-Mates; nor none be at mine; for the survivors, the Rev'd Mr. Samuel Mather at Windsor, and the Rev^d Mr. Taylor at Westfield [are] one Hundred Miles off, and are entirely enfeebled." But he did note with satisfaction on this, his last dispatch of a classmate, "Had a good pair of Gloves, and a gold Ring."[10]

After burying their dead, the Puritans immediately reverted to the problems of the living, and there was no long, brooding turning away from the practical demands of life. This was particularly important to Josiah Franklin. When Anne Child Franklin died in 1689, Franklin was just beginning to make his way in Boston and, as a result of diligence, tactfulness, and good sense, was doing well enough to support his family and to earn for himself small places of responsibility in the life of his community and his church. Now, at the death of Anne, he was thirty-one years old and the father of four young children, ranging in age from Elizabeth at eleven, Samuel at eight, Hannah at six, to little Josiah at nearly four. The tallow rendering, the soapmaking, and the candle pouring had to go on for long hours of the day and sometimes into the night. The house had to be kept, meals prepared, and clothing made. There was no alternative to a prompt second marriage. He could not afford to hire help, and even if he could there was no place for a servant to sleep except in his bed.

Everyone understood his position, and many had been through it. Sentiment or feelings of devotion to the dead partner did not enter it. Certainly there was no implication of callousness or indifference; on the contrary, it was assumed to be a tribute to a good marriage to seek an early second one and somewhat puzzling behavior to wait too long or never remarry at all. Michael Wigglesworth, physician, preacher, and a chronic and calamitous versifier, who occasionally rose to the level of poet, bewildered his clerical brethren when, bereaved at twenty-eight, by the death of his wife after only four years of marriage and one child, he waited for twenty years before choosing a second wife. When he at length made a choice, his selection at forty-eight of his seventeen-year-old servant girl, Martha Mudge, appalled them, and Increase Mather, who often assumed the pastoral role of a bishop in his relationship to other parsons, felt it his duty to admonish Wigglesworth and persuade him to alter his course: "The Report is, that you are designing to marry with your servant mayd, & that she is one of obscure parentage, & not 20 years old, & of no Chch, nor so much as Baptised. If it be as is related, I w^ld hubly entreat you (before it be too late) to consid^r of these arg^ts in oppositio. . . . It useth to be said *nube pari* [marry an equal], but to marry with one so much your Inferio^r on all accounts is not *nubere pari*. And to take one that was never baptised into such neerness of Relacon, seemeth contrary to the Gospel;

[10] Ibid., III, 388–89.

esplly for a Minist^r of Ct to doe it. The like never was in N.E. Nay, I questio wheth^r the like hath bin known in the chr^n world."[11] Wigglesworth went ahead and married her anyway. When she died, after eleven years and six children, Wigglesworth waited only five months to propose to his third wife, the widow of a respected physician, who accepted. The Reverend Joseph Moss, of the Harvard class of 1699, who was given to ordering madeira by the gallon, married his second wife six weeks after his first died and his third six months after his second died; and Jonathan Law, of the class of 1695, took five wives within the space of thirty-two years. Bereaved women were no less eager to marry anew than were men and largely for the same reason: Life was just too difficult if one was unmarried in a frontier society that was sheerly physically demanding. The relict of John Glover, an opulent merchant, married her second husband within three months of his death in 1696 and her third two months after the second's death in 1703. And Mehitabel Willis, daughter of Samuel Willis, of the class of 1653 at Harvard, joined with three Harvard men in connubial succession, with the classes of 1669, 1671, and 1675 each being represented within a period of eight years.

So essential did the community regard the remarriage of widows and widowers, particularly if children were involved, that benevolent conspiracies were immediately entered into to find new mates for them if the bereaved were slow in taking the initiative. Among the clergy, the church was frequently the conduit. Esther Warham was only fifteen when she married Eleazar Mather, Increase's brother, in 1659 and only twenty-five when he died. She simply stayed in the parsonage and married Mather's successor, Solomon Stoddard, four days after he was formally extended the call to Mather's parish. If not by calculated spontaneity, matches were often arranged by outright planning. The same Solomon Stoddard was blessed, in his marriage to his predecessor's widow, with no fewer than thirteen children, had six unmarried daughters resident in his house, and when a young colleague from a neighboring town sought his advice in finding a suitable wife, ushered him into an adjacent room and told him to take his choice. The widow of James Alling, the minister at Salisbury, called upon Caleb Cushing, as soon as he was named her husband's successor, and simply told him that his single state was inconsistent with his ministerial duties and suggested that he marry her to correct the situation, and he did.[12]

With the speed and purposiveness of his time, Josiah Franklin sought a new wife almost immediately after Anne's death. He found one, Abiah Folger, twenty-two—just ten years his junior—and lost no time in marrying her, on November 29, 1689, five months after he had become a widower. It was an inspired choice, and the marriage was to be prolific, long,

[11] Cited in Sibley, *Biographical Sketches*, I, 281.
[12] The Harvard data are taken from Sibley, *Biographical Sketches*.

and felicitous. Ten children—six boys and four girls—were to be born over the next twenty-two years, not one of them a still or even a troubled birth. Both Josiah and Abiah were to live to venerable ages, and as Benjamin Franklin, their eighth child and youngest son, was to write on their tombstone, "They lived lovingly together in Wedlock/Fifty-five Years." He also recalled that, like his father, "My Mother had likewise an excellent Constitution. She suckled all her 10 children."[13] But there was more than physical sturdiness about the marriage. Abiah Folger brought to the Franklin line the zest, vitality, curiosity, and articulateness of a comparable breed, originating in the tenacious Low Countries, nurtured in the sedulous climate of seventeenth-century Norwich in Norfolk, and settling on the determinedly independent island of Nantucket.

* * *

At the approximate time that the names of the first Franklynes, the ancestors of Josiah, were appearing in the register of the parish church at Ecton in the last half of the sixteenth century, the forebears of Abiah Folger, then with the surname Foulgier, were beginning to bristle when their Protestant beliefs and inclinations were increasingly frustrated as the liberties of such ancient feudal duchies as Flanders and Walloon were left gasping for survival amid the rampant theopolitics of Charles V's Holy Roman Empire, itself blindly striking out in every direction to regain its waning strength. When Charles abdicated and his son Philip II, King of Spain, succeeded him, and the Tyrannical Council of Blood was established in 1567 to extinguish all Protestant opposition to the Church of Rome, the fate of the refugees from Flanders and the other Low Countries was sealed. Those who could migrated to the Protestant England of Queen Elizabeth.

The Flemish and the Walloons brought to their new home qualities of character and of temperament that made certain their easy absorption into a host society. They were industrious, independent, resolute, given to common sense, and highly expressive, as their rich contributions to the arts during and before the Renaissance amply demonstrated. Probably of more immediate value to a society rapidly changing from agricultural to commercial, they also brought consummate skillfulness in a trade—the weaving of cloth. Since the reign of Henry I, in the twelfth century, the cathedral city of Norwich in East Anglia had been the weaving capital of England due to the arrival of some enterprising Dutch who, having been driven from their native land by one of its periodic inundations, set out to make their living by doing the only thing that they knew how to do: making cloth. Then in 1328, the sixteen-year-old King Edward III married Philippa, daughter of William, Count of Holland and Hainaut (Flanders), whereupon "great numbers of Flemings came over and settled at Worsted, Norwich, Lavensham, Sudbury, &c. insomuch that Norwich,

[13] *Autobiography*, 56.

in a few years, became the most flourishing city in England, by reason of its extensive trade, in worsteds, fustians, freezes, and other woolen manufactures: and so much hath the government thought this trade worth protecting, that there have been no less than fourteen statutes made, besides divers writs, and proclamations issued, and ordinances established to guard and nourish it. This, Edward III. took very proper measures to effect, by prohibiting any unwrought wool to be carried out of the kingdom, and by granting great privileges and liberties to all artificers, who should come over and settle here: at the same time enacting, that none should wear any other than English cloth, or use any facing of silk or furs, except the king, queen, or their children, unless they could afford to spend 100l a year: and this is the first sumptuary law [i.e., regulation of food or apparel] we meet with in our history."[14]

Then, second only to London among the cities of England in size, and jealously guarding the health of the weaving industry that gave it a size and prosperity that elevated it above such rival cities as Bristol and York, Norwich moved swiftly and decisively to countervene any condition arising that might weaken it. Fortunately for the Flemish Protestants who, once the Duke of Alva was turned loose on them to enforce Philip II's harsh repressions, had to yield, die, or leave their homeland, Norwich saw its worsted industry (i.e., the making of cloth from wool combed so that the fibers lay parallel, named for a village to the north of Norwich called Worthstead, later Worstead) endangered by the rise in popularity of the "new drapery," a lighter fabric similar to worsted, produced in Flemish towns in the mid-1500s. In 1564, three years before Alva's Council of Blood began its ruthless program, Norwich noticed that its worsted industry was "much decayed." The town fathers looked longingly to the new woolen cloths being woven some hundred miles across the North Sea in Flanders. In 1565, sensing the inevitable dislocation of Flemish weavers of Protestant convictions by the headstrong persecutions of Philip and his henchman, the Duke of Alva, they took action. "In 1565," an anonymous local historian of Norwich wrote two centuries later, "the worsted manufacture being much decayed, the mayor, sheriffs &c. waited upon the duke of Norfolk at his palace, to consult with him what were the properest steps to be taken on this occasion; when it was resolved to invite hither some of the strangers who had fled from the persecution raised against them in the Netherlands by the Duke of Alva, and settled themselves at London and Sandwich [nearest port to Flanders] under the queen's protection; who had granted them a license for the making Flanders commodities of wool in her majesty's dominions. Upon the duke's [i.e., of Norfolk] application, and at his own charge, the queen granted letters patent for the fixing here thirty master workmen, with ten servants to each of them, in the whole three hundred and thirty Dutch and

14 *The History of the City and Country of Norwich* (Norwich, 1768), 73.

Walloons; who immediately on their arrival set up manufactures of bayers, says, arras, mockades, &c. and in a very short time their number increased to three thousand and upwards."[15]

Norwich, with the permission of the crown, did more; linking economic prudence with religious conviction in the emerging tradition of Protestantism, it exempted those who made the Flemish new drapery from the long and hard terms of apprenticeship imposed by statute upon all other weavers. And to assure them freedom of worship "the choir of the friers preachers church" was assigned the Dutch and the chapel of the Bishop of Norwich to the Walloons for their religious assemblies. In response to these hospitable measures, by 1582 there were in Norwich 3,300 Netherlands migrants and nearly 1,400 children born of them in England—the total representing well over a fourth of the city's total population.

Among this throng of Flemish weavers was the first of the Foulgiers to live in England, and in 1593 or near it there was born to him, a son, John, who grew up an Englishman, the patronym gradually changing from Foulgier to Foulger to Folger, and who married an English girl, Meribah Gibbs. To them, in 1617, was born in Norwich an only son, Peter, who would become Abiah Folger Franklin's father and Benjamin Franklin's grandfather. The Folger family which also included a daughter, apparently prospered in Norwich, but their stay was destined to be short-lived when Queen Elizabeth died and was succeeded by James I, who denounced the nonconforming Protestants when he met his first Parliament in 1603. The situation, for the Flemish immigrants as for most other nonconformists, was worrisome but endurable, though some of them left with the Pilgrims for the Netherlands in an ironic move to regain the liberties the deprivation of which had forced them to leave that land only two generations earlier. Among them was John Robinson, the young Cambridge-educated curate of St. Andrew's Church, second largest among Norwich's forty-five parishes, who joined the Pilgrims and became their pastor during their twelve years of exile in Amsterdam and Leiden before the settlement by them of the Plymouth colony in New England in 1620. In the years that followed, after the rise of Bishop Laud to power and the succession to the monarchy of Charles I, the plight of the dissenters worsened; and the migrations to New England in the path of the Pilgrims increased. The drift toward civil war was becoming clearer, and the elevation of Laud to the primacy of all England when Charles named him Archbishop of Canterbury in 1633 rendered the prospects to many dissenters even more hopeless. John Folger was among them; and with his wife and two children he left his home for a second time in pursuit of freedom, setting sail for Boston on the ship *Abigail* in the summer of 1635 and arriving there in October. Though old enough at eighteen to stay behind had he wished or to go elsewhere, his son Peter went with him.

[15] *Ibid.*, 225.

Sailing on the same ship with the Folgers were John Winthrop, Jr., son of the first governor of the Massachusetts Bay Colony, and his second wife, Elizabeth Reade; Sir Henry Vane, a gifted young layman, who had left Oxford to continue his studies on the Continent rather than take the oath of conformity imposed when Bishop Laud became chancellor of Oxford in 1630; and the Reverend Hugh Peter, Elizabeth Reade Winthrop's stepfather, who had left England in 1628 when Laud in his swift sweep to the primacy was named Bishop of London, the diocese in which the dissenting Peter served at St. Sepulchre's. Hugh Peter ministered for seven years in Holland to a congregation of English separatists who, rather than move on to Plymouth with their brethren in 1620, had elected to stay in the Netherlands. But Laud's ubiquitous agents kept a harassing eye on his activities even there, and in 1635 he concluded to sail for New England on the *Abigail*. His wife, possibly not sufficiently well to undertake the rigorous voyage, since she died shortly afterward, did not accompany Hugh Peter on his journey. He consequently brought along a young bond servant, Mary Morrill, with whom young Peter Folger became enchanted and whose freedom he later bought for twenty pounds from Hugh Peter. They were married in New England, though how soon after their arrival is not known.

The ship *Abigail* arrived in Boston, October 6, 1635, in the midst of some breaking crises. Adherents of Governor Winthrop and those of his successor, Thomas Dudley, were locked in a series of political disputes, which Vane and Hugh Peter undertook to resolve. Vane, at the age of twenty-three, was elected governor, after being in the colony only seven months. Roger Williams, minister of the church at Salem, was raising disturbing questions of autocracy in the church, imperialism in the treatment of the Indians, and usurpation of powers by the civil authorities, and for expressing such views was banished from the colony three days after the *Abigail*'s arrival. Hugh Peter succeeded him at the Salem church. The Folgers, father, mother, daughter, and son, did not linger in Boston with their distinguished shipmates or participate in the critical events with which they became involved. They went on to Dedham to practice the weaver's trade and to feel out the mood and the direction of the new land to which they had come.

* * *

Unlike Josiah Franklin, who quickly settled into a position in the social and economic structure of the town of Boston when he arrived from Banbury, Oxfordshire, in 1683 and retained it substantially unchanged until his death sixty-three years later, the Folgers, when they arrived from Norwich, Norfolk, in 1635, nearly half a century ahead of the Franklins, had an exploratory attitude about the new land and society to which they had come. All the evidence suggests that they were a more spirited people than the Franklins, more on the move, more impatient perhaps. Certainly they had been brisker in their resistance to restrictions imposed upon their dissenting practices during the reign of Charles I. In 1635, when Thomas Franklin, Josiah's father, no more than "inclined to the presbyterian Government and discipline"[16] of the church, was, at forty-two years of age, living agreeably and pleasantly in the established parish of St. Mary Magdalen in Ecton, with no intention, despite his leanings, of letting the ecclesiastical disputes upset his idyllic life, John Folger, five years older, was leaving Norwalk with wife and children for a distant wilderness, because he would not put up with repression, as his father before had refused to do in Flanders. The very fact that the Folgers were a refugee family in Norwich made them both less inclined to stay there in the face of repression (England wasn't really home to them—home lay across the North Sea amid the beautiful meadows of Flanders, the decision to leave which for their principles having long since been faced) and less tolerant of an oppressiveness which, having been unwilling to put up with it in their homeland, they were not likely to accept passively in an adopted land. Moreover, Norwich was a teeming city of thousands, given a cosmopolitan character by the large number of immigrants from the Low Countries, and the inhabitants did not take the restrictive measures of Archbishop Laud with the pastoral patience of those "inclined to the presbyterian Government and discipline" in the little village of Ecton.

The aggressively dissenting elements of Norwich's population were as old as the Reformation in England and its rebellious spirit. The ancestors of John Folger's Norwich-born wife, Meribah Gibbs, were rebelling against what they regarded as forms of tyranny as early as the 1230s, when Henry III had to come to the city to settle a dispute between the citizens and the monks of an ancient Benedictine abbey possessed of special privileges and exemptions since the reign of the Anglo-Saxon monarchs in the first millennium. In subsequent years, the conflicts centering on the resentment of poor and disgruntled citizens and the power and wealth of the 122 monasteries, in a city where the only abbot in England was the Bishop of Norwich, erupted periodically, and no number of exemplary executions, punishings of ringleaders, and removals of sympathetic mayors from office could subdue the citizens for long. And three thousand Norwich rebels died resisting the enclosure of lands to which they had previously had access during the reign of Edward VI in 1549; and seventeen thousand more saw, in sullen defeat, their leaders, the brothers Robert and William Kett hanged in chains, one from the parapet of Norwich Castle and the other from the tower of Wymondham Church.

Rebellion against religious oppression was no more unthinkable to the Norwich citizen than economic and civil rebellion. Thomas Bilney, a young Cantabrigian clergyman born in a hamlet named for his family on

---

[16] Benjamin Franklin the Elder, "A short account of the Family of Thomas Franklin," MS, Yale University Library.

the edge of Norwich, infuriated Cardinal Wolsey by urging that "the kings and princes of these times destroy and burn the images of saints set up in their churches." "Our Saviour Christ is our mediator between us and the Father, what need have we therefore to seek for any remedy from saints?"[17] His question was answered ultimately—but only after he had been repeatedly dragged from the pulpit for his views, stood in penance at St. Paul's Cathedral in London during the preacher's sermon, and endured a year's imprisonment in the Tower of London only to return to Norwich to repeat his reservations about the saints—by his burning at the stake in a bleak spot called Lollard's Pit outside the Bishopgate in Norwich on the eve of an August Sabbath in 1531. A century later, William Laud, Archbishop of Canterbury and master of the conscience of Charles I, directed one of the first of his edicts to destroy Puritanism to the refugees from religious repression in other lands who had come to England. An order went out that all foreign refugees were to conform to the Church of England in their beliefs and practices. When the bewildered refugees, commanded to conform to a church they had never been in, petitioned the King that all former sovereigns had provided them safe asylum from papal persecution without condition, he amended Laud's order to provide that surviving original refugees could continue their own form of worship but their English-born progeny must attend the Church of England. This meant John Folger and his family, and it was this that induced them to leave their homes and their work to escape oppression, with 140 other families who left Norwich for either Holland or New England. The Folgers, with the majority of them, chose New England.

In 1635, when they arrived, Boston was only five years old, a little huddle of houses on the edge of the sea with but one church—John Cotton's —no schools, no commerce, and dependent, as a peninsula that was an island at high tide, for its sustenance upon the farm lands to the southwest. Just four weeks before the *Abigail* bearing the Folgers arrived in Boston, twelve men from the settlement Watertown, adjacent on the west to Boston, secured from the General Court a free grant for a plantation up the Charles River ten miles from Boston. The Folgers, instead of staying in Boston, joined the new settlement, later called Dedham, but only as passing tenants; and they seemed not to have tarried long, for their names do not appear among the eighteen freemen of the town in either August 1636, when the first recorded public meeting was held, or again in July 1637, when twelve more freemen were added to the town's roster. Dedham was a rude frontier community concentrated in a row of tiny cottages on the edge of a meadow, each on a long and narrow lot, stretching back into the meadow from a common street, and each pegged together for lack of nails, with thatched roofs and no window glass. But it was

[17] From a sermon preached in 1527, cited in *The History of the City and County of Norwich*, 174.

peaceful, and the first settlers had called it "Contentment"—a name the General Court apparently thought frivolous and changed to Dedham when the town was legally organized in 1636. Whatever the cause of their restlessness at Dedham, which would be explicable enough considering that the Folgers were a gregarious, urban family, they moved to Watertown, three miles downriver toward Boston, probably under the sponsorship of one of the Watertown families who had settled Dedham.

Watertown was as old as Boston itself, having been settled by Sir Richard Saltonstall, the Reverend George Phillips, and others who came in Winthrop's fleet before the first winter made probings farther up the river implausible. Saltonstall, whose uncle was lord mayor of London and father the first citizen of Halifax in Yorkshire, was distinguished among the founding Puritans of New England for his outspoken contempt for the spirit of intolerance that John Cotton and his brethren felt essential to the inviolability of the Bible Commonwealth. After establishing the Watertown settlement, Saltonstall returned to England to restore his failing health and by letter admonished his colleagues in New England, "Doe not assume to yourselves infallibilitie of judgment, when the most learned of the apostles confesseth he knew but in part and saw but darkly as through a glass, for God is light, and no farther than he doth illumine us can we see, be our parts and learning never so great."[18] By 1635 Watertown was a flourishing little town, with over a hundred families, its own church, and an expansionist spirit that led to the acquisition of lands in Connecticut where the town proposed to send settlers. The community was lively, venturesome, and looking to the future. Among its 108 freemen was Thomas Mayhew, an enterprising emigrant from Wiltshire, who was exactly the same age as John Folger and had come to New England sometime before 1632, when he was already engaging at Medford in various commercial activities, none of which seemed to have flourished. By 1637 Mayhew was in Watertown, where he was operating a gristmill, which he later bought, for a London merchant whose colonial interests he supervised. Mayhew's affairs prospered rather more at Watertown than at Medford, and he was an impressive and substantial citizen when the Folgers— John, his contemporary in his late forties, and Peter, the contemporary of Thomas Mayhew, Jr., in his early twenties—arrived. The Mayhews and the Folgers shared an appetite for adventure that was within another generation to combine with the stolid spirit of the Franklins in the marriage of Josiah Franklin to Abiah Folger years later.

* * *

When James I in 1621 created the "Council for the Affaires of New England," he lumped together virtually all those northern lands that had originally been granted the Virginia Company, whose efforts at settling

[18] Letter quoted in Samuel Eliot Morison, *Builders of the Bay Colony* (Boston, 1930), 155.

them under Sir Ferdinando Gorges came to nothing in 1607. In 1635 Charles I concluded to separate the islands between Cape Cod and the Hudson River from the mainland in making future grants, and he conveyed them to the Earl of Stirling, Secretary of the Kingdom of Scotland, to dispose of as he saw fit. In 1641 the earl sold Nantucket to Thomas Mayhew and his son for forty pounds. Having some reservations, possibly because of its relatively small size and its distance, some thirty miles, from the mainland, Mayhew and his son had doubts about the practicality of settling Nantucket, and they went back to Stirling's agent and bought the proprietary rights to Martha's Vineyard and the Elizabeth Isles as well. While Thomas Mayhew, Sr., remained in Watertown to take care of his growing business interests and engage in local and colony politics, Thomas, Jr., organized a small group in 1642 to plant a settlement in Martha's Vineyard at Edgartown. The maternal grandfather of Benjamin Franklin, Peter Folger, then twenty-five, four years young Mayhew's senior, went with him.

Young Mayhew was inspired less by the profit motive than his father was and more by a strong sense of Christian mission. He organized a church immediately at Edgartown and became its pastor. To Peter Folger he assigned the function of schoolmaster and surveyor. Since, aside from his own tiny colony, all the residents of Martha's Vineyard were Indians, there were few to whom Mayhew could preach in the English language and fewer that Folger could teach. Touched by the plight of the Indians laboring in ignorance and superstition to wrest a sustenance from the sandy soil of the island, Mayhew learned their language and decided to commit his life largely to converting them to Chistianity, becoming the first apostle to the Indians some four years before John Eliot set out from his Roxbury parish to preach to the inhabitants of Nonantum, a village of Indians upstream on the Charles. Under Mayhew's benevolent influence, Peter Folger also learned the language of the Indians and, in addition to his teaching and surveying, aided Mayhew in his missionary work—"an able godly Englishman, nam'd Peter Foulger," Cotton Mather recorded in his history of New England, "who was imploy'd in teaching the youth in reading, writing, and the principles of religion, by catechising. . . ."[19]

The work of Mayhew and Folger in Martha's Vineyard progressed effectively. The principal Indian sagamores being won over to Christianity, Mayhew got over the early hurdles of suspicion and hostility, and by 1652 there was a full-time school exclusively for the Indians. Meanwhile his father left Watertown in 1646 and moved to the Vineyard, where he set himself up as chief magistrate and governor, which he had every right to do under the terms of the deed with Stirling. Young Mayhew thereafter devoted all his time and most of his personal funds to his missionary work, which had become such a financial drain by 1657 that he sailed for Eng-

[19] Mather, *Magnalia Christi Americana*, II, 429–30.

land to stimulate support there and to oversee the disposing of his father-in-law's estate. The ship on which he sailed was never heard from again, and that recurring epitaph in New England family records, "Lost at sea," was entered after the name of Thomas Mayhew, Jr., thirty-six. "Thus came to an immature death, Mr. Mayhew," Cotton Mather wrote years later, "who was so affectionately esteem'd of the Indians that many years after he was seldom named without tears."[20] Old Governor Mayhew, deeply saddened by the death of his only son, who was one of the purest of Christian spirits in an age beset more with the letter of the faith than its essence, undertook at the age of sixty-five to continue his son's work, devoting the rest of his long life and much of his means to this labor.

Peter Folger, who was forty years old and the father of five by the time his friend, the younger Mayhew, disappeared at sea, evidently did not have his heart in teaching and converting Indians for the rest of his life. Two years after Mayhew's disappearance, Folger was ready for a new enterprise. It came when Tristram Coffin and a friend, Edward Starbuck, of Salisbury, a little settlement far north of Boston, put into the harbor at Edgartown in a shallop, with only Isaac Coleman, a cabin boy, as crew, having in mind the exploring of some of the smaller islands as possible places of settlement for themselves and some of their friends, many of whom were becoming increasingly distressed at the harsh measures being taken by the Massachusetts magistrates against the Quakers and other "heretics." On learning that Thomas Mayhew, the governor and principal proprietor of Martha's Vineyard, also owned the island of Nantucket, Coffin determined to sail on to the smaller island to study its possibilities, for it—like Martha's Vineyard and the rest of Lord Stirling's grant to Mayhew—was not a part of Massachusetts but an independent colony having "the same powers of government which the Massachusetts people enjoyed by their charter."[21] He enlisted Peter Folger to go along as an interpreter to deal with the Indians, who would have to agree to the sale of any land to the settlers and be compensated for it, and also as a surveyor to advise them on the possible divisions and uses of the land. The former function was of particular importance and not a little delicacy, for Nantucket was a small island long inhabited by the Indians, who, in the absence of any frontier to retreat to, could not simply be pushed into the sea. Moreover, though for his forty pounds Mayhew had acquired proprietary title to Nantucket, the resident Indian sachems and their people were under the impression that they had a substantial claim to the land; and terms would have to be arrived at with them. Folger, who had come to know the Indians well during his seventeen years of work among them on the Vineyard and who was always on the side of the underdog, dealt effectively with them on behalf of his principal, Coffin. As a result, a practical scheme for a settlement

[20] Ibid., 430.
[21] Hutchinson, *History of Massachusetts Bay*, I, 151n.

on Nantucket was worked out, and Coffin went back to Martha's Vineyard to come to an agreement with Thomas Mayhew.

Committed to carrying on his lost son's work on Martha's Vineyard, Mayhew had no interest in himself actively participating in a Nantucket settlement, and he readily agreed to very reasonable terms through which Coffin and eight of his friends could acquire Nantucket "to Injoy their heirs and assigns for Ever with all the privilidges thereunto belonging for and in Consideration of the sum of Thirty pounds of Currant pay unto whomsoever I the sd Thomas Mayhew mine heirs or assigns shall appoint and also two bever hats one for myself and one for my wife. . . ."[22] Since eighteen years earlier Mayhew had paid the Earl of Stirling forty pounds for Nantucket, he could hardly have had a profit uppermost in mind, unless there was an extraordinary shortage of beaver hats on Martha's Vineyard. He did, however, as an integral part of the deed, retain a one-twentieth share in the venture, probably so that he could have some voice in the fate of an island in such close proximity to the one to which he and his son had committed so much of their lives. Tristram Coffin, for his part, went back to Salisbury, sailing the long arc around Cape Cod, across Massachusetts Bay and past Boston Harbor and its islands, around the rocky promontory of Cape Ann and into Salisbury. There his eight partners ratified his agreement with Mayhew, and ten new partners, including Edward Starbuck, and ten tenant inhabitants were admitted to the company. Peter Folger executed a formal deed with Wanackmamack and Nickanoose, the head sachems of the Nantucket Indians in 1660, and by 1662 the Salisbury company had divided the land among twenty-one landowners and several tradesmen and artisans whose services were essential and who were given a half-share in the venture rather than the full share given to those who had invested their money. Among the "half-share men," as they came to be called, was Peter Folger, who had presided over most of the land allocations and was "excepted as a Tradesman namely as a Surveyor, Interpretor and Millar"[23] in March 1664, getting two quarts out of every bushel ground at the town mill in return for his labors.

Though there is no concrete evidence that Nantucket was settled by its company of some thirty original families as a specific rebellion against the rigid authority of the Bible Commonwealth, there is little doubt that they were all independent-minded people who had difficulty swallowing the absolutist edicts handed down by the Puritan magistrates and accepted when not encouraged by the Puritan priests. Of the ten original proprietors who came to live on the island, two—Thomas Macy and Richard Swayne—had been fined and disenfranchised or admonished for giving

---

[22] The deed is in Alexander Starbuck, The History of Nantucket, Tuttle edition (Rutland, 1969), 18, "From a copy made and certified to by Eleazor Folger, and to which is appended the following note—'A true Coppy of the Record so much as is legible but Time has Defaced some part thereof.'"

[23] Franklin B. Hough, ed., Papers Relating to the Island of Nantucket (Albany, 1856), 14.

shelter to Quakers (in Macy's case, for forty-five minutes during a rainstorm), although they were neither banished nor imprisoned for their
offenses. But Macy was a Baptist and therefore never wholly acceptable to
Puritan orthodoxy, and Edward Starbuck was his friend and his partner in
a proprietary share of the Nantucket company. Two other original proprietors, Christopher Hussey and Robert Pike, whose holdings were occupied
and their interests represented by Hussey's son, Stephen, were in chronic
trouble with the Massachusetts authorities. Pike, a deputy in the General
Court, was disenfranchised for denouncing a law prohibiting preaching
without a license and Christopher Hussey for petitioning the court to re-
scind its punishment of Pike.

The atmosphere of freedom induced by the independence of Nantucket
from the Massachusetts Bay Colony and its unyielding magistracy was
highly congenial to the instincts and temperament of Peter Folger. Since
it had been unsettled since being claimed by the British after Bartholomew
Gosnold's voyage along the New England coast in 1602, the island was
clearly assigned to no jurisdiction. Sir Ferdinando Gorges, "Lord Proprietor" of the Province of Maine, had claimed jurisdiction, under the terms
of his grant from King Charles, over all the islands Lord Stirling held, but
he died in 1647, twelve years before Nantucket was settled. By 1670 New
York, under the authority of the Duke of York, had been claiming that
"The Patent of the Duke includes Martha's Vineyard and those other
Isles" and serving notice that the "Plymouth Colony, Rhode Island or any
other that have any Pretences, or lay Clayme to any of those Islands"
would be resisted by the governor of New York, Francis Lovelace. The inhabitants of Nantucket readily recognized the jurisdiction of New York
and the authority of Governor Lovelace, with whom they made an
agreement which virtually gave them autonomy. Tristram Coffin and
Thomas Macy were the principal spokesmen for the settlement; and the
former was appointed by Lovelace as chief magistrate of Nantucket, having been nominated for the post by his townsmen, the town itself naming
all other officers, civil and military, except the chief military officer who
was to be selected by Governor Lovelace from two nominees of the town.
All things considered, Nantucket was, with Martha's Vineyard and Rhode
Island, the freest society in the realm. There was, moreover, a genuine
freedom of religion that took expression not in doctrinal statements or
political declarations but in the undisturbed exercise of such freedom by
sects still condemned and banned as heretics in the Bible Commonwealth.
Nantucket's first historian, Thomas Macy's great-grandson, wrote, "During the first fifty years of the settlement, the people were mostly Baptists;
there were some Presbyterians, and a few of the Society of Friends. The
little community was kind and courteous to each other and hospitable to
strangers. The prevalence of good feeling was remarked and felt by all who
came among them."[24] To Peter Folger, whose family had twice moved to

[24] Obed Macy, *History of Nantucket* (Boston, 1686), 29.

strange lands to find religious tolerance and not to deny it, the liberality of Nantucket must have been a matter of primary importance—more vital than even the right to exercise his own religion—and he was to make this clear throughout his life by both his actions and his words, albeit sometimes in a way that seemed more mischievous than saintly.

Dominated by no strong or oppressive government, self-imposed or from without, and imbued with a sense of freedom in their island aloofness from the Bible Commonwealth, of which all of them had had a not wholly palatable taste, the Nantucketers' Elysium was nevertheless shaken severely by the inherently troublesome structure of first-class and second-class citizens. The first class was made up of the "First Purchasers"—the twenty who had originally compacted to buy full shares in the settlement plus a few others to whom they had subsequently voted partnerships. The second class was constituted of scores of tradesmen who were invited to the island because their services were necessary to the settlement and who were given a half-share, including a homesite, as an inducement to leave the mainland and start anew. Some of these "half-share men" were associated with the island from its first settlement. Peter Folger, who was, of course, involved in the first probings of Nantucket as a suitable spot for a new community and had, in fact, been the chief planner of its first planting, had no stake and apparently no residence on the island until he was given his half-share in 1664. Since the prosperity of the new colony was dependent largely upon its maritime commerce, half-shares were distributed from the beginning to seamen—anyone who agreed, like William Worth, "To come and Dwell on the Island and to Imploy himself or be Imployed on sea affairs." Other early grants of half-shares were made, for example, to Joseph Gardner, who agreed to "supply the occasions of the Island in way of a Shoemaker"; to Nanthaniel Holland as "a Taylor on the Island"; to James Loper "to Carry on a Designe of Whale Catching"; and to Peter Folger's twenty-two-year-old son, Eleazor, who had witnessed the deeds that his father had helped negotiate with the Indians, for agreeing to learn the trade of a blacksmith and to practice it. Much to their later regret, the first purchasers also gave Joseph Gardner's brother, John, of Salem, a half-share "upon Conditions that he come to Inhabit and set up the trade of fishing with sufficient vessel fit for the taking of codfish."[25]

For the first decade of Nantucket's history, the Folgers and their fellow half-share men lived in sufficient accord with the first purchasers. But they were Englishmen, and it went against their grain that more than half of them were second-class citizens with a voice in their government less than equal to that of some of their peers, and with their personal rights abridged by the commitment to practice only the trade meted out to them by the first purchasers at the time of their receiving their half-shares. There is no

[25] Ibid., passim.

The first known portrait of Benjamin Franklin was painted when he was in his thirties, some fifteen years after he left Boston, and was prospering as printer, publisher, bookseller, and postmaster in Philadelphia. FOGG ART MUSEUM, HARVARD UNIVERSITY

At least as early as the parish register of the Church of St. Mary Magdalen, in Ecton, Northamptonshire, begins, in 1559, Franklin's ancestors lived in the village, and some lie buried in its churchyard. PHOTO BY ARTHUR B. TOURTELLOT

Josiah Franklin was baptized at the ancient Saxon font in the Ecton parish church, as were six of his eight brothers (two, twins, died at birth) and his sister. PHOTO BY ARTHUR B. TOURTELLOT

The ancestral home and smithy of the Franklins was on the principal street of the village, just beyond the three-story building in the center. PHOTO BY ARTHUR B. TOURTELLOT

The site of the Franklin house in Ecton is now occupied by a public house called Three Horseshoes, a name probably inspired by the Franklin smithy. PHOTO BY ARTHUR B. TOURTELLOT

The house directly across the street from the Franklin house in Ecton, as generations of the family looked out on it, still stands. PHOTO BY T. R. BONSEY, RECTOR OF ECTON

W Rought Things, Printed *Englifh* or *India* Calico's; Cloth, Silk, and Stuff, Scoured; Linen, Cloth, Silk, and Stuff, Dyed, Printed, or Watred; AND Black Cloth, Silk, and Stuff, Dyed into Colours: BY Benjamin Franklin, At the *Indian Queen* in *Princes-Street* near *Leicefter-Fields*.

Josiah Franklin and two of his older brothers, John and Benjamin, became dyers. But Josiah and Benjamin (known as "the Elder," to distinguish him from his famous nephew) had to abandon their trade in Puritan Boston for lack of demand. AMERICAN ANTIQUARIAN SOCIETY

The Boston of the early eighteenth century, when Benjamin Franklin was growing up in it, was a peninsula town, jutting out into Massachusetts Bay, its life attuned to the sea.
SCENOGRAPHIC AMERICANA, 1768, NEW YORK PUBLIC LIBRARY COLLECTIONS

Benjamin Franklin was born in a small rented cottage, near the corner of Marlborough (now Washington) and Milk streets, across from the Old South Church, close to Boston Harbor. PICTURE COLLECTION, NEW YORK PUBLIC LIBRARY

The sign that Josiah Franklin adopted for his tallow shop, which made and sold soap and candles, was "The Blue Ball." BOSTONIAN SOCIETY

Samuel Willard (1640–1707), for thirty years pastor of the Third (Old South) Church and, for seven, acting president of Harvard College, baptized Benjamin Franklin. PICTURE COLLECTION, NEW YORK PUBLIC LIBRARY

Increase Mather (1639–1723) was the influential pastor of Boston's Second Church, a political emissary to London in 1688 to negotiate a new charter for the colony, and president of Harvard for sixteen years, being replaced, to the bitterness of the Mathers, in 1701 by Samuel Willard. CULVER PICTURES

question that, for all practical purposes and under English law, they had entered into a contract to provide specified services in return for land and rights to common pastures, woodlands, and water sources. They also had escape clauses, permitting them to leave after three years, at which time the departing half-share man had the right to sell his land back to the town "at a Valluable price and if the Town do not buy it then he may sell it to whom he pleases."[26] The economic conditions were hardly oppressive, certainly far from enslaving. And [civilly] the sources of their political discontent could not have included disqualification for public office, for John Gardner and William Worth were elected selectmen along with three purchasers in January 1672/3—within months of their having been given their half-shares.

Whatever the specific causes of the half-shares men's uneasiness, Tristram Coffin and Matthew Mayhew, Thomas Mayhew's grandson and agent on Nantucket, sent a letter to Major Edmund Andros, Lovelace's successor as governor of New York, petitioning him to reaffirm the rights of the first purchasers, who ". . . and not without Cause, have feared a Disturbance in their Quiet and Peaceable Injoiment of their said Interest; by those they had formerly admitted in among them. . . ."[27] The context of the complaint suggests that the basic trouble was that half-shares men were only conditional owners of their land, despite whatever improvements they had made on it through their own earnings and efforts, whereas the first purchasers were full and unconditional owners and that the half-shares men took advantage of the Dutch incursion of New York, which occasioned Lovelace's dismissal, to stage an insurrection against the authority of Tristram Coffin and his fellow first purchasers, claiming that the old Stirling grant and the Duke of York's charter leading to it were invalid and that therefore all the land allocations and all the laws made since were also invalid. What in essence was happening was that a thorough land reform policy was being demanded, the laws sustaining the old system were being challenged, and some ringleaders among the half-shares men were openly urging revolt by ignoring the lawful processes of the priority of the first purchasers, the validity of all charters, grants, and transactions leading to their authority to impose conditions on the titles of half-shares men to their land and the right of the island's courts to try and punish the insurrectionists. Thomas Macy was commissioned Chief magistrate by Andros for a one-year term, beginning October 1, 1675. Presumably, it was his responsibility to preside over the legal proceedings dealing with the rebellious half-shares men's leaders, and apparently he went about it with enthusiasm. But his commission, according to the half-shares men, expired on October 1, 1676, since no reappointment was re-

26 Town Records, under date of August 5, 1671.
27 Hough, *Papers Relating to Nantucket*, 60.

ceived from Andros. Although an order of Lovelace in 1673 had specifically provided that the chief magistrate remain in office until a successor was named, the half-shares men refused to recognize Macy's authority after the expiration date of his commission. The leader in opposing him was John Gardner, who had been the rallying point of the insurrection all along and saw now a good chance to revive it. In league with him was that perpetual champion of the underdog, Peter Folger.

As clerk of the court over which Macy presided, Folger was in a peculiarly advantageous position to be obnoxious to an authority with which he had no sympathy, and he expressed his views by refusing, after October 1, 1676, either to record any more proceedings of the court or to deliver to Macy any of the court records—all this despite the fact that the town had voted to recognize the automatic continuance of Thomas Macy in office until a successor was named or his own reappointment received from Andros in New York. It was Folger's somewhat strained reasoning that since his position and hence his custody of the records emanated from the authority of the court as an institution and not a particular magistrate, he should not release the records to the magistrate. He was indicted for contempt but refused to respond to the summons. Instead he went to John Gardner's house for refuge, and the constable appeared with a warrant for his arrest, the court record showing that "Tis the Order of the Court that the Constable be sent to Peter Ffoulger for the Court Booke, and all records of that Nature and this is to impower the Constable herein, and to bring them to ye Court forthwith, and Peter Ffoulger is hereby required to deliver them."[28] Dramatizing with the pen in a long letter to, of all people, Governor Andros, Folger narrated the rough treatment to which he was put thereafter:

"The sayd Constable by the Help of other Men, haled and draged me out of the Cap't [Gardner] House and caried me to the Place where they were met. I Spake not a Word to the Constable, nor resisted him in the least. When I cam at the House I saw none of the Court, but the Constable told me that the Court was adjourned to Wednesday next and that I was committed into his Hands and must give Bond to appeare then.

"Feb. 19th, I cam before them and carried myself every way as civilly as I could, only I spake never a Word, for I was fully persuaded that if I spake anything at al, they would turn it against me. I remembered also the old Saying that of nothing comes nothing."

The disingenuousness of an experienced clerk of court's feigning hurt surprise that refusing to answer a magistrate in a legal proceeding could be construed as contempt of court is more appealing than convincing. But Folger was stubborn about it and refused to yield. Macy accordingly sentenced him to appear before the court of assize in New York. "After my sentence," Folger continued in his exercise in pathos to Governor Andros,

[28] Starbuck, *History of Nantucket*, 53n.

for he and his friends could easily have raised bond as property owners, "The Constable called for Twenty Pound Bond, or to Prison I must go presently, when they al know that I am a poore old Man [he was fifty-nine, and his foe, Macy, was sixty-five], and not able to maintayne my Family [he had only two daughters still at home]. All my Estate, if my Debts were payed, will not amount to half so much, and as for making use of Friends, they all know that I have more Need of any Helpe that way for the Supply of my Family. For want of a Bond away the Constable carried me to Prison, a Place where never any English-man was put, and where the Neighbors Hogs had layed but the Night before, and in a bitter cold Frost and deep Snow. They had only thrown out most of the Durt, Hogs Dung and Snow. The rest the Constable told me I might ly upon if I would, that is upon the Boards in that Case, and without Victuals or Fire. Indeed I persuaded him to fetch a little Hay, and he did so, and some Friend did presently bring Beding and Victuals."[29]

The case against Folger was indefinitely suspended, and Folger and Gardner continued to bedevil the authorities but stayed clear of jail. Folger's old friendship with the Indians and his compulsive sympathy for the underdog seem to have put him on the side of the Indians during King Philip's sad and futile struggle to make a last stand against the forces that were inevitably and at a rapidly accelerating rate pushing his people to the west. Folger also became a Baptist, probably less out of conviction than because Baptists were underdogs in New England, in the process hopelessly confusing some of his older Indian converts whom he attempted to rebaptize through total immersion—a rite possibly assumed by the bewildered Indians, insensitive to the niceties of the doctrinal disputes then so popular in New England on the nature of baptism, to be a clear intent to drown them.

In 1676, when King Philip's War burst out in its greatest violence, Folger took pen in hand and wrote a strong pamphlet in which he lectured New England on why God had permitted the Bible Commonwealth to be visited with such a devastating affliction as to wipe out whole towns and more than decimate the population. Though addressed to the people of the New England colonies generally, it was clearly meant for the particular eyes of the Puritan ministers and magistrates, from whom, as a resident of the New York province, Folger was safe—though there is little in his life to suggest that he would not have done the same thing even if he were not beyond the reach of Puritan wrath.

Because versification was construed as giving any document more dignity and authority, Folger laboriously set forth his thesis in verse—four prefatory couplets and no fewer than 105 quatrains, ending fearlesssly, but perhaps somewhat anticlimactically and surely with the most tortured of rhymes, with his own name, for Peter Folger was never one to hide his light under a bushel. He began his statement, entitled "A Looking Glass for the Times or the Former Spirit of New England Revived in this Generation," with the highest confidence:

> Let all that read these Verses know,
> That I intend something to show
> About our War, how it hath been,
> And also what is the chief Sin,
> That God doth so with us Contend,
> And when these Wars are like to end.
> Read them in Love; do not despise
> What here is set before thine Eyes.[30]

The appeal of this to colonists who went to bed in stark fear of being wiped out before morning, who had seen entire villages of their fellows leveled and among whom not one family had escaped, by some bond of blood or marriage, some loss, must have been vast, for since time immemorial men have asked, in response to disaster, "Why?" and "When will it end?"

Folger absolved the Indians of any blame or responsibility, though he thought them "very foolish." "Yet God doth make of them a Rod/to punish us for Sin." The sin of the Puritans? Intolerance and the persecution of those who disagreed with them—particularly the Baptists "for the Witness that they bare/against Babes Sprinkling," i.e., infant baptism. The chief culprits? "They were the Tribe of Ministers,/as they are said to be,/Who always to our Magistrates/must be the Eyes to see./These are the Men that by their Wits,/have spun so fair a Thread,/That now themselves and others are/of Natives in a Dread." The cure? "Let Magistrates and Ministers/consider what they do;/Let them repeal those evil Laws,/and break those Bonds in two,/Which have been made as Traps and Snares/to catch the Innocents,/And whereby it has gone so far,/to acts of Violence." Expecting no such change of heart in "our College Men"—that was to say, the products of the repository of the Puritan intellect, Harvard College—Folger, in good democratic fashion, called upon the people to turn to God but, in league with Him, to keep the courts in their place. "Let us then seek for help from God,/and turn to him that smite;/Let us take heed, that at no time,/we sin against our Light./Let's bear our testimony plain/'gainst Sin in High and Low;/And see that we no Cowards be,/to hide the Light we know./When *Jonathan* [i.e., any man] is call'd to Court/shall we as Stander's by,/Be still and have no Words to speak,/but suffer him to die?" Resolving to seek no refuge in anonymity and having made about as grave a charge against the Puritan establishment as was conceivable—violating the laws of God—Folger concluded, "Because to be

[30] The excerpts are taken, not from the original edition printed in Boston by John Foster in 1676, but from an edition in the John Carter Brown Library at Brown University, "Printed in the Year 1763."

a Libeller, I hate it with my heart,/From Sherbon Town [then the name of the town of Nantucket], where now I dwell,/my Name I do put here,/ Without Offence your real Friend,/it is Peter Folger."

This incredible document was printed, even more incredibly, in the very citadel of the Heavenly City, Boston, in the same year that it was written —1676—by the young printer John Foster, a close friend and parishioner of the Mathers and printer of their sermons, a protégé of Increase Mather, who as one of the licensers of Boston's first press got him the post of printer, and a graduate of Harvard College in the class of 1667. There is no record that, despite Folger's blatant attack on the ministers and the college, Foster suffered the slightest reprisal or even rebuke for his boldness in printing it; in fact, he continued to be the Mathers' favorite printer, and when he died, at thirty-three, he left remembrances for the Mathers in his will. And on Folger's broad indictment of them, which really denounced what John Cotton had rightly pronounced the basic assumption of Puritanism—the danger of tolerating dissenting beliefs—and Harvard College, of which Increase Mather was president, the Mathers were inexplicably silent. In the case of Increase, as a matter of fact, he had to be an accessory in its publication, for, as one of the licensers of the Boston printing press, he was charged with approving all that was printed. After Philip's death in battle, in any case, the war drifted toward an end as the superior arms of the colonists repulsed the Indian; and there was no such uprising as Peter Folger called for against the magistrates.

Folger and Gardner both appear to have kept up their crusade on behalf of the half-shares men. In 1686 Folger was in some sort of minor difficulty, for a constable took a beast away from him in lieu of a fine, but for his pains was ordered by a court friendly to Folger "forthwith to deliver unto Peter Folger that beast that was killed at Poatpis, there to deliver it to him, it being the beast that was formerly taken from him as a fine. You having liberty to way [weigh] the quarters, hide and tallow and to take a receipt accordingly."[31]

Peter and Mary Folger had nine children, eight before moving to Nantucket, where only the last, Abiah, Benjamin Franklin's mother, was born, on August 16, 1667. All of them survived to adulthood. Of the two sons, Eleazor and John, both stayed in Nantucket, Eleazor achieving distinction as a public servant (he was witnessing deeds executed by his father with the Indians when he was eleven years old), as register of deeds, clerk of court, envoy to deal with the Indians, public schoolmaster, and deputy to the Great and General Court in Boston. Eleazor married John Gardner's niece, Sarah Gardner, thus cementing a strong political alliance. John, eleven years his junior, a farmer, who was also the town's miller, married into the opposition, with Mary Barnard, granddaughter of a first purchaser, whose cousin John Barnard had married Bethiah Folger, John's

31 Starbuck, *History of Nantucket*, 73.

older sister. (In June 1669 John and Bethiah, with Eleazor Folger, Isaac Coleman, and an Indian, went to Martha's Vineyard by canoe to buy furniture for their new home the year after their marriage. All but Eleazor perished on their return when the canoe capsized.) Of the other six sisters, two married Nantucket men and stayed on the island. Two married residents of Charlestown and Salem. A fifth, Patience, married Ebenezer Harker, of Nantucket, but they left the island and went to Boston where Patience Folger Harker was accepted into the Old South Church in 1684. Her youngest sister Abiah—last of Peter Folger's brood of daughters— followed Patience to Boston, where she received adult baptism on August 19, 1688, her father apparently having already been seized with his Baptist persuasions when she was born in 1667. When Josiah Franklin was bereaved in 1689, then, she had been, for a year, a fellow parishioner. In his unhappy autumn of 1689, Abiah Folger was close to him, and they were married.

The Folger line brought spirit, zest, rebellion, and thoroughgoing independence to the sturdiness, sense of responsibility, self-reliance, and incorruptible integrity of the Franklins. In his maturity, Benjamin Franklin wrote appreciatively of the character of his maternal grandfather, characterizing that outspoken poem of protest Peter Folger wrote "as written with a good deal of Decent Plainness and manly Freedom,"[32] and he treasured Cotton Mather's tribute to Peter Folger in his *Magnalia Christi Americana*. Certainly, Folger's remarkable liveliness, his enormous versatility, his energy, his boisterous resistance to authority which he thought errant or abrasive, his love of the written word, his essential skepticism (evidenced, often to the distress of his more acquiescent townsmen, by his repeated challenges to the law), his joyous learning of new trades when the need arose, his enterprise in mastering the language of the Indians, his defiance of the wrong and the wrongheaded as he recognized them, his delight and uninhibitedness in trying his hand at both poetry and prose, his qualities of character and intelligence that led the settlers to depend on his skill and fairness in dividing the land among them, his high sense of understanding of the fundamental injustice being dealt the Indians and his willingness to risk his own privileged position to do something about it—all this constituted a powerful and opulent heritage to his children and to his grandchildren, one that was to surface over and over again in the values, interests, and ways of the sixty-second of his grandchildren and the thirty-eighth of his grandsons, born sixteen years after his death, Benjamin Franklin.

* * *

The marriage of Josiah Franklin and Abiah Folger was a felicitous one, destined to last until 1744, when Josiah died at the age of eighty-seven to be followed five years later by Abiah's death at eighty-four—neither of

[32] *Autobiography*, 52.

them, as Benjamin wrote, having ever suffered "any sickness but that of which they dy'd."[33] Nine children, six boys and three girls, were born to them over a period of eighteen years between 1690 and 1708. Josiah, who had "owned the covenant" at the South Church in 1685 two years after his arrival, became a communicant in 1694. It speaks well for the regard in which Abiah was held that she was made a communicant at the same time—a remarkable achievement for a young woman in view of the length of time it took most parishioners of the Puritan churches to progress to full communion with the church.

Within the South Church family, Josiah was an increasingly respected force, moving under the benevolent eye of Judge Sewall into a position of leadership among the communicants. The judge noted in his diary whenever the midweek meeting of the neighborhood parishioners took place at "Mr. Josiah Franklin's" and whenever Franklin, because of the judge's hoarseness from a cold, was called upon to "set the tune" for the psalms or to offer the closing prayer. And as in his civil life, Josiah served as a tithingman, a clerk of the market, and a constable, so in his ecclesiastical life the diligent, intelligent soapmaker of Milk Street sought and assumed responsibility, offering his simple cottage across from the South Church for prayer meetings, and probably serving generously cider, beer, and victuals, for there was something in the Puritan temperament that associated hearty eating with religiosity. He filled in on occasion as precentor for the husky-voiced Sewall, and eventually stood for the lofty office of deacon, losing by twenty-seven votes to Bartholomew Green, the most noted of early New England printers, and by nine votes to Daniel Henchman, a prominent bookseller and the first paper manufacturer in Boston, who represented the third generation of his family to belong to the South Church, with which they were associated from its beginning.

That Josiah Franklin—a young tradesman, a relative newcomer to Boston as compared to the earliest families and one without any pre-established connections in the town—could rival, in the regard of those who knew him best and with whom, aside from his family, he spent the most time, is persuasive substantiation of the recollection that Benjamin Franklin had of his father as a man of "sound Understanding and solid Judgement in prudential Matters."[34] It is more. For it provides a convincing example of the nonaristocratic nature of New England Puritanism, expressed not in any instinct for commonality for its own sake but rather in the higher importance attached to qualities of intelligence and character

[33] Ibid., 56. Benjamin Franklin was in error, however, in fixing his father's age at his death as eighty-nine. Josiah Franklin was born December 23, 1657. In reporting Josiah's death, *The Boston News-Letter* of January 17, 1744/5, had his age correct: "Last night died Mr. Josiah Franklin, tallow chandler and soapmaker: By the force of a steady Temperance, he made a Constitution, none of the strongest, last with comfort to the age of Eighty-seven years. . . ." Benjamin Franklin also put the wrong date, 1655, for his father's birth, on his parents' epitaph in the Granary Burial Ground in Boston.

[34] Ibid., 54.

than to family associations and wealth. Josiah Franklin, largely through the South Church, became the familiar, on terms of total equality, with some of the best minds of the Bible Commonwealth—the clergy, the educators, the lawyers, the emerging class of well-read merchants, the leaders of the civic life of the community. It was possibly the least stratified of any society planted by a European power in the New World and, except for the inherent closed-mindedness on other paths to salvation than that promulgated by Puritanism, the most open-ended. But by the turn of the century, when Josiah and Abiah Franklin were raising a family, the town of Boston, with Baptist, Quaker, and Church of England churches openly established and an increasingly bold body of skeptics asserting their views, was also becoming a lively center of contrasting views. The printing press, though subject to license and to regulation by the authorities, was in many instances surprisingly unmolested. Not only had Peter Folger's assault on the Boston Puritan priests been published as early as 1676 by a printer who owed his job to the most powerful of them, but the following year a mariner named George Jay had published by Samuel Green at the press at Harvard an attack on the magistrates, bearing the fortright title, *Innocency's Complaint against Tyrannical Court Faction in New-england*, and charging flatly:

> The *Massachusetts* is alike for Crime
> Unto Judea, in Christ Jesus' Time
> Here Laws are extant, that doth terrify
> Well meaning men, and Liberty deny
> In serving God, except in their own way.[35]

Moving into a new century, taking to new ways, no longer shutting out new views and new values, the Boston in which Josiah and Abiah Franklin lived was touched with a sense of freedom—not merely from a tyrannical crown three thousand miles across the sea but from the tyrannical minister and magistrate around the corner.

The material affairs of the little Franklin household prospered sufficiently, without in any measure laying a foundation for a family fortune. Processing tallow and making soap and candles continued, all through Josiah Franklin's lifetime, to be a grueling and demanding way of making a living; and since it was the most time-consuming and exhausting of hard labor, there was no way to build it into an affluent industry by spending more time and more effort at it. The trade simply by its nature had a ceiling on it; but it was a living—and a reliable one—and Josiah was able to support a family that totaled sixteen children and that, for a period extending over forty years of his life, always included at least one child under sixteen and at one time numbered ten children under that age. Setbacks were visited upon him, but he had resources of determi-

[35] Broadside in the collection of the Massachusetts Historical Society.

nation and judgment that enabled him to overcome them and to go on very much as though they had never happened.

Such an episode occurred in Milk Street on the night of Tuesday, September 16, 1690, ten months after Josiah and Abiah were married and when she was six months into her first pregnancy. A fire broke out in the house of their neighbor, John Allen, a worsted comber by trade, and spread rapidly down the street.

Fires were a constant problem in Boston. The little peninsular town, with its closely packed wooden houses and churches often with faultily built chimneys and exposed on all sides to the winds, had been plagued with disastrous fires as the town grew and its buildings were built closer and closer to one another. In 1654 a fire swept through the town and was of such alarming proportions that the building of a conduit was authorized to bring water down from the top of Seaborne Cotton's hill to a wooden reservoir in the market place. Captain Robert Keayne, always on the alert for a public service project to atone for his questionable mercantile practices, when composing his will some months after the fire of 1654, wrote, "Having thought of the want of some necessary things for the Towne of Boston, as a Market-place [house] and Condit; the one a good helpe in danger of fyre, the want of which we have found of sad and costly experience, not only in other parts of the Town, where possibly they have better supply of water but in the heart of the Town about the Market-place—and many fair buildings there be round about it."[36] And shortly after this first of a chain of "Great Fires" in Boston, it was ordered by the town "that thear be a ladder or ladders to every house within this Town, that shall rech to the ridg of the house, which every househowlder shall provide for his house by the last day of the 3d. mo. next, one the penaltie of 6s.8d.; that every householder shall provide a pole of about 12 foot long with a good large swob at the end of it, to rech the rofe of his house to quench fire; that the seleckt men shall provide six good and large ladders for the Towne's use, which shall hang at the outside of the Meetinghouse, to be branded with the Town mark; that a bell man goes about the Town in the night, from 10 unto 5 a cloke in the morning."[37] New regulations were also made that authorized the pulling down of houses to stop fires and forbade the carrying of firebrands or fire pans from one building to another. But the tinderbox town could not be protected from all human error, and on November 27, 1676, the second "Great Fire" occurred, "accidentally kindled by the carelessness of an apprentice that sat up too late over night, as was conceived; which began an hour before day, continuing three or four, in which time it burned down to the ground forty-six dwelling-houses, besides other buildings, together with a meeting-

[36] *Antiquarian Journal*, VI, 90.
[37] Drake, *History and Antiquities of Boston*, 334n.

house of considerable bigness."[38] The apprentice, a tailor's helper, lit his candle on arising and then, falling asleep, let it set fire to his lodgings in a house at the north end of the peninsula. Among the dwellings was the house of the Reverend Increase Mather, who rejoiced in the fact that of his library of over a thousand books, he was able to rescue all but less than a hundred. Only a fierce southeast rainstorm saved the town even greater devastation, and once again the authorities sought to alleviate the potential danger from fires—this time by widening and straightening the streets when the burned-out area was rebuilt. The third "Great Fire," in a town still built primarily of wood, and the worst of all, broke out at midnight on a sultry summer night early in August, in 1679, in an alehouse called the Three Mariners, located in the very heart of Boston near a drawbridge over Mill Creek, an artificial waterway that led from the Mill Pond on the north side of the peninsula to the town cove on the southeast side. The fire, raging until noon the next day, consumed virtually the entire trading part of Boston, leveling eighty houses and seventy warehouses. The ships at the Town Dock, the largest in the harbor, were also destroyed with their cargoes. In a town then of 4,500 with some seven hundred houses, the proportions of the disaster were impressive enough with over a tenth of its housing destroyed; but the real effect can be gauged only by the overwhelming destruction of its commercial establishment. After this conflagration, the General Court for the first time got to the real cause of the repeated disasters—wooden construction: "This Court, having a sense of the great ruines in Boston by fire, and hazard still of the same, by reason of the joyning and neereness of their buildings, for prevention of damage & losse thereby for future, doe order & enact, that henceforth no dwelling house in Boston shall be errected & sett up except of stone or bricke, & covered with slate or tyle, on penalty of forfeiting double the value of such buildings. . . ."[39]

But the Allen house, like the other cottages in Milk Street and like the South Meetinghouse across the street, was built long before the mandatory reform in building materials; and when the fire broke out at eleven o'clock that September night in 1690, the entire household and the neighboring ones were sound asleep. Samuel Worster, an apprentice who lived in the Allen house and probably slept in the garret, was burned to death in the fire as the house was destroyed. Quickly the fire leaped across narrow passageways to the neighboring houses of Lieutenant Reynolds, occupied by the Franklin family; of Thomas Bligh, who had lived in the town since 1652; of Benjamin Langden, a small manufacturer; and of Savil Simpson, a warden of King's Chapel. According to the diary of Judge Sewall, whose house was at the foot of Cotton Hill close to the area of the fire, the Reynolds, Bligh, and Langden houses were destroyed, "and a

[38] William Hubbard, *Narrative of the Troubles with the Indians* (Boston, 1677), 115.
[39] Shurtleff, *Description of Boston*, 642.

great part of Savil Simson's." Sparks and embers flew across the street and settled on the roof of the brooding cedar meetinghouse of the South Church. "The wind being Sou-west," Sewall recorded, "the South-Meeting-House was preserv'd with very much difficulty, being in a flame in diverse places of it."[40]

What happened to the Franklin household, at that time consisting of, in addition to Abiah and Josiah, three of Josiah's daughters and two of his sons by Anne Child, the oldest twelve and the youngest three, can only be conjectured. The seven undoubtedly were extended lodgings by neighbors or friends in the South Church, but there is no record of where they went until the little house was restored. In any case, Reynolds had a mortgage to Simeon Stoddard for fifty pounds on the house in 1691, indicating that it had been rebuilt by then. In the following year, on April 27, the town "Granted Libertie to Josiah Frankline to erect a buildinge of Eight foote square upon the Land belonging to Lt Natha: Reynolds, neere the South Meetinge house."[41] By that time their first child, a son, John, had been born to Abiah and Josiah, and the additional space was undoubtedly needed to accommodate the supplies and equipment for Josiah's trade; tiny as the projected structure was, it could relieve significantly the pressures on space made by a family of eight on a modest cottage. The permit also indicated that Josiah's trade had not suffered from the fire and that, if anything, it had prospered even more.

During the last eight years of the seventeenth century and the first three of the eighteenth, the Franklin family grew. A second son, Peter, was born in 1692; a daughter, Mary, in 1694; a son, James, in 1697; and a daughter, Sarah, in 1699. All lived to adulthood. Then in 1701, Abiah and Josiah had a fourth son, Ebenezer; in little more than a year afterward, the toddler met with a fatal accident, duly recorded by Judge Sewall: "Ebenezer Franklin of the South Church, a male-Infant of 16 months old, was drown'd in a Tub of Suds, Feb. 5, 1702/3."[42] Ten months later, another son, Thomas, named for the first of the recorded Franklins, was born. And then on the January Sunday, in 1705/6, Josiah Franklin's last and tenth—Abiah's fifth—son was born, and called Benjamin, after Josiah's brother, who of all his siblings was to remain closest to Josiah and to the boy named for him.

Meanwhile, the sixteenth century had ended, and with it the vision of the Heavenly City as seen by John Winthrop and articulated by John Cotton. Boston was no longer a Puritan outpost but a town growing in diversity and in contrasts. And its children were to be a new breed—English and yet American. Of them all, Benjamin Franklin was to be most strongly molded by the city into a principal architect of a new era—in letters, in politics, and in science.

[40] Sewall, *Diary*, I, 330.
[41] Shurtleff, *Description of Boston*, 619.
[42] Sewall, *Diary*, II, 73.

PART THREE

The Education of Benjamin Franklin

And, ye fathers, provoke not your children to wrath;
but bring them up in the nurture and admonition of
the Lord.

> —The Epistle of Paul the Apostle
> to the Ephesians, A.D. ca. 59–61

But he that shall take time to Pause upon what he
reads (especially where great Truths are but in a few
words hinted at) with intermixed meditations and
ejaculations suitable to the matter in hand, shall
find such Truths concisely delivered, to be like mar-
row and fatness, whereof a little goes far, and does
feed and nourish much.

> —A Discourse of the Last Judgment,
> John Wise and Jonathan Mitchell, A.D. 1664

VII

The Education at Home

> I have from my Youth been indefatigably studious to gain and treasure up in my Mind all useful and desirable Knowledge. . . .
> —Benjamin Franklin[1]

The child of the tallow chandler was a long way, in time and in distance, from the cottage in Boston when he left the only record of the first and probably the most significant force in the shaping of the mind and the values that were to govern his long life. It was in the summer of 1771, at the country house of his friend, Jonathan Shipley, the Bishop of St. Asaph, at Twyford, a little village nearly midway between Winchester and Southampton in Hampshire (the diocese of St. Asaph is in northern Wales), when Benjamin Franklin reconstructed, wholly from his recollection, the role that his father, Josiah, played in his earliest education. He was speaking freely, intimately ". . . in rambling Digressions. . . . But one does not dress for private Company as for a publick Ball."[2]

Josiah Franklin was a versatile man, and he apparently took seriously, and put into daily practice, a fundamental principle of Puritanism—once pithily asserted by his pastor, Samuel Willard, in the declaration that "*without knowledge* the mind of Man cannot be *good*, and that a people are *destroyed* for lack of Knowledge."[3] In bringing up to adulthood the twelve of his sixteen children who survived, he brought to bear upon their training the little graces of his talents, the deftness of his skills, the open candour of his mind, and the solid example of his character, and these

---

[1] "Silence Dogood," No. 3 (April 30, 1722), in *Papers*, I, 13.
[2] *Autobiography*, 56–57.
[3] Samuel Willard, *A Compleat Body of Divinity* (Boston, 1726), 12.

were the things that Benjamin Franklin was to recall to his own son all those years later:

I think you may like to know Something of his Person and Character. He had an excellent Constitution of Body, was of middle Stature, but well set and very strong. He was ingenius, could draw prettily, was skill'd a little in Music and had a clear pleasing Voice, so that when he play'd Psalm Tunes on his Violin and sung withal as he sometimes did in an Evening after the Business of the Day was over, it was extreamly agreeable to hear. He had a mechanical Genius too, and on occasion was very handy in the Use of other Tradesmen's Tools. But his great Excellence lay in a sound Understanding, and solid Judgment in prudential Matters, both in private and publick Affairs. In the latter indeed he was never employed [he did, however, serve in the civic posts of tithingman, constable, and clerk of the market; see pp. 105ff. *ante*] the numerous Family he had to educate and the straitness of his Circumstances, keeping him close to his Trade, but I remember well his being frequently visited by leading People, who consulted him for his Opinion in Affairs of the Town or of the Church he belong'd to and show'd a good deal of Respect for his Judgment and Advice. He was also much consulted by private Persons about their Affairs when any Difficulty occur'd, and frequently chosen an Arbitrator between contending Parties. At his Table he lik'd to have as often as he could, some sensible Friend or Neighbour, to converse with, and always took care to start some ingenious or useful Topic for Discourse, which might tend to improve the Minds of his Children. By this means he turn'd our Attention to what was good, just and prudent in the Conduct of Life. . . .[4]

The "sensible Friends or Neighbours" of Josiah Franklin, though his son never recorded their names, were undoubtedly primarily members of the Old South Church, and their character and their values can be educed from the nature and significance of the Old South community during the years of Benjamin Franklin's earliest recollections, probably from 1710, when he was four years old, until he left his father's house in 1718, at the age of twelve, to become apprenticed to his brother. And the South Church was almost wholly the product of the intellect and convictions of Samuel Willard, who was for nearly three decades its minister; for twenty-four of those years he was the pastor, the neighbor, and the friend of Josiah Franklin, seventeen years his junior—young enough to be his pupil and yet old enough to share his perspective. The whole temper of Josiah Franklin's brand of Puritanism reflected the logical bend of the mind of Willard, its sturdy if somewhat contradictory combination of theological conservatism and religious liberalism, its flexibility in public affairs, and its totally independent attitude. "He's well furnish'd with Learning and solid Notion, has a Natural fluency of Speech, and can say what he pleases," the London bookseller and author John Dunton commented, after visiting

[4] *Autobiography*, 54–55.

Willard three years after Josiah Franklin's arrival in Boston.[5] Given the imperatives of his time and locus in history, Willard could reduce—as neither of the Mathers could—the institutions of mankind to their essentials, though he was always the orthodox Puritan in what he saw as the central purpose of the human odyssey. And so he could write of civil governments in an age and a place where their presumptions sorely tried the Puritan priesthood: "Government is to prevent and cure the disorders that are apt to break forth among the Societies of men; and to promote the civil peace and prosperity of such a people, as well as to suppress impiety, and nourish Religion"[6]—a definition which, deleted of its extension, would have satisfied the Constitution makers among whom Benjamin Franklin sat nearly a century later.

Willard also expressed man's constant and inevitable dependence on reason—even in theological matters—as Franklin and his contemporaries were to do through the Enlightenment of the century that saw the beginning of Franklin's life and the end of Willard's: "It is impossible for us to know or understand things but by some rule of reason or other. Reason is nothing else but the manner of a Being, whereby it is acted upon our Understanding. We know nothing of God but by putting some Logical Notion upon him. All things are conveyed to us in a Logical way, and bear some stamp of reason upon them, or else we should know nothing of them."[7] And the optimism that infected the lives of Benjamin Franklin and his contemporaries also distinguished the utterances of Samuel Willard from those of most Puritan preachers, despite the heavy context: "Of all knowledge, that which concerns our selves is the most profitable, and of our selves, that which informes us about our eternity is the most desirable. . . . He, therefore, and only he can enjoy solid comfort, who hath an hope grounded in knowledge that it shall at last go well with him."[8] The strain of pragmatism is apparent—the first clause could have been written a quarter of a century later for *Poor Richard*.

The pragmatism of Dr. Willard was apparent, too, in the approach that he took to accepting the presidency of Harvard College at a time when the Mathers for all practical purposes regarded it as their own proprietorship. Increase Mather, of the class of 1656, in which he was ranked second only to his brother Eleazar (and that only because he was two years younger), had been a fellow of the college since 1675 and was elected president ten years later—after having declined the office in 1681 because his Second Church parishioners would not consent to his resigning his pastorate to live in Cambridge, then an uncertain journey across the bridgeless Charles River from Boston. In 1685, after two other clergymen had

[5] Sibley, *Biographical Sketches*, II, 17.
[6] Samuel Willard, *The Character of a Good Ruler* (Boston, 1694), 10.
[7] Willard, *Compleat Body of Divinity*, 44.
[8] Miller, *New England Mind*, I, 50.

turned it down, Increase Mather accepted the presidency but only with the understanding that he be allowed to retain his pastorate and not be required to live in Cambridge. For sixteen years he ran the college *in absentia*, visiting it for weekly sermons to the students, acquiring for himself the only doctorate given by Harvard during the first 135 years of its history, and irritating more than a few members of the General Court by his obstinate view of Harvard as an adjunct of seventeenth-century Congregationalism and his steadfast conviction that the mission of the college was to perpetuate the past and resist the future. Despite a series of enactments by the General Court to dislodge him by requiring that the president of Harvard College be required to reside in Cambridge, he clung tenaciously to the office, adroitly side-stepping the residence requirement by one means or another until 1701 when, after a somewhat grudging experiment in living in Cambridge that lasted only for a few months, he flatly wrote the legislature, "I am determined (if the Lord will) to return to Boston the next week, and no more to return to reside in Cambridge."[9] He added later in person that he would, however, be willing to go on running the college on the same terms as he had in the past. Not rising to this offer, the General Court declared the office vacant and, although Cotton Mather confidently expected to be named his father's successor, invited Samuel Willard, who had held the largely honorary office of vice-president since 1700, to reside in Cambridge and become president. Willard asked for some time to think it over and to consult his congregation, during which time the Mather faction, to keep the seat warm for the dynasty, introduced a resolution "that Mr. Increase Mather be desired to take the care of and reside at the Colledge."[10] Before this was acted upon, Willard gave his reply and said that he was ready to assume charge of the college—not, however, to reside in Cambridge and give up his parish. He would visit the college once or twice a week and stay overnight. The General Court accepted his proposal, despite the fact that he rejected Cambridge residency as Mather had, and turned down the Mather resolution—an offense for which the Mathers never forgave Willard and which occasioned one of Cotton Mather's least admirable public tantrums. (Samuel Sewall noted, some weeks after the General Court's action, that "Mr. Cotton Mather came to Mr. Wilkins's [book]shop, and there talked very sharply against me as if I had used his father worse than a Neger [Sewall had the year before published a pamphlet against slavery]; spake so loud that people in the street might hear him."[11])

Samuel Willard served as president of Harvard for six years, but to circumvent the residency requirement used the title only of vice-president. He presided over the college with eminent good sense and steered it back onto its broad course as an educational institution, rescuing it from the

[9] Sibley, *Biographical Sketches*, I, 428.
[10] Ibid., 429.
[11] Sewall, *Diary*, II, 45.

narrow way that Mather had plotted for it as a Congregational seminary. On August 14, 1707, he resigned the post, having had a series of convulsive seizures and, a month later, "after he had cut his finger, while eating oysters, went up to his study, called his wife, prayed to God to bless them all then fell into a convulsion about noon,"[12] and two hours later died, still the pastor of the Old South after nearly thirty years and having been for a quarter of a century the largest single influence on the life of the household of Josiah Franklin, baptizing the newly born, burying the dead, teaching, preaching, counseling, and constituting more than anyone else the long bridge between the Puritanism of Samuel Welles's seventeenth-century Banbury and that of Cotton Mather's eighteenth-century Boston.

*   *   *

Samuel Willard was succeeded at the South Church by his hand-chosen colleague pastor, thirty-six-year-old Ebenezer Pemberton, a former tutor at Harvard and a sharp-tempered liberal in his convictions. In choosing Pemberton as his colleague for almost ten years before his death, Willard had twice gone against the will of his church members, including the most influential of them, Judge Sewall. The members of the church, through their leading representatives, meeting at Judge Sewall's house, had first expressed a desire to call Simon Bradstreet, another young Harvard liberal. Willard, having unsuccessfully proposed Pemberton two years earlier, vetoed their choice, because (according to Sewall) he resented the "disorderly carriage" of the twelve members "in striving to bring in Mr. Bradstreet, after only thrice preaching." But Willard also made clear more generally "his dislike of the Person and his preaching, inferiour to the ministerial gifts of others." This seemed unfair to the honest judge; and though he had not been an original proposer of Bradstreet, he sprang to his defense and challenged Willard's right to veto his congregation's choice; but Willard, a strong-minded man, would have none of it, dismissing Bradstreet as having no qualities "but a Memory, and the Greek Tongue, with a Little poesy."[13] The following year the members elected yet another liberal Harvard tutor, Jabez Fitch, as colleague pastor, choosing him over Pemberton by a vote of thirty-seven to twenty-three, but "Mr. Willard in an angry manner told them they did not know what they were about, and by his authority dismissed the assembly."[14] Willard thereupon postponed all action, for over a year, until the parish called Pemberton unanimously to be its associate minister.

As a member of the Old South, Josiah Franklin probably participated in these remarkable exercises in the democratic processes of Congregationalism, but it is likely that he yielded to the wisdom of Willard. In any case, in Ebenezer Pemberton the Franklin family got as their pastor for ten years, 1707 to 1717, a youthful, if physically frail, independent-

[12] Joseph Sewall, in Sibley, *Biographical Sketches*, I, 13.
[13] Sewall, *Diary*, I, 148, 150.
[14] Sibley, *Biographical Sketches*, IV, 202.

minded scholar of somewhat spirited disposition, which may have been what attracted Willard to him in the first place. He carried on the latitudinarian practices of the Old South Church as established by Willard, going too far in the judgment of such conservative fundamentalists as Judge Sewall when he arbitrarily restored to the church a woman, expelled for adultery, without first posting notice to the congregation. At the same time Pemberton was capable of displays of temper, often triggered by one of the Mathers' persistent ventures to free Harvard College from the usurping liberals and restore their own authority over that erring custodian of the Puritan future. To fend off the Mathers, Pemberton, along with thirty-eight other ministers, petitioned the General Court to approve, by appropriating a salary, the election by the Harvard Corporation of John Leverett, a liberal, as president of the college to succeed Willard. Leverett, though by scholarship, temperament, and natural wisdom the best qualified man ever up to then to have been elected to the office, was to the fury of the Mathers not only a liberal but also a layman—the first in the history of the college to be selected president. Moreover, Leverett showed other alarming tendencies. Among other things, he urged the teaching of French at the college and the study of Anglican theologians, causing Cotton Mather to complain bitterly that the college might just as well be turned over to the charge of the Bishop of London. Aided by a political stratagem, Governor Dudley eased the legislative approval of Leverett's election through the General Court and the Council, so angering the Mathers that they shot off letters to Dudley, accusing him of, *inter alia*, "gross untruth . . . barbarous murder . . . covetousness . . . unhallowed hunger of riches . . . bribery."[15] Ebenezer Pemberton's temper exploded at the Mathers' annoyance, and he told Judge Sewall that, if he were the governor, he would "humble" Cotton Mather, "though it cost him his head." And when Sewall, carrying out his judicial responsibilities in a case involving the libel of the Mathers by Dudley's defenders, fined the libelers, Pemberton, encountering the judge at a public dinner, "with extraordinary Vehemency said (capering with his feet) If the Mathers order'd it, I would shoot him thorow. I told him he was in a passion. He said he was not in a Passion. I said, it was so much the worse. . . . Mr. [Experience] Mayhew told me afterward, that I said his Carriage was neither becoming a Scholar nor Minister. The truth is I was surpris'd to see myself insulted with such extraordinary Fierceness, by my Pastor, just when I had been vindicating two worthy Embassadors of Christ (his own usual Phrase) from most villanous Libels."[16]

Startling as was the spectacle of Samuel Willard's successor's so losing control over himself as to get quite literally hopping mad at his most distinguished parishioner, who was also a loyal friend and benefactor,

[15] The quoted charges are from Cotton Mather's letter, dated January 20, 1708, printed in part in Silverman, *Letters of Cotton Mather*, 77.
[16] Sewall, *Diary*, II, 291.

Ebenezer Pemberton nevertheless had qualities of commanding merit to everyone with the possible exception of Cotton Mather, who characterized him as "a man of a strangely choleric and envious Temper, and one who had created unto me more Trials of my Patience, and more Clogs upon my Opportunities to do good, than almost any other Man in the World."[17] But to Josiah Franklin and his other parishioners, as to his Harvard contemporaries, Pemberton was an exceptional intellect and a strong influence. One of his most brilliant contemporaries, who was in the class behind him at Harvard, Benjamin Colman, thought Pemberton the equal in scholarship of his teacher, William Brattle, one of the first four American inhabitants to be elected a fellow of the Royal Society. Pemberton attached determining importance to learning and particularly to acquaintance with good literature: "The more of good literature civil rulers are furnished with, the more capable they are to discharge their trust to the honour and safety of their people. And learning is no less necessary, as an ordinary medium to secure the glory of Christ's visible kingdom."[18] It was central to the Pemberton theory of the role of learning that the unlearned go to school to the learned, that they should know and keep their place, and that, getting to the heart of the matter, erudition was greater to be desired than religious ardor.

Pemberton was the first clergyman whose life could have had any direct effect upon the young Benjamin Franklin. Willard was dead within little more than a year of baptizing Benjamin, but Pemberton was unquestionably a familiar figure to the growing boy until his eleventh year. The health of the young pastor, however, never afforded him the opportunity to make the impression on the Old South that his great predecessor had. The first meeting of Old South members to be held at Josiah Franklin's house during the first year of Pemberton's pastorate moved, according to Judge Sewall, that "a Day of Prayer may be kept respecting his [Pemberton's] health."[19] Largely because of his uncertain health, the ministry of Pemberton was not a consistently powerful one, and the Old South seems to have lacked the command over its parishioners' lives that it had in Willard's days. Judge Sewall noted an occasional absence of Josiah Franklin from the informal weekly meetings that were held at the houses of various church members. As for Pemberton, as his health worsened, his temper became sharpened and his insight blunted. When Governor Dudley and his Council moved to relieve members of the Church of England, by then an accepted institution in Boston for a generation, of the obligation to support by direct assessment the dissenting churches, "Mr. Pemberton spake very fiercely against the Govr and Council's meddling with suspension of Laws." On the same occasion "he spake very fiercely" also

---

[17] Mather, *Diary*, II, 436.
[18] Ebenezer Pemberton, *Sermons and Discourses on Several Occasions* (London, 1727), 212.
[19] Sewall, *Diary*, II, 236.

of his own church's overseers of seating, whose function was to assign pews, clearly implying that Judge Sewall, for one, was using undue influence in his capacity as an overseer. He stormed from the pulpit against the old practice, born of bitterly cold hours in the wintertime, of the men putting their hats on after the prayers at meeting to keep their pates warm during the interminable sermons. And when Sewall expressed some sympathy for a demonstration by some of the populace—"God's people"—against the export of grain in a time of shortage, "Mr. Pemberton said, with much fierceness, they were not God's people but the Devil's people that wanted Corn. There was Corn to be had; if they had not impoverish'd themselves by Rum, they might buy Corn," and the good judge "was stricken with this furious Expression."[20] The pastor quarreled with the civic authorities because, after he opened the Council's session with prayer, "No body went with him to the door" and "No body asked him whether he were out of breath."[21] And he complained inordinately about such trifles as not being "sent for" by his hosts when he was invited to dinner.

Pemberton seemed to have a particular bitterness toward Judge Sewall, partly no doubt because the judge was, as a communicant of his church, a convenient target representing the civil authority, partly because there was a certain contradictory attitude of admiration and distrust of Sewall that Pemberton showed from his first arrival at the church, and partly because Sewall's religion was of a less intellectualized and more fundamentalist brand than that of his younger pastor. Sewall was nevertheless patient and generous toward the cantankerous preacher (after Pemberton berated him for fining the Mathers' libelers, he went out of his way to call on Mrs. Pemberton after the birth of her son and give her nurse a gift of money). But the judge was most deeply offended when, after his son Joseph Sewall was called by the Old South to be colleague pastor (with no help from Pemberton), the pastor pointedly neglected to pray for the young Sewall before the latter's first sermon—an inveterate custom among Congregational clergy, who never missed any opportunity to indulge themselves in orisons. The succession of Pemberton's ailments kept Sewall the diarist busy recording them—"sore eyes," "lame Leggs," and "piles," among them; and although Pemberton was always striking out at the judge, it was Sewall for whom he sent as he approached his end. In the cold and snow of a February afternoon in 1716/17, Pemberton "call'd me," Sewall recorded, "to sit down by him, held me by the hand and spake pertinently to me, though had some difficulty to hear him. Mr. [Joseph] Sewall pray'd fervently, and quickly after he expired, bolstered up in his Bed, about ¾ past 3. after noon in the best Chamber."[22]

* * *

The Old South then passed into the stewardship of the Sewalls, father

[20] Ibid., 281.
[21] Ibid., III, 7.
[22] Ibid., 119–20.

and son, leading layman and youthful pastor—learned, conservative, doctrinal, believing, traditional, pious. They were kindly, enormously gregarious, fond of good food and good drink, in their way far more democratic than either Samuel Willard or Ebenezer Pemberton. To Josiah Franklin, Judge Sewall was probably much closer than was his son, Joseph, the twenty-nine-year-old new paster of the Old South. By 1717, when the earnest young man succeeded Pemberton, Josiah had known his father for thirty-four years. He and the judge had been born in England only five years and sixty-five miles apart (Samuel Sewall was the older, having been born in Hampshire in 1652); and although Sewall had been graduated from Harvard, had taken his master's degree, had served as tutor and librarian of the college, had tried and abandoned preaching, had married the daughter of the richest man in Boston, had become an officer of the elite Ancient and Honorable Artillery Company, had launched a profitable mercantile business, had been appointed manager of the colony's printing press, and had been elected a deputy to the Great and General Court—all by 1683, when he was thirty-one and Josiah Franklin arrived in Boston— Samuel Sewall and Josiah Franklin, through the only leveler (with the possible exception of the countinghouse) known to Puritan society—the meetinghouse—became as close as was likely in the case of two men of such diverse situations. Although Sewall as a magistrate and Franklin as a constable walked the streets of Boston together "to visit disorderly poor,"[23] it was Franklin's joining the small inner group of Old South parishioners which met privately at the house of one of them each week to discuss sermons that really made the judge and the tallow chandler friends. Josiah Franklin seems to have been a regular attendant, or Sewall would not have noted in his *Diary* the occasional absences of Josiah; and sometimes, on a blizzardy winter night, he noted that he and Josiah were the only members present. Often Franklin was the host for the meetings, and the rich and influential Sewall went to the cottage of the tallow chandler for the most important engagement of his week: "I go to the meeting at Mr. Franklin's" recurs in the judge's *Diary*. Judge Sewall liked to read the published sermon of some distinguished cleric at the meetings, which included also the singing of psalms and listening to a prayer composed by one of the members. Children of the host family were usually privileged, in a manner of speaking, to attend the sessions, provided that they remained quiet—a gesture which in the Franklin family may well have accounted for a signal lack of religious fervor in later years.

The elder Sewall was undoubtedly a powerful religious as well as civic force in the lives of his contemporaries, particularly those of the Old South. He kept a sharp eye on any evidence of unorthodoxy within the congregation or for that matter within Congregationalism generally, tolerant as he was with regard to the practitioners of other denominations, the friendship of many of whom he prized. But he would put up with no in-

[23] Ibid., II, 93.

trusions of Anglicanism in the unadorned exercises of his own church. He wrote a letter to the Reverend Henry Flint, berating him for referring to the apostle Luke as "Saint" Luke, and later on encountering Flint in the street invited him to dinner to argue the matter on the somewhat extraneous grounds—but not without sound Puritan devotion to Judaism's idea of Jehovah—that if one called Luke or Matthew "Saint" he would also have to refer to "Saint" Moses and "Saint" Jeremiah. When a twenty-one-year-old visiting preacher from Harvard to the Old South, Nathaniel Gookin, baited the judge a few weeks later by repeatedly referring to "Saint" James, Sewall said, "It had better becom'd a person of some Age and Authority to have intermeddled in things of such a nature," adding in Latin that sometimes confidence, far from being a virtue, is merely audacity.[24] He also waged war against the Book of Common Prayer, and much as he loved funerals refused to attend any conducted in the liturgy of the Church of England (". . . at the Grave Mr. Myles [rector of King's Chapel] Read Comon-Prayer; which I reckon an indignity and affront. . . . I was much surpris'd and grieved at it, and went not into the burying place"[25]). He rebuked his daughter for wearing gloves while receiving communion rather than receiving it "by the naked Hand of Faith" and without concern for "outward Order and Comeliness."[26] He stormed against wigs and had the same delusive preoccupation with hirsute determinism as a force in history and with hirsute adornment as a symbol of rectitude that generations before and since him have had, and he once went so far as to absent himself from his beloved Old South at Sunday service to attend another church "out of dislike of Mr. Josiah Willard's [the pastor's son] cutting off his Hair, and wearing a Wigg."[27] And he fought a constant battle against using the sign of the cross in baptism, maintaining stoutly that "One great end for which the first Planters came over into New-England, was to fly from the Cross in Baptisme" but also admitting that "I had rather have Baptisme administered with the incumbrance of the Cross, than not to have it Administered at all."[28] But the judge's orthodoxy was not wholly negative or full of fears of ungodly incursions. He supported missionaries to the Indians, repeatedly bought four or five hundred copies of books which he thought of sufficient importance to distribute to his friends and acquaintances, and entertained an altogether absorbed attitude toward the earthy as well as the spiritual affairs of the town. Essentially benevolent in spirit and in action, he may well have had more effect upon Josiah Franklin and his family and the rest of his contemporaries through the strength of his character than through the steadfastness of his convictions.

24 Ibid., 233.
25 Ibid., 244.
26 Ibid., III, 279.
27 Ibid., II, 48.
28 Ibid., III, 298.

As to his son, chosen at twenty-four as a colleague to the pastor of the Old South and destined at twenty-nine to be his successor, even Cotton Mather, whose dislike of Willard and Pemberton was at times soaring, thought of Joseph Sewall as "a dear Son, and one of an excellent Spirit"[29] —at least until the Harvard Corporation once again ran roughshod over Mather's chronic ambition to be president of the college and instead chose Joseph Sewall, whom Mather forthwith dismissed, along with the corporation itself, with contempt: ". . . yesterday the six Men, who call themselves the Corporation of the College mett, and Contrary to the epidemical Expectation of the Countrey, chose a modest young Man, of whose Piety (and little else) every one gives a laudable Character."[30] Because his congregation would not release him, Sewall did not accept the presidency (fortunately for Harvard, since he ruled out intellectual inquiry as an appropriate activity for the Christian mind) but earnestly went among his Old South parishioners dispensing his orthodoxy; and, in the words of a Harvard biographer, he "dreaded the propagation of any opinions in this country, which were contrary to the principles of our fathers . . . he was no friend to free inquiries . . . never entered into any curious speculations. . . ."[31] During his ministry, which lasted until long after Josiah Franklin's death and Benjamin Franklin had been away from Boston nearly half a century, Joseph Sewall was an influence only on the preservation of orthodoxy in Massachusetts, and left no great stamp on his times, really personifying the end of an era and outliving it by nearly a century.

The effect of the change in character of the Old South upon the Franklin household can only be conjectured, but judging by the religious odysseys of the Franklin male offspring, who grew into adulthood largely during the ministry of Sewall, the latter's thought and words had little influence on them. Indeed, Cotton Mather was the only Boston cleric whom Benjamin recalled, more than once, as having influenced him in his boyhood. But there were also, in his father's house, the dinner table discussions of "some ingenius or useful" subjects, and they probably reflected the congenial orthodoxy of the Sewalls. Such of Josiah Franklin's fellow members of the Old South who would be likely to be invited and to come to his table were probably, like Josiah, "leather aprons," tradesmen whose demanding lives made for simplicity of conviction and who were comforted rather than distressed by the predictability of Joseph Sewall's sermons and lectures. Once doctrinal matters were certain, time was left for the uncertainties of human relationships, and so Josiah Franklin was "frequently chosen an Arbitrator between contending Parties" where the requirement was good sense rather than intellectual agility. And "what was good, just and prudent in the Conduct of Life" became the substance of

[29] Mather, *Diary*, II, 436.
[30] Ibid., 748.
[31] John Eliot, *Biographical Dictionary* (Boston, 1809), 422–23.

the conversations at the Franklin table. For the rest of his life, Benjamin Franklin, always uninterested in fine points of theology, was always interested primarily in what was "good, just and prudent," all of which became favored and much-used words in his lexicon as a writer, a diplomat, and a statesman. Moreover, consistent with Puritan practice, Josiah Franklin surrounded his family with the paraphernalia of learning. Besides his slender library, there were on the walls of the living room of his house four large maps of the world. In the summer of 1789, a year before his death, Benjamin Franklin still remembered at eighty-three how he had learned geography. His friend and fellow member of the American Philosophical Society, Dr. Benjamin Rush, the Philadelphia physician who was surgeon general of the Continental Army and an experienced, observant reporter, visited his venerable friend and recorded in his journal their conversation about education. Franklin, he wrote, "highly approved of learning Geography in early life, & said he had taught himself it, when a boy, while his father was at prayers, by looking over four large maps which hung in his father's parlour." Dr. Rush added, enigmatically and enticingly, without transition or explanation, "Time misspent, & time spending itself."[32] Though the incessant prayer sessions obviously did nothing to fortify Benjamin's religious devotion, they did provide him with a respectable education in a subject which did not appear on the curriculum of the Boston Public Latin School until nearly a century later in 1814.

* * *

Benjamin Franklin was the youngest of Josiah's sons and the youngest but two of his eighteen children. Because of this and because he was intended for "the Service of the Church" and was a prodigious child who learned to read very early, he was the object of special attention in the household. The fact that he learned to read so early—probably by the age of four—indicates that someone took the trouble to teach him: his father, his mother, or one of the older sisters or brothers who populated the house when he was a young child. He also learned from the household teeming with children older than he some of the practical aspects of life—lessons that stayed with him all his days and cropped up among strange circumstances. At the age of seventy-three, when he was the American envoy to France during the Revolutionary War, he diverted himself by writing brief, light essays, for the amusement largely of his French friends and which he addressed usually to one of the Paris ladies who so delighted him and so distressed John Adams when he became part of the mission. One of these trifles or "Bagatelles," as Franklin thought of them, was addressed to the gifted and beautiful young harpsichordist Madame Anne-Louise d'Hardancourt Brillon de Jouy, in response to her curiosity about an expression—that people would be better off "if we would but take care *not to give too much for our Whistles*"—used by Franklin, somewhat

---

[32] "Excerpts from the Papers of Dr. Benjamin Rush," in *Pennsylvania Magazine of History*, XIX (1905), 27.

cryptically, in corresponding with her about her concept of Paradise. "You ask what I mean?—You love Stories, and I will excuse my telling you one of myself. When I was a Child of seven Years old, my Friends on a Holiday fill'd my little Pocket with Half-pence. I went directly to a Shop where they sold Toys for Children; and being charm'd with the Sound of a Whistle that I met by the way, in the hands of another Boy, I voluntarily offer'd and gave all my Money for it. When I came home, whistling all over the House, much pleas'd with my Whistle, but disturbing all the Family, my Brothers, Sisters and Cousins, understanding the Bargain I had made, told me I had given four times as much for it as it was worth, put me in mind what good Things I might have bought with the rest of the Money, and laught at me so much for my Folly that I cry'd with Vexation; and the Reflection gave me more Chagrin than the Whistle gave me Pleasure. . . . As I grew up, came into the World, and observed the Actions of Men, I thought I met *many who gave too much for the Whistle.*"[33] Franklin made some minor revisions in the piece and some expansions upon its moral and printed it, as he did other of his bagatelles, on the press that he had set up in his villa, for distribution to his friends. Among those closest to him was the Abbé Pierre Louis Lefebvre de la Roche, who read more than economic caution into the whistle incident and attributed to it Franklin's determination all through his long life not to pay the price of violating rationalism for any pleasure, pursuit or property. "In short, I conceive," said Franklin in the printed version of his boyhood misadventure, "that great part of the miseries of mankind are brought upon them by the false estimates they have made of the value of things, and by their *giving too much for their whistles.*"[34]

By the time of the whistle episode in 1713, "all the Family, my Brothers, Sisters and Cousins," who teased the seven-year-old Benjamin Franklin into his memorable lesson, were no longer housed in the little Milk Street cottage rented from Lieutenant Reynolds by Josiah Franklin since shortly after his arrival in 1683. In 1708 Lieutenant Reynolds died and left the property to his three sons, one of whom wanted eventually to occupy it himself. Nearly thirty years of diligent labor at his tallow business and the prudent management of his affairs made it possible for Josiah Franklin at that time to take a monumental step and become a property owner. On January 25, 1712, when young Benjamin was six years old and just two months before Jane, the last of Josiah's children, was born, he bought a property whose history dated back to 1643 and which had since then passed through the possession of six successive owners, one of whom was Lieutenant Governor William Stoughton, who left it to his niece Mehitabel Cooper in 1705, along with the neighboring Green Dragon

[33] The text, from the written version sent by Franklin to Mme. Brillon for her corrections, differs from the printed version, and is in Richard E. Amacher, *Franklin's Wit and Folly* (New Brunswick, 1953), 42ff.

[34] Smyth, *Writings of Benjamin Franklin*, VII, 414–16.

Tavern, the Starr Tavern, and three other dwellings. After the death of her husband at sea in 1705 and her prompt marriage to a rich merchant from London, Peter Sergeant, the property was divided and sold in separate parcels. The part of the Stoughton property purchased by Josiah Franklin was known as the "corner estate" from its location on the southwest corner of Hanover and Union streets. Compared to the humble Milk Street cottage on its tiny lot of little more than 600 square feet, the property acquired by Josiah in Hanover Street was impressive in dimensions— over 3,500 square feet—and ideally situated, just across Union Street from the Boston Stone that marked the center of the town, for a business dealing directly with retail customers. It fronted for ninety-three feet along Hanover Street, the major cross street of the crowded North End, and for thirty-eight feet along Union Street that ran vaguely north and south across the narrowest part of the peninsula and connected the tidal Mill Pond to the harbor at the Town Dock. The major building on the property was on the corner, facing Union Street. This was the house to which Josiah, now fifty-five years old, moved his family, his trade, and his sign, the "Blue Ball" that he had first hung as his trademark on his Milk Street shop in 1698.

Josiah Franklin paid Peter Sergeant, who lived in the most massive house in Boston, a huge brick mansion, across Marlborough Street from the head of Milk Street, which was to become Province House, the residence of the royal governors after 1714, £320 for the Union Street property—£70 in cash and £250 in a mortgage loan unquestionably taken back by Sergeant. It speaks extremely highly of Josiah Franklin's standing in Boston that he could acquire what was a very considerable property very largely on his credit and his ability to liquidate a sizable debt. The investment was a wise one for Josiah, for it was made at the beginning of a long period of inflation that saw the price of silver, the basis of the currency, rise from 8s. 6d. per ounce in 1713 to 13s. in 1722, when he paid off the mortgage and took out a new and lesser one with Simeon Stoddard, who had married Sergeant's widow. There is no known description of the house at the sign of the Blue Ball in Union Street, except that it was built of wood and consequently had to have been built before 1679, when frame houses were outlawed because of fire risk. The house was demolished sometime in the last half of the eighteenth century to make way for a new brick house, which was in turn torn down, under condemnation proceedings for the widening of Union Street, revealing that the old Franklin house had in its cellar a huge oven—a characteristic in its time of a relatively large and well appointed house, a probability borne out by the fact that Josiah's will indicated that in his later years he and Abiah had sufficient rooms in the house to take lodgers.

To Josiah and Abiah Franklin, who had reared from infancy, between them, thirteen children in a cottage of two rooms and a garret, the new house must have been a great deliverance, particularly as they themselves were well into middle age (Abiah was forty-five in 1712 when Jane Franklin, her last child, was born) and as the age gap between the oldest and youngest of their children still at home widened. To have an increased degree of privacy, even though it was far from total, was, amid a people to whom moments of ease were rare, one of the few small luxuries that years of struggle could earn. Young Franklin, blowing his overpriced whistle all through the Union Street house and driving his siblings and parents to distraction, was probably regarded as having got no worse than he deserved when he was bilked of all his coppers in his obnoxious purchase.

To the boy himself the house that was to be the home of his boyhood was probably of less importance than its surroundings. Boston boys were attuned to the sea—to the wharves and the ships, the tidal ponds and sluices, the salt marshes and the creeks. For a third of the year they lived as much in the water as on the land. Most of them dreamed of going to sea, of the sea as the way to the future and to the world. There was no place in Boston where a boy could live in closer rapport with the sea than at the corner of Union and Hanover streets. Two hundred feet to the north was the Mill Pond, a salt marsh on the edge of the broad mouth of the Charles that had been dammed to trap the sea water at high tide so that, spilling out at low tide, it could be used to power gristmills. In front of the house, a hundred feet east of Union Street, was Mill Creek, an artificial canal that carried the Mill Pond's waters, after they had turned the mill wheels, southerly across the peninsula to Boston Harbor by the Town Dock, dividing the town into the "North End" and the "South End" at the narrowest point of the entire peninsula.

Some four hundred feet to the south from the Franklin house, if one followed the creek, and a few yards farther if one took the more meandering Union Street, was the very center of the harbor front, with a score of wharves stretching out into the harbor, dominated by a remarkable structure that enchanted English mariners; it was a broad elongated pier, with buildings on one side and on the other a roadway thirty feet wide, "which goes by the name of the Long Wharf, and may well be called so," a London shipmaster wrote admiringly, "it running 800 foot into the harbour, where large ships, with great ease, may both lade and unlade: on one side of which are warehouses, almost the whole length of the wharf."[35] The shipping served by the wharves was enormous. By the time that Franklin was eight years old there were well over a thousand ships of Boston registry alone using the port—ranging in size from the great ocean-crossing ship of up to six hundred tons down through the smaller, faster brigantines and barks, averaging some fifty tons, to the coastal running sloops and ketches, of from thirty to forty tons. This impressive fleet was five

[35] Nathaniel Uring, "Boston and New England," in New Hampshire Historical Society, *Collections*, III.

times in number and almost three times in tonnage that registered in all
the ports of the British Islands combined, and it represented the greater
part by far of the total American merchant fleet, for Boston's relative
proximity to England very early tended to create for it a virtual monopoly
on English shipping; even such nearby ports as Salem and New Haven saw
their once promising fleets shrink in both number and tonnage while Boston's grew.[36] To the boys of Boston the wonder of this crowded port lay
no more in the forest of towering masts and the rows of imposing
bowsprits along the waterfront than in the remote and bizarre lands from
which the ships had come, bearing their goods, their aromas, and their
stains: Guinea, Madagascar, Alexandretta, Brazil, Madeira, the ports of
the Mediterranean, and of the American coast from Nova Scotia to the
Carolinas. The schoolboy came closer to geography by a walk along the
waterfront than by all the data that could be fed him in the classroom,
and his life was infused with the lore and the lure of the sea. Franklin's
generation of Bostonians was rarely agrarian in its instincts, never really attuned to the land, seldom lured away by the countryside to the west of
them. It was always seaward that they turned, always the harbor with
which they were in league, always the ocean that drew them like an irresistible rip tide to the outer world.

As enticing as the sea itself was the busy clutter of the paraphernalia,
and those supplying it, necessary to sustaining the seafaring life. Twelve
shipyards were within easy reach of Benjamin Franklin's boyhood home,
many of them within sight of his windows. Except on the Sabbath and in
the extremest weather, for all ships were built out in the open, the yards
never rested. Larger than most buildings and infinitely more intricate,
thirty-three ships a year on the average were launched in the Boston
shipyards—one of the vast, shapely hulls sliding down the ways into the
harbor every week during the ice-free months from April to December.
The shipyards were bustling places, marvelously varied in the spell they
cast over boys. In the saw pits, two men, one above and one below, used
long, tough ripsaws to slit huge oak logs into deck beams; with heavy
broadaxes and sharp adzes, others shaped natural curves and forks from
the oak trees into the gently curved framing that gave the hulls their superb contours; and still others bored holes through the planking and framing with massive augers so that they could be fastened together with
oaken treenails—wooden pegs, thicker than broomsticks, that could wedge
the ship together below the waterline far more enduringly than iron bolts
and nails. After the launching, the most spectacular step was "stepping
the mast," planting the towering trunks of resinous trees into the finished

[36] The shipping figures are based on the admirable tables compiled by Bernard and
Lotte Bailyn in *Massachusetts Shipping 1697–1714* (Cambridge, 1959), 78–133; they
are necessarily approximations because they represent cumulative new registrations over
a seventeen-year period but provide no evidence of individual ships' longevity of service.

hull, by means of a huge block-and-tackle derrick mounted on a sheer hulk brought alongside the new vessel.

The necessary adjunct wonderlands of the shipyards—the ropewalks and sail lofts—were supposed to be forbidden territory to casual visitors, particularly the young, because they presented a constant possibility of physical danger. Yet there was probably not a schoolboy in Boston who was not familiar with the long ropewalks and the wondrous tools and gear that accomplished the staggering task of combing fibers, spinning them into yarn and laying the strands into the miles of rope it took to rig a single ship. Though the sail lofts, where hundreds of bolts of linen were stretched out, cut and sewn by the sailmakers with spikelike needles and leather palm-thimbles into the acres of sails necessary to move a hundred-ton ship before the wind, were unauthorized fields of exploration for the boys of the town, they were often welcomed by gregarious and perhaps somewhat bored workmen. And more fascinating than toy stores were the shops of ship chandlers with their intriguing and provocative collections of the gracefully utilitarian instruments of the sea: compasses, ship's bells, spyglasses, belaying pins, mast hoops, deadeyes, blocks—the scores of implements and fittings that in accord with the disciplined economy of a ship's space were designed and made with a simplicity forthrightly true to their function and, therefore, possessed of a beauty wholly in themselves.

Exploratory rather than contemplative as a boy (as he was able to be in manhood), Franklin was peculiarly suited to making the most of this transient, mobile, concentrated world of the colonial Boston waterfront. He was given to expressing himself physically and through a compelling curiosity into the practical spheres of social and physical phenomena; and there appears to have been little emotional about him and of the introspective almost nothing. To one of his temperament, the bustling compact town at his doorstep, which—despite the spiritual objective its founders intended for it—had become increasingly keenly and even happily acclimatized to the life of commerce, was a wholly congenial initiation into a life that was to be devoted in great measure to the world of commerce and the forces that governed it—a world in which the mature Franklin would be as fully at home as he was in the Boston of his boyhood.

* * *

Three years after Josiah Franklin bought the Union Street house and when Benjamin was nine years old, there arrived to take up residence in the household—then consisting at most of Josiah and Abiah, possibly their unmarried daughter, Sarah (sixteen), and their three youngest children, Benjamin, Lydia (seven), and Jane (three)—Josiah's older and only surviving brother, Benjamin Franklin the Elder, as he became known, who was to exert a mild, diverting influence on the younger Benjamin's largely self education and an inauspicious, though fortunately transient, influence on his development of a literary style.

Of Josiah Franklin's eight siblings, two of whom had died in infancy, Benjamin the Elder, seven years his senior, had always been closest to him. Even though the two had not seen one another for thirty-two years, they seemed to have corresponded with some regularity between Boston and London. As an additional link to New England, Benjamin's only son, Samuel, thirty-one years old in 1715, had already been in Boston for some time before then and was setting himself up in trade as a cutler by the time his father arrived on October 15, 1715. Six months later, Samuel wrote to his sister, Elizabeth, in London, "I was much surprized to hear of My Fathers coming to Boston. Thinking I should never have seen him More on this side the Grave, But Much More When I saw him, tho. Uncle [i.e., Josiah] used to say I was his fore runner. Father has his health here very Well, I should be glad if a Mean[s] May be found to bring you also over, and then I shall be Easie. . . ."[37] But Samuel was a bachelor and, like most of the unmarried tradesmen, did not keep a house and consequently could not offer his aging father accommodations. So the elder Benjamin moved in temporarily with Josiah, until he could find employment and provide for himself. He stayed for four years. In his amiable, interested way he became a companion to his young namesake and nephew, balancing perhaps the stronger, more resolute disposition of the boy's father.

Josiah Franklin was in 1715, at fifty-eight, a modestly successful man, well established in his trade, a property owner, a respected member of the town's most intellectual and liberal congregation (the Old South), and a minor officeholder trusted by his neighbors. Hard-working, persevering, obviously of an intellectual capacity beyond the demands of his drudging craft, Josiah was in his life and in his religion a highly responsible, somewhat cerebral man, quite thoroughly at home in the total Puritan experience without being its captive. And though life had not dealt with him softly, neither had it dealt with him unkindly. Both his marriages were happy, and the second long and fulfilling. All but four of his eighteen children grew to adulthood, though only six survived him. Moreover, he had planted deep roots during his thirty-two years in the colony, and he was at peace with his environment, as he was with his heritage and his prospects. Benjamin the Elder, by contrast, was in 1715, at sixty-five, a failure. Drifting from ill luck to ill luck in his constant shifts of trade associations as a dyer in London, he seemed to have an occupational compulsion to fall in with the wrong people at the wrong time, losing money or status or both at every turn and ending up in bankruptcy. The 124 quatrains of his versified autobiography, which has survived, unfinished, in the remarkably precise handwriting of his commonplace books, constitute a pathetic chronicle, in rhymes and meter often no less pathetic, of

[37] Colonial Society of Massachusetts, *Publications*, 1906, 203.

an endless series of misadventures, misunderstandings, and misfortunes.[38]
He was falsely accused of theft by the first master dyer to whom he was
apprenticed in London in 1666, and it was in his nature passively to pay
the penalty exacted by his master until his older brother, John, also a
London dyer, intervened:

> My Brother Near me could not bear
> The Gross Abuses on me Laid
> We to the Chamberlaine Repair
> My cause was Good yet sore afraid
>
> Seven Weeks it was, Long time I thought
> Ere the cause to an Issue came
> For to Lord Mayor's court it was brought
> There they my Innocence proclame.

If Mr. Pratt, his villainous first master, was too severe, his second, Mr.
Payne, gave him "too Much Liberty," which sent

> Me into Danger into Sin
> I'de been Destroyed and Folly wrought
> Had not God my kind preserver been.

Fully half the verses are preoccupied with old Benjamin's struggles with
unspecified offenses against the Lord and collaborations with the devil,
and, alternating with these, divinely inspired assertions of conscience that
rescued him at the last minute. He similarly recounted, in his relentless
rhymes, a succession of physical ailments—"malignant fevers" and
"aques"—that brought him close to the grave, only, again repeatedly, to
be rescued by a benevolent God with whom he maintained a sort of consulting internist relationship:

[38] There are three commonplace books known to have been written by Benjamin
Franklin the Elder. The originals of two of them are in the library of the American
Antiquarian Society. The first of these consists of 231 pages, all in the author's handwriting and paginated by the odd-numbered pages; it begins in 1674, when Franklin
was twenty-four and had just completed his apprenticeship as a dyer in London, and it
concludes with entries for 1714, except for six quatrains ending a long autobiographical
poem carrying him into the year 1719, when he moved from his brother Josiah's house
in Boston to his son Samuel's. The second volume has 203 pages, of which only the
first 33 are in Franklin's handwriting; this volume also appears to be missing some
pages since the front cover end paper notes that it contains 236 pages; the extant pages
include entries from 1719 until 1725.
  A third commonplace book consists of 16 pages, the original of which was, in 1906,
in the possession of Dr. Edward A. Whiston of Newtonville, Massachusetts, who permitted a copy to be read at the January 25, 1906, meeting of the Colonial Society of
Massachusetts. The entries appear to begin in 1719 and to end in 1724. The pages are
numbered but begin with page 41 and end with page 56. The dates and the few pages
involved suggest that these might be part of the pages possibly missing from the second
AAS volume—except that these pages bear pagination figures, which the second AAS
volume does not, and that each page bears the running heading "Memorand," which
the AAS volume also lacks.
  Unless otherwise noted, all excerpts from the commonplace books are from the AAS
manuscript volumes.

My God Directs to me a Nurse
And she a Famed physician found
My God Averts the Threatened Curse
and with Success Endeavours crowned.

Obviously lonely, bewildered, ill used, and unhappy during his youthful years in a city brutal in its treatment of apprenticed labor and little better off in the lot dealt out to him as a journeyman, the elder Benjamin Franklin was a forlorn figure groping his way through the London of the Restoration, which seemed not to have touched him in his lowly state with either exuberation or indignation. Life was merely a battle, from his sixteenth to his twenty-third year, against injustice, poverty, and loneliness —all of it narrated in the verses with a curious mixture of self-pity and acceptance, with a lack of bitterness and at the same time with a resignation unimaginable in what is known of the Franklins who came before him and those who followed after him. In 1683, again at the intervention of his attentive brother, John, who had moved to Banbury in Oxfordshire because he did not find London conducive to his health, Benjamin's loneliness and to some extent the pointlessness of his life were relieved:

My Brother for a wife comends
One much above my hope and tho't
Both take advice of both their friends
And providence to pass it brought.

The woman "much above" this genuinely and justly unassuming man was Hannah, youngest of the twelve children of Samuel Wells, the dissenting minister of Banbury, whose views quickened the inclination of John and Josiah Franklin toward Puritanism during their formative years as young men in the 1680s. Following the death of Wells, his widow moved to London in 1682, and there Benjamin married Hannah in November 1683.

But everything always turned to ashes in Uncle Benjamin's hands and, following closely, in his verses, on his joyous discovery of Hannah Wells, were two stanzas, plaintive in their sparseness, on the deaths, within a span of twenty-two years, of his wife and eight of their ten children:

Happy was I in this my Wife
In her Relations Good and kind
She was the comfort of my life
Dear Soull she's Gone, I left behind

Ten Children by her God me Gave
Of Eight saw Good me to Deprive
May those two Double blessings have
I shall Rejoyce they are alive.

From the death of Hannah Wells Franklin in 1705, old Benjamin's life lost whatever impetus it ever had; and when his favorite daughter, named Hannah for her mother, died on "the last day and the last hour of the old year"—1710—the wearied and sad drift of his affairs culminated in his abandoning hope. "I have now tho'ts of laying down my business," he wrote a niece in Northamptonshire, "tho I know not what to turn to not being able to doe as when I was young for I run into debt and see no likelyhood of recovering it and what will be the issue God only knows. . . ."[39] And so alone, without funds, he put his broken fiscal affairs in the hands of solictors, took his last few shillings, and, unnoticed, set sail for Boston and Josiah's house in Union Street:

In Seventeen hundred and fifteen
of Augusts calends twenty-sixt
Bound for America unseen
On board Nantucket sloop I fixt.

We lanced forth on the Abyss
And oft behold Great Wonders there,
Where Nought but sky and water is
And onley sun and stars Appear

October seventh or Eight We made
Distant Discov'ry of cape Codd
At this Good News we are all Glad
and I gave Thanks unto my God.

At Marblehead We Anchor'd first
There the first house, Grass, Apple saw
And there with Syder Queucht my Thirst
Good, as from Apples they could draw.

But unto Boston we were bound
On Lord's Day eve I saw that place
And there a Kind, kind Brother found
Bless't with a Wife and Num'rous Race.

When Uncle Benjamin took up residence with Josiah's now relatively small family, he sought, probably earnestly enough, a means to support himself; but dyers of silk were still not at all in demand in Boston, and he lacked conspicuously the kind of self-starting power which Josiah had exhibited under the same circumstances, and which was an almost essential aptitude of new arrivals, even at relatively advanced ages, in a new land. So he took to the pen to occupy himself—indeed, he seemed more content with writing than doing anything else, mercifully turning more often to prose than he was given to do in London. He wrote a long and invaluable "Short Account of the Family of Thomas Franklin of Ecton in Northamptonshire,"[40] which is strikingly accurate, on the whole, as to names and dates. His prose was clear, economical, uncluttered; for when he resisted his compulsion to rhyme, at which he was extraordinarily awkward, and to sustain a meter, at which he was brutally mechanistic, old

Benjamin could manage the language reasonably well, and his writings were no small achievement within the obvious limitations of a comparatively uninstructed man. Moreover, he was not an imperceptive reporter and, once again when free from his addiction to versifying, a rather tidy and concise writer. He could, for example, characterize three of his nieces —the daughters of his sister Hannah—neatly and with an impressive vividness of which he was, with rare exceptions, incapable when stirred to verse. "Elenor has a charming tongue, is of a very obliging cariage free in her promises but far from endeavours to perform them. Jane is of few words and many deeds, yet guilty of the above named fault—these two speak and write and read french near as fluently as English, are rosy, witty and highly for the church of England. Hannah is of very few words—you must draw them out or goe without them—of a bashful countenance and a weak constitution, they are all 3 of very smal Appetites. I know some one woman that would eat more than they all."[41]

Another literary pursuit in which Uncle Benjamin, whose accounts of himself from earliest youth reveal a strong and somewhat fond hypochondriac strain, engaged himself to occupy his idle years in Josiah's house, was the compiling of his lifelong medical history, consisting of the dates and symptoms that were visited upon him since "I was a little child," to which he added addenda covering the years in Boston, up until a few months before his death at seventy-seven—a life of the creditable length that is often a concomitant of hypochondria and an ironic compensation for the long, brooding thoughts of death. He also amused himself by transcribing from the Town Book of Boston the names of all the streets, lanes, and alleys in town—intrigued, perhaps by such suggestible items as Turn Again Alley, Beer Lane, and Princes Street, the namesake of the London street in which he had labored so vainly to establish his dyeing business. And he copied arresting items from the Boston and English newspapers that came his way—some of such momentous events as the abortive expedition of the Spanish fleet to return James Francis Edward Stuart, the Old Pretender, to Scotland, and others more bizarre than significant, such as the appearance in Cape Cod waters of "a strange creature, His head like a Lyons, with very large Teeth, Ears hanging Down, a large Beard, a long beard [sic], with curled hair on his head, his Body about 16 foot long, a round buttock, with a short Tayle of a yellowish colour. . . ."[42]

A more systematic effort of Benjamin the Elder was a treatise on "Dyeing and Coloring." The section devoted to making the dyes was actually a catalogue of specific recipes, largely based on material derived from other sources, for the making of variously colored inks and dyes, the directions being given in crisp, brief, clear language, without a wasted or superfluous word. The material on the process of dyeing threads and cloths, though in-

[41] Yale MS, p. 10 (unnumbered). See Chapter II, *ante*.
[42] Colonial Society of Massachusetts, *Publications*, January 1906, 192.

complete in the extant version, appears, however, to be directed particularly to a New England audience, as revealed by an observation somewhat yearning for a craftsman in a community inhospitable to his craft: "Dying of skeyn, Raw or unwrought silk, I presume will not be practiced here in N.E. in this century, but Time May come When it Will. . . ."[43]

But Uncle Benjamin could not resist very long the urge to versify, and since he seemed to regard it as a form more of literary exercises than of literary expression, he was given to tricking it up by such devices, which could not possibly achieve anything but making it even more strained and mechanical, as acronyms, acrostics, abecedaries, anagrams, mazes, and stanzas consisting of word crosses, letter ladders, and a variety of structural graphics that intrigued the attention for their own sake rather than that of the content they were designed to serve. So thoroughly could he lose himself in words and so enchanted could he become in ingeniously deploying them that on the day of Hannah's death, he consoled himself by writing seven stanzas, the initial letters in the lines of each spelling out her name. He composed acrostics on the names of his brothers and sisters, his sons and daughters, and his nieces and nephews. In the summer of 1710, five years before he came to Boston, one had been duly dispatched to his namesake Benjamin, then in his fifth year; full of avuncular counsel and inverting sentences, torturing tenses, and dropping articles mercilessly to accommodate the acrostic and the coupled rhymes—all with the magnificent disdain of any punctuation whatsoever that characterized all his verses:

> Be to thy parents an Obedient son
> Each Day let Duty constantly be Done
> Never give Way to sloth or lust or pride
> If[44] free you'd be from Thousand Ills beside
> Above all Ills be sure Avoide the shelfe:
> Man's Danger lyes in Satan, sin and selfe.
> In vertue, Learning, Wisdome progress make
> Nere shrink at suffering, for thy saviours sake
> Fraud and all Falshood in thy Dealings Flee
> Religious Always in thy station be
> Adore the Maker of thy Inward part
> Now's the Accepted time Give him thy Heart
> Keep a Good Conscience, 'tis a constant Frind
> Like Judge and Witness This Thy Acts Attend
> In Heart with bended knee Alone Adore
> None but the Three in One Forevermore

A week earlier he had composed another poem for his young nephew. Obviously disturbed by some comment sent from the Boston Franklins

[43] Ibid., 222. The treatise on dyeing and coloring is appended to the commonplace book excerpts and was also in the possession of Dr. Whiston in 1906.

[44] In early typography, the capital "I" was also used as a capital "J." Consequently, the acrostic—though loose at this point—is sustained.

that gave him to understand that his namesake had an "Inclineation to Martial affaires" (since the younger Franklin was then four and a half years old, it must have taken no graver form than playing soldier), Uncle Benjamin had abandoned any abecedarian adornment of his work and sent the little boy a forthright indictment of the military:

> Believe me Ben It is a Dangerous Trade
> The Sword has Many Marr'd as well as Made
> By it doe many fall, Not Many Rise
> Makes Many poor, few Rich, fewer Wise
> Fills towns with Ruin, fields with blood beside
> Tis Sloth's Maintainer, And the Shield of pride
> Fair Citties Rich to Day, in plenty flow
> War fills with want Tomorrow and with woe
> Ruin'd Estates The Nurse of Vice broke limbs and scarrs
> Are the Effects of Desolating Warrs

Though pacifism was no strong characteristic of Puritanism (as a matter of fact the pulpit literature of Calvinism is replete with militaristic terminology and analogies), Benjamin the Elder clearly felt very strongly about wars and making one's way, either as an individual or as a nation, by the sword. As a consequence, the lines have an uncontrived quality that reflects deep conviction rather than the sense of occasion that so often lay behind Uncle Benjamin's rhymes. Their immediate absorption by a four-year-old, however, prodigious, may have been limited, but their lasting impact could be persuasively hypothesized: No statesman of his time was less given to urging war as an instrument of policy or resolver of disputes than he, and none did more to avert war than Benjamin Franklin.

In addition to visiting his verses upon his nephew, Uncle Benjamin encouraged the boy's own scribblings. Young Benjamin took to the pen at a very early age as readily and as zestfully as he took to the water; and by the age of seven he was apparently sending copies of his writings to his uncle. The old man was delighted and moved to compose, in response, what was technically the best of his poems to survive. There is a consistency of image, a grace of words, an intimation of lyricism, and a closing note of prophecy that did not ordinarily distinguish his didactic outpourings:

> Tis time for me to Throw Asside my pen
> When Hanging-sleeves [i.e., children] Read, Write and Rhime Like Men
> This Forward Spring Foretells a plentious crop;
> For if the Bud bear Graine, what will the Top?
> If plenty in the verdant blade Appear
> What may we not soon hope for in the Ear?
> When Flow'rs are Beautiful before they're Blown
> What Rarities will afterward be shown?
> If Tree's Good fruit unoculated bear

You May be sure 'Twill afterward be Rare.
If fruits are Sweet before th'ave time to Yellow
How Luscious will they be when they are Mellow.
If first years Shoots such Noble clusters send
 What Laden boughs, Engedi like, May We Expect I'th End?
Goe on, My Name, and be progressive still
Till thou Excell Great [Edward] Cocker with thy Quill.
Soe Imitate and [hi]s Excellence Reherse
Till thou Excell His cyphers, Writing, Verse;
And show us here that your young Western chime
Out Does all Down unto our present Time.
With choycer Measure put his poesie Down;
And I will vote for thee the Lawrell Crown.[45]

After Benjamin the Elder took up residence in Josiah Franklin's household in Union Street, he fell eagerly into the design of his brother to designate the apt boy who was his namesake for the ministry. For Uncle Benjamin was an unaffectedly religious man, full of daily devotion and a constant awareness of his faith. Much of his commonplace books is taken up with his own rendering of the Psalms, in effect a disastrous diminishment of the King James Version but in intent a dedicated purifying of it, as though to strip the paeans of David from the liturgical corruptions of the Church of England. Soon after his arrival in Boston, he undertook a revision of Psalm 107 and presented himself to sing it "at First Meeting with my nephew Josiah Franklin"—this had to be in 1715, the year of the elder Benjamin's arrival, because his nephew Josiah is known to have been lost at sea not much later than 1715. The effort, which took place undoubtedly at the Old South, was a failure. Uncle Benjamin probably underestimated the extraordinary emphasis that the New England Puritans placed on the psalter and did not appreciate that it constituted the sole concession to liturgical music, albeit *a cappella*, that the meeting permitted itself and that, therefore, one did not alter its language lightly. No book of the Old Testament or of the New was more central to the dour order of Calvinist worship than the Book of Psalms. Perhaps nothing could be more offensive to the community of the saints than a newcomer among them presuming to offer his own version of ancient orisons. And Old Benjamin's choice of the 107th was, for a New England congregation, an unfortunate one with which to tamper, containing as it did the verses graven in the minds of every family with seafaring men, "They that go down to the sea in ships, that do business in great waters; these see the works of the Lord, and his wonders in the deep." The memorable passage went on to say of the plunging of the men aboard their craft, from the crests to the troughs of the waves, "They reel to and fro and stagger like a drunken man, and are at their wit's end. Then they cry to the Lord in their trouble, and he bringeth them out of their distress." Benjamin the Elder felt that the

---

[45] Punctuation provided.

timeless language could be improved by his inexorable rhyming couplets, and he treated the Old South meeting, very likely in the presence of that stern custodian of the Psalms, Judge Samuel Sewall, to his own version:

> They stagger Like a Drunkard Who
> Bereav'd of Sense Reels fro and Too
> Brought almost to Distraction They
> To God With fervent cryes doe pray.

The improvement fell upon unresponsive ears: ". . . being unaffected by God's Great Goodness in his many Preservations and Deliverances," old Benjamin wrote in his commonplace book, "It was coldly entertain'd."

Somewhat sensitive about his failure in life and not really close to his surviving son, Samuel, the Boston cutler, Uncle Benjamin had hoped to realize himself through aiding the career of his youngest nephew and namesake. When the latter was writing his recollections of his boyhood, only Uncle Benjamin among his relatives not in his immediate family was singled out for special mention. "He was an ingenious man," Franklin recalled, "I remember him well."[46] An inveterate reader and "a great Attender of Sermons of the best Preachers," Uncle Benjamin invented his own form of shorthand, partly to save paper, doubtlessly, but probably largely to keep up with the delivery of the preachers. He taught his nephew the system, but since the latter was never addicted to sermons, it shortly vanished from his mind through disuse. Years later, in the summer of 1771, when in London on his second diplomatic mission as an agent for four of the colonies, Benjamin Franklin encountered quite by chance a collection of thirty-two volumes of political pamphlets, which a book dealer called to his attention. Franklin browsed through the collection, and immediately—after half a century—recognized Uncle Benjamin's handwriting and bought the volumes on the spot. "It seems my Uncle must have left them here [i.e., London] when he went to America."[47] Apparently, Uncle Benjamin was a dabbler in political matters—an inclination not wholly approved in retrospect by his politically inclined nephew: "He was also much of a Politician, too much perhaps for his Station."[48]

All the sermons that Uncle Benjamin had assiduously taken down in his shorthand he proposed to give to the younger Benjamin, when it was expected that he would in due course go to the Boston Grammar School, then matriculate at Harvard and at length enter the ministry. In later years, the younger Benjamin seemed more amused than touched by the

---

[46] *Autobiography*, 53.

[47] Franklin's *Autobiography* was weak in dates. He said the collection covered "all the principal Pamphlets relating to Publick Affairs from 1641 to 1717" (p. 49), but Uncle Benjamin left London for Boston in 1715. Since Franklin was writing the *Autobiography* in the country and had probably left the collection in London, he may have erred in his recollection of the dates; or perhaps an interim owner of the collection had added the pamphlets of the two later years.

[48] *Autobiography*, 49.

old man's intention. "My Uncle Benjamin," he wrote in his *Autobiography*, "too approv'd of it [i.e., Josiah Franklin's purpose in educating his son for a clerical career] and propos'd to give me all his Shorthand Volumes of Sermons I suppose as a Stock to set up with. . . ."[49]

Benjamin Franklin's choice of words in characterizing the body of homilies prized by his devout uncle, who had painstakingly assembled them over decades, reflected the contained view that he took of the theological content of Puritanism from the earliest recollections of his boyhood. The nephew had outgrown his uncle. In time the latter left the Union Street house when his son Samuel married Hannah Kellineck in the summer of 1719 and set up a household that could accommodate the old gentleman. His departure from the Union Street house did not occur a moment too soon. As his visit stretched on into its fourth year, the constant presence of the impractical, loquacious, perpetually childlike old man wore heavily on the nerves of Josiah, who was working at a demanding trade, raising a large family and trying to fulfill his duties as a member of the Old South. "Our Father, who was a very wise Man," Benjamin, the younger, wrote fifty years later to his sister Jane, "us'd to say nothing was more common than for those who lov'd one another at a distance, to find many Causes of Dislike when they came together; and therefore he did not approve of Visits to Relations in distant Places, which could not well be short enough for them to part good Friends. I saw Proof of it, in the Disgusts between him and his Brother Benjamin; and tho' I was a Child I still remember how affectionate their Correspondence was while they were separated, and the Disputes and Misunderstandings they had when they came to live sometime together in the same House."[50]

By the time of Uncle Benjamin's departure, the young Franklin had left the Union Street house, too, and was well embarked upon a career as lively in its enterprise and as confident in its assumptions as his old uncle's was lugubrious and timorous.

[49] Ibid., 53.
[50] Carl Van Doren, ed., *The Letters of Benjamin Franklin and Jane Mecum* (Princeton, 1950), 126.

VIII

The Education in Schools

The good Education of Youth has been esteemed by wise Men in all Ages, as the surest Foundation of the Happiness both of private Families and of Common-wealths.
—Benjamin Franklin[1]

No more important calling existed in the Puritan state than the ministry, and no decision that Josiah Franklin made with regard to a member of his family was arrived at with a graver sense of responsibility than that to "devote" Benjamin "as the tithe of his Sons to the Service of the Church."[2]

Any profession, vocation, or trade—the employment by which a man not only sustained a living for himself and his family but also demonstrated his worth to his community and evidenced his respect for himself —was a serious matter to the Puritan male and not entered into lightly. Moreover, as the earliest New England teachers insisted, a man's outward and temporal life was lived as much as an affirmation of his faith as was his spiritual life. "A Christian would no sooner have his sinne pardoned [i.e., attach no more importance to it], than his estate to be setled in some good calling, though not as a mercenary slave, but he would offer it up to God as a free-will Offering, he would have its condition and heart setled in Gods peace, but his life setled in a good calling, though it but of a daylabourer, yet make me as one that may doe thee some service," John Cotton wrote.[3] This high view of a man's occupation, however humble, accounted in considerable measure for there being no elitism except the spiritual in Puritan life and for the readiness and ease with which Samuel Sewall, the chief justice, and Josiah Franklin, the tallow chandler, visited in one another's homes and regarded one another as full equals.

[1] *Proposals Relating to the Education of Youth in Pennsylvania*, (1749), in *Papers*, III, 399.
[2] *Autobiography*, 52.
[3] John Cotton, *The Way of Life* (London, 1651), 437.

The practical strain in Puritanism, the marriage of pragmatism with doctrine that accounted for its essential, social egalitarianism, was nowhere more apparent than in the paradoxical significance and lack of significance that was read into the choice or the acceptance and the responsible practice of one's vocation. To Cotton and to the heirs of his principles as New England's first teacher, faith sanctified the calling and it also fused the spiritual and temporal lives into common purpose: "But now as soone as ever faith purifies the heart, it makes us cleane creatures . . . and our callings doe not interfeire one upon another, but both goe an end evenly together, he drives both these plowes at once. . . . This is the cleane worke of faith, hee would have some imployment to fill the head and hand with."[4]

When Benjamin Franklin reported in his *Autobiography* his father's decision to prepare him for the ministry, he indicated that, "Tithe of his Sons" or not, Josiah Franklin made not a sentimental but a deliberative decision, following Cotton's injunction that "a warrantable calling . . . not onely aime at our own, but at the publike good, that a man "hath gifts of body and minde suitable to it," and that "hee would not come unto it by deceit and undermining of others, but he would see the *providence and ordinance* of God leading him unto it, the counsell of friends, and encouragement of neighbors. . . ."[5] And so Josiah Franklin, conscious of the depth and dimensions of his commitment of his tenth-born son to the ministry, considered other factors than his own inclination. "My early Readiness in learning to read . . . and the Opinion of all his Friends that I should certainly make a good scholar encourag'd him in this Purpose of his. My Uncle Benjamin too approv'd of it. . . ."[6]

The compulsion of Josiah Franklin to have his gifted child prepared for the ministry was in accord with the aspirations of all good men in his Boston to enhance their lives by devoting a son "to the service of the Church." Alone among callings, it was wholly centered on the next world and wholly acclaimed in the present. "They whose hearts are pierced by the Ministry of the word," said Thomas Hooker to his followers in Hartford, "they are carried with love and respect to the Ministers of it."[7] No one was placed so high in Puritan life, no one so accomplished or so renowned in his own right, that he did not derive the vastest satisfaction from a son's having the gifts and capacity to enter the ministry, for it was the highest use to which intelligence and erudition could be put. During the seventy-eight years between the founding of Harvard College in 1636 and the decision, in 1714, of Josiah Franklin to commit Benjamin to the church, 607 students attended the college; 366 of them—nearly 6 out of 10—became ministers or preachers, though several were never ordained be-

---

[4] Ibid.
[5] Ibid., 438–39.
[6] *Autobiography*, 53.
[7] Thomas Hooker, *The Application of Redemption by the Effectual Work of the Word* (London, 1659), 453.

cause the Congregational clergy were not ordained as ministers generally but as pastors or teachers in specific parishes. (The next most common profession, medicine, lagged far behind, thirty-two graduates becoming physicians during the same period, although several of the clergymen were also trained and practiced as physicians.) This was, of course, in accord with a historic awareness of the founders of the college, "dreading to leave an illiterate Ministry to the Churches, when our present Ministers shall lie in the Dust,"[8] but the language of the Great and General Court had simply appropriated four hundred pounds "towards a schoale or colledge" and made no mention of its being a training school of ministers. Nevertheless, for well over a century, Harvard's major contribution to the New Jerusalem was to fill its pulpits; and as for its alumni, lay and clerical alike, few saw any loftier achievement of the college. The delight of Judge Sewall's life was the entrance of his sixth and youngest son, Joseph, the only to survive infancy, into the ministry as a pastor of his own church, the Old South; and he carefully recorded in his diary the congratulations of gracious fellow parishioners: "Col. Checkley very cheerfully Congratulated me on account of my Son's very good Sermon. Capt. Hill congratulated me, coming in first."[9] And Cotton Mather, who was profoundly anguished by the profligate life of his oldest son, Increase ("I am within these few hours, astonished with an Information, that an Harlot big with a Bastard, accuses my poor Son *Cresy*, and layes her Belly to him . . . what shall I do now for the foolish Youth!"[10]), was as clearly elated when his youngest son, Samuel, first preached at the Second Church—the "Church of the Mathers"—and no less moved, perhaps, by the text that his son chose for the occasion: "This Day, my son *Samuel*, (while yett short of eighteen) appeared in the Pulpit where his Father and Grandfather before him, have served our Glorious Lord; and preached on Exod. XV. 2. *He is my Father's God and I will exalt Him.*"[11]

* * *

With a very few exceptions, the Sewalls among them, Boston's families during its first century accumulated little wealth. Accordingly, the decision to prepare a boy for a career in the church could involve an economic commitment of very considerable dimensions. Cotton Mather, though he received a comfortable salary for the time, was always financially embarrassed. Six of his fifteen children lived to adulthood and were supported by him, in the case of the four girls, until the marriages of two of them and the deaths of the other two, and, in the case of the two boys, Increase and Samuel, until the first was lost at sea after a rebellious and wild youth,

[8] The language, renowned as it is, comes from no official document but from an anonymous tract, New England's First Fruits, published in London in 1643, and has been attributed to Henry Dunster, Harvard's first president, who succeeded its original "master" in 1640.
[9] Sewall, *Diary*, II, 287.
[10] Mather, *Diary*, II, 484.
[11] Ibid., 770.

and the second was safely ensconced as his father's colleague in the Second Church. Mather probably exaggerated his financial crises, but while Samuel was awaiting his master's degree, his father was complaining that the only prospect that he had of freeing himself of financial vexations was "by selling all my Goods to pay the Debts and breaking up my Family," and when a creditor threatened to take his large library, his most precious possession, "A little Number of my Flock, generously joined for my Deliverance out of my Entanglements."[12] When his son, Samuel, entered Harvard at the age of twelve, he was awarded the first Thomas Hollis scholarship for poor students, though one of its curators admitted that Samuel was "not properly poor"[13]; it provided him with ten pounds a year, and the college gave him from other funds the rest of his expenses.

When Josiah Franklin faced the prospect of financing six years at the Latin School and at least four at Harvard for Benjamin, the demands on his hard-earned and slender resources were the lowest that they had been since his arrival in Boston three decades earlier. Besides Benjamin, there were only three dependent children, his sisters Sarah, fifteen, Lydia, six, and Jane, two. Josiah himself was, at fifty-seven, sturdy and healthy, and so was his wife Abiah at forty-seven. The little business was prospering and unlike Dr. Mather, Josiah was a prudent manager who would under no circumstances have gotten beyond his financial depths in the conduct of his affairs. Unlike Dr. Mather, too, he did not consider that every decision he made was in itself a visitation from the Almighty. Accordingly, he consulted with his friends, as Benjamin noted in his *Autobiography*.

Prominent among these would have been the clergy and lay leaders of the Old South. Ebenezer Pemberton had spent ten years as librarian and tutor at Harvard, and from 1707 was a fellow of the Corporation; he knew something of the qualities in a boy that made for scholarship. By 1714 Pemberton and Josiah Franklin had known one another for fourteen years, and though his physical frailty at times made him cantankerous particularly with theological conservatives, Pemberton was a good and concerned pastor, held in admiration and affection by his flock. His advice would have been of commanding, perhaps of determining, importance to Josiah Franklin. So also would have been Judge Sewall's. A large-hearted man, generous in his impulses and genuinely democratic in his practices, the judge had a consistently high regard for Josiah Franklin, who would have sought and heeded his counsel. Sewall was always a friend to learning and a friend also to those who prized it. He had also been a tutor at Harvard and keeper of the college library and had resolved a dispute between the college and the town of Cambridge concerning the sometimes disruptive practice of Cambridge schoolboys sitting in the rear seats of college classes

[12] Ibid., 703, 745.
[13] Benjamin Colman, Harvard, 1692, in Colman Manuscripts, Massachusetts Historical Society, July 1720.

when "some sober youths for the present might be seated there."[14] Although he had himself abandoned thoughts of a ministerial career after having delivered a maiden sermon two hours and a half in duration because he was afraid to look at the hour glass, and later turned to a mercantile and legal career, he became a stout pillar of the church and adopted an avuncular role toward the care and feeding of young ministers and students. His highly advantageous marriage brought him great wealth, which he used to a large extent to strengthen the ministries to the Indians (whom he regarded, with John Eliot, as descendants of the ten lost tribes of Israel), to teach the Indians English and grammar, and to fortify the feeble finances of Harvard College. He conducted a far-flung correspondence with learned men, and he bought and distributed, free, hundreds of copies of books that impressed him. The judge unquestionably knew all the Franklin children from their earliest childhoods and would have had a strong influence on Josiah's decision regarding the future of Benjamin. Finally, the master of the Latin School (known commonly before 1698 as the Grammar School), Nathaniel Williams, was the son of Deacon Nathaniel Williams and had attended the Old South since boyhood and was therefore known to Josiah Franklin. In fact, he and Josiah became full members of the church within a month of each other in 1693 —Nathaniel on January 7, when he was in his last year as a student in Harvard College and his father was elected a deacon of the church, and Josiah, with Abiah, on February 4, after he had been attending the Old South for almost ten years. For all practical purposes, Josiah was turning Benjamin over to Nathaniel Williams' care, for the Latin School was the lengthened shadow of its master and, as an institution, it became strong and effective because of the competence and devotion of those who directed it, who governed its values, and who determined its curriculum.

* * *

The "Free Grammar School of Boston" had its origins in 1635, five years after Winthrop's settlement, not through the establishment of an institution, but in the action "At a Generall meeting upon publique notice" of Boston residents "yt oᵣ brother Mr. Philemon Pormort shalbe intreated to become scholemaster for the teaching & nourtering of children wᵗʰ us."[15] In the following year, a voluntary group of forty-five of the inhabitants contributed the money, some forty-five pounds, to maintain the school, but gradually public funds were appropriated from revenues realized by rentals of islands in Boston Harbor and other tracts owned by the town, by income from public docks and ferries, and, eventually, by general taxation. For the next thirty-two years, the school was taught by Cambridge and Oxford alumni, then for three years (from 1667 to 1670) by a

[14] Sibley, *Biographical Sketches*, II, 346.
[15] Recorded by Thomas Leverett, elder of the First Church, April 13, 1635, in Winsor, *Memorial History*, IV, 237.

Harvard graduate and, thereafter for thirty-eight years, by the first great schoolmaster in America, Ezekiel Cheever, who was paid by the town an annual competence of sixty pounds and for whom a residence was built and in due time an usher or assistant was provided. The first schoolhouse was built behind King's Chapel but by 1704 it was outgrown, and a new building capable of housing a hundred boys was constructed. A well-proportioned gambrel-roofed, clapboard structure, some forty by twenty-five feet, it was located on the southeast corner of the old burying ground almost adjacent to the first building of King's Chapel and in pleasant architectural accord with that unpretentious frame edifice with its small-paned windows, gently peaked roof, and modest steeple. Surrounded by trees and surmounted by a cupola and bell, the schoolhouse was agreeable, light and airy, with eight windows on the ground floor and five dormers on the second. In warm weather, when the windows were raised, the sounds and smells of the surrounding houseyards and of the bustling waterfront less than a thousand feet distant lured the attention of the hundred boys from their benches, aligned in rows of three on each side of the four rooms, to the great, diverting world outside, but not at the price of their learning, which achieved a level of distinction unsurpassed in secondary education anywhere in the colonies through the combined strengths of the school's teachers and curriculum.

The teaching skills of the master, Ezekiel Cheever, were memorialized by Cotton Mather in one of his mercifully few ventures in verse, distinguished more for its generosity of feeling than for any literary merit ("Were grammar quite extinct, yet at his brain/The candle might have well been lit again"[16]). Living to the vast age of ninety-four and teaching at the Latin School until the end, Cheever undertook, even on his death-bed, to instruct Judge Sewall, when the latter with characteristic consideration went to visit him, telling him that, in sending afflictions upon His people, "God by them did as a Goldsmith, Knock, knock, knock; knock, knock, knock, to finish the plate: It was to perfect them not to punish them." Sewall was so impressed that he went immediately to tell Ebenezer Pemberton and thence to take to the dying Cheever "the best Figs I could get, and a dish Marmalet."[17] When he died in 1708, Cheever left behind, besides the largest number of Harvard men ever prepared by a single individual, a small book called *Accidence, a Short Introduction to the Latin Tongue,* which remained the most widely used elementary text on Latin for well over a century in America.

The venerable Cheever, who was the principal architect of the Boston Latin School's theory and practice of classical education, had agreed, five years before his death, to the appointment of Nathaniel Williams, a

[16] Cotton Mather, *Corderius Americanus. An Essay upon the Good Education of Children* (Boston, 1708), 28.
[17] Sewall, *Diary,* II, 230–31.

twenty-eight-year-old clergyman and physician recently returned from two years as a missionary in Barbados, as his assistant. Williams and Cheever got along admirably, and Williams was immediately invited to succeed Cheever as master on the latter's death. After some stately negotiations with the selectmen raising his salary from £80 to £150, Dr. Williams settled into the mastership, practicing medicine, preaching occasionally at the Old South (on which occasions courtly old Judge Sewall yielded his pew to Mrs. Williams), and declining, with fine discrimination between the best of Latin schools and the second best of colleges, an invitation of the Corporation of Yale to become its rector.

Nathaniel Williams was Benjamin Franklin's first and probably most important teacher. Unlike many schoolmasters, he was neither a menacing nor an authoritarian figure. For one thing, he did not look fearful, being "of a middling Size, enclining to Fatness; His Countenance Fresh and Comely, with a mixture of Majesty and smiling Sweetness." His manner, too, was such as to be reassuring to young boys subject for the first time to authority outside the home: "His Conversation mingled with Chearfulness and Gravity," and Thomas Prince, colleague pastor with his classmate, Joseph Sewall, of the Old South and first among the early historians of New England, said that, to his patients, Dr. Williams' "lively Voice and Countenance . . . did good like a Medicine, reviv'd our Spirits, and lighten'd our Maladies."[18] One of the terms under which he accepted the mastership was that he be given a competent assistant. The second to hold this post of usher under Williams was Edward Wigglesworth, who began his duties in 1713, the year before Benjamin Franklin entered. Born the year that Williams was graduated from Harvard, 1693, Wigglesworth was himself graduated at the age of seventeen. He had been orphaned at fifteen, the child of the chronically ailing physician-minister-poet, Michael Wigglesworth, by his second marriage when he was sixty-two. Edward Wigglesworth placed first in his class and, between his bachelor's and master's degrees, taught school at Casco Bay Fort. Wigglesworth was by temperament more scholarly than Williams (he was later the choice of the Harvard Corporation to hold the college's first endowed professorship). Physically slight and unimpressive, he was hard of hearing and suffered a speech impediment that cause him to lisp and to speak in a soft, restrained voice. His principal power was intellectual, and he brought to his discipline of theology a broad and catholic outlook. It is likely that Dr. Williams turned over to his junior colleague the routine instruction of the younger boys, but the curriculum remained firmly in the hands of the master.

For boys of eight years, as Benjamin Franklin and most of his classmates were on entering the Latin School, the curriculum was a demanding

---

[18] The quotes from Prince's funeral sermon on Dr. Williams and from the obituary in the *New England Weekly Journal*, January 17, 1738, are in Sibley, *Biographical Sketches*, IV, 184–85.

though not an unmanageable one, directed quite simply at meeting Harvard's requirements that its entering students be able to use Latin as the language of all instruction and be familiar with the principal Greek authors in the original. Three years before Franklin entered the Latin School, the selectmen presented a proposal to a meeting of inhabitants of the town that an inquiry be made by the school inspectors and ministers as to whether, for those students who had no intention of becoming scholars and going on to college, the teaching methods and curriculum were adequate. Calling attention "to the Information of Some of the Learned, who have made Observation of the easie & pleasant Rules and Methods used in Some Schools in Europe, were Scollars, p'haps within the compass of one year, have attained to a Competent Proficiency So as to be able to read and discourse in Lattin," the selectmen suggested that while the Latin School's "more Tedious and burthensome methode" may have been good for potential scholars, for the run-of-the-mill students it might be desirable that "Some more easie and delightfull methodes be there attended and put in practice."[19]

The townspeople adopted the selectmen's proposal, and a list of "those Gentlem[en] whom they shall chuse as Inspectors of the School," according to the selectmen's recommendation, appeared for the first time on the roster of town officials following the town meeting of March 12, 1710/11, among the five chosen being Judge Sewall. But the somewhat disingenuous proposal to find a short cut to the mastery of Latin apparently did not galvanize Nathaniel Williams into action. After nearly a year went by, he reported, not to the school inspectors, but to whom he would have regarded as a more concerned individual, the senior fellow of Harvard College and "an excellent scholar, in the *Latin, Greek and Hebrew*,"[20] Nehemiah Hobart. He sent a detailed curriculum of the school's Latin and Greek for Hobart's "Correction, alteratiō or advancemᵗ as you shall see meet." The curriculum, if it differed in any significant particular from that he inherited from Ezekiel Cheever (which is most doubtful according to the recollections of Cheever's curriculum by his former students), was certainly far from radically innovative; certainly it indicated no "Competent Proficiency" within a year or even three. But it did prescribe an assiduous course of study, especially for the young boys of eight, nine, and ten. "The three first years," Williams reported, "are spent first in Learning by heart & then acc: to their capacities understanding the Accidence [i.e., Cheever's short introduction to Latin, which was still being printed in Boston as late as 1838] and Nomenclator [or *Nomenclatura*, a Latin-English vocabulary of common words and phrases used in the public schools of England and imported by Boston booksellers since the mid-seventeenth century] in construing & parsing acc: to the English rules of

[19] Colonial Society of Massachusetts, *Proceedings*, XXVII, 22.
[20] Massachusetts Historical Society, *Collections*, X, 168.

Syntax Sententiae Pueriles [a book of sentences for children in Latin with English translations by a prolific seventeenth-century London teacher, Charles Hoole] Cato [Dionysius Cato, the author of a collection of moral precepts, *Disticha de Moribus ad Filium*, was particularly appetizing to a Puritan community and was regularly used in all New England Latin quarterlies] & Corderius [a book of dialogues in Latin written for young students by an early French schoolmaster, Mathurin Cordier, after whom Cotton Mather dubbed Ezekiel Cheever "Cordierus Americanus"] & AEsop's Fables." (There was nothing new about this as a part of the curriculum; John Barnard, a beginner at the school in 1689, said, "Master put our class upon turning Aesop's Fables into Latin verse."[21]).

Young Benjamin Franklin's scholarly gifts, as estimated by his father and his friends, turned out to have been soundly estimated. During his first—and, as it developed, his only—year at the Latin School, "I had risen gradually from the Middle of the Class of that Year to be the Head of it, and farther was remov'd into the next Class above it, in order to go with that into the Third [class] at the End of the Year."[22] This was a most remarkable accomplishment for the child of the candlemaker's cottage, for many of his classmates came from backgrounds much more privileged in terms of formal learning or of wealth or of social position. With whom, specifically, Franklin had to compete in order to achieve his superior record is known only in part. Probably his class consisted of fourteen or fifteen, since it was recorded in 1709—five years before Franklin entered the Latin School—that there were "Frequently one hundred scholars in the school[23] and the curriculum consisted of a seven-year program. Three boys known to have entered with Franklin were Mather Byles, Samuel Freeman, and Jeremiah Gridley, all of whom, with Franklin, were born during the first three months of 1706.[24] All three finished their courses at the school and were graduated from Harvard College in the class of 1725. Of them, Mather Byles, the nephew of Cotton Mather and grandson of Increase Mather, the repudiated president of Harvard, who later left the boy "a fourth" of his considerable library, was probably Franklin's keenest scholastic rival; he had high native intelligence, a sharp wit, and outstanding and original literary ability. His path was to cross Franklin's soon

21 John Barnard, *Autobiography*, in Massachusetts Historical Society, *Collections*, 3rd Ser., V, 177–243.

22 *Autobiography*, 53.

23 *Materials for a Catalogue of the Masters and Scholars Who have belonged to the Public Latin School, Boston, Massachusetts, from 1635 to 1846* (Boston, 1847), 10.

24 In *Catalogue of the Masters and Scholars Who Have Belonged to the Boston Latin School 1635–1879* (Boston; 1878), Benjamin Gibson is attributed to the class entering in 1714 (p. 6). This is improbable. Gibson was graduated from Harvard in 1719 (six years ahead of the others in that Latin School class), and he was born in 1700 (six years ahead of those others known to be in the class). Gibson probably was graduated from the Latin School in 1714 rather than entering, in 1714, since he was the valedictorian that year. This catalogue was a not wholly successful attempt to update the 1847 catalogue cited in the note preceding.

after the Latin School years of both, and the youthful acquaintance of the two was to be renewed by their correspondence in their aged years when the humor and civility of both bridged differences and strengthened accords, as Byles became a somewhat unorthodox preacher, inclined toward doctrinal liberalism, Anglican taste, and Tory convictions, and a noted poet given to humor and improbable but workable puns (on being put under constant observation in virtual house arrest during the Revolution for his Tory views, he referred to his guard as an "observe-a-Tory" and, at seventy-eight, being unable to stand to welcome a guest, he remarked that he was not a member of "the rising generation").[25]

Of Franklin's other two known Latin School classmates, Samuel Freeman was the son of a brewer, who was a member of the Mathers' Second Church, but Samuel went back to the Church of England and left an estate of impressive proportions, earned as an able and shrewd merchant, to "the College and Christ Church [after King's Chapel, the second Church of England parish in Boston], in Boston, that for the Colledge, in order to assist the maintenance of some of the Poor Scholars of the Episcopal Persuasion."[26] Freeman did not take his second degree at Harvard and left no evidence of any particularly scholarly interests. As to Jeremiah Gridley, he was probably much more of a competitor with young Franklin for the distinction of leading their class at the Latin School. Gridley took his master's degree, became an usher at the Latin School for six years, under Nathaniel Williams, founded a weekly newspaper, and became one of the most eminent lawyers of his time. He was unorthodox and mercurial in his religious views, and John Adams, who became one of his law protégés, commented on "his great learning, his great parts, and his majestic manner . . . a bold spirited manner of speaking . . . his words seem to pierce and search, to have something quick and animating; he is a great reasoner, and has a very vivid imagination."[27] Adams also noted that Gridley had his limitations ("stiffness and affectation"), but for half a century or more he was held up as the model of a skilled advocate, and he must have been a school-days contender with Franklin for scholastic leadership.

Whatever the degree and quality of his classmates' rivalry, Benjamin's prodigious reading and native intelligence stood him in good stead, and he evidently raced effortlessly through a curriculum the selectmen had thought "Tedious and burthensome." Moreover, the sturdiness of Nathaniel Williams' methods, in Franklin's case, stood the test of time. Benjamin Franklin never gave up being a student, even enlisting contemporaries into voluntary associations to advance their knowledge when their formal schooling was over. And almost twenty years after his single, triumphant year at the Latin School, at the age of twenty-seven, busy with his printer's trade and supporting a family, he resumed the study of languages. "I soon

[25] Arthur W. H. Eaton, *The Famous Mather Byles* (Boston; 1914), 173, 199.
[26] Suffolk Probate Records, XXVIII, 247.
[27] John Adams, *Works*, ed. C. F. Adams (Boston, 1850–56), II, 46.

made myself so much a Master of the French as to be able to read the Books with Ease. I then undertook the Italian. . . . I afterwards with a little Painstaking acquir'd as much of the Spanish as to read their Books also," he wrote in his *Autobiography*. "I have already mention'd that I had only one Years Instruction in a Latin School, and that when very young, after which I neglected the Language entirely. But when I had attained an Acquaintance with the French, Italian and Spanish, I was surpriz'd to find, on looking over a Latin Testament, that I understood so much more of the Language than I had imagined . . ."[28]—which speaks eloquently for the effectiveness of Nathaniel Williams' teaching methods.

At the end of Benjamin Franklin's first year—despite his impressive progress—Josiah Franklin took him out of the Latin School and abandoned the idea of educating him for the ministry. Recounting this revision of his father's plans in later years, Franklin expressed no bitterness, only a simple acceptance that implied a basic respect for the reasoning that led his father to the decision and perhaps also enormous relief that he was spared being launched on a clerical career for which by temperament he was uniquely unfitted, by intellect poorly geared, and by conviction wholly unequipped. He also, later in life, expressed some considerable doubt as to the value of emphasizing the classics at the outset of the educational process, despite the clear aptitude that his year at the Latin School showed that he himself had for them. After resuming the study of Latin following learning the modern romantic languages in 1733, he ascribed his rapid progress with Latin to his way's being "smoothed" by his newly acquired acquaintance with French, Italian, and Spanish. "From these Circumstances I have thought that there is some Inconsistency in our common Mode of Teaching Languages. We are told that it is proper to begin first with the Latin, and having acquir'd that it will be more easy to attain those modern Languages which are deriv'd from it; and yet we do not begin with the Greek in order more easily to acquire the Latin."[29] It could, of course, be as plausibly postulated that the ease with which he acquired his knowledge of French, Italian, and Spanish in his maturity may have been due in considerable measure to his boyhood training in Latin. In any case, his own first writings, the Silence Dogood papers, written when he was fifteen, were embellished with Latin quotations and references. And when he came, in 1749, after thirty years of writing and editing, to composing and publishing his *Proposals Relating to the Education of Youth in Pensilvania*, leading to the founding of the University of Pennsylvania, he wrote in eloquent defense of the study of Latin and Greek, though he was careful not to specify it as necessarily his own view:

When Youth are told, that the Great Men whose Lives and Actions they read in History, spoke two of the best Languages that ever were, the

[28] *Autobiography*, 168.
[29] Ibid., 169.

most expressive, copious, beautiful; and that the finest Writings, the most correct Compositions, the most perfect Productions of human Wit and Wisdom, are in those Languages, which have endured for Ages, and will endure while there are Men; that no translation can do them Justice, or give the Pleasure found in Reading the Originals; that those Languages contain all science; that one of them is become almost universal, being the Language of Learned Men in all Countries; that to understand them is a distinguishing Ornament, &c. They may be thereby made desirous of learning those Languages, and their Industry sharpen'd in the Acquisition of them. . . . And though all should not be compell'd to learn Latin, Greek, or the modern Languages; yet none that have an ardent Desire to learn them should be refused; their English, Arithmetick, and other Studies absolutely necessary, being at the same Time not neglected.[30]

In accounting for his leaving the Boston Latin School after a single outstanding year, he attributed the decision made by his father to the latter's "view of the Expence of a College Education, which, having so large a Family, he could not well afford, and the mean Living many so educated were able to obtain, Reasons that he gave to his Friends, in my Hearing. . . ."[31] It is not likely that Josiah Franklin would have, in Benjamin's presence, given as his reason any second thoughts on the boy's suitability for the ministry, but the economic reasoning does not hold up very impressively on examination. It is true that Josiah Franklin had raised a large family, but it was not at all exceptional in size and was raised, moreover, over a long period of time. Of his thirteen children that survived early childhood, the first was thirty-four when the last was born, and at no time did Josiah have more than four sons under the age of apprenticeship and more than three daughters under sixteen, the ages beyond which colonial children were usually independent of their parents. By the time Benjamin was in the Latin School, he was the only boy left at home; and all his sisters and half-sisters, except for the two younger sisters, were either married or of an age to be domestically employed. At the Latin School, tuition was free, and the only charge expected to be met was six shillings a year "fire money" to pay for wood to heat the school, though even that modest sum was not required of boys from poor parents. The boys apparently owned their books, but these were in widespread supply from students of previous years and also among Boston booksellers, and it was obvious from his small library that Josiah Franklin was quite accustomed to spending money on books and the slight cost of slender school texts would not have been burdensome to him. As for the expenses at Harvard College, Josiah Franklin had, through the Old South, the closest of ties to those who were running the college, and he would have known very well that boys of such outstanding ability as Benjamin demonstrated at the Latin School would be provided with scholarship funds, supplemented by

[30] *Papers*, III, 415.
[31] *Autobiography*, 53.

compensation as waiters, to defray their college expenses. Had Benjamin continued at the Latin School, he would have entered Harvard with the class of 1724—a year ahead of those who entered the school with him because of his having been advanced a year—and the class with which his name was listed in the college catalogue after he received an honorary master's degree in 1753. Of the forty-three members of the class, ten were the sons of tradesmen and artisans—carpenters, blacksmiths, tailors, tanners, brewers, and glovers among them—similar in their economic resources to Josiah Franklin. Nine others were sons of farmers. Five were the sons of ministers or schoolmasters. Four were orphans. Only seven of the forty-three are known to have come from families of some wealth—all of them the sons of merchants. There is little evidence, therefore, that Josiah would have been obliged to terminate the classical education of the leader of his class at the Boston Latin School solely because he could see little prospects of meeting the costs of a Harvard education.

What probably moved the shrewd, observant, and practical Josiah, who in his thirty-one years in Boston had come to know the town, its ways, and its values thoroughly and, through his membership in the Old South, the citadel of the Boston learned community once Harvard rid itself of the Mather influence, was his thorough understanding of the relationship between Harvard and the church establishment. Unquestionably, he realized that although Benjamin qualified, so far as intelligence and scholastic aptitude went, for a Harvard education with scholarship support, the boy could hardly have withstood very searching inquiry into the degree of his piety—and most scholarship aid was intended to help educate students for the ministry. An incident that occurred in Benjamin's boyhood, very probably at the approximate time of his year at the Latin School, for it would have been a little too precocious earlier and a little too artless later, may well have furnished conclusive evidence to Josiah Franklin that the tithe of his sons was just not destined for service to the church. Benjamin Franklin narrated the episode, which he did not include in his *Autobiography*, to his grandson, William Temple Franklin, who appended it to his edition (the first) of his grandfather's writings: "Dr. Franklin, when a child, found the long graces used by his father before and after meals very tedious. One day after the winter's provisions had been salted,—'I think, Father,' said Benjamin, 'if you were to say *Grace* over the whole cask— once for all—it would be a vast *saving of time.*' "[32] The significance of this remark in a society where wordiness in religious exercises was counted a virtue much to be desired would not have been lost on Josiah Franklin. It is most likely, then, that Josiah Franklin simply had sufficient insight into his son's interests as they began to manifest themselves to know that a bend toward devotions and theology was not among them. And so he took

[32] William Temple Franklin, ed., *Memoirs of the Life and Writings of Benjamin Franklin, LL.D.,* 3 vols. (London; 1818), I, 447.

a more practical outlook as to the boy's future and "sent me to a school for Writing and Arithmetic kept by a then famous Man, Mr. Geo. Brownell. . . ."[33]

* * *

George Brownell's was one of eight "writing schools" conducted for the children of Boston's two thousand familes in 1715. Two of them were supported by public funds, the Queen Street Writing School, at the foot of the eastern slope of Beacon Hill, and the North Writing School in the North End. Though the Queen Street school was not far from the Franklin house, Benjamin was probably not eligible for it because the purpose of the Queen Street school was specifically "to teach ye Children of the Towne to read & write."[34] Of the six private writing schools, one was conducted in French for the Huguenots by John Rawlins, a friend of Judge Sewall. Of the remaining five schoolmasters, the best qualified academically were Edward Mills and Ames Angier, both of whom held both bachelor's and master's degrees from Harvard. Mills, however, was not only a communicant of the Church of England but also a vestryman of King's Chapel, which provided his school with an annual sum to teach the children of any indigent members; it is unlikely that Josiah Franklin would have given any thought at all to sending his son to such an establishment, which in any case was relatively distant from Hanover and Union streets, being located on the northwest edge of town in Sudbury Street. As for Ames Angier, he lacked prudence in his private affairs, constantly being in trouble with the sheriff for nonpayment of debts, which would have aroused grave doubts about his desirability as an influence on the young in the mind of an honest and prudent tradesman like Josiah Franklin. George Brownell, on the other hand, was enterprising and businesslike; and his schoolroom was conveniently located in Wings Lane, just two streets west of the Franklin house off Hanover Street. Brownell was also easily the most versatile of the Boston schoolmasters of 1715. The announcement of the opening of his school, for which, like all schoolmasters in Boston, he had to be granted a license, showed a remarkable range of versatility, even assuming his wife aided in the conduct of the school: "At the house of Mr. George Brownell in Wings-Lane Boston, is taught Writing, Cyphering, Dancing, Treble Violin, Flute, Spinnet, &c. Also English and French Quilting, Imbroidery, Florishing, Plain Work, Marking in several sorts of Stitches and several other works where Scholars may board."[35]

The achievement of the Boston writing schools was far more precise, on the whole, than the encyclopedic notice of Brownell might suggest. They accounted in great measure for a most extraordinarily high rate of literacy for a colonial outpost still primarily occupied with keeping itself physically

[33] *Autobiography*, 53.
[34] *Boston Records*, VII, 171.
[35] *Boston News-Letter*, March 2 to March 9, 1712.

and economically viable. The turn of the century, from the outbreak in 1675 of King Philip's War, which spread death and destruction through southern New England, to the Treaty of Utrecht in 1713, ending eleven years of Queen Anne's War and, for a time at least, the colonial struggle with France and Spain, was a bleak era, with considerable demands upon the colonists' resources. But with some grumbling they kept the free schools open and supported the private schools. As early as 1680 the literacy rate in Massachusetts among males called upon to sign documents was as high as 98 per cent,[36] and in the seaports it was 99 per cent; among women it was 62 per cent during the same general period.[37] But the writing schools could, and frequently did, do more. Edward Wigglesworth, the usher at the Boston Latin School who instructed Benjamin Franklin and became the first Hollis professor at Harvard, said of the hapless Ames Angier, "I was under Mr. Angier's Instruction, to my great Delight & Satisfaction, about a Twelvemonth (as I remember) before my admission into the Colledge. If I was in any Measure fitted for the College, before I was Admitted into it, I have Reason thankfully to Acknowledge Myself Indebted Entirely to Mr. Angier for it."[38] In the case of girls, for whom there were neither public grammar schools nor a college, their entire institutional education came from the writing schools. In 1711 Cotton Mather was determined that his daughters would be educated, "that they may do good unto others; and if they should be reduced into Necessities, unto themselves also." For his daughter, Katharine, when eighteen, he prescribed, "Knowledge in Physic, and the Preparation, and the Dispensation of noble Medicines," and for his younger daughters, Abigail, seventeen, and Hannah, fourteen, "I will consult their Inclinations."[39] Less ambitious parents were required by law, as a minimum, where there were no free schools, themselves to teach their children to read, and Josiah Franklin's daughters all could read and write. Though there is evidence that less conscientious parents were not sufficiently deterred by threats of fines from avoiding this duty, since the literacy rate of women was consistently, though not dramatically, lower than that of men, that the vast majority of parents took their obligation seriously is indicated by the fact that in 1700, when there were fewer than two hundred students in the writing schools, one Boston bookseller alone, according to John Dunton, carried a stock of over seven hundred primers.

Though called writing schools, the private proprietary schools—as Brownell's announcement and Edward Wigglesworth's testimony indicate— were really comprehensive elementary schools, in most cases ranging up-

[36] From studies of Clifford K. Shipton cited by Samuel Eliot Morison, *The Intellectual Life of Colonial New England* [*the Puritan Pronaos*] (Ithaca, 1956), 83–84.
[37] William H. Kilpatrick, *The Dutch Schools of New Netherland* (1912), 229, which uses Suffolk County, Massachusetts, as a basis of comparison.
[38] Sibley, *Biographical Sketches*, V, 28.
[39] Mather, *Diary*, II, 112.

ward into the secondary level. The major emphasis was on writing, because, aside from direct oral utterances, writing was the only form of communication that existed, and it was the sole form of communication for the record and was therefore as essential for tradesmen as it was for scholars. By writing, the schoolmasters meant both penmanship and composition, and spelling was also taught. The masters took enormous pride in their own skills at penmanship and labored for years compiling slim copy books of splendidly embellished examples of their craftsmanship which, while they bore little relationship to the real world of eighteenth-century communications, set standards of elegance and excellence for their pupils that could not fail to impress them. The students were also taught the principles of the quill pen, the shaping of them from goose feathers and the sharpening and maintenance of them. Teaching was by constant drill in an endless and demanding quest for perfection, and the indications are that far more attention was directed to the craft of penmanship than to the art of composition. In writing, Benjamin Franklin said that he acquired a fair degree of competence quite promptly, and he paid tribute to George Brownell as "very successful in his Profession generally, and that by mild encouraging Methods."[40]

With arithmetic, Benjamin was less successful. Though there were several elementary arithmetic textbooks published in London (none were published in Boston until 1729) that were available at Boston booksellers, inventory figures of the latter indicate that they were bought only by the masters as guides in instructing their pupils. The subject was taught by "cyphering," i.e., by copying down figures and working out problems in a mathematical vacuum. Students were provided with copy books in which they copied out problems in figures after the correct solution had been worked out in the classroom. Probably, during the first year, the substance of the subject as taught in the writing schools was limited to the basic procedures of adding, subtracting, multiplying, and dividing. Benjamin said, "I fail'd in the Arithmetic, and made no Progress in it"[41]—which testifies less to George Brownell's being "very successful in his Profession generally" than to his having "mild encouraging Methods," since a few years later Franklin, "asham'd of my Ignorance in Figures, which I had twice failed in learning when at School [the usher at Boston Latin School probably also gave first-year boys extracurricular elementary instruction in arithmetic], I took [Edward] Cocker's Book of Arithmetick [published in London in 1677 and sold in Boston by John Ive, bookseller], and went thro' the whole by my self with great Ease."[42]

Altogether the year at Brownell's writing school probably failed in Josiah Franklin's evident purpose in sending the boy there, which was to

[40] *Autobiography*, 53.
[41] Ibid.
[42] Ibid., 63–64.

supplement his taste of the classics with the practical knowledge, particularly of elementary arithmetic, that was essential to the success of any self-employed artisan, who could not even render bills without such knowledge. But it did give him a year of "writing" and a year of experience with his contemporaries in a fairly relaxed atmosphere—and the latter may have been the major achievement of the year

* * *

Schoolboys go to school not only to their masters and their textbooks but also to their peers. It is through and with them that boys discover their surroundings and their relationships to them; and, to a considerable extent, the tones and the interests of their whole lives are set by these early, impressionable exposures. The young Franklin grew up in a town which, though by modern standards was small, was so densely populated as to have the nature of a bustling city. The lively spirit of the harbor, with ships coming in every day from distant ports, with the shipwrights and corders always busy, with the wharves crowded with familiar goods to be shipped out and the unfamiliar shipped in, and with all the rub of the human diversity and contrast of a seaport's transient population, imbued the town with a spirit of adventure, of practicality, and of zest for larger, broader, more speculative awarenesses. And the day of the Bible Commonwealth was over, the lofty vision of John Winthrop of a community dedicated solely to the realization of God's will on earth lost in the pulsating world of ships and merchandise and a society made up increasingly of the skeptical, the ungodly, or merely the spiritually unconcerned. The Puritan experiment was dependent upon isolation, and with the rise of Boston as a seaport isolation was gone forever.

All this, to the boy Franklin and most of his contemporaries, meant an orientation toward the sea rather than the meetinghouse, toward the concrete rather than the abstract, and toward the active rather than the contemplative. Their fathers were, in a sense, seeking a retreat *from* the world when they came to Boston; the sons saw the port of Boston as a gateway *to* the world. The boys explored the wharves, the marshs, the shipyards, and the ropewalks; they listened to the stories of mariners; they became absorbed in the world at their doorstep, in its hubbub, its changing restlessness, and its sheer physical exuberance. At the same time, there was a sturdy practicality about them, an extraordinary sense of self-reliance, and a persistent integrity that sprang from both their heritage and their surroundings. The eyes of the young Franklin looked longingly seaward, but the year that he attended Mr. Brownell's writing school was the year that Josiah Franklin, Jr., his second oldest half-brother, was lost at sea, at twenty-nine, after a nine-year absence on a previous journey to the East Indies; even as a boy, Benjamin had enough sense of human relations to know that his father would never permit his going to sea. I "had a strong Inclination for the Sea," he recalled, "but my Father declar'd against it. . . ." He went on, however, to record how, without violating his father's wishes by running away, as Josiah, Jr., had done, he did get in league with the ocean waters surrounding his peninsula home: "living near the Water, I was much in and about it, learnt early to swim well, and to manage Boats, and when in a Boat or Canoe with other Boys I was commonly allow'd to govern, especially in any case of Difficulty."[43]

During his boyhood, Franklin developed into a powerful swimmer, and the inventiveness that characterized his mind all his life first manifested itself in connection with his love of swimming. After he had mastered conventional swimming, he sought various means of accelerating the speed at which a human body could propel itself through water. Understanding quite thoroughly the theory of swimming, which he regarded as natural as walking, he realized that there was a limit to the capacity of the human hands and feet to generate speed in the water because of the limited size of the palms and of the soles of the feet—the two sets of propellents employed in swimming. Accordingly, Franklin wrote, "I made two oval palettes, each about two inches long, and six broad, with a hole for the thumb, in order to retain it fast in the palm of my hand. They much resembled a painter's palettes. In swimming I pushed the edges of these forward, and I struck the water with their flat surfaces as I drew them back. I remember I swam faster by means of these palettes, but they fatigued my wrists." Franklin was probably also among the first aquatic performers to contrive and use flippers, although he apparently made them of a rigid material, as he had the hard paddles: "I also fitted to the soles of my feet a kind of sandals; but I was not satisfied with them, because I observed that the stroke is partly given by the inside of the feet and the ankles, and not entirely with the soles of the feet."[44]

Franklin, whose inventive career was more than once to involve the use of kites, also experimented with that ancient device as a means of increasing his speed and decreasing his expenditure of energy as a swimmer, confident fifty years later that he had hit upon a way of crossing the English Channel. He was flying a paper kite one day by the Mill Pond when he was moved to go swimming and so tied the string of his kite to a stake in the ground. "In a little time being desirous of amusing myself with my kite and enjoying at the same time the pleasure of swimming, I returned; and, loosing from the stake the string with the little stick which was fastened to it, went again into the water, where I found that, lying on my back and holding the stick in my hands, I was drawn along the surface of the water in a very agreeable manner. Having then engaged another boy to carry my clothes round the pond, to a place which I pointed out to him on the other side, I began to cross the pond with my kite, which carried

[43] *Autobiography*, 53.
[44] Undated letter to Barbeu Dubourg, ed., *Oeuvres de M. Franklin* (Paris, 1773), II, 310. Retranslation given is in Smyth, *Writings of Benjamin Franklin*, V, 543.

me quite over without the least fatigue, and with the greatest pleasure imaginable. . . . I think it not impossible to cross in this manner from Dover to Calais."[45]

As a result of his swimming prowess, Franklin developed exceptional strength in his arms and shoulders, which served him in good stead all his life. When he was nineteen and working at John Watts's printing house near Lincoln's Inn Fields in London, he found that he could carry up and down the stairs of the great printing house a large, heavy form of type in each hand, while the other fifty workmen could manage only one in both hands. Having fallen in with another young employee of Watts, John Wygate, Franklin "taught him, and a Friend of his, to swim, at twice going into the River [Thames], and they soon became good Swimmers. They introduc'd me to some Gentlemen from the Country who went to Chelsea by Water [i.e., up the Thames by barge, probably from Black-friars] to see the College and Don Salter's [museum of] Curiosities. In our Return, at the Request of the Company, whose Curiosity Wygate had excited, I stript and leapt into the River, and swam from near Chelsea to Blackfryars [almost four miles] performing on the Way many Feats of Activity both upon and under Water, that surpriz'd and pleas'd those to whom they were Novelties. I had from a Child ever been delighted with this Exercise, had studied and practis'd all Thevenot's Motions and Positions [from the French swimming teacher's book, *The Art of Swimming*, which had been translated into English, published in London, and sold in Boston], added some of my own, aiming at the graceful and easy, as well as the Useful."[46] Word of Franklin's extraordinary swimming skills spread through London so that a former Chancellor of the Exchequer, Sir William Wyndham, sought to engage him to teach his sons to swim, and Franklin himself "thought it likely, that if I were to remain in England and open a Swimming School, I might get a good deal of Money."[47] And when Franklin later set forth his proposals for the establishment of the academy in Philadelphia, he included swimming in the curriculum, quoting John Locke's *Treatise on Education:* " 'Tis that saves many a Man's Life; and the Romans thought it so necessary, that they rank'd it with Letters; and it was the common Phrase to mark one ill educated, and good for nothing, that he had neither learnt to read nor to swim. . . ."[48]

The command that Franklin said he was yielded by his friends in his boyhood he did not hesitate on occasion to assert in order to advance some project, as he was wont to do all his life, that he was persuaded was in the common interest. The Boston of the first quarter of the eighteenth century offered sufficient opportunities for an imaginative lad. Always in-

[45] Ibid., 545.
[46] *Autobiography*, 103.
[47] Ibid., 106.
[48] *Papers*, III, 403.

trigued by the possibility of channeling natural forces and conditions to serve the needs of man, young Franklin during his school days launched a project in the Mill Pond that proved instructive. The Mill Pond was a tidal basin about two hundred feet up Union Street from the Franklin house, and it represented a benevolent conspiracy of man and nature to lure young boys into visionary projects. Originally the North Cove, a natural inlet of about fifty acres on the Charles River side of the Shawmut peninsula, the Mill Pond was formed by constructing a dam or causeway across its mouth so that the waters were trapped in it at high tide and then, as the tide receded, spilled out of a sluice with sufficient force to turn the gears of the corn mills and later of a sawmill. The edges of the Mill Pond were, of course, salt marshes, full of readily accessible fish at high tide but, at low tide, exposed bottom lands, without water but also too sodden to be usable as land. Small boys always fish from the land, and young Franklin and his friends went to the rim of the marsh to catch minnows at high tide; but with the venturesomeness of youth, they used to follow the tide out, with what Franklin regarded as unsatisfactory results, and he used his position of leadership among the boys to correct the situation. "I was generally a Leader among the Boys," he reported, "and sometimes led them into Scrapes, of which I will mention one Instance, as it shows an early projecting public Spirit, tho' not then justly conducted. There was a Salt Marsh that bounded part of the Mill Pond, on the Edge of which at Highwater we us'd to fish for Minews. By much trampling, we had made it a mere Quaqmire. My Proposal was to build a Wharf there fit for us to stand upon, and I show'd my Comrades a large Heap of Stones which were intended for a new House near the Marsh, and which would very well suit our Purpose. Accordingly in the Evening when the Workmen were gone, I assembled a Number of my Playfellows, and working with them diligently like so many Emmets, sometimes two or three to a Stone, we brought them all away and built our little Wharff. The next Morning the Workmen were surpriz'd at Missing the Stones; which were found in our Wharff; Enquiry was made after the Removers; we were discovered and complain'd of; several of us were corrected by our Fathers; and tho' I pleaded the Usefulness of the Work, mine convinc'd me that nothing was useful which was not honest."[49] And the busy emmets undoubtedly spent some time and labor undoing their ill-advised construction.

The boyhood of Benjamin Franklin ended, so far as responsibility and activity went, when he began at the age of ten, his two years of school over, to work for his father in the tallow shop, succeeding his brother John, sixteen years his senior, who had married during Benjamin's last year at school and left his father to set up his own candle and soap business in Rhode Island. They were days of drudgery for the boy—"cutting Wick for

[49] *Autobiography*, 54.

the Candles, filling the Dipping Mold, and the Molds for cast Candles, attending the Shop, going of Errands, &c."[50] And yet the education of Benjamin Franklin continued apace. An observant lad, older than his years as a result in part of being the youngest boy in a sizable family and in part of his precocity, he learned much of the personalities and institutions of the busy provincial capital as he went his rounds of errands and deliveries. He came to know the town, the forces that were shaping its future, and some of the limitations of the establishment that governed it. Equally importantly, relieved of formal scholastic assignments, he had time, when the long day's work amid the vats and the molds was over and the walking through the streets and lanes of Boston was done, to explore the greater world beyond, in time and space, the tight little peninsula that housed the first Bible Commonwealth.

[50] Ibid., 53.

IX

The Education
from Books

> . . . I do not remember when I could not read.
> —Benjamin Franklin[1]

Although it meant the end of his schooling, Benjamin Franklin's employment in his father's tallow shop marked a new beginning to his education. The purposive colloquies around the family table, the amiable intellectual ramblings and primitive literary exercises of his Uncle Benjamin, the hard and syllogistic sermons and lectures of Samuel Willard at the South Church, and occasional exposures to the prodigious, quote-ridden exhortations of Cotton Mather—all these were persistent factors in honing the mind and awarenesses of a boy who prized learning above all else. But, as he attested throughout his long and varied life and as many of his major public achievements lastingly demonstrated, the chief force in shaping the latent genius in Franklin was his insatiable appetite for books. Reading was not a peripheral part of Franklin's boyhood. Books were central to it —as central, indeed, as they were to the active exercise of the Puritan discipline in the Boston of the Mathers. Perhaps the most salient fact in Franklin's life, certainly the most propitious, was that he was born in a bookish community, a little town where books had an importance and a permeating presence all out of proportion to its size but in direct proportion to the commitment of intellectual fervor that Puritanism presupposed. And it was his reading more than any other single force that turned Benjamin Franklin, at an incredibly early age, from the Puritanism, to which he was born, to the Enlightenment, of which he was to be the major American exponent and a principal world emissary, just as it was to a very large extent the unquenchable thirst for books that brought the Bible Commonwealth to its decline, as deism—the simple acknowl-

[1] *Autobiography*, 5.

edgment of the existence of one God uncluttered by dogma and sacraments—accorded more and more with the knowledge and thought spread by books.

The seeds of the attrition of the Bible Commonwealth were thus sown at its inception when the founders gave first priority to books in a society of men who "honored study and revered the symbols and instruments of learning."[2] For Boston had a library even before it was settled in 1630 by John Winthrop and his resolute company. On April 13, 1629, very nearly a full year before the *Arabella* set sail for New England, the Massachusetts Bay Company acquired in London a library of some fifty volumes, largely theological in content but containing also grammars, Greek and Latin as well as English, such odd volumes as "A booke called The French Country Farme," and, despite the total disfavor in which it was held, the Book of Common Prayer. No greater evidence of the Puritans' respect for books and, more particularly, for prose style of the most superior order of excellence could exist than the inclusion of the latter in a library carefully selected by a Puritan minister, the Reverend Samuel Skelton, for shipment on a crowded vessel where not an inch of space was occupied by a superfluous bit of cargo. Of less literary but greater doctrinal discrimination were New England mice; it was reported of the library of the younger John Winthrop, that "many books in a chamber where there was corn of divers sorts, had among them one wherein the Greek testament, the psalms and the common prayer were bound together. He found the common prayer eaten with mice, every leaf of it, and not any of the two other touched, nor any other of his books, though there were above a thousand."[3]

Before there was a college or even a school in Massachusetts and before there were any public buildings, there were several private libraries in addition to the governmental one selected by Skelton that was housed in the governor's residence. The recluse William Blackstone, the Church of England cleric living in isolation in Boston from 1623 until the incursion of the elect, had as his sole intellectual company a library of 160 printed and 10 manuscript volumes. After Blackstone left Boston, three years following the Puritans' arrival, for the solitude of Rhode Island and took his library with him, but with the succeeding influx of clergy in a colony that was, within a few decades, to have one minister for every two hundred inhabitants, the number of private libraries multiplied rapidly. Following the example of Elder William Brewster, who brought a library of 400 books with him to Plymouth in 1620, most of the religious leaders who migrated to Boston from England brought libraries with them, and those produced

[2] Julius Herbert Tuttle, "The Libraries of the Mathers," *American Antiquarian Society, Proceedings*, XX, 271.

[3] John Winthrop, *The History of New England*, ed. James Savage (Boston, 1853), II, 24.

by Harvard, beginning with the class of 1642, acquired theirs through Boston booksellers. John Cotton brought a considerable library with him from Boston, England. "Indeed," his grandson wrote, "his Library was vast, and vast was his acquaintance with it."[4] John Harvard brought with him from Cambridge 373 books, a versatile collection comprised of classical and Renaissance authors as well as of contemporary theologians, which on his death in 1638 he left, with £779, to the college established by the colony two years earlier. A larger but less celebrated private library was left to the college by the Reverend Theophilus Gale, fortunately for the nomenclature of the college, years after John Harvard's bequest, or there would have been an unseemly rhyming of the names of New England's two earliest academic outposts of Puritanism.

The private libraries of clergy less generous to the college were often listed as the major assets of their estates and were sold, on their deaths, to younger ministers, though not infrequently their widows hung on to them for they often proved a powerful lure in attracting new husbands of the cloth, one of whom, the Reverend John Oxenbridge, minister of the First Church, in Boston, was moved to bequeath his wife nine of his own books, "besides ye books she had in her former widow hood."[5] Usually consisting of from 150 to 400 works, the ministerial libraries were naturally heavy in theology, particularly in polemical theology which so particularly delighted the Puritan priests, who brought to disputation all the dedication that the Anglican priests brought to the liturgy. But the earliest New England libraries were also rich in classical works and, because of the Puritan conviction that all knowledge was in league with rather than in conflict with religion, in works of science, medicine, and natural history, some of which lent slender support to Calvinist doctrine and even less to Calvinist emphases. Thus, Brewster's library contained the essays of Bacon; Myles Standish's the *Commentaries* of Caesar; Winthrop's *The Prince* of Machiavelli; Daniel Russell's the works of Seneca, Homer, and Chaucer; Benjamin Bunker's the essays of Montaigne, the works of Descartes, and the minor Greek poets.

Cotton Mather, who was graduated from Harvard in 1678 at the age of sixteen, had, in his own words, "A library exceeding any man's, in all this Land,"[6] which was no exaggeration for it also exceeded in size that of any institution in the land. Mather's study, the dominant room of his great brick house in Hanover Street, was lined with "boxes with between two and three thousand Books in them."[7] His library was as diversified as were the intellectual interests of its owner and reflected the enormous range of his curiosity. Few subjects escaped his attention. Besides hundreds of theological works, with a heavy concentration of the scholastics, he owned sev-

[4] Mather, *Magnalia Christi Americana*, I, 274.
[5] *New England Historical and Genealogical Register*, XLIV, 86.
[6] Mather, *Diary*, VII, 77.
[7] Ibid., 447.

eral volumes on geography; on medicine (in which he was better read than most physicians of his time); on physics, astronomy, botany, and zoology (one of the first three Americans to be elected a fellow of the Royal Society of London, the principal academy of the sciences in the English-speaking world, Mather was a regular correspondent of the society, providing it with reports of scientific advances in America); on political and military history; on the classics, including the Greek and Roman philosophers, historians, dramatists, and poets; and on virtually all such practical subjects as navigation, trade, and commerce. Nor did Cotton Mather ever lose an opportunity to enlarge his library. By 1682 the Harvard College Library was sufficiently advanced in size and scope to encounter the comfortable problem of duplicates, as more and more private libraries were given to the college; accordingly, the college adopted a policy of selling the duplicates in order to finance other acquisitions. The major share of the disposed books went to the college fellows, and among the fellows Increase Mather got the major portion. But Cotton Mather outdid them all: of 365 books sold by the college in 1682, he acquired 100, a considerable part of them classical works in large folio editions.[8] Mather was also known to beg and borrow books almost shamelessly. "Tho' I am furnished with a very great Library yett seeing a Library of a late Minister in the Town to be sold, and a certain Collection of Books there, which had it may be above six hundred single Sermons in them; I could not forbear wishing myself made able to compass such a treasure. I could not forbear mentioning my Wishes in my Prayers before the Lord; that in case it might be a Service to His Interests, He would enable me in His good Providence, to purchase the Treasure now before me. But I left the Matter before Him with the profoundest Resignation willing to be without every thing that He should not order for me. Behold, a Gentleman, who a year ago treated me very ill; but I cheerfully forgave him! carried me home to dine with him; and upon an accidental Mention of the Library aforesaid, He to my Surprise, compelled me to accept of him a Summ of Money, which enabled me to come at what I had been desirous of."[9] It was in the blood of the Mathers to give the Lord strong assistance, and the "accidental Mention" was no doubt pointed.

Long before Josiah Franklin arrived in Boston, there was a public library, as distinguished from the governmental library acquired before the Massachusetts Bay Company left England. In 1656 a rich merchant of questionable ethics (he was fined by the General Court for profiteering on imports and was once publicly castigated, as he stood in meeting, by John Cotton, for his elastic business practices), Robert Keayne, left the town money to build a Town House and books from his collection to start a li-

---

[8] The list of titles is in Colonial Society of Massachusetts, *Publications*, XVIII, 407–17.
[9] Mather, *Diary*, I, 2.

brary, provided the town included in the Town House "a handsome roome for a Library & another for the Eld^rs and Scholl^rs to walke and meete in,"[10] a condition which the town met within the three years that Keayne specified. The new library could not compete, however, with Harvard for gifts and bequests (although John Oxenbridge left it nine volumes in 1674); and it did not become a common source of reading materials for the townspeople generally until well over a century later, its room serving chiefly as a meeting place for gatherings, such as those of the first Episcopalians, that had no home of their own. Nevertheless, it had a sufficient collection to engage a young Harvard graduate, John Barnard of the class of 1700, to catalogue and arrange it in 1702, compensating him with "two of those books of which there are in the Said Library two of a Sorte."[11]

A more general source of reading and referential materials, resorted to by those lacking either the resources or the brazenness of a Cotton Mather to build a personal library, were the books that they simply created by the arduous task of copying whatever fell into their hands temporarily, writing down summaries of sermons and lectures and maintaining commonplace books of curious facts, maxims, and quotations. The elder Benjamin Franklin's commonplace books were certainly a constant wellspring of wonder and interest to his young nephew, for the uncle retained all through his long life the curiosity, the sense of surprise, and the joy of discovery of a schoolboy. The poorer country clergy depended upon copying books that they borrowed, or excerpts from them, for professional tools, frequently binding them expertly in parchment or pigskin. Even Cotton Mather on occasion was forced to turn to the laborious business of copying if he wanted a permanent record of writings that interested him. "Seldome any *new Book* of Consequence finds the way from beyond-Sea, to these parts of *America*, but I bestow the Perusal upon it. And, still as I read, I note curiosities in my blank Books, which I entitle Quotidiana."[12]

* * *

At the opposite extreme of the size and variety of Cotton Mather's library in Hanover Street, just south of Prince Street, was the modest shelf of books that occupied a corner of the common room of Benjamin Franklin's father's house at the sign of the Blue Ball in Union Street some four hundred yards distant from Mather's. But the significance lay less in the contrast than in the fact that the hard-working tallow chandler, toiling from the rising to the setting of the sun at his soap and candle making, had any library at all. As recalled by Benjamin Franklin, it was small enough, but not the narrowest; and it was of sufficient importance to him

[10] Suffolk Probate, VI, 75.
[11] *Records of Boston Selectmen, 1701–1715,* 26. Cited in Sibley, *Biographical Sketches,* IV, 504.
[12] Mather, *Diary,* I, 548.

that he remembered it in detail over fifty years later. "My father's little Library consisted chiefly of Books in polemic Divinity . . . Plutarch's Lives there was, in which I read abundantly, and I still think that time spent to great Advantage. There was also a Book of Defoe's, called an Essay on Projects, and another of Dr. Mather's, called Essays to do Good which perhaps gave me a Turn of Thinking that had an Influence on some of the principal future events of my *Life*."[13]

His congenital appetite for books committed Franklin to reading "most" of his father's works in polemic theology, consisting on the whole of the pedantic, hair-splitting dissertations that characterized the most disputatious religious species that had ever emerged from the minds of men. Thousands of tracts were published by Puritan divines, arguing fine points of doctrine or practice with each other or joining rhetorical battle, in far more devastating language, with the willfully imperceptive apologists of the Church of England and those diabolically inspired deviationists, the Quakers and Baptists. By far, the major volume of such literature was imported from England, a steady flood of it flowing through prospering Boston booksellers all through the colony's first hundred years and reaching a huge crest during the last two decades of the seventeenth and the first two of the eighteenth centuries. The outpourings of the American Puritans were very apt to be exegetical, expounding the Bible, the doctrines adopted by the synods, and the discipline implicit in the suppositions of Congregationalism. Consequently, most New England theological works were pulpit literature, simply published sermons and lectures; but because these were a minimum of an hour and often two hours or more in the length of delivery, they amounted to substantial publications. They were also, in many cases, works of considerable literary merit—a form of literature *sui generis*, with an architectural structure, rhetorical values, and syllogistic order. Many a Puritan layman who could not afford to buy published sermons, like Uncle Benjamin, devised systems of shorthand to record them as delivered. In any case, they were read and discussed as literature, and it was no part of Puritan reasoning to attribute to them any qualities of mysticism or infallibility. The Puritan clergyman was, with regard to his flock, merely the first among equals. And his sermons constituted the last word on nothing; if they were any good, in fact, they were no more than points of departure for further discussion. Even as gargantuan an ego as Cotton Mather, who saw no contradiction in extolling what he took to be his own humility, regarded his sermons as contributions to a perpetual, infinite dialogue and not as *ex cathedra* pronouncements, and he eagerly read all the sermons of others on which he could get his hands.

The Franklins' own pastor, Samuel Willard, made no inconsiderable contribution to the pulpit literature of New England, with only the

13 *Autobiography*, 58.

Mathers exceeding him in published output. Sermons preached by him during his thirty-four years at the South Church were published in no fewer than forty volumes, the last running to over a thousand pages. The inventory of the slender estate of Josiah Franklin revealed that he had on his bookshelf, in addition to his "Books in polemic Divinity," some of Dr. Willard's sermons. Bearing, in some cases, such forbidding titles as *The Mourners Cordial Against Excessive Sorrow* and such inviting ones as *Love's Pedigree*, the sermons showed a very considerable degree of literary skill: ". . . though it [saintliness] be now grown a Nickname of contempt among wicked and prophane Men, yet count it the most orient Jewel in their Crown, the most odoriferous and pleasant Flower in their Garland, that we can say of them that they lived and died Saints; all other Escutcheons will either wear away, or be taken down, every other monument will become old and grow over with the Moss of time, and their Titles, though cut in Brass, will be Canker-eaten and illegible: This onely will endure and be fresh and Flourishing, when Marble it self shall be turned into common dust."[14]

It is likely that Willard's sermons, many of them expounding the good life, made more of an impression on the young Franklin than the polemic theology into which he dipped. Religious controversy always struck him as wasteful and quite pointless. ". . . I imagine a Man must have a good deal of Vanity who believes, and a good deal of Boldness who affirms, that all the Doctrines he holds are true; and all he rejects are false," he was to write his parents years later.[15] From his childhood, there was a certain purity, a clarity, about Franklin's religious belief ("Serving God is doing Good to Man"[16]); and it lasted through his long life, the end of which, when it became imminent, he approached "chearfully, with filial Confidence."[17] But with his father's polemic divinity works, the boy who years earlier had suggested the logic of wholesale grace was impatient. He said plaintively that he had "since often regretted that at a time when I had such a Thirst for Knowledge, more proper Books had not fallen in my Way since it was now resolv'd I should not be a Clergyman."[18]

* * *

A "more proper" book that did fall in Franklin's way was John Bunyan's awesome narrative *The Pilgrim's Progress*. It was the first book, among those that he read in his childhood, to which he referred by specific title in his *Autobiography*, recalling that he was so "pleas'd" with it that, since "all the little Money that came into my Hands was ever laid

---

[14] Samuel Willard, *The High Esteem Which God hath of the Death of His Saints*, (Boston, 1683), 16. In *The Puritan Pronaos*, Samuel Eliot Morison discusses the literary quality of colonial sermons, especially Willard's (Chap. 7, passim).

[15] To Josiah and Abiah Franklin, April 13, 1738, in *Papers*, II, 203.

[16] *Poor Richard*, 1753, in *Papers*, VI, 406.

[17] Smyth, *Writings of Benjamin Franklin*, IX, 491.

[18] *Autobiography*, 58.

out in Books," the very first collection he bought "was of John Bunyan's Works, in separate little volumes."[19] The clear, idiomatic language of the dramatic story of Christian's hazardous odyssey to Celestial City stood out in memorable contrast to all the petulant polemics through which the book-hungry boy Franklin had plowed his way, impressing him so deeply that more than fifty years later he referred to it as "my old favourite Author Bunyan's Pilgrim Progress."[20] The edition to which Franklin had access, as part of his father's small collection, was very likely that printed in 1681, three years after the book was published in London and two years before Josiah Franklin arrived in Boston, by Samuel Green, for Judge Sewall, who among his many activities was manager of the printing press in Boston, having been appointed by the General Court in October 1681 and serving until September 1684. It is quite possible that Sewall, who was fond of Josiah Franklin and whose diaries reveal him as frequently performing little acts of generosity, gave Josiah a copy of the book, by then already second only to the Bible in popularity among dissenters everywhere. Its circulation rapidly spread to other readers, regardless of their religious beliefs; and translations into most European languages made it, again second only to the Bible, the most ubiquitous publication in the Western world.

The imaginative and visionary creation of an exceptional literary talent, *The Pilgrim's Progress* was an innovative work of such dimensions as to constitute a landmark in the history of English literature towering in lasting significance far above its transient force as a powerful promulgation of the Puritan faith. Written in the grimness of a Restoration prison out of the deep conviction of the simple tinker turned preacher that John Bunyan was, the lean, chaste style breathed new life and spirit into English prose. The golden age of the Elizabethans gone and that of the Augustans not yet begun, English literature had become heavy, weary, and at times bogged down, as though by the sheer burden, like that which Bunyan's Christian carried on his tenacious pilgrimage, of the conflicts and strife of an England that moved within the space of less than a generation from the disruptive war of Cromwell to the excesses of the Restoration. Bunyan restored the language to the possession of the English people to a degree to which it had not been theirs since the days of Elizabeth. The rhymed preface of the book had the idiomatic freshness, the quality of unaffected literary primitiveness, that some of the less strained verses of

[19] Ibid.

[20] Franklin was recalling in 1771 an episode on his journey from Boston to Philadelphia in 1723. During a squall in the channel of Arthur Kill off New Jersey, a drunken Dutchman fell overboard, and Franklin reached into the water and hauled him back aboard. Sobered by the cold water, the Dutchman took a copy of Bunyan's book out of his pocket and asked Franklin to dry it for him while he slept off what remained of his stupor. Always the printer, Franklin recalled that the Dutch edition was "finely printed on good Paper with copper Cuts, a Dress better than I had ever seen it wear in its own Language."—*Autobiography*, 72.

Benjamin Franklin's Grandfather Peter Folger and his Uncle Benjamin occasionally reached:

> This book it chalketh out before thine eyes
> The man that seeks the everlasting prize;
> It shows you whence he comes, whither he goes;
> What he leaves undone, also what he does;
> It also shows you he runs and runs
> Till he unto the gate of glory comes.[21]

But if Bunyan was simple in his language, he was knowing in his style. "Honest John," Benjamin Franklin wrote in recalling his youthful reading to his son, "was the first that I know of who mix'd Narration and Dialogue, a Method of Writing very engaging to the Reader, who in the most interesting Parts finds himself as it were brought into the Company and present at the Discourse."[22] The first prose writer in English to combine narrative and dialogue, Bunyan did not hit upon the innovation by accident. He was well aware of what he was doing and of the striking impact that his inventive style was likely to have upon an age whose prose was, whatever else its merits, dismally lacking in any qualities of vitality. A stout Puritan, he had it very much on his mind that he had devised a literary form that would entertain as well as inspire his readers, and as a conscientious believer he anticipated criticism from his more somber brethren —charges that he answered in his preface with good Puritan functionalism:

> May I not write in such a style as this?
> In such a method, too, and yet not miss
> My end—thy good? . . .
>   You see the ways the fisherman doth take
> To catch the fish; what engines doth he make!
> Also his snares, lines, angles, hooks, and nets:
> Yet fish there be that neither hook, nor line,
> Nor snare, not net, nor engine can make Thine:
> They must be groped for, and be tickled, too,
> Or they will not be catched, whate'er you do.[23]

But it was neither the novelty of the form nor its idiomatic language alone that gave *The Pilgrim's Progress* its high literary distinction. For all its simplicity—perhaps, in great measure, because of it—there is a haunting poetic quality about the telling of the noble tale of the pilgrim that touches in grace the King James Version, as when the wearied Christian pauses against his better judgment, during his steep ascent of the Hill Difficulty, to sleep in the daytime: "Oh wretched man that I am, that I should sleep in the daytime; that I should sleep in the midst of difficulty!

[21] John Bunyan, *The Pilgrim's Progress*, Puritan edition (London, 1903), 15.
[22] *Autobiography*, 72.
[23] Bunyan, *Pilgrim's Progress*, 11.

that I should so indulge the flesh, as to use that rest for ease to my flesh which the Lord of the Hill hath erected only for the relief of the spirits of pilgrims! How many steps have I taken in vain! Thus it happened to Israel; for their sins they were sent back again by the way of the Red Sea; and I am made to tread those steps with sorrow which I might have trod with delight, had it not been for this sinful sleep. How far might I have been on my way by this time! I am made to tread those steps thrice over which I needed not to have trod but once; yea, also, now I am like to be beknighted, for the day is almost spent. Oh, that I had not slept."[24] The story is, moreover, remarkably concise. Few words are wasted as Christian encounters one menacing obstacle after another and a succession of diversive characters who would impede his way. Bunyan lingers over none of them. Their natures are revealed, their purposes disclosed, their fate sealed —and Bunyan has Christian once more on his way to the Celestial City.

The appeal of this odyssey to a young boy of Franklin's intuitive gift for words is clear. Equally so is the effect on him of the dramatic content of the book: the basic adventurousness of the plot, the vivid scenes, and the very real characters, epitomes of human weaknesses and failures, masteries and triumphs, that would not have escaped observation in real life even by the young, particularly by one of Franklin's prodigious aptitude. Like the fisherman that he cited with his hooks, his lines, and his nets, Bunyan used the mystery of the unknown, the suspense of the uncertain, and the conflict of the irreconcilable to lure his readers from page to page, beginning with Chapter I, page 1, and paragraph one: "As I walked through the wilderness of this world, I lighted on a certain place where was a den, and laid me down in that place to sleep; and, as I slept, I dreamed a dream. I dreamed, and behold, I saw a man clothed with rags, standing in a certain place, with his face from his own house, a book in his hand, and a great burden upon his back. I looked and saw him open the book, and read therein; and as he read, he wept and trembled; and, not being able longer to contain, he brake out with a lamentable cry, saying, 'What shall I do?' "[25] There followed, in skillfully paced succession, suspense ("for just before us lie a couple of lions in the way, whether sleeping or waking we know not; and we could not think, if we came within reach, but they would presently pull us in pieces"); mystery ("for he had gone but a little way before he espied a foul fiend coming over the field to meet him. . . . Then did Christian begin to be afraid, and to cast his mind whether to go back or to stand his ground"); and conflict (". . . first they scourged him, then they buffeted him, then they lanced his flesh with knives; after that they stoned him with stones, then pricked him with their swords, and last of all they burned him to ashes at the stake. Thus came Faithful to his end").[26]

[24] Ibid., 52.
[25] Ibid., 17.
[26] Ibid., 51, 64, 105.

The strong command that Bunyan had over the power of words—particularly when they were combined in proper names of wondrous places—added dramatically to the vividness of Christian's odyssey: the Valley of Humiliation, the Wall of Salvation, the Delectable Mountains, Vanity Fair, the Town of Fair Speech, the County of Conceit, and the River of Death. Through this engrossing countryside went a memorable procession of characters, some aiding Christian on his arduous pilgrimage and some obstructing him, none of them complex and all of them dominated by a single human quality somewhere apparent in every community of Christendom. In the first chapter alone, there are Evangelist, whose conviction is tempered with compassion; Obstinate, who attempted to discourage Christian at the outset of his pilgrimage; Pliable, willing to go along but yielding to the first obstacle encountered; Help, who pulled the enmired Christian out of the Slough of Despond and set him once more on his way; Mr. Worldly Wiseman, who knew all the answers and directed an overly trusting Christian to a more easily reached and more comfortable village than the Celestial City; Mr. Legality, "a cheat"; and his son, Civility ("notwithstanding his simpering looks, he is but an hypocrite"). And so, throughout the book, scores of characters are introduced, make their points with sharpness and directness, have their effect for better or worse on Christian and his perilous journey, and finally, though usually disappearing from the narrative as fast as they entered it, lingering unforgettably in the mind of the reader, the very names—Watchful the Porter, Lord Hategood, Giant Despair of Doubting Castle and his wife, Diffidence, Mr. Great-heart—animating their characters and accentuating their characteristics.

Impressive to a young mind as were the strength of the story of *The Pilgrim's Progress*, its graphic scenes, and the credibility of its characters, there was implicit in the work a view of life, an attitude that was peculiarly congenial to the values beginning to take shape in the mind of the young Franklin—values that were clearly the product of the Puritan creed but in the convictions and perceptions of Franklin from his earliest years never dominated by it. Chief among these was the idea of progress, that a man could move forward, whether through the allegorical obstacles that beset the resolute path of Christian or the real hardships confronting a poor and obscure boy in Puritan Boston. A sense of progress was to become the central motif of Franklin's life, the force behind it, the object before it, the very substance of it. Nor was progress, either to the Bedford tinker turned storyteller and preacher or to the eager son of the Boston tallow chandler, a gift from heaven; it was to be wholly believed in, to be sought, and to be shaped and advanced by man, aided by faith and reason. And so the axiomatic quality of *The Pilgrim's Progress*, its deft incorporation of lines from the Scriptures, and its imbuing religion with life, in an age ceaselessly determined to imbue life with religion, combined to make it Franklin's favorite of all his early reading, and its essentially optimistic theme was to illumine his whole experience and influence his whole achievement.

Bunyan's life, as a magnetic preacher as well as the most widely read author in the language, ended when he was sixty in 1688, ten years after *The Pilgrim's Progress* was first published; the first edition of his collected works was published four years later. But his fame was so far-flung and the appetite for his writings so vast that many editions appeared in rapid succession, and the bibliographical evidence suggests that Franklin bought an inclusive collection "in separate little volumes." Of these, inspirational to the devout as many of them were, only three approached, and none equaled, *The Pilgrim's Progress* in literary distinction. One was Bunyan's immensely moving autobiography, written during the first of his two imprisonments, *Grace Abounding to the Chief of Sinners, or a Brief and Faithful Relation of the Exceeding Mercy of God in Christ to His Poor Servant John Bunyan.* The narration of a profoundly personal spiritual experience in terms relating to the turmoil of daily life rather than solely to doctrinal principles was a vigorous, original, and powerful composition in itself; but it was also, in both substance and style, the prototype of his later masterpiece, the publication of which it anticipated by six years. Its qualities of spontaneity, directness, and immediacy would inevitably have had a strong impact upon a young reader who, like Franklin, had been brought up in a home where religion was the center of life and yet was somehow oddly depersonalized. The other two major works in Benjamin Franklin's collection were *The Life and Death of Mr. Badman* (1680), which was the allegory of Christian told in reverse as it recounted the utterly disastrous path of its well-named protagonist to total perdition. But the realistic eye of Bunyan, his earthiness, his grasp of the brawling everyday life surrounding his own spiritual longings and agony, and his mastery of the narrative form made *Mr. Badman* enormously gripping reading, powerful, robust, and above all convincing. Similarly, the fourth of Bunyan's major works, the allegory *The Holy War or The Losing and Taking of the Town of Mansoul* (1682) had such a vigor and so pervading an atmosphere of the conflict between good and evil that, heavier and more laborious as it was than its predecessors, it still had a strength and vitality of very strong appeal, in the context of the body of Puritan literature, to the new generation of dissenters. The remainder of Bunyan's collected works which Franklin acquired were less impressive, many of them homilies probably more effective in the hearing than in the reading. In any case, the young Franklin apparently found little in them over which he wanted to linger or to which he wanted to return, for he sold the lot in order, with the funds realized, "to enable me to buy R. Burton's Historical Collections; they were small Chapman's Books and cheap, 40 or 50 in all."[27]

[27] *Autobiography*, 57–58.

"R. Burton" was really one Nathaniel Crouch, a skillful literary artisan, who having been apprenticed to a London printer, Livewell Chapman, from 1656 to 1663, was inspired with the idea of compiling a series of little books, to sell at a shilling each, that would parcel out in agreeably brief form great events, personalities, and oddities, largely of British history. Crouch was a competent, deft craftsman who understood the popular taste of his time, and met the demands of that taste without pandering to it. He wrote crisply, instructively, and with eclectic flair, making no claim to originality of substance and relying solely and frankly on other publications for the material he used. His style and his purpose were essentially journalistic, and at twelve pennies each his books found an avid audience both in Britain and in the colonies. Dr. Johnson, not given to effusive or casual praise, was impressed by the usefulness of Crouch's little books to those whose formal instruction or reading in history was limited. In 1784, an old man in the last year of a strangely imperishable life, he ordered a set for himself in a letter to his bookseller with an ironical non sequitur on "backward readers," among whom he surely did not count himself: "There is in the world a set of books which used to be sold by the book-sellers on the bridge, and which I must entreat you to procure me. They are called *Burton's Books*; the Title of one is *Admirable Curiosities, Rarities, and Wonders in England*. I believe that there are five or six of them; they seem very proper to allure backward readers; be so kind as to get them for me. . . ."[28]

Both the number and range of the volumes far exceeded Dr. Johnson's expectations. There were forty-five volumes in all, and the scope of their contents is suggested by titles an admiring rival publisher of Crouch's, John Dunton, called "a little swelling." Among them, and characteristic of them, were *Wonderful Prodigies of Judgment and Mercy, discovered in Three Hundred Historians* (1681); *Female Excellency, or the Ladies' Glory; worthy Lives and memorable Actions of nine famous Women* (1688); *The General History of Earthquakes* (1694); and *Unfortunate Court Favourites of England* (1695). The facts incorporated in these shrewdly marketed compilations and distillations were, in accord with the standards of the time, generally accurate. Their pace was spirited, and their tone lively. Undoubtedly, they vastly broadened young Franklin's knowledge, enlarging the store of information that he was early in life to draw on in journalistic pursuits not incomparable to those of Crouch. But they apparently had neither a profound impact on his thinking nor a strong influence. He seemed merely to have eagerly devoured them and moved on to a much more significant phase of his boyhood reading.

* * *

What Burton's little books did achieve for young Franklin was to open his eyes to an English-speaking world that went far beyond the wharves

---

[28] Dr. Johnson to Mr. Dilly, Bookseller, in the Poultry, January 6, 1784, in James Boswell, *The Life of Dr. Johnson*, ed. Edmund Malone, Modern Library edition, 1080.

jutting out into Boston Harbor and far beyond the canons of Puritanism. The work that by his own testimony appealed most to him after Bunyan's, Plutarch's *Parallel Lives of the Noble Greeks and Romans*, did more: It introduced the boy to a human experience that went far back before the history of England began. This, the celebrated progenitor of all biographies in all languages, is a massive work—forty-six lives in all—of a grand and majestic design and as noble in motive as it is in title. The learned world of Puritanism was deeply engrossed with the classical world, wholly at home with its languages, distilling meaning and principles from its copious lore and modeling much of its own expressionism on the patterns of the ancients. The classics, in addition to occupying a large place in the curricula of the Boston Grammar School and Harvard College, also occupied a large place on the private bookshelves of the clerical and lay gentry. But it was an alliance which, while old and familiar, was not immune from moments of acute discomfort. Thus, Cotton Mather, as well instructed a classicist as his times had to offer and who peppered his prose as liberally with classical references as most of his contemporaries did with commas, could complain, in discussing the duties of schoolmasters, "of little boys learning the filthy actions of the pagan gods,"[29] in the same piece of writing in which he offered four quotations in classical Latin in as many paragraphs. To such a paradoxical attitude, Plutarch brought great comfort, as the Puritan mind sought to reconcile the classical manner, all of which it admired, with classical matter, much of which it deplored. For Plutarch set out to do what Cotton Mather would have made the major criterion of the merit of all human activity: conveying moral instruction and example. The first paragraph of Plutarch's life of Timoleon the Corinthian certainly had the enthusiastic approval of Mather, who included Plutarch's *Parallel Lives* among the Harvard College Library duplicates that he bought in 1682:

"It was for the sake of others," Plutarch wrote at the beginning of *Timoleon*, "that I first commenced writing biographies; but I find myself proceeding and attaching myself to it for my own; the virtues of these great men serving me as a sort of looking-glass, in which I may see how to adjust and adorn my own life. Indeed, it can be compared to nothing but daily living and associating together; we receive, as it were, in our inquiry, and entertain each successive guest, view 'their stature and their qualities,' and select from their actions all that is noblest and worthiest to know. 'Ah, and what greater pleasure can one have?' or what more effective means to one's moral improvement? Democritus tells us we ought to pray that of the phantoms appearing in the circumambient air, such may present themselves to us as are propitious, and that we may rather meet with those that are agreeable to our natures and are good than the evil and un-

---

[29] Cotton Mather, *Bonifacius. An Essay upon the Good*, John Harvard Library edition (Cambridge, 1966), 85.

fortunate; which is simply introducing into philosophy a doctrine untrue in itself, and leading to endless superstitions. My method, on the contrary, is, by the study of history, and by the familiarity acquired in writing, to habituate my memory to receive and retain images of the best and worthiest characters. I thus am enabled to free myself from any ignoble, base, or vicious impressions, contracted from the contagion of ill company that I may be unavoidably engaged in; by the remedy of turning my thoughts in a happy and calm temper to view these noble examples."[30]

In reporting his boyhood acquaintance with Plutarch's *Lives*, Benjamin Franklin said he read in them "abundantly, and I still [i.e., at the age of sixty-five, when he wrote the *Autobiography* in 1771] think that time spent to great Advantage."[31] The highly sophisticated craftsmanship of Plutarch made the *Lives* exciting and lively reading, engrossing to all ages and of particular fascination to the young. Running through the *Lives* is Plutarch's repeated demonstration that the boy is father to the man—a judgment not likely to have been lost on the young Franklin. There was the child Alcibiades, playing at dice with other boys in an Athens street, as "a loaded cart came that way, when it was his turn to throw; at first he called to the driver to stop, because he was to throw in the way over which the cart was to pass; but the man giving him no attention and driving on, when the rest of the boys divided and gave way, Alcibiades threw himself on his face before the cart and, stretching himself out, bade the carter pass on now if he would; which so startled the man, that he put back his horses, while all that saw it were terrified, and, crying out, ran to assist Alcibiades."[32] To a boy, all of whose play had taken place in the narrow, cart-laden streets of Boston, Alcibiades was thenceforth no remote figure from a distant age in a distant land but a new companion in whose destiny one had a deep and immediate interest. Adventure, too, permeated the *Lives*, as in Pompey's routing of the pirates from their domination of Mediterranean commerce with his mighty fleet of five hundred ships. This, too, had immediacy and reality to a boy who grew up in a town where pirate-hangings were a common occurrence and piracy a constant problem, and Pompey could as well have lived in colonial Boston as in ancient Rome.

In essence, Plutarch personalized history by narrating it through the lives of great men—much as two of the most prominent heirs of the Puritans, Carlyle in England and Emerson in America, insisted biography was the true nature of history. In doing so, aside from infusing it with human interest rather than imposing upon it institutional generalities, Plutarch also, and inevitably, evoked such elements in the Puritan consciousness as practicality, a drive toward productive lives, and a respect for science.

[30] Plutarch, *Parallel Lives of the Noble Greeks and Romans*, trans. John Dryden, Modern Library edition, 293–94.
[31] *Autobiography*, 58.
[32] Plutarch, *Lives*, 234.

Again, these were presented not as abstract desiderata but as wholly attainable and concrete objectives, proved by the actions of actual figures from the past. There is something clearly Franklinian in the practicality of the episode of the young Alexander's undertaking, with youthful assurance, the training of the spirited horse Bucephalus, after his father's most skilled horsemen had failed—and then succeeding, turning his elders' scornful laughter to applause, by having observed that the horse was disturbed and frightened by his own moving shadow, turning him to face into the sun and then mounting and mastering him with absolute command. And the productiveness of the lives of such men as Demosthenes and Cicero as eminent orators, who despite strong odds and "from small and obscure beginnings, became so great and powerful,"[33] would have sound meaning to a Boston whose major forum was the orator's platform or the preacher's pulpit. Similarly, that constant quest for scientific knowledge that so occupied Cotton Mather and for scientific experiment that was to intrigue Benjamin Franklin was personified by such of Plutarch's noble ancients as Numa Pompilius' attempts "not without some scientific knowledge" at reforming the calendar with remarkable prescience, as no one could have appreciated more than the English and their colonies, who were still in Franklin's boyhood functioning under the burden of a calendar, abandoned as obsolete by the rest of the world, that began the year in March.

Great, however, as Plutarch's *Lives* was a fascinating reading, Franklin's recollection of his reading in it as "time spent to great Advantage" clearly indicates that sheer enjoyment was not enough for him. Even in his boyhood he was always highly purposeful in his reading; and although he derived great pleasure from a felicitous style as well as from absorbing subject matter, he was always eager that his reading be turned to good account so far as his own development went. Through his reading, he undertook quite seriously to instruct himself, to make his perceptions more acute, and to develop whatever latent abilities he might have had. He wanted his reading to count for something other than mere entertainment. In this driving quest, it is little wonder that he attached so much importance to Plutarch, which he very probably read in the superb, straightforward translation supervised by John Dryden, who wrote a prefatory life of Plutarch for it in 1683. For "goodness" and "the good," in the best and most admirable sense of the Greek *agathos* and *aretē*, spring from every page of Plutarch not as abstractions but in the triumphs of living men of honorable motives over the conflicts of contentious forces or individuals in massive efforts and combinations of efforts to defeat them. The morality inherent in living useful lives and, by contrast, the inherent evil of living uselessly emerge not in jeremiads, too many of which the Franklin children probably endured in the South Church, but in arresting examples taken from the experience of great men whose lives, though

[33] Ibid., 1023.

good, were full of drama, ingenuity, and achievement. And so the ten-year-old boy, toiling amid the fetid boredom of the tallow vats, was witness to the monumental accomplishments of Pericles during the golden age of Athens. The significance of Pericles' life was made specific enough: ". . . in the exercise of his mental perception, every man, if he chooses, has a natural power to turn himself upon all occasions, and to change and shift with the greatest ease to what he himself shall judge desirable."[34] But the point does not stand by itself, to be accepted or turned down as doctrine —an exercise totally repellent to young boys; the point is demonstrated, the significance clinched, by the valorous life of a man exemplary in his ideals, his abilities, and his wisdom and by the grace with which he lived it. Some of those qualities in Pericles' character and disposition that Plutarch most effectively summarized were incipient in the character and disposition of the boy Franklin—different in so many feats and emphases as his life was to be from that of the Athenian. "When he was now near his end," Plutarch wrote of Pericles, "the best of the citizens and those of his friends who were left alive, sitting about him, were speaking of the greatness of his merit, and his power, and reckoning up his famous actions and the number of his victories; for there were no less than nine trophies, which, as their chief commander and conqueror of their enemies, he had set up for the honour of the city. They talked thus together among themselves, as though he were unable to understand or mind what they said, but had now lost his consciousness. He had listened, however, all the while, and attended to all, and speaking out among them, said that he wondered they should commend and take notice of things which were as much owing to fortune as to anything else, and had happened to many other commanders, and, at the same time, should not speak or make mention of that which was the most excellent and greatest thing of all. 'For,' said he, 'no Athenian, through my means, ever wore mourning.'" And Plutarch went on with words which, read by the young Franklin in 1716, could well have been applied to the venerable Franklin at the close of a life, three quarters of a century later, no less illustrious in many respects than that of Pericles: "He was indeed a character deserving our high admiration not only for his equitable and mild temper, which all along in the many affairs of his life, and the great animosities which he incurred, he constantly maintained; but also for the high spirit and feeling which made him regard it the noblest of all his honours that, in the exercise of such immense power, he had never gratified his envy or his passion, nor ever had treated any enemy as irreconcilably opposed to him."[35]

* * *

The idea and the ideal of progress, dramatized so memorably in the avid young mind of Franklin by Bunyan and endowed with boundless dimension by Plutarch, were to be advanced in his scheme of things im-

[34] Ibid., 182.
[35] Ibid., 211–12.

measurably and lastingly by an extraordinarily bold and propulsive book by the ablest journalist in post-Restoration England, the first of the great reform journalists in the language, Daniel Defoe. The book bore the dull title *An Essay upon Projects*, not helped much by an enigmatic subtitle, "Effectual Ways for Advancing the Interests of the Nation"; but it was an enormously strong book. Defoe was a realist, knowledgeable and perceptive about the society and the times in which he lived. As such of his novels as *Moll Flanders* and of his historical reports as *The Plague* testify, he had a sharp insight both into human character and into the social conditions that molded it. He had also the clarity and the soundness of judgment that could differentiate without quibbling between the significant and the trivial, the sensible and the fallacious, and the intrinsically right and the intrinsically wrong.

Like Franklin's mother's family, of Flemish stock (the name was variously spelled De Faux, De Vaux, and De Foe), and like his father's, of long residence in Northamptonshire (in Peterborough, the see of the diocese), the Defoes were independent-minded yeomen, who dissented less under the compulsion of strong religious fervor than in stolid resentment of being told what they could or could not do. Though educated at the seminary in Newington for the nonconformist ministry, Defoe really felt no call and, as an outlet for his talents, turned first to the mercantile world, in which he suffered a succession of misfortunes in maritime insurance, and later to pamphleteering and politics, combining the two to the distress of the Establishment.

Essentially a humanist in his values and outlook, Defoe had as little patience with the sectarian disputes among dissenters as he did with those between the dissenters and the Church of England and addressed some of his most brilliantly scathing articles to their bickerings. He really saw, as did Franklin, the kingdom of God on earth best advanced by equitable and decent behavior among men. And since he was a product of the city, his perceptions and his concerns were largely urban, as Franklin's also were. From his earliest boyhood, Franklin knew the busy port town of Boston with as much instinctive insight as Defoe, his father's contemporary, knew London; and he sensed, with Defoe, where the sore spots were. No more than five years after reading Defoe's *An Essay upon Projects*, he was to apply to Boston many of the cures Defoe prescribed for social and economic ills in London.

An Essay upon Projects, the seventh of the 254 books and tracts that Defoe published in his lifetime, was first published in May 1698, almost twenty years before it fell into Franklin's hands. But it was so far ahead of its time, so prophetic in its vision, and so sound in the "projects" it urged that for many decades—in fact, long after Franklin as a mature man was launching some of Defoe's projects in Philadelphia—it went through repeated editions and remained a vade mecum to those on both sides of the Atlantic who were by temperament or conviction committed to the advancement of man's social well-being either for its own sake or as a responsible way of glorifying his God. The appeal of Defoe to the young Franklin seems self-evident. There was no affectation in Defoe, no posing, no patience with glitter or ancestor-worship ("For fame of families is all a cheat,/'Tis personal virtue only makes us great"[36]). But there was a freshness of view, an inventiveness, and a daring forthrightness in him that surfaced on every page of his writing and made him irresistible to the young and venturesome who were not content with their world as it was. His appeal to reason, which he once called "First Monarch of the World,"[37] was unconditional and basic to all his thought and all his writings. He put it forthrightly and explicitly at the outset of the *Essay*, offering no theoretic defense of reason that may have turned away a young reader but getting to the heart of the matter: "Man is the worst of all God's creatures to shift for himself: no other animal is ever starved to death; nature without has provided them with both food and clothes, and nature within has placed an instinct that never fails to direct them to proper means for a supply; but man must either work or starve, slave or die; he has indeed reason given him to direct him, and few who follow the dictates of that reason come to such unhappy exigencies; but when by the errors of a man's youth he has reduced himself to such a degree of distress as to be absolutely without three things, money, friends, and health, he dies in a ditch or in some worse place—an hospital."[38]

The final barb was characteristic. Defoe sought neither to conceal nor to dwell upon his contempt for inadequacies among men or their institutions; he dealt with them in a word or a phrase, and then went on to what could be done to improve them. He despised brokers, who profit upon the risks taken by others: "those exchange mountebanks we very properly call brokers" and "those vermin of trade."[39] Clergymen who preached moral improvement while they walked a social treadmill fared no better: "I am not about to argue anything of their [i.e., curses' and oaths', to which Defoe objected because of their meaningless stupidity and debasement of the language] being sinful and unlawful, as forbid by divine rules; let the parson alone to tell you that, who has, no question, said as much to as little purpose in this case as in any other."[40] But if Defoe could deal curtly and harshly with some whom he counted obstacles to progress, he could deal at length and eloquently with those whom he saw as the victims of injustice. The oppressed treatment of the merchant seamen, who were the

---

[36] Daniel Defoe, *The True-Born Englishman*, Reynell, Clements edition (London, 1842), 16.

[37] In the dedication of the devastating satire on the divine right of Kings, *Jure Divino*.

[38] Daniel Defoe, *An Essay upon Projects*, Reynell, Clements edition (London, 1841), 10.

[39] Ibid., 7, 28.

[40] Ibid., 36.

principal drudges in England's prosperous trade, was a harsh reality to the
reportorial eye of Defoe: "Sailors are *les enfans perdue*, the forlorn hope
of the world; they are fellows that bid defiance to terror, and maintain a
constant war with the elements; who, by the magic of their art, trade in
the very confines of death and are always posted within shot, as I may say,
of the grave." Defoe, however, was far too much a social realist to leave
the impression that a hazardous occupation bred a special class of upright
and dedicated men. "'Tis true," he added, "their familiarity with danger
makes them despise it, for which, I hope, nobody will say they are the
wiser; and custom has so hardened them, that we find them the worst of
men, though always in view of their last moment."[41]

The Franklin family, like virtually every family in every New England
port town, knew enough of that rough subculture of the sea to recognize
the truth in the unminced words of Defoe. The family Bibles of few families were without the sad entry, "Lost at sea," as the Franklin family's was
with the junior Josiah's disappearance in 1715. And yet it was not the
physical danger alone that led a duteous father like Josiah Franklin to
frown upon a seaman's life for his sons. He knew, with Defoe, that with the
necessary peril of death in the seaman's work went an inevitable contempt of life. To young Benjamin, who was wise beyond his years in the
ways of the waterfront, the reality of the seaman's plight and of their
nature as men, as Defoe summarized them, would have been entirely convincing. But the grip that Defoe's *Essays* had on him, in respect of the seamen as well as in other areas of town life of the time, was the imaginative,
plausible means Defoe suggested of improving the situation. Franklin was
never interested in analysis for its own sake, and neither was Defoe. The
point was to see the problem clearly, realistically, and without any bias
save toward the good, and then to find a means that was workable to
achieve that good. In the case of the seamen, Defoe saw the unjust economics that was their lot as the key to their oppressed state and to the
hard-bitten quality of their characters as men. He pointed out that, if a
sailor was disabled through service in the Royal Navy, he was pensioned
for life in proportion to the degree of disablement; merchant seamen were
not, leading to an inordinate loss of merchant ships to pirates because the
seamen could see no advantage to them in resisting. With an effective and
strategic use of dialogue that greatly impressed Franklin, Defoe let the
case be put in the words of a crewman to the captain of a merchantman
accosted by pirates: "Noble captain, we are all willing to fight, and don't
question but to beat him off; but here is the case—if we are taken we shall
be set on shore, and then sent home, and lose, perhaps, our clothes, and a
little pay; but if we Fight and beat the privateer, perhaps half a score of us
may be wounded and lose our limbs, and then we are undone and our
families. . . ."[42] Defoe then proposed a scheme of workmen's compen-

---

[41] Ibid., 22.
[42] Ibid.

sation, to which merchant seamen would each contribute a shilling per quarter, that would assure them an outright sum or a pension for life if they were maimed or, if killed, a payment to their widows. This would be achieved by a mutual or "friendly" society and set forth a pattern that Franklin was to apply very early and often in attacking a multiplicity of socioeconomic problems throughout his life.

An Essay upon Projects probed with comparable directness a score of other problems, in each instance projecting a device or method to bring about a solution or at least a significant alleviation of the problem. And although the teeming London of William and Mary and Anne and of the beginning of the House of Hanover—the battleground of Defoe's half-century-long war against injustice, inequity, and sheer social callousness—was three thousand miles and six weeks' time away from Boston, the colonial outpost had a stake in the quality of life in London as the ultimate seat of its government and the ultimate architect of its destiny. Moreover, the local social problems of the port town on the Charles were approaching more and more closely, in nature if not in degree, those of its massive counterpart on the Thames. The problems and projects that commanded Defoe's attention, all of them treated crisply, incisively, and uncompromisingly, included stock swindles; the regulation of banking; tax reform; the establishment of highway commissions; insurance against losses, fire, and faulty real estate titles; co-operatives to aid widows; pensions to provide security for the aged; organized medical aid for the afflicted; reforms against bankruptcy procedures that left debtors to die in prison; an academy "to polish and refine the English tongue . . . the noblest and most comprehensive of all the vulgar languages of the world"; a royal academy to provide properly educated personnel for the military; quasi-judicial commissions to deal with problems requiring expertise beyond the competence of ordinary courts; a central source of man power to recruit seamen without resort to bribery in the case of merchantmen and the gross evils of impressment in the case of the navy; and, with an ironic humor recurring in Defoe's writing, that those who were born idiots be taken care of in houses maintained at public expense, the funds to be provided by authors on the grounds that they got, by chance, a greater amount of brains than normal just as the idiots, by chance, got less.

All of Defoe's projects sprang from the hard realities of life in a society that was becoming far more complicated and interdependent than it had ever been before—realities that were as quickly and as clearly recognizable to the people of Boston as to those of London. And Defoe's solutions were astonishing in their soundness and their prophetic powers—some of them anticipating with remarkable precision the economic reforms and social innovations of both the English and American experience of the twentieth century.

For the young Benjamin Franklin, all of them were fascinating ventures in progress. All of them, in one form or another, engaged his attention over and over again as his life advanced. None of them, however, made as immediate and deep an impression upon Franklin as yet another area that occupied Defoe's interest and occasioned some of his most perceptive and oracular writing: the position of women. In the most male-oriented age thus far in Britain's history, he began his assault upon the unjust treatment of women with characteristic forthrightness: "I have often thought of it as one of the most barbarous customs in the world, considering us as a civilized and christian country, that we deny the advantages of learning to our women. We reproach the sex every day with folly and impertinence, while I am confident, had they the advantages of education equal to us, they would be guilty of less than ourselves. One should wonder, indeed, how it should happen that women are conversible at all, since they are only beholden to natural parts for all their knowledge. Their youth is spent to teach them to stitch and sew, or make baubles: they are taught to read, indeed, and perhaps to write their names, or so, and that is the height of a woman's education: and I would but ask any who slight the sex for their understanding, what is a man (a gentleman I mean) good for, that is taught no more."

Probably the first to assert the natural superiority of women, Defoe added: "The capacities of women are supposed to be greater and their senses quicker than those of the men; and what they might be capable of being bred to is plain from some instances of female wit which this age is not without; which upbraids us with injustice, and looks as if we denied women the advantages of education for fear they should vie with the men in their improvements." Defoe's solution: the prompt establishment of academies to furnish young women with an education fully equal to that offered young males of the time, with limitations as to the scope and level of study fixed only by the capacities and interests of the students. After offering details for such an academy to correct what he regarded as an outrageous injustice in his own land, Defoe aimed a dart at the rest of the world: ". . . I take upon me to make such a bold assertion, that all the world are mistaken in their practice about women: for I cannot think that God Almighty ever made them so delicate, so glorious creatures, and furnished them with such charms, so agreeable and so delightful to mankind, with souls capable of the same accomplishments as men, and all only to be stewards of our houses, cooks and slaves."[43]

The impact that Defoe's essay on the education of women had upon the young Franklin is clear from the *Autobiography*. He records, as the first debate in which, while still an apprentice, he participated, a private dialogue with "another Bookish Lad in Town" on "the propriety of educating the Female Sex in Learning, and their Abilities for Study."[44] Franklin was for it, and his friend against it. And for the rest of his life, Franklin

[43] Ibid., 44.
[44] *Autobiography*, 60.

delighted in the company of women. His closest friend among the thirteen of sixteen siblings that he knew (three others had died before he was born) was his younger sister, Jane. Among the women in whose education he was to have a voice—for example, his daughter, Sally, and the daughter of his landlady in London, Polly Stevenson—he urged and made possible a versatile education that would make the most of their capacities. In short, he went to school to Defoe, and the lessons he learned were lasting.

* * *

Benjamin Franklin's early reading—that which in the *Autobiography* he recalls having read before he was twelve years old—culminated in a volume by no such distant authors in a London he had never seen as Bunyan, Burton, and Defoe or by an ancient figure from the past like Plutarch. It was written in a study less than half a mile from the Franklin house on Union Street by the Reverend Cotton Mather, whom Benjamin had undoubtedly seen personally many times in his rounds of delivering candles for his father and some of whose sermons or lectures he could not have escaped hearing in a town of little more than ten thousand, among whom Cotton Mather was easily the most vocal and permeating presence. The book—the 205th among Mather's 455 published works—was written when Mather was forty-eight years old and Franklin a child of four. But six or seven years later the chasm of the years was bridged between the famous cleric and the unknown child of the tallowshop by a common instinct "to do good"—i.e., to live lives of usefulness to their fellow man, in the case of the Puritan priest as a form of tribute to his Maker, and in the case of the eager boy, as the essential ingredient in his individual progress through a life intent even then on formulating a value system and a pattern of living that would give the fullest expression to his determination to "do good."

The book, Franklin wrote in the *Autobiography*, "perhaps gave me a Turn of Thinking that had an Influence on some of the principal future Events of my Life"[45]—a degree of acknowledgment that far exceeded his appreciative comment on the importance that Plutarch and Bunyan had been to him. The reason is clear: The little book distilled from the vast reservoir of Puritan doctrine and rhetoric and aspiration those elements of social behavior that had high value not in some distant, celestial future but that bore immediate fruit, produced immediate results, and advanced the progress of any man and his fellows toward a better world. The book was not easy going for a young boy. Even the title was formidable: *Bonifacius, an Essay upon the Good, that is to be Devised and Designed, by Those Who Desire to Answer the Great End of Life, and to Do Good while They Live.* The implication of the title, of course, is that Mather regarded the good done in this life as a way of preparing for the next—a proposition that, had its full meaning been clear to him, would not have

[45] Ibid., 58.

been arresting to a young boy who had shown no evidence of preoccupation with the hereafter. At the same time, neither was Cotton Mather so obsessed with the hereafter not to have a lively interest in temporal and terrestrial affairs, delving as he did in his life and works into virtually all of them.

Cotton Mather was capable also of a really generous dedication to the Boston community. Despite the long exercises in solitary devotions, the endless fasting, and the alternating extremes of private ecstasy and lonely despair, he was a community-minded man, anxious that Boston, with its lofty raison d'être, realize its great destiny of proving God's kingdom on earth. He took Boston seriously. It was not just another place in which to live but, if one wanted to glorify God and not merely save one's own soul by the good that one did, the best and perhaps the only place to live. Yet he had increasingly grave reservations as to what was happening to Boston. Thoroughly convinced of John Donne's no man's being an island unto himself, he urged *"brethren to dwell together in unity,* and carry on every good design with *united endeavors."*[46] Benjamin Franklin had a similarly deep and constant sense of community. Everything except reading he preferred to do in fellowship with others both as a boy and throughout his life. Always willing to assume leadership, as in his boyhood organizing of swimming classes and dam-building, he attached primary importance to the welfare and progress of the community. Moreover, Boston was still an outpost—a frontier still in many respects—and there was a necessary interdependence among its people.

Although arriving at it by different routes and certainly through opposite extremes of intellectual complexity, the emerging temperament of Benjamin Franklin and the fixed character of Cotton Mather were attuned to the practical. No religion has ever been less hostile to science than Puritanism, particularly in its New England manifestation, for the Puritans wholly believed in established principles of physical action in the universe—principles laid down by the mind of God and inherent in the orderly universe created by Him, as for example, in the revolution of the planets around the sun and the gravitational force of the earth. Far from contesting or even disputing such scientific facts, the Puritans held it a firm duty to explore, to study, to experiment with, and to understand them. It was neither accident nor perversity that made Mather an outstanding student of science in his time; nor was it coincidence that of the nine American colonials elected to the Royal Society from the first settlements to 1734, eight were Puritans. Scientific knowledge and study were to them a way of appreciating the greatness of God and His works—and consequently of glorifying Him. In the case of the young Franklin, with his far simpler concept of a Supreme Being, his fascination with the world of physical principles and the working of things found expression in an in-

[46] Mather, *Bonifacius,* 5.

ventiveness that was to lead to some of his most enduring achievements, his most satisfactory pleasures, and, above all, his most concrete contributions to the progress that he regarded as the theme of life.

Essays to Do Good, as *Bonifacius* came to be known,[47] represents Mather's great, swarming mind at its best, as it also represented his religion at its best. It is not always easy, in the tangled prolixity of Puritan literature, to find any clear reassertion of the Christian ethic. Through the pages of this small book, it radiates from and is reflected in the very style of the writing, as if the author had been as clearly relieved of his heavily brooding nature as Bunyan's Christian was of his burden. There is no dwelling on man's essential baseness, no groveling in humiliation, no haranguing of the devil. The mood is optimistic, the substance affirmative— even joyous. "It is an invaluable *honor*, to do *good*; it is an incomparable *pleasure*. A man must look upon himself as *dignified* and *gratified* by God, when an *opportunity* to do good is put into his hands. He must embrace it with *rapture*, as enabling him directly to answer the great End of his being. He must manage it with *rapturous delight*, as a most suitable business, as a most precious privilege."[48]

For the young reader, the tone of *Essays to Do Good* is gentle and often avuncular—a factor which may well have made it a particularly warm recollection by Franklin of his early reading. Instead of showering his readers with blame for their inadequacies and imperceptions, Mather showed a desire to understand and to give thoughtful guidance. "It is to be feared," he wrote with a total lack of the tantrum note that he had been known to sound, "that we too seldom *inquire* after our opportunities to do good. . . . We do not *use* our *opportunities*, many times because we do not *know* what they are; and many times, the reason why we do not *know*, is because we do not *think*."[49] In his spirit of geniality, Mather even indulged his congenital weakness for puns. A good place for a person to begin to do good, he suggested, was to devise ways to improve the lives of his own relatives. "One great way to prove ourselves *really good*," he added, "is to be *relatively good*."[50]

A fundamental appeal of Mather's manual to the child of a "leather apron" was that it was rooted in the Puritan assumption that social and economic status had nothing to do with prospects of salvation or even of temporal preferment within the church, as was amply demonstrated by the influential Judge Sewall's suggesting that he be succeeded in the high and conspicuous post of precentor (chant leader) at the South Church by the tradesman Josiah Franklin.[51] Even the loftiest figures among the Puri-

[47] For brief but perceptive comments on the corruption of the title of Bonifacius, see David Levin's generally informative introduction to the John Harvard Library edition.
[48] Mather, *Bonifacius*, 19.
[49] Ibid., 41.
[50] Ibid.
[51] Sewall, *Diary*, III, 171.

tan patriarchy were wholly committed, both in theory and in practice, to the basically democratic nature of Congregationalism, unwilling as they were—as John Cotton made so clear—to entertain the idea of democracy in the state. It may have been an implicit supposition of Puritanism that godliness was in league with riches and distinction, but it was never a part of its case that riches and distinction were necessarily in league with godliness, as some of the most renowned personages associated with the Church of England or the crown were reminded more than once. Mather asserted these principles in *Essays to Do Good* in such a direct way as to make an indelible impression on the mind of young Franklin and crop up over and over again in his own writings, especially in the earlier years of his maturity, although in less righteous language. "I take notice," Mather wrote, "that our Apostle [i.e., St. James], casting a just contempt on the *endless genealogies*, and long, intricate, perplexed pedigrees, which the *Jews* of his time, stood so much upon; proposes instead thereof to be studied, *charity, out of a pure heart*, and a *good conscience, and faith unfeigned*. As if he had said, I will give you a *genealogy* worth ten thousand of theirs, first, from *faith unfeigned* proceeds a good conscience: from a *good conscience* proceeds a *pure heart*: from a *pure heart* proceeds a *charity* to all about us."[52]

From Franklin's position at about the bottom of any scale—of age, for example, or of position as a helper (beneath even an apprentice) in a grimy trade, and of family influence—the prospect put by Mather had an inevitable appeal, sounding almost as though addressed directly to him, even touching upon his mechanical interests: "My friend, thou art one that makes but a *little figure* in the world, and a *brother of low degree*; behold, a vast encouragement! A *little* man may do a great deal of *hurt*. And then, why may not a *little* man, do a great deal of *good*! It is possible the *wisdom of a poor man* may start a proposal, that may *save a city*, serve a nation! A *single hair* applied unto a flyer [i.e., flywheel] that has other wheels depending on it, may pull up an *oak*, or pull down an *house*."[53]

To Franklin, the young inveterate reader who would read theological polemics, to which he had an aversion bordering on disdain, rather than read nothing at all, the Mather volume would have been most reassuring had he had any doubts of the value of reading. "There are not a few persons, who have many hours of leisure in the way of their *personal callings*. When the *weather* takes them off their business, or when their *shops* are not full of customers, they have *little* or *nothing* to do; now, Sirs, the proposal is, *Be not fools*, but *redeem* this *time* to your own advantage, to the best advantage. To the *man of leisure*, as well as to the *minister*, it is an advice of wisdom, *Give thyself unto reading*. Good Books of all sorts may

[52] Mather, *Bonifacius*, 31.
[53] Ibid., 25.

employ your *leisure*, and enrich you with treasures more valuable than those which the way and work of your callings would have purchased."[54]

The importance of books ran throughout Mather's text as it did throughout his life and that of his young reader in Union Street. Not only would he have had more men reading books, he would have more men collecting them and more men writing them. "It is no rare thing for men of quality to accomplish themselves in *languages* and *sciences*, until they have been prodigies of literature. Their *libraries*, too, have been stupendous collections; approaching towards *Vatican* or *Bodleian* dimensions. An *English gentleman* has been sometimes the most accomplished thing in the whole world. How many of them (besides a [Edward] Leigh, a [Charles] Wolsel[e]y, or a [Edward] Polhil[l]) have been benefactors to mankind by their incomparable writings? It were mightily to be wished that *rich men*, and persons of an elevated condition, would qualify themselves for the use of the pen, as well as the sword; and by their pen deserve to have it said of them, 'They have written excellent things.' "[55] Though neither rich nor of elevated condition, the young Franklin did, while still a child, both build a library and write excellent things.

In his suggestions of specific projects to do good, there is evidence that Mather had read with profit Defoe's *An Essay upon Projects*, which had been published thirteen years earlier. Voluntary associations (of young men, of families, of neighborhood groups) were proposed for the purpose of mutual improvement and social reform. But many of the proposals were heavily laden with Mather's homilies and references, often of strained relevance, to no fewer than 151 figures from classical and medieval times and to church fathers and preachers. For all of that, it got down to specifics and to reality, as Mather addressed himself to readers of specific callings or conditions. His fellow ministers he urged, among other things, to "uphold and cherish good *schools* in your towns"; to form societies for the suppression of disorders; to "Give thyself unto reading"; to educate themselves in medicine, so that in physician-less country congregations they could practice medicine as part of their ministries and in larger towns work with the physician and "*unite counsels* with him, for the good of his patients."[56] He entreated schoolmasters to teach writing by the copying of "the brightest maxims of wisdom," instead of meaningless lists of words; and "to turn such things into Latin"; and to punish gently and with instructive intent: ". . . let nothing be done in a *passion*; all be done with all the evidence of compassion that may be. . . . Fitter to have the conduct of *bears* than of ingenuous *boys* are the masters that can't give a *bit* of learning but they must give a knock with it."[57]

54 Ibid., 39–40.
55 Ibid., 118.
56 Ibid., 77–82.
57 Ibid., 87.

In his counsel to the magistrates, for whom he had little love because of their gradual wresting away of authority from the ministers and of their generally lesser degree of learning, Mather adopted a glacial tone. He doubted, in the first place, that there was any desire to do good in them: "'Oh! when will *wisdom* visit *princes and nobles*, and all the *judges of the earth*; and inspire them to preserve the due lustre of their character by a desire to do good in the earth. . . .*" He then addressed to them a stern lecture on the nature of their responsibilities and their common avoidance of their duties, culminating, by way of explanation as to how such deficient men could ever have attained the eminence of magistrates in the first place, with the gods' accounting for the elevation of the incompetent centurion Phocas to East Roman Emperor: "Non inveni pejorem [I couldn't find anyone worse]." The only practical advice that he could give the wretched lot was to consult and support their ministers. The real solution, Mather concluded, was for the people to keep an eye on them, his encyclopedic mind summoning the words of the ancient Greek Theognis, "When the administration of affairs, is placed in the hands of men, proud of command, and bent to their own private gain, be sure the people will soon be a miserable people."[58] Even to a young contemporary of Cotton Mather, the point was not lost, and very early in life Benjamin Franklin, as did his brothers, had a healthy but at times so belligerent a skepticism of the magistrates that they were in danger of the judgment.

Physicians were, to Cotton Mather, a wholly different matter. Exceptionally well versed in medicine himself, he was more skilled in its diagnostic and therapeutic aspects than most of the physicians of his time, and he was a medical theorist of well-proved brilliance. He admired men of medicine, respecting their calling and elaborating on their vital importance to the community. When he came to them in his roster of recommendations to the professions as to doing good, he addressed them as "your noble profession," and "men universally learned." And he spoke their language, addressing to them an incredibly sound lesson on psychosomatic medicine nearly two centuries ahead of its time, citing European medical authorities of the highest competence with whose works he made a point of keeping *au courant*. Nobody, layman or physician, knew better than Mather, who was shortly to risk his life and reputation in advocating inoculation against smallpox, the physiological nature of bodily disease. But he knew also, before most physicians, that there was more to perils to health than physical afflictions. "*Tranquility of mind* will do strange things towards the relief of bodily maladies. . . . I propound then, let the *physician* with all possible ingenuity of *conversation*, find out, what matter of *anxiety*, what there is, that has made his life *uneasy* to him. Having discussed the *burden*, let him use all the ways he can devise to take it off."[59] Although, to his later distress, young Franklin was to find himself

---

[58] Ibid., 93, 96.
[59] Ibid., 103.

with his brother aligned against Mather on inoculation, he became deeply interested in medicine and in his maturity was to make significant contributions to its progress.

Perhaps nothing in Mather's book influenced Franklin as much as his advocacy of voluntary association, both for the common good of all and for the improvement of the individual members. Both Mather and Franklin were gregarious personalities, and associative action was a natural inclination to them. But it was more. Neither man could see any significant and directed progress being achieved without the sense of mutual responsibility and mutual inspiration that can spring only from activated concern for one another's welfare and from the free exchange of ideas. Mather himself launched neighborhood associations in Boston called Associated Families; and Josiah Franklin, himself a highly gregarious man, belonged to one of them. In *Essays to Do Good*, Mather set forth the formula for conducting such associations, incorporating a decalogue of suitable principles, objectives, and procedures for them.

The ten guidelines spelled out were to be principal criteria for the forming and functioning of Franklin's earliest venture into associative activity, his founding of the "Junto" in Philadelphia when he was twenty-one, with the distinction that, while Mather's proposals were ultimately directed at the better exercise of the Christian religion, Franklin's were aimed at the advancement and improvement of philosophic discussion. Mather also proposed the creation of societies called Young Men Associated—again centered on the strengthening of religious practices but again advocating the approaches of exchange and mutuality that were to characterize a major part of Franklin's civic and political activity all his life.

Mather's "Reforming Societies, or Societies for the Suppression of Disorders," though at first glance they might seem essentially vigilante, were, as proposed by Mather, surprisingly enlightened in their objectives and more democratic than otherwise in their methods: "If any *laws* to regulate what is amiss be yet wanting, the *Society* may procure the *legislative power* to be so addressed, that all due provision will soon be made by our law-givers. What is defective in the by-laws of the town may be by the Society so observed, that the town shall be soon advised, and the thing redressed." The reform societies were also charitable associations, charged to "find out who are in extreme necessities, and may either by their own liberality, or by that of others to whom they may commend the matter, obtain succors for the necessitous."[60]

All of Mather's societal proposals had in common procedures of full and open discussion, which held an exceptionally strong appeal for Franklin all his life. In addition to their being the very heart of his youthful "Junto," their sway over him was to be asserted amid great causes and great events. The spirit of constructive discussion informed the pages of his *Proposal*

[60] Ibid., 134.

for Promoting Useful Knowledge, advocating the creation of the American Philosophical Society when he was thirty-seven; it animated his influence in the Convention of 1787, leading to the framing and adoption of the Constitution of the United States, when he was eighty-one; and it governed his motives and his actions in scores of matters affecting his community and his country between those ages.

In *Essays to Do Good*, Cotton Mather, the chief advocate of God and the principal prosecutor of Satan in the Boston of Benjamin Franklin's boyhood, wrote, "The *sluggards* who do no good in the world are *wise in their own conceits*; but the men who are diligent in *doing of good* can give such *a reason* for what they do, as proves them to be *really wise*. Men *leave off to be wise* when they *leave off to do good*. The *wisdom* of it appears in this: 't is the best way of spending our *time*; 't is *well-spent*, when spent in *doing of good*. It is also a sure way, a sweet way, effectually to bespeak the *blessings* of God on ourselves. Who so likely to *find blessings* as the men that *are blessings?*"[61] When Benjamin Franklin was an old man, fondly recalling the town of his boyhood, he wrote Cotton Mather's son, "When I was a boy, I met with a book, entitled '*Essays to Do Good*', which I think was written by your father [it was published anonymously, though its authorship was no secret in Boston]. It had been so little regarded by a former possessor, that several leaves of it were torn out; but the remainder gave me such a turn of thinking, as to have an influence on my conduct through life; for I have always set a greater value on the character of a *doer of good*, than on any other kind of reputation; and if I have been, as you seem to think, a useful citizen, the public owes the advantage of it to that book."[62]

The letter was an extravagant tribute, written out of a kindness no doubt deepened because addressed to the son, born the same year as Franklin, of a renowned and often abused man then dead for fifty-six years. But the essential point of the letter was demonstrated even more convincingly in the life of its author, Benjamin Franklin, than in his words.

[61] Ibid., 149.
[62] Benjamin Franklin to the Reverend Samuel Mather, May 12, 1784, in Smyth, *Writings of Benjamin Franklin*, IX, 208.

PART FOUR

The Education of New England: The Courant

Declare ye among the nations, and publish, and set up a standard; publish, and conceal not. . . .
—The Book of the Prophet Jeremiah, 595 B.C.

I must observe to you that wee have been so unhappy of late as to have many Factious & Scandalous papers printed, & publickly sold at Boston, highly reflecting upon the Government, & tending to disquiet the minds of his Majestie's Good Subjects. . . .
—Speech to the Great and General Court, Governor Samuel Shute, A.D. 1724

X

The Printing House

> ... 'tis impossible any Man should know
> what he would do if he was a Printer.
> —Benjamin Franklin[1]

Once Josiah Franklin had perceived that "the tithe of his sons" was not
destined, by temperament or conviction, for the ministry, a new decision
had to be made as to the boy's future. Benjamin was bright, practical, and
venturesome. He was also independent, strong-willed, and cheerfully overconfident. If left alone—further schooling being out of the question—he
would unquestionably have shipped out as a cabin boy on one of the three
or four hundred great, alluring ships that set out from Boston every year.
But his father, already having gone through that ordeal with his son
Josiah, would have none of it, and Benjamin at ten was too young to manage it on his own. And so what became of him was dictated by the only alternative left to a town boy with neither a predilection for farming nor
any familial access to it: apprenticing himself to an artisan, learning his
trade, and then setting up for himself either in Boston or in one of the
newer and growing towns to the west, north, and south of Boston.

Boston itself was largely a community of artisans. The learned pursuits
were limited to the ministry, teaching, a few magistracies, and, to an
equally minor extent, the practice of medicine. Mercantilism provided rich
livings for a few at the top of the economic scale, but aside from the laborers on the wharves most of the many dependent for a livelihood on importing and exporting were mariners who were away at sea most of their
working lives. (Benjamin's brother, Josiah, Jr., twenty-nine, was for nine
years gone on his first voyage.) On the other hand, there were virtually no
jobs in manufacturing. Conditions were inhospitable to the growth of any
manufacturing on a sizable scale, for aside from the essential deter-
rent inherent in the colonial economy, which assumed the export of raw
materials to a manufacturing motherland, labor was scarce and consequently expensive—too expensive in New England to compete with Eng-

[1] "Apology for Printers," 1731, in *Papers*, I, 198.

land or the European continent. But there was more to it. The kind of spirited, enterprising people induced to sail across the sea and start anew in strange and remote places were not likely to hire themselves out as factory hands dependent upon someone else's will and orders and plans. They wanted to be their own masters. This some of the later Boston arrivals did by moving out to the near frontier of western New England and starting farms. If they were townsmen by nature and by choice, they also became artisans, for mastering a craft represented lifetime security in the economy, a respected position in the community, and a creative role in the society. In fact, many of those who left Boston to become farmers were often lured by grants of land in return for their agreeing to practice trades, as Benjamin Franklin's mother's forebears were in the case of the islands of Martha's Vineyard and Nantucket.[2]

In deciding to bring his youngest and last son into his own trade of tallow chandler, candlemaker, and soapmaker, Josiah Franklin was making not only a practical judgment but one that would seem to him a benevolent one as well. There was nothing material that he had more precious to give his son than his experience and the business he had built, particularly since, approaching the beginning of his seventh decade, he had every prospect of early admitting the boy to full partnership and to his ultimate succession as sole proprietor. It was possible also that Josiah had the survival and health of his little business in mind. Good apprentices were hard to come by and often, despite stern contractual obligations, difficult to hold. Moreover, he had taken Benjamin's older brother, John, as an apprentice, and the experiment worked well, John having left to start his own business in Rhode Island. As for the nonmaterial aspects of the situation, Josiah Franklin was far too perceptive a man not to have known that in Benjamin he had an exceptional child on his hands—one whose singular gifts could develop into great powers for good or be precipitated, by unfortunate associations or indifferent guidance, into dangerous channels. Working in his father's shop, Benjamin would be by his side, where Josiah could watch him grow into manhood, help to shape his character, and influence the development of his mind.

For all of his intentions, however, the trade into which Josiah was initiating his son was one of the least inspiring, least imaginative, and least innovative in eighteenth-century life; and no craft could have been less responsive to the analytical, inventive, and inquiring mind that was already apparent in the young Franklin or less conducive to the development of his expressive talents. Soap and candlemaking was just a trade—a way of making an honest living and of occupying a serviceable place in the community—and it was a smelly, dreary, oppressive trade at that. In 1716 soap and candles were still made from tallow essentially as they were when

[2] For further examples, see Robert E. Brown, *Middle-Class Democracy and the Revolution in Massachusetts, 1691–1780* (Ithaca, 1955), Chap. 1, passim.

Josiah opened his first shop in Boston more than thirty years earlier. It was not until 1750 that the crystalline spermaceti of the sperm whale was introduced into candlemaking, vastly simplifying the laborious and odiferous task of rendering the tallow from beef and mutton fat; bayberry bushes, which grew flourishingly all over New England, were early discovered to have a berry that could be reduced to wax by boiling and skimming, furnishing a far more agreeable, less oily, and more fragrant substance than tallow; but it took hours to gather enough bayberries—up to fifteen pounds —to make a single pound of wax, and consequently bayberry candles were a luxury, usually homemade, for the few. And there had been no major innovation in the technique of candlemaking since the Sieur de Brex in Paris contrived the candle mold in the fifteenth century, replacing in the commercial production of candles the hand-dipping methods dating back to the Greeks and Romans in Pliny's time. In Boston, when Benjamin Franklin entered his father's trade, the great mass of candles was made, as was soap, from animal fats rendered into tallow by a process so offensive to the nostrils as to have long been declared in England, like slaughtering, as one of the "noxious" trades. The fatty tissues of oxen and sheep were chopped into bits and then heated over open fires. After reaching a temperature of 109° to 114°, the exuded fats collected on the surface of the water, the remaining membranes sinking to the bottom, and were skimmed off to be used as the principal materials for candles and soap. It took some acquired skill, but neither talent nor intellect, to do this proficiently. But the quality of the product—the candle or soap—resulting from the manufacturing process varied with the skill, experience, and attentiveness of the artisan; and since materials were money—especially tallow, which was still scarce in the colonies—the artisan could not afford to squander them on poorly rendered end products. A good craftsman was conscientious, watchful, and demanding of himself and his employees, seldom working less than twelve to fourteen hours a day and less than six days a week. Straining the tallow to eliminate unevenness in the candle's melting, the twisting of the cotton or flax fibers into wicks of the right thickness and tightness, the even pouring of the molten tallow into the molds, the withdrawing of the candles from the mold at the proper degree of solidification, and, in the case of the dipping method, by which wicks were dipped into a bath of hot tallow rather than the tallow's being poured around the wicks, the timing and frequency of the dips, building up the body of the candles—these skills constituted the craft of candlemaking. Any candles that sputtered or guttered because of faulty wicks or that burned unevenly because of uneven pouring or dipping of the body of tallow would bring complaints and loss of customers.

Benjamin Franklin recalled being employed in the elementary phases of this process: ". . . cutting Wick for the Candles, filling the Dipping Mold, and the Molds for cast Candles [i.e., those made by pouring]. . . ."[3] Oddly enough, aside from describing his father as also a "Sope-Boiler,"[4] Franklin recalled in his *Autobiography* nothing of the soap side of the business, though he was intrigued all his life by soapmaking formulas evolved by his family over the years and often, when on diplomatic missions to Europe, sent to his younger sister, Jane Mecum in Boston, for cakes of the "Crown Soap"—and the recipe for it—that became a Franklin family institution. (Jane Mecum wrote, ". . . it would be a great help when we could convince people they have been decved by a miserable Imitation, & that no won Els can make the trew soap. . . ."[5]) The making of soap, nevertheless, was an even less engaging process than making candles. Fundamentally, it involved boiling the fatty acids from tallow with caustic alkalies; economically, it was a tandem trade to candlemaking, not merely because both candles and soap were made of tallow, but also because the oleic acid content of the tallow, useless for making candles, was valuable for soapmaking. The soap was boiled hard in great "soap pans" or "coppers" and then allowed to cool either in a mass to be dispensed as "soft soap" or in molds to be sold as cakes. The success of the product depended upon the skill with which the alkali, usually obtained from slaking, or hydrating, ashes, and the fatty acid were mixed, upon the temperature and duration of the boiling, and upon the timing of the steps in the post-boiling process. But the whole procedure was dull, formularized, predictable, without variation, and unsusceptible, given the materials of the time, of innovations. And though Franklin all his life was extremly fussy about soap (he took the trouble at eighty years old to send some cakes that had crumbled back from Philadelphia, to his sister in Boston to get her "Advice whether to re-melt it all, &. in what manner"[6]), soapmaking bored him so much as a boy that he made no specific mention of it when he recalled the days in his father's shop beyond that minimal reference to his father as a soap boiler.

"I dislik'd the Trade," Franklin said flatly,[7] and he kept his dislike no secret from his father for the two years that he worked for him. Josiah Franklin made no attempt to force his son to stay and concluded in 1718, when Benjamin was twelve, that he had to do something about getting his son into a trade more congenial to his tastes, interests, and instincts. Despite Benjamin's "strong Inclination for the Sea,"[8] Josiah ruled that out absolutely, it being scarcely three years since his second son, Josiah, Jr., was lost at sea. And so Josiah did an imaginative and wise thing: He took Benjamin on long walks through the streets and lanes of Boston so that he could observe at first hand any interest that the boy might show in any trade that they encountered among the scores that made the town of

[3] *Autobiography*, 53.
[4] Ibid.
[5] Van Doren, *Letters of Benjamin Franklin and Jane Mecum*, 196.
[6] Ibid., 264.
[7] *Autobiography*, 53.
[8] Ibid.

Boston, so far as most finished goods went, almost a wholly self-sufficient community. As early as 1650, Edward Johnson, originally himself a joiner by trade but by choice an early and wondering chronicler of the way of life in New England, catalogued no fewer than thirty trades at which men made their entire livings, without engaging in farming or fishing, winding up his list with a curiously appreciative tribute to one that he apparently prized above the others: "Carpenters, joiners, glaziers, painters, follow their trades only; gemsmiths, locksmiths, blacksmiths, nailers, cutlers, have left [it to] the husbandmen to follow the plow and cart, and they [follow] their trades; weavers, brewers, bakers, costermongers, feltmakers, braziers, pewterers and tinkers, rope makers, masons, lime, brick, and tile makers, card makers to work and not to play [i.e., cards for weaving and not for whist], turners, pump makers, and wheelers, glovers, fellmungers [sheepskin workers, who separated wool and pelt], and furriers are orderly turned to their trades, besides divers sorts of shopkeepers, and some who have a mystery beyond others, as have the vintners."[9]

In the walks with his father, Benjamin had the opportunity "to see good Workmen handle their Tools."[10] In an age of artisans, when everything from a ship built of the wood of three thousand oak trees to the nails used in its superstructure were made by hand, tools—themselves made by hand—were the most prized of a man's possessions, the instruments of his expression and the symbols of his achievement. For the most part, specific tools were peculiar to specific trades, usually having been devised in the first place by an artisan engaged in the trade and sometimes having been adapted from these by artisans in other trades to their own special requirements. Colonial tools were creative, ingenius extensions of man's natural tools—his hands and fingers primarily but also his arms, his legs, his muscles, and his sense. But because the daily test of their worthiness was their functionalism, they were uncluttered and forthright in design and were made to express their purpose rather than to conceal it. The subtle curve of an ax handle came not from an appeal to the eyes but to the arms of the man swinging the ax; and the ax head, the blade, was a remarkable combination of sheer weight, to furnish momentum and impact for the downward swing, and of tapering grace, to form a sharp wedge that could cut its way cleanly through the hardest woods. A universal tool, its use being the first step in clearing the forests, building the hull of a ship, erecting a house, constructing furniture, and providing fuel, the ax was gradually adapted to the special needs of individual woodworkers so that the range of axes extended from the heavy broadax used in hewing great timbers into ship beams to the narrow-bladed joiner's ax as precise as

---

[9] The passage occurs in *The Wonder-Working Providence of Sion's Saviour in New England*, Bk. III, Chap. 6. The book, designed to encourage migrators to New England, was first published anonymously in London, dated 1654, and was somewhat loosely entitled *A Hist. of New Eng.* Later editions were published in 1867, edited by William F. Poole, and in 1910, edited by J. F. Jameson, both with the longer title.

[10] *Autobiography*, 57.

a chisel in cutting out mortise holes. The design of hammers and mallets, too, accorded with the varying needs of different artisans—carpenters, coopers, cobblers, wheelwrights, bricklayers, millers, printers—all having both heads and handles as diversified in size and shapes as the works they produced. There were also the tools unique to particular crafts—the punches and awls of the leatherworkers, the soldering lamps of the metalworkers, the treadle lathes of the turner.

Not only in the tools that they employed but in the work that they did with such basic materials as wood, leather, and metal, colonial artisans were highly specialized. In Josiah Franklin's Boston, for example, there were no fewer than fourteen categories of woodworkers: cabinetmakers, carpenters, carvers, chairmakers, coachmakers, coopers, gunstockers, joiners, millwrights, sawyers, shipwrights, turners, wheelwrights, and woodcutters. Within these categories there was even more specialization, shipwrights, for example, being further divided between framers and plankers. These specialist-artisans became expert not only with specialized versions of such tools as axes and hammers but also in the kind of wood used in their specialties, birch for the cabinetmakers, for example, and oak for the shipwrights.

All this made a lasting impression on the young Franklin, not merely in the general terms of educational field trips in the material life of a colonial society but more particularly as instruction in how to use tools and how things were fashioned and put together: ". . . it has been useful to me, having learnt so much by it, as to be able to do little Jobs my self in my House, when a Workman could not readily be got; and to construct little Machines for my Experiments while the Intention of making the Experiment was fresh and warm in my Mind."[11] The number of contrivances known to have been originated in his lifetime by Franklin—not to mention those he may well have improvised during his early printing days in Philadelphia, where his printing house took on the kaleidoscopic aspect of a general store and center of general services—summoned into use many of the tools that he observed in use on those walks in Boston. He made clocks, stoves, lightning rods, astronomical instruments, eyeglasses, a chair that could be converted into a ladder, a clothes-pressing machine, a pole with a manipulable grasp at the end to take books down from high shelves, laboratory equipment, and a musical instrument—an armonica— for which Beethoven and Mozart, among other Europeans, composed. (Franklin inherited his father's talent for music; aside from being an acceptable singer, he played the violin, the harp, and the guitar, wrote lyrics for songs, composed a quartet for three violins and cello, and was a perceptive and articulate critic of music.)

Instructive as Benjamin said that these tours of the artisans were to him in later years, they resulted in no immediate solution to the problem his father faced with an enterprising, strong-minded boy who despised the

[11] Ibid.

trade to which he was being bred and who, he feared, "should break away and get to sea."[12] Consequently, Josiah turned, as he and his brothers had in Ecton, London, and Banbury, inward to the family for help. His nephew, Samuel Franklin, was now established in Boston as a cutler, with his own shop, and Josiah made arrangements for Benjamin to be apprenticed to him to learn the cutler's trade. Cutlery was infinitely more varied than rendering soap and candles and more responsive to mechanical ingenuity; and every artifact produced by a cutler was a distinctive piece of craftsmanship. As ancient as the sharp-edged fragments of flint that primitive man used in the Stone Age, cutlery had become an art by the Bronze Age, when knives of bronze contributed to the age's name. In England cutlery was one of the oldest of crafts, Sheffield having been a center of its manufacture before the time of Chaucer ("A Sheffeld thwitel [whittling knife] baar he in his hose"); and the Cutlers' Company of London was incorporated in 1654. As time passed and alloys progressed in their capacity for honing with the development of steel, cutlery became one of the most sophisticated of crafts. Though by 1624 in England, blades were required to be made of steel, handles could be made of any material, giving the artisan full range to his imagination, his taste, and his originality. The scope of the instruments he produced also gave free rein to his skills: knives of every size and purpose, razors, scissors, daggers, saws, cutting tools for other trades among them. It was a trade that Josiah Franklin, at the lowest point in the artisan scale, could well wish his son to learn and practice.

But after a few days, Benjamin was back on his father's hands again. Samuel had decided that he wanted to be paid to teach his young cousin the trade. Benjamin's recollection that his father found this proposal "displeasing" was probably an understatement tempered by the passage of time. Josiah Franklin may very well have been bitterly resentful. For four years he had given lodging and food to Samuel's aging father, who was still living in his house, still partaking of his hospitality. He refused to pay Samuel and would find a place for his son elsewhere.

Josiah turned again to the family, this time even closer—to his twenty-one-year-old son, James, who had returned in 1717 from England, where he had learned the printer's trade, and set up a press in Queen Street. Benjamin, when he was twelve years old in 1718, went to work for James Franklin, the printer.

* * *

Relieved to get away from the vats of molten grease, the young Franklin apparently turned with pleasure to the world of types and inks and composing sticks in his brother's small printing house. But it was not an easy life to which he had turned; and, as he put it, he "still had a Hankering for the Sea."[13] For some time, he refused to sign the rigidly binding ar-

12 Ibid.
13 Ibid., 58.

ticles of indenture, which for all practical purposes would have made him wholly subservient to his brother for nine years—a prospect probably made all the more forbidding to him because at twenty-one James lacked the wisdom and maturity that Josiah had as a taskmaster and lacked also, of course, the sense of paternal concern and protection that Josiah had toward the boy. Moreover, Benjamin was a precocious boy and seems to have had some of the more irritating characteristics of one fully aware of his exceptional gifts. There is little evidence either that James had much affection for Benjamin, young men of twenty-one not being inclined to adore twelve-year-old brothers, or that Benjamin had much respect for James, forward twelve-year-olds not being apt to yield with grace to taking orders day in and day out from an older brother. Nevertheless, the solid instinct for making the right judgment that governed Franklin all his life triumphed over both his longing for the sea and his annoyance at the thought of his brother's having absolute command over him. And he signed the indentured agreement. The term of nine years was rather longer than was common (apprentice seamen were indentured for only four, and the average trade apprenticeship was for seven years). Benjamin was also relatively old at twelve to begin an apprenticeship, having, unlike most apprentices, spent two years at school and two years hating soap and candle-making while reading Plutarch and Bunyan. The indenture was also exceptional in that James Franklin did not have to assume duties common in most master-apprentice relationships: He did not have to instruct him in reading, writing, and arithemtic or provide for any special attention to problems of health, as many masters did; one surviving apprenticeship agreement in New England specifically required a cooper to teach his seven-year-old apprentice not only barrelmaking but also "to write and read English, and cast accounts, and be at the cost and use his best endeavours to get his scurf head cured. Also to learn [sic] him the trade of a cooper, and at the end of his time to let him go free and give him double apparel, a musket, sword and bandoliers and 20 s[hillings]."[14] James did, however, have to teach his young brother the art of printing and provide him with lodging, food, drink, clothing, laundering, and, during the last year of his apprenticeship a journeyman's wages. In return, Benjamin simply turned his life over to his brother's rule: He, Benjamin, ". . . shall truly and faithfully serve, his [James's] Counsels lawful and honest obay, his seacretts shall keep, hurt to his master he shall not doe nor consent to be done, at unlawful games he shall not play, nor from his master's business absent himselfe by night or day, his masters goods he shall not wast nor imbezzell, nor them lend without his masters Consent. Taverns and ale Howses he shall not frequent except about his masters business there

[14] Cited in William B. Weeden, *Economic and Social History of New England,* 1620–1789 (Boston, 1890), I, 84f.

to be done but as a true and faithful servant ought to behave himself in word and deed during the said terme. . . ."[15]

James Franklin's printing house stood across the narrow passage of Queen Street from the gloomy pile of the town prison, which had given the street its original name of Prison Lane. It was not one of the more desirable sites in Boston, but it was cheap for the young printer, whose struggling business consisted almost entirely of printing small editions of pamphlets for booksellers, who were Boston's only publishers, and occasionally a piece of cloth for a rich merchant's wife. Nearby in Queen Street, separated by Dorsett Alley, was one of James Franklin's three competitors, Samuel Kneeland, also twenty-one years old, whose great-grandfather, Samuel Green, in 1650 succeeded America's first printer, Stephen Daye, as the printer of the colony's official printing press at Harvard College. James's other two competitors were Bartholomew Green, more than thirty years James's senior, who was a son of Samuel by his second wife and taught the trade to Kneeland, and Thomas Fleet, thirty-three, who, having left London under some pressure for annoying the High-Churchmen, set up a printing house in Pudding Lane in 1712, five years ahead of James's, and prospered greatly. The press in Cambridge having been sold some fifteen years earlier (Thomas Hollis gave Harvard fonts of Greek and Hebrew type in 1718, but they went unused until 1761), these four constituted the only presses not only in Massachusetts but also, with the exception of one set up in New London, Connecticut, by another descendant of Samuel Green, in all New England.

Modest as was James Franklin's printing house, it had to be a reasonably sturdy building with strong sleepers supporting the floor because of the heavy weight of the press. Franklin's press was a Blaeu wooden handpress, virtually unchanged since a Dutch map maker developed it early in the seventeenth century, and was to remain unchanged until Lord Stanhope devised an iron press nearly two hundred years later. The other furnishings of the trade were described by Joseph Moxon, printer, member of the Royal Society and "Hydrographer to the King's Most Excellent Majesty," in a book, *Mechanick Exercises: Or, the Doctrine of Handy-Works. Applied to the Art of Printing*, which since its publication in 1683 became the vocational bible of printers everywhere. This accumulation of tools— and not the building housing them—was what constituted a "printing house." Moxon gave the printer specific directions for the setting up of the printing house. "Having consider'd what number of *Presses* [Boston printers had only one each] and *Cases* he shall use, he makes it his business to furnish himself with a Room or Rooms well-lighted, and of convenient capacity for his number of *Presses* and *Cases*, allowing for each Press about Seven Foot square upon the Floor, and for every *Frame* of

[15] The language is in Weeden, I, 274n.

Cases which holds Two pair of *Cases, viz.* one pair *Romain* [i.e., roman] and one pair *Itallica* [italics], Five Foot and an half in length (for so much they contain) and Four Foot and an half in breadth, though they contain but Two Foot and Nine Inches: But the room will be left to pass freely between two *Frames*." Moxon gave stern advice as to the placement of the equipment in the rooms. "He places the Cases on that side the Room where they will most conveniently stand, so, as when the *Compositer* is at work the Light may come in on his Left-hand; for else his Right-hand plying between the Window-light and his Eye might shadow the *Letter* he would pick up: and the *Presses* he places so, as the Light may fall from a Window right before the *Form* [the type locked in a frame ready for printing] and the *Tinpan* [i.e., the tympan, a framed piece of cloth placed between the platen and the paper to soften the pressure of the latter upon the inked type]: And if situation will allow it, on the North-side the Room, that the *Press-men*, when at their hard labour in *Summer* time, may be the less uncommoded with the heat of the *Sun*: And also that they may the better see by the constancy of that Light, to keep the whole Heap [of pages] in equal Colour. He is also to take care that his *Presses* have a solid and firm Foundation, and an even Horizontal Floor to stand on, that when the *Presses* are set up their Feet shall need no Underlays, which both damage a *Press*, are often apt to work out [of position], and consequently subject it to an unstable and loose position. . . . He is also to take care that the Room have a clear, free and pretty lofty Light, not impeded with the shadow of other Houses, or with Trees. . . ."[16]

In addition to his press and cases of type, the printer had to provide space for "correcting" stones, lye, and rinsing troughs for cleaning type forms before they went to press, distributing frames on which forms of type awaiting breaking up for distribution were kept, benches for stacking unused paper, racks with lines of string on which to hang printed sheets for drying, jugs in which to mix inks, tables on which to apply them to the type forms, other tables to take trial impressions or proofs, and sloping counters at which compositors could set type.

Printing was hard and slow physical labor, but it was never dull, never wholly predictable, and infinitely varied in its productions. Every signature of pages was a separate piece of work, having to be composed entirely by hand with no tool but a composing stick that guided the compositor in adhering to fixed length for each line. Each form, usually consisting of four pages, was then locked up in a frame, inked by two inking balls, one held in each hand, and first rubbed or "brayed" together to make sure that the degree of ink in them matched. The form was then locked into the stone bed of the press, the tympan was folded over the type, a single sheet of

[16] Joseph Moxon, *Mechanick Exercises: Or, the Doctrine of Handy-Works. Applied to the Art of Printing* (London, 1683; reprinted in literal facsimile, New York, 1896), I, 10f.

paper was inserted, and then the whole rolled under the platen. The printer then pulled the spindle lever, pressing the paper on the type. All these operations were involved in the production of every single individual sheet printed—that is, for every set of single copies of the four different pages on the form. Thus, if a forty-page pamphlet was being printed, it would take ten operations of inking the type, preparing the sheet of paper and tympan, pulling the lever, rolling back the bed to take off the printed sheet, and hanging up the sheet to dry. If the print order was for five hundred copies of the pamphlet, it would take five thousand such series of operations on the press to produce them even before sorting, cutting, and binding the sheets into the finished product. It was estimated that two pressmen of equal ability operating a press—one inking the type and one handling the sheet, tympan, and platen lever—could at best print two hundred and forty sheets an hour once the slower tasks of setting and proofing the type were accomplished. This amounted to the equal of six copies of a forty-page publication, and an edition of five hundred copies would take over eighty hours to produce, plus the time for composing, cutting, and binding, all of which was also done by hand. For a printing house's output to reach a profitable level at this rate, a twelve-hour day was a necessity, and in summertime the additional daylight was often used to stretch the working day to fourteen or fifteen hours. Physical strength was, consequently, a necessity, and this young Benjamin Franklin had in abundance, his naturally sturdy body being further strengthened by the great amount of swimming that he had done since early childhood. His powerful arms and shoulders made the lifting of the heavy forms of little effort, and he never recalled being so fatigued that he was not ready for several hours of reading "the greatest Part of the Night," when he went up to his sleeping quarters after the long day of labor, or for composing ballads in stanzas not appreciably beyond Uncle Benjamin's in literary distinction.

Like most new businesses—particularly one imbued with an extra-material quality like printing—James Franklin's Queen Street establishment had a struggling time of it for the first year or two of its existence. Having no ties with the Green family, which amounted to a printing dynasty in New England for the first century of its printing history, and neither the influence nor the means of the mature, assured Thomas Fleet, James apparently made a hand-to-mouth existence with job printing for the booksellers, although his family ties with the Old South Church seemed of some help, for among the earliest of Franklin's publications was *A Discourse had By the late Reverend and learned Mr. Ebenezer Pemberton Previous to the Ordination of the Reverend Mr.* Joseph Sewall . . . *Affirming and Proving the* Validity *of Presbyterial Ordination*—the imprint being "Boston: Printed by J. Franklin for S. Gerrish and Sold at his Shop near the Old Meeting-House. 1718." Reading some of his young apprentice's ballads, he got the notion that he could print them and then Benjamin could go out and hawk them in the streets of Boston, much as he had seen Grub Street balladeers sell their effusions in the coffeehouses of London while he was learning his trade there—a brisk business which Thomas Fleet transported from England when he arrived in 1712. All it required, in addition to a contriving facility with rhyming and a lesser one with meter, was a topic much in the public attention, preferably with a dramatic or emotional content. Young Benjamin, during the first year of his apprenticeship, was visited with two such inspirations.

The first occasion was on a gale-stricken Monday early in November 1718, when George Worthylake, his wife Ann, and his daughter Ruth were swept to their deaths in the turbulent waters of Boston Harbor, culminating Worthylake's brief and unhappy experience as first keeper of the lighthouse that had been built in 1716 on a rocky promontory, connected to one of the Brewster Islands by a sand bar that disappeared at high tide, called Beacon Island. Situated at the entrance to the Outer Harbor, the light guided ships through a deep, narrow channel past the rocks and shoals into the safety of the Inner Harbor. George Worthylake, forty-five years old in 1718, knew the harbor well, having grown up on Pemberton Island and owning a farm on Lovell's Island; he also had grazing land on Great Brewster Island, next to Beacon Island, where he kept a flock of sheep. His pay in 1716–17 as keeper of the lighthouse was fifty pounds a year—a generous sum, since he continued to farm; but in 1717–18, at his pleading, his pay was raised to seventy pounds, partly in compensation for the loss of fifty-nine of his sheep which, during a storm the previous winter, had wandered lemminglike into the sea and to their deaths. On the day that he himself came to an end, with his wife and daughter, the Worthylakes were attempting to land on the precipitous, rocky edge of Beacon Island in a canoelike open boat, which a slave, one Shadwell, had taken out to bring ashore the Worthylakes and a friend, John Edge, after drinks and a meal on board the sloop of another friend. As the boat approached the shore, another Worthylake daughter, Anne, was horrified to see it capsize and all five passengers drown.

It was the kind of event that had all the elements that capture public imagination: the terror of sudden death, father, mother, and child dying together, a young girl among them, an act of nature, man against the sea and losing. Cotton Mather, ever eager to exploit a disaster for the glory of God, dropped any previous prospects for his sermon the following Sunday and wrote a sermon entitled, incongruously perhaps to George Worthylake's surviving son and daughter Anne, "Providence Asserted and Adored. *In a Sermon Occasioned by the Tragical Death of several, who were unhappily drowned, near the Light-house, at the Entrance of* Boston-Harbour. *With a Relation of the unhappy Accident.*" Within two months

Mather had his sermon in print with his customary missionary zeal to capture the attention of those unable to hear his words in person.[17]

The Franklin brothers moved with equal speed if under less spiritual compulsion. Benjamin set to work. The twelve-year-old apprentice sat down and strung together his verses, and apparently James dropped all other work to get them in print. "They were wretched Stuff, in the Grubstreet Ballad Stile. . . ." But it "sold wonderfully, the event being recent, having made a great Noise. This flattered my Vanity."[18] None of the verses are known to have survived, which is probably just as well for their young author's place in letters. Eleven stanzas, written in a Victorian hand and ascribed to Franklin, were found on Middle Brewster Island, near the site of the lighthouse, in 1940; but their style, locutions, punctuations, capitalization, and faintly romantic gothic tone are much more suggestive of the nineteenth century than of the eighteenth. On the other hand, the version did bear the same title that Franklin recalled, "The Lighthouse Tragedy" and the clear by-line, "by Benjamin Franklin." And it is not at all impossible that some later resident of those lonely islands, often taking the brunt of fierce northeastern storms, could have copied the poem from a prized but faded original printed by James Franklin. Some excerpts, however, suggest some fictionalizing of the facts, but no balladeer before or since has been known to have been inhibited in that direction:

> Oh, George, this wild November
> We must not pass with you
> For Ruth, our fragile daughter,
> Its chilly gales will rue.
>
> So, home to Lovell's Island,
> Take us when falls the sea
> To the old house where comfort
> And better shelter be.
>
> Now they reach the open channel
> Where the flood tide breasts the gale
> Rears a toppling wall of water,
> Making Anne's cheeks grow pale.
>
> Quick the prow is upward borne.
> George in Anne's arms is tossed
> Husband, wife and child together
> In the chilly waves are lost.[19]

[17] No copy was known to Sibley (*Biographical Sketches*, III, 129) to have survived, but it is listed in Samuel Mather's catalogue of books by his father and in Thomas Prince's manuscript catalogue.

[18] *Autobiography*, 59f.

[19] Cited by Edward Rowe Snow in *Boston Herald*, August 13, 1971.

Whether quite so sentimental as these presumed excerpts, Franklin's verses were popular, their sales probably stimulated by the drowning of Captain Robert Saunders, who had been appointed to succeed Worthylake, scarcely a week after his predecessor had gone to his death. Writing his diary entry for November 17, 1718, Cotton Mather, more inspired than distressed, responded with characteristic professional expedience, "Another Master of the *Light-House* is (with another Person) already drowned. So surprising a Dispensation gives me an Opportunity to Lett fall such Passages on the Sea-faring part of my Flock, as may have a mighty Tendency to excite the Motions of Piety in them. God prosper these Endeavours."[20] In any case, the sales of the ballad, which probably, temporarily at least, elevated James's regard for his brother-apprentice, were sufficiently impressive (there is some evidence that it was translated and sold overseas—e.g., in France as "La Tragédie du Phare"[21]) that the Franklins seized upon the next extraordinary event of a sensational nature to publish another epoch by Benjamin, early in 1719.

The occasion for this second and last ballad was a vivid account, appearing in the *Boston News-Letter*, of March 2, 1719, of the capture and death of the British pirate Edward Teach (also known as Thatch or Thach) at the hands of a brave young Virginia lieutenant in the Royal Navy named Robert Maynard. Teach was the scourge of the southeastern coast of the American colonies for five years—a heinous figure, indeed, made all the more unpalatable by his formidable appearance, dominated by a long, heavy black beard, which he parted in the middle, tying the ends with ribbons and curling them behind his ears. His predations upon legitimate shipping and his raids on the coastal towns of North Carolina became legendary after the end of the War of the Spanish Succession in 1713 brought an end also to his privateering, and reports of his ferocious visage gave him the name of "Blackbeard," by which he was popularly known throughout the colonies. In 1717 he captured a sizable French merchantman, renamed it *Queen Anne's Revenge*, armed it with forty heavy guns, and promptly terrified the Spanish Main and its neighboring waters. His notorious thievery and murders were matched by his brazenness. He received a royal pardon and thereafter simply continued his criminal maraudings, boldly putting into North Carolina coves to spend the winter. He entered into stately negotiations with the royal governor of North Carolina, Charles Eden, who stoutly denied that he had shared in any of Blackbeard's ill-gotten gains, but he attended the pirate's marriage to a sixteen-year-old Carolinian. However, Eden did nothing to apprehend the pirate; accordingly, the governor of neighboring Virginia, Alexander Spotswood, heartily tired of Blackbeard's assaults on Virginia shipping, sent out

[20] Mather, *Diary*, II, 568.
[21] See Worthington C. Ford in Massachusetts Historical Society, *Collections*, 7th Ser., VIII, 566n., and *Papers*, I, 6.

a sloop of twenty guns under the command of Lieutenant Maynard, with orders to capture or kill Blackbeard. Maynard found Blackbeard's ship taking refuge in the friendly waters of Ocracoke Inlet in North Carolina's jurisdiction, but the Virginian, ignoring legal scruples, if in fact any valid regulations against the ship of one British province pursuing a pirate into another's province's waters existed, went into the inlet after him. The night was spent by the two ships jockeying for position, neither willing to attack in the dark among the dangers of sand bars and shoals. According to reports, Blackbeard spent the night belowdecks drinking, in full confidence that when daylight came he could summarily obliterate the Virginian upstarts. He succeeded in an attack on Maynard's sloop that resulted in twenty-nine casualties. When the smoke cleared, only Maynard was left on the sloop's deck. Blackbeard boarded it with a boarding party to take Maynard and turn his sloop over to a pirate crew. No sooner had he gotten aboard to take what he thought the sole survivor, than the remaining crewmen of the sloop, who, unhurt, had hidden below, swarmed from the hatches and after a bloody struggle overcame the pirates, Maynard reserving to himself the honor of administering the *coup de grâce* to the almost indestructible Blackbeard, who had suffered twenty sword slashes and as many superficial wounds, by firing a pistol ball through his head, which was then severed and hung on the *Revenge*'s bowsprit as Maynard proudly sailed it home. Aside from his monumental villainy, Blackbeard inevitably became a legend because of a spirited personal life, including polygamy (fourteen wives) and his capacity for hobnobbing with the great, such as Governor Eden, and using them to his own advantage.

A balladeer could not have invented a likelier subject, particularly for a maritime community like Boston where the fact of piracy was an ever-present reality (six had been hanged on Boston Common in 1704) and public interest and concern were widespread and deep.[22] Apparently, the Franklin brothers had scored another commercial success; and if assumed fragments surviving are valid evidence, the ballad was at least somewhat more vigorous and less cloying than its predecessor. In the form of a "Sailor Song," common to the time, the verses had a genuine feel of the sea about them, a youthful bounce, and far more of the spirit and temperament of the young Franklin in them than "Ruth, our fragile daughter" bore witness to:

> Will you hear of a bloody Battle,
>   Lately fought upon the seas,
> It will make your Ears to rattle,
>   And your Admiration cease:

[22] For the *News-Letter*'s account of Blackbeard see Hugh R. Awtry in *Regional Review*, II (June 1939), 11–19. Daniel Defoe, under the pseudonym Charles Johnson, includes Blackbeard in his *General History of the Pyrates* (London, 1724–28).

> Have you heard of Teach the Rover,
> And his Knavery on the Main;
> How of Gold he was a Lover.
> How he loved ill got Gain.[23]

The excursions of his young son into narrative verse left Josiah Franklin not only unimpressed but also somewhat rankled—probably as much by the vanity to which its commercial success was giving rise in Benjamin as by literary deformities that could not fail to cause anguish in a devotee of the Psalms of David. He might also have suffered from a vision of his son ending up his days composing doggerel in the fashion of Uncle Benjamin, and so he took steps to nip his son's career in versifying in the bud. Speaking of his success, Benjamin amended it by writing, "But my Father discourag'd me, by ridiculing my Performances, and telling me Verse-makers were generally Beggars; so I escap'd being a Poet, most probably a very bad one."[24] Had the exercises of Benjamin been genuine attempts at poetry, at expressing his feelings or perceptions or experiences, limited as they may have been at the time, his father's handling of the situation would no doubt have been cruel; but they were inspired by none of these things—they were no more than contrived rhymings to exploit sensational news stories—and his father's forthright reaction was honest, direct, and effective. Moreover, he knew the boy's temperament and fully realized that ridicule would not wound him nor intimations of perpetual poverty be lost on him. And so he put a crisp, final stop to this line of activity and probably not a moment too soon.

* * *

His fledgling literary efforts having been effectively terminated by his father's forthright intervention, Benjamin Franklin resumed his reading "at Night, after Work or before Work began in the Morning; or on Sundays, when I contrived to be in the Printing House alone, evading as much I could the common Attendance on publick Worship, which my Father used to exact of me when I was under his care: And which indeed I still thought a Duty; tho' I could not, as it seemed to me, afford the Time to practise it."[25] Sensing the inadequacy of his formal education, he repaired his fractured experience with arithmetic at Mr. Brownell's school by going through one of Edward Cocker's many arithmetical books. Cocker, a Northamptonshireman like the Franklins, a scrivener and an engraver, taught writing and arithmetic at his own school near St. Paul's in London and was known to his contemporary, Samuel Pepys, as "by his discourse very ingenous and well read in all our English poets."[26] The arithmetic

---

[23] The lines, in *Papers*, I, 7, are from a ballad published in the later eighteenth century in England, "The Downfal of Pyracy," which Edward Everett Hale thought was the Franklin ballad (*New England Magazine*, XXIV, 505–7).

[24] *Autobiography*, 60.

[25] Ibid., 62–63.

[26] H. B. Wheatley, ed., *The Diary of Samuel Pepys* (London, 1893–99), IV, 199–200.

which Franklin studied was unquestionably, of the more than thirty works in calligraphy, writing, and arithmetic attributed to him, the posthumous work called *Cocker's Arithmetick, being a Plain and Easy Method*, which was edited, published, and possibly wholly written by John Hawkins, also a schoolmaster who succeeded Cocker. The textbooks of Cocker were extremely popular, selling widely for well over a generation after his death in 1675. Under the facile instruction of the *Arithmetick*, Franklin mastered the subject without difficulty, and then pressed on to John Seller's *An Epitome of the Art of Navigation* and Samuel Sturmy's *The Mariner's Magazine; or, Sturmy's Mathematical and Practical Arts*.[27] John Seller was hydrographer to the crown, under whose patronage he had a monopoly for thirty years on selling navigational charts and maps. He also wrote and published books on surveying and gunnery, and unquestionably whatever tutelage in mathematics Franklin got from his book was elementary and functional. Samuel Sturmy's book was also a practical guide, designed as a vade mecum for working mariners, and by the time that Franklin perused it in 1720 it had attained the status of a kind of working classic, dating back to 1669, in navigation. By 1720 Franklin had pretty much abandoned his yearning for the sea; and he read these works not for vocational purposes but to become "acquainted with the little Geometry they contained," which apparently was enough, for he added that he "never proceeded far in that Science."[28]

Always ambitious to write with competence, Franklin also studied *An Essay towards a Practical English Grammar, Describing the Genius and Nature of the English Tongue*, by James Greenwood, a schoolteacher at Hackney and later surmaster at St. Paul's School in London. The book was highly praised by such critics as Isaac Watts and was, throughout the eighteenth century and many editions, a standard grammar on both sides of the Atlantic. To Franklin, now in the printing house and taking so readily to the written word, the book was particularly valuable because it dealt not with criticism but with the actual craft of writing that Franklin was determined to master.

Franklin also plowed his way through a volume by a popular food faddist of the late seventeenth century, Thomas Tryon, called *The Way to Health, Long Life and Happiness, or a Discourse of Temperance*, which advocated vegetarianism and included a variety of recipes for dishes without flesh. Tryon was a shepherd in his youth but tired of it by the time that he was eighteen and walked the eighty miles from Cirencester to London, where he apprenticed himself to a hatter. There in his free time he studied astrology and medicine, went through some religious conversions, and was suddenly visited with the conviction that he should drink only water and eat only bread and fruit. After marrying, building a prosperous trade in hats, and establishing a seat in Hackney, he felt compelled

[27] Published in London in 1681 and 1669 respectively.
[28] *Autobiography*, 64.

to instruct the world in his exemplary dietary way of life, which he did in the fifteen publications that issued from his pen between 1682 and 1700. The book Franklin read was actually the second edition (1691) or third edition (1697) of his 1682 book, *Health's Grand Preservative; or the Women's Best Doctor*; and it dealt as much with "the Ill-Consequences of drinking Distilled Spirits and smoaking Tobacco" as it did with vegetables and "the excellency of Herbs." "Tryonism" was taken up, usually with perishable enthusiasm, by hundreds of followers, for whom Tryon constructed a book of rules; but his lasting effect, which reached well into the nineteenth century, consisted less in any body of individual Tryonites than on a few influential leaders, like Joseph Ritson, the nineteenth-century apostle of vegetarianism, and Lewis Gompertz, founder of the Society for the Prevention of Cruelty to Animals, including eating them. Franklin seemed to be motivated more by an instinct to save money than to achieve the blessings catalogued in Tryon's title, for he really wanted money to buy books and hit upon a scheme to convert his conversion to vegetarianism to a fiscal savings system that became his book-buying fund. The significance to him of this accomplishment was considerable since, like all apprentices, he was paid nothing and could not expect to be for nine years. Had his brother been married, however, his whole plan would have collapsed because he would have been expected to eat what was supplied in the household, whether animal or vegetable. As it was, however, James Franklin paid another family to provide meals for himself and his apprentice. And so Benjamin "propos'd to my Brother, that if he would give me Weekly half the Money he paid for my Board I would board myself. He instantly agreed to it. And I presently found that I could save half what he paid me. This was an additional Fund for buying Books: But I had another Advantage in it. My brother and the rest going from the Printing House to their Meals, I remain'd there alone, and dispatching presently my light Repast, (which often was no more than a Bisket or a Slice of Bread, a Handful of Raisins or a Tart from the Pastry Cook's, and a Glass of Water) had the Rest of the Time till their Return, for Study, in which I made the greater Progress from that greater Clearness of Head and quicker Apprehension which usually attends Temperance in Eating and Drinking."[29] His vegetarianism did not survive the five years he was to spend as an apprentice to his brother. His repudiation of it, he said, was due to his observation that fish eat one another and he saw no reason, therefore, that he shouldn't eat fish, too. A more likely cause of his change of heart was that there was no longer any economic consequence of his vegetarianism.

Physically inconsequential as his eating habits seemed to be, their indirect effect on his thinking, through the books he was able to acquire, was deep and lasting. The most fundamental was John Locke's monumental

[29] Ibid., 63.

work, *An Essay Concerning Human Understanding*,[30] first published
nearly thirty years earlier but still the point of departure of deistic thinking and still the bête noire of the orthodox clergy of both the established
and dissenting churches. John Locke was born in 1632, fourteen years before Josiah Franklin, and he died in 1704, almost two years before Benjamin was born. Despite the gap of nearly three quarters of a century in
their times, the lives of Locke and Benjamin Franklin had some odd parallels as they had also dramatic contrasts. Both were by nature compro-
misers, moderates, conciliators. Both were meant by their fathers—Locke's
a village attorney and Franklin's a Boston artisan—for the ministry, but
neither showed any inclination for clerical careers. Both, born into Calvinism, ended up in the Church of England, but neither so much through
any convictions as on the wholly practical grounds that it was less contentious than the constantly bickering dissenting churches and therefore
probably a more promising source of conciliation. Both were gregarious,
Locke happily immersed in his friendships in London and Oates and
Franklin in those of his in London and Passy. Both strongly favored the
intellectual company of women—Locke delighting in the salon of Lady
Masham, daughter of a celebrated Cambridge classicist, and Franklin in
that of Madame Helvétius. Both were impatient to the point of embarrassment and distress with pedantic theological disputes that led nowhere.
Both were, by instinct and by belief, empiricists, who were given to practical experimentation in the natural world—Locke as a physician, and
Franklin as a natural philosopher. Both differentiated between scholarship
and education, each having strong views for example, of the limited use of
the study of Latin to those who were going to spend their lives in practical pursuits but each convinced, too, that a comprehensive education was
essential to personal fulfillment and to effective citizenship. Both spent
time in political and diplomatic posts—Franklin, of course, in roles of historic import but Locke's limited to some months as a secretary in Branden-
burg and fifteen years as adviser and secretary to the First Earl of Shaftesbury, perhaps the most vigorous politician in the reign of Charles II. The
lives of both were, in a very central way, rooted in a deep and commanding spirit of tolerance and dominated by a quest for compromise without

[30] Originally published as *An Essay Concerning Humane Understanding* (London,
1690) by Thomas Basset in Fleet Street. Three subsequent editions appeared before the
author's death in 1704, and he made some significant changes in these. Since his death
there have been hundreds of editions—many of them, unfortunately, severely edited,
largely for reasons of space. There is a complete edition, published originally by the Oxford University Press in 1894, and republished by Dover Publications, New York, in
1959. The work in this edition was perceptively and carefully collated and fully anno-
tated by the late Alexander Campbell Fraser, onetime professor of philosophy at the
University of Edinburgh. Professor Fraser also wrote long biographical, critical, and historical essays on Locke and the work, which appear in whole in the Dover edition.
  For convenience of readers of other editions, the citations for quotations from
Locke's *Essay* are given in book, chapter, and sections rather than in page numbers,
which, of course, vary widely.

defying principle—in Locke's case, demonstrated by his influential pen and, in Franklin's, by his imperturbable diplomacy. Politically, both rejected revolution against legitimate and just authority, but both advocated effective protest against tyranny.

The contrasts between Locke and Franklin were less striking and, in many respects, less significant—dramatic as they may have been on the surface. Locke's bend was really intellectual and academic. His association with Oxford lasted altogether thirty-two years—terminating only when he lost his fellowship at the mandate of Charles II, though he did not much enjoy the curricular formalities of his undergraduate years of participating in what he regarded as the ostentatious display of public disputations. But he delighted in the world of ideas. In fact, his whole philosophic system centers on the reality and fundamental, even basic, role of ideas in the individual human experience, of which, indeed, he regarded the forming of ideas as the beginning: "If it shall be demanded then, *when* a man *begins* to have any ideas, I think the true answer is—*when he first has any sensation.*"[31] Nor did Locke believe that man could live without having ideas even if he chose to: "These simple ideas [i.e., derived from sensation, such as solidity, odor, taste, motion, and space], when offered to the mind, the understanding can no more refuse to have, nor alter when they are imprinted, nor blot them out and make new ones itself, than a mirror can refuse, alter, or obliterate the images or ideas which the objects set before it do therein produce."[32] Franklin was, on the other hand, not at all academic by nature. He loved to be in the midst of worldly and practical affairs, and the roster of the fields of activity in which he occupied himself was enormous: business, legislation, diplomacy, administration, organization, education, experimentation, and, of course, politics on every level from running for assemblyman to constitution making. Locke's political career was limited to his years as adviser to Shaftesbury, and his brief diplomatic career ended when he declined appointment to the first secretariat of the important embassy in Spain. Franklin also lacked the subtlety of Locke's distinctions and the depths of his perceptions. And yet the infectiousness of Locke's thought to Franklin and the congeniality of its expression must be apparent from the relish with which the youth of fifteen read that mammoth, sprawling work of some quarter million words, written but certainly not composed over a period of nearly two decades and assailing concepts and a milieu that had been bred in the boy since his birth. Over the years, Locke spoke to him to a point and with the words he was not to get in the Old South Meetinghouse or at the table of his father.

This was in a way as Locke had intended. He resolved at the beginning

[31] *An Essay Concerning Human Understanding*, Bk. II, Chap. 1, Sec. 23.
[32] Ibid., Sec. 25. A mirror can, of course, distort, but so can the senses and so also can the will of the artist; but Locke had no difficulty with this—his skeptical rationalism's hard core of subjectivism was an essential element in his lifelong battle against all forms of dogmatism.

of the *Essay* to eschew the language of the scholars and so write as to be readily understandable to the average man. And he succeeded. Here was a boy of fifteen—a printer's apprentice in a colonial port town with two years of schooling—taking to the *Essay* with enthusiasm and so absorbing it that the direction of his intellectual development was to be impelled by it and the values that saw him through a long and varied life were to be set by it. The directness of the dedication to Locke's friend and patron, the Earl of Pembroke and Montgomery, president of the Royal Society, could only be reassuring to a youth brought up in an atmosphere strangely ambivalent, as its chief priest Cotton Mather was, in its hospitality to the new in the physical sciences and its rigid resistance to change in theology. Said Locke: "The imputation of Novelty is a terrible charge amongst those who judge of men's heads, as they do of their perukes, by the fashion, and can allow none to be right but the received doctrines. Truth scarce ever yet carried it by vote anywhere at its first appearance: new opinions are always suspected, and usually opposed, without any reason but because they are not already common. But truth, like gold, is not the less so for being newly brought out of the mine."[33] The lack of pretension and any semblance of categorical authority in Locke's preface to his readers must also have been as a refreshing wind from the sea on an August afternoon to a youth that squirmed through the endless homilies of the Puritan preachers: "I have put into thy hands what has been the diversion of some of my idle and heavy hours. If it has the good luck to prove so of any of thine, and thou hast but half so much pleasure in reading as I had in writing it, thou wilt as little think thy money, as I do my pains, ill bestowed.[34] Locke's implicit style—insofar as in a literarily graceless and ill-constructed work there was any at all—of conferring with his readers rather than lecturing them was a captivating feature in the polemics of its time and made the *Essay* the most widely read work up to then written in English philosophy—heady matter as it was for the community of the saints.

But it was the substance of Locke that took seed so deeply in Franklin's youthful awarenesses and was to nurture the enlargement of his thought in religion and science, in politics and education, in ethics and philosophy. Locke begins, of course, with the rejection of any doctrine of innate principles and universal assent, which was totally destructive of the very bedrock of Puritan thought and belief. But Franklin was never primarily negative (he was always in search of the affirmative), and neither was Locke. That aspect of his philosophy insisting that there were limits to the reach of human knowledge was put with such homely positivism as to give encouragement rather than trouble to an artisan's apprentice, particularly in a seaport: "It is of great use to the sailor to know the length of his line, though he cannot with it fathom all the depths of the ocean. It is well he knows that it is long enough to reach the bottom, at such places as are

[33] Ibid., The Epistle Dedicatory.
[34] Ibid., The Epistle to the Reader.

necessary to direct his voyage, and caution him against running upon shoals that may ruin him. Our business here is not to know all things, but those which concern our conduct."[35] The last sentence, which has often been said to be the motto of Locke's entire *Essay*, really put into perspective and, probably equally important, lent respect to the inclination of Franklin's own still groping mind. Whether the soul was salvageable naturally or from baptism or not at all and whether evil was redeemed by faith, grace, or works really did not interest Franklin, who could not believe such matters, after spending his whole childhood listening to their being debated by the ablest Puritan thinkers, of any consequence in the ordinary affairs of life, and in Locke he found confirmation with this drift of his own thinking.

He found more. He found that skepticism, far from being a great evil, could be a great good—probably with some relief, for, despite a certain brashness that he had in his youth, Franklin must have been troubled from time to time, in the Boston of the Mathers, by his doubts, his questionings, his inability simply to accept what he had been taught. Locke showed that out of genuine skepticism grew genuine knowledge and not merely bland assumptions. But his skepticism was wholly lacking in cynicism, primitivism, or negativism. He had a basic faith in the rational order of the world and the universe, and skepticism—extreme and for its own sake—not only did not interest him but repelled him as absurd: "I think it is beyond question, that man has a clear idea of his own being; he knows certainly he exists, and that he is something. He that can doubt, whether he be anything or no, I speak not to; no more than I would argue with pure nothing, or endeavour to convince nonentity, that it were something. If any one intends to be so sceptical, as to deny his own existence (for really no doubt of it is manifestly impossible) let him for me enjoy his beloved happiness of being nothing, until hunger, or some other pain, convince him of the contrary."[36] And if the role of skepticism was the beginning and method of Locke's philosophy, the rule of reason was its end and its triumph: "Reason," Locke concluded, with an eloquence rare in his writing, "is natural revelation, whereby the Eternal Father of light, and Fountain of all knowledge, communicates to mankind that portion of truth which he has laid within the reach of their natural faculties: revelation is natural reason enlarged by a new set of discoveries communicated by God immediately, which reason vouches the truth of, by the testimony and proofs it gives, that they come from God. So that he that takes away reason, to make way for revelation, puts out the light of both, and does much-what the same, as if he would persuade a man to put out his eyes, the better to receive the remote light of an invisible star by a telescope. . . . Reason must be our last judge and guide in everything."[37]

[35] Ibid., Introduction, Sec. 6.
[36] Ibid., Bk. IV, Chap. 10, Sec. 2.
[37] Ibid., Chap. 18, Sec. 10.

Always suspicious of dogma and always distrustful that mystical revelations, unreasoned and unreasonable, should condition man's thinking, Franklin's mind began its maturing with the readings of Locke, and the influence of Locke upon him surfaced over and over again throughout his life, almost with directness in his design for the establishment of the academy that became the University of Pennsylvania and certainly with consistency until the end of his days in his religious thinking.

Franklin's conviction that theological dogma had far less to do with true religion than did conscionable behavior that had its seeds in the skepticism implicit in Locke's writings, found its fuller development and final formulation in the works of Anthony Ashley Cooper, the Third Earl of Shaftesbury the grandson of Locke's patron and friend. Shaftesbury's education as a very young boy was, in fact, overseen by Locke, who chose his governess because of her proficiency in the classical languages, which thus became familiar to Shaftesbury from his childhood. He was further educated at Winchester and by tutors on the Continent. In 1695, when he was twenty-five years old, he was elected to Parliament and showed considerable political skill, but his health was unequal to the demands of a political career; and although when he succeeded to the earldom in 1699, he attended sessions of the House of Lords regularly, he abandoned politics after the accession of Queen Anne in 1702. Wandering from London to the countryside to France to Holland to Naples in search of relief from a chronic asthma, he devoted himself to letters primarily in the fields of philosophy and ethics and became, next to Locke and perhaps in some respects more than he, the outstanding force of the transitional period between the seventeenth and eighteenth centuries, the most influential thinker and writer of England, his influence extending also to the Continent and to America. His major writings were published collectively in a volume with the omnibus title *Characteristicks of Men, Manners, Opinions, and Times*,[38] a work characterized by Alexander Pope in a letter to William Warburton the Bishop of Gloucester, as having "done more harm to revealed religion in England than all the works of infidelity put together."[39] A collection of essays, inquiries, and treatises, most published earlier as individual anonymous volumes, the book contained his reflections and observations on a wide range of subjects, such as enthusiasm, wit and humor, advice to authors and students, virtue, moralists. A liberal Whig in politics, he was despised by the cynical "practical politician" version of apostate Whigs, who claimed that he was "too bookish, because not given to play, nor assiduous at Court; that he was no good companion, because not a rake nor a hard drinker; and that he was no

[38] Two editions were prepared in Shaftesbury's lifetime (London, 1711 and 1714), but he did not live to see the second edition in print.
[39] See C. A. Moore, "Shaftesbury and the Ethical Poets of England 1700–1760," in *Publications of the Modern Language Association*, XXXI (June 1916), 276

man of the world, because not selfish nor open to bribes."[40] In temperament he was gentle, generous, benign, and, despite poor health, courageous and optimistic. In character he was a man of both implicit and explicit goodness, which was recognized and respected by the enemies he made by his political rectitude and the churchmen he aroused by his religious freethinking. Intellectually, he was a Platonist, and to him beauty, affection, integrity, and virtue were all the same thing—all the instrument of man's living his life in harmony with divine design and in realization of his own distinctions. His benevolence and his grace were simultaneously revealed in the incident of his maiden speech in Commons, where a bill assuring counsel to defendants in cases of treason was being debated. The young member was flustered and lost track of the argument; but he impressed the House thoroughly by his apologetic recovery: "If I am so confounded by a first speech that I cannot express my thoughts, what must be the condition of a man pleading for his life without assistance."[41]

With regard to religion, Shaftesbury regarded its whole use and purpose as related not to theological disputations nor to ecclesiastical paraphernalia but to man's conduct and his relationship with his fellows. A deist rather than an atheist, as Franklin was from the time he read Shaftesbury and was to remain all his life, he prized the body of Christian principles and ethics. But he took a very light view of such Christian doctrine, sacred to priestcraft, as mystical revelation, miracles, life after death, and all that assemblage of dogma, occupying the more scholarly clergy of the Church of England and nearly all the Puritan divines of New England their entire lifetimes—matters with which Benjamin Franklin had so little patience. His moral philosophy had both the practical sense that Franklin was seeking in those solitary hours at his brothers' printing house after his scanty meals and the benevolence which, as he matured, he made the cardinal principle of his life. Shaftesbury's comments identifying love with beauty and both with goodness nurtured and strengthened the thoughts planted in Franklin's mind by Locke. The "beauty" Shaftesbury was talking about, he said, "views communities, friendships, relations, duties, and considers by what harmony of particular minds the general harmony is composed and commonweal established. Not satisfied even with public good in one community of men, it frames itself a nobler object, and with enlarged affection seeks the good of mankind. . . . Laws, constitutions, civil and religious rites; whatever civilises or polishes rude mankind; the sciences and arts, philosophy, morals, virtue; the flourishing state of hu-

---

[40] From an account of Shaftesbury by his son, the fourth earl, quoted in Edmund Gosse, *English Literature* (London, 1903), III, 188.

[41] Erroneously attributed by Samuel Johnson in his *Lives of the Poets* to Charles Montagu, Earl of Halifax (1661–1715); Johnson took it from *The Works and Life of the Right Hon. Charles, late Earl of Halifax* (London, 1715). Horace Walpole has it correctly ascribed in his *Royal and Noble Authors*, Park edition (London, 1806), IV, 55.

man affairs, and the perfection of human nature—these are the delight prospects, and this the charm of beauty which attracts it."[42]

This principle of harmony pervaded the writing of Shaftesbury, and its articulation, in terms both of his style and of the examples he evoked, certainly was appealing to the youth in Boston sifting through the clutter of the Bible Commonwealth to find something not only in which he could believe but also by which he could live. Thoughts stirred in him by Locke must have been fortified by such equations as "conscience, or a natural sense of the odiousness of crime and injustice"; that, as from external objects "there necessarily results a beauty or deformity, according to the different measure, arrangement, and disposition of their parts; so, in behaviour and actions, there must be found, of necessity, an apparent difference, according to the regularity and irregularity of the subjects"; and, of the mind, "however false or corrupt it be within itself, it . . . in all disinterested cases must approve in some measure of what is natural and honest, and disapprove what is dishonest and corrupt."[43] And though Franklin was never so sublimely optimistic as Shaftesbury and though what, even at sixteen, he had seen of life in a colonial port outpost could hardly have led him to share Shaftesbury's gentle trust in the inherent goodness of mankind, the humanistic thrust of Shaftesbury's doctrine of virtue and above all his convincing demonstrations that holiness should not be equated with rigid adherence to dogma nor religion with righteousness stayed with Franklin all his life and shaped the humanitarianism toward which Franklin was first moved by the *Bonifacius* of Cotton Mather and the *Essay upon Projects* of Daniel Defoe. Moreover, the language, if possibly not the style, of Shaftesbury reached him. Like Locke, his earliest mentor, who insisted on using words as simple as possible and who dreaded the possibility inadvertently of sinking into the intellectual jargon of his time, Shaftesbury was determined to avoid the locutions of the pedants and the theologians, and his writings abound with short, classically rooted words that were part of the language of all Englishmen and not the distillation of a specialized lexicon. For Franklin, however, Shaftesbury's style, so far as can be judged by the effect that it had on his own, was a different matter. Steeped as he was in aesthetics and fluent as he was in Greek, Latin, Italian, and French, Shaftesbury was inclined toward elegance, flights of overrefinement, and curious bursts of bombast— none of which afflicted Franklin's writing. Yet he was one of the most widely read of all the moral philosophers of his time, in large part because all literate people could clearly understand him, and his influence extended to the whole succession of Enlightenment figures that followed him, including the poets as well as the philosophers and the printer's ap-

---

[42] From "The Moralists," in *Characteristics*, quoted in Gosse, *English Literature*, III, 189.
[43] The examples are from Robert Chambers, ed., *Cyclopedia of English Literature*, I, 669.

prentice in Queen Street, Boston. Though both Locke and Shaftesbury remained churchmen—one gets the impression that Locke did so in the belief that, for all its fallacies, man was better off ethically and socially with the church than without it and Shaftesbury because of a temperamental yearning for the liturgy and an aesthetic satisfaction with the poetry of, for example, the collects—both were essentially deists and were so labeled by their critics. Deism, almost entirely a concept of the late seventeenth and early eighteenth centuries, was as lean a religious belief possible outside of atheism and really had its root less in a priori thought than in reaction to the excesses of Catholicism and High Church practices in the Church of England, on the one hand, and of fanatic Protestantism, particularly Calvinism, on the other. It accepted the idea of the existence of a supreme being responsible for the creation of the universe and the natural laws by which it is governed. That such a being would intervene thereafter in the affairs either of nature or of man was a wholly untenable and even a silly view to the deists, even the soft-spoken Shaftesbury not only rejecting but also ridiculing any such notion. The deists claimed that the newly discovered principles of physics of the time—particularly those of Sir Isaac Newton—supported their view and they could not believe that having constructed such orderly principles any supreme being deserving the designation would intervene at will and suspend, distort, or amend them for the sake of advancing any one or another of the hundreds of faiths, churches, sects, or denominations that claimed exclusive access to the truth through implausible revelations.

This simplistic theology naturally aroused the ire and fears of churchmen and other orthodox religious thinkers, for it dispensed with any need alike of priesthoods and of theologians. The most influential Presbyterian voice in London, Robert Trail, called deists "nothing else but a new court word for Atheist."[44] Edward Stillingfleet, onetime dean of St. Paul's and the Bishop of Worcester, aging and in bad health, launched a battle against the deistic implications of Locke's *Essay Concerning Human Understanding* and lent the weight of his prodigious reputation in three publications, all of them answered by Locke, to put a prompt stop to the spreading of Locke's theories.[45] Even the scientific world, largely through the person of a founder and president of the Royal Society, Robert Boyle, the eminent chemist and physicist whose skepticism brought significant innovations to those disciplines, provided fifty pounds in order to establish at Oxford a series of annual lectures in defense of Christianity against "notorious infidels," in which Boyle lumped together indiscriminately "atheists, theists [including deists], pagans, Jews and Mahommedans" but carefully specified that the lectures "not descend" to discussing differences

---

[44] R. Trail, *Selected Writings* (Edinburgh, 1845), VI, 107.
[45] The pamphlets are in the sixth volume of Richard Bentley, ed., *Life and Works of . . . Edward Stillingfleet* (London, 1710).

The dominant but fast-waning ecclesiastical influence in Benjamin Franklin's Boston was Cotton Mather (1663–1728), son and colleague of Increase. He had a lasting influence on Franklin's social thought. PICTURE COLLECTION, NEW YORK PUBLIC LIBRARY

"The Church of the Mathers," Boston's Second Church, was, for sixty-four years under their charge, the defender of the Puritan faith against the liberal drift of other Boston churches, and for many years it dominated the civil establishment. BOSTONIAN SOCIETY

A continuous force in the affairs of Benjamin Franklin's Boston was the chief justice of Massachusetts, Samuel Sewall (1652–1730), friend and fellow communicant of Josiah Franklin at the Old South Church and defender of "authority," both spiritual and temporal.

As a young boy Benjamin Franklin was intended by his father for an education at Harvard College and a career in the ministry—plans abandoned when he showed little religious inclination. FOGG ART MUSEUM, HARVARD UNIVERSITY

The first public building in Boston, the Town House, built in 1657, housed the first public library in America and was the center of the town's civic life for fifty-four years, until it was destroyed in the great fire of 1711. NEW YORK PUBLIC LIBRARY

The Old State House, still standing, was built in 1712 to replace the Town House and was for the rest of the century the center of the colony's political life. BOSTONIAN SOCIETY

The Province House (1679–1864
across old Marlborough (now Washin,
ton) Street from Franklin's birthplace
was long the handsomest building i
Boston and served as the residence of th
royal governors during Franklin's bo
hood. BOSTONIAN SOCIETY

The first Church of England parish in
Boston was King's Chapel, which stood
next to the Boston (Latin) Grammar
School, where Benjamin Franklin dis-
tinguished himself for a year as a scholar.
Most contributors to James Franklin's
newspaper were associated with King's
Chapel. (In the background is the
beacon that gave Beacon Hill its name.)
BOSTONIAN SOCIETY

Benjamin Franklin bought and read all
the works of John Bunyan (1628-88).
PICTURE COLLECTION, NEW YORK PUBLIC
LIBRARY

The Pilgrim's Progress of John Bunyan was the
first book that Franklin recalled reading, and it
remained a favorite among his books all his life.
RARE BOOK DIVISION, NEW YORK PUBLIC LIBRARY

THE
Pilgrim's Progress
FROM
THIS WORLD,
TO
That which is to come:

Delivered under the Similitude of a

DREAM

Wherein is Discovered,
The manner of his setting out,
His Dangerous Journey; And safe
Arrival at the Desired Countrey.

I have used Similitudes, Hos. 12. 10.

By *John Bunyan.*

Licensed and Entred according to Order.

LONDON,
Printed for *Nath. Ponder* at the *Peacock*
in the *Poultrey* near *Cornhil,* 1678.

Through his *Parallel Lives of the Noble Greeks and Romans*, Plutarch (first century A.D.) made a lasting impression on the young Franklin, who years later regarded his reading Plutarch as "time spent to great Advantage." PICTURE COLLECTION, NEW YORK PUBLIC LIBRARY

Cotton Mather's *Bonifacius*, first published when Franklin was four years old, was widely read for a century and a half as a guide to individual and social improvement under the more familiar title, *Essays to Do Good*. RARE BOOK DIVISION, NEW YORK PUBLIC LIBRARY

BONIFACIUS.

AN ESSAY
Upon the GOOD, that is to be
Devifed and Defigned,
BY THOSE
Who Defire to Anfwer the Great END
of *Life*, and to DO GOOD
While they *Live*.
A BOOK Offered,
Firft, in General, unto all CHRISTIANS,
in a PERSONAL Capacity, or in
a RELATIVE.
Then more Particularly,
Unto MAGISTRATES, unto MINISTERS,
unto PHYSICIANS, unto LAWYERS,
unto SCHOLEMASTERS, unto Wealthy
GENTLEMEN, unto feveral Sorts of
OFFICERS, unto CHURCHES, and
unto all SOCIETIES of a Religious
Character and Intention. With Humble
PROPOSALS, of Unexceptionable
METHODS, to *Do Good* in the World.

Eph. VI. 18 *Knowing that whatfoever Good thing any
man does, the fame fhall he receive of the Lord.*

BOSTON in N. England: Printed by B. Green, for
Samuel Gerrifh at his Shop in Corn Hill. 1710

among Christian believers.[46] The first of the lectures after Boyle's death in 1692 was eight discourses that same year by a protégé and chaplain of Bishop Stillingfleet, Richard Bentley, later the royal librarian at St. James's and chaplain in ordinary to the King. In one of his lectures, Bentley declared, "Some infidels . . . to avoid the odious name of atheists, would shelter and screen themselves under the new name of deists, which is not quite so obnoxious."[47] The last three of Bentley's lectures attempted to use the *Principia* of Newton—still, only five years after their appearance, a subject of intense interest—to prove the orthodox Christian concept of an all-powerful, anthropomorphic, intervening God, and he lashed out against the deists in "taverns and coffee-houses, nay, Westminster Hall and the very churches" who would argue otherwise.[48] Bentley's Oxford lectures were immediately printed individually as tracts, not only in English but in Latin and Dutch, and had an enormous circulation as organized Christendom sought to stem the free thinking of a new and skeptical generation.

Various copies of the Boyle lectures fell into Benjamin Franklin's hands ("when I was scarce 15") very possibly at the instigation of his father, who by this time could clearly see his son's religious heritage slipping away and these lectures as a possible road to its restoration. They had the opposite result: "It happened that they wrought an Effect on me quite contrary to what was intended by them: For the Arguments of the Deists that were quoted to be refuted, appeared to me much stronger than the Refutations. In short I soon became a thorough Deist."[49] The substance of his doubts was further enlarged by a chronic disputer of the Boyle lecturers, a disciple of Locke, Anthony Collins, whom Franklin also read. A graduate of Eton and King's College, Cambridge, and a student of law in the Temple, Collins had an orderly, syllogistic mind, although he lacked the hair-splitting theological scholarship of some of his opponents. One of his books most objectionable to the Boyle lecturers was *Discourse of Freethinking* published in 1713 advocating that if religious belief were based on free inquiry, as it ought to be, orthodoxy would fall of its own dead weight. Bentley published a prompt and punishing reply centered on what he regarded as Collins's lapses in theological discriminations. (In subsequent editions of his book, Collins corrected some of the more egregious—e.g. translating "*idiotis* [i.e., lay] *evangelistes*" as "idiot evangelists.") Collins also took on in published debate another distinguished scholar-divine, the 1704–5 Boyle lecturer, Samuel Clarke, on the question of the natural immortality of the soul. Clarke, a metaphysician, was actually a liberal theologian, whose speculative rationalism was regarded by

---

[46] Published in the fifth volume of Robert Boyle, *Works* (London, 1744).
[47] Boyle Lecture 6, in *Works* (London, 1836–38).
[48] Lectures 7, 8, 9, ibid.
[49] *Autobiography*, 113–14.

some of his reverend brethren as itself but a step removed from deism. (When he was proposed by Queen Anne for the Canterbury see, she was told by the Bishop of London that he was the most learned and honest of men but he lacked one qualification: he was not a Christian.) The Collins-Clarke controversy resulted in four tracts by Collins against the idea of natural superiority.[50] In addition to these, to which Franklin could have had access, Collins had written *An Essay Concerning the Use of Reason* (1707), in some respects a preface, distinguishing between what is above reason and what is contrary to it, to the *Discourse on Freethinking*, and this, too, may have fallen into Franklin's eager hands.

Though Franklin lacked the intellectual depth and persistence of Locke, the somewhat innocent optimism of Shaftesbury, and the head-on cerebral attack of Collins, much of the thinking of each rubbed off on him ineradicably. Though he went through a brief period of extreme ethical nihilism—". . . Vice and Virtue were empty Distinctions . . ."[51]—which was very soon corrected—"I grew convinc'd that *Truth, Sincerity and Integrity* in Dealings between Man and Man, were of the utmost Importance to the Felicity of Life . . ."[52]—the basic tenets of Franklin's deistic belief were at this period formed, with but few later modifications, for life.

With the certainty of youth compounding the zeal of the neophyte, Franklin set out to convert his best friend, "another Bookish Lad in the Town, John Collins by Name with whom I was intimately acquainted. We sometimes disputed, and very fond we were of Argument, and very desirous of confuting one another."[53]

During this period, Franklin was reading the most ubiquitous and enduring work on logic of the time, one of two books in the *Courant's* library that emanated from the French thinkers resident in the mid-seventeenth century at the Cistercian abbey in the Yvette valley near Paris known as Port Royal. The two books were, in their English translations, *Logic: or the Art of Thinking* and *Rhetoric: or the Art of Speaking*, both popularly known by their subtitles alone.

Though he may well have read the second of these (he both practiced and preached the rubrics of good, classical writing—simplicity, clarity, and order—laid down by its author, Bernard Lamy,) Franklin mentions only the first as having been among those he read at the printing house. *Logic: or the Art of Thinking* was the joint production, in the early 1660s, of two eminent French lay theologians, Antoine Arnauld and Pierre Nicole. Arnauld was also a gifted mathematician and a lawyer, and Nicole a skilled literary craftsman. The two were thorns in the sides of both the Roman Church, particularly the Jesuits, and the Calvinists. They lived in uneasy

---

[50] Texts are extant, with the answers of Clarke, in the latter's *Works* (London, 1738), III. Clarke's Boyle lectures are in Vol. II.

[51] *Autobiography*, 114.

[52] Ibid.

[53] Ibid., 59.

residence at the semideserted abbey, not daring for long stretches of time to venture into Paris for fear of harassment because of their unorthodox views, before finally being exiled to Brussels. Philosophically, the Port Royal authors could have accomplished little more for Benjamin Franklin than confirm his opinion that theological polemics were largely a matter of straining at gnats. Arnauld and Nicole were the chief expositors of the doctrines of the Dutch Catholic reformer, the Bishop of Ypres, Cornelius Jansen, whose disdain for the Jesuits was almost matched by his contempt for the Presbyterians and whose one hero was St. Augustine, an exegesis of whose theology constituted his major works and provided the Port Royal writers the substance of their case that theology had little to do with religion, that the Church of Rome was in dire need of reform, and that Calvinism was no salvation, however closely some Jansenist principles seem to coincide with Calvinist doctrine. There was a curious and, as it eventuated, an unresolved ambivalence about Jansenism centering on the conflict that it saw but did not really recognize between the institutional authority of the Church and the individual conscience of the believer. Antoine Arnauld came from a long and learned line of French lawyers, and his exposition of Jansenism in his book *De la fréquente Communion*, published in 1643, made of it a cause célèbre in France. He sought to avoid, through legal tactics and stately syllogisms, any real confrontation of the accusation by Pope Innocent X that Jansenism was heretical due to its Calvinistic leaning toward predestination. Having gone in hiding after the storm broke with the papal declaration, Arnauld set himself to the task of composing tightly written but less closely reasoned pamphlets in defense of Jansenism and attacking the Jesuits. Nicole was the principal editor of the Jansenist apologia. The weakness of their case notwithstanding, the two men developed some very sound principles for building and advancing an argument.

These principles, the substance of *Logic: or the Art of Thinking*, were almost certainly the only aspect of a century-old theological dispute that interested the young Franklin, whose own religious views were by then quite fully formed and forever resistant to dogmatic disputes. But since he never suffered much from a sense of tentativeness or insecurity about the validity of his religious views, he was much more concerned with an ability to express his convictions and win a hearing for them than he was in probing and revising them. For this purpose, he unquestionably turned to Arnauld and Nicole with great hopes.

To an extent his expectations were well placed. Logic, a methodology peculiarly congenial to Franklin's temperament, had gone through a sometimes lean period of transition during the century before Franklin was born. The old scholasticism that had dominated logic for over three centuries had run its course, and the humanists were proving far more responsive to the realities of man's position and outlook. A new system of logic was developing on the Continent and was to influence English thought, as

Pierre de la Rarnée's *Dialecticae of 1556,* for example, served as the prototype, in fact the original, of Milton's treatise on logic over a century later.
The "Port Royal Logic," as it came to be known, of Arnauld and Nicole,
first published in 1662, was the next major French influence on English
thinkers and writers, and it was altogether a healthful one. A fundamental
element in the Port Royal philosophy was careful and precise definition.
Arnauld and Nicole went to great pains to emphasize the critical role that
definition, or the lack of it, played in the construction of faulty syllogisms,
in the confusion of thought, and in the evasion or even outright contradiction of logic. From this it followed that excess verbiage, linguistic trap-
pings, and loose expansions served, despite the surface temptation to use
them as diversionary tactics in debate, only to confuse and weaken one's
basic argument. The Port Royal prescription made for discipline in arguing, but, as practiced by Arnauld, it also made for a certain exasperation in
opponents, because it tended to be so forbidding in its precision and
thoroughness as to fence in an opponent and leave him no place to go,
however valid his contention. It was a logic untempered by any imaginative insight; and though it unquestionably helped Franklin to use words
with caution and to state a proposition with care, it did little to make him
an agreeable and persuasive conversationalist.

Franklin discovered that he could get nowhere in his debates with
Collins, whom he described as naturally more fluent, by the kind of argumentative rhetoric that he derived from his reading of Arnauld and
Nicole. Entirely by chance, he came across the more persuasive and less assertive method of Socrates in James Greenwood's *Essay towards a Practical English Grammar,* which included an example of Socratic dialogue
among its appendices. He determined to find out more about Socrates and
got a copy of Xenophon's *Memorabilia Socratis,* probably in the 1715 edition translated by Edward Bysshe, who rendered the title *The Memorable
Things of Socrates,* as Franklin has it in his *Autobiography.* Though for
the fullest, richest impression of Socrates, it was perhaps unfortunate that
Franklin did not first encounter him in the pages of Plato (who might
also have tempered some of the youth's coarser generalizations), and
though Xenophon, a professional soldier, was not as skilled or as experienced a student of rhetoric as Plato (he probably, for that reason, reported Socrates' dialogues with less of Xenophon in them [even though
much more sketchily] than Plato did of Plato in them), the simple directness of Xenophon's reporting of Socrates provided Franklin with a superbly useful tool for improving dramatically his handling of his end of a
discussion. *Memorable Things* contains, in four short "Books," examples
of over fifty dialogues—most of them rendered as brief and to the point as
Xenophon could manage. Clearly, they could make quite vivid to Franklin,
already eager from Greenwood to learn the secret of the Socratic method,
the ageless effectiveness of the salient question as contrasted to the unilat-
eral assertion—the effectiveness that so troubled the prosecutors of Soc-

rates. "But, you know, Socrates," Charicles, one of the "Thirty Tyrants," complained, "most of the questions you like to ask are ones to which you know the answers. That is the kind you must stop asking."[54] And they were the kind that persuaded the young Franklin that he could press his views more convincingly and also more amiably if he adopted the Socratic rather than the Matherian method of promulgating them. Xenophon's examples, somewhat elemental as contrasted to Plato's exposition and elaboration of Socrates' views, were persuasive and wholly comprehensible with the largely self-instructed youth who read them: ". . . Antiphon asked him how it was that he expected to make others politicians when he himself did not take part in politics, if indeed he was capable of doing so. Socrates retorted: 'Which would be the more effective way for me to take part in politics—by doing so alone, or by making it my business to see that as many persons as possible are capable of taking part in them?' "[55] It impressed Franklin deeply that Socrates had won the argument without making a single assertion, as did also Socrates' genius for inculcating among men what seemed to Franklin, all his life, as the highest principles (*Poor Richard* is full of them) governing conduct without resorting to the kind of sermonizing and voicing of threats of damnation that emanated so constantly, with rare exceptions, from the Puritan pulpits:

"Don't you think [Socrates asked Euthydemus, a young Athenian in whom he wanted to promote a guardedness against self-indulgence without lecturing him] that self-indulgence debars people from wisdom, which is the greatest good, and drives them into the opposite state? Don't you think that, by dragging them off in pursuit of pleasure, it prevents them from studying and apprehending their real interests; and that it often confuses their perception of good and bad alternatives and makes them choose the worse instead of the better?"

"That does happen," said he.

"And who, Euthydemus, can we say has less concern with self-discipline than the self-indulgent man? because surely the effects of self-discipline and of self-indulgence are directly opposed?"

"I admit that, too," he said.

"Do you think that anything is more likely to hinder one from devoting oneself to the proper objects than self-indulgence."

"No, I don't."

"Do you think there is anything worse for a man than that which makes him choose what is bad for him instead of what is good, and persuades him to cultivate the former and disregard the latter, and compels him to behave in the opposite way to that which is adopted by sensible people?"

"No, nothing," said he.

"Isn't it likely that self-discipline brings results, for those who practice it, which are opposite to those of self-indulgence?"

"Certainly."

[54] Xenophon, *Memoirs of Socrates*, trans. Hugh Tredinnick (London, 1970), 40–41.
[55] Ibid., 63.

"Isn't it also likely the cause of these opposite results is supremely good?"

"Yes, it is," he said.

"So it looks as if self-discipline were the best thing for a man."

"Very likely, Socrates," he said.[56]

The effect upon Franklin of his discovery of Socrates was swift and compelling, modifying his attitude, which was on its way to becoming obnoxiously assertive, as well as reforming his rhetoric. Of the Socratic method, he recalled, "I was charm'd with it, adopted it, dropt my abrupt Contradiction, and positive Argumentation, and put on the humbler Enquirer and Doubter. And being then, from reading Shaftsbury [sic] and Collins, become a real Doubter in many Points of our Religious Doctrine, I found this Method safest for my self and very embarassing to those against whom I used it, therefore I took a Delight in it, practis'd it continually and grew very artful and expert in drawing People even of superior Knowledge into Concessions the Consequences of which they did not foresee, entangling them in Difficulties out of which they could not extricate themselves, and so obtaining Victories that neither my self nor my Cause always deserved."[57]

The youthful triumphs were, no doubt, ephemeral, but the exercises were of lasting value; and though as time went on Franklin abandoned the leading questions, the temper of Socrates, his total lack of belligerence, his moderation of utterance, his patient trust in the inevitable evoking of the truth ("Very likely, Socrates")—all these stayed with Franklin through the nearly seven decades, of counseling his friends, representing his countrymen, and conciliating his enemies, that were left to him.

* * *

The fortunes of James Franklin's struggling printing house took an upward turn in 1719, when a degree of financial predictability was achieved through his employment by the publisher of a new weekly newspaper to print the journal. Called *The Boston Gazette*, it was the third newspaper to be established in the American colonies, the first *Publick Occurrences both Foreign and Domestick*, having been launched twenty-nine years earlier by Benjamin Harris, a Boston bookseller of volatile and venturesome temperament, and the second, *The Boston News-Letter*, having been started by John Campbell, a Scottish bookseller, who was also postmaster of Boston. (The fourth American newspaper was the *American Weekly Mercury*, which began publication in Philadelphia by Andrew Bradford, one day, December 22, 1719, after *The Boston Gazette* began publication.)

The atmosphere for publishing a newspaper in Boston in 1719 was considerably less oppressive—though far from wholly salubrious—than it was when Benjamin Harris began his short-lived *Publick Occurrences* in 1690.

[56] Ibid., 212–13.
[57] *Autobiography*, 64–65.

Harris, a refugee from chronic arrests in London for his aggressive journalism, arrived in Boston in 1686, three years after Josiah Franklin's emigration, in search of a more hospitable climate for the kind of publications which had, in the London of the Restoration, landed him first in the pillory and then in King's Bench Prison. He suffered from an overweening phobia of papism, having been an alumnus of Titus Oates's fraudulent plot to "expose" an alleged conspiracy of the Jesuits to assassinate Charles II (at the same time burning London and massacring its inhabitants), in order to assure the succession of James Stuart, the Catholic Duke of York, to the throne and the consequent restoration of England to Rome. His London paper, *The Protestant* (Domestick) *Intelligence*, was suppressed in 1681, but the accession of James, upon the death of Charles in 1685, so fired him with alarm that he published an inflammatory exposition called *English Liberties*, which was promptly seized by the authorities and induced him to follow the counsel of John Dunton to leave England for Boston. He brought with him a stock of books and opened a bookshop at the Town Pump near the Old South Meetinghouse. He also brought with him a fiery disposition and a mercurial temperament. "To speak the truth," wrote his friend, Dunton, "Mr. Benj. Harris has had many good thoughts, though he has wanted the art of impressing them: and could he fix his mercury a little, and not be so volatile, he would do well enough."[58] He immediately resumed his publishing activities, but in a much mellower mood, hiring Samuel Green to print "An Almanack for the Year of Our Lord MDCLXXXVII. By John Tulley," which turned out to be a highly successful venture and brought many of the customers of Boston's other seven booksellers to his shop, including Judge Sewall and the Mathers. By 1690 he was prospering, having made two return visits to England to replenish his stock, published a widely sold copy of the old Massachusetts Bay Charter of 1628 and expanded his bookshop into a convivial spot called the London Coffee House, where in addition to books and his own publications he dispensed coffee, tea, and chocolate. As soon as a Protestant was restored to the British throne on the deposing of James II, Harris sped up his publishing activities, producing no fewer than ten titles, including two by the prolific Cotton Mather, in the year 1690 alone. During that summer, Harris was visited with the idea of publishing a newsletter, derived no doubt from the newsletters that Henry Muddiman had issued in London, under various titles, since the 1660s to supplement the dull routine proclamations published in the official *London Gazette*. Harris was gifted with a sprightly, concise style, and he recognized what was newsworthy and what was merely filler.

This first of American newspapers was published as a four-page pamphlet, with three of its 6″ by 9½″ pages printed in double columns and the fourth left blank. Most of the first column of the first page was taken

[58] John Dunton to George Larkin, cited in George Emory Littlefield, *Early Boston Booksellers* (Boston, 1900), 148.

up by a clear and forthright statement of the publisher's intention: ". . . that the Countrey shall be furnished once a moneth (or if any Glut of Occurrences happen, oftener,) with an Account of such considerable things as have arrived unto our Notice . . . That Memorable Occurrents of Divine Providence may not be neglected . . . that some thing may be done towards the Curing . . . of that spirit of Lying, which prevails among us. . . ."[59] Despite these high motives, Benjamin Harris's newspaper lasted exactly one issue and four days before it was suppressed and any future issues strictly forbidden by the governor and Council on the grounds, first, that it was printed "Without the least Privity or Countenance of Authority," and, second, that it "contained Reflections of a very high nature."[60] The latter charge was directed at the longest of Harris's ten news stories, concerning the Western Expedition in the French and Indian War against Canada, during which Indian allies of the British were reported to have butchered some of their French captives. Harris was not above injecting his editorial opinion in the body of his news reports, and he concluded, "And if Almighty God will have *Canada* to be subdued without the assistance of those miserable Salvages, in whom we have too much confided, we shall be glad, that there will be no sacrifice offered up to the Devil, upon this occasion. . . ." The suggestion that the government of Massachusetts could be in league with the devil was, of course, preposterous—even though the populace had thrown out of office and imprisoned the governor, Sir Edmund Andros, "the grand author of our miseries," not seventeen months earlier and there was only a provisional government and no governor at all until Sir William Phips was appointed to the office in 1692. Harris, who did not persist in his attempt to publish a newspaper, was appointed by Phips as official printer of the acts and laws of the province, and with characteristic enterprise returned to the relatively safe London of William and Mary in 1695 and resumed the cantankerous career that he had abandoned nine years earlier, founding the *London Post* and engaging in public quarrels even with such old friends as Dunton.

Boston and the American colonies were without any newspaper at all for fourteen years, until 1704 when the canny Scot, John Campbell, started publication of *The Boston News-Letter*. Unlike Harris's spirited *Publick Occurrences*, the *News-Letter* was "Published by Authority" and was a cautious business enterprise rather than a journal with a sense of mission. Campbell was over forty years old when he arrived in Boston in the mid-1690s and opened a bookshop. His brother, Duncan, had preceded him by nearly a decade and by 1693 already had a prosperous book-

[59] The only known surviving copy of *Publick Occurrences* is in the Public Record Office in London. Facsimiles and reprints of the text appear in part in several histories of American journalism, and the entire text is in Frederic Hudson, *Journalism in the United States from 1690 to 1872* (New York, 1873), 44–48.
[60] Littlefield, *Early Boston Booksellers*, 153.

selling and publishing business. John Dunton described him as "a brisk young fellow that dresses a-la-mode, and sets himself off to the best advantage; and yet thrives apace."[61] He was appointed postmaster in 1693 and with Andrew Hamilton started a mail service as a private monopoly running from Portsmouth, New Hampshire, to Jamestown, Virginia. Campbell used his franking privilege to distribute his own books, and he used all the postmasters along the route to send him news items about their towns and regions. When John Campbell succeeded his brother as postmaster in 1702, he decided the news items were salable, he started sending, for a price, handwritten summaries of the news he collected to various public men and merchants who could use them to advantage. In 1704 he got the idea of printing the items, using his postal franking privilege to mail it and his status as postmaster to proclaim it as "Published by Authority." Modeled on the innocuous *London Gazette*, the *News-Letter* was a uniformly dull repository of such things as months-old excerpts from British papers, shipping news, reports of sermons, governmental proclamations, appointments, and court judgments. Occasionally, it verged on the sensational, with stories of suicides, crimes, and fake kidnapings; but when it did so, Campbell with innate caution pointed out the moral of the story so explicitly that he ran no risk of government censure and, as a matter of fact, was able to solicit and get a government subsidy. Accurate, reliable, stolidly reporting what he regarded as useful information, Campbell could never capture the public attention and seldom fanned any real interest in what was going on either in the world or in the colonies; his paper was a kind of holding operation, and he frequently published complaints about the difficulty he had keeping it financially afloat, being unable, he said, to dispose of three hundred copies per impression as late as 1719 when he was ousted from the postmastership but still kept his paper alive.

So firmly had John Campbell associated the publication of the *News-Letter* with the postmastership that his successor to the office, William Brooker, assumed that proprietorship of the newspaper went with the job. On finding out otherwise, as Campbell took his paper with him when he left the office, Brooker started his own paper and, after its London model, called it *The Boston Gazette*. Following the precedent set by Campbell, he proclaimed, in an imprimatur at the masthead, "Published by Authority." He engaged James Franklin, who was at the time the poorest and probably, therefore, the cheapest and most available of Boston's four printers, to print it for him. Franklin was neither publisher nor editor of the new paper, being employed solely as its printer; but he turned out an attractive sheet, visually more inviting than the *News-Letter*, bearing on the left of the masthead a picture of a square-rigger in full sail and, on the right, a postal rider on a galloping horse, blowing his horn to announce his arrival as he approached a village. Compared to seeing the sedate *News-*

[61] Ibid., 133.

Letter, the immediate reaction of the reader to the *Gazette* was an impression of speed, importance, and urgency. Brooker was also a better journalist than Campbell, the dour, persevering Scot who stoutly maintained that no news should be wasted, however old and delayed it was, and who at one time was more than a year behind on the news he was dispensing. The *Gazette*, on the other hand, remained as current as the pace of land and sea communications made possible, and, unlike Campbell, refused to hold up fresh news in order first to get unused stale news out of the way. Brooker also introduced a competitive spirit into newspaper publishing, making for livelier reading and creating a personality for his paper. Campbell, who had been postmaster for fifteen years, was so bitter at being removed from office that he refused to patronize the postal service by sending the *News-Letter* through the mails. In the first issue of his *Gazette*, Brooker made it clear to his readers that Campbell had been "removed" from his office, which so infuriated Campbell that the next issue of the *News-Letter* referred directly and in unflattering terms to the new rival paper. "I pity the readers of the new paper," Campbell wrote. "Its sheets smell stronger of beer than of midnight oil. It is not reading fit for people."[62] In his next issue, Brooker replied, "Mr. Campbell seems somewhat displeased that the author says he was *removed* from being Postmaster. I . . . think I could not have given his being *turned out* a softer epithet."[63] Public interest in the personal dispute, however, was short-lived, and the *Gazette* became pretty much the same sort of passive chronicler of events as the *News-Letter* had been for fifteen years. Within thirty weeks of his appointment, Brooker was out of office, and Philip Musgrave succeeded him. True to his conviction that the paper should be a perquisite of the postmaster, Brooker let Musgrave have the *Gazette*, the printing of which the new proprietor promptly took away from James Franklin and gave to Samuel Kneeland, James Franklin's young contemporary and a member of the Green printing dynasty in Boston dating back to 1650.

With remarkable enterprise and confidence for a young man of twenty-four, with little resources, and with no important connections, James Franklin decided to print a newspaper of his own. On August 7, 1721, he launched *The New-England Courant*, the first really independent newspaper in the American colonies and the first since Benjamin Harris's ill-fated, one-issue *Publick Occurrences* not to be "published by authority," i.e., by a postmaster. It was the most important thing that he was to do in his short life, and it was to have a most significant effect upon the life and achievements of his brother, Benjamin.

62 *Boston News-Letter*, January 4, 1720.
63 *Boston Gazette*, January 11, 1720.

XI

The Controversy

... what they want in Knowledge they endeavour to supply by Obstinacy, Noise and
Fury: and when you press hard upon them, instead of Argument, they fly to personal Re-
proaches and Invectives.

—Benjamin Franklin[1]

When the first issue of James Franklin's *New-England Courant* appeared,
it marked the real beginning of the long battle for a free press in America,
for its two rivals, "published by authority," were mere chroniclers of old,
stale, and usually remote items that had nothing to do with the events, issues, and personalities that were shaping the character and destiny of the
town of Boston. Perhaps the most underestimated figure in the history of
American journalism so far as his pioneering significance goes, James
Franklin was to become also its first martyr. Ironically, the impact and
meaning of his brief but striking career as the first practitioner of a free
press in the colonies who flew directly and knowingly into the face of the
authorities (Benjamin Harris had simply folded up at the first rebuke)
have unquestionably been diminished by the dazzling glare of the subsequent career of his young brother, who almost literally went to school at
this brother's newspaper and certainly there began his professional life as
printer, as writer, as editor and publisher. Indeed, although he was to rally
with noble loyalty and firm sense of principle to his brother's support
when trouble came, Benjamin seems not to have fully appreciated his
brother's enterprise, his courage, and his spirit of independence; and in
general a great disservice was done, not so much to James Franklin, as to
history, by the paltriness of Benjamin's account of James in the *Autobiography*—however understandable this might be from the incisiveness
of his recollection of his brother's less attractive qualties, his irascibility,
his slave-master attitude, and his generally grudging nature. But if nothing
more were known of James Franklin (and there is little else to know, for
he died at thirty-eight in Newport, Rhode Island, where he moved his

---

[1] "On Conversation," *Pennsylvania Gazette*, October 15, 1730, in *Papers*, I, 180.

printing house in 1726) than his launching, publishing, and sticking with the *Courant* in spite of the most vigorous opposition, his place in the development of the free press in America would remain secure.

James Franklin's total disregard for the sanctity of the Boston establishment was apparent to the point of scintillation on the first page of the first issue of the *Courant*. It was the opening shot in the *Courant*'s first battle in a five-year war to survive and to make its point in a society whose leadership was wholly hostile to freedom of the press. Unfortunately, the opening battle was, though for the right principle, in the wrong cause. It declared war on Cotton Mather, who, though constantly complaining—and rightly enough—of his diminishing influence, was still the most influential single individual not only in the town but probably also in the province, in a context which was easily Mather's finest hour and the largest genuine triumph of a career that was uniquely agonized and agonizing even in an often dolorous society.

The occasion was the most devastating epidemic of the smallpox that Boston had seen in a series of epidemics that had darkened its history from the very beginning, when one of the ships in John Winthrop's fleet carried the dreaded affliction from England, with one child dying of it en route. The history of smallpox was a westward-moving phenomenon from its introduction into European life. Throughout history man's military ventures have brought in their wake scourges of disease, and smallpox was no exception. The lethal contagion, first recorded in China in the third century, was unknown in northern Europe until the Crusades, when the liberators of the Holy Land brought it home with them as one symbol of their achievement, and in southern Europe until the spread of Islam by the sword introduced it into every country that the sprawling Moslem crescent engulfed. By the seventeenth century, it was an omnipresent dread in Britain—the "pox" becoming such a commonplace that it was by far the most rampant cause of death and left those who survived pock-marked for life. Four out of every five Englishmen had smallpox. Millions died of it—children, adolescents, and adults. Scores of millions were blinded by it. Scores more were crippled or left with residuary chronic ailments that conditioned the rest of their lives. The fortunate escaped with pock pits all over their faces. The Spanish conquistadores, to whose forebears the disease was brought by the Moslems, brought it in turn to the New World in 1520 when an African slave in Pánfilo de Narváez's expedition to Mexico was seized with it, having contracted it in Spain, and landed with it in full, communicable flowering in Mexico. The disease spread more rapidly than the efficacy of Spanish arms under Cortez, making the military conquest of one population center after another unnecessary, for within six months half of their inhabitants had died and the others fled to the hill in wondering anguish.

The earliest known epidemic (as compared to a sprinkling of cases here and there) in New England occurred in the Connecticut River valley in 1634, when some Dutch ships ventured upstream from Long Island Sound, carrying aboard infected crewmen. Soon after the English settled in the Massachusetts Bay Colony, however, the disease began to recur, with devastating regularity, in epidemic proportions. In 1644, in 1649, in 1665–66, in 1677–78, and in 1689–90, there were major outbreaks, which, John Josselyn wrote, "hath carried away abundance of their children."[2] It also carried away abundance of their "enemies," bacteriological warfare having been employed against troublesome Indians by giving them blankets, towels, and handkerchiefs that had been used by smallpox victims as a means "that can serve to extirpate this execrable race,"[3] and in some Indian communities the mortality neared 100 per cent because the proportion of nonimmunes was so high as compared to the white communities. The 1677–78 epidemic in Boston was of fearful proportions, taking the lives of as many as thirty people of a population of less than six thousand in a single day; Cotton Mather, then a young cleric, claimed to have foreseen and prophesied the tragedy a year earlier when he declared, in language so general that it could have covered any disastrous occurrence, that "very soon God will lift up his hand against Boston,"[4] and he wrote ruefully, as he saw his prophecy fulfilled, "Never was it such a time in Boston . . . burying-places never filled so fast . . . corpses following each other close at their heels. . . . Above 340 have died of the Small Pox in Boston since it first assaulted the place. To attempt a Bill of Mortality, and number the very spires of grass in a Burying Place seem to have a parity of difficulty and in accomplishment."[5] Before it was over at the end of 1678, Mather's estimate of the deaths turned out to be moderate, for some seven hundred—about 12 per cent of the population—were dead of the disease. Despite the conviction of the clergy that smallpox was a visitation from the Almighty, the governor and Council were convinced that man could intervene and at least minimize its devastating effects: God also visited rain upon the townspeople, but they took shelter; fires but they extinguished them; and cold but they lit fires. And so quarantine was first introduced, it being the general experience that most epidemics started with infections borne by ship from Europe; in July 1677 an incoming ship, of which it was known "that God's Afflicting hand has been upon them by the Infectious Disease of the Small Pox," was ordered not to dock but to lie in quarantine at Lovell's Island in the Outer Harbor "for the prevention of the further spreading of that Infectious & noysome Disease

[2] John Josselyn, *An Account of Two Voyages to New-England*, Massachusetts Historical Society, *Collections*, 3rd Ser., III, 333.

[3] Though the practice may not have been widespread, cases are documented in W. E. and A. E. Stearn, *The Effect of Smallpox on the Destiny of the American Indian* (New York, 1945).

[4] O. E. Winslow, *A Destroying Angel* (Boston, 1974), 26.

[5] Cotton Mather to John Cotton, November 1678, in Massachusetts Historical Society, *Collections*, 4th Ser., VIII, 383.

amongst the Inhabitants."[6] Because the disease was known to be infectious without direct contact, other measures were taken to control its spread. Households with diseased occupants were not allowed to hang out laundry in their yards. Victims were prohibited from leaving their houses until a fixed quarantine time had passed. Infected articles of clothing and bedding had to be deposited in supervised centers. Watches of a dozen men each were appointed to enforce regulations. And the Reverend Thomas Thacher, the first pastor of the South Church, who was also a physician, published a broadside called "A Brief Rule to Guide the Common People of New-England How to order themselves and theirs in the Small Pocks, or Measels." Thacher, who practiced medicine in Boston while pastor of the Old South, kept himself well informed on medical developments in England and took the substance of his publication from the pioneering English clinician Thomas Sydenham, whose innovations in the diagnosis and treatment of the most prevalent ailments in England revolutionized the practice of medicine by such empirical steps as letting fresh air into the rooms of the sick instead of sealing them and throwing out the more impausible lore of the pharmacopeia of his time. The text was widely distributed and made as simple for the layman to understand as possible. Since there was neither a preventive nor a cure for the disease, all that Thacher could offer were measures to control its progress, relieve its symptoms, and minimize its effects. His major point was to help the body's self-healing properties to have a chance, and the steps he advocated were really for the dietary and practical management of the disease rather than for any claimed cure. His directions simply told the reader the signs of the progress of the disease—signs that any lay person could readily recognize—and precise measures to take to give the patient the best prospect of recovery. He regarded the control of the disease as the central objective and catalogued specifically the courses to be avoided—heightening the fever "by too much clothes, too hot a room, hot *Cordials*," or attempts to eradicate the fever and its natural curative powers "by preposterous cooling . . . by *blood letting, Clysters* [enemas], V*omits, purges* or *cooling* medicines." But Thacher was himself too skilled and experienced a physician to advocate self-treatment of so calamitous a disease: ". . . the season of the year, Age of the sick, and their manner of life here require a discreet and different Consideration, requiring the Counsel of an expert Physitian." He sensibly urged keeping the patient as normally cool as possible and in winter as normally warm and urged a moderate diet of "water-gruel, water-pottage, and other things having no manifest hot quality, easy of digestion, boild Apples, and milk sometimes for change, but the coldness taken off." But he was forthright about the terminal signs when all efforts had failed: "if the Urine be bloody, or black, or the *Ordure* of that Colour; or if pure blood be cast out by the Belly or Gumms: These signs are for the most part deadly."

[6] In Massachusetts Archives, LXI, 155.

Aware of the sensibilities of the physicians and the resentful attitude of some at ministers intruding upon their field, Thacher—even though he was thoroughly trained as a physician himself and had practiced medicine in Weymouth as well as in Boston—was careful to conclude his publication (the first medical paper published in the colonies) by a disclaimer addressed to the "Candid Reader" but clearly meant for the "Learned Physitians," among whom he was careful to exclude himself: *"These things have I written Candid Reader not to inform the Learned Physitian that hath much more cause to understand what pertains to this disease than I, but to give some light to those that hath not such advantages, leaving the difficulty of this disease to the Physitians Art, wisdom, and Faithfulness: for the right managing of them in the whole Course of the disease tends both to the Patients safety, and the Physitians desired Success in his Administrations: For in vain is the Physitians Art imployed, if they are not under a Regular Regiment. I am, though no Physitian, yet a well wisher to the sick. . . ."*[7]

For forty-four years, through three major epidemics and countless outbreaks of lesser extent, Thacher's broadside, published also as a pamphlet, remained the basic therapeutic literature on the subject for both the layman and the physician. In the epidemic of 1702, twenty-four years after Thacher's death, his treatment was still heavily relied upon as the disease spread through the hot summer, into the autumn, and reached its peak in the early winter. In July, Cotton Mather wrote that he kept a vigil "with respect unto the Condition of the Town, where the Small-pox begins to spread."[8] In October, he wrote, "The dreadful Disease, which is raging in the Neighborhood, is now gott into my poor Family."[9] Three of his four children and his housemaid contracted the disease in rapid succession, while Mather's thirty-two-year-old wife, Abigail, lay dying of tuberculosis. Mather took the radical and sacrificial step of converting his library into a hospital: "My Study, is tho' a large, yett a warm chamber, (the hangings whereof, are Boxes with between two and three thousand Books in them;) and we are so circumstanced, that my House, tho' none of the smallest, cannot afford a safe Hospital now for my sick Folks, any where so well as there. So I resigned my Study, for an Hospital to my little Folks, that are falling sick of a loathsome Disease."[10] And as the sad year drew toward its end, "More than fourscore people [1 per cent of the population] were in this black Month of *December*, carried from this Town to their long Home."[11]

---

[7] The Thacher broadside was first printed in Boston in 1677 and was reissued during the epidemics of 1702 and 1721. The full text is in Henry R. Viets, *Medicine in Massachusetts* (Boston, 1930), 29–34. A copy of the original broadside is in the collections of the Massachusetts Historical Society.

[8] Mather, *Diary*, I, 435.

[9] Ibid., 445.

[10] Ibid., 447.

[11] Ibid., 451.

The epidemic, in which his own children "came alive out of the fiery Furnace of the Small Pox which almost consumed them,"[12] deepened Mather's scientific interest in the disease as the enormously well read man of science that he was since his student days, when what seemed an incurable stammer induced him to put aside thoughts of the ministry and study medicine. Possessed of a remarkable insight into psychosomatics, he successfully treated his own speech affliction but continued his reading, methodical observations, and speculative inquiries in science generally and in medicine particularly the rest of his life. At least as early as 1712 he was a principal American correspondent of scientific data to the Royal Society and in the following year, he "was proposed, balloted for, and approved to be a Member of the Society," by its Council, an action subsequently confirmed by the full membership, though he was not able to go through the ritual in London traditionally formalizing the admission of elected candidates.[13] The same year he published in Boston the instructive *A Letter About a Good Management under the Distemper of the Measles, at this time Spreading in the Country. Here Published for the Benefit of the Poor, and such as may want the help of Able Physicians.* Measles was often fatal, Mather's second wife, three of his children, and his housemaid having died of it in 1713; and his pamphlet was the only guide to its treatment available to laymen. Unlike Thacher and many other less qualified ministers, however, he never practiced medicine, although he did devote considerable time and attention to public health activities, virtually founding preventive medicine in Boston, but never in the process attempting to discredit the professional medical men. He had probed and to some extent adopted the organic mechanistic theory of disease—i.e., the malfunctioning of the vital organs mechanically—and he was familiar with the chemistic approach—i.e., the cause of disease being the imbalance of the body's chemical constituents.

In both inductive and speculative thought on the nature of disease and particularly smallpox, Mather was far out ahead of the overwhelming majority of physicians. And his observations, theorizing, and acquaintance with some unique case histories, coupled with the results of a long and assiduous correspondence with German and English scientists convinced him of the animalcular cause of smallpox and that pathogenic animal bodies, microscopic in dimensions, could decimate entire cities. The theory was, of course, not original and was inevitable from the Renaissance, when the classical concept of disease specificity began to make scientific inroads on generalized pathology, which stemmed from the notion, more theological than medical, that all diseases are but varying symptoms of one inclu-

[12] Ibid.

[13] The election and accreditation of Cotton Mather as a fellow of the Royal Society is carefully reconstructed by George Lyman Kittredge in "Cotton Mather's Election into the Royal Society," *Colonial Society of Massachusetts, Proceedings*, December 1911, 81–114, and in his "Further Notes on Cotton Mather and the Royal Society," *Ibid.*, April 1912, 281–92.

sive disease attributable to divine interventions. Though Mather skillfully reconciled his advanced medical thinking with his tenacious theology, he became the most original and venturesome medical commentator in the colonies in the first quarter of the eighteenth century. As the most common scourge of his time (he lived through four major epidemics by the time he was elected to the Royal Society), smallpox was of particular significance to Mather. He was persuaded, no later than 1716, that the spread of smallpox could be controlled if its animalcular nature were understood. And understanding it, he was a most implausible, even if a popular, target for James Franklin's *New England Courant* to select for attack in 1721, when the worst smallpox epidemic in Boston's history was ravaging the population.

By 1721 there had been no epidemic of the disease for nineteen years: Children had been born and in turn borne children, with a consequent reduction in natural immunity to the disease through an inexposure to it for the longest period since the colony was settled ninety years earlier. Quarantine measures instigated by the epidemics of 1677, 1689, and 1702—each of which occurred within fairly immediate memory of the preceding—fell into disuse; recognition of symptoms and the early employment of therapy were all but forgotten; an air of relaxed safety from the predator permeated the town. Then, on April 22, 1721, H.M.S. *Seahorse* arrived from Saltertuda in the West Indies. In the false sense of security encouraged by the absence of any epidemic for nearly two decades, there was no longer any quarantine of incoming ships, and *Seahorse*'s crew came into Boston, took up lodgings where they liked, and circulated freely among the townspeople. On May 8 one of the ship's company came down with the fateful malady, and the alarmed authorities posted a watch outside his lodging house to see that no one entered or left. Shortly another case was discovered at Captain Wentworth Paxton's house, another watch was posted, other cases traceable to the same ship were reported, and *Seahorse* with her entire complement was ordered to an island in the Outer Harbor to prevent further infections. Workmen were sent out to clean the streets. Watches were established at every house known to have been exposed. Burials at night on the day of decease were required in the case of all victims. Never had the town been quicker to recognize the threat of impending disaster or prompter to take steps to avert it. Despite all that could be done, however, the disease was already let loose, uncontrolled and uncontrollable, and destined, as summertime friendly to the spread of such epidemics was just a few weeks away, to hit Boston, science, and the small world of Franklin's infant newspaper with memorable impact.

Cotton Mather, easily the most sophisticated man in Boston regarding the disease, was slow to see the import of the 1721 invasion, not so much because of any lack of scientific recognition of the possible repercussions

of the eight cases eventually reported among *Seahorse*'s company as because of the kind of hectic family and personal distractions that were always contending with God, his quest of knowledge, and his compulsion to
"do good" for Mather's attention. This time it was his intractable son Increase again: "My miserable, miserable, miserable Son Increase!" he wrote
that inexorable April. "The Wretch has brought himself under public
Trouble and Infamy by bearing a Part in a Night-Riot, with some detestable Rakes in the Town. . . . And what is my Duty in relation to this incorrigible Prodigal."[14] He was also troubled by the infirmities of old age
afflicting the father whom he venerated: "My aged Father, too much
laies to Heart; the withdraw of a vain, proud, foolish People from Him in
His Age. . . . Lett me comfort him what I can. . . . My aged Parent is
under Infirmities, what shall I do for his Releef?"[15] And finally, but not
least to him, he could see his own great influence in decline this fifty-
fourth year of his age as "I must now more than ever look on my Flock
with a sacrificing Eye. 'Tis incredible what Numbers are swarming off into
the New Brick Meetinghouse in the Neighborhood" and his colossal vanity
deeply wounded by the "Diminution of my Flock, and the wicked Spirit
manifested by them, who for the Pride of Pues, and such vile Motives, are
gone out from us. . . ."[16] Inevitably, his private woes were pre-empted by
his public concerns, and soon the deadly sprawling of the smallpox around
him was commanding his attention, his solicitude, and the noblest efforts
of a strangely busy, tortuous, and thwarted life. On May 26, 1721, little
more than a month after *Seahorse*'s arrival, he recorded, "The grievous
Calamity of the *Small-Pox* has now entered the Town."[17]

The epidemic was, by all quantitative standards, calamitous indeed.
During a nine-month period, of a population in Boston of 10,500, nearly
6,000 were victims or had already had it; and of these, some 900 died—
close to one out of seven of those afflicted. (The dimensions of the epidemic can be gauged in modern terms if one envisions a city of 1 million
people, with 600,000 afflicted and 90,000 dead.) The disease was particularly ravaging among those born since the last epidemic of 1702, but it
also struck down many of maturer years. The pen of Judge Sewall, whose
diaries sometimes take on the character of a necrology of his times, was
kept busy recording the deaths and funerals of relatives, neighbors, and
notables. During the course of the epidemic, the judge took to writing obit-
uaries of the more distinguished victims for *The Boston News-Letter*—
among them a thirty-eight-year-old fellow of the Harvard Corporation,
the Reverend Joseph Stevens, who was buried along with his four-year-old
daughter and his wife's sister, both also victims; the merchant Joseph Ap-
pleton, fifty-nine; John White, fifty-two, treasurer of Harvard; Peter Cut-

14 Mather, *Diary*, II, 612.
15 Ibid., 617, 629.
16 Ibid., 616, 621.
17 Ibid., 620.

ler, forty-one; and Captain Zecheriah Tuthill, fifty-two, for nineteen years commander of the guard at Castle William. Sewall, who loved sermons almost as much as funerals, also recorded his distress at the necessity, on Thanksgiving Day in 1721, which would ordinarily have been marked by three or four sermons at as many services in every church, of there being "But one Sermon in most Congregations by reason of the Distress of the Small Pox"—an action that he considered decided upon all too casually, for he added, "Note. I think so great an Alteration should not have been made; without the Knowledge and Agreement of the Councillors and other Justices in Town, met together for that purpose."[18] Toward the end of the year, though he noted wistfully the death of an old retainer of the smallpox ("About 7 m. Susan falls asleep. . . . She had served me and my family faithfully fifteen years, and now I hope she is gon to Heavenly Rest." Next day, the good judge "went next the hearse" accompanying Susan to the burying ground[19]), Judge Sewall was almost wholly preoccupied with his ultimately successful but fiscally complicated marriage agreement with the Newton widow of a Boston merchant's son, Mary Shrimpton Gibbs, and dropped all references to the epidemic.

Cotton Mather, on the other hand, had become increasingly disturbed by the relentlessness of the epidemic. It was the better side of the Mather of *Bonifacius*,[20] genuinely intent on making this world a better place, and of Mather, the inexhaustibly curious student of the natural world, that rose to the surface to command his actions during that memorable year, rather than the thundering Mather of the pulpit or the groveling Mather of the study floor. Though not wholly ignoring God's role in the matter—"Because of the destroying Angel standing over the Town, and the grievous Consternation on the Minds of the People, I move the Ministers who are the Lecturers of the City, to turn the next Lecture into a Day of Prayer that we may prepare to meet out God"[21]—he placed his reliance on science and his trust in his own scientific knowledge and instincts. He determined to propose a step that was to shake the town to its roots and to set James Franklin's *New-England Courant* out with a first issue that was to give it instantly a degree of notoriety that it might otherwise have taken weeks to achieve. What Cotton Mather, who knew more about it than any physician in New England and most in England, proposed was inoculation, which was the intentional infection of a person with a small case to immunize him against a natural infection with a large and possibly lethal case.

"The Practice of conveying and suffering the *Small-pox* by *Inoculation*, has never been used in *America*, nor indeed in our Nation [i.e. Britain]," Mather noted in his diary in May of 1721. "But how many Lives might be

18 Ibid., III, 294.
19 Ibid., 296.
20 Mather, Pp. 306–19, *supra*.
21 Mather, *Diary*, II, 625.

saved by it, if it were practiced? I will procure a Consult of our Physicians, and lay the matter before them."[22] On June 23, 1721, he wrote "a Letter unto the Physicians, entreating them to take into consideration the important Affair of preventing the *Small-pox*, in the way of Inoculation,"[23] urging upon them the introduction of inoculation to check the rampant spread of the disease, which had by then crossed the Charles to infest Cambridge and Charlestown and was beginning to take its toll not of isolated but of virtually all households in Boston. Mather was first introduced to the idea of inoculation years earlier, in 1707, by a black slave who had been given him by his parishioners. Mather, presiding over a household of children and always conscious of disease, was interested in his new servant's medical history. "Enquiring of my Negro-man, *Onesimus*, who is a pretty Intelligent Fellow, Whether he had had y^e *Small-Pox*; he answered, both, *Yes*, and *No*; and then told me, that he had undergone an Operation, which had given him something of y^e *Small-Pox*, & would forever praeserve him from it; adding that it was often used among ye Guarumantese [a nomadic Sahara people], & whoever had ye Courage to use it, was forever free from ye fear of the Contagion. He described ye Operation to me, and shew'd me in his Arm ye Scar, which it had left upon him. . . ."[24] Reports from other Boston blacks confirmed the existence of a primitive but effective inoculation practice among Africans. But since Boston had been without an epidemic for six years, Mather noted it at the time only as a bit of curiosa peculiarly congenial to his animalcular theory of the disease. Seven years later, in 1713, reports of the practice of inoculation in Turkey began to filter into the Royal Society, through a fellow, Dr. John Woodward, Professor of Physic at Gresham College, Oxford. Another of the ubiquitous fellows of the Royal Society, Dr. Emanuel Timonius, a medical graduate of Padua and also an alumnus of Oxford, was practicing medicine in Constantinople, and sent Woodward details of the inoculation method for publication in the society's *Philosophical Transactions*. Dr. Woodward, one of Mather's regular Royal Society's correspondents, sent him Dr. Timonius' account, and in return Mather sent Woodward his intelligence about inoculations among the Africans. Another account of successful inoculations against the smallpox in Turkey later reached the society, through Sir Hans Sloane, from Dr. Jacobus Plylarinus, a physician who observed it while serving as Venetian consul in Smyrna. The two letters, though written three years apart, appeared in the same volume (XXIX, published in 1717) of the *Philosophical Transactions*, a copy of which Dr. William Douglass, Boston's leading physician and the only one holding a doctorate in medicine, lent Mather.

---

[22] Ibid., 620–21.
[23] Ibid., 628.
[24] In George Lyman Kittredge, "Some Lost Works of Cotton Mather," Massachusetts Historical Society, *Proceedings*, XLV (February 1912), 422. The text is from Mather's letter report of July 12, 1716, to Dr. Woodward for conveyance to the Royal Society.

(Meanwhile, Lady Mary Wortley Montagu, a celebrated wit and beauty who had lost her brother in a London smallpox epidemic and herself been disfigured by it, accompanied her husband, the British ambassador, to Constantinople, and there had her six-year-old son inoculated with such success that she later launched a campaign for the inoculation against smallpox in England, persuading the Princess Caroline to have two daughters inoculated during an epidemic in London coeval with the Boston epidemic of 1721.) In his 1716 report to Dr. Woodward, Mather had wondered, "How does it come to pass, that no more is done to bring this operation, into Experiment & into Fashion—in *England?* When there are so many Thousands of People, that would give so many Thousands of Pounds, to have ye Danger and Horror of this frightful Disease well over with y^m. I beseech you, syr, to move it and save more lives than Dr. *Sydenham* [from whose work Thacher's broadside had been derived]. For my own part, if I should live to see y^e *Small-Pox* again enter into o^r City, I would immediately procure a Consult of o^r Physicians, to Introduce a Practice, which may be of so very happy a Tendency."[25] Mather's June 1721 appeal to the physicians of Boston carried out that resolve, not guaranteeing that inoculation would be invariably or even occasionally successful but urging only that the physicians consider it:

> I will only say that inasmuch as the practice of suffering the Small-Pox, in the way of *Inoculation,* has never yet, as far as I have heard, been introduced into our Nation where there are so many that would give great Sums to have their Lives ensured for an Escape from the Dangers of this dreadful Distemper; nor has ever anyone in *America,* ever yet made the tryal of it, (tho' we have several *Africans* among us, as I now find, who tryed it in their own Country,) I *cannot but move,* that it be WARILY proceeded in.
>
> I durst not yet engage that, the Success of the Trial here, will be the Same, that has hitherto been in the other Hemisphere: But I am very confident, no Person would miscarry in it, but what would most certainly have miscarried taking the Contagion the *Common Way:* And I would *humbly Advise,* that it be never made but under the management of a Skilful PHYSICIAN, who will wisely *prepare the Body* for it, before he performs the Operation. *Gentlemen,* My request is, That you would meet for a *Consultation* upon this Occasion, and so deliberate upon it, that whoever first begin the practice, (*if you Approve it should be begun at all*) may have the countenance of his worthy Brethren to fortify him in it.[26]

The main body of the letter, which was never published but was distributed by hand to ten practicing physicians in the town, contained a digest of his own knowledge of African inoculations, Dr. Timonius' observations on inoculation in Turkey, specifics of the operational procedure involved,

---

[25] Ibid.
[26] Ibid., 434.

Dr. Pylarinus' observations, and more instructions on how to carry out the procedure and on the treatment of postoperative symptoms, which were carefully listed in a day-by-day account of the progress of a patient's recovery.[27] The tone of the letter was instructive and—as Mather simply could not help sounding even when he was most earnestly entreating— superior and condescending. And his letter fell with a dead silence on the medical community, who neither held the recommended consultation nor even extended the courtesy of acknowledging it—a fearful affront to Boston's leading cleric and most encyclopedic mind—and Dr. Douglass, infuriated because Mather conveyed the impression that Drs. Timonius and Pylarinus had written directly to him (the kind of vanity Mather could not resist), demanded from the cleric, and got, the return of his volume of the *Philosophical Transactions*, from which Mather had abstracted the Timonius and Pylarinus reports. Though Mather did nothing to prevent such a chilly reception of what was essentially a humane and informed labor (it is doubtful that he was temperamentally capable even of imagining such a reaction), he was outraged at the treatment he received from a profession for which he really had the highest respect and into which, by sending such a pedagogic communication, he had no sense of intruding: ". . . I proposed unto the Physicians of the Town, the unfailing Method of preventing death, and many other grievous miseries, from a tremendous Distemper, by Receiving and Managing the *Small-Pox*, in the way of *Inoculation*. One of the Physicians had the Courage to begin the Practice upon his own Children and Servants; and another Expressed his Good Will unto it. But the rest of the Practitioners treated the Proposal with an Incivility and an Inhumanity not well to be accounted for."[28]

The "one Physician" was Zabdiel Boylston a forty-two-year-old physician and surgeon, who lived with his wife and children in the very heart of town in Dock Square. He had been educated by his father, also a physician and surgeon, and by Dr. John Cutler, Boston's leading physician until his death in 1717 and for a generation the leading teacher and trainer of Boston's medical men. Boylston came from an old family in the colony, his grandfather having arrived in 1635, and he himself had gained respect for his character, his professional competence, and a special surgical skill in the removal of stones from the bladder. There is no evidence that he was the Mathers' personal physician, but Mather felt free to write him an individual, personal letter two or three weeks after his communication to the profession had fallen with such a dull thud. Somewhat more tactful and less lofty than in his circulated letter, he first complimented Dr. Boylston and then urged him to give the most serious thought to practicing

---

[27] The text of the actual letter has not been preserved; but Professor Kittredge, ibid., established beyond any doubt that it was essentially the same language and content of the appendix to Chap. 20 of Mather's posthumous book, *The Angel of Bethesda*, ed. Gordon W. Jones, M.D. (Barre, Mass. 1972).

[28] Ibid., 112–13.

inoculation and repeated all that he knew about the procedure, unable to refrain from adding that such knowledge was "all that was ever published in the world."[29] Himself an alumnus of the 1702 epidemic, Boylston was already naturally immune, but on June 26, two days after receiving Mather's letter, he inoculated the three members of his household who had not already left town to avoid contamination. The three were his six-year-old son, Thomas, a thirty-six-year-old slave, and the latter's two-and-a half-year-old son. After a few days passed, Boylston was fully persuaded of its practical effectiveness, having already been convinced by Mather of its theoretic plausibility. Accordingly during the first two weeks in July, he inoculated three more and, in the next five days, another four, including his thirteen-year-old son, John—a total of ten. It was the first venture in immunology in the Western Hemisphere.

Word rapidly spread around the compact little town that Dr. Boylston was deliberately giving people the disease from which all prayed to be spared and that, far from fulfilling his professional duty to do all in his power to arrest the epidemic, he was intentionally spreading it. The whole notion of inoculation, that one could prevent disease by causing it, seemed to the laity, as to virtually all the profession, outrageously illogical. It also seemed to the religious a shameless invasion of a decision reserved to the Almighty: whom and where a disease will strike. Finally, enough was known of the primitive method, and even more was rumored, to generate the widespread view that as well as flying into the face of logic and religion—two staples of the Puritan mind—the practice of inoculation was brutal: the deliberate opening up of several wounds in the skin until some drops of blood appear; the dropping into the wounds the matter pressed out from the pustules of people desperately ill of a fatal disease; then the subsequent occurrence of the disease in the patient thus infected with the pox and the attendant fever. That the disease in the inoculated ran a mild and swift course, resulting in lifelong immunization, was a concept untenable even to the medical profession let alone the laymen, since the existence of pathogenic microcosms was unknown to them. And so the full fury of the town of Boston was let loose on Boylston for his unconscionable acts, abusing his profession and his trust and further threatening the lives of his townsmen already in mortal fear from the rampaging natural spreading of the disease. In July the people of Boston, Mather reported, probably with customary hyperbole, began to "rave, they rail, they blaspheme; they talk not only like Ideots but also like *Franticks*, And not only the Physician [Boylston], who began the Experiment, but I also am an Object of their Fury; their furious Obloquies and Invectives." Mather was

[29] *Massachusetts Magazine*, I (1789), 788. Mather may have written a similar letter to other physicians. His *Diary* (II, 628) records for June 23: "I write a letter unto the Physicians, entreating them to take into consideration the important Affair of preventing the *Small-Pox*, in the way of Inoculation." The letter to Boylston was dated June 24.

particularly concerned that the public outcry was such that he did not dare to have his nonimmune second son, Samuel, a student at Harvard, in whom he put all his hopes after his first son's, Increase's, lapses, inoculated for fear of public uprising. "The cursed Clamour of a People strangely and fiercely possessed of the Devil, will probably prevent my saving the Lives of my two Children, from the Small-pox in the way of Transplantation."[30]

Boylston was reportedly forced to go into secret hiding, and parties were reportedly organized to hang him—both of them doubtful rumors, for on July 17, at the height of the public fury, he published a notice in the *Gazette*, vindicating his actions and promising further evidence of their effectiveness and that he did not fear public resentment. But there was swift political reaction as the spread of the disease continued unabated and the deaths rose from eight in June to eleven in July (they were to peak at 411 in October); the selectmen of Boston convened a public hearing on July 21, bringing together the physicians, officials, and citizens of the town to consider the issue of inoculation. At the meeting a French physician, Dr. Lawrence Dalhonde, a veteran of practice in the French Army which had taken him into the Near East, read an unfavorable report, composed in French but the English translation of which was certified by Dr. Douglass. The report, a strange piece of medical literature so far as cause-and-effect goes, used three collections of case histories, totaling seventeen individual cases, suggesting among other things that deaths from ulcers twenty years after inoculation and from parotidean tumors twenty-five years after were due to the inoculation. Astonished at this scientific methodology, Dr. Boylston gave a calm report on the successful progress of the seven that he had inoculated, and he invited all the other physicians in the town to examine the patients and to make their own reports on the progress of their cases. All of them refused, but then submitted, and the selectmen adopted and caused to be published, a report accepting Dr. Dalhonde's strangely documented contention that earlier inoculations in Belgium, Italy, and Spain had occasioned "The Death of many Persons," tended to "spread and continue the Infection," and could "prove of most dangerous consequence."[31] The officials, moreover, publicly rebuked Boylston for spreading the disease and warned him against continuing the practice. Three days later, Dr. Douglass, still seething at Mather—the more so because he had persuaded Boylston to undertake, alone among Boston physicians, the practice of inoculating—sat down and wrote a letter of bitter invective to *The Boston News-Letter*, signed with the clearly transparent signature "W. Philanthropos." Douglass's letter was a vicious personal attack upon a colleague, "a certain cutter for the Stone" whom he called illiterate and ignorant, making allegations of professional incompetence in "not preparing the Bodies of his Subjects, unfit to manage any of their

[30] Mather, *Diary*, II, 632. Mather repeated the substance of the entry in *The Angel of Bethesda*, 112–13.
[31] Zabdiel Boylston, *An Historical Account of the Small Pox Inoculated in New England* (London, 1726), 3–4.

Symptoms." It also appealed to the religious emotions of the populace: Boylston was "trusting more the extra groundless *Machinations of Men* than to our Preserver in the ordinary course of Nature," and he, Douglass, questioned whether Boylston's conduct was "consistent with that Devotion and Subjection we owe to the *all-wise Providence* of GOD Almighty." Finally, with fine insensitivity to professional brotherhood, the letter suggested that Boylston's practicing inoculation could legally "be construed a *Propagating of Infection and Criminal*" and that, should one of his inoculated patients die, "the Operator will be indicted for Felony."[32] The attack was an uncalled-for, unscientific, and not uniformly informed attack upon an able and conscionable physician by a lesser and junior colleague, whose major claim to preferment was that he held a doctorate degree in medicine while the object of his attack had only "read" medicine, learned it through apprenticeship to a great physician, and practiced it with distinction for two decades.

Strangely enough, it was not the medical profession that sprang to Dr. Boylston's defense. It was the Boston clergy, through a joint letter of six leading ministers covering the whole spectrum of theological conservatism and liberalism: Increase and Cotton Mather, copastors of the conservative Second Church; Thomas Prince, pastor of the moderate Old South; Benjamin Colman, pastor of the liberal Brattle Street Church, and his associate, William Cooper; and John Webb, pastor of the fundamentalist New North Church, whose young wife was to die in the epidemic. They repudiated, first, Douglass's personal and professional attack on Boylston: "He is a son of the Town [pointedly—Douglass was an immigrant Scot] whom Heaven (as we all know) has adorned with some very peculiar Gifts for Service to his Country, and hath signally own'd in the Successes he has had . . . tho' he has not had the honour and advantage of an Academical Education, and consequently not the letters of some Physicians in the Town [pointedly—William Douglass was, of course, the only M.D. among them], yet he ought by no means to be called Illiterate, ignorant, etc. Would the Town bear that Dr. Cutler or Dr. William Davis should be so treated [thus equating Boylston with the two best men of medicine the colony had produced]." Secondly, they disposed of Douglass's somehow fawning and sanctimonious religious argument: "For what hand or art of Man is there in this Operation more than in bleeding, blistering and a Score more things in Medical use? which are all consistent with a humble trust in our Great preserver, and a due Subjection to His All-Wise Providence [flinging Douglass's own language back to him]."

But, unjust as it was to charge Dr. Boylston with possible criminal conduct in administering inoculation, Dr. Douglass did have a clinical point, which the six clerics did not answer, in his argument that inoculation tended to spread the infection. It unquestionably did, for Dr. Boylston put no restrictions on the patients he infected by inoculation. Unlike

[32] *Boston News-Letter*, July 24, 1721.

those who acquired the infection naturally, whose houses were put under watch, those inoculated circulated around the town, received guests, and otherwise behaved as though presupposing that the inoculation made them not only immune but also not even carriers—which was not the case, since the primitive inoculation techniques made them really ill of the disease (though usually much less desperately than those who were naturally infected) and fully capable of transmitting it to someone else. And it went very much against the scientific grain of Douglass that Boylston exercised no control over those he had infected and, although carefully observing and recording their progress, never restricted their movements or contacts during the period of their contagion, when obviously they should have been isolated and under quarantine. As a trained physician, too, he was fully aware of the dangers implicit in leaping at conclusions on scanty evidence, and he knew that the evidence on the efficacy and safety of inoculation was quite scanty and—as far as the accounts in the *Philosophical Transactions* went—based on undocumented secondary reports upon which the avidly inquisitive mind of Cotton Mather might seize uncritically but which a disciplined, trained professional attitude might find dangerous and abhorrent. Douglass's difficulty, however, despite all this, was that he was just flatly negative, and his professional failure was that, rather than working with Boylston to minimize any risks involved, he attacked him ungenerously, even unfairly and certainly with more professional jealousy than with any sense of professional responsibility. Moreover, Boylston, undeterred by the Douglass onslaught and fully convinced that he was doing what was right and necessary, ignored Douglass, his other opposing medical colleagues, the selectmen, and the public outcry: ". . . if any think to go on with their Calumnies and Fooleries, I shall not think to take any notice of them. What I do (I hope as it has hitherto done) will vindicate itself with People of Thought and Probity."[33] The professional assurance and the maturity of Boylston's attitude carried him through the repeated and increasingly vituperative attacks on him. The principal author of those immoderate assaults was Dr. Douglass, and the principal vehicle of them was James Franklin's new paper, *The New-England Courant*.

* * *

When James Franklin, a young, poor, and uninfluential printer, probably in the spring of 1721, first talked about starting a newspaper in a town which already had two—*The Boston News-Letter* of John Campbell and *The Boston Gazette* of incumbent postmasters—struggling to survive, some of his friends, Benjamin Franklin recalled, tried to persuade him to abandon the idea as commercially a risky venture "not likely to succeed."[34] Josiah Franklin, it would seem from everything known of his pru-

---

[33] Zabdiel Boylston, *Some Account of what is said of Inoculating or Transplanting the Small Pox* (Boston, 1721), 11.
[34] *Autobiography*, 67.

dent, cautious nature, probably shared this view. But James was recently returned from the England of the "new" journalism of Addison and Steele, of the coffeehouse repartee, and of a rising generation of quizzical wits not given to an unquestioning acceptance of the established institutions or to uncritical respect for their spokesmen. When he came back to Boston and opened his printing house, the little building in Queen Street began to attract—as printing houses everywhere tended to do—a little group of like-minded men, most of them young, largely because of their interest in the printed word and what emanated from the presses. James Franklin's shop was no exception, and a coterie of articulate, faintly rebellious, and, as Benjamin described them, "ingenius" men sprang up around him—some of them of a challenging attitude to the Puritan establishment because they themselves favored the Church of England (the associate rector of King's Chapel, Henry Harris, was among them, as were three lay members of the Anglican chapel); three physicians, not enamored of the Puritan ministers; and a couple of booksellers, who found Franklin's a livelier place for discussion than the older Boston printers and who very possibly thought it an easier one to influence, booksellers being the publishers of their time and printers, therefore, being essential to them but also constituting an extremely independent breed of artisans with minds of their own and a tendency to assert them through what they chose to print. Among this group of Franklin's friends were two who seemed to have been most vigorous in urging him to undertake publication of the paper: John Checkley and Dr. William Douglass.

John Checkley, at forty-one one of the oldest of the coterie, was a sophisticated bookseller—at "The Sign of the Crown and Blue Gate against the Town-House"—who, though born in Boston and a product of Ezekiel Cheever at the Latin School, had his collegiate education at Oxford, studied and collected art on the Continent for some ten years, became "a ripe scholar in Latin, Greek and Hebrew,"[35] returned to Boston about 1710, married a good dissenter from Milton, and acquired the brick house next to the Town House—the very heart of public affairs in Boston. He became an Anglican, slightly contemptuous after his long European sojourn of Boston provincialism, and a steady thorn in the side of the Puritan ministers. He was the leading lay expounder of Church of England doctrine and practices (eventually he was ordained and was for over a decade the rector of King's Church in Providence); in 1719 he published a reprint edition of a defense of Christianity, Church of England version, against deism[36]; and in 1720 he wrote a dialogue critical of the Puritan doctrine

[35] E. F. Slafter, ed., *Memoir of John Checkley* (Boston, 1897), I, 2.

[36] *The Religion of Jesus Christ the only True Religion, or a Short and easie Method with the Deists . . . In a Letter to a Friend.* The Seventh Edition. Boston: Printed by J. Fleet, and are to be sold by John Checkley, at the Sign of the *Crown* and *Blue Gate* over against the *West* End of the Town-House. 1719.

The author was the Reverend Charles Leslie (1650–1722), a son of the Bishop of Clogher and a major apologistic writer in England.

of election and of the concept of predestination.[37] A man of superior intellect and learning, a man of the world in background, a rich conversationalist, and a sharp humorist, Checkley was an impressive, supremely self-confident personality and capable of scathing innuendo, bound to appeal to the young printer so lately exposed to his type in London. Checkley represented, in fact, an extension to Boston of approaches and attitudes that James Franklin had seen for the first time in London.

Dr. Douglass, too, had an extra-Boston, Old World air of authority and experience about him. He was born in Gifford, Scotland, of a family of distinguished lineage, and was educated, leading to his degree in medicine, at the universities of Edinburgh, Leyden, and Paris. Douglass was a man of brilliant mind and intellectual acumen, whose interests were wide. He was an able linguist, one of the first botanists to classify American plants, a meteorologist of some skill; wrote as an astronomer, an economist, and a geographer; and as a cartographer, made surveys and drew maps. He wrote a two-volume work of provocative, though highly prejudiced and often erroneous, observations of the British colonies.[38] He did not take a kindly view, or even a fair one, of any authority, ecclesiastical or civil; and all forms of censorship were anathema to him. He hated Indians ("man-brutes"), Bishop Berkeley and his philosophy ("tar water"), George Whitfield, the evangelist ("vagrant"), the French ("common nuisance"), and paper money ("this cheating game"),[39] to the condemnation of which he devoted the major part of his *A Discourse Concerning the Currencies of the British Plantations in America*.[40] Douglass was a bachelor, acquired some wealth, and was a kind of medical counterpart of Cotton Mather in that there were few areas of life into which he did not intrude his attention and his presence, often with the same degree of sublime self-confidence and total disdain of opposing views. Altogether, the coming together of such a personality as Douglass with James Franklin, the publisher of a new paper intent against dullness, could not have been more conducive to the paper's making a provocative debut—or a riskier one.

Douglass first came to Boston in 1716, and then left to travel for a year in the West Indies. When he came to Boston, he brought with him letters of introduction to both Increase and Cotton Mather and to Benjamin

[37] *Choice Dialogues between a Godly Minister and an Honest Country Man, Concerning Election & Predestination*. (No place or date of publication.) This dialogue, was charged on its appearance to Checkley. It was answered anonymously shortly after its publication by a friend of Checkley, the Reverend Thomas Walter, of Roxbury, a nephew of Cotton Mather, in *A Choice Dialogue Between John Faustus, a Conjurer and Jack Tory, His Friend* . . . Boston: Printed for N. Boone at the Sign of the Bible in *Cornhill*: B. Gray and J. Edwards at their Shops in *King-street*. 1720.

[38] *A Summary, Historical and Political, of the First Planting, Progressive Improvements, and Present State of the British Settlements in North America* (Boston, 1749 and 1751).

[39] The characterizations are from the *Summary*, I, 116; I, 149; I, 250; I, 2; and I, 359.

[40] *Discourse Concerning the Currencies* was published in London in 1739 and in Boston in 1740. It was since reprinted in several editions.

Colman, the pastor of the liberal Brattle Street Church. He apparently had, before the inoculation crisis of 1721, a warm relationship with Cotton Mather and went to great pains, in his recriminatory letter to *The Boston News-Letter*, to attribute to Mather "a Pious & Charitable design of doing good"—however misdirected the effort and however sardonic Douglass meant to be. Douglass was by nature methodical rather than intuitive, somewhat coldly clinical in his approach to medicine rather than humanistic, and given to a kind of objective thoroughness in the reporting of his patients as case histories rather than to a primary concern with them as troubled human beings. Once the controversy over the inoculation began, his great conceit was on a collision course with Mather's vast vanity, with the conscientious, dedicated Boylston the object of Douglass's attack and Mather's defense. Douglass's major interest in Franklin's new paper was obviously the direct forum it would furnish him for asserting his anti-inoculation view. And he wrote the lead piece in the first issue, taking up a column and a half out of the four that made up the single sheet, to continue the castigation of Boylston that he had started in the *News-Letter* three weeks earlier and, in addition, to denounce the "Six Gentlemen of Piety" for defending Boylston. It seems likely that Douglass (with whom Checkley agreed) had little difficulty persuading James Franklin that, by leaping into the controversy, his paper could get off to a conspicuous start and at the same time satisfy his intention of avoiding the dullness of his competitors and his instinct to shake up the establishment. (In the third issue of the *Courant*, two weeks later, Checkley went so far as to say of the *Courant*'s founding, ". . . the chief design of which Paper was to oppose the *doubtful* and *dangerous* Practice of inoculating the *Small-Pox*. . . ."[41]

In his contribution to the *Courant*'s first issue, Douglass reported "at the Request of Several Gentlemen in Town" what had happened in Boston with regard to inoculation since his *News-Letter* diatribe. In substance, he characterized it as "the Practice of Greek old Women" and said that "notwithstanding the Terror and Confusion from his Son's Inoculation-Fever," Boylston went right on inoculating people—and this in spite of the selectmen's acceptance of the opinion of "all the practicioners in Town," who "*unanimously agreed that* it *was rash and dubious*, being entirely new, not in the least vouched or recommended (being meerly published, in the Philosophick Transactions by way of Amusement) from Britain." (This was possibly the most cavalier disparagement of the learned publication ever voiced by a provincial practicioner.) "B---n," as he subtly designated Boylston, was still inoculating people. Douglass then turned to the clergy supporting Boylston, thus assuring a much more verbose battle than would have been the case had he limited his attack to the taciturn Boylston. His lashing of the distinguished ministers was broad and stinging. "Notwithstanding the general Aversion of the Town

[41] *New-England Courant*, No. 3 (August 14 to August 21, 1721).

[to inoculation], in Contradition to the declared Opinion of the Practitioners, *in Opposition* to the Selectmen, and *in Spite* of the discouraging Evidences relating to this Practice, *Six Gentlemen of Piety and Learning profoundly ignorant of the Matter*, after serious consideration of a Disease one of the most intricate practical Cases in Physick, do on the Merits of their Characters, and for no other, with a V*ox praeteriag; nihil*, assert, &c. If this Argument, *viz.* Their Character, should prevail with the Populace (tho' here I think they have missed of Their Aim) who knows but it might oblige some prophane Person to canvas that sort of Argument. I think their [i.e., the ministers'] Character ought to be sacred, and they themselves ought not to give the least Occasion to have it called in question. They set up for Judges of a Man's Qualifications in the Practice of Physick, and very lavishly bestow all the fullsome common Place of *Quack* Advertisements. One would think they meant some *Romantick Character*, something beyond that of candid [Dr. Thomas] *Sydenham*, the sagacious [Dr. John] Radcliff, or the celebrated [Dr. Richard] Meade: They might indeed in respect of his moral and religious Qualifications, which lay properly under their Cognizance, have said, That he was a modest, humble Man, a Man of Continency, Probity, &c."

Douglass's piece then degenerated into a name-calling squabble with Boylston and the ministerial six. But in publishing the communication, James Franklin had launched the first really free press in America. He had criticized the ultimate instrument of authority in the Bible Commonwealth: the ministers of the state church. For the first time in public debate their authority and even their competence in fields other than morals and religion were challenged by a learned man of recognized professional standing, the leading physician in the town, who had, in fact, been more or less sponsored by the Mathers and Benjamin Colman when he first started his practice in Boston and who was born and bred in the Calvinist tradition, although himself a deist. It was true that Douglass disputed the authority of the ministers, not as a critic of the concept of a coalescent church and state, but only because he was frankly alarmed at a layman's interpreting professional medical papers and took a dim view, too, of admitting to practice physicians without academic training and without meeting the formal requirements of a medical education. (All his life, Douglass fought, on sufficiently valid grounds, for higher standards for admission to the profession, offering to endow a medical professorship and still complaining, as he neared the end of his life, "A young man without any liberal education, by living a year or two in any quality with a practicioner of some sort, apothecary, cancer-doctor, cutter for the stone, bonesetters, tooth drawer, etc., with the essential fundamental of ignorance and impudence, is esteemed to qualify himself for all the branches of the medical arts . . . there are more die of the practicioner than of the natural course of the distemper under proper regimen."[42] There is little doubt that Douglass was willing and eager to use young Franklin's paper to express a somewhat arrogant professionalism. But Franklin was certainly smart enough to recognize it, and so was Checkley, who was probably awaiting his turn to use the *Courant* to strike a blow for the apostolic origin of the episcopacy. The fact is that, whatever the merits of the immediate cause, the *Courant* was out to establish the practice and the principle of a press free to do more than publish either "under authority" or so blandly as not even to interest authority. Its very name was borrowed from the paper most notorious in London for its insistence upon the freedom of the press and its willingness to suffer for it—*The London Daily Courant*, whose publisher, Samuel Buckley, was brought to the bar of the House of Commons in 1712 for unfavorable reports on its proceedings.

* * *

The *Courant* succeeded in what it set out to do. The Mathers were infuriated at the impudence of the upstart paper and its principal contributor, Douglass; they were also familiar, of course, with the Anglican views of Checkley. In a town as small as Boston it seems most unlikely that Franklin's associates in the venture could be unknown. The patriarchal Increase could see nothing but the collapse of the Bible Commonwealth and its whole mission, and Cotton's vanity of learning was hurt to the quick by the work of a man whose scientific status he respected. Possibly after a family conference, the bright young grandson of Increase and nephew of Cotton, Thomas Walter, Checkley's disputant about election and predestination of two years earlier, immediately set to the task of composing an answer. Wit being one of his most reputed gifts, another being invective, he did it in the form of a satire. It was ready for the press before the next edition of the *Courant*. The title, in small letters, was *The Little-Compton Scourge*, with the subtitle, in the largest letters on the page, *The Anti-Courant*, set in exactly the same type as the masthead of the first number of *The New-England Courant*. The imprint was, of all things, "Boston: Printed and Sold by *J. Franklin*, over against *Mr. Sheaf's* School in Queen-Street," and the price was three pence—half the price of the *Courant*, probably because it was printed on only one side of the sheet. It appeared on the morning of Monday, August 14, and the second number of the *Courant*, published the same day, carried an announcement that the satirical broadside "by Zechariah Touchstone" would be published "This Forenoon" and "Sold by the Printer hereof"—i.e., Franklin. It was all a little too tidy to seem the work of the Mathers, who had plenty of associations with Boston printers without encouraging Franklin under the circumstances; yet, when the inoculation controversy first began, weeks before the *Courant* appeared, Cotton Mather had said, "I will employ the Witt

[42] *Summary . . . of the British Settlements*, II, 383.

and Pen of my Kinsman at Roxbury, to serve the Cause of Truth and Right on the present Occasion."[43] Nevertheless, the suggestion arises that Walter's old friendly contender, Checkley, put him up to the satire and that Franklin, with the family's talent for shrewd publicity, agreed to publish it, convinced that it was just what was needed to give the *Courant's* second issue the extra push that would make it less of an anticlimax to the opening issue.

If this possibility, in some particulars remote, was actually the case, the scheme boomeranged badly on Checkley, for he had shared the first page of the first issue with Douglass; and, while it was Douglass who attacked the clergy, Checkley had composed a rather innocent piece, in the vein of the journalistic wit of England at the time, designed primarily to personalize the new paper and invite an informal relationship with its readers, the only offensive part, so far as the inoculation dispute went, consisting of the last line of a triplet that took clear and sharp aim at the six ministers who defended Boylston. The rest of Checkley's column was a facetious complaint that "a Man can't appear in Print now a Days" without first answering a lot of irrelevant questions about his background and education. Speaking as the *Courant* personified, he then volunteered that he was forty-three—old enough for flights of wit; but if any complained that he was too young for sagacity, he argued that "beards do not make wisdom." He promised that in the third issue he would furnish his "gentle Readers," who were probably "impatient" to know more about him, with more information. Meanwhile, he assured them that he was one of "the good Company of a certain set of men . . . ," leading into the offending triplet:

> Who like faithful Shepherds take care of their *Flocks*,
> By teaching and practising what's Orthodox,
> Pray hard against Sickness, yet preach up the POX.

He concluded with a rather heavy-handed note about his intentionally being "very, very dull" on occasion so that his fellow writers would not be made to look so bad.

Checkley, who regarded himself as considerably brighter and more polished than the local, non-Oxford wits, obviously thought the piece full of innocuous humor, though he was intentionally goading the Puritan ministers with his rhyme. He was shocked when his old friend Walter, himself a Puritan minister, devoted practically his whole Anti-Courant, not to Douglass's serious, open, but nonpersonal attack on the minister, but to his, Checkley's, rather good-natured rambling. Walter's piece said, in substance, that the *Courant* spokesman was worrying about the wrong thing if he thought anyone was curious about his pedigree, education, or age and that his real trouble was that he knew nothing about wit and wouldn't recognize it if he encountered it. He then instructed the *Courant*

[43] Mather, *Diary*, II, 636.

on what wit was and how to recognize it, lectured it on Latin versification, criticized its language and "wretched writing," characterized it as
brainless and superficial, and concluded:

> Go on, Monsieur Courant, and prosper; Fear not to please your Stupid
> Admirers, which will be an easy Task, if you will but consult your own
> heavy *Genius,* and write in your native Stile, of which you have been so
> sharp and discerning as to give us the apt and proper Character, VERY,
> VERY DULL . . .

> Go on, dull Soul, labour in Spite
> Of Nature, and your Stars to write.

Walter hit Checkley where he was most sensitive: his pride as a man of
the world, a wit, and a writer. So stung as to lose any sense of humor or of
occasion, Checkley lost control of himself in the third issue of the *Courant*
and descended to an attack on Walter, whom he described as the "Tom-
Bully for the Cause" of his grandfather, uncle, and four other pro-inoculation clergy. (Checkley meant the "Tom" to reveal the identity of the author of the *Anti-Courant* and also used the initials "T.W." for the same
purpose.) He attributed the presence of the author in Little Compton to
his taste for hard cider, because that's where the largest orchards were; he
accused Walter of having written a scurrilous letter to a clergyman-patron
(his uncle, Cotton Mather, was probably intended, for the two had a brief
falling-out during Walter's college days); of having been discovered "with
another *Debauchee,* at a Lodging with two Sisters, of not the best Reputation in the World, upon the Bed with them Several Hours"; and of
chronic drunkenness:

> No Wonder *Tom* thou wert so wroth
> Since *Bacchus* did inspire,
> 'Twas *Rum, raw Rum* and *Cyder* both
> That rous'd thy *Grubstreet* Ire.

James Franklin had not been either perceptive or quick enough to stop
this vilification from being published; or what is more probable, as a relatively uneducated young printer, he stood in too great awe of the worldly
Oxonian, nearly twice his years in age and even more in experience, to stay
his wild pen. But as soon as the issue had been in circulation for a few
days, he realized that this kind of personal opprobrium was not what he
intended when he sought to establish in Boston the kind of lighthearted
but useful journalism with which he had become acquainted during his
apprenticeship in London. Realizing it a bit late for the publisher of a
journal identifying him as such and apparently having been rebuked by his
own pastors at the Old South,[44] he showed his command of the paper by
closing its columns thenceforth to Checkley and by inserting an apology

[44] See James Franklin in *New-England Courant,* No. 18 (November 27 to December
4, 1721).

for the vulgar diatribe at the end of his news column in the *Courant*'s fifth edition: "Several Gentlemen in Town believing that this Paper (by what was inserted in No. 3) was published with a Design to bring the Persons of the Clergy in Contempt, the Publisher thinks himself oblig'd to give Notice, that he has chang'd his Author; and promises, that nothing for the future shall be inserted, anyways reflecting on the Clergy or Government, and nothing but what is innocently Diverting. N.B. Any short Piece declaring either for or against Inoculation, may be inserted in this Paper, provided it be free from malicious Reflections." And when Walter, some months later, lectured in Boston, the *Courant* went out of its way to pronounce it "excellent."[45]

"Innocent" diversion may have been the original intent of Franklin—and subsequent issues leave no doubt that he put a stop to the kind of scurrilous expression of personal vendetta that reached its low with Checkley's attack on Walter. But the Courant was, necessarily from its very nature as a weekly paper, too deeply involved with the life, the events, the attitudes, and the personalities of the town to carry innocence to the point of excluding topicality. But, without going to the extreme of such blandness, Franklin did succeed in getting his paper back on the track—and he meant his addendum to the apology in the Checkley-Walter matter when he promised impartiality in the smallpox inoculation controversy. Meanwhile, however, Douglass had plunged the *Courant* deeper into the role of opposition to inoculation and, therefore, to its chief promulgators and defenders, the Mathers.

The lead piece in the second issue of the *Courant* was by Dr. Douglass, over the pseudonym "Horat[io]." The previous issue of the *Courant* had carried a news item about the departure of sixty soldiers from Castle William on board a transport to join an expedition against Indians in Maine who had been harassing the settlers. Douglass's piece consisted entirely of a satirical suggestion that the expedition include a company of inoculators, armed with incision lances, their ammunition being "the best Proof, that is, a composition of Negro Yaws and confluent Small Pox," and headed by a "Major General Inoculator," and that their function be to reduce the Indian population by inoculating them. The piece had genuine wit; and—in a less volatile atmosphere and perhaps if it did not involve the sensitive egos of the Mathers—it would certainly have qualified as one of James Franklin's prescribed "innocent Diversions." There was nothing personal in it at all, but it held up to ridicule the idea, so contradictory to most of the townspeople, that a disease could be controlled by willfully spreading it through artificial infection of the unafflicted. Douglass implied that the major general inoculator, "who in Quality of a Field Officer may do Duty on Horseback," should be Cotton Mather, and that his inoculating troops follow the methods outlined by Dr. Timonius,

[45] *New-England Courant*, No. 31 (February 26 to March 5, 1722).

whom—in a gibe at the erroneous impression that Mather had created in his letter to the physicians that Timonius was a personal correspondent—Douglass described as "our Inoculator General's good Friend and intimate Acquaintance." Deriding Mather's apparent inattention to details in medical literature, he suggested of his proposed germ warfare, ". . . tho' Timonius such Expeditions [i.e., inoculation attempts generally] be made only in Winter and Spring, ours shall be in Summer, as in all Probability like to do most Execution in that Season." In criticism of what he chose to regard as the irony of the taking of fees, by his own profession of healing, for spreading disease, he further suggested that the inoculators ". . . be allowed a Gratuity of 10 l. per Head, of each Indian who survives, conveys and spreads the Infection among his Tribe; and of 5 l. per Head for those who blow up too soon [i.e., become contagious] (or die) before they reach the Place where Execution is intended." Douglass also injected the religious and moral issues; although he put it in a nonpersonal way, any indictment of inoculation on these grounds could, of course, be most painful to the clergy who supported it, particularly when a nonbeliever like Douglass managed to sound so righteous: "The three greatest Evils incident to Mankind are the *Sword, Famine* and *Pestilence.* The first, or *Jus Belli,* hath been allowed and practiced by all Nations in all Ages. The second is also made Use of to annoy an Enemy; as in the Instance of Blockading or *starving strong Towns:* But the doing of Execution by *Infection or Pestilence,* seems reserved for the Honour of the Inoculator [Boylston] and his *six Directors* [the six ministers signing the letter]. That it is righteous and lawful we have had it lately sufficiently attested, and henceforth can be *no case of conscience to a* Christian. . . ." The first page of the second issue was shared with Douglass by another Boston practitioner, George Steward, who objected in strong language to inoculation on the medical grounds that the correspondents of the Royal Society in Turkey had reported some cases of inoculated patients' breaking out with abscesses symptomatic of the plague, and he appended a letter from a visitor to Aix-en-Provence describing the horrors of the plague outbreak there in 1720. Why a paper of which Douglass was the principal medical adviser and writer should accept the authority of the Turkey correspondents on the abscesses but not on the positive results of inoculation was not stated; and the indignation of his clerical opponents was too seething for them to take the time to call attention to the inconsistency, while Dr. Boylston probably felt that it would be a waste of time anyhow.

Douglass's mild satire evoked a letter to one of Franklin's rival papers, *The Boston News-Letter,* that bore all the stylistic and verbal earmarks of Cotton Mather. The letter compared the contributors of the *Courant* to England's Hell-Fire Club—a notorious collection of cynical young fops who amused themselves by taking such sacred names as the persons of the Trinity and the apostles and holding black masses in tribute to the devil.

"Notwithstanding God's hand is against us in his Visitation of the Small-Pox, and the threatening Aspect of the wet Weather," the letter said, "we find a notorious, scandalous Paper, called the *Courant*, full freighted with Nonsense, Unmanliness, Railery, Prophaneness, Immorality, Arrogance, Calumnies, Lies, Contradictions, and what not all tending to Quarrels and Divisions, and to debauch and corrupt the minds and Manners of New England." It found the paper all the more deplorable because among its contributors were ". . . Practicioners of Physic, several of whom we know to be Gentlemen by Birth, Education, Probity, and good Manners."[46]

Though the *Courant*'s attacks wounded, they did not deter either Cotton Mather or Zabdiel Boylston. Mather had been personally indecisive as to whether to accede to his son Samuel's entreaties to be inoculated or not, and his dilemma continued: If Samuel died of it through contracting it naturally, he would feel privately guilty; and if he died because inoculation miscarried, he would feel "my Condition would be unsupportable." Old Increase had the solution: "His Grandfather advises that I keep the whole Proceeding private [i.e., secret], and that I bring the Lad into this Method of Safety."[47] On August 15, the day after Franklin published Douglass's satire, Cotton Mather showed the courage of his convictions by having Dr. Boylston come to his house and inoculate the son in whom, Increase the second seeming hell-bent on disaster, he put all his hopes for the future. On the same day, Samuel's Harvard roommate died of the disease through natural contagion—a coincidence that led to some difficulties because the subsequent progress of Samuel's case, which took over two weeks before he was out of symptomatic difficulties, was much more suggestive of his already having contracted it from his roommate or others than of the seven or eight days' mild symptoms encountered by Dr. Boylston in the case of his inoculations. Two days afterward, Mather, still troubled about whether he had done the right thing with regard to Samuel but still convinced that, scientifically, humanely, and, by some theological gymnastics, even religiously, inoculation was the only right course, resorted again to the pen and wrote a long exposition of the inoculation method being used in Boston, to be sent to England for publication in the "hope it may be introduced into the English Nation, and a World of good may be done to the miserable Children of Men."[48]

Boylston, who resisted from the beginning getting involved in rhetorical and emotional arguments about inoculation, by now felt that there were sufficient case histories to present a reasonably well documented account, on which he and Mather collaborated, with the latter doing most of the actual writing, Boylston not feeling fully at home putting words on paper, though the pamphlet bore his name as publisher. The account sum-

[46] *Boston News-Letter*, No. 916 (August 14 to August 21, 1721).
[47] Mather, *Diary*, II, 635.
[48] Ibid., 638.

marized the observations of Timonius and Pylarinus to the Royal Society,
reported Mather's interviews with Boston slaves on the African practice
and Boylston's firsthand accounts of his own Boston inoculations and a
defense of the religious and moral validity of the technique—altogether a
compact and useful account.[49] Perhaps partly as a result of Boylston's rising above the emotional and contentious clamor, Douglass's piece in the
third *Courant* occupied the entire first page and part of the second in
discussing for the most part the medical aspects of inoculation, although
he also took occasion to note that the practice was "countenanced *by
Some* [i.e., the clergy], whose proper Business is of another nature," and to
do a little rabble-rousing by suggesting that the Mathers were calling the
townspeople liars in claiming that most of them had no real scruples
of conscience about the practice. And that was the end of Douglass's appearances in the pages of the *Courant* for over four months, Franklin apparently having decided upon a more moderate path with regard to inoculation.

In the fourth *Courant*, the issue was kept alive by a pseudonymous article by the associate rector of King's Chapel, Henry Harris, that was moderate in tone, although he took the personal position that it was the
religious duty and a dictate of the sixth commandment for all men to
preserve health and therefore that deliberate infection was not to be condoned. The only other words on the matter were in a set of seven quatrains by James Franklin, "On the Distress of the Town of Boston, occasioned by the Small Pox," the only achievement of which was proof that a
gift for poetry did not run in the Franklin family, if any further proof
were needed after the exercises of his uncle and his young brother. And in
the fifth issue of the *Courant*, Franklin ran as the lead item a letter entreating the paper to drop the whole issue of inoculation. The letter was
lighhearted, written with grace and spark, and it must have come, on that
first Monday in September, as a welcome relief to readers when the town,
with the malady still unabated after all the bitter words, was as tired of
squabbles as it was of death. Pseudonymously, signed "Zerubbabel Tindal"
and attributed by Benjamin Franklin to a Mr. Gardner, whose further
identity is lost to history but who turned out to become the *Courant's*
most prolific contributor, it pointed out "that too much of one thing is
good for nothing" and that the author, representing a talented group of
"Honest Wags," could produce an infinite variety of diverting material if
the *Courant* was continuing the inoculation dispute merely to fill space.
James Franklin wrote an answer in the same light spirit, explaining some
deletions that he had made, and then turned to resuming his running professional vendetta with John Campbell and his *News-Letter*.

But the respite could not last. Inoculation or not, as the dreary summer
ended, the disease got worse rather than better, with the twenty-six deaths
of August rising to over a hundred in September and soaring to over four

[49] Boylston, *Some Account*, 12.

hundred in October. The economic life of the town came to a stop, as merchants closed their stores, incoming vessels lay in the outer harbor in halfhearted efforts at quarantine, and provisions for the peninsula town, dependent on the countryside for almost daily supplies of food and other essentials, stopped as wagons and sloops from outside Boston refused to make deliveries for fear of contamination. The funeral bells tolled incessantly, and an order by the town's selectmen to limit the tolling of bells, a measure taken to reduce public despair, proved unenforceable. Military companies ceased their drills on the Common, and all societies except the churches eliminated public meetings. Yet the theory of quarantine was imperfectly understood. Watches over infected houses proved impractical, there just not being enough guards to go around, and those exposed to the contagious circulated freely around the town and sat through the long hours of church services in direct contact with those as yet unexposed. The epidemic not yet reaching the surrounding countryside, the towns around Boston sent relief in the form of money, wood, and provisions, one town gathering "several Hogsheads of Tallow, which is to be sent hither and made up into Candles, to be distributed among the Poor"[50] after possibly being processed in Josiah Franklin's shop. Castle's Island was designated as a depository for supplies coming into Boston by ship so that their crewmen would not be exposed to the disease at the town's wharves, and parties of volunteers within the town were organized to meet at a tavern on the edge of the town all from outside who "come with or send Cord-Wood, Billets, Faggots, &c. Butter, Cheese, Geese, Dunghill Fowls, Eggs, Bees-wax, or in short, any Commodity that may be brought. Our Inducements are to Screen our Brethren in the Country from receiving or carrying the Distemper among them. . . ."[51]

* * *

Dr. Boylston went on with his inoculations: in August, seventeen; in September, thirty-one; in October, eighteen. All the patients, with the exception of young Samuel Mather, were treated without any secrecy about it, throughout the entire epidemic, cresting in October and almost entirely over by the end of December, with deaths declining to 249 in November and to 31 in December. Dr. Boylston inoculated a total of 242 people, 6 of whom died, while during the epidemic 5,759 people (roughly half the entire population of Boston) contracted the disease through natural contagion, with 842 dying and almost the same number fleeing the town for safety. Clearly, the statistical evidence was on the side of inoculation, with the death rate 2.5 per cent for the inoculated patients and 14.6 per cent for the natural victims. But the atmosphere, as the morbid fall dragged on into winter, was not conducive to the acceptance or even the consideration of such evidence. While a hundred deaths from natural causes of the disease could be accepted as the will of God, a single death from inoc-

[50] *New-England Courant*, No. 14, (October 30 to November 6, 1721).
[51] Ibid., No. 10 (October 2 to October 9, 1721).

ulation was the result of man's intervention into God's affairs—the opinions and reassurances of the six distinguished ministers to the contrary notwithstanding. The tone of the debate got more recriminatory, articulated on both sides in the most hyperbolic phrases, Cotton Mather contributing some of the most vehement language but his opponents doing all that they could to inspire him to greater verbal assaults. October 30, 1721, Mather published anonymously in *The Boston Gazette* a report to supplement the pamphlet on which he had collaborated with Dr. Boylston. He managed to insult his opponents even before the text began by his belligerent title for the piece: "A Faithful Account of what has occur'd under the late Experiments of the *Small-Pox* managed and governed in the way of *Inoculation*. Published, partly to put a stop unto that unaccountable way of Lying, which fills the Town & Country on this occasion; and partly for the Information & Satisfaction of our Friends in other places."[52] In the November 6 issue of *The New-England Courant*, Franklin published a letter, signed "Peter Hakins" but written by John Eyre, a young Harvard graduate, who began by saying that he didn't think his brief letter would violate Franklin's promise in September to keep the *Courant* neutral. Eyre then proceeded to attempt to discredit Mather's *Gazette* report, "wherein the Reverend Author publishes to the World what abundances of Lying and false Reports have been spread concerning that New and Safe Way, as esteem'd by some." He then ignored the factual data offered by Mather, to whom it had obviously been supplied by Boylston, but took up the lying issue, implying that, as far as he could see, the lying consisted mainly of Mather's own "Equivocations, mental Reservations, and Jesuitical Evasions." This sort of rhetoric, of which he was a skilled contriver, Mather could take perhaps, but then Eyre went on to reopen that chronically sore spot of the Puritan minister: the theory of the inclusively encompassing range of his concerns, of his influence, and of his moral, even if not of his direct, authority. Quoting Dr. Gumble, he wrote, "'Doubtless, a Clergyman, while he keeps within the Sphere of his Duty to God and his People, is an Angel of Heaven; but when he shall degenerate from his own Calling, and fall into the Intriegues of State and Time-Serving, he becomes a Devil; and from a Star in the Firma-Ment of Heaven, he becomes a sooty Coal in the blackest Hell, and receiveth the greatest damnation.'"[53] The insult was gratuitous, underserved, irrational, and ever unrealistic, since a large proportion of Massachusetts ministers had always practiced medicine, including such luminaries as Thomas Thacher of the Old South, Charles Chauncy, president of Harvard, and the cleric-poet of Malden, Michael Wigglesworth. Since James Franklin had reasserted his control of the paper when he stopped Checkley's contributions, he could hardly evade responsibility for the appearance of the Eyre letter in his columns. In any case, the Mathers and

[52] *Boston Gazette*, No. 101 (October 23 to October 30, 1721).
[53] *New-England Courant*, No. 14 (October 30 to November 6, 1721).

their supporters held him responsible. Cotton Mather, encountering Franklin in the street on November 13, a week after the letter appeared, told him so in severe terms: "You make it your Business, in the paper call'd the *Courant*, to villify and abuse the Ministers of this Town. There are many curses which await those that do so. The Lord will smite thro' the Loins of them that rise up against the Levites [i.e., the priestly tribe of Israel]. I would have you consider of it, I have no more to say to you."[54]

Mather's outburst was, if inexcusable, quite explicable. The mood of the town on the inoculation issue had been getting even uglier as the natural threats of winter neared and the November days grew shorter and the hours of darkness longer. On November 1, Cotton Mather took his nephew, Thomas Walter, the minister of Roxbury, who had so infuriated John Checkley with his *Anti-Courant*, into his house so that he could be inoculated by Dr. Boylston and go through his recovery there. But nothing was secret in Boston, and word soon got around town that, not satisfied with advocating the spread of the disease by willfully infecting healthy Bostonians with it, Mather was now making matters worse by bringing outsiders into town and getting them infected. The contumely and clamor against him mounted. "This abominable Town, treats me in most malicious and murderous Manner, for my doing as CHRIST would have me to do, in saving the lives of the People from an horrible Death."[55] On November 4 the freeholders of Boston at a town meeting voted not to allow inoculated individuals to come into town or to come for the purpose of receiving inoculation—a step clearly directed at Mather. On the ninth, he complained again of "The scottish Errors and cursed Clamours, that fill the Town and Countrey, raging against the astonishing Success of the *Small-Pox* Inoculated. . . ."[56] Four days later, as Thomas Walter lay recovering in Mather's bedroom from the mild case induced by his inoculation, at three o'clock in the morning, someone threw a bomb through the window of Mather's chamber, assuming that he was sleeping there. "The Weight of the Iron Ball alone, had it fallen on his Head, would have been enough to have done Part of the Business designed. But the *Granado* [grenade] was charged, the upper part with dried Powder, the lower Part with a Mixture of Oil of Turpentine and Powder and what else I know not, in such a Manner, that upon its going off, it must have splitt, and have probably killed the Persons in the Room, and certainly fired the Chamber, and speedily laid the House in Ashes. But, *this Night there*

---

[54] Ibid., No. 18 (November 27 to December 4, 1721). From Franklin's comments and the context of his defense, there is little doubt that Cotton Mather was the deliverer of this rebuke. (See p. 438 *infra*.) In his introduction to *The New-England Courant, A Selection of Certain Issues* (Boston, The American Academy of Arts and Sciences; 1956), Perry Miller identifies Mather as Franklin's accuser.

[55] Mather, *Diary*, II, 655.

[56] Ibid., 656.

stood by me the Angel of the GOD, whose I am and whom I serve; and the merciful Providence of GOD my SAVIOUR, so ordered it, that the Granado passing thro' the Window, had by the Iron in the Middle of the Casement, such a Turn given to it, that in falling on the Floor . . . the Fuse was violently shaken out . . . without firing the Granado. When the *Granado* was taken up, there was found a Paper so tied with String upon the Fuse, that it might out-Live the breaking of the Shell, which had these words in it; COTTON MATHER. You Dog, Dam you: I'l inoculated you with this, with a Pox to you."[57]

It was just the kind of incident that, with his constant flirting with martyrdom but always somehow avoiding it, inspired Mather and refortified his sense of personal partnership with God, and he saw in it both divine approval of his inoculation advocacy and convincing evidence that he was marked, like many of the other of God's most intimate and effective colleagues, for inevitable martyrdom, the ecstasies of which by November 19 he was already experiencing: "I have communicated a never-failing and a most allowable Method, of preventing Death and other grievous Mysteries by a terrible Distemper among my Neighbours. Every day demonstrates that if I had been hearken'd to, many precious Lives (many Hundreds) had been saved. The Opposition to it, has been carried on, with senseless Ignorance and raging Wickedness. But the growing Triumphs of Truth over it, throw a possessed People into a Fury, which will probably cost my Life. I have Proofs, that there are people who approve and applaud the Action of *Tuesday* Morning: and who give out Words, that tho' the first Blow miscarried, there will quickly come another, that shall doe the Business more effectually."[58]

Grave as such violence was in its implications of the alarming trend that the controversy was taking as well as in its direct threat to human lives already sadly enough imperiled, and genuinely as Mather saw the epidemic as part of a divine pattern with him at the center, he saw also its temporal publicity value and composed an account of it for the newspapers, with an additional sentence ascribed to the note attached to the bomb that involved a former parishioner disgruntled because of a lie he accused Mather of telling about a friend. Franklin published Mather's version verbatim "To prevent wrong Representations that may be made of a late Occurrence much talked of,"[59] adding only that the governor had offered a fifty-pound award for anyone discovering the culprit. Meanwhile, Cotton Mather prepared once again in a life that endured a thousand deaths to meet his maker: ". . . I am filled with unutterable Joy at the Prospect of my approaching Martyrdom."[60]

[57] Ibid., 657–58.
[58] Ibid., 52.
[59] *New-England Courant*, No. 16, (November 13 to November 20, 1721).
[60] Mather, *Diary*, II, 661.

The martyrdom, of course, did not come in the form of a vengeful death, and although James Franklin had been deeply disturbed by his encounter with Mather, he refrained for two weeks from replying to it. And then, Franklin, who seems to have had very real convictions about the right of a free people to say, print, and read what they wanted, still outraged by the invocation of the clerical curse upon him, gave a full account of the entire affair to his readers, signing it with his name—the first piece he had ever written for attribution to appear in his own paper. He reprinted verbatim the Eyre ("Peter Hakins") letter that had occasioned the Mather outburst. Franklin's comment was, in the frantic context of the time, extraordinarily level-headed. Certainly, it was the first, and possibly it was one of the most genuine, defenses of the freedom of the press in America. And for a struggling twenty-four-year-old printer locked in battle with the most powerful voice in the province, it was a judicious piece that stands well the test of time:

> Nothing is more certain than that great and good Men may sometimes give so great a Loose to their *Passion* and *Opinion*, as to load those whom they apprehend to differ from them with unjust and groundless Charges: and the Law of Nature, not only *allows*, but *obliges* every Man to defend himself against his Enemies, how great and good soever they may appear.
>
> The severe Treatment I have met with on account of some late Pieces inserted in this Paper, is known to all who know any thing of the present unhappy Divisions of the Town: and since by the Industry of some Persons, the charge against me is made publick, I hope by being publick in my Vindication will find a Pardon.
>
> About Three Weeks since, a certain Gentleman stopt me in the Street, and with an air of great Displeasure attack'd me in Words to this Effect: [There follows the language, quoted above, of Mather's public rebuke of Franklin.]
>
> This heinous Charge and heavy curse would have been more surprizing to me, if it had not come from one who is ever as groundless in his Invictives as in his *Pangyricks*. I confess there were two pieces inserted in the Courant (No. 3) in Answer to the Anti-Courant, which I have since wish'd had been left out; but my Printing the Anti-Courant, laid me under some Obligation to publish them; tho' I believe, if I had took more Time to peruse them, I should not have done it. But this Gentleman has endeavour'd to make me an object of *publick Odium*, for no other Reason than my publishing an Answer to a piece in the *Gazette* of October 30, wherein the greatest Part of the Town are represented as unaccountable Lyars and Self-Destroyers, for opposing the Practice of Inoculation. I speak not only my own Opinion in this, but that of the Town in General, who were so exasperated that at a Town Meeting soon after, they mov'd, that a Committee might be appointed to find out the Author; but the Moderator telling them, that he believ'd it was not their Province to enquire into the Matter, and, besides the difficulty of finding out the Author [i.e., of *proving* the authorship—everyone knew that it could be no

one but Mather],[61] the Piece was too scandalous to deserve their Notice, they were persuaded to desist. [At this point, Franklin reprinted the Eyre-Hakins letter in its entirety.]

The Person [John Eyre, Harvard College, 1718] who brought this Letter to me, is a Schollar and a Gentleman, and (to undeceive some who think it came from a Tory [i.e., John Checkley]) one who was never suspected to have imbib'd any Tory Principles. Now I leave the World to judge, whether any particular Person, or the Ministers of the Town in general are reflected on in it. Here is no Name mention'd, nor would so many have thought the *Coat fitted* the suppos'd Author of the aforesaid Piece in the *Gazette,* if he had not *challeng'd it* by a Curse on the *Taylor* [i.e., Franklin] in the open Street, and afterwards so often in private Conversation: He confidently affirms that I either employ some Persons to write Things on purpose to abuse and vilify the Ministers, or write them my self. I beg leave to say, that in this way he is very much misinform'd, I neither have wrote any one Letter my self, nor employ'd any other Person to write anything relating to the Ministers; nor do I know the Authors of many of the Letters sent to me. Several Ministers both in Town and Country constantly take the *Courant,* which I believe they wou'd not do, if they thought it publish'd on purpose to bring their Persons into Disesteem. As, in Controversies of Religion, nothing is more frequent than for Divines themselves to press the *same Texts* for *opposite Tenets,* they cannot fairly condemn a man for dissenting from them in Matters of Religion; much less can any Man be thought to hinder the Success of the Work of a Minister, by opposing him in that which is not *properly a Minister's Work:* And, "to attempt to reduce all Men to the same Standard of thinking, is (as the British *Cato* [in the *London Journal*] observes) absurd in Philosophy, impious in Religion, and Faction in the State." Even Errors made publick, and afterwards publickly expos'd, less endanger the Constitution of Church or State, than when they are (without Opposition) industriously propagated in private Conversation.

Hence to anathematize a Printer for publishing the different Opinions of Men, is as injudicious as it is wicked. To use Curses without a Cause, is to throw them away as if they were *Nothing Worth,* and to rob them of their Force, when there is Occasion for them.

The *Courant* was never design'd for a Party Paper. I have once and again given out, that both Inoculators and Anti-Inoculators are welcome to speak their Minds in it; and those that have read the Courants must know, that I have not only publish'd Pieces wrote among ourselves in favour of Inoculation, but have given as full an Account of the Success of it in England, as the other Papers have done; Yet the Envy of some Men has represented me as a Tool to the Anti-Inoculators. What my own Sentiments of things are, is of no Consequence, nor any matter to any Body. I hereby invite all Men, who have Leisure, Inclination and Ability, to speak their Minds, with Freedom, Sense and Moderation, and their Pieces shall be welcome to a Place in my Paper.

[61] The assumption's validity was demonstrated by Professor Kittredge in "Lost Works," 460.

I hope I have now given full Proof of my Impartiality: But if the Gentleman above-mention'd, or those influenc'd by him, think themselves wrong'd at any time, and will not be at the Pains to defend themselves, they are welcome to treat me as they please; I shall give my self nor the Town any further Trouble in my Defence.

JAMES FRANKLIN[62]

Franklin's defense against being bullied in the public streets and having the curse of a clergyman called down upon him (James Franklin was not so far removed from regard for the spiritual power of an ordained minister that such a curse was not an awesome matter) was clear and convincing. The evidence that his paper had been impartial is far less so. In twenty-two of the first twenty-three issues of the *Courant* (No. 7 is missing) published between August 7, 1721, and January 8, 1722, when the epidemic was virtually over, there were forty-seven editorials, letters, and news items involving the subject of inoculation. Of these, twenty-five were neutral news items—obituary notices, accounts of town actions of a quarantine nature, reports of relief supplies arriving. Twenty-one, and most of these were the longest and most prominent pieces, were clearly and, in most cases, strongly either anti-inoculation or anti-inoculators. Only two of the forty-seven even tended to give a favorable view of inoculation. One of these was a report in December of successful inoculations in London—which is the only case that Franklin cited in his quite far-fetched claim of impartiality. The other was a letter by Gardner urging everyone to be inoculated but so overstating the case, in what Benjamin Franklin described, in a notation on his copy of the issue, "in imitation of Dr. Mather," as to make it to the knowing reader a satirical comment on the confidence of the pro-inoculators in the practice. Actually, of course, the *Courant*'s lack of partiality was not a valid consideration in the issue of a free press, the test of which is the freedom to be partial, not to be impartial. The *Courant* was not primarily a newspaper. It was primarily an organ of the views and perspectives of a group of youngish men, gathered around James Franklin, who was, however, their conduit rather than their leader, although he apparently did exercise exclusive editorial control except for the first three issues, when Checkley, "his Author," seemed in his aggressive way to have assumed that power.

Franklin was on far sounder and certainly more relevant grounds when he argued against condemning printers "for publishing the different Opinions of Men." However, he did not stop there. In the same issue of the *Courant*, in which he published and signed his notable defense, he allowed himself to be drawn into the tangential dispute about whether the ministers were wandering out of their proper fields and became mere "meddlers" when they concerned themselves with other than spiritual affairs—a question the very raising of which was still an outrageous heresy

[62] *New-England Courant*, No. 18 (November 27 to December 4, 1721).

to many of the heirs of John Cotton, for whom there were *no* affairs that were not or should not be spiritually oriented, and it was also a threat to the authority and status of the ministers, who were seeing their position in the structure of the provincial society being gradually but steadily and pronouncedly eroded by the growth of civil authority. It did not set easily with them to see "young Franklin" speeding up this process by attacks upon their general influence in the community. It was this in the John Eyre—"Peter Hakins" letter that so aroused the ire of Cotton Mather, prompting his public tongue-lashing of Franklin. The latter ignored the matter in his defense, and then Cotton Mather proceeded with his customary ineptness to correct the omission and to agitate Franklin to attack him directly as a clergyman.

On December 2, 1721—the Saturday before the *Courant*'s publication on Monday, the fourth—James Franklin was setting the type for the paper, the major part of which consisted of his self-defense. That same day, Cotton Mather was writing in his diary, "Some very wicked Persons, must have suitable Admonitions dispensed unto them."[63] Then, as Franklin recounted the episode, without naming the principal although clearly enough identifying him, Mather set out to dispense his admonition—an account which Franklin then appended to his defense, publishing it over his initials:

> On Saturday in the Afternoon, soon after I had set my Types for the above Vindication, I received my Curse *at Large*, inclos'd in the following Letter, & since it comes so earnestly recommended, I shall insert it *Verbatim*.
>
> To Mr. *Franklin*, Author of the *Courant*.
>
> Sir, You have given out that you refuse nothing that is sent to you, therefore I presume that you will insert the inclosed in your next Courant, which will no doubt much Please and Edify your Candid Readers, I am sure it will one who subscribes himself
>
> Your constant Reader,
Castalio
>
> Dec. 2, 1721.
>
> The words that were spoken to young *Franklin* the Printer, Nov. 13, 1721 (of which there have been many Lies raised as the manner of them is on all Occasions)
>
> "Young man: You Entertain, and no doubt you think you Edify, the Publick with a weekly Paper, called *The Courant*. The Plain Design of your Paper, is to Banter and Abuse the Ministers of God, and if you can, to defeat all the good Effects of their Ministry on the Minds of the People. You may do well to Remember that it is a Passage in the Blessing on the Tribe of *Levi, Smite thro' the Loins of them that shall rise against him and of them that irate him*. I would have you to know, that the Faithful Ministers of Christ in this Place, are as honest, and useful, Men

---

[63] Mather, *Diary*, II, 662.

as the Ancient *Levites* were, and are as Dear to their Glorious Lord as the Ancient *Levites* were: And if you Resolve to go in Serving their Great Adversary as you do, you must expect the Consequences."

The Reason of this faithful Admonition was, because the Practice of supporting and publishing every Week, a Libel, on purpose to lessen and Blacken, and Burlesque the Vertuous, and Principal Ministers of Religion in a Country, and render all the Services of their Ministry Despicable, and even Detestable to the People, *is a Wickedness that was never known before*, in any Country, Christian, Turkish or Pagan, on the face of the Earth, and some Good Men are afraid it may provoke Heaven, to deal with this Place in some regards as never any place has yet been dealt withal, and a Charity to this Young Man, and his Accomplices might render such a Waring proper for them.

The conveying letter was obviously written by someone acting at Mather's request, for the tone is not Matherian and the punctuation, capitalization, and choice of words, including the subscription, do not accord with those in Mather's books, letters, and diaries. "Castalio" merely conveyed to Franklin a written version of substantially what the young printer had been told on the street, and the grammatical, rhetorical, and orthographic specifics in that version *do* accord with those of the other writings of Mather, who was, alone among the Boston ministers of 1721, capable of equating himself with Levi, of characterizing himself as a "principal" (as opposed to what?) minister, and of such exaggerations as to say that the *Courant* "every week" attacked the clergy, when as a matter of fact, after Douglass's opening salvos there was no attack on the clergy for twelve weeks until John Eyre's letter in November. James Franklin, in any case, answered the admonition, immediately following his printing of it, in such a manner as to alienate the clergy generally without strengthening the case he had already put in the paragraphs of his defense. It was, by then, late on Saturday; he had to lock up his type and have the press ready to start printing on Monday morning. Angry and in a hurry, he struck out bitterly at Mather and his ilk.

"The Author of this *faithful Admonition*, is certainly under a Degree of Distraction, or he would never desire a Thing to be made publick so much to his own Confusion: Nor wou'd the best Friend I have in the World, have done more to clear up my Reputation," Franklin began, with an assurance somewhat strained in the light of what he was to say later in his comments.

Is this the *manner of you*, Sir, to curse young Franklin in the Street, without proving any Thing against him, and then to send *The Words that were spoken* to him to the Press? You say the *Courant* is a *Libel, supported and publish'd every Week*, ON PURPOSE, *to lessen, and blacken, and burlesque the* PRINCIPAL *Ministers of Religion*, &c. Pray, Sir, When were the Ministers mentioned in the *Courant*, but when they themselves first occasion'd it, by zealously recommending the doubtful Practice of Inoculation? Again, This *is a Wickedness that was never known before in any Country, Christian, Turkish, or Pagan, on the Face of the Earth.* Here, Sir, You oblige me to insert a short Paragraph of News and a Scrap of Poetry, which I never to now intended to have made publick. The News is from a *London* paper I have by me, and the Poetry in a Letter to the *St. James's Post*, published in *England* some time since, on the News of Mr. [Gershon] W[oode]l's being expell'd the House of Representatives of this Province, for his ill Treatment of the Ministers. [The representative from Tiverton was expelled July 15, 1720, having "Exprest himself with great Enmity to the Ministers of this Province."[64]]

London, *August* 12. They write from Cambridge [England] that the Head of a certain College has lately lost his Interest very much there, through his Pride, Avarice and other Priestly Endowments.

The Poetry concludes the Letter, which is too long to insert here.

> Thus Priests by strict Rules
> May be call'd the Edge-Tools,
> Which the People, *poor Fools,*
>   Are forbidden to touch.
> Be a Villain, a Traytor,
> Affront your Creator,
> Or glory in Satyr,
>   It safer is much.
> Nay, be lewd, drunk, or swear,
> Proud, Covetous as they're;
>   You may escape the holy Snare,
> But if a P[rie]st once you've thoroughly vext,
> He'll stick by You closer than e'er to his Text,
> You're plagued for't in this World, and d[am]n'd in the Next.

Now, Sir, Your Knowledge of Christian Countries, obliges you to own, that far worse Libels than these are frequently publish'd in *England,* and none of the PRINCIPAL *Ministers of Religion, are lessen'd, or blacken'd or burlesqu'd* by them, tho' some zealous *State-Divines,* and Meddlers in other Men's Matters, are sometimes so unwise as to discover their *Guilt* by their *Resentments:* And if you will for once impartially compare these Things with the *Courant's,* you can't for Shame but take your Curse again, and make use of it yourself, for endeavouring to *lessen, and blacken, and burlesque* young *Franklin* and his Accomplices.

I confess, I have not treated this Gentleman as his Character deserves; but (whatever is the Matter with me) I can't help being so metaphysical as to separate his Person from his Character. He has no Business to curse anybody out[side] of his own Congregation. My own Pastors [i.e., Joseph Sewall and Thomas Prince of the Old South] are as faithful to their Flock as he can be to his; and they have not yet thought proper so much as to

[64] *Journals of The House of Representatives of Massachusetts* (Boston, 1921), II, 240.

reprove me for inserting anything in the *Courant* since No. 3 [when Checkley made his crude attack on Thomas Walter].   J.F

As young Benjamin Franklin had learned of Socratic dialectics from his reading of Xenophon, exchanges of such assertions got no one anywhere, changed no minds, mitigated no wrath. Five days afterward, Cotton Mather privately pronounced, "Warnings are to be given unto the wicked Printer, and his Accomplices, who every week publish a vile Paper to lessen and blacken the Ministers of the Town, and render their Ministry ineffectual."[66] But affairs in the kingdom of Holland began to preoccupy him, and he busied himself to preparing papers and letters to send the Dutch to save them from the smallpox, from themselves, and from any lessening of the religious spirit among them. So Mather ended his troubled year of 1721.

But James Franklin was not going to let the conflict end. In the *Courant* of December 11, he announced on the first page that the next issue would have a letter against inoculation, adding inflammatorily, "giving an Account of the Number of Persons who have dy'd under that operation."[67] The letter signed "Absinthium," was written by Dr. George Steward. It is a long letter, occupying all of the first page and part of the second, objecting calmly to inoculation on medical grounds, until the last paragraph when Dr. Steward accused Dr. Boylston of spreading the infection by inoculating people at his Dock Square house "in the Heart of the Town" and then turning them loose to infect others; nobody answered it. In the same issue, the prolific Mr. Gardner contributed a letter, as from someone—"Tom Penshallow"—in the Plymouth Colony, complaining that they did not enjoy the same freedom of speech that the people in Boston did and that it was being rumored that a law was to be passed in Plymouth specifically banning the *Courant;* Gardner answered his own letter in the next issue, saying that it was Plymouth's own fault if they elected to office men who made bad laws and the remedy was to elect better men. It was the last *Courant* issue of the year, dated Christmas Day, and the acrimony of the great inoculation controversy appeared spent. The year—one of the gloomiest in Boston's history—was ending, as were also the dreadful epidemic that afflicted the town and the bitter dispute to which it gave rise. The Mathers, insomuch as it was temperamentally possible for them, appeared to be drifting back to spiritual concerns. The atmosphere was quieter. Then the *Courant* let loose a blast, in its second issue of 1722, that sent old Increase Mather into a seizure of righteous indignation, opening up all the wounds of 1721 and rubbing salt into them.

By then Franklin's most frequent and lengthiest contributor (he had

[65] *New-England Courant,* No. 18 (November 27 to December 4, 1721).
[66] Mather, *Diary,* II, 663.
[67] *New-England Courant,* No. 19 (December 4 to December 11, 1721).

contributed major pieces to six of the past seven issues of the *Courant*),
Gardner was an extremely skilled writer and a first-class mind. His January
contribution was in the form of a dialogue between a clergyman, obviously
of the Mather persuasion, concerning inoculation, and a skeptical layman,
who did not believe that ministers, however great and good, were not fallible. The great heresy of the piece occurred, however, in response to a comment made by the clergyman, substantially the same as one that Cotton
Mather had, in fact, made:

"*Cl.* But I find all the Rakes in Town are against Inoculation, and that
induces me to believe it is a right way.

"*Laym.* Most of the Ministers are for it, and that induces me to think it
is from the D[evi]l; for he often makes Use of good Men as Instruments
to obtrude his Delusions on the World."[68]

Completely ignoring the last clause, the aged Increase Mather inserted
an advertisement, over his signature, in both the *News-Letter* and the *Gazette*, denouncing the *Courant* in the harshest terms that had yet been
publicly applied to it. After quarreling with the authenticity of the
Courant's reporting of a *London Mercury* account of inoculations in England and denying that he was for long a subscriber to the *Courant*
(whether a subscriber or not, he and his son certainly never missed reading an issue, and, as James Franklin pointed out, by sending his grandson,
Mather Byles, to Franklin's shop to pick up individual copies, Mather
"paid more for the paper, and became more of a Supporter of it"[69] than if
he remained a subscriber), the patriarch condemned both the *Courant*
and Franklin personally for publishing it: "In special, because in one of his
Vile Courants he insinuates, that if *the Ministers of God approve of a
Thing, it is a Sign it is of the Devil*; which is a horrid thing to be related!
And he doth frequently abuse the Ministers of Religion, and many other
worthy Persons in a manner, which is intolerable. For these and such like
Reasons I signified to the Printer, that I would have no more of their
Wicked Courants." The old man longed for the censorship of his earlier
days that suppressed *Publick Occurrences* once and for all after the first
and only issue. "I that have known what New England was from the Beginning, cannot but be troubled to see the Degeneracy of this Place. I can
well remember when the Civil Government would have taken an effectual
Course to suppress such a *Cursed Libel!* which if it be not done I am
afraid that some *Awful Judgment* will come upon this Land, and the
Wrath of God will arise, and there will be no Remedy, I cannot but pity
poor *Franklin*, who tho' but a *Young Man* it may be Speedily he must appear before the Judgment Seat of God, and what answer will he give for
printing things so vile and abominable? And I cannot but Advise the Supporters of this Courant to Consider the Consequences of being *Partakers*

[68] Ibid., No. 23 (January 1 to January 8, 1721–2).
[69] Ibid., No. 27 (January 20 to February 5, 1722).

in Other Mens Sins, and no more Countenance such a Wicked *Paper.*"[70]

James Franklin devoted the entire first page of his next issue to a fairly competent and responsive reply, with no vituperation, to "This Charge I now lye under from the oldest Minister in the Country," implying that the old cleric had been put up to lending his name to the advertisement by others (he could have had Cotton Mather in mind): ". . . some Persons have been so undutiful to the Reverend Dr. *Increase Mather* as to perswade him to prefix his Name to an advertisement. . . ." The central complaints, that the ministers were the tools of the devil and that the paper ought to be suppressed, Franklin answered succinctly and calmly enough. Of the first, he simply pointed out that the dialogue with the comment on ministers and the devil added significantly that the devil "often makes Use of good Men" and gave David as a biblical example. Of the question of suppression, he claimed that the very fact that the *Courant* had not been suppressed proved that it had done nothing against the law. Finally, as to his own salvation, he concluded, "I expect and Hope to appear before God with safety in the Righteousness of Christ."[71]

* * *

Although the *Courant* and more particularly James Franklin as an individual were to face more serious conflicts with the establishment, the smallpox controversy in Boston, epitomized by the strong, old Mathers on the one side and the brash, young paper on the other, was over. Cotton Mather bewailed at a meeting of Boston ministers that it had left him so slandered that he could no longer introduce measures to improve life in Boston but would limit himself to supporting the proposals of others—a declaration that got shouted down by his colleagues, as he no doubt fully expected. Dr. Douglass wrote, in the form of a letter to a British friend, Alexander Stuart, M.D., a fellow of the Royal Society, a critique of *Inoculation of the Small Pox as Practised in Boston,* which James Franklin published and for which he wrote an introduction renewing his attack on the clergy. It created no great stir nor did other pamphlets Franklin published designed to keep the controversy alive less because there was any longer any danger of inoculation's spreading the infection than to keep up his attack on the Mathers. In time, Douglass modified his view and was persuaded that, rightly administered, inoculation had proved to be a useful means of combating the disease.

Dr. Boylston wrote an excellent *Historical Account of the Small-Pox Inoculated in New England,* which was published in London in 1726. He had been invited in 1724 by the Royal Society to visit London as its guest and, before returning to Boston eighteen months later, was elected to the society, the twelfth American and eighth New Englander so honored. While he was in London he was visited by a young man of twenty, who

[70] *Boston News-Letter,* No. 939 (January 22 to January 29, 1722).
[71] *New-England Courant,* No. 27 (January 29 to February 5, 1722).

had gone there under false promises of an important association but found himself stranded "without money, friends or counsel. I applied in my extreme distress to him, who supplied me with twenty guineas, and relying on his judgment, I visited him as opportunities offered, and by his faithful counsels and encouragements I was saved from the abyss of destruction which awaited me, and my future fortune was based on his timely assistance."[72] The youth was, according to Boylston's grandnephew, Benjamin Franklin.

The episode is not mentioned in the *Autobiography*. But neither did Franklin mention the entire smallpox controversy of 1721, though he was present at the very center of it, in the printing house of the *Courant*, which was launched in the midst of it and was the central conduit of the opposition to inoculation, keeping the issue alive long after the problem ceased to be acute. That Franklin would not have remembered it is inconceivable. His *Autobiography* contains much earlier details of much lesser events in his life. Moreover, Franklin had taken his own file of copies of the *Courant*, and beginning with the first issue and continuing through the forty-third marked the authorship of virtually every article and letter that appeared, including all those dealing with the inoculation controversy.[73] The probability is that Benjamin omitted all reference to it because the subject was on several grounds a painful one to him. First, the method of discussion, vituperative and argumentative, went wholly against his grain; moreover he had read Xenophon and was convinced that it was no way to conduct an argument. Secondly, he knew at the time of writing the *Autobiography* that his brother and his coterie had taken the wrong side, for subsequent history proved Boylston and the Mathers overwhelmingly right, and Benjamin himself, even as a boy, had a real respect for Cotton Mather's learning and sense of community responsibility. But the most persuasive reason that suggests itself is more profoundly human than either of these: In 1736, when Franklin was thirty and had been away from Boston and the *Courant* for thirteen years, the second of his two sons, Francis Folger Franklin, a child of magical beauty and charm and his father's delight, died of smallpox. Ironically, it was rumored all over Philadelphia that the child came to his end because his father had had him inoculated. To Franklin's lasting sorrow, the opposite was true, and he sought compensation for his grief in publicly urging inoculation on others. In his *Pennsylvania Gazette* of December 30, 1736, he published a rare signed paragraph: "Understanding 'tis a current Report, that my Son Francis, who died lately of the Small Pox, had it by Inoculation; and

---

[72] *New England Historical and Genealogical Register*, XXXV, 129, according to an account assumed to be by Ward Nicholas Boylston, grandnephew of Dr. Boylston, who met Franklin in Paris in 1783.

[73] For an account of the discovery of this file in the British Museum, see Worthington C. Ford, Massachusetts Historical Society, *Proceedings*, April 1924, 336ff.

being desired to satisfy the Publick in that Particular; inasmuch as some People are, by that Report (join'd with others of the like kind and perhaps equally) deter'd from having that Operation perform'd on their Children, I do hereby sincerely declare, that he was not inoculated, but receiv'd the Distemper in the common Way of Infection: and I suppose the Report could only arise from its being my known Opinion, that Inoculation was a safe and beneficial Practice; and from my having said among my Acquaintance, that I intended to have my Child inoculated, as soon as he should have recovered sufficient Strength from a Flux with which he had been long afflicted."[74] In 1771, by then a grandfather and writing the *Autobiography* in England, Franklin wrote that he "long regretted bitterly and still regret"[75] not inoculating his son, and a year later, in response to accounts sent to him of his three-year-old grandson, Benjamin Franklin Bache, he wrote ruefully of the son who had died so many years earlier, "All, who have seen my grandson, agree with you in their accounts of his being an uncommonly fine boy, which brings often afresh to my mind the idea of my son Franky, though now dead thirty-six years, whom I have seldom since seen equalled in every thing, and whom to this day I cannot think of without a sigh."[76]

Whatever his attitude in later life, or even at the time, toward the substance of the smallpox controversy in Boston and whatever his views of the manner in which it was conducted, the dispute lasting well over half a year and occurring in the awesome context of sudden death, demonstrated in life much of what Benjamin Franklin, fifteen years old the year of the epidemic, had been reading in books for as long as he could remember. His instinct, traceable to some of the earliest episodes in his life, to questioning authority, indeed to questioning all things, was fortified. His respect for freedom, particularly the freedom to inquire, to report, to circulate ideas and opinions, was strengthened. His resolve to be effective in his discourse and his writing was invigorated. And through that argumentative, overpositive, but indomitable cluster of *Courant* contributors, he was initiated into the contentious, fallible, but principled nature of the democratic experiment which was to occupy so much of his life.

[74] *Papers*, II, 114.
[75] *Autobiography*, 170.
[76] Van Doren, *Letters of Benjamin Franklin and Jane Mecum*, 134.

XII

The Contributors

> . . . the Opinions of Men are almost as varied
> as their Faces.
>
> —Benjamin Franklin[1]

Essentially, perhaps at times inordinately, gregarious in temperament, Benjamin Franklin probably welcomed the conversations and debates among James Franklin's "ingenious Men among his Friends who amus'd themselves by writing little Pieces for this Paper [the *Courant*], which gain'd it Credit and made it more in Demand . . ."[2] —particularly in contrast to the loneliness of the tallowshop and the solitary meals that he took after beginning his apprenticeship to his brother in order to save money for buying books. As his eager embracement of Cotton Mather's idea of "voluntary associations" for discussing matters of religion and morals and, when he was twenty-one, his adaptation of the idea to the establishment of the "Junto" to discuss "any Point of Morals, Politics or Natural Philosophy"[3] demonstrated, the process of learning and intellectual growth was not to Franklin an isolated one but rather stimulated and nourished by social contacts. His instinct and gift for informed discussion would have made him an ideal and provocative member of a university community, and yet at the same time there was a self-pacing, desultory quality about Franklin's intellectual development that did not accord agreeably with many of the rubrics and much of the discipline of academic scholarship. The young Franklin was far more attuned to the give-and-take of a colloquy than to the listening and reciting of the pedagogic method. Even though his lowly status as an apprentice permitted him no active role in the conversations of the Couranteers, he had an attentive ear, a retentive memory, and a racing mind that kept well abreast and often ahead of the dialogue to which he listened as he went about his menial chores.

Miserable as Franklin's apprenticeship—any apprenticeship—was, it had enormous advantages to one of his talents and capacities because it

---

[1] "Apology for Printers," 1731, in *Papers*, I, 194.
[2] *Autobiography*, 67.
[3] Ibid., 117.

was in a printing house and, even more, because it was a printing house publishing a newspaper. With the possible exception of a bookseller's, there was no shop in which a youth of Franklin's nature could have been more felicitiously placed. Had it been, like most artisans' shops, including his father's, a shop where master and apprentice were alone nearly all the time, doing routine and repetitive tasks, the combination of sibling rivalry and master-apprentice relationship, compounded by an assertive spirit of independence on both sides, would necessarily have been disastrous. But such explosive tension was markedly alleviated, and made bearable to Benjamin, who was characteristically short of patience as a youth, by the constantly changing atmosphere engendered by the comings and goings of the contributors to the *Courant*, by the undoubtedly spirited arguments as to what went into the paper and what stayed out, and by the unpredictable mix of divergent minds and backgrounds seeking to make common cause: the snide, assured, but erudite Checkley; the stubborn, professional Douglass; the urbane, wise Gardner; the bookish, well-disposed Adams; and the peaceable, youthful Oxonian curate Harris, among them. No less appealing to the young, exploring mind of Franklin was the spirit of questioning old ideas and old authorities that bound the contributors together despite the differences as to some of their immediate interests. The methods of their questioning, too, were wholly new to Boston and essentially youthful: ridicule, an impudent logic, an irreverence that guarded against offending religion but considered the extra-religious activities of its exponents fair game, and an amused if impatient and relentless skepticism of the old and the habitual.

All this was apparent from the animated way that James Franklin and his earliest contributors undertook, from the beginning, to make the *Courant* a lively alternative to the dull irrelevance of the weekly disseminations of the *News-Letter* of John Campbell and the *Gazette* of Philip Musgrave, whose proprietors were, respectively, fifty-six and forty years James Franklin's seniors, while their newspapers had antedated his by seventeen years and nineteen months respectively. In the very first issue of the *Courant*, Checkley, in his introduction to the new paper, had referred obliquely to the dullness of its rivals: ". . . *out of mere Kindness to my* Brother-Writers, *I intend now and then to be* (*like them*) *very, very dull* . . ."[4]—on which gibe the old Scot, John Campbell, leapt in fury, obviously falling into a trap carefully prepared by the *Courant* to gain the benefit of attention in the competing papers. In the next issue of the *News-Letter*, Campbell published a long advertisement, verbose and disconnected, which took seriously the *Courant's*

---

[4] *New-England Courant*, No. 1 (August 7 to August 14, 1721). Frederic Hudson, *Journalism in the United States* (New York, 1873), 61, gives the offending reference as specifically applied to the *News-Letter* and the phrase as "a dull vehicle of intelligence." These were both assumptions, since no early copies of the *Courant* were available to Hudson. No such specific reference or phrase appeared in the *Courant*.

promise to be "very, very dull" in fairness to its competitors—a promise compared by Campbell, in the only bright phrase in the interminable complaint, to "soure Ale in Summer"[5]—and ended with the odd and pathetic plea that, if the *Courant* were to charge him with dullness, it should first have warned him, told him in what respects and given him a chance to mend his style, even providing him with an imitable example.

James Franklin was delighted with the space, amounting to nearly an entire column in the eight columns of the *News-Letter*, and promptly responded in the next issue of the *Courant* in twenty-seven lines of verse, very probably of his own authorship since, of the seven contributors to the first ten issues of the *Courant*, only Franklin is known to have contributed verse and, of his six contributions, all but the last were in verse.[6] Styling himself "Jack Dulman" (a pseudonym which the somewhat haughty Checkley could never have brought himself to use), Franklin dashed off a series of rhymes that, for all their awkwardness, had sufficiently sprightly turns to make it the most animated passage that had yet appeared in American journalism. Addressed openly "to John Campbell," it had the insolence that was to grate upon competitors, clergy, and magistrates until they all in succession locked horns with the *Courant*'s contributors; but there was no malice to it—rather the good-natured, if quite rowdy, initiation of a purposive feud. "Jack Dulman by Design may Dulman be; /But you by Fate are duller far than he," the younger publisher addressed his venerable adversary; and he rudely disposed both of Campbell's bucolic image of "soure Ale in Summer," suggesting that the *Courant*'s "*Ale* grows better, yours is *too, too* stale," and of his plea that the *Courant*'s author help him identify the sources of his dullness rather than publicly censure it, declaring, "He need not tell you where you're *flat and dull*;/Your Works declare, 'tis in your empty Skull. . . ."[7] Poor, plodding Campbell ground out a meandering, sputtering reply in *his* next issue, in which he seemed to lose control of his indignation as well as his syntax in conjecturing a source of inspiration for James Franklin's verses: ". . . as a little before the Composure you had been Rakeing in the Dunghill, its more probably the corrupt Stearns got into your Brains and your Dullcold Skul precipitate them into Ribaldry. . . ." And he made a desperate effort to rescue his now slightly sodden symbol of the ale: ". . . you say your Ale grows better but have a Care you do not Bottle it too New, lest the Bottles fly and wet your Toyes."[8]

This stately dialogue ended with John Campbell's fetid contribution,

[5] *Boston News-Letter*, No. 915 (August 7 to August 14, 1721).

[6] As reported by Worthington C. Ford, Massachusetts Historical Society, *Proceedings*, LVII (April 1924), 336–53, the verses were attributed in Benjamin Franklin's marked copy to James Franklin and then the name was scratched out, though it remains visible. Moreover, only James used the pseudonym Jack Dulman.

[7] *New-England Courant*, No. 3 (August 14 to August 21, 1721).

[8] *Boston News-Letter*, No. 917 (August 21 to August 28, 1721).

not because James Franklin or his contributors conceded that the old gentleman had got the better of it, but because the same issue of the *News-Letter* carried another reference to the *Courant* and its authors that had far more serious implications than anything that Campbell had to say and that clearly indicated that Franklin had initiated something far more significant than a newspaper rivalry. It was the letter, sent to the *News-Letter* at the outset of the inoculation controversy, accusing the whole cabal of *Courant* writers of constituting something as outrageously contemptuous of all religion and morals as the infamous Hell-Fire Club of England. Though it was signed "Your [i.e., Campbell's] Friends and Well-wishers to Our Country and all Good-Men," it was widely accepted as the work of Cotton Mather. Franklin wisely left Mather's contentions on inoculation to the three physicians among his contributors, but he himself took charge of the counteroffensive to the scurrilous Hell-Fire Club allegation—an allegation that he was not sufficiently removed from the Puritan heritage and influence of Josiah, his father, to regard calmly or treat lightly. Characteristically, James resorted to verse,[9] his lines less directed at the *News-Letter* or its publisher than to the author of the letter and less concerned with the substantive issue than with the Hell-Fire Club reference, which went deeply against the grain of the more orthodox side of James's nature:

> *The Club you mention did their GOD deny*
> *And Hell exceed in horrid Blasphemy:*
> *Yet such you deem the Men who you oppose,*
> *And dare to call them Hellish Men as those.*
> *You* take for granted *others think the same,*
> *And make the* People (*like your selves*) *profane.*
> *Why will you thus* admonish, warn, advise.
> *The Town to see with your Ill-natur'd Eyes?*
> Lot's Wife remember *when you write again;*
> 'Twill help to season your envenom'd Brain.[10]

For months, as well it might have, the Hell-Fire label plagued the *Courant*'s contributors, as Mather latched onto it as a usefully sensational device to discredit his inoculation opposition and also the critics of the clergy, of whom Mather suspected that Checkley was still a ringleader. Six months after the *News-Letter* communication, reports of the diabolic character of the *Courant* were still being circulated. "That the *Courants* are carry'd on by a *Hell-Fire Club* with a *Nonjuror* [i.e., a Jacobite communicant of the Church of England, *viz.*, Checkley] at the Head of them, has been asserted by a certain Clergyman in his common Conversation,

---

[9] Again Benjamin Franklin had ascribed the piece to James in his marked copy of the *Courant* and again scratched it out. Ford did not mention this in his account of the marked copies cited in Note 6, *supra*.

[10] *New-England Courant*, No. 5 (August 28 to September 4, 1721).

with as much Zeal as ever he discover'd in the Application of a sermon on the most awakening Subject. This is one of the malicious Acts used by him, and his hot-headed Trumpeters, to spoil the Credit of the *Courant*, that he may reign Detractor General over the whole Province, and do all the Mischief his ill Nature prompts him to, with hearing of it. . . . It is a Pleasure to me, that I have never inserted any thing in the Courant, which charg'd any Man, or Society of Men, with being Guilty of the Crimes which were peculiar to the *Hell-Fire Club* in *London,* and which the Devils themselves are not capable of perpetrating."[11] The piece—the leading article of the *Courant's* fourth issue of 1721/2—was one of James Franklin's best and most perceptive writings. In it, the exceptional young printer—exceptional for both his courage and his insight—got much closer to the heart of what was the basic trouble with the lost yearning of the Mathers and what was bothering them in their dynasty's twilight than any of the Mathers ever came close to doing with regard to the emergence of a Franklin or a *Courant* or to the very existence of the group of commentators who found a place in its columns. For the deep worry of the Mathers was not the decline of religion in Boston or even the decline of Puritanism. It was the decline of the power of the ministers—which, to the Mathers, might very well be equated with the collapse not only of religion and Puritanism but of all civilization. In his columns, James Franklin read them a singularly perspicacious and pertinent lecture on what was wrong with their wistful, hard-dying dream of the authoritative role of the Calvinist clergy: "For a Man to give up his Right and Title to his Senses, and allow his whimsical Minister (for some such there are in all Countries) to dispose of him Body and Soul, *just as the Humour takes him,* is no Argument of Love, but on the contrary opens a Door for a dangerous Prejudice, if not an irreconcilable Hatred between them. *The best of Men are but Men at the best,* and if of ambitious Tempers are apt to receive all the Honour *given* them, without considering whether it is due to them *for their Works sake.* And if, after a Minister has kept an open Breast to receive *Honours of all Sorts,* he begins to demand them as a *Duty* from his Hearers, 'tis not always necessary to *please* him in order to *love* him: This is so far from being a Duty, that the contrary is one great Proof of our being good Protestants, & the Subjects of a King who allows us Liberty of Conscience." Compared to the Mathers' wild, wholly unfounded ravings about a club of devil worshipers making their headquarters in a Queen Street printing house, this was one of the most lucid comments on the dilemma of the Puritan priests, as the Englightenment dawned in the New World, that was apt to be made in a Boston standing astride the old theocratic state and the new civil politics of the province. Franklin and his Couranteers were a pace ahead of their times; and the Mathers

---

[11] *Ibid.*, No. 25 (January 15 to January 22, 1722).

were still looking back longingly to John Cotton, who had written so assuredly to Lord Saye and Sele about God's flat rejection of democracy "as a fitt government."[12]

* * *

Benjamin Franklin, who knew and heard and read all the Couranteers, and who also knew, had heard, and had read at least some of Mather, left no record of his views as to the conflict between them. It was unlikely that it would have been a matter of overriding concern to the fifteen-year-old youth, who was probably more interested in the issues raised in the conversations around him than in the personalities. He may well have had some difficulty refraining from blurting out his own rapidly forming opinions, but he left sufficient record of the likelihood that he would have gotten a box on the ears for his outburst if he had. In any case, his good sense certainly told him that the youngish but mature group of quite respectable Boston townsmen that drifted in and out of his brother's printing house was not a very likely assortment of devil worshipers given to conducting black masses in the middle of the night and assuming the names of the prophets, of the saints (whom the Puritans did not recognize as such anyhow), and of the more arresting sins. Attractive as this sort of fantasy may have been to some young people, particularly in a society where they could play a major role in such an extravagant fantasy as witchcraft, to Franklin, whose mind from earliest boyhood completely balked at the irrational, it would have been the kind of nonsense to be expected of the overzealous. Since the worship of God had been pretty well defined in his mind as "doing Good to Man," he undoubtedly would have dismissed devil worship as no more mysterious or alluring than doing evil to man—which Franklin, albeit imperfectly, sought to avoid all his life. In any case, to him the appeal of the Couranteers, whether merrily dubbed "Honest Wags," as by Gardner, or demoniacal conspirers out to "corrupt the minds and morals of the people," was much more likely the forthrightness of their expression, the concatenation of their arguments, and the very fact that, in a wholly—or at least apparently—nondenominational context, they were challenging an establishment that to the young Franklin's generation had had its day and represented rather an obstacle than an avenue to progress.

The initial core of the group was constituted, of course, of John Checkley, hardly bereft of any denominational motive, and of Dr. Douglass, whose arrogance as to medicine could easily match the Mathers' as to theology. But to Benjamin Franklin, knowing them was a wholly new experience. Brought up in the solid if unimpassioned orthodoxy of the cottage in the shadow of the Old South Church, the alumnus of hundreds of Sunday meetings and thousands of family prayers, his exposure to formal learning was limited to the single year under the benevolent, effec-

12 See Chap. V, Note 2, *supra.*

tive tutelage of Nathaniel Williams at the Latin School and a rather mechanical, half-successful year at the writing school, and then the dreary two years of soap and candles. Now here was John Checkley, a somewhat dashing fellow in his early forties, who had been educated at Oxford and had traveled throughout Europe, at home with the classics, completely repudiating the premises of the Bible Commonwealth by becoming confirmed in the Church of England, writer, bookseller, publisher. And William Douglass, for all his vanity, was no less impressive a figure in the provincial seaport—skilled in modern languages, one of the most versatile of scientists, whose mind roamed competently and knowingly among half a dozen of the natural sciences, an amateur historian who made up in vivacity what he lacked in accuracy, and totally resistant to any authority, in large measure because he could conceive of no one's being his superior in any respect. To Checkley, with his Anglican devotion to the liturgy and his appreciation of the saints, a Hell-Fire Club, ridiculing and blaspheming both, would have been even more repugnant than it was to Mather, and it would have been equally so to Douglass, with his contempt for anything that flew in the face of the scientific method.

Checkley, the founding "author" of the *Courant*, had a very brief tenure as a contributor, his appearances having been terminated with the third issue, after his sorry attack on the drunken and rakish habits of his old friend, Mather's nephew, the Reverend Thomas Walter. But he was still a friend of many of the other contributors, perhaps indeed a recruiter of some of them, since he was easily the most articulate advocate of the Church of England in Boston and at least five of the thirteen contributors acquired by James Franklin were members of King's Chapel, the only Anglican church in the town. And it is not likely that this supremely self-confident, irrepressible, magnetic anti-Puritan would have disappeared wholly from the house of the only publication that dared to question Puritan authority in temporal matters; but even if he had, he had already become known to Benjamin, he still had his bookshop, situated like a magnet to the "bookish lad," Franklin, next to the Town House, and he still was one of the lively, insurgent personalities that were surfacing in town to challenge old acceptances and to advance new prospects. Moreover, Checkley, partly because of his pivotal location at the crossroads of Boston life at the Town House and partly because of his highly visible role in Boston Anglicanism, was something of a hero to those growing restless under the heavy hand of Calvinism; he had been twice fined by the Court of General Sessions of the Peace—once for selling a pamphlet that advocated the apostolic origin of the episcopacy and another for flatly refusing to take a loyalty oath which was imposed by an act passed by the General Court but for the swearing of which he alone was singled out among all Bostonians.[13]

[13] See *John Checkley, or the Evolution of Religious Tolerance in Massachusetts Bay* (Boston, 1897), I, 32–40.

As for the other of the two contributors to the first issue of the *Courant*, Dr. Douglass remained a steady contributor, though nothing from his pen appeared for some months after James Franklin, in the autumn of 1721, sought to broaden the base of his new paper from a single-purpose (anti-inoculation) publication to a journal of general comment and intelligence. After his contributions to the first three issues—each of them disputing Dr. Boylston's practice of inoculation—Douglass was absent from the columns of the *Courant* from August 21, 1721, until January 22, 1722, at which time he resumed where he left off, again attacking the proponents of inoculation. Of the eight contributions that he made to the first forty-two issues of the *Courant*, only one had to do with anything except inoculation, and that one was a complaint that Philip Musgrave, the postmaster, who published the *Gazette*, had printed a carping note about the selectmen simply because they would not do his bidding; and with the disdain that he usually reserved for Dr. Boylston and Mather, he likened Musgrave, a dullish fellow, an inept, inefficient postmaster, and the most uninspired of editors, to a "dunghill cock" or "peevish mongrel" who strutted and crowed and barked and snarled but then turned tail and ran away. In May 1727 he was allowed the last word on inoculation in the *Courant*. It speaks well for him and his scientific spirit that he indicated a modification of his once obdurate stand and was willing to admit inoculation as a desirable experiment; and he went on to become an epidemiologist of the highest order of distinction, one of whose published works became a classical authority on scarlet fever. Douglass was a constant visitor to the *Courant* and, next to Gardner and James Franklin himself, its most frequent contributor, and young Benjamin was repeatedly exposed to his crisp logic and his disciplined, scientific approach to affairs—qualities that served strongly to abet his own intellectual leanings.

Like Checkley but with far less interest in theological dispute, Dr. Douglass was a member of the Church of England and of King's Chapel. The two men were therefore at least acquaintances and very possibly friends before they fell in with James Franklin and seized upon his *Courant* as a convenient vehicle to air their views. But the two shared little real interests, except their impatience with the grasp that the Congregational clergy still labored to exert on the total life of the province, and Dr. Douglass, who, like everyone else, knew of Checkley's Jacobite sympathies, came to suspect him of a strong bend toward Romanism in his High Church persuasions: ". . . to sum up all, as, not afraid to own his principles, he wears a crucifix."[14]

Next in order to Checkley and Douglass to appear as contributors to James Franklin's *Courant* were two other men of medicine, Dr. John Gib-

[14] Dr. William Douglass to Cadwallader Colden. Massachusetts Historical Society, *Collections*, 4th Ser., II, 182.

bins and Dr. George Steward. Both of the latter may have been induced by the inoculation controversy to enter the public prints, but it is probably not insignificant that they were fellow parishioners, with Checkley and Douglass, of King's Chapel and members of the Church of England; and they may have been equally attracted to the prospect of challenging the authority of the Mathers—much more likely in the case of John Gibbins than it was in that of George Steward. Gibbins was, in 1721, a young apothecary-physician of thirty-three. He was graduated in the class of 1706 from Harvard College, where he distinguished himself for having to pay more fines than any other member of his class, the charges against him for breaking windows costing him more than what he paid for his quarters. In a class of six, he had entered at the top of the class, was reduced to second place when a new member of the class who outranked him socially was given first place by the faculty, was temporarily dropped to fifth place as a result of his window-breaking escapades, and finally graduated second in rank. His father was a soldier, and he himself went off in Queen Anne's War to fight the French in Acadia and then returned to Harvard to take his master's degree. During his military service, he apparently picked up some medical knowledge and some experience from an army surgeon. He opened an apothecary in Boston, prospered, served in a couple of petty town offices, and became a member and supporter of King's Chapel, contributing ten pounds in 1718 to help build a gallery and a new pulpit and to pave the walk in front of the chapel—an amount exceeded only by that given by Governor Samuel Shute. He became successively a vestryman and warden of the parish, and he served as a bondsman for John Checkley when the latter got into trouble for some of his rebellious publications. A friend of Checkley, Gibbins was probably introduced to James Franklin as a potential contributor to the *Courant* for the purpose of providing further answer to the *"Anti-Courant,"* Thomas Walter's *Little-Compton Scourge*. His contribution did Gibbins no particular credit; it was based entirely on rumors that Walter drank too much, though Gibbins had some difficulty determining whether the offending beverage was "Cyder," rum, "rectified Spirit of Wine," or "other Dram."[15] The major purpose of Dr. Gibbins, as an Anglican who had departed the dissenting fold of Benjamin Colman's liberal and Anglican-leaning Brattle Street Church, where he was baptized and married, seems to have been to achieve the satisfaction of putting the old guard Congregational clergy in its place—and his victim, Thomas Walter, *was* the great-grandson of John Cotton, the grandson of Increase Mather, the nephew of Cotton Mather, and the minister of the church at Roxbury, which was exceeded in seniority only by the First Church among Boston churches. Though Dr. Gibbins, despite his profession, had nothing to say on the merits of inoculation against smallpox, he did have a most unprofessional comment, of ques-

[15] *New-England Courant*, No. 3 (August 14 to August 21, 1721).

tionable medical soundness, to make on the generally well known "consumptive" condition suffered, with extraordinary good cheer, by young Thomas Walter and that was shortly to be charged with his death at the age of twenty-eight. Gibbins suggested that a fondness for the bottle was "the Cause of his [Walton's] Body's being so weak, and his Mind so very vicious."

Dr. George Steward, like Zabdiel Boylston, had learned medicine through an apprenticeship. By 1721 he had achieved a solid reputation in Boston, having practiced medicine there for twenty years. He was a much more serious writer than Gibbins and of an apparently far higher sense of professionalism in his choice of words and material. His writings for the Courant were thoughtful and restrained and stuck closely to the medical aspects of the inoculation controversy, making allegations about no one's motives or morals and staying wholly clear of the role of the ministers in the advocacy of inoculation. He warned that there was some evidence, reported in the Royal Society's Transactions, that the practice might spread some symptoms of the plague, and he emphasized the futility of any step against the plague, such as the quarantine of vessels ordered by the governor, if other measures were permitted that were suspected of spreading it. As the controversy neared its close, Steward wrote another long piece, occupying all of the first and a quarter of the second page of the Courant, with a summary of medical reasons why inoculation should be avoided; these were soundly rooted in the medical knowledge of the time and in the logic of what was very clearly a closely reasoning and impassionate mind, matching the high level of medical forensics exemplified by Boylston but compromised no little by both Douglass and Mather in their irrelevant indulgence in personalities. The gist of Dr. Steward's argument was that inoculation was far from infallible (people did die from it) and that the argument frequently advanced to counter this point, "that there is nothing infallible in Physick," true as it was, was not wholly applicable because one had to distinguish between uncertainty attached to "making a well man sick and endeavouring to make a sick Man well." The only moral query that Steward put was whether a practice which, even if it saved some lives, occasioned the loss of others, accorded with the dictate of the sixth commandment, but that matter he was willing to leave to the ministers favoring inoculation, "who are certainly excellent Commentators on the Sixth Commandment"[16] —the gentlest reproof of the pro-inoculation clergy that appeared at any time in the Courant's long obsession with the subject.

With Drs. Douglass, Gibbins, and Steward dominating the pages of the first three issues of the Courant (among them, they wrote all the pieces, except for two by Checkley and one by James Franklin), young Benjamin Franklin was exposed to a fairly steady diet of medical discussion, both in

16 Ibid., No. 20 (December 11 to December 18, 1721).

the columns of type that he helped to set and print and in the conversations prevalent in the printing house. Franklin's aggressive curiosity would have prevented any boredom on his part and, if the situation followed the pattern characterizing his general intellectual development during his adolescence and early maturity, would, on the contrary, have stimulated him to seek even more knowledge of the subject. His interest in the medical sciences, in any case, manifested itself at a very early age. Questions relating to medicine occurred with some frequency among those proposed for study and discussion by his Junto; and he developed from his Boston years a lifelong interest in the effects of diets upon health, compiling and putting into practice many of them. He seldom had an ailment. He was interested in the effects of habits of exercise and sleep on general health. He practiced and preached hydrotherapy long before most general practitioners recognized its value. He wrote wisely about the common cold and was among the first to attribute its spreading to closed, stuffy rooms; and he advocated fresh air as a factor in the treatment of respiratory ailments a century or more ahead of the medical profession generally. He prescribed medicinals freely for his family and his friends, and he had a thorough understanding of the pharmacology of his time. He invented a flexible catheter, anticipated electrotherapy with his experiments with the use of electricity to treat nervous disorders, and was recognized by the physicians of America and Europe as a specialist on lead poisoning. Every ailment that he had—the gout, kidney stones, sprains, diarrhea, near fatal episodes of pneumonia—he studied, charted symptoms, made astonishingly exact prognoses, all with the calm air of scientific detachment that made it appear in his written records that the distress was happening to someone else, and all without the least trace of either hypochondria or self-pity, but with the kind of confident trust in his own ability to cope with his body that permitted him to refer casually to the age of eighty-three, when he suffered a skin complaint at that advanced age, as "the age of commencing creptitude,"[17] quickly dropping the matter and turning his attention to John Fitch's steamboat. He was elected to membership in several professional medical societies, and the most eminent physicians in England, France, and America treated him as a colleague in their correspondence, conversations, and travels with him. The boy in the printing house, during those early medically preoccupied days of his brother's *Courant*, was seeing only the smallest beginning of a lifetime alliance with the medical profession, though fortunately for the only time, on the side of reaction and the status quo.

* * *

Besides the practice of medicine, the three physicians who for all practical purposes constituted James Franklin's board of editors for his fledgling newspaper's first three issues, had little in common by way of background,

17 Jared Sparks, ed., *The Works of Benjamin Franklin* (Boston, 1840), X, 363.

personality, education, or prose style—except for one thing: They were all parishioners at King's Chapel of the Reverend Henry Harris, who was the sole contributor, except for James Franklin himself, to that fourth issue of the *Courant*, when the paper seemed to Franklin to be getting out of hand under the fervid direction of Checkley and Douglass. The entire issue was actually turned over to Harris, with Franklin saving space only for six quatrains of unaccustomedly devout verse from his own pen. This was in itself an affront to the clerical establishment of Boston, since Henry Harris was associate rector of King's Chapel, the first and still the only parish of the Church of England in Boston. Twelve years earlier, Harris had been dispatched by Henry Compton, the Bishop of London, to Boston to succeed Christopher Bridge, who had left Boston, first for Rhode Island and then for New York. Harris was still a fellow of Jesus College, Oxford, and remained such after he settled in Boston. The combined stipend of his fellowship and the King's grant for his ministerial services amounted to nearly half again the competence paid the Congregational pastors by most Massachusetts parishes—a fact that did not rest easily on the Puritan awareness that there was a strong and just association between righteousness and this world's goods. Moreover, Harris, who had scarcely reached his twenties and had been out of college barely two years when he came to Boston, was entirely independent of the local parish for his compensation, deriving it wholly from the royal bounty and the Oxford fellowship perpetually endowed by Sir Leoline Jenkins. He was married and had a small family of two sons and a daughter, and they lived in a house in Queen Street which he rented from Captain Christopher Taylor, later also a contributor to the *Courant*. A man of gentle and tolerant spirit but also of strong personal independence, who declined to subordinate himself to his rector, Harris was a liberal both politically (a Whig) and theologically (a low churchman). When the advocate general of the province, John Valentine, a man much respected "for his Knowledge and Integrity, most eminent in his Profession, Clear in his Conceptions, and Distinguishable happy in his Expressions,"[18] and a warden and vestryman of King's Chapel, hanged himself in a fit of melancholy, the rector, Samuel Myles, refused to conduct the burial service (although he attended it); Harris read the office.

The character and enlightened mind of Harris shone through his long and civilized letter-essay in the fourth issue of the *Courant*[19]; and although it is unknown whether he made other contributions to the paper (the authors of the contributions made to the issues after that of May 28, 1723, were not identified by Benjamin Franklin, in his marked file of the paper), it is clear from later issues of the *Courant* that Harris continued to be the only clergyman who had any influence on the paper. This was

[18] Ibid., I, 247.
[19] He used the pseudonym "Frank Scammony."

strongly evidenced when a second Church of England parish was established in Boston in 1722, and, aided to no small extent by the mischievous churchmanship of John Checkley, a split as between the low and high wings of the church became sharp and deep. The *Courant* devoted much attention and space to the breach, strongly adhering to the latitudinarian views of Harris. Moreover, a relationship existed between the *Courant* and King's Chapel all out of proportion to the latter's size or influence in the general Boston community. Of the thirteen individuals whose contributions James Franklin published in the first ten months of the *Courant*'s publication, eight (including five members) had King's Chapel associations and a ninth became a founder of the Church of England parish in Portsmouth, New Hampshire, the home of his wife.[20] Obviously, these men were attracted to the *Courant* because it was the only Boston newspaper likely to furnish space for their views, both the *Gazette* of John Campbell and the *News-Letter* of Philip Musgrave being wholly and unconditionally subservient to the established Congregational clergy and considered by the latter as duty-bound to carry their views and bespeak their interests. Corollary to this, James Franklin, who never became a member of the Old South, the church of his father, but who never abandoned organized religion, gravitated toward a church that was not aligned with the political establishment and claimed no authority over the temporal affairs of the province. Furthermore, he had only a few years earlier returned from a long stay in London, where he unquestionably fell in far more with members of the Church of England than with the dwindling number of dissenters left in London. Just as Addison and Steele had liberated him from the dreary prose of the Puritans, surcease from the tyrannizing presence of the theocracy of Boston probably freed him from any automatic devotion to the paternal faith.

Much of the hospitable attitude of the *Courant* and of James Franklin, its proprietor, toward the Church of England communicated itself to Benjamin. Most of those "Men of some Character among us for Learning and Ingenuity,"[21] whose approval he so earnestly sought in his brother's printing house, were Anglicans, completely free from the kind of daily pressures of their religion that beset his father's household and the families of the boys with whom he had gone to school and grown up. The only church with which he himself ever became even informally affiliated (he supported it regularly and was buried in its churchyard, though he never became a communicant) was the Church of England, later the Protestant Episcopal, parish of Christ Church in Philadelphia; and his closest friend in the United Kingdom was the Bishop of St. Asaph, Jonathan Shipley,

---

[20] Five of the *Courant* contributors were members of the King's Chapel parish: the Reverend Henry Harris, John Checkley, Dr. William Douglass, Dr. John Gibbins, and Dr. George Steward. Two others were contributors and possible members: Thomas Lane and John Williams. And one was the King's Chapel printer: Thomas Fleet.

[21] *Autobiography*, 68.

who remained in correspondence a close intimate of Franklin even during the Revolution. The introduction of Anglicanism in Boston was in no sense a deeply religious movement. The transplanting to New England of the Church of England, never a highly zealous arm of Christendom, was, before an imprimatur was put upon it by the royal governors largely for politicosocial reasons, really a quite gradual process, largely instigated by those with social attachments to the old institutions of England. This yearning for the stateliness, the order, and the literary quality of the liturgy was a far more commanding force in their gravitation to the church than was any doctrinal enthusiasm for the saints or any preoccupation with the Thirty-nine Articles. There was also a temperamental element involved in the decision of many of the townspeople who saw fit, after King's Chapel was founded, to cast their spiritual lot with the Anglicans; they simply found uncongenial an order of presbyters, who did not even have any ordination except as ministers of their own individual parishes (if a Puritan minister in New England resigned, or was thrown out of, his pastorate, he ceased to be an ordained minister, and if he left one parish for another, he was required, in an inexplicable theory of the fragility of holy orders, to be ordained all over again) and yet claimed authority over the moral life of the entire community. Certainly it was such qualities of resistance to the Puritan proposition that, to the Franklins, made the somewhat cavalier young Anglicans attractive alternatives to Mather, Sewall, and their breed of moral categorists; if any body of theological distinctions was involved, Benjamin Franklin remained silent on it.

Of the other contributors to the *Courant* who had Church of England associations, none revealed much passionate commitment about his beliefs. John Eyre, twenty-one, who contributed four pieces to the early *Courants*, alone among the contributors shared with the Franklins familial ties with the Old South, of which his father had been a member from 1683 until his death in 1700, shortly before John's birth, and his maternal grandfather, the merchant, Thomas Brattle, had been a founding member and benefactor. John was the last of twelve children, all but three of whom died in childhood. He entered Harvard College at the age of fourteen, the second of his generation to bear the name of John Eyre, his older brother, a member of the class of 1700 having died of drowning in a skating accident during his freshman year. Eyre had just taken his master's degree in 1721, but seemed otherwise occupied in living a merry life of dancing, drinking, and outings in the company of Benjamin Lynde, a classmate, who also descended from rich merchants. The Old South and its teachings had little to do with him, and he drifted away from it. Seven years after his father's death, his mother had married, in 1707, Wait Still Winthrop, later chief justice of the province; and on *his* death in 1717, Judge Sewall, who succeeded him, sought the widow's hand and, in the process, tried to get the support of young John, to no avail, the son being indifferent to the judge's quest and his mother expressing some distress that the judge owned neither a coach nor a periwig. John Eyre obviously took up with the Couranteers for the purpose of having something to do befitting his somewhat jaunty way of life, his swaggering disregard for Puritan repressions, and his love of less ascetic ways (when he joined the siege of Louisbourg years later as adjutant of a regiment, he sent home for "a keg of pickled oysters, put up in vinegar"[22]). But he also had about him a gently reflective side, and perhaps no sentence ever emanated from the sons of the Puritans that touched more sensitively upon a central weakness in their credenda than a line from his correspondence: "It does not seem an unchristian thought to think that departed Souls laugh at our stile, to compare our groans with their triumphs."[23]

The youngest of the contributors and, aside from Dr. Gibbins, the only one to have attended Harvard, Eyre achieved the distinction of seeing his first letter to the *Courant*, signed Peter Hakins, appear twice, as it precipitated that dramatic outburst from Cotton Mather against James Franklin in the street. His second contribution, which did not appear until March 5, 1722, was a lighthearted letter, purportedly written by a Frenchman named Anthony De Potsherd and affecting a salutation and complimentary close in French, characteristic of the humor of the eighteenth century but somewhat less provincial in tone than Boston was accustomed to reading. The author's complaint was a wife—"a Creature call'd Woman"—with whom he "had not had one Hours Quiet or Peace. . . . She is continually railing and reviling me at a most intolerable Rate, and all the Reason she assigns for it is, as she says, because I don't perform the Duty of an Husband rightly towards her. She is so inveterate in her Envy and Jealousie, that she won't allow me to stir abroad without her leave, and yet she leaves me sometimes Two or three Hours together, and a Gossiping she goes with some of her She Companions, and when their Frolick is over, they come home, and make me their laughing Stock and Ridicule. . . . When any thing abroad or at home has displeased her, all her Resentments are cast on me, and I am nothing but *Rascal, Cuckold*, & c. I have endeavoured by all the means I can to reclaim her, but all won't do. I have sometimes endeavoured to reduce her to a moderate Dyet (for she lives on the Fat of the Land) but that won't take Effect. I once attempted to beat her into good Humor, but she came off Conqueror. If you can prescribe any Remedy whereby I may reduce this Scolding Hag to any good Humour, or how I may get rid of her, it will lay an Infinite Obligation on V*ous tres homble Serviteur*."[24]

Eyre's third contribution to the *Courant* was, on the surface, an improbable sequel to a public airing of the marital plight of M. De Potsherd. Occupying the leading position in the issue of April 9, 1722, the letter was obviously aimed as a satirical dart at the stale, remote, and irrelevant con-

[22] Sibley, *Biographical Sketches*, VI, 242.
[23] Ibid., 243.
[24] *New-England Courant*, No. 31 (February 26 to March 5, 1722).

tents of the *Courant*'s rival newspapers with their constant phobia of offending the clergy or even of venturing an opinion on any matter of current controversy. Eyre suggested that the *Courant* publish excerpts from sermons from time to time to "bring your Paper in greater Repute, if possible: And I doubt not, but the Reproach which has been cast on you and the Readers of your Papers will soon wear off. . . ."[25] To start off the new righteousness of the *Courant*, Eyre furnished a passage from a sermon of somewhat less than pressing immediacy, delivered before Edward VI, by the Right Reverend Hugh Latimer, the sixteenth-century Bishop of Worcester martyred in the reign of Queen Mary, in which the bishop sternly warned that greed on the part of judges led to the perversion of justice, and urged that the next step in the progression should be hanging even if it were "my Lord chief Judge of *England*, yea, and were it my Lord Chancellor himself, to *Tyburn* with him." And, Eyre concluded, "These are Father *Latimer's* own Words, and so let him pass." That Eyre did not choose the passage wholly by chance is suggested by the fact that his next contribution to the *Courant*, a month later, advanced a cynical view of public office holding that "Men can hardly rise to Preferment and be honest. . . . No covetous Person will use more Water to fetch the Pump, than he designs to pump out again."[26]

Five years Benjamin Franklin's senior, John Eyre was, of all the "Honest Wags" frequenting the Queen Street printing house, closest to him not only in age but also in writing style and, though not at all gifted as compared to the apprentice whom he may well have not so much as noticed, to some extent in temperament. Eyre's first contribution to the *Courant*, in particular, clearly influenced both the direction and the tone that Benjamin's first writing efforts for the *Courant* were to take. For all of Eyre's high social position (he ranked first in his class on graduation from Harvard), his De Potsherd letter—in comparison to *The Spectator*, to which in more than one respect it was indebted—had a provincial rawness, an unpolished heartiness, and a broad humor that was characteristic of a colonial outpost shaking off old repressions and beginning to acquire a buoyancy and boisterousness as it began to assume a character of its own. Eyre's other contributions suggested the range of topics that even a young man could discuss in the columns of the *Courant*, and—whether John Eyre ever noticed Benjamin Franklin or not—Franklin certainly noticed *him* and was no doubt encouraged by the youthful Eyre's acceptance into that company of "ingenious Men" surrounding the proprietor of the *Courant*.

* * *

Of the nine contributors to the *Courant* who had some association with early Anglicanism in Boston, the names of four do not occur on King's

[25] Ibid., No. 36 (April 2 to April 9, 1722).
[26] Ibid., No. 41 (May 7 to May 14, 1722).

Chapel's roll of members; but one, Thomas Fleet, was the printer to King's Chapel, two others, Thomas Lane and John Williams, contributed to its building fund, and a fourth, Christopher Taylor, who was never designed for any formal church ties, was a friend of the associate rector, Henry Harris, to whom he rented a house in Queen Street not far from Franklin's printing house.

Except for the Franklins themselves and the prolific Mr. Gardner, Taylor was the most frequent contributor to the first forty-three issues of the *Courant*—the only issues for which a list of contributors survives. In 1721 Captain Taylor was forty-four years old, a mariner, the father of a son by his servant maid, Anne Bell, whom he never married (though he bestowed his name on his son and made him his heir), and the proprietor of considerable property and wealth. His father, James Taylor, was also once a mariner and became a prosperous manufacturer, who owned an ironworks in Lynn and extensive residential properties in Boston, where he was a respected member of the First Church. James Taylor was for over two decades treasurer of both the province of Massachusetts Bay and the town of Boston, sometimes, when the exchequer was thin, paying pressing public bills out of his own pocket. When on his death in 1716, he left Christopher, first-born of his sons, only fifty pounds, "which with what I have formerly given (whereby he hath acquired a good estate) is the full of what I shall give him,"[27] the captain instituted a long series of litigations against the executors of his father's estate—an occupation that he was carrying on at the time of his writing for the *Courant*. Taylor was a self-confident, but somewhat mystifying and contradictory, independent character, defiant of the mores of the community in his own conduct but watchful of them in others' and somehow rising above any widespread criticism for it—in March 1721, in fact, he was designated a constable (it was characteristic of his self-assurance that he refused to serve) and yet he was in some difficulty, though cleared by the grand jury the next month.

Captain Taylor wrote seven pieces for the *Courant* between December 1721 and May 1722, or more than one a month, and apparently continued for some time afterward, since in 1723 he was denying authorship of a specific *Courant* piece that distressed the establishment because it raised the question as to whether Governor Shute, when he embarked secretively for a voyage to London, had it in mind to advance, at Whitehall, his own interests or those of the province.[28] Taylor's first contribution consisted of some scathing comments on the residents of New Hampshire for "their immoderate Pursuit of Gambling," about which the captain seemed to know a great deal and bear some personal resentment. The following week Taylor had another gossipy piece in the *Courant*, in which he reported

[27] Essex Wills, *lib.* xi f. 208.
[28] The offending piece was in the *Courant*, No. 76 (January 7 to January 14, 1722), and Taylor's denial was in the *News-Letter*, No. 990 (January 14 to January 21, 1723).

that an unnamed Boston lawyer, who was frequently referred to by the *Courant* as "cohabiting with a certain French lady as his Wife," financed and participated in an elaborate wedding ceremony and subsequent dinner for two Africans, one of whom was said to be his slave; the point of the piece, according to Taylor, was to put the question as to whether the lawyer was attempting, by such an ostentatious wedding for his servant, to taunt the magistrates with his own living arrangements or to invite them to investigate his marital status. Whatever the point of the contribution, it is difficult to imagine what Taylor's own point was in view of his relationship with Anne Bell. However, the lawyer with the French mistress apparently intrigued him, for a few weeks later he wrote a critical account of the lawyer's defense when he was finally haled before the Quarter Sessions to explain his marital status, or lack of it, and Taylor added—again with a purpose difficult to fix—that "a Woman who was presented by the Grand-Jury (at the same Sessions) for having a Bastard Child declared in open Court that he was the Father of it."[29] Taylor seemed to derive some sort of satisfaction from teasing the establishment by opening their eyes to sexual irregularities going on all about them and devoted his fourth *Courant* piece to a description of activities that were going on in a bawdy house operating within hearing distance of Joseph Sewall's pulpit at the Old South Church.[30]

Occasionally—at least, on three occasions—Captain Taylor's attention was diverted, in his contributions, from his vigilance over the town's sexual morals to other matters. When the Hell-Fire Club charge was being aired by the Mather faction against the Couranteers, Taylor was one of the targets of the charge who answered it. After attributing a letter in the *Gazette* of January 15, 1721, repeating the charge, to "some scurrilous hireling" of Philip Musgrave, the postmaster and proprietor of the *Gazette*, Taylor put a very convincing, if somewhat heated, case, that if Musgrave and his correspondent had knowledge of any such "destestable" club, they "*pluck up their Courage* and give a *List of the Names* of the Persons that are pointed at in that Letter, as a Hell Fire Club; that, if any such there be, they may be rooted up and banished. . . ."[31] Taylor also had a stern message for those who loitered around the market place during the Thursday weekly lectures instead of attending the lectures, "where it is much more likely for them to profit, than to saunter from one Place to another, until the *Lecture* is over, and then stand in the Street with a Pinch of Snuff between their Fingers, making Remarks on, and ridiculing those that frequent that sacred Place."[32] Unless the purpose of this contribution was to throw, not the loiterers, but the lecturers off guard, the concern of

[29] *New-England Courant*, No. 37 (April 9 to April 16, 1722).
[30] See p. 654, *infra*.
[31] *New-England Courant*, No. 25 (January 15 to January 22, 1722).
[32] Ibid., No. 33 (March 12 to March 19, 1722).

Captain Taylor, who is nowhere recorded as a devout church member, is almost impossible to discern. The captain also submitted (with an introductory comment, of what on the surface seems a strained relevance, on an act of Parliament giving the Admiralty regulatory power over the sale of white pine, which was used for ship masts) a well-written essay, from the *London Journal* of Thomas Gordon and John Trenchard, on the natural versus legislative law. As a mariner, Taylor undoubtedly was resentful of the Admiralty's pre-empting a resource of New England so essential to shipping as its towering white pines, and while the matter was on his mind he was probably poking through the *Courant's* library, which contained a file of the *London Journal*, and came upon the essay, a significant point in which—"that Laws are not always the measure of Right or Wrong"—accorded with his views of the Parliament's naval stores act.

To the young apprentice, not long since greatly enamored of the sea, and himself an independent and somewhat rebellious spirit, Captain Taylor, the proximity of whose house to the Franklin printing house made it easy for him to stop by often, was a dashing, strong figure—enough of the defiant in him to make him interesting and enough of Boston in him to make him explicable. It was no secret that he was the father of a bastard child, a fact which would have lent him an additional aura in the eyes of a boy who was to show some precociousness in his tolerance of casual sexual activity. But it is not likely that, among the *Courant's* contributors, Taylor had much of an intellectual influence on Benjamin through the latter's exposure to his personality on his visits to the printing house or even through his writings. Except possibly the Hell-Fire Club defense and the *London Journal* excerpt, which Benjamin might well have read in its original form, none of Taylor's writings would have impressed him as ringing true or carrying much force by way of either reasoning or prose style.

Of a wholly different cut of cloth was the printer Thomas Fleet, one of James Franklin's three competitors in the printing business. Like Franklin, Fleet was a young man who had the courage to establish a press in spite of the entrenched rivalry of Samuel Green's two heirs, Samuel Kneeland and Bartholomew Green, the first of whom in 1721 was printing the *Gazette* for the postmaster, Philip Musgrave, and the second the *News-Letter* for John Campbell, the ex-postmaster. Between them, Kneeland and Green had a firm grasp on the printing business within the power of the Boston establishment to bestow. Bartholomew Green was at fifty-five the most firmly established of the Boston printers, the printer to Harvard College and also the governor and Council of Massachusetts; in addition he shared with his kinsman, Kneeland, the commission of printer to the House of Representatives, though the enterprising bookseller Nicholas Boone was, for a time, the titular printer, actually functioning as publisher. Though he was a deacon of the Old South, Green, known for his piety, was a stalwart defender of Mather, to whom he succeeded his father, Samuel Green, as principal printer, a post which provided him with a volume of work about equal to that required by the college and government together. Of the 370 titles published by Mather through 1721, Bartholomew Green printed close to 100. Kneeland was also a beneficiary of the influence and reputation of Samuel Green, his great-grandfather, and could be assured a reasonable amount of the printing business of the Boston establishment when he started operating his press in Prison Lane, close to Franklin's, in 1718, just a year after Franklin started operations. He, too, had printed a score of Cotton Mather's publications. Fleet had also benefited from Mather's fecundity, having printed a total of sixteen of the cleric's books by 1721, three of them the first year that Fleet was in business, 1713—a fairly prolific year even for Mather, during which he published twenty books.

Despite the competition among them, the printers of Boston were a fraternal group, sometimes farming work out to each other and sometimes sharing a project rather than hiring an extra journeyman to help them. Fleet had arrived in Boston from England in 1713, when he was in his middle twenties. He had learned his trade in London, having migrated thence from his native Shropshire, and acquired a reputation for skill, industriousness, and conscientiousness at a time when the printing business was, under the influence of the Augustan literary revival and the proliferation of newspapers and reviews, undergoing a period of great prosperity. A Low-churchman, he fell into some difficulty when he publicly demonstrated against the Tory High Church preacher, Henry Sacheverell, thus infuriating some of the latter's politically powerful London supporters and making his own departure from London desirable. He made a good impression among Anglicans in Boston, King's Chapel being Low Church, and his industriousness at a greatly respected trade attracted the support of the Puritan majority as well. By the time that he became a contributor to the *Courant*, he was comfortably established in Pudding Lane, not far from the Old South Church, and obviously had friendly feelings for his junior colleague, James Franklin, who may very well have owed to Fleet his introduction to the London printer from whom he learned his trade. The only printer left in Boston who did not have a weekly newspaper to print, Fleet unquestionably kept an interested eye on the bold project of Franklin—the only man in Boston who was both printer and publisher, as well as editor, of his own newspaper—an undertaking upon which even the Green dynasty did not venture until 1723, when Campbell relinquished the dreary *News-Letter* and turned it over to Bartholomew Green.

Fleet's first contribution to the *Courant* was in January 1722, when Franklin's paper was in the midst of its feud with the postmaster, Philip Musgrave. The real complaint of the *Courant* against Musgrave was, of course, that he permitted his *Boston Gazette* (which still bore the legend

"Published by Authority" prominently on its masthead, thus implying that its news somehow had its origin in official places when as a matter of fact it meant merely that its contents were subject to approval by the governor and Council) to become the organ of the Mathers in their vendetta with the *Courant*. But rather than limit its battle with Musgrave to the *Gazette*'s offenses—a battle which the *Courant* by no means abandoned— Franklin and his contributors concluded to go after Musgrave for the incompetency and inefficiency of the post office, rather an easy target since no postal system has ever been known to be wholly satisfactory to its constituents. Since the *Gazette* and its demeaning "Published by Authority" claim to preferment, which somehow went against the grain of any printer who was a freeman, was regarded as an adjunct and added emolument of the postmastership, the thought was that discrediting the one would help to discredit the other. The post office, originally a locally appointed agency answerable to the colonial council, became in 1710 an agency of the General Post Office created by Parliament; it was really a little independent empire of the postmaster, whose nearest superior was over three thousand miles and six weeks' voyage away, and he ran it very much more to suit his convenience than the public's. The post office was originally open only on Monday mornings "to deliver out all letters that do come by post," and since virtually all the arriving mail came by ship, it was not open even for those brief hours during the winter; and it was open "from two o'clock in the afternoon to six o'clock" to accept outgoing mail. But by 1722 it was supposed to be a generally available service, though Musgrave was apparently somewhat arbitrary and whimsical in dispensing its services. James Franklin himself fired the opening gun in the *Courant*'s attack on Musgrave in his edition of January 8, 1722, accusing him of refusing the delivery of letters when they were called for, of opening letters enclosing money and removing the money from them, and of falsely claiming that such openings were due to faulty sealing wax. Thomas Fleet pressed the case against Musgrave's postmastership in the next issue, revealing a more imaginative and less heavy-handed style of attack than Franklin's. Fleet cast himself in the role of a visitor from the moon who came to Boston and "found the People in a terrible Uproar, fretting and complaining against some body that had abus'd and injur'd them." After the exchange of some pleasant chitchat on terrestrial and lunar affairs, Fleet reported, he listened to the complaints of "about a half dozen of the most Moderate" Boston inhabitants, who claimed that they had "a poor careless, lazy, gump-headed" postmaster with a "crabbed, surly, snappish Temper." Fleet then cast into dialogue case histories of various abuses suffered by patrons of the Boston post office so that they emerged not as abstract accusations but as little dramas of individual people suffering small tragedies as a result of the postmaster's inefficiency, laziness, or ill nature: ". . . a Man that had a Letter sent him from a neighbouring Province, to invite him to go Master of a Vessel; but the Letter was detained by the Post-Master several Weeks, tho' often asked for, so that the poor Man lost his Bi[e]rth . . . a poor Taylor, being at some distance from home, sent *Forty Shillings* to his Wife, who was then Sick; and because he would be sure it should come safe to her Hands, he directed his Letter to the Post-Master, requesting him to deliver the Money safe to his Wife, but the poor Woman has never receiv'd a peny of it."[33]

The device was innovative in Boston journalism, and it was effective. Personalizing a situation or an issue, however simply, in order to gain and hold the interest of readers not really interested in abstractions, was one of the artifices of the writing craft that Benjamin Franklin learned in the rooms of the *Courant* and put to good use for many years as a writer and publisher of essentially popularized newspapers and almanacs. In Thomas Fleet's first effort for the *Courant*, he found a quite workable model. Fleet, whose career as a printer in many other respects resembled Franklin's (he, too, became a quite successful businessman and publisher, though he did not write extensively), also shared some of the young Franklin's social convictions—the tendency, for example, to redress what he regarded as unfair or excessive criticism of women by men. Using the pseudonym "Ann Careful," Fleet said that it was high time that the "old rusty Batchelors" who ran the *Courant* and appointed themselves "Women's Monitors" listened to the exposure of some of their own faults. "Ann Careful" proceeded to sketch a very convincing picture of her own husband, who "is so taken up with Inoculation and State Affairs, that he spends most of his Time in going from House to House, and from Shop to Shop, loitering and chattering, about that which no ways concerns him, and neglects his own Business at Home, by which we are reduced almost to penury."[34] There was probably not a *Courant* reader who had not encountered such a universal expert given to addressing himself at length to every public problem, no matter how intricate, and incapable of paying the least attention to his private problems, however elemental. Similarly, Fleet looked into a rampant social evil of the time—the raiding of estates before a corpse was cold by predatory creditors—and he used the same technique of not preaching against the evil in the abstract, but of constructing a situation through the homely details of which the reader could himself see the inherent injustice. Fleet shrewdly rejected any portrait of a rich man's estate's being pillaged by a swarm of claimants and instead chose the death of a young husband and father and the descent upon his wife of creditors insisting that "the Widow's clouts [swaddling clothes of her infant] and other Child-bed Linen" was attachable for the settling of her late husband's accounts. "We desire these hungry Creditors to consider, whether they act like Gentlemen or like Christians in their Proceedings against a distress'd Widow . . ." he concluded.[35] Again, the lesson in popular writing was clearly not lost on the apprentice to Fleet's trade, who also yearned to write effectively and who was to achieve his objective on a scale that, until his time, was unknown in the American colonies.

The eighth of the *Courant* contributors with King's Chapel associations was Thomas Lane, who contributed the then not inconsiderable sum of twenty pounds toward the erection of a new edifice some years later in 1752 when Dr. Gibbins was a vestryman. Little else is known of him or the Lane family, which apparently had a rather obscure history in Boston. One William Lane is recorded as having been appointed a chimney sweeper as early as 1655, a John Lane was granted a license to run an ordinary in 1702, and an Edward Lane married a niece of Governor Joseph Dudley. Thomas Lane emerged from his obscurity to write two pieces for the *Courant*,[36] both written in an affected rustic tone, not wholly convincing, about the need for the voters to reject candidates for public offices when their purposes in running were less to serve the public than to enrich themselves and to advance their own ambitions. He also repudiated the claims of incumbent officeholders that, if they aided a voter as, for example, in procuring a license, they should necessarily be rewarded with the voter's vote in the next election; and he warned against ruthless men who desired power only to misuse it: "Let us consider how it will be with us, if a haughty, covetous, revengeful Man should get in Power, he may wheedle us to choose his Relations and Tools into Places of Trust, by a species Pretence of Piety, in giving a Piece of Plate to the Church, and making large Promises of doing Justice to all; but when his Sycophants are at hand to support him, if he should invert Justice by drawing up an Indictment against any one of us, and be a JUDGE of it himself; or if he or his Relations should think fit to assault us, and we for defending our selves shall be prosecuted for it, and try'd by him; if he should take it upon him to examine such Matters as no way belong to him, and is directly an Infringement of our Priviledges."[37]

Lane's long piece, appearing the day before the town meeting of May 15, 1722, which was to elect Boston's representatives to the Great and General Court, was the first time that the *Courant*, two weeks earlier the first newspaper in America to publish an editorial opinion on a forthcoming election, cast doubt on the high motives of those aspiring to or achieving public office and suggested—rather pointedly, given the theocratic heritage—that overt religiosity could be a masquerade for cynical ma-

---

[35] Ibid., No. 38 (April 16 to April 23, 1722).

[36] Worthington C. Ford, "Franklin's *New-England Courant*," Massachusetts Historical Society, *Proceedings*, LVII, 336, has Lane as the author only of a piece signed "Elisha Trueman" in the *Courant* of May 7 to May 14, 1722. However, there was in the edition of April 23 to April 30, 1722, another piece signed "Elisha Trueman" on the same subject, unattributed by Franklin to anyone else, which was undoubtedly by Lane. Both pieces were date-lined "Woodstock."

[37] *New-England Courant*, No. 41 (May 7 to May 14, 1722).

terial interests. The unknown Thomas Lane, perhaps a close contemporary of James Franklin, was politically knowledgeable, skeptical, and sufficiently facile with his words and broad in his references to manage to combine, in the pseudonymous Elisha Trueman, both some of the sapient, astute qualities of the country bumpkin that, by the time of the Revolution, evolved into a New England type, however apocryphal, and some of the intellectual comfort that the Puritans derived from resorting to the ancient Greeks and Romans for precedents of exemplary or reprehensible behavior. His two pieces were shrewdly calculated to alert the voter to be wary of candidates and the office seeker to watch his step, without saying a thing with which any good man, in or out of office, could disagree, at the same time asserting the power of the press to be a third factor in the electoral process, aligned on the side of the voter and, though not necessarily against the officeholder or the office seeker, at least skeptical of him. It was intrinsically, of course, the role that the press was destined to fill in the American democracy, but that the *Courant* was far ahead of its time became quite clear before Benjamin Franklin's brief career in Boston's primogenous journalism came to its early close.

* * *

Of all the contributors to the *Courant* whose names Benjamin Franklin recorded on his file copies of the paper, the only name that he also recorded as he began the *Autobiography* half a century later at Bishop Shipley's house in Twyford was that of Matthew Adams. The recollection, however, was in connection, not with Adams's contributions to the *Courant*, but with his generosity to Franklin in inviting him to his personal library and lending him books to read.

Matthew Adams was not one of the Braintree dynasty but one of three brothers, who were sons of Scotch-Irish immigrants, Hugh and Avis Adams, who arrived in Boston in 1684, the year after Josiah Franklin arrived. Hugh Adams set up in the trade of cordwainer, or shoemaker, in Boston and prospered sufficiently to buy a house and to send the eldest of his sons, also named Hugh, to Harvard. The senior Adams apparently died young, since Hugh, Jr., complained, during the first of three catastrophic pastorates ranging from South Carolina to New Hampshire, that he was having great difficulty supporting his wife and two younger brothers and two younger sisters on his stipend of only seventy pounds a year, particularly since his parishioners had actually, over a two-year period, paid him only half that amount. Hugh was a mournful, despairing, tactless man, a hypochondriac and whiner ("I was sick of a Putrid Feaver, and of the Tertian Ague and Feaver, the Dropsie, Scurvy, Pestilence, Hypochondriack Melancholy, and Gonagra Gout . . . a Splenetick Fermentation of Melancholick-chyle working Wind in my Stomach, and then circulating Rheumatick Pains, like Swords Piercing through me, Sometimes Strangling my breath, and constantly overclouding my head with Such black Vapours that I could scarce exercise grace or Reason . . ."[38]). It speaks well for the strength of character of Matthew Adams and his siblings that they survived this *locum parentis*, Matthew becoming a fairly successful merchant in Boston and his brother, John, a prosperous mariner and influential member of the provincial council in Nova Scotia. Matthew Adams was married in Dr. Colman's liberal Brattle Street Church in 1715 to Katherine Brigdon, by whom he had three sons and a daughter.

The Adamses, like their more renowned Braintree namesakes, were a tribe of compulsive writers. The melancholy, disaster-prone Hugh composed verse while he was at Harvard and later, during his tempestuous ministerial career, when he was always feuding with either his parishioners or his clerical colleagues; wrote legal briefs in lawsuits that he brought (once when Adams won a defamation action, Judge Sewall said, "Seeing you have Justice done you, [I] hope it will incline you to Govern your Tongue and your Pen"[39]); constructed wretched verses deploring periwigs and hoop skirts, which Sewall suggested that he "keep still"; and authored long, factious, somewhat bizarre theological theses, which Sewall urged him to send to his fellow ministers before he published them, knowing full well that the ministerial council would suppress them. In December 1722, probably through his brother, Matthew, he contributed to the *Courant* a rhymed argument that Christmas was really in September and appended a lethal warning, by way of postscript, to a Jesuit missionary to hostile Indians that he was flirting with certain death by inciting them against the English. John Adams, the son of the Nova Scotian mariner and a great favorite of his uncle, the Couranteer, Matthew, was finishing his senior year at Harvard when the *Courant* started; he was a brilliant scholar and very widely recognized as one of a handful of colonial poets worthy of survival (a verdict subjected to some subsequent critical revision) and a prolific writer of prose, whom his uncle said he once witnessed dictating simultaneously to three scribes on three different subjects. His clerical career, like his uncle Hugh's, however, was a miserable failure, and he ended up a relatively short life of thirty-five years in sedentary study and writing at Harvard under a grant raised by some admiring alumni. (His Uncle Matthew had his collected poems published in a volume to which he contributed a preface highly appreciative of his departed nephew's exceptional gifts as both a scholar and a poet.) Matthew himself, though assiduous in his business and sufficiently prestigious to refuse to serve as a constable, was a devoted amateur of letters and a voluminous reader, who built an impressive collection of books. His enthusiasm was contagious, and that the *Courant* was planned by James Franklin to have a literary character and a variety of prose and verse interested him as a reader and supporter and stimulated his tribal instinct himself to take to

[38] MS autobiography in Massachusetts Historical Society, 33.
[39] Sewall, *Diary*, III, 76.

the pen. In May 1721, six months before the *Courant* was started, he had written a poem, which he called "An Evening Retirement." The great epidemic of smallpox had just begun four days earlier, no one realizing the vast dimensions that it would take and no one aware even that there was more than the single case of the West Indies sailor in the entire town. Matthew Adams, however, had some vague feeling that the shadow of death and a vengeful Lord hung over the town, and he was moved to commit his feelings to heroic couplets that turned out to be all too prophetic: "See! now th' infectious Clouds began to rise/With sickly Gloom to vail the healthful Skies." Attributing the impending disaster to "an angry God," irked by "a black and awful List of all our Crimes," Adams revealed a gentle, passive, and somehow non-Puritanical side of his nature in a personal epode: "I'll hide me in Love's Chamber, till his Rage/Is overblown, and Mercy mount the Stage./Then of his sparing Grace I'll gladly sing;/My rescu'd Life to him a thankful Tribute bring."[40] In the deepening gloom of the following November, when the disease was running rampant through the town and the inoculation controversy was raging just as wildly, he gave the verses to James Franklin, who printed them, with a modest and graceful introduction by Adams, as the lead piece in an issue of his paper that had a curiously placid tone throughout, just before, in the next issue, Franklin opened fire on the Mathers, over the curse incident, with a fury that neither he nor anyone else had ever shown before.

Matthew Adams stayed above the fray. His next contribution, a month later, was an evocative selection from his reading on the nature of eternity, followed after an interval of two months by a piece that demonstrated Adams's versatility and disclosed a lively sense of humor, as he led up to a plea for a restoration of some sense of brotherhood and serenity to life in the town, as the smallpox epidemic, which he did not mention, ebbed dramatically. He began with a spirited response to letters supposedly from women readers, but actually written by James Franklin and his friends, which complained about the *Courant*'s treatment of the sex and said that he was distressed "to see the *Courant* arraign'd at the Bar of Female Impudence, before a pair of supercilious bottle-nos'd Gossips, and (without a fair Hearing) condemn'd and offer'd a Sacrifice to their imperious Rage . . . summonsed up before their Mighty Saucinesses, to answer for the Capital Crimes of unmasking the Villainous, and exposing the domineering Practice of some masculine Females towards their goodnatur'd Husbands." Adams went on to point out that contentiousness had been besetting the whole town on all sides: ". . . a certain Gentleman steps in, (who it seems is a silent Mourner for the Loss of his Breeches,) and made a learned Harangue on the Subject . . . exclaiming bitterly against the Supporters of that Weekly Libel [the *Courant*], which infests the sober Part of the Town, and tends to debauch the Minds of unthinking youth,

[40] *New-England Courant*, No. 17 (November 20 to November 27, 1722).

and set us all in a Flame: Crying out, *Oh! The Divisions, the Quarrelings, the backbitings of the Times.*" Such accusations of the *Courant*'s sowing dissent reminded Adams of the fat man in a crowd in Leicester Fields who complained about all the room everyone else was taking up until someone said to him, "Bring your own Guts to a reasonable Compass, and then I'll engage we shall have Room enough for us all." Adams applied the example to the storm that had burst around the *Courant* amid demands that it reform. "For who does more to blow up this Fire of Contention, (which threatens to consume the very Remains of Brotherly Love and Agreement) than those who *cry down their neighbours* to *cry up Reformation.*" Adams then proceeded to the dilemma always faced by the censor. "If the *Courant* deserves the horrid Names which some have given it, what shall we say of those Gentlemen who are with Egg [i.e., still at breakfast] to read it (tho' *Incognito*) every Monday, and can hardly digest their *Chocolate*, till they have swallow'd a Dose of *Courant Hellebore!* 'T is strange it should be too vile and scandalous to be printed, and yet full good enough to be faithfully perus'd as often as it appears. In fine, if Persons would not see their own Irregularities, let them beware of peeping into magnifying glasses: Let Hen-peckt Husbands and boisterous Wives refrain dipping into the *Courant* for the future, and I dare forfeit a Title to their Esteem if they ever see any Thing in it against themselves. And should the Sworn Enemies of the *Courant* once leave off their Railings and bitter Invectives against *Couranto*, and move harmoniously in their proper Spheres, they will soon see the happy Effects therof."[41]

The avuncular manner of Matthew Adams extended not only to nourishing Benjamin Franklin's interest in reading and his nephew's in writing but also to his fellow townsmen's in voting. It was he who launched the *Courant* on its path of political action by writing a piece highly critical of a property owner who had made it known to his tenants "that they should vote for good Honest men for Representatives, such men as he would have them vote for, or else he would turn them out of his Tenements." Although the piece did not name the culprit, it identified him to the knowing reader through what must have been somewhat conspicuous and possibly unique facial characteristics: ". . . he commonly goes with one eye half shut, and his mouth screwed up in a whistling posture."[42] Adams was one of the more senior members of James Franklin's little company of ingenious men, whose average age was in the twenties or early thirties, and his writing style suggests a rather easygoing, temperate man as compared to some of his more fiery fellow contributors. The brother, father, and uncle of Puritan ministers, he understood the church and the clergy, including their limitations; yet he had at the same time that implicit independence that constantly surfaced in the Puritan

41 Ibid., No. 30 (February 19 to February 26, 1722).
42 Ibid., No. 39 (April 23 to April 30, 1722).

character and sometimes in the face of Puritan practices. And he had also, to a noteworthy extent, the Puritan love of learning and a lifelong fascination with books. He was in an admirable position to have been the doyen of the Couranteers and perhaps, alone among them, felt perfectly free to "take notice of" the young apprentice, even though James Franklin, according to Benjamin's version of their relationship, made it sufficiently clear that he was to be seen and not heard—an apprentice in the strictest sense of that lowly berth. In the printing house, which was rather self-consciously determined to be iconoclastic about the Puritan priests and the civil establishment and at times was somewhat impulsive and rash in expressing its attitude, Adams was a moderating influence, without the veneer of the young Anglicans and with some sympathetic understanding of the more affirmative side of the Puritan proposition and experience. Fifty years afterward, Benjamin Franklin could recall his name, could recall visiting with him, and could recall borrowing his books—obviously a man with whom he felt at home and from whom he gained some surcease from the uncomfortable atmosphere of hostility that he felt enveloped his relationship with his brother.

Always enamored of learning and vicariously attached to Harvard, Matthew Adams would have taken satisfaction, had he known it, that the year of his death, 1749, his young protégé, Benjamin Franklin, was the founder and the first president of the fourth college in the American colonies, which was to become the University of Pennsylvania.

* * *

There were, aside from the Franklins, fourteen contributors to the *Courant*'s first forty-three issues (with only the seventh issue unaccounted for—no copy was found in Benjamin Franklin's marked file), who wrote a total of seventy-one pieces. Two of those individuals, in addition to Dr. Gibbins, the Reverend Henry Harris of King's Chapel, and Cotton Mather, who furnished the account of the grenade attack on his house during the inoculation bitterness, wrote only one piece each—a woman, identified only as Madam Staples, who wrote a pert twelve-line poem in response to James Franklin's "Caution to Batchellors," and John Williams, who wrote a satirical attack on the illiteracy prevailing at "Harfet Coleg." Of the remaining sixty-six known contributions, thirty-two—very nearly half—were written by one man, "Mr. Gardner," who first appeared in the fifth issue, after James Franklin had become abruptly disillusioned with John Checkley's headlong aggressiveness and had begun also to have some reservations about his *Courant*'s becoming primarily a spokesman for the anti-inoculation medical community, with the strong-willed Dr. Douglass calling the turns. James Franklin's new "author," as he called Gardner, was, with Franklin, the sole author of the fifth, sixth, and eighth issues—possibly also of the missing seventh. Of the subsequent thirty-two issues whose authors were marked by Benjamin Franklin, eighteen had contributions by Mr. Gardner, three issues with three pieces by Gardner and four issues with two by him. During those first forty weeks of the *Courant*, Gardner used nineteen different pseudonyms and roamed comfortably, dispassionately, and competently through the whole range of subjects, trivial and significant, superficial and penetrating, transitory and persistent, that preoccupied the Boston of Cotton Mather and the emerging challenge to the Puritan prerogative. He wrote masterly Socratic dialogues, familiar essays, illuminating expositions, sharp satires, pointed editorials, facetious parodies, lyrical poetry, and homely letters. His talent was both versatile in its style and divergent in its range. He did not keep the *Courant* out of trouble, but he helped James Franklin to keep it responsibly critical and clear of shrill belligerence.

No figure of comparable significance in the provincial literature of New England is more totally veiled in the unknown, so far as his background, his personality, and, indeed, his very identity go, than "Mr. Gardner." Unfortunately, when Benjamin Franklin went through his collection of the *Courants* published during his association with his brother and marked on them the authors of all the pseudonymous and anonymous contributions, he seemed to be doing it for his own future recollection rather than to leave a record for posterity, and he consequently omitted some first names or initials, possibly because he did not know them in all cases and would have heard them addressed in the printing house, in cases where the men were senior to his brother, only as "Mr." Of the contributors, John Checkley, who was by 1721 already a notorious writer whose full name was well known in Boston, John Eyre, youngest of the contributors, Matthew Adams, Benjamin's special friend and benefactor among the contributors, Thomas Fleet, an established printer whose imprint was familiar to everyone in Boston, and John Williams were all identified by their first names; T. Lane by his first initial; and the Reverend Henry Harris, Captain Taylor, and Doctors Douglass, Steward, and Gibbins by their titles. Only Mr. Gardner and Madam Staples were identified solely by their last names, and Madam Staples had written only one minor piece for the paper. The name Gardner, spelled also as Gardiner, occurred in the Massachusetts Bay Colony even before the Winthrop settlement, Sir Christopher Gardiner having arrived, a month before the Puritans, with some servants and a concubine. His stay in Massachusetts was brief, however, after it became known that he had two wives living abroad; the colony first put him in jail and then let him go to Maine, upon learning that he was an agent of Sir Ferdinando Gorges, who held a grant from James I for what became the Province of Maine. Sir Christopher disappeared from New England history shortly thereafter. A George Gardiner arrived from Bristol in 1637, but his family retained the old spelling of his name; one of his descendants, Sylvester, became a noted physician and the husband of a daughter of Dr. John Gibbins. Sylvester Gardiner was only thirteen years old in 1721; were it not for his age, his Anglicanism, his liberalness, and his enterprise would have made him a likely possibility as the prolific and quite exceptional "Mr. Gardner" of the *Courant*.

No other Gardner in the civil or church records of Boston qualifies as the *Courant*'s contributor as closely or even at all suggestibly. The Gardeners who were graduated from Harvard prior to 1721 either had died by then or were holding quiet rural pastorates outside of Boston. Patience Folger Harker, the older sister of Franklin's mother, married a man named James Gardner, after the death of her first husband, but his first name was surely known to Benjamin, who would have used it in any mention of him; and it is, moreover, not known that James Gardner survived his wife, who died in 1717, or that he ever went with her to Boston. And Patience's brother, Eleazar Folger, Benjamin's uncle, married Sarah Gardner, also of Nantucket, where, however, they both stayed. A Samuel Gardner whose name recurs in the lists of Boston officeholders from 1702 to 1716 would qualify chronologically, but in no other respect; he was one of the fourteen "mechanicks" from the Mathers' church, who with their pastors' blessings started the conservative New North Church and whose new pastor, John Webb, was a cosigner with the Mathers of the letter to the *Gazette* in defense of Dr. Boylston and inoculation.[43]

One or two facts about the elusive Mr. Gardner, nevertheless, surface through his writings. First of these is that he was a Congregationalist and not an Anglican, for he wrote critically of the tendency of ladies "to sit down in Time of publick prayer" and again, quite sharply, of off-beat singing of the psalms: "Whereas several Persons sitting together in a Pew, in a Church at the South Part of Boston, some Time past by their irregular singing, have considerably disturb'd that Part of Divine Service. This is to advertise them, that for the future they keep Time with the rest of the Congregation. . . ."[44] And it can be deduced from his first contribution's tone of joyousness and dash that, though probably quite senior to James Franklin, he was still a relatively young man, as his lines on his own capacities as a contributor tend to affirm: "Above the Heav'ns which terminate our Sight,/We'll soar.—The rolling, whirling Orbs of Light,/In their mysterious, rapid Dance we'll sing;/And to DULL mortals we'll new Wonders bring."[45] These were not the words of an elderly gentleman facing his decline. Finally, the extent of his knowledge and the range of his references, disclosed in his writings, firmly establish that he was a man of learning, even of erudition.

The wit of Gardner shone through several of his contributions. He characterized a "penurious Miser" as "a Sort of Tantaliz'd Creature, whose

[43] James Savage, *A Genealogical Dictionary of the First Settlers of New England* (Boston, 1860), has several Gardner entries, II, 226–31. None suggests the identity of the "Mr. Gardner" of the *Courant*.

[44] *New-England Courant*, No. 36 (April 2 to April 9, 1722).

[45] Ibid., No. 5(August 28 to September 4, 1721).

Belly is forever Lank and Empty, while his coffers are Crowded with *Glittering Dust*, and it is harder to draw it thence, (tho' to supply his own Wants) then to dig it out of its native Mine."[46] And in response to the use, by Increase and Cotton Mather and their four clerical colleagues, of syllogisms to confirm the infallibility of their judgment, Gardner reduced the syllogism to a shred in a devastating attack on the limitations of logic: "A Method of preventing *Death*, which Dr. I-----e M---r and his Son, and several other Ministers say is the *right Way*, is not only lawful but a Duty. But Dr. I-----e M---r and his Son, &c. do say, That Inoculation is the right Way, *Therefore*, Inoculation is not only lawful but a Duty."[47] And when he could no longer stand the almost sadistic dullness and irrelevance of stories with which the *Gazette*'s publisher, Philip Musgrave, afflicted his readers (two successive issues of the paper in January 1722 featured as the front-page leads a ceremonial address by the Anglican clergy of South Carolina welcoming the province's new governor and another, a week later, by the Presbyterian ministers), Gardner published an advertisement in the *Courant* purporting to be the consensus of those who wrote for all three Boston newspapers: "At a full Meeting of the Couranteers, Gazeteers, &c. *Unanimously Voted*, that the Thanks of this Society be given to Mr. *Philip Musgrave*, for his late Services, in gratifying them and the whole Town and Country with several Humble Addresses from the Inhabitants of South *Carolina* to their present Governour; and that he be desired, if any Thing of the same Nature should offer, further to communicate."[48]

Gardner was also capable of writing a kind of homely human-interest letter, in a somewhat mocking tone, that was used by James Franklin and several of his contemporaries in London to enliven their endless columns of shipping news and official acts of the government. A scolding, stingy wife is complained of in one communication, and a scolding, spendthrift wife in another. As the vernal juices were stirring in midspring of 1722, Gardner wrote in the guise of a disappointed suitor whose love flatly refused to sign over all her wealth to him, and he consequently attached an advertisement for "Any young Gentlewoman" who had at least five or six hundred pounds that she would be willing to give him as part of a marriage agreement; but in the next issue he published another advertisement advising "Any young Gentlewoman who . . . has taken it into her Head to marry me upon the Terms" proposed to abandon the thought, because, as he explained in an accompanying letter, he had come to see the folly of his proposal to his original love and had made peace with her by withdrawing the mercenary condition that he had imposed on it.

Gardner also had a lyrical gift of a superior order. Perhaps he had no equal in this respect in colonial literature other than Edward Taylor,

---

[46] Ibid., No. 6 (September 4 to September 11, 1721).
[47] Ibid., No. 17 (November 20 to November 27, 1721).
[48] Ibid., No. 31 (February 26 to March 5, 1722).

whose remarkable work did not appear until the mid-twentieth century, that pastor-physician of the frontier village of Westfield having left orders with his heirs that his four hundred pages of poetry not be published, lest their rich, sensuous warmth corrupt his brethren or his own reputation. But Gardner felt no such bounds, and the asperity of many a Puritan parson must have been inflamed by a contribution of Gardner to a midwinter *Courant* on the delights of one Eliza. An excerpt:

> Her rosie Cheeks, with modest blushes crown'd,
> Inspire the Soul, and make the nimble Spirits bound.
> What rapturous Accents from her Lips I hear,
> Which warm the Breast, and charm the ravish'd Ear!
> Her pleasing Smiles, her every Grace combin'd,
> Do feast the Senses, and regale the Mind.
> Who can withstand the Lightening of her Eyes;
> For there the loveliest Charm of Beauty Lies.[49]

The emotional intensity and the physical fervor of Gardner's poems were quite alien, if not to the Puritan spirit, at least to Puritan utterances. Signing his verse "Corydon," for Vergil's rustic swain, Gardner asked that the *Courant* print it in "Emphatick Italick"—which James Franklin did, thereby further weakening his shaky standing among the ministers.

Gardner, however, was at his most eloquent and at his best when he dealt as an essayist with the problems, the contradictions, the aspirations, and the disquietudes of an age in transition. If some of the subjects that he chose reflected no more than conventional wisdom, he stated the case with such freshness, clarity, and close reasoning that he brought a new dimension to the Boston dialogue of the time. It was nothing new, for example, for self-appointed prophets to declare with remarkable precision the date of the second coming, the end of the world, and the day of judgment. Among the fears and awful sense of doom propagated by the Puritan insistence on a vengeful God, such dire prophecies rose to more than normal proportions. Gardner brought to those prophecies a calm, analytical look and a systematic refutation of the fake prophets "who because they would fain be thought wiser than Christ our Saviour, have ventured to mark out the exact Time of his coming to Judgment, whose Error Time has long since confuted." Thus, by the example of history, he sought to set at rest an omnibus prophecy current at the time of his writing, "That Wars and Pestilence shall be all over the World, and Constantinople shall be destroyed in 1721. That Christ shall be known to all Nations in 1722. That a great Man shall rise from the Dead in 1723. That *Affrica* shall be burnt in 1725. That all the World shall be astonied [i.e., stunned] in 1726. That the General Judgment of Quick and Dead shall be in 1727."[50] Such notions, "which sometimes Captivate whole Herds of the Vulgar,"

---

[49] Ibid., No. 16 (January 22 to January 29, 1722).
[50] Ibid., No. 8 (September 18 to September 25, 1721).

Gardner subjected to "the publick Scorn" that he persuasively demonstrated they deserved.

In an age given to prolixity, often very clumsy, Gardner had an engaging conciseness to his style—brief but graceful and sharply to the point.
Of honor, for example, he wrote, "He is the Honourable Man, who is
Influenc'd and Acted by a Publick Spirit and fir'd with a Generous Love
of Mankind in the worst of Times; who lays aside his private Views, and
foregoes his own Interest, when it comes in Competition with the
Publick: Who dare adhere to the Cause of Truth, and Manfully Defend
the Liberties of his Country when boldly Invaded, and Labour to retrieve
them when they are Lost." And of certainly one of the most direct and
pithy distinctions ever attempted in the language: "The Religious Man
fears, the Man of Honour, scorns to do an ill Action."[51] Of conversation:
". . . the more open, free and ingenuous any Conversation is, the greater
Pleasure and Satisfaction arises to the Persons engaged in it; for till we arrive at some Degree of *Freedom*, we cannot find a delightful Gust and
Relish, but converse only as Strangers, under Restraints and Uneasiness
. . . but sincere Friends not only converse with, but dwell IN each other,
and by Consequence, cannot but take Pleasure in beautifying those Minds
they delight and chuse to dwell in; now will they ever be wanting in their
Endeavours, to purge them from all Pollutions and render them as pure,
immaculate and splendid as is possible."[52] And of the ancient instinct to
believe in a supreme being: "Indeed, the heathen were so far from
disbelieving a Deity, that they were wont to worship a Plurality of Gods:
But it is observable, that in their Devotions they address'd themselves to
them, only as Mediators between them and the most high Sovereign
Numen; for tho' they talk'd of a Multitude of Gods, which were believ'd
and Worship'd by the common People, yet the Philosophers and Sages
among them always look'd upon the numerous Rabble of distinct Deities,
to have been but different Names, and various Representations, of One
Supream Incomprehensible Nature, exhibiting and manifesting his Divine
Power thro' the whole World."[53] But Gardner brought up, in the
Courant's columns, a more immediate problem, somewhat ahead of its
time, when he wrote a letter, as from a resident of Portsmouth in New
Hampshire, after some repressive laws had been passed in that province,
stating, "Ever since the New Laws have been Enacted, there is not a private Man among us who dare open his Lips, unless it be to Flatter. As for
Freedom of Speech, it is utterly suppress'd among us, and I suppose
quickly we shall be hang'd for our Thoughts."[54] Gardner answered his
own complaint pointedly in the *Courant*'s next issue: "But have you any
Laws that deprive you of Priviledges, which belong to you as *Men*, and

[51] Ibid., No. 35 (March 26 to April 2, 1722).
[52] Ibid., No. 38 (April 16 to April 23, 1722).
[53] Ibid., No. 29 (February 12 to February 19, 1722).
[54] Ibid., No. 20 (December 11 to December 18, 1721).

Englishmen, which you did not Consent to by your *Representatives?* And if they will enact Laws to enslave you and your Posterity, Cannot you *Ease your selves of such Adversaries*, and elect better Men in their Room?"[55]

The *Courant* was feeling its way: It had no precedent to follow in carving out for itself a useful role as a journal published independently "of authority," the closest prototype being the two-year-old *American Weekly Mercury* in Philadelphia, whose publisher Andrew Bradford was called before the Pennsylvania Provincial Council, was rebuked, and apologized for some skeptical comments on the state of the province's credit. But there was no theoretic, let alone any functional, sense of the purpose of independent journalism. Both *The Boston Gazette* and *The Boston News-Letter* were nonentities, in this respect, with no sense of mission at all and without any real feeling of independence or even any desire for it. James Franklin had a groping instinct as to what a newspaper should be doing, but he was young and inexperienced and was arriving at conclusions brought about by trial and error. But it was Gardner who brought to the free press in America the first definition of its responsibility and of its high purpose in language as exact as it was soaring:

> *As it is a fundamental Maxim in Politicks* that the Government ought to be of no Party at all; *so, he who engages in such a Task* [i.e., publishing a newspaper], *should if possible, conceal his Own private Opinion in things that are* controverted, *and not suffer the Fire of* Party-Zeal *to make an Eruption on any Occasion whatsoever. Indeed, the whole managery of such an Affair requires the greatest Prudence imaginable. A Man . . . must not expect to please all men. . . . He ought to view Men's Vertues and Crimes abstracted from their Persons, and commend and censure them accordingly. . . .*
>
> Go on; *And let* Impartiality *be your constant Motto, and* Truth *the Compass by which you Steer. Go on; and check the Follies and Extravagancies of a fantastick Age: Describe the Proud, the Envious and Ambitious in their odious Hue; and paint the Usurer and the Oppressor in their Infernal Colours. Here let your Whips be turn'd into Scorpions,*
>
> And Let pointed Satyr speak for injur'd Right,
>
> *Proceed; And cause the Idolatrous Miser to shrink his wrinkled Brow, beneath his adored Pile; and let the scoffing Atheist and hellish Blasphemer know, that they deserve not Arguments but Anathema's; nor fear to rebuke the Lying Spirit, which like the Pestilence, walketh in Darkness.*
>
> *Detect the vile Impostor, and shake the tottering Basis of his fake Greatness: Expose him to the World in his fallacious Tricks, and sordid Acts; portray the whole Mistery of his Iniquity, and discover his Sham Qualifications for Posts of Honour.*
>
> *Briefly, promote Enquiries after Truth, quicken and rouse the Slothful, animate and inspire the Dull: and however, the World has been impos'd on, it will soon appear, that Crimes are not lessen'd and sanctifi'd because*

[55] *Ibid.*, No. 21 (December 18 to December 25, 1721).

committed by Men in High Station, or of Reverend Name; nor are they enhanced because they are perpetrated by the Obscure and Mean.[56]

Written before any tradition of a free press had evolved, before indeed any clear theory of the function of journalism in a free society had emerged, Gardner's prescient declaration of the high mission of the newspaper and his realistic appraisal of the inevitable plight of the conscientious editor were the most brilliant of the works of the Honest Wags. Their authority alone implies the position of leadership that Gardner occupied at the *Courant*; that his presence on its premises was as constant as his influence can be inferred from the frequency of his contributions and their span in time, extending from the *Courant*'s fifth issue in September, 1721, when James Franklin was disturbed by the vehemence of Checkley and Douglass, to at least the fortieth issue in May 1722, and quite possibly for several months longer in the six-year history of the *Courant*. Benjamin Franklin, who was a silent witness to the conversations that took place in the printing house except when he was out delivering the paper on Mondays, very probably heard more from Gardner than the other Couranteers. But there was no period when Gardner exclusively was James Franklin's writing colleague; nor was he necessarily the most durable. And there is no evidence anywhere to suggest that he or anyone else, except James Franklin, had any authority over the other contributors or that the latter constituted any organized club at all, "Hell-Fire" or otherwise. The Couranteers were a motley, highly individualized group, not susceptible of organization or of domination even by one who seemed so clearly the superior intellect and writing talent among them, as Gardner did. Far from a raucous, rebellious gang of "leather aprons," the group included men with impressive educational credentials, such as Douglass, Harris, and Eyre, of responsible entrepreneurial character, like Thomas Fleet, and of solid Puritan associations like Matthew Adams, whose great pride, like Mather's, was his library. Captain Taylor was, to be sure, something of a stormy petrel, but he was the son of a man who was for twenty-one years treasurer of the province and hardly an obscure insurgent. And most of the Couranteers were not given to striking out at the establishment and then retreating into a cautious silence. Dr. Douglass, who had written for the first issue, was still writing for the forty-second; and John Eyre, Thomas Lane, Thomas Fleet, Captain Taylor, and Matthew Adams were also contributing pieces for as long as Benjamin Franklin's file of copies identified contributions by their author's names. Altogether the Couranteers were a cross section of the new Boston, the center of the commonwealth of the future. Though often fumbling and self-conscious in their wit, at times shallow in their satire, and occasionally imperceptive and unfair in their aggressiveness, the "most generous clan of Honest Wags" were the harbingers of the changes that were in time to overcome the old

[56] Ibid., No. 16 (November 13 to November 20, 1721).

order socially, economically, politically, and ecclesiastically. They set out quite unabashedly to "educate" New England; and if their impact was far from being widespread, it was nevertheless felt. And it was feared, because, in a seminal way and perhaps also in an evidentiary way, it repeated something valid and inevitable in the odyssey of the Bible Commonwealth.

Benjamin Franklin was well qualified, by his reading and by his concentrated and determined study of forensics, to participate in the discussions of the Couranteers. The rules of apprenticeship and the despotic role that James Franklin read into the master-apprentice relationship, however, imposed silence upon him. But he had seen that, despite the animation, the daring, and the intoxication of the iconoclastic and skeptical conversation that he heard in the printing house, it was the *written* word promulgated by the *Courant* that was stirring the town and alarming the establishment. And there was no rule against an apprentice's writing.

PART FIVE

The Liberation of Benjamin Franklin

But whoso looketh into the perfect law of liberty, and continueth therein, he being not a forgetful hearer, but a doer of the work, this man shall be blessed in his deed.
—The General Epistle of James, A.D. ca. 50

Though arguments be never so plaine, and Scriptures never so pregnant; yet a carnall wretch will carry himselfe against all, and say, it is not my judgement, I am not of that mind.
—*The Soules Humiliation*
Thomas Hooker, A.D. 1638

XIII

The Emergence of Silence Dogood

> . . . it seems to me that there is scarce any Accomplishment more necessary to a Man of Sense, than that of *Writing well* in his Mother Tongue. . . .
>
> —Benjamin Franklin[1]

By the spring of 1772, Benjamin Franklin was sixteen years old. He had been apprenticed to his brother for four years and knew quite thoroughly the printer's trade. He had read widely and prodigiously. He had come to know intimately the streets, the characters, the institutions, the attitudes, and the misgivings of the town of Boston. He began to achieve an understanding of his heritage and an enlightened perspective on his surroundings, sifting out what he found of validity to him and brushing aside the rest as he constructed, with the boldness of youth but with considerable flexibility, a religious belief of his own—deistic but essentially a philosophy of social pragmatism governed rather than inspired by the Christian ethic. He had been an eyewitness to the most vehement controversy thus far in Boston's history—the inoculation conflict. And he had seen, and (to the extent of helping to print it, delivering it to subscribers, and hawking it in the streets) he had participated in, the publication of a kind of journal wholly new to Boston and to the colonies, a paper that had literary ambition, that sought to acquire a character, that aimed to be both diverting and critical in its reports and observations, that refused to be subservient or, for that matter, necessarily responsive to "authority," and that, in pursuing these purposes, brought about the real beginnings of a free press in America and fumbled toward a native American literature. He had been in the company daily of all of the principal protagonists in this preludial venture, *The New-England Courant*. He had a special rela-

---

[1] *Pennsylvania Gazette*, August 2, 1733, in *Papers*, I, 138.

tionship, of course, with James Franklin, its founder, and, before it was over, he himself was to become a principal protagonist.

The brothers, however, were to constitute a strained alliance: James, the enterprising, somewhat irritable printer, who had the vision—and, when the printing of the *Gazette* was taken away from him, the economic incentive—to conceive the project of the *Courant* and the courage to undertake it; and Benjamin, the avidly learning, somewhat impatient boy, who had the insight to go to school, as it were, to the *Courant*'s bookshelves, to his brother, however badly they got along, and to that motley company of contributors who had such buoyant independence in their views and such radiant confidence in their ability to express them. If James was influenced considerably by the more polished and brittle minds of some of the Couranteers around him, it was, nevertheless, he who selected those minds, admitted their writings to his columns, and, in some cases, threw them out. As for Benjamin, at sixteen and with the kind of sprightly assurance that he showed all through his life, he was eager to be a central and accepted figure among the Couranteers rather than a tangental observer. "Hearing their Conversations, and their accounts of the Approbation their Papers were receiv'd with, I was excited to try my Hand among them."[2]

What Benjamin was seeking was, very naturally, a liberation from the subjugation which is the lot of boyhood and of apprenticeship—subjugation to parents, to schoolmasters, to taskmasters, and to an order of things and a system of values arrived at by others and in the shaping of which he had no voice. The instrument of his liberation was to be the pen, to which his high regard for the written word and his close acquaintance with books had led him, and the incentives were powerful: the keenness of his yearning to report his observations of the miniature world around him, the force of his eagerness to assert the convictions that took shape so lastingly at such an early period in his life, and the dynamism of his drive to improve society—to "do good," in the Mather lexicon. The result of these irrepressible stirrings in the young Franklin was the launching by Franklin, as, in David Hume's words, "the first great man of letters for whom we are beholden to her [America],"[3] of the series of fourteen familiar essays, published in *The New-England Courant* pseudonymously, at two- or three-week intervals from April 24 to October 8, 1722, that came to be known as the Dogood papers.

As Franklin could not remember a time when he did not want to read, he seemed also from the earliest age to have a compulsion to write that went beyond the mere desire or inclination that occasionally stirs many "bookish" young people. There was some of this compulsive writing in the blood: His great-grandfather, Henry Franklin, landed in prison for writing verses attacking some local potentate; his grandfather, the second Thomas

---

[2] *Autobiography*, 67.
[3] David Hume, *Writings* (London, 1874–75), IV, 154.

Franklin, was a scrivener with a bend toward writing notes on local history; his uncle, Benjamin, in addition to his interminable verses, wrote a brief but creditable family history and had a lifelong love affair with the written word, whose magic never failed to intrigue him; his maternal grandfather, Peter Folger, also took to the pen to make political points in his running battle with the Puritan establishment; James Franklin, his brother, revealed in his writings for the *Courant* an impressive competence and ease with the writing craft, even though his work neither aspired to nor attained the level of literature; and his father, Josiah, had an instinct for letters, took a very active and enlightened interest in Benjamin's early writing efforts, and proved himself to be both a sound and an effective critic. In addition to these hereditary factors, there was also a compelling external consideration that put Benjamin in league with the written word: A major fact of his age was that, aside from oratory in the pulpit or the legislature, the written word was the principal means of influencing one's social, intellectual, and political world. This Benjamin Franklin clearly intended to do, at least from the time that he entered his brother's printing house, where he witnessed with awe the power of the Couranteers to stir up the town of Boston and where he experienced the power of Locke and Shaftesbury to influence his own thinking and of the Port Royal logicians and Xenophon to recast the form and style of his expression. Benjamin was determined to write well, and he was willing—indeed, he was eager—to work at it.

Josiah Franklin, who seemed to have made no explicit effort—in any case, none recalled by his son—to revitalize Benjamin's attention to his religious duties, which sagged deeply once he was out of his father's care and apprenticed in the printing house (". . . evading as much as I could the common Attendance on publick Worship . . ."[4]), intervened, on his own initiative, in the direction that Benjamin's literary activity was taking. Nothing perhaps was more revealing of Josiah's moderation as a Puritan and of his intuitive grasping that the colonial venture in New England had implications and promise of far wider horizons than those envisioned by the Bible Commonwealth. It was as though, having concluded that Benjamin was not destined for a career in the church, he saw it as his paternal duty to recognize the area in which the last of his sons was to make the most of his capacities, and to step in and help when a significant occasion presented itself, as it did early in Benjamin's apprenticeship. The situation arose from the debate that Benjamin had, after reading Defoe's attack on depriving women of an education equal to that accorded men, with his boyhood friend, John Collins, on the subject. Collins, Franklin recalled, maintained that educating women "was improper; and that they were naturally unequal to it." Franklin said that he took the opposite side —"perhaps a little for Dispute sake," he added, although there is extensive

[4] *Autobiography*, 63.

evidence, including an early Dogood paper, that he thoroughly believed in his case then and all his life. Collins apparently got the better of the oral argument, or so Franklin thought, but the two boys parted leaving the question up in the air. "He [Collins] was naturally more eloquent," Franklin remembered, "had a ready Plenty of Words, and sometimes as I thought bore me down more by his Fluency than by the Strength of his Reasons. As we parted without settling the Point, and were not to see one another again for some time, I sat down to put my Arguments in Writing, which I copied fair and sent to him. He answer'd and I reply'd. Three or four Letters of a Side had pass'd, when my Father happened to find my Papers, and read them. Without entring into the discussion, he took occasion to talk to me about the Manner of my Writing, observ'd tho' I had the Advantage of my Antagonist in correct Spelling and pointing [i.e., punctuation] (which I ow'd to the Printing House) I fell far short in elegance of Expression, in Method and in Perspicuity, of which he convinc'd me by several Instances. I saw the Justice of his Remarks, and thence grew more attentive to the *Manner* in Writing, and determin'd to endeavour at Improvement."[5]

Determined as he was to achieve an effective literary style, Franklin inevitably turned to the books available to him for instruction and example. Most of the reading of his early boyhood, and some of that which he had done during his first years at the printing house, was undertaken for its substance rather than its style, the Port Royal authors and Xenophon being exceptions. But as time went on during his apprenticeship, the works of more and more authors became accessible to him. Not only was he permitted to borrow at will from the "pretty Collection of Books" of Couranteer Matthew Adams, but he made it a point to strike up friendships with the apprentices of Boston's numerous booksellers so that they would smuggle books out to him at night when the shops closed; and having stayed up most of the night to read them, he would rise early the next morning to get them back again before the shops opened. At the same time, James Franklin's printing house, which, like most printing houses of the eighteenth century, was really a publishing house as well, was building up a varied and extensive library, a partial catalogue of which James Franklin printed in the *Courant* on one occasion to prove, after the paper had been criticized by "restless, uneasy Spirits" for being "saucy" and "impudent," that at least it was literate. Thirty-eight works or authors were listed, and the range was impressive. The classical works included Pliny the Elder's scientific encyclopedia, *Natural History*; Flavius Josephus' twenty-book history of the ancient Jewish people, *Antiquities of the Jews*; Aristotle's *Politics*; Vergil's works; a four-volume *Athenian Oracle*; and a history of Rome. English literary figures were represented by the works of Shakespeare and Milton; *The Spectator* of Joseph Addison and Richard Steele;

⁵ Ibid., 60–61.

and the latter's short-lived daily, *The Guardian;* the briefly popular but unenduring works of the seventeenth-century poet, essayist, and pamphleteer Abraham Cowley, whose purist and best work (the last of eleven *Discourses by way of Essays, in Verse and Prose*), an autobiography called "Of My Self," may have been, in its forthright, simple style as well as the frankness of its content, a model Franklin had in mind when undertaking his own autobiography; the satirical poems, aimed at the Jesuits, of John Oldham; and Samuel Butler's long, impudent, and bitter satire against the Puritans, the Don Quixotic *Hudibras;* the allegorical work—perhaps the masterpiece of all English satire—Jonathan Swift's *A Tale of a Tub,* which the venerable dean himself declared years later the work of a genius and to which Benjamin Franklin's friend, Matthew Adams, was so devoted that he lifted a paragraph from it verbatim, ascribing it only to a source "I had somewhere read," in the third of his four contributions to the Courant[6]; the two essay series, *The Reader,* edited by Steele in 1714, two years after *The Spectator* ended, and *The Lover,* also derivative of Addison and Steele; the English periodical of "Curious Amusements for the Ingenious" called *The British Apollo;* and such current London imports as *The Ladies Pacquet* and *The Ladies Calling.* Trivia were limited (*The Turkish Spy* appears, for example), and great works exemplifying both high literary standards and lasting substantive significance were the rule rather than the exception, the choices on the whole sophisticated and far from parochial: There were the works of the Huguenot poet Guillaume de Salluste du Bartas (probably in Josuah Sylvester's translation of 1608), who had had a pronounced influence on Ben Jonson and Milton; St. Augustine's works, the inspiration of the Port Royal theologians; the *History of the Reformation,* by Gilbert Burnet, the Bishop of Salisbury; Thomas Burnet's *Theory of the Earth,* which held that, before the biblical flood, the earth was egg-shaped and became round only when the internal waters burst out; the superbly written polemics of John Tillotson, eightieth Archbishop of Canterbury; the gently nonconformist writings of William Bates, who, though he declined succession to the post once held by Addison's father as Dean of Lichfield, took communion with the Anglicans in a spirit of Christian conciliation; the writings of Robert South, the rector of Islip, whose debates with the dean of St. Paul's on the nature of the Trinity were so animated that William III told them both to stop them; the more pragmatic works of the English Presbyterian preacher John Flavel, whose *Husbandry Spiritualized* was a vade mecum to thousands of dissenting yeomen; and the theological treatises of Stephen Charnock, the Cantabridgian nonconformist cleric, which were basic Calvinist pulpit literature. Of general informational or referential works, the *Courant* had a good working library, James Franklin singling out for mention a history of France; Moll's *Geography;* Peter Heylin's *Cosmography*

---

[6] *New-England Courant,* No. 30 (February 26 to March 4, 1722).

and his compendium called *The Sum of Christian Theology*; Cotton Mather's *Magnalia Christi Americana*, which Franklin listed under its subtitle, "The Ecclesiastical History of New England"; John Oldmixon's history, *The British Empire in America*, which Franklin referred to as the "History of the American Colonies"; the accounts by George Sandys of his travels, which covered Asia Minor, Palestine, Egypt, and Greece; and the two Port Royal books on the arts of thinking and speaking.

* * *

Of all the works in the *Courant* library, none made so deep an impression on the young apprentice as *The Spectator*, the creation of Joseph Addison, aided and abetted by his friend from boarding-school days, Richard Steele. The language of his autobiography suggests that Franklin discovered *The Spectator* before the *Courant* was started and before the full set of eight volumes was available to him in the printing house library: "About this time [i.e., early in his apprenticeship, when he was having his written exchanges with Collins] I met with an odd Volume of the Spectator. It was the third. I had never before seen any of them. I bought it, read it over and over, and was much delighted with it. I thought the Writing excellent, and wish'd if possible to imitate it."[7] The third volume of *The Spectator* consists of eighty-one essays: thirty-nine of them by Addison; thirty-five by Steele; three by Addison's cousin, Eustace Budgell, a twenty-five-year-old miscellaneous writer and also a miscellaneous rogue, who eventually drowned himself in the Thames; one by John Hughes, a minor dramatist, librettist, and translator; and three of uncertain authorship. The papers appeared daily, except Sundays, between September 14, 1711, and December 18, 1711, when Benjamin Franklin was five years old and three years before he entered the Latin School. But the substance of *The Spectator* was not perishable with the passage of time, nor was it vulnerable to differences between the ages of the authors and those of their readers. *The Spectator* papers, though their locale was London, were concerned largely with human characteristics and propensities, the vanities and follies, the triumphs and graces, the values and hopes, the manners and customs of people; and they stayed clear of topicality, religious, political, or economic, as Addison earnestly sought to restore human values both to literature and to society. He steadily ignored all forms of institutional and traditional conflicts, distinctions, and doctrines, as the third volume of *The Spectator* rambled amiably through subjects of universal interest—among them, jealousy, the misuse of talents, henpecking wives, excessive zeal, parents' hardness to children, ambition, discretion, flattery, laughter, seduction, and good nature as a moral virtue. Addison and his friend, Steele, who so admirably supplemented the cheerfully scholarly and gently moralistic temperament of Addison with his deeper insight into human relationships and his earthier knowledge, reached across the

[7] *Autobiography*, 61–62.

seas and the years and brought the young Franklin, in the deft, lucid, urbane pages of *The Spectator*, a view of society fundamentally generous, humanistic, moderate, unconcerned with creeds and the clashes between them but enchantingly concerned with the behavior of people, their treatment of one another, and the ways, trivial and consequential, through which they revealed and expressed themselves.

The communion between two London men of letters, each of them in his fortieth year when *The Spectator* papers appeared, and the Boston printer's apprentice, in his thirteenth year when he first read them, was not as improbable as might seem on the surface. There were, of course, other contrasts between the authors and their young reader than the generation of difference in ages. Addison and Steele were the children of the upper-middle, educated class—Addision of a Church of England vicar and Steele of a Dublin attorney—and Franklin the child of a provincial artisan. Addison and Steele spent five years at Charterhouse, in preparation for Oxford, where Addison stayed fifteen years as undergraduate at Queens and scholar and fellow at Magdalen, and Steele stayed for three years, first at Christ Church and then at Merton; Benjamin Franklin, on the other hand, had but a single year at the Latin School in aborted preparation for Harvard, which he never entered. Addison was a sensitive, reticent boy, the child of the country rectory at Milston in Wiltshire and of the deanery at Lichfield, his father a scholar and prolific writer, while Steele, a somewhat irresolute, frothy lad, orphaned at the age of six, grew up in the comfortable, worldly seat of a maternal uncle, who was the agent of the militant Dukes of Ormande; Franklin, hearty and bold by nature, the ambitious, self-instructing son of the tallow chandler, grew up in the modest, frugal cottage-shop in Union Street. Addison and Steele both came to their literary work discriminating in their tastes, at home with the theater (both wrote plays of accomplished professionalism), thoroughly grounded in the classics (Addision was recognized as one of the best Latin poets since the classical age of Augustus), personally acquainted with such luminous figures as John Dryden and William Congreve, self-confident and highly originative in their style; Franklin was on his own, a fumbling experimenter, who had to get an easy bend toward doggerel out of his system, and then an imitator, struggling to find a literary form that would accommodate his native and innovative talents, somehow dissatisfied with the traditional but lacking the foundation, the literary poise, to originate a form wholly his own. Yet, for all these contrasts, the similarities of outlook, of values, and of the vision of the human situation and its prospects between the gregarious London essayists' in their prime and the solitary Boston apprentice's in his artless youth were more striking. *The Spectator* authors were, in a sense, the conciliators of Puritanism and the Restoration, the literary architects of a new humanism, the benevolent agents of a new age, a new order, and a new approach to an appraisal of the plight and promise of mankind, that was fresh and uncluttered even if neither philosophically profound nor broadly realistic. All this was to be also the theme and the point of much of Franklin's long life. But there were more specific similarities. *The Spectator* belonged to a city and looked at society, for the most part, through the lens of the social epitomizing that occurs most commonly in cities. Benjamin Franklin, too, belonged to the cities all his life—Boston, Philadelphia, London, Paris. He was most at home where there was the ferment of human life. All of them, Addison, Steele, and Franklin, also had in common a taste for public office, and they all held both elective and appointive offices (though Steele was expelled from Parliament for writing a "seditious" tract attacking, among others, Queen Anne).

When Addison first went to live in London, he lived in the heart of the city, in a Haymarket garret, no better probably than the garret lodgings of Franklin in Boston; and as Franklin developed a sense of thrift through the example of a frugal father, Addison practiced thrift in reaction to a somewhat extravagant one. Though at a later age than Franklin, Addison drifted away from the church as a possible career, but like Franklin he felt the strong need to be a good if not a devout layman; and, also like Franklin, he had a distrust of piety for its own sake. Both, too, had a major preoccupation with the improvement of men and their institutions, not through exhortation but through lively illustrations and evocative characters. Addison and Franklin shared an impatience with pedantry and at the same time an appetite for the calm pushing forward of the frontiers of thought by courageous, independent thought. Locke had an influence on both that contributed significantly to the shaping of both their thought and their lives. Finally, Franklin's aims as a thinker and as a writer, not in his youth only but throughout his life, were the same as those asserted by Addison in the tenth *Spectator:* ". . . I shall endeavour to enliven Morality with Wit, and to temper Wit with Morality. . . . It was said of *Socrates,* that he brought Philosophy down from Heaven, to inhabit among Men; and I shall be ambitious to have it said of me, that I have brought Philosophy out of Closets and Libraries, Schools and Colleges, to dwell in Clubs and Assemblies, at Tea-Tables and in Coffee-Houses."[8]

With Steele, Franklin's similarities were of a somewhat different order. Steele and Franklin both were boys and men of great good nature. Both had a lifelong interest in the components and quality of institutional education. Both were genuinely and deeply interested in the nature of conversation as the basic form of human communications. Each was inclined to school himself quite thoroughly in the more raucous side of town life, and each with as much zest and enjoyment as curiosity about the world in which he lived. Each had less of Addison's sensitivity, a brasher spirit,

[8] *Spectator,* I, No. 10 (March 13, 1711).

and a less polished way. Steele, who frequently troubled Addison with his political excesses, his improvidence, and his somewhat unscrupulous conduct of his personal affairs, did not have any of Franklin's prudence or sense of moderation, no more than Cotton Mather's Boston, in which Franklin grew up, had any outward and visible signs of the grace of Queen Anne's London, in which the authors of *The Spectator* flourished.

By the time that Franklin first came across *The Spectator*, its principal authors had become estranged, Addison ultimately dying of asthma and an edema at the manor of his wife, the Dowager Countess of Warwick, and Steele, immersed in politics and knighted by George I, undergoing a temporary political eclipse induced largely by the vehement spirit which he brought to public affairs. Both Addison and Steele had, for all practical purposes, abandoned the literary activities that radiated such bright promise less than a decade earlier, but the slender quantity of their best work was enough to launch the familiar essay as a literary form on both sides of the Atlantic. Certainly they inspired the first serious writing efforts of Benjamin Franklin. There is some reason to believe that, in his later satirical writings, he was more influenced by Jonathan Swift, but there is no mention at all of the Dublin dean in the autobiography, even though *A Tale of a Tub*, which was in the *Courant*'s library, antedated *The Spectator* by seven years, and no mention of Swift in Franklin's other known writings until 1733, when Swift was quoted in a piece by Franklin "On Literary Style" in his *Pennsylvania Gazette*.[9] But in his early years, he clearly used Addison and Steele's *Spectator* papers as his models and their authors as his tutors. There are few passages in all autobiographical literature more touching and more revealing, and more undiminished in its poignancy by the fame it later achieved, than Franklin's account of the determination of a young boy, schooled far below his capacity to learn and his gifts to make the most of his learning, to write well and the travail that he went through, after the long day's work in the printing house, to realize that resolve:

> . . . I took some of the Papers, and making short Hints of the Sentiment in each sentence, laid them by a few Days, and then without looking at the Book, try'd to compleat the Papers again, by expressing each hidden Sentiment at length and as fully as it had been express'd before, in any suitable Words, that should come to hand.
>
> Then I compar'd my Spectator with the Original, discover'd some of my Faults and corrected them. But I found I wanted a Stock of Words or a Readiness in recollecting or using them, which I thought I should have acquir'd before that time, if I had gone on making Verses, since the continued Occasion for Words, of the same Import but of different Length, to suit the Measure, or of different Sound for the Rhyme, would have laid me under a constant Necessity of searching for Variety, and also have tended to fix that Variety in my Mind, and make me Master of it. There-

9 *Papers*, I, 328.

fore I took some of the Tales and turn'd them into Verse: And after a time, when I had pretty well forgotten the Prose, turn'd them back again. I also sometimes jumbled my Collections of Hints into Confusion, and after some Weeks, Endeavour'd to reduce them into the best Order; before I began to form the full Sentences, and compleat the Paper. This was to teach me Method in the Arrangement of Thoughts. By comparing my work afterwards with the original, I discover'd many faults and amended them; but I sometimes had the Pleasure of Fancying that in certain Particulars of small Import, I had been lucky enough to improve the Method or the Language and this encourag'd me to think I might possibly in time come to be a tolerable English Writer, of which I was extreamly ambitious.

My Time for these exercises and for Reading, was at Night, after Work or before Work in the Morning; or on Sundays, when I contrived to be in the Printing House alone. . . .[10]

Franklin left no record as to which of the eighty-one papers in the third volume of *The Spectator* he used in his exercises, but most any of them would have served his purpose. The first paper in the volume was concerned with the phenomenon of jealousy. Written by Addison, it had those qualities of directness, clarity, good sense, and inherent benevolence for which the young writer was striving: "*Jealousie is that Pain which a Man feels from the Apprehension that he is not equally beloved by the Person whom he entirely loves*. . . . The jealous Man's Disease is of so malignant a nature that it converts all he takes into its own Nourishment. . . . But the great Unhappiness of this Passion is that it naturally tends to alienate the Affection which it is so solicitous to engross. . . ."[11] Another of Addison's papers struck close to home to anyone in Cotton Mather's Boston: "There is nothing in which Men more deceive themselves than in what the World calls Zeal. There are so many Passions which hide themselves under it, and so many Mischiefs arising from it, that some have gone so far as to say it would have been for the Benefit of Mankind if it had never been reckoned in the Catalogue of Virtues."[12] And yet another struck close to the heart of Franklin's own character as it was fast evolving during his apprenticeship: "When a Man is made up wholly of the Dove, without the least Grain of the Serpent in his Composition, he becomes ridiculous in many Circumstances of Life, and very often discredits his best Actions. . . . I am heartily concerned when I see a Virtuous Man without a competent Knowledge of the World. . . ."[13] Steele was less polished and less engaging than Addison as a literary model for Franklin; but as an *in absentia* tutor in the society of the age of Queen Anne, he was more realistic, more practical, less patient with the

[10] *Autobiography*, 62–63.
[11] *Spectator*, III, No. 170 (September 14, 1711).
[12] Ibid., No. 185 (October 2, 1711).
[13] Ibid., No. 245 (December 11, 1711).

heartless and hypocritical but more profound in his social insights, probing below the surface of manners to get at the root of the situation. His contributions to *The Spectator* were incisive and pungent, but without abrasiveness, abuse, or malice. And though the provincial New England port town may have lacked some of the refined postures of London, and most of the affectations that were imported from the French to *The Spectator's* distress, there were still to be seen in Hanover Street, in Marlborough Street, in Summer and Winter streets, and along the bawdy waterfront of Fish and Ship streets, all the conditions and sorts of men and women that gave Boston's life, as they did London's, its pace and conflicts. The types familiar to Steele were not unfamiliar to the young Franklin: "I am a Man of Pleasure about Town," Steele had a *Spectator* correspondent write, "but by the Stupidity of a dull Rogue of a Justice of Peace and an insolent Constable, upon the Oath of an old Harridan, am imprisoned here for Theft when I designed only Fornication."[14] But there was also in Steele a vision of life that characterized the humanistic instincts of the Enlightenment. It was magnificently expressed in a passage (in that third volume of *The Spectator* over which Franklin labored so hard to emulate its style) of the highest order of Augustan prose: "Human Nature appears a very deformed, or a very beautiful Object, according to the different Lights in which it is view'd. When we see Men of inflamed Passions, or of wicked Designs, tearing one another to Pieces by open Violence, or undermining each other by secret Treachery; when we observe base and narrow Ends pursued by ignominious and dishonest Means; when we behold Men mix'd in Society as if it were for the Destruction of it; we are even ashamed of our Species, and out of Humour with our own Being: But in another Light, when we behold them mild, good, and benevolent, full of a generous Regard for the publick Prosperity, compassionating each other's Distresses and relieving each other's Wants, we can hardly believe they are Creatures of the same Kind. In this View they appear Gods to each other, in the Exercise of the noblest Power, that of doing Good; and the greatest Compliment we have ever been able to make to our own Being, has been by calling this Disposition of Mind, Humanity."[15] Whether this was one of the passages that the intrepid Boston apprentice transformed to verse and then recast in his own prose version is uncertain. It is certain that Steele's humanistic distinction between good and evil—man's making the most of himself and his kind rather than the least—rather than the distinction springing from the Puritan concept of a good but fiercely jealous God locked in perpetual conflict with an evil but indestructible Satan, with man a craven pawn in the struggle, was the essence of the human quest as Franklin had come to see it then and was to continue to see it the rest of his life. He had made up

14 Ibid., No. 182 (September 28, 1711).
15 Ibid., No. 230 (November 23, 1711).

his mind that a basically humanist creed was to be the point and guide of his life, as his future writings and actions made clear. He had obviously made up his mind, too, to write in the vein of *The Spectator*. The vehicle was to be the letters of one "Silence Dogood," addressed to *The New-England Courant*; and they were to leave their mark both on Franklin's own development and on the development of an American literature as contrasted with the colonial and provincial English literature that antedated them.

* * *

A combination of factors accounted for the genesis of the Dogood papers. The most immediate, though perhaps the least compelling, among them was, as Franklin stated in his autobiography, the stimulating example of the Couranteers around him and the contagion of excitement and satisfaction that their writings generated among those valorous scribblers, to whose company Benjamin wanted so desperately to be admitted. The literary progenitor of the Dogood papers was unquestionably *The Spectator*, though not so much substantively as in literary devices, format, and nomenclature. The ethical contents of the Dogood papers obviously had their roots and frequently their whole substance largely, though not wholly, in Daniel Defoe's *An Essay upon Projects*, which Franklin had absorbed before he went to James Franklin's printing house. But the material of the essays—the characters and characterizations, the incidents, the dialogue, the vignettes, the points of view expressed—was right out of Dock Square, the center of life in the town, not two hundred yards from the *Courant's* headquarters in Queen Street, and out of Boston Neck, the narrow link between Boston and the mainland where town and country met. And the context was the new, restless, rapidly growing, rapidly changing Boston that was slipping away from the governance of the Puritan dynasties and was already severed from the resolve of the Bible Commonwealth. Doubts were surfacing, and with them new outlooks. The old unanimity of thought had gone, and in its place arose dissent from dissent, not monolithically but in a whole spectrum of views ranging from deism at one end to high Anglican churchmanship at the other. And a cauldron of simmering social ingredients made for a cauldron, too, of social outlooks. It was this new Boston, this concentrated corner of an emerging America, to which young Benjamin Franklin was assigning himself the roles of reporter, interpreter, and, within the bounds of an essentially moderate temperament, agitator.

From his own earliest recollections and from the earliest evidences of his life, Franklin had a fundamentally social outlook. Life to him was not a solitary odyssey, but a gregarious adventure. He had few inward compulsions and swarmed with outward drives. And the qualities of mind and disposition that limited the depth of his intellectual interests were the same qualities that widened their breadth. While still a youth, he had an uncommon range of social vision, a prophetic appreciation of the social drift of mankind, and a rather sharp instinct for the direction that it ought to be taking—in his judgment, a co-operative, voluntary association. In the fabric of life in the miniature world of the port town of Boston, Franklin read into its warp and woof testimony of the predicament and promise of man in general as the rays of the Enlightenment began to touch the craggy, gray shores of New England.

It was not a deliberative process for him at all but rather a perceptive one inspired by a driving curiosity, which led him into the way of journalism and later into the natural sciences. The child born across from the South meetinghouse on one street and from the governor's mansion on another was worldly wise at a very early age. Delivering candles from his father's tallowshop, when he was no more than ten, took him into the houses, shops, taverns, and public buildings of the town, and after he was twelve he was in the streets, around the squares, at the market places and along the wharves, hawking broadsides, tracts, and the newspaper that trickled from his brother's printing press. From all this he had gained, by the age of sixteen, a realistic and unfiltered familiarity with the many facets of Boston life which had neither chroniclers nor spokesmen in the town's civil, religious, or commercial establishments. The thought certainly must have more than once crossed Franklin's mind, steeped as he was in *An Essay upon Projects,* that what Boston needed was a Daniel Defoe to articulate the facts of life beyond the meetinghouse, the countinghouse, the rooms of the governor and his Council, and the chamber of the lower house of the Great and General Court, and to respond to those facts with imagination and some sympathetic insight. Franklin, who was not a somber or brooding youth, also shared the common conclusion of the Couranteers that it was time for Boston to laugh at itself occasionally, to recognize the fallacies always present in community life, to ridicule the pompous and hypocritical, and to take a light view of outmoded conventions and anachronistic attitudes. That this could be done with the good humor and kindliness that were basic aspects of his nature, Franklin, having read *The Spectator* of Addison and Steele, could have had little doubt. Nor did he seem to have much doubt that he was ready to fill the gap left by the absence of an American Addison and Steele and of an American Defoe. He knew the weak spots to be revealed and the accepted strengths to be questioned; and he had an awareness, even if no profound understanding, of the irreversible changes that were taking place and had taken place in Boston even during his brief lifetime.

These changes were apparent in virtually every aspect of life in the fading years of Cotton Mather's Boston, as worldly intrusions disturbed the utopian design plotted by John Winthrop and articulated by John Cotton. In no area were these intrusions more inevitable and more persistent than in the economic life of the province, bringing about changes that were neither anticipated as certain to come by the founders of the Puritan state nor recognized for what they meant, when they did come, by the heirs of the founders.

The Bible Commonwealth had never turned its back on the practical business of the material life, and the opportunity to make a respectable living rather than an intense religious spirit accounted for the migration of hundreds of artisans like the Franklins. But as the population became larger, more varied, and more complex, so did the relatively simple economic life envisioned by the first settlers. The rise of the merchants created a class not only of commanding wealth but also with its own political interests and influences. At times it achieved the force of a plutocracy and, to serve its own ends, sought to ally itself with the representatives of the crown and their councilors rather than the representatives in the legislature; and it looked always anxiously to London and Whitehall for the preservation and aggrandizement of its fortunes, accordingly strengthening Anglican institutions in the New World (the Church of England, for example) rather than building upon the peculiarly American institutions initiated by the founders. Other hallmarks of an emerging class society appeared. Luxury trades, unknown as late as the end of the first decade of the eighteenth century, had opened up and prospered by the beginning of the 1720s, to serve the small but discriminating clienteles that could increasingly afford such imports as Mantua silks, Irish linens, Dutch wallpaper, and English boots; and an endless assortment of wines and preserved delicacies from western Europe turned up in highly specialized vintners' and grocers' shops along Marlborough Street. Inevitably, these highly visible signs of an upper economic class led to a social cleavage which revealed itself in conflicts over such issues as the mercurial monetary system patched together arbitrarily and extemporaneously by royal governors, by the legislators, and sometimes by the financiers themselves. A wedge was driven, by diversive economic and monetary interests, between the country people beyond Boston Neck and the merchants and shippers, who had little concern with the rural economy. Even within the city, the artisans fell into collision, on economic grounds, with the plutocracy, and an alliance between country farmers and town artisans prevented for years the opening of a produce market in Boston for fear of its control by the upper stratum. Moreover, where extremes of wealth and poverty in seventeenth-century Boston had been rare, by the 1720s they had become commonplace and dramatic, as the Scotch-Irish, with slender stakes and no jobs waiting, arrived by the shiploads; as Queen Anne's War and the constant perils of the sea steadily swelled the number of destitute widows and orphaned children; and as periodical "depressions" occurred as a result of natural disasters, war dislocations, and the repeated tolls of fires and plagues. The economy, in essence, was restless, unpredictable, and changing faster than it could be managed; and the same process of change, in part a consequence of the changing economy and in part a cause of it, was being visited upon the society as a whole.

The troubled economy of Boston gave rise, too, to increased crime and to a scrubby borderline world centered on the waterfront. Unemployment instigated much of this, but much, too, was inherent in the flow of a new kind of immigrant—seamen jumping ship, predatory if petty adventurers, opportunists looking for a quick economic killing, the generally restless, who drifted from one port city to another in endless futile search for point and fulfillment, and the social outcasts of Boston itself, never able to adjust themselves to their surroundings and after some trial and error abandoning hope and taking to drink, brawling, and keeping alive by scavenging and shady dealings. With legitimate paths to economic survival closed to them, an inevitable proportion of the unskilled and the inadequate turned to parasitical lives of crime, feeding one way or another on the society that rejected them. Burglary and robbery, crimes against property most common in societies with extremes of wealth, were the most frequent offenses, but more sophisticated crimes also began to occur as the economy and the social situation became more intricate. No sooner was paper money issued than counterfeiters went to work printing spurious certificates and selling or spending them. Commercial rivalries made for corrupt practices in trade at a high level, and the abuse and criminal exploitation of indentured labor was erosive at the lower. With frustrations in the face of economic and social injustices, mobbism appeared and with it some impassioned and some cynical manipulators of mobs. Gangs, raiding warehouses and waylaying the watch, sprang up, and the criminal as a chronic offender became a characteristic of town life. By the time that he was sixteen, Franklin knew them all—the drifters, the drunks, the harlots, the shifty, the unwilling debris of any society moving aimlessly and without purpose.

Problems fundamentally economic gave rise, too, to the emergence of social distinctions as between town and country that the dissipation of the leveling force of a dominant Puritanism left unchecked. The people of the rural area had less and less in common with the townspeople, particularly those of the port towns who looked to trade for their sustenance rather than to the land and were far less satisfied than their rural countrymen with mere sustenance in any case. Moreover, the smallness of the rural centers and, in the case of many, the remaining characteristics of the near frontier made for greater homogeneity and greater interdependence. Life was simpler, more innocent, more unified and uniform. Country and village people knew one another, trusted one another, and shared participation in the same institutions. In contrast to the port towns, the population was stable, the wealth more evenly distributed, and the atmosphere consequently less conducive to tensions, conflict, and frustrations. As a result, the country residents looked with some suspicion and with a moral superiority upon the townspeople. The lavishness of the town's wealthy and the rebelliousness of its deprived were alike, to the rural populace, culpable and unnecessary, and the conditions of life that spawned such extremes of behavior were thought lacking both in virtue and in common sense.

Within the town of Boston, as inner social stratifications were forming, the kind of cohesiveness that bound together the disparate lives of Judge Sewall and Josiah Franklin was dissolving, as the vision of Boston as a celestial kingdom on earth paled among the elect and never inspired at all the later arrivals, the compulsion behind whose migration was amost entirely economic, professional, or, in any case, extra-religious. Not only were most of the new immigrants indifferent to the premises of the Bible Commonwealth, but those who were not were frequently at best bemused by them and at worst openly derogatory of them and even outrightly hostile. Of such a breed were the Couranteers, particularly that third of them known to have been members of the Church of England, the intensity of whose devotion to the Book of Common Prayer and the Thirty-nine Articles was, with the exception of John Checkley, never close to the depth of condescension in their attitude toward the rustication of the Puritan social position after the Restoration. And so social distinctions in Boston, in the seventeenth century virtually obliterated by religious unanimity, were propagated by religious diversity in the eighteenth. Congregationalism had not only been at the top of the heap but *was* the heap, jealously guarding itself from contamination. Ever since the beginning of the royal governors, when James II consolidated the American northeast colonies into a single "Dominion of New England" in 1686 and Sir Edmund Andros, the first royal governor, hammered on the doors of the Old South and commandeered it for Anglican services while its own outcast and outraged communicants milled about in the street, the Church of England grew steadily in social prestige. Successive royal governors and their entourages were followed into the Church of England by the rich merchants seeking either social advantage or influence with the governor, for the Anglican church itself in Boston had no influence as an institution at all nor was it in search of any. The merchant class, however, was interested in establishing firm economic ties with England, and the church was a convenient symbol of all ties with the homeland. But the Episcopalians saw religion as an adjunct to life rather than, as the Puritans did, its core—a view not altogether uncongenial to Anglicanism generally in the eighteenth century. At the opposite end of the class stratifications induced by denominationalism were the Baptists and the Quakers, who were concerned neither with the growing wealth that preoccupied the Episcopalians or the waning authority that haunted the Congregationalists. The Baptists and the Quakers turned from both in quest of a simpler, deintellectualized religion that would give them comfort and direction from its inspirational content rather than its institutional power. Fundamentally spin-offs of Congre-

gationalism, these sects attracted largely the poorer, the less educated, and
the less worldly townsmen, thus becoming a divisive factor. And yet
though the diversity of religions stimulated a diversity of classes, it was at
the same time a democratizing influence in that it tended to reduce the
domination of the political life of the community by a privileged denom-
ination—even though it was not until after the American Revolution
that Congregationalism ceased to be Massachusetts' established church,
supported by public funds and by an impenetrable inner group whose position was secured largely by hereditary influences.

The political changes that occurred since the granting in 1691 of a new
royal charter for Massachusetts by William and Mary also disrupted
significantly the social texture of life in Boston and the province. Ironically enough the charter was engineered by old Increase Mather, who had
gone to London for that purpose in 1688 and had come back to a cold reception in 1692, with his new charter and his hand-picked new governor,
Sir William Phips. The effect of the new charter was to strengthen considerably the authority of the crown over the life of the province and to reduce proportionately the control of the people over their own affairs—particularly those with limited real or personal property. In the Bible
Commonwealth, though it may have appeared tellingly discriminating on
the surface, membership in the church as the sole qualification for voting
was essentially democratic in a one-church community; besides it made for
no economic or social distinctions—Judge Sewall and Josiah Franklin were
equals. The new property requirements eliminated hundreds of voters
from any participation in the electoral process at all. Even those who
remained eligible saw the reach of their franchise seriously reduced. They
could vote for members of the House of Representatives, the lower body
of the Great and General Court; but the upper body, the Governor's
Council, was elected jointly by its outgoing members and by the incoming
representatives, and the governor, appointed by the crown to serve at its
pleasure, could veto the election of any councilor, thus assuring himself a
compliant upper house. Moreover, the House of Representatives, the only
remaining direct link with the people, had its wings seriously clipped. The
House's political weight had been felt and its will realized by its power to
appoint all the officials in the counties who presided over the courts, administered the pubic institutions, and commanded the militia. These
were now appointed by the governor subject only to confirmation by a
Council whose members' elections were all approved by him. A ruling few,
an autocracy, was established, with the Mathers, through access to their
friend Phips, making sure that the powerful Council consisted primarily of
their parishioners. Though Phips was a total disaster as a governor and
recalled to London after two years and though the Mathers' direct grasp
on the government was thus short-lived, the damage was done, so far as
dividing the people went.

The cleavage between the wealthy and powerful, in league with the governor and his Council, and the artisan and rural population, who still looked to the House for protection of their rights and interests, was further broadened in 1720, when the House elected Elisha Cooke, a Boston physician and a political foe of the Mathers as its speaker, and Governor Samuel Shute vetoed the choice. Cooke published a pamphlet defending the right of the House to elect its own speaker, but after a long-drawn-out dispute the Privy Council in London was to affirm the governor's veto power. The governor and his Council were, as a result of these and other affronts to the democratic instincts of a British community, the objects of scorn, suspicion, and resentment by the majority of the populace, while the House remained their one source of hope for a fairer share of participation in public affairs—the more so because, while the Governor's Council's proceedings tended to be as much *in camera* as possible, the House of Representatives began printing its proceedings in 1715, when Governor Joseph Dudley publicly misrepresented its actions. Altogether the political climate was such as inevitably to give rise to a journalism of contention in the 1720s, and the young Franklin, ingrained with both an interest in political affairs and a feeling for them, was in the right place at the right time to make the most of the opportunity.

* * *

Having determined that the raw material of his proposed anonymous contributions to the *Courant* would be the economic, social, religious, and political situations and attitudes around him and that he would also attempt to advance some Defoe-like projects to better the lot of his countrymen, Franklin had to invent a personality as the author of his papers, partly in order to give them continuity, which was essential to his purpose, but also to give them human interest by personifying the views he wanted to convey, the points he sought to make, and the ground he intended to cover. He had, of course, to eliminate immediately any thought of such a personality's being a Boston apprentice. In the first place, it would hint too strongly at the real authorship, and he suspected—no doubt correctly since James Franklin thought his apprentice troublesome enough without the added obnoxiousness of an author's vanity—"that my Brother would object to printing any thing of mine in his Paper if he knew it to be mine."[16] Consequently, a character as far removed from a town boy as possible had to be used. Secondly, he was far too realistic to assume that the views of a youth of sixteen would carry any weight or even get a fair hearing. And yet he wanted a freshness of outlook—not related to the Boston establishment, not even to the extent of being a predictable critic of every aspect of it, which some of the Couranteers were beginning to sound like—and he wanted a real, full-bodied character, not merely the kind of clever or facetious pseudonym, suggesting only a single dominant characteristic, that sprinkled the pages of *The Spectator* ("Jack Modish,"

[16] *Autobiography*, 67.

for example, or "James Easy") and the *Courant* ("Zechariah Hearwell," or "Philanthropos"). Finally, he wanted one whose history and position in life would be inherently susceptible of the respect of the *Courant* reader, no apologist of the establishment but without being subject automatically to the categorical censure of the establishment, and someone who would be in a position to know Boston but not to be of it. What Franklin was after was a sympathetic but not weak character, independent but not abrasive, articulate but not glib.

For all these purposes, Franklin hit upon an inspired notion: a country widow of limited means, animated interests, and fundamentally benevolent outlook. She could be critical without being an upstart, concerned without sounding self-serving, reformist without appearing officious. For another of his purposes in creating the character, which was to incorporate into it some of his own enthusiasms, tastes, and predilections, a country widow was hardly an appropriate or convincing mask for a quite earthy Boston boy of a rather uninhibited nature, and there were consequently passages and points that occurred in some of the papers that left considerable doubt that they emanated from a widow anywhere or, for that matter, from any rural character. This, however, was a minor matter, because Benjamin made his widow so convincingly sensible and good-natured, so alert and ubiquitous in her interest, that the reader was lured into believing her capable of discussing anything, providing she was not stupid, trite, or doctrinaire about it—and she never was, though there is no impression, on the other hand, of infallibility or omniscience.

As a name for his character, Franklin went directly to the works of Cotton Mather. He was probably quite aware that his brother and the Couranteers would recognize and enjoy the irony of a Mather-inspired pseudonym in the *Courant*. But Benjamin himself was being both jocular and serious in contriving the name Silence Dogood for his widow-author. "Dogood" obviously came from the subtitle of Mather's *Bonifacius, or Essays to Do Good*, which had left such a lifelong impression on Franklin when he read it four or five years earlier. Moreover, he seriously intended the imaginary author of his papers to do good, and he was himself at heart a reformer, this driving part of his nature furnishing a major incentive of his undertaking the papers. He did not use the term either facetiously or pejoratively, with the kind of implication of soft-headed or meddlesome charitability that "do-goodism" was to acquire in later times. He meant it as a clear indication to the reader that the papers were intended to improve as well as to divert their audience.

The widow Dogood's first name was another matter. Franklin no doubt meant it to be sardonic, since the whole purpose of the character he was creating was *not* to be silent, and he may have had also the sardonic thought that neither was Cotton Mather ever afflicted with a passion for silence. Moreover, Mather had recently published a lecture and a sermon which had been delivered, as the smallpox epidemic was approaching its crest, during the autumn of 1721, and which bore the title *Silentiarius*.[17] (Though the publication was a somber one, on the occasion of the death of his daughter, and the title referred to the silence of suffering, the association of the word "silence" in connection with any aspect of Cotton Mather struck his contemporaries as ludicrously incongruous, in view of the verbosity which was legendary during his lifetime and little short of unbelievable in retrospect. The tragic circumstances of the lecture—Mather's personal bereavement—would never have induced Benjamin Franklin to take advantage of Mather when he was vulnerable; and if there were any element of insensitivity involved, it was due to the thoughtlessness of youth rather than to any intention. Franklin was simply never inclined to vindictiveness, and there is no evidence at all—rather more evidence suggestive of the contrary—that he shared in the personal animosity that had developed between his brother and Cotton Mather during the smallpox controversy.) Franklin also had an ear for a memorable phrase, and "Silence Dogood" was memorable.

Having invented his character and after informing his readers that they would have every fortnight "a short Epistle, which I presume will add somewhat to their Entertainment," Franklin followed the example, set by Addison in the first issue of *The Spectator* and by Checkley in the first issue of *The New-England Courant*, of having the author identify himself lest the reader ignore an unknown quantity—a misgiving for which there is little justification in early eighteenth-century literature, since most identifications of authors were more preposterous than uncertainty would have been forbidding. The device was almost a formula:

Addison in *Spectator*, No. 1 (March 1, 1711)	Checkley in *Courant*, No. 1 (August 7, 1721)	Franklin in *Dogood*, No. 1 (April 2, 1722)
I have observed that a Reader seldom peruses a Book with Pleasure until the Writer of it be a black [i.e., dark-complexioned] or a fair Man, of a mild or a choleric Disposition, Married or a Batchelor, with other Particulars of the like nature, that	*It's an hard Case, that a Man can't appear in Print now a Days, unless he'll undergo the Mortification of Answering to ten thousand senseless and Impertinent Questions like these,* Pray Sir, from whence came you? And what Age may you be of,	And since it is observ'd, that the Generality of People, now a days, are unwilling either to commend or dispraise what they read, until they are in some measure informed who or what the author of it is, whether he be poor or rich, old or

17 Cotton Mather, *Silentiarius. A Brief Essay on the Holy Silence and Godly Patience, that Sad Things are to be Entertained withal* was published in 1721, in Boston, by S. Kneeland.

Addison in *Spectator*, No. 1 (March 1, 1711)	Checkley in *Courant*, No. 1 (August 7, 1721)	Franklin in *Dogood*, No. 1 (April 2, 1722)
conduce very much to the right understanding of an Author. To gratifie this Curiosity, which is so natural to a Reader, I design this Paper, and my next, as Prefatory Discourses to my following Writings, and shall give some Account of them of the several Persons that engaged in this Work.	may I be so bold? Was you bred at Colledge Sir? And can you (like some of them) square the Circle, and cypher as far as the *Black Art?* &c. *Now, tho' I must confess it's something irksome to a Man in hast, thus to be stop'd at his first setting-out, yet in Compliance to the Custom of the Country where I now set up for an Author, I'll immediately stop short, and give my gentle Reader some Account of my Person and my rare Endowments.*	young, a Schollar or a Leather Apron Man, &c. and give their Opinion of the Performance, according to the Knowledge which they have of the Author's Circumstances, it may not be amiss to begin with a short account of my past life and present Condition, that the Reader may not be at a loss to judge whether or no my Lucubrations are worth his reading.[18]

Alone among the three apologists, Franklin seemed to mean what he said, whereas Addison/Steele was merely being polite and Checkley simply cantankerous; and Franklin let Mrs. Dogood, in a style that was uniquely hers however derivative the form, reveal enough of herself in the first of her communications to the *Courant* to create an appetite for more information about her in subsequent issues. It was all in a tone of such disingenuous cordiality as to engage the affections of the reader and at the same time with a humor that was, far from being disingenuous, quite knowingly satirical in its pointedness, albeit gently so. Striking, too, was Franklin's economy as a writer—revealing the most in the least words. Silence Dogood's account of her origins, improbable because so close to probable, is impressive evidence that a sense of the folk humor in the American experience was already well developed in Franklin, as were a

18 The quote passages are from *The Spectator*, No. 1 (March 1, 1711), *The New-England Courant*, No. 1 (August 7, 1721), and ibid., No. 35 (April 2, 1722). In *Literary Influences on Colonial Newspapers, 1704–1750* (Port Washington, N.Y., 1966; originally published, 1912), 29, Elizabeth C. Cooke pressed the parallels to include, quite interestingly, the opening paragraph of the first literary essay to appear in *The New England Weekly Journal* (founded in 1727 by Samuel Kneeland) attributed to Mather Byles, the Boston Grammar (Latin) School classmate of Benjamin Franklin. "An ingenius Author has observed that a Reader seldom peruses a book with pleasure, till he has a tolerable Notion of the Physiognomy of the Author, the year of his Birth and his Manner of Living. . . ." As Miss Cooke suggested, it lacked the fiber of Franklin; it also lacked the grace of *The Spectator* and the brashness of the *Courant*.

talent and a zest in expressing it: "At the time of my Birth, my Parents were on Ship-board in their Way from *London* to *N. England.* My entry into this troublesome World was attended with the Death of my Father, a Misfortune, which tho' I was not then capable of knowing, I shall never be able to forget; for as he, poor Man, stood upon the Deck rejoycing at my Birth, a merciless Wave entred the Ship, and in one Moment carry'd him beyond Reprieve. Thus, was the *first Day* which I saw, the *last* that was seen by my Father; and thus was my disconsolate Mother at once made both a Parent and a Widow."[19]

Recollections, by now bemused and detached, of his dreadful ballad on the deaths of the lighthouse keeper, his wife, and his daughter and of similar maudlin outpourings by others probably moved Franklin to the most improbable scene of a new father being swept off deck by a wave at the very moment of exultation at his child's birth. He meant, of course, for it not to be quite believed, but it got Silence Dogood off to a good-natured start by its amiable, uncomplaining tone. More important for Franklin's purposes, the implausible circumstances of Silence's birth fairly guaranteed her indigence; and she could therefore speak for the poor and unprivileged. The latter included women, who, Franklin had been wholly and permanently persuaded by his reading of Defoe, were treated both unjustly and stupidly by a power cartel of males, in some respects their inferiors. Having carefully conceived his principal to make her a plausible voice for the poor and for women, his next purpose was to gain for her acceptance among the rural inhabitants and a position of respectability. The former were important because the "leather aprons" of Boston—the artisans, tradesmen, and laborers—had much more in common with them economically, politically, and socially than they did with their upper-strata townsmen. And although, so far as is known, Franklin had not spent a single day of his life in the country, he felt a rapprochement with country dwellers and shared much of their outlook. As for respectability, Franklin had seen enough of the boomeranging effect of the somewhat determined iconoclasm of the Couranteers to realize that one could get nowhere, by way of influencing opinion, by displaying built-in prejudices, and by confusing expressions of heated contempt with dispassionate critical observations. By moving Silence to the country ("at a small Distance from the Town," so that she would know what was going on there) and, after

[19] *New-England Courant*, No. 35 (March 26 to April 2, 1722); punctuation, italicizing, and capitalizing follow the text as printed in the *Courant* original files in the Massachusetts Historical Society, fifty-five issues of which were published in facsimile by the American Academy of Arts and Sciences, including all fourteen issues containing the Dogood papers, in 1956 on the occasion of Franklin's 250th birth anniversary. In this and the following chapters, the Dogood papers are treated according to categories of subject rather than chronologically. The chronological order of the papers as published, all in 1722, was: No. I, April 2; No. II, April 16; No. III, April 30; No. IV, May 14; No. V, May 28; No. VI, June 11; No. VII, June 25; No. VIII, July 9; No. IX, July 23; No. X, August 13; No. XI, August 20; No. XII, September 10; No. XIII, September 24; No. XIV, October 8.

schooling apparently no more extensive than Franklin's and having her apprenticed, as a housekeeper, to "a County Minister, a pious good-natured young Man and a Batchelor," Franklin managed in one stroke to achieve both rural credentials and respectability-by-association for his creation. It remained for him, in the first introductory Dogood paper, to make it possible for Silence to act as an advocate of his own views, many of which had been derived from his extensive reading. Apprenticing Silence to a clergyman was an added advantage in this respect, since the best private libraries in New England at the time were still those of the clergy; and just as Benjamin had had access to the library of the *Courant* as an apprentice and, through the older man's kindly interest, to that of Matthew Adams, Silence's master, "observing that I took a more than ordinary Delight in reading ingenius Books, he gave me the free Use of his Library, which tho' it was but small, yet it was well chose, to inform the Understanding rightly, and enable the Mind to frame great and noble Ideas." A little later in the introductory paper, Silence referred to the hours that she spent, as Franklin did in the deserted printing house on Sundays, "with the best of Company, *Books.*" Lest his Silence seem too admirable a woman to be convincing, Benjamin imposed on her one limitation in a bit of obiter dicta on the nature of women, bearing all the authority of a sixteen-year-old boy, but nevertheless well and gently put: "Thus I past away the Time with a Mixture of Profit and Pleasure, having no affliction but what was imaginary, and created in my own Fancy; as nothing is more common with us Women, than to be grieving for nothing, when we have nothing else to grieve for." Franklin closed the paper, about a thousand words in length, with what had become a ritual in Augustan familiar essays: "I am not insensible of the Impossibility of pleasing all, but I would not willingly displease any. . . ."[20]

As a literary performance, the paper was an extraordinary achievement for a young boy. Though it owed its form to *The Spectator* and perhaps something of its spirit, it was in an idiom of its own—an idiom of provincial New England, more town than country, less feminine but not more transparently so than Franklin may have suspected, and full of warmth, good humor, and good sense. To a town for nearly a year beset with anger, bitter recriminations, ugly epithets, and a dialogue of accusation, it was like a breath of fresh air in the pestilence-ridden town. Both in substance and in tone, it came far closer to what James Franklin had originally had in mind when he started the paper as a New England counterpart of *The Spectator*, insofar as his major purpose had been to divert its readers and not to harangue them. There was, of course, an innocence about the first Dogood paper (it touched upon no controversial issues and cast doubts on no established institutions) that was not to last very long, but it succeeded

---

[20] The quotes are all from the first Dogood paper, in *New-England Courant*, No. 35 (April 12 to April 19, 1722). Subsequent Dogood papers were numbered *seriatim* in the *Courant*. All the Dogood pieces are in *Papers*, I, 8–45.

clearly in introducing a personality of contagious interest and charm into a paper that James Franklin had somehow never gotten wholly along the path he had intended.

Having composed the paper, Benjamin copied it in a disguised handwriting so that his brother, who from the nature of their work together must have been completely familiar with Benjamin's hand, would not recognize it, and "put it in at Night under the Door of the Printing House. It was found in the Morning and communicated to his Writing Friends when they call'd in as usual. They read it, commented on it in my Hearing, and I had the exquisite Pleasure, of finding it met with their Approbation, and that in their different Guesses at the Author none were named but Men of some Character among us for Learning and Ingenuity."[21] Knowing the typesetting schedule of the *Courant* thoroughly, Benjamin probably timed his paper's delivery to get it into the next issue, new authors being generally impatient about seeing their work vested with the authority of print. In any case, on the morning of Monday, April 2, 1721, Franklin's literary career was launched on the front page of the *Courant*, in second position only to the lead piece by the paper's chief contributor, Mr. Gardner, a rather spiritless homily on the nature of honor. It was the first, last, and only time that Silence Dogood's communications were not given the lead position, in most cases occupying the entire first page of the paper.

James Franklin added an editor's note following the text: "*As the Favour of Mrs. Dogood's Correspondence is acknowledged by the Publisher of this Paper, lest any of her letters should miscarry, they may be deliver'd at his Printing-House, or at the Blue Ball in Union Street, and no Questions shall be ask'd of the Bearer.*" The youthful delight of Benjamin at the total success of his dissemblance must have been almost equal to his great satisfaction in its literary reception among the Couranteers. Not only did he have the exceptional opportunity of being both the author of the mysterious communications and a witness to their reception and publication but he had the ludicrous pleasure of being offered, as a means of delivering the manuscripts without revealing their source, the use of his own father's house in Union Street as a depository. The triumph was complete, and he started composing the second Dogood paper (April 16, 1722), slightly longer, equally animated, and adding a few gentle barbs at some of the vanities of the time.

In continuing her autobiographical account, Silence told her readers of an interesting development in the life of the young servant girl of the benign country parson: "My Reverend Master who had hitherto remained a Batchelor . . . took up a Resolution to marry . . ." and, of course, he married Silence. Her account of this major event in her life was utterly lacking in romanticism and, for that matter, in femininity. But what it lacked

---

[21] *Autobiography*, 67–68.

in those directions, it made up for in humor and authenticity. For one thing, his housemaid was not the minister's first choice, and there seemed an air of functionalism about the whole affair—as in fact, as Judge Sewall's records of his matrimonial ventures convincingly demonstrate, there was generally about New England marriages. Silence reported of her proposer, ". . . having made several unsuccessful fruitless Attempts on the more topping Sort of our Sex, and being tir'd of making troublesome Journeys and Visits to no Purpose, he began unexpectedly to cast a loving Eye upon Me, whom he had brought up cleverly to his Hand."

The marriage of master with servant was not at all uncommon, and there was virtually no gap between the classes in the country in any case. Benjamin Franklin's own maternal grandfather, Peter Folger, had married Mary Morrill, the bond servant whose freedom he bought from the Reverend Hugh Peter. And the marriage of the learned and gifted Reverend Michael Wigglesworth to his maidservant, which so annoyed Increase Mather, was a well-known bit of Massachusetts social lore. Franklin was here striking a blow for the old egalitarianism of which, he could see all around him, Boston was fast losing sight. Perhaps not unmindful of Wigglesworth, he had Silence report, "This unexpected Match was very astonishing to all the Country round about, and served to furnish them with Discourse for a long Time after; some approving it, other disliking it, as they were led by their various Fancies and Inclinations." Obviously, however, Silence could neither have a wholly independent voice nor arouse much sympathy among her readers if she had simply remained a lucky orphan who had married above her station into the comfortable security of a country parsonage. Accordingly, he had Silence's bright situation plunged into gloom, after seven years of marriage and three children, by "inexorable unrelenting Death, as if he had envy'd my Happiness and Tranquility. . . ."

In the second Dogood paper, Silence reports that she took the minister succeeding her husband into her house as a lodger, "by whose Assistance I intend now and then to beautify my Writings with a Sentence or two in the learned Languages, which will not only be fashionable, and pleasing to those who do not understand it, but will likewise be very ornamental." Franklin thus achieved, in the kind of incident wholly plausible in the New England of the early eighteenth century (newly ordained country clergy were usually bachelors and very commonly boarded or lodged with their predecessors' widows), the remarkable feat of making Silence a widow, thus enlisting for her some sympathy in Boston where a quarter of all adults were widows, nearly half of them requiring charitable support,[22] and at the same time keeping her in such close association with the learned community that she would be qualified, and likely now and then, to speak out on matters that might otherwise seem unlikely concerns of a

[22] *Report of the Record Commissioners*, X, passim.

country widow. With regard to his intention to "beautify my Writings with a Sentence or two in the learned Languages, Franklin was, of course, having some fun at the expense both of the town clergy—particularly Cotton Mather, who could barely complete a paragraph without injecting some Latin or Greek quotation—and of some of the Couranteers, who, in imitation of the *Spectator* and probably also to keep the Mathers in their place, were also inclined to sprinkle a few classical quotes throughout their writings, as well as of James Franklin, who often put one at the masthead. Of the fourteen Dogood papers, eight had Latin dicta as headings—three from Cicero, three proverbial, and one each from Seneca and Terence—all of which would have been sufficiently familiar to Benjamin from his Latin School days; if they had not been, he would not have dared consulting any of the Couranteers for fear of revealing his identity. In concluding the second Dogood paper, Franklin had Silence report some of her qualities of character and areas of conviction. Most of these were entirely probable self-revelations for a country widow: ". . . I am an Enemy to Vice, and a Friend to Vertue . . . of an extensive Charity, and a great forgiver of *private* Injuries: a hearty Lover of the Clergy and all good Men. . . ." The underscoring of "private" is significant but would hardly be characteristic of Silence Dogood. Its import was that she would feel less forgiving, or not at all, about injuries from public sources, but it is unlikely that it would occur to her to make any such distinction. It would, however, occur to Benjamin Franklin, who had seen the *Courant* and his brother maligned publicly. Even less likely coming from the country woman, and more likely from Benjamin Franklin, was Silence's declaration that she is "a mortal Enemy to arbitrary Government and unlimited Power. I am naturally for the Rights and Liberties of my Country; and the least appearance of an Incroachment on those invaluable Priviledges, is apt to make my Blood boil exceedingly." This was, of course, completely a Franklin and a Couranteer talking, and not a woman living in a rural village beyond the interest if not the reach of any arbitrary government at the time. But it was useful and necessary for Benjamin to introduce the thought, and somewhat emphatically, for he had it firmly in mind for Silence Dogood to have her say in the area of public affairs and, as events developed, rather more pointedly and to more immediate ends than he envisioned at the time of writing the second Dogood.

Having made clear all that he thought interesting and necessary for his readers to know about Silence's background, Franklin devoted the third Dogood paper (April 30, 1722), somewhat briefer than the first two, to the nature of the proposed contents of Silence Dogood's writings. She asserted that, having found the acquisition of a small stock of knowledge and understanding useful to her over the years, she proposed to pass some of it along "by Peace-meal to the Publick." Franklin then went directly to an eleven-year-old issue of *The Spectator*, published on September 25, 1711, and borrowed from it wholesale to provide Silence Dogood with an explanation as to how she was going to manage to meet the divergent emphases and interests of her readers. Addison, in *The Spectator*, had written, with characteristic urbanity:

> I may cast my Readers under two general Divisions, the *Mercurial* and the *Saturnine*. The first are the gay part of my Disciples, who require Speculations of Wit and Humour; the others are those of a more solid and sober Turn, who find no Pleasure but in Papers of Morality and sound Sense; the former call everything that is Serious Stupid. The latter look upon everything as Impertinent that is Ludicrous. Were I always Grave one half of my Readers would fall off from me: Were I always Merry I should lose the other. I make it therefore my endeavour to find out Entertainments of both kinds, and by that means perhaps consult the good of both more than I should do, did I always write to the particular Taste of either.[23]

Benjamin Franklin, in the *Courant*, wrote, both with greater simplicity and with greater economy, obviously indebted as he was for the thought:

> I am very sensible that it is impossible for me, or indeed any *one* Writer to please *all* Readers at once. Various Persons have different Sentiments; and that which is pleasant and delightful to one, gives another a Disgust. He that would (in this Way of Writing) please all, is under a Necessity to make his Themes almost as numerous as his Letters. He must one while be merry and diverting, then more solid and serious; one while sharp and satyrical, then (to mollify that) be sober and religious; at one time let the Subject be Politicks, then let the next Theme be Love: Thus will everyone, one Time or other find some thing agreeable to his own Fancy, and in his Turn be delighted.

Franklin, in the same paper, invited his readers, particularly the women among them, to enter into correspondence with him, and James Franklin added an editor's note that any letters intended for Mrs. Dogood be dropped at his printing house, "directed to her." Diverting as may have been the prospect of the women of Boston confiding their views, problems, and concerns to a sixteen-year-old apprentice, the invitation was an obvious stratagem for future issues of the Dogood papers to publish letters (in *The Spectator* manner, pseudonymously written by the authors themselves to stimulate interest or to introduce new subjects)—a device to which Franklin resorted in the fifth Dogood paper. Franklin then closed the third paper with a peculiarly masculine and town-sounding analogy for a lady in the country. Indicating that she was now finished with information about her background and intentions, Silence Dogood said, "I think I have now finish'd the Foundation, and I intend in my next to begin to raise the Building." It was a very neat analogy and wholly suitable to the

[23] *Spectator*, No. 179, Everyman's Library edition (London, 1945), II, 32.

literary structure of the Dogood papers as a whole, but it would have hardly sprung readily or naturally to the mind of a rural widow. It made no difference, however; everybody at the *Courant* knew that Silence Dogood was either one of their own number (except, of course, the apprentice) or a witty kindred spirit. And Silence Dogood turned with zest to the phenomena surrounding and characterizing life in Boston.

* * *

Of the eleven ensuing Dogood papers, no more than four could be said to have a content of particular relevance to women as women or one to which Silence Dogood might have been presumed to bring somewhat more authority than a man might. First among these was the fifth Dogood paper (May 28, 1722) that unquestionably owed its origin to Franklin's reading of Defoe's *An Essay upon Projects* in his preapprentice days. The paper was headed with one of those fashionable and ornamental quotations from the classics that Silence Dogood had promised her readers: "*Mulier Mulieri magis congruet*"—"Women understand women"—from Terence's *Phormio*.[24] The occasion was ostensibly a letter, not from a woman, whose correspondence had been particularly invited, but from a man who subscribed himself, in good *Spectator-Courant* style, "Ephraim Censorius," which advised Silence, before she took on the task of straightening out the human race generally, that the "first Volley of Resentments be directed against *Female* Vice; let Female Idleness, Ignorance and Folly, (which are Vices more peculiar to your Sex than to our's) be the Subject of your Satyrs, but more especially Female Pride, which I think is intollerable."

In Silence Dogood's response to her purposefully churlish correspondent, Franklin set forth the convictions, which he had first set forth in his early debates with Collins, on the indefensible position of women, and to which he subscribed all his life. Franklin always liked women, enjoyed their company, and flatly rejected any notion that they were in any sense, other possibly than the physical, the "weaker" sex. His fifth Silence Dogood paper in the *Courant* of May 28, 1722, set forth his view, shaped and clarified by his early reading of Defoe but strengthened by his own observations and conclusions with the passage of the years, that, if women were in fact given to any inclinations in the directions specified by his alleged correspondent (which he himself never believed), then the men had no one but themselves to blame. One by one, he disposed of the observations of "Ephraim Censorius."

To answer the charge of idleness, Silence Dogood resorted to the

---

[24] The translation is freely rendered. Franklin, in his employment of Latin quotations in the Dogood papers, took them out of context, sometimes in the process making the original meaning inapposite. The Terence quote, from *Phormio*, IV, v, 14, is literally, "A woman will rather [i.e. tend to] agree with a woman," and in the original context could be translated, "Women understand each other better [than men understand them]."

Socratic method that Franklin had absorbed from his reading of Xenophon and the dialogues appended to his grammars, and he raised questions, some of which were self-answering and to some of which he provided the only answers that struck him as responsive: "As for Idleness, if I should Quaere, Where are the greatest Number of its Votaries to be found with us [i.e., the women] or the Men? it might be I believe be easily and truly answer'd, *With the latter.* For notwithstanding the Men are commonly complaining how hard they are forc'd to labour, only to maintain their Wives in Pomp and Idleness, yet if you go among the Women, you will learn, that *they have always more Work upon Their Hands than they are able to do; and that a Woman's Work is never done,* &c.[25] But however, Suppose we should grant for once, that we are generally more idle than the Men, (without making any Allowance for the *Weakness of the Sex,*) I desire to know whose Fault it is? Are not the Men to blame for their Folly in maintaining us in Idleness?"

The same question was raised with regard to the allegations of ignorance and folly: ". . . let us see (if we are Fools and Ignoramus's) whose is the Fault, the Men's or our's." For the answer, Franklin had Silence turn for a direct quote, constituting about a fifth of the paper, to Defoe's *An Essay upon Projects.*[26] It was a forceful and judiciously chosen excerpt, in which Defoe bore down heavily on the self-defeating stupidity of men in refusing to provide for the education of women. It was, of course, a favorite subject of Franklin's during his apprentice days and the one which, in his oral and written debates with John Collins, led to his father's inducing him to improve his style of discourse. In the fifth Dogood paper, he wisely let Defoe, whom, in the manner of the time, he identified only as "An ingenious Writer," carry the argument, ending it with Defoe's devastatingly conclusive question, "Shall we upbraid Women with Folly, when 'tis only the Error of this inhumane Custom [i.e., denying them equal educational opportunity with men] that hindred them being made wiser?"

Silence Dogood finished her defense of women against her censorius correspondent's categorical charges by flatly rejecting, in an un-Socratic manner, the accusation of "intollerable" pride: ". . . there are more Instances of extravagant Pride to be found among Men than among Women, and this Fault is certainly more hainous in the former than in the latter." A postscript was added to the paper, obviously preparatory to qualifying Silence to comment more specifically on the scene in Boston: "*Mrs. Dogood has lately left her Seat in the Country, and come to Boston, where she intends to tarry for the Summer Season, in order to compleat her Observations of the present reigning Vices of the Town.*"

The first "reigning Vice" was hardly a vice, but it was of particular in-

[25] The origin of this, a line in a rhyme already well known in Franklin's youth, is not known.
[26] Daniel Defoe, *Essay upon Projects,* 42.

terest to a woman. In her sixth contribution (June 11, 1722) to the *Courant*, headed by a quotation from Seneca's *Thyestes*, "*Quem Dies videt veniens Superbum, Hunc Dies vidit fugiens jacentem*"—Whom the rising sun sees proud, the setting sun sees humbled[27]—Silence Dogood discussed what she regarded as "Pride of Apparel" as exemplified particularly by the fashion of hooped petticoats introduced in England as early as Queen Elizabeth's time, when "wheel" farthingales were first used and were reintroduced, after the Puritan interregnum, and which in Queen Anne's reign were just beginning to appear in Boston, threatening a controversy for a while as heated as that over inoculation. Before proceeding to condemn them by ridicule in terms much more suggestive of an adolescent boy than a mature woman, Silence relieved herself of some general dicta about pride of apparel. The first of these was that "The *Pride of Apparel* has begot and nourish'd in us a *Pride of Heart*, which portends the Ruin of Church and State." Franklin certainly believed no such thing, but it was just as certainly a likely and credible attitude for a rural widow under the direct and continuous influence of country parsons. And Silence proceeded to a more practical consideration of pride, with the recollection that "my late Reverend Husband" maintained that, in accord with the proverb, "a Fall was the *natural Consequence*, as well as *Punishment* of Pride." From then on Silence Dogood was pure Benjamin Franklin, concerned with the practical effects that pride of apparel could have: "persons of Small Fortune under the Dominion of this Vice, seldom consider their Inability to maintain themselves in it, but strive to imitate their Superiors in Estate, or Equals in Folly, until one Misfortune comes upon the Neck of another, and every Step they take is a Step backwards. By striving to appear rich they become really poor, and deprive themselves of that Pity and Charity which is due to the humble poor Man, who is made so more immediately by Providence."

In using the current enthusiasm for hooped skirts as an example, Franklin was at his zestful, down-to-earth best, but he so phrased his case as to make it appear that he had completely forgotten that it was supposed to be the language of a country widow: "These monstrous topsy-turvy *Mortar-Pieces*, are neither fit for the Church, the Hall, or the Kitchen; and if a number of them were well mounted on Noddles-Island, they would look more like Engines of War for bombarding the Town, than Ornaments of the Fair Sex." He then put it to the women that they at least "lessen the Circumference of their Hoops," on the facetious grounds that it was highly questionable "Whether they, who pay no Rates or Taxes, ought to take up more Room in the King's High-way, than the Men, who yearly contribute to the Support of the Government."

In the Boston of only seven years earlier, when Uncle Benjamin arrived

[27] Literally, "Whom the coming day sees powerful,/The fleeing day sees laid low," from *Thyestes*, 613–14.

A pioneer among social reformers, Daniel Defoe (1660–1731), through his *Essay upon Projects*, planted in Franklin's mind several schemes for voluntary action that he later brought to fruition. PICTURE COLLECTION, NEW YORK PUBLIC LIBRARY

While an apprentice to his brother, Franklin read the monumental treatise on the nature of knowledge, *An Essay Concerning Human Understanding,* by John Locke (1632–1704), which deeply influenced the shaping of his own philosophy.

The Third Earl of Shaftesbury, Anthony Ashley Cooper (1671–1713), a pupil of Locke's, strengthened, through his *Characteristics of Men, Manners, Opinions and Times*, the deistic leanings in religion that Franklin never abandoned. PICTURE COLLECTION, NEW YORK PUBLIC LIBRARY

Zenophon (430–c. 355 B.C.) in his accounts of Socrates' dialogues in *Recollections of Socrates* convinced Franklin that argumentativeness in a discussion was self-defeating.

The wooden printing press used by Franklin was entirely hand-operated and remained virtually unchanged for almost two hundred years, from the early seventeenth to the early nineteenth centuries. NATIONAL MUSEUM OF HISTORY AND TECHNOLOGY, SMITHSONIAN INSTITUTION

A. 537.   [N° 1]

THE
New-England Courant.

MONDAY August 7. 1721.

Homo non unius Negotii: Or, Jack of all Trades.

IT'S an hard Case, that a Man can't appear in Print now a Days, unless he'll undergo the Mortification of Answering to ten thousand senseless and Impertinent Questions like these, Pray Sir, from whence came you? And what Age may you be of, may I be so bold? Was you bred at Colledge Sir? And can you (like some of them) square the Circle, and cypher as far as the Black Art? &c. Now tho' I must confess it's something irksome to a Man in my case, thus to be stop'd at his first setting-out, yet in Compliance to the Custom of the Country where I now am up for an Author, I'll immediately stop short, and give my gentle Reader some Account of my Person and my rare Endowments.

As for my Age, I'm some odd Years and a few Days under twice twenty and three, therefore I hope no One will hereafter object against my soaring now and then with the grave Wits of the Age, since I have dropt my callow Feathers, and am pretty well fledg'd: but if they should tell me that I am not yet nor worthy to keep Company with such Illustrious Sages, for my Beard do'n't yet reach down to my Girdle, I shall make them no other Answer than this, Barba non facit Philosophum.

I make no Question my gentle Readers, but that you're very Impatient to see me intirely dissected, and to have a full View of my outward as well as inward Man, but as I stops short just now, meerly to oblige you, so I shall Hop as short here, and give no farther Account of my self until this Day fortnight; when you shall have a farther Account of this useful Design, and of my great Endowments of Body and Mind.

And to engage the World to converse farther with me, I'll find me in the good Company of a certain Sort of Men, of whom I hope to give a very good Account.

Who like faithful Shepherds take care of their Flocks,
By teaching and practising what's Orthodox,
Pray hard against Sickness, yet preach up the POX!

N. B. This Paper will be published once a Fortnight, and out of meer Kindness to my Brother-Writers, I intend now and then to be (like them) very, very dull; for I have a strong Fancy, that unless I am sometimes flat and low, this Paper will not be very grateful to them.

abnormit sapiens.—— Hor.

At the Request of several Gentlemen in Town: A Continuation of the History of Inoculation in *Boston*, by a Society of the Practitioners in Physick.

THe bold undertaker of the Practice of the Greek old Women, notwithstanding the Terror and Confusion from his Son's Inoculation-Fever, proceeds to inoculate Persons from Seventy Years of Age and downwards.

The Select Men (or Managers of the Town Affairs) in duty bound to take Cognizance of the Matter, desire a Meeting of all the Practitioners in Town, to have their Opinion whether the Practice ought to be allowed or not; they unanimously agreed that it was rash and dubious, being entirely new, not in the least vouched or recommended (being meerly published, in the Philosophick Transactions by way of Amusement) from Britain, tho' it came to us via London from the Turks, and by a strong viva voce Evidence, was proved to be of fatal & dangerous Consequence. B——n is desired by the Select Men to desist.

Notwithstanding the general Aversion of the Town, in Contradiction to the declared Opinion of the Practitioners, in Opposition to the Selectmen, and in Spite of the discouraging Evidences relating to this Practice, Six Gentlemen of Piety and Learning, profoundly ignorant of the Matter, after serious Consideration of a Disease one of the most intricate practical Cases in Physick, do on the Merits of their Characters, and for no other reason, with a Vox praterias; nihil, assert, &c. If this Argument, viz. their Character, should prevail with the Populace (tho' here I think they have missed of their Aim) who knows but it may oblige some prophane Person to canvas that sort of Argument. I think their Character ought to be sacred, and that they themselves ought not to give the least Occasion to have it called in question. They set up for Judges of a Man's Qualifications in the Practice of Physick, and very lavishly bestow all the fulsome common Place of Quack Advertisements. One would think they meant some Romantick Character, something beyond that of candid Sydenham, the sagacious Radcliff, or the celebrated Mead: They might indeed in respect of his moral and religious Qualifications, which lay properly under their Cognizance, have said, That he was a modest, humble Man, a Man of Continency, Probity, &c. At first reading of this Composure, many were perswaded, that it was only a Piece of Humour, Banter, Burlesque.

The New-England Courant, the fourth newspaper to be published in Boston, was one of three that survived and competed for public attention. The *Courant,* founded by James Franklin in 1721, was by far the most spirited and independent. THE NEW-YORK HISTORICAL SOCIETY

The Spectator's cofounder, Joseph Addison (1672–1719), created the form of familiar essay that was the model for Franklin's earliest published writings, which he undertook only after the most careful study of *The Spectator*. PICTURE COLLECTION, NEW YORK PUBLIC LIBRARY

Richard Steele (1672-1729) wrote in an earthier vein than his collaborator, Addison, and his writings served Franklin as prototypes for his probings of the seamier side of Boston. PICTURE COLLECTION, NEW YORK PUBLIC LIBRARY

On Union Street, the home of Franklin's boyhood was a neighbor of the Green Dragon Tavern, the most noted of the scores of taverns that served the hard-drinking inhabitants of Cotton Mather's Boston. CULVER PICTURES

to discover that fashions were so drab—predominantly still the colorless homespun of the settlers' day—that there was no need of his trade as a silk dyer, the introduction of hooped skirts would have been so outrageous an example of worldly vanity as to be treated with expressions of the gravest concern rather than with levity. As it was even in 1722, Benjamin's Silence Dogood paper on the subject evoked a response from an anonymous commentator, subscribing himself "Hypercarpus," in the next issue of the *Courant*. It was his view, stated more gently than his choice of words might imply, that Silence was guilty of "an Absurdity so gross that it should not pass unobserved" in stating that "*The Pride of Apparel has begot and nourish'd in us a Pride of Heart.*" Hypercarpus thought that Silence had gotten the cart before the horse and that "The Sins of Men are originally in the Heart, and from thence brought forth into Acts . . . that out of the *Heart* of Man proceeded evil thoughts &c, even every Abomination. But I ask Mrs. Dogood's pardon for this Observation."[28] It speaks well for Franklin's success in creating Silence Dogood as an affable rather than a bitter critic that, despite the apparently strong view of her correspondent, his letter was in tone kindly to her. In any case, she had opened up a subject that sparked some interest, undoubtedly was the subject of a sermon or two, and seemed to James Franklin worth exploiting, for in an issue of the *Courant* four months later he was advertising a three-pence tract, published and sold by him, with the alarmist title, HOOP-PET-TICOATS *Arraigned and Condemned, by the Light of Nature, and the Law of God.*"[29] As for Hypercarpus, Silence Dogood disposed of him in an equivocatory, one-sentence postscript in Latin to her next letter: "*Mater me genuit, peperit mox filia matrem*"—loosely, "Mother produces daughter; daughter soon produces mother."

It was not until the tenth issue of her papers (August 13, 1722) that Silence Dogood returned once more to the specific world of the eighteenth-century woman. In it she took up a subject upon which she could be expected to be as fully qualified as anyone to speak: the need to do something to provide systematic relief for indigent widows. Heading her letter with a quote in the original from Cicero's *De Officiis*: "*Optime societas hominum servabitur*"—"A society of men is best watched over"[30]—she said that she had been turning the problem over in her own mind for some time and had thought of some projects, but that an "intimate Friend of mine . . . put into my Hands a Book, wherein the ingenius Author proposes (I think) a certain [i.e., a sure] Method for their Relief." The always "ingenius Author" was, of course, Defoe, and the book, again, *An Essay upon Projects*. Silence turned over virtually her entire letter to a

---

[28] *New-England Courant*, No. 46 (June 18 to June 25, 1722).

[29] Ibid., No. 69 (November 26 to December 3, 1722).

[30] The Cicero quotation is abridged, from *De Officiis*, I, 16, omitting a significant conditional clause in the original: "A society of men is best preserved if the greatest kindness is shown where there is the nearest relation."

fifteen-hundred word excerpt from Defoe's proposal to start an insurance plan for widows, on the grounds that it would be vain of her to draft one of her own in view of the soundness of that of the "ingenius Author." The fact is, however, that Benjamin Franklin and the *Courant* were just emerging from a tempestuous summer[31] and Franklin probably did not have the time to write a wholly original Dogood paper. In fact, it was the first time that he did not meet his fortnightly schedule. A week later, therefore, he took the opportunity to advance an idea of Defoe with which he had for years been intrigued. He did, however, personalize very convincingly the Defoe proposal by having Silence add some thoughts of her own. One was that similar insurance plans could be worked out among other categories of individuals who needed to aid one another. "But above all, the Clergy have the most need of coming into some such Project as this. They as well as poor Men (according to the Proverb) generally abound in Children; and how many Clergymen in the Country are forc'd to labour in their Fields, to keep themselves in a Condition above Want? How then shall they be able to leave any thing to their forsaken, dejected and almost forgotten Wives and Children. For my own Part [it will be recalled that Silence was left a clergyman's widow with three minor children], I have nothing left to live on, but Contentment and a few Cows. . . ."

In the next of her papers, the eleventh (August 20, 1722), which Franklin finished fast enough to have it printed after only a week's interval, Silence Dogood continued her interest in insurance projects, but both widows and clergymen were dropped as either beneficiaries or insured. Instead, young Franklin set forth a remarkable scheme for insuring young women against unwanted virginity. The paper is striking and charming evidence of Franklin's total lack of fanaticism about his enthusiasms, one of the most fervent and persistent of which was the provision of some degree of economic security for those plunged into difficult circumstances through such devices as voluntary co-operative savings and insurance plans and "friendly societies," whose members could make economic provisions for emergencies together that were beyond their means separately. In quoting Defoe, the strongest and most persuasive proponent of the idea at such length, on behalf of widows, in the tenth Dogood, he was then moved to poke gentle fun at the idea of such social security projects in the eleventh, published a week later. The result was probably the most delightful and humorous of the Dogood papers and the only wholly whimsical one; and despite the subject's inherent possibility for ribaldry and vulgarity, of which the mass of Franklin's writings were less than barren, there is no trace of either in his discussion of the plight of attractive young ladies who clung to their virginity too long in the constant hope that someone better than their succession of wooers would turn up sooner or

[31] Chap. XV, *infra.*

later. He headed the piece with a Latin quotation, of undetected source but possibly written by himself if he could find no more apt citation from his limited store of Latin, for his subject was one he would most likely have wanted dignified by one of the learned language references he had promised at the outset of the papers. Accordingly there appeared, in stately Latin, the pronouncement: *"Neque licitum interea est meam amicam visere"*—"Nor is it permitted meanwhile to visit my friend."[32]

To get into the subject and also to add ironically a context of formality and legalism, Franklin began the paper with "The Humble Petition of Margaret Aftercast," speaking "in the forlorn State of a Virgin well stricken in Years and Repentance." The background of her situation had a notable similarity, in reverse, to that of Benjamin's Uncle John Franklin in Banbury, about which Uncle Benjamin had written in the family chronicle[33] and which had unquestionably been the subject of much reminiscing in the Josiah Franklin household. The significantly named Margaret Aftercast submitted that "being puff'd up in her younger Years" with too many suitors, assumed that her wit and beauty would attract such a constant and lasting flow of them that she could discard them at her pleasure. This, she conceded, was her own fault, due to vanity. Some of them, however, she claimed, were rejected for the perfectly justifiable reason that they were "to all Appearance in a dying Condition," only to recover and marry someone else—which Margaret regarded as unfaithful since several of them had averred "that they should die or run distracted for her." Finally, she pointed out that "no new Offers appearing for some Years past, she has been industriously contracting Acquaintance with several Families in Town and Country, where any young Gentlemen or Widowers have resided, and Endeavoured to appear as conversable as possible before them . . . and the better to restore her decay'd Beauty, she has consumed above Fifty Pound's Worth of the most approved *Cosmeticks*. But all won't do." The petition concluded with a plea to Silence Dogood, who had expressed such sympathetic and helpful concern for widows, "to form a Project for the Relief of all those penitent Mortals of the fair Sex, that are like to be punished with their Virginity until old Age, for the Pride and Insolence of their Youth."

Silence Dogood replied that her first instinct would be to start a matchmaking service for such ladies as Margaret Aftercast, but Franklin amused himself by having Silence declare that any such attempt was prevented by her "extream Modesty and Taciturnity," both of which qualities had been thus far conspicuous by their absence in her writings. So she proposed instead a loose adaptation of the friendly society plan for widows projected in her previous paper, "whereby every single Woman, upon full proof of

[32] The relevance of this quotation to the text that follows is elusive. Since it was unascribed, Franklin may very well have written it himself and been somewhat overconfident of his Latin.

[33] Pp. 37, 63, *supra*.

her continuing a Virgin for the Space of Eighteen Years, (dating her Virginity from the Age of Twelve,) should be entitled to £500 in ready Cash." The paper then proceeded to specify some circumstances under which the award would be either denied or reduced. These included women who, after reaching the age of twenty-five, turned down any suitor "without sufficient Reason for so doing, until she has manifested her Repentance in Writing under her Hand." No member of the society who had turned down proposals since becoming a member "shall be entituled to the £500 when she comes of Age; that is to say, *Thirty Years* [i.e., twelve years of childhood plus eighteen additional years of virginity]." Apparently any member who had the good fortune to marry after receiving the award at thirty could keep the money—unless, for more than an hour, in any company, she held forth in praise of her husband, in which case she had to return half the £500, and if she did it a second time she would have to return the rest.

* * *

The seven Dogood papers relating particularly to aspects of the position of women in Boston life certainly put the writing skills of a sixteen-year-old boy to an exceptional and demanding test. Not only the gap of years but also the deeper chasm of sex had to be bridged between the printer's apprentice and the country parson's widow. That it was done convincingly was perhaps the result less of a persuasive literary style than the creation of a persuasive personality, for Silence Dogood, like Benjamin Franklin, emerged as that rarity of all ages and of both sexes—the reformer tempered by wit and a dash of irreverence, whose concern is genuinely benevolent but whose manner is wholly relaxed. Conversely, the greater significance of the Dogood papers to Franklin's later development may well have consisted less in their representing, through the exercise of his pen, a beginning to the evolution of a literary style, a peculiarly American style, than in their liberating him through the exercise of his mind, from rubrics of thought and limits of visions imposed upon him and his generation by possibly the most rigid society ever organized on other than a communal scale by the English-speaking people. Nor was this liberation of the young Franklin merely a passive thing, simply freeing him from responsibilities and burdens that his father's generation and most of his own contemporaries took more or less for granted in Matherian Boston. It was essentially an active phase through which he was going, in that for the first time in his young life, albeit at an exceptionally early age, Franklin was beginning to shape the world around him rather than to be shaped by it. All the indications are that he found the experience rewarding and exhilarating, and he led Silence Dogood zestfully into far broader fields, as the spirit moved him, than her actual counterparts were likely to invade.

XIV

Silence Dogood
on the Offense

> ... if all Printers were determin'd not to
> print any thing till they were sure it would
> offend no body, there would be very little
> printed.
>
> —Benjamin Franklin[1]

Silence Dogood was launched as a country innocent who, by a timely removal to Boston, could make some observations from the comfortable detachment of her position on some of the follies of the times and a few of
the problems faced especially by women. Before the fourth issue of the
Dogood papers had passed, however, she was making excursions into areas
that were less probable concerns of an aging rural widow than those of a
prodigious young townsman. The shift in subject matter was inevitable,
even if not constant. His age, his interests, and his values were bound to
separate Benjamin Franklin from the good woman he had created to express his views. The situation, however, did not frustrate or repress him.
He knew some of the areas of life in the provincial capital that he wanted
to touch upon, and others were to occur to him with some forcefulness as
events in Boston, during the brief span of Silence Dogood's literary output, touched tellingly on his own life and immediate surroundings. It was
not in Franklin's nature to hesitate to take on these subjects simply because he had hit upon a literary device not ideally suited to handle the
matter. He simply adjusted the device to the subject. The first such topic
dumped into Silence Dogood's matronly lap was Harvard College, the
quality of education it supplied and the quality of the students it attracted. It was not to show Silence Dogood at her most benevolent nor
Benjamin Franklin at his most perceptive. But it had a point to make—
and made it forcibly enough to draw blood.

[1] "Apology for Printers," 1731, in *Papers*, I, 195.

When Franklin attacked Harvard in no uncertain terms, in the fourth Dogood paper (May 14, 1722), Harvard College was eighty-six years old, six years younger than the Massachusetts Bay Company; and Benjamin Franklin was sixteen years old, the average age of the forty-nine freshmen at Harvard in the class of 1725. (But if Franklin had finished at the Latin School and gone on to Harvard, as his father had originally intended, he would have been a sophomore in 1722 because of his having been advanced a year at the school, although even at fifteen he would have been far from the youngest member of the entering class of 1724, that distinction falling to Thomas Baker, a blacksmith's son, who was twelve—which was itself not uncommon, the youngest student to have been admitted having been Paul Dudley, class of 1690, at the age of ten.) The image is easily evoked of the brightest boy in his class sitting in the garret of a small printing house, after a twelve-hour day of labor, lambasting the college which he was deprived of attending and ridiculing the contemporaries who, though his inferiors, were lucky enough to be there. But there is little evidence to support such a conceit, and pathos was no part of the Franklin character or experience then or later. On the other hand, there is much to be inferred from his life, and his account of it, and from his temperament and the particular path that his genius took, that strongly suggests the opposite—that he would not have been very much at home at Harvard, even under the liberalizing presidency of John Leverett.

In the first place, Franklin never expressed any disappointment, much less any resentment, at his father's decision to take him out of the Latin School. Since Harvard was still to a great extent a collegiate training center for the Puritan clergy (of the thirty-nine survivors of the class of 1724, seventeen became ministers) and since his father would have expected him to enter the ministry, Franklin may very well have experienced a great sense of relief to have that uncongenial prospect firmly and finally closed to him. In the second place, he always resisted authority, at least from his apprentice days (perhaps earlier, since he succeeded in the study of arithmetic very well on his own not more than a year after he failed it at Mr. Browning's school) and throughout the rest of his life, doing his best and most significant work when wholly in command of himself and of his own time and pacing. Any educational institution is necessarily to a degree authoritarian, and those in Puritan New England were quite markedly so. Franklin preferred a desultory program of reading, at first being left entirely to what was at hand and later more eclectic but bent entirely to his own interests and discoveries. There was, of course, also something broadly and healthily characteristic of all youthful reading in this: More pleasure is derived from a book that is discovered by the reader than by any that is prescribed for him. This is particularly true of a lad who is essentially a self-starter and not a shirker, and one who questions authority rather than surrenders to it. Finally, as his vast curiosity about man and nature mounted, Franklin's approach to knowledge was, far from being systematic, teleological in some respects and, in others, largely pragmatic. Intellectual inquiry or intellectual activity of any sort for its own sake or that dealt principally in abstractions was neither a source of delight to him nor, in his judgment throughout his life, a promising investment of his time or mind; indeed it was the interminable intellectual straining of Puritan theology as much as anything that alienated him from the faith of his fathers at exactly the same time that he was leading Silence Dogood into her free-swinging attack upon Harvard College, still the principal if wavering custodian of Puritan thought. When Franklin drew up his "Proposals Relating to the Education of Youth in Pennsylvania," urging the creation of the "academy" in Philadelphia that was to become the University of Pennsylvania, he was careful to emphasize the practical approach to a liberal education at the outset, preparing the way of the reader by an eloquent prefatory statement on the place of education in a free society, which declared, "The good Education of Youth has been esteemed by wise Men in all Ages, as the sweet Foundation of the Happiness both of private Families and of Common-wealths.*" The asterisk referred to a footnote, of considerable significance and not a little prescience: "As some Things here propos'd may be found to differ a little from the Forms of Education in common Use, the following Quotations [they were in annotations throughout the pamphlet] are to shew the Opinions of several learned Men, who have carefully considered and wrote expresly on the Subject; such as Milton, Locke, [Charles] Rollin [French rhetorician, historian, and rector of the University of Paris], [George] Turnbull [chaplain to the uneducatable Prince of Wales who became George III], and others. They generally complain, that the *old Method* [i.e., that practiced by, among others, Harvard] is in many Respects wrong; but long settled forms are not easily changed. For us, who are now to make a Beginning, 't is, at least, as easy to set out right as wrong. . . ."[2] The introductory passage on the curriculum followed by the students then got to the point which Franklin from his youth both preached and practiced: "As to their Studies, it would be well if they could be taught *every Thing* that is useful, and every *Thing* that is ornamental: But Art is long, and their Time is short. It is therefore propos'd that they learn those Things that are likely to be *most useful* and *most ornamental*, Regard being had to the several Professions for which they are intended."[3]

Given these premises, it is not likely that Franklin would have rejoiced in the curriculum of Harvard College of the 1720s. It is doubtful that he would have gotten far in the first year without bolting from Cambridge to seek his fortune elsewhere. President Benjamin Wadsworth copied down in his diary the program of studies for Harvard freshmen as contracted by

[2] Ibid., III, 399.
[3] Ibid., 404.

a tutor, Henry Flynt, in 1723: "The first year the Freshmen recite the Classick Authours Learn't at School viz Tully Isocrates, Homer, Virgil, with the greek Testamt on Mondays, Tuesdays, wenesdays and Thursdays in the morning and forenoon; . . . and on Saturday morning the greek Catechism and on Friday mornings Dugard or Farnabys Rhetoricke, and the Latter part of the year the Hebrew Grammar and Psalter [Petrus] Ramus and Burgesdicius's Logick and towards the latter end of the year they dispute on Ramus's Definitions, mondays and Tuesdays in the Forenoon." Moreover, students, as a matter of fixed routine, translated passages of the Old Testament from Hebrew to Latin and of the New from Greek to Latin at morning and evening prayer every day—a custom that would hardly have enchanted Franklin. In addition, "All the [Thomas Hollis] Profess^{rs} publick Lectures [on divinity, every Tuesday afternoon] and that the Monitors add a Column in their Bill to note the Absent & Tardy."[4] Not until the third year of the curriculum did any subjects that may conceivably have held a particular interest to Franklin turn up ("Mr. Mortons Physicks, Dr. Mores Ethics, a System of Geography"[5]), although a twenty-four-foot-long telescope mounted on the roof of Massachusetts Hall in 1722 may have intrigued him. Virtually all the work of the students was done orally, with no written examinations or papers; declamations and disputions in Latin were engaged in by every student as often as twice a week. To Franklin, who discovered in his debates with John Collins that he was much more effective with the pen than with the tongue, this may have been at best a perpetual ordeal, and it was the sort of thing at which, when fifteen, he may have simply rebelled. A further cause for rebellion was that there was absolutely no Oxonian or Cantabridgian elasticity, variability, or relaxation about the curriculum. It is not unlikely that, had he been exposed to it, Franklin would have written an even more farcical account of Harvard than his fourth Dogood paper, though unquestionably a better informed one.

Further evidence, aside from the fact that it was intrinsically against Franklin's benign nature to bear a grudge, that he wrote the Dogood lampoon out of no personal pique is clear from the agreeable relations he always had with the institution and also with the Boston Latin School contemporaries with whom he kept in touch until toward the end of his life. And he seemed always to have appreciated the honorary Master of Arts degree that Harvard bestowed on him in 1753—the first honorary degree of five, three masters (Harvard, Yale, and William and Mary) and two doctorates (St. Andrew's and Oxford), that he received when such honors

---

[4] The Wadsworth *Diary* version is in the Colonial Society of Massachusetts, *Publications*, XXXI (1930), 455–56. The curriculum also appears in Samuel Eliot Morison, *Harvard College in the Seventeenth Century* (Cambridge, 1936), I, 146, which compares the Wadsworth draft with Tutor Flynt's.

[5] Harvard College Records in the Colonial Society of Massachusetts, *Publications*, XVI (1925), Pt. II, 476.

were rare ("Thus without Studying in any College I came to partake of their Honours"[6]), although in his autobiography he mistakenly ascribed priority to Yale's (September 1753) over Harvard's (July 1753). Though Franklin could not have known it, four years at Harvard might well have been much less conducive to the polymorphous career that distinguished him among all his contemporaries than were his apprentice years in the printing house and, at his own pace and in his own way, his reading, his poking about the busy port town, his listening to his brother's "clan of Honest Wags," and his probing, through observation and experience, the merits and the failings of the Boston establishment. Very possibly, had he spent four years at Harvard as an undergraduate and then another two or three awaiting his master's degree (which all serious students did), much of the genius of Franklin, with its remarkable quality of spontaneity rather than quiet persistence, would have been blighted, his literary style would have lost its intuitive and its improvised characteristics, and his life probably would have taken a more premeditated course, more centripetal and less diffusive. What he lost by not pursuing a longer academic career was possibly a greater degree of intellectual discipline, a profounder rationalism, and a more synergistic mobilization of his wide and diverse interests and aptitudes. But these surely are minor matters when compared to the freshness, the unclutteredness, and the zest of the thought and utterances springing from his own nature and perceptions, unpolished and unshaped by a direct institutional influence of any continuity in his young life.

If Franklin himself, then, seemed to have had no feelings of bitterness about not matriculating at Harvard, the *Courant*, in at least two issues preceding Silence Dogood's satirical anatomizing of the college, showed signs of seeking a feud with it—signs not diminished by the fact that at least two of the Couranteers, John Gibbins, A.B. 1706, and John Eyre, A.B. 1718 and M.A. 1721, were graduates of Harvard and that a considerable proportion of the *Courant's* subscribers were also graduates. And the *Courant* never forgot that, at least up until the presidency of John Leverett and for seventy-two of its eighty-six years, Harvard was the creature of the Puritan ministers, and was convinced that this was not so much by intent of its founders as by the ecclesiocentric drift of its administrative control up to the point where, by the seventeenth century, it had come under the firm domination of the Mathers. The references to Harvard that occurred in the *Courant* prior to Benjamin Franklin's satirical blast were couched in such terms as to cast ridicule on individuals associated with the college as well as the values of the college itself. At the height of the smallpox epidemic, for example, the *Courant* took it amiss that a Harvard student undertook to reproach it for the dressings down which it more than once administered in its columns to Cotton Mather

[6] *Autobiography*, 209.

and which were in their tone wholly appalling in a society of theocratic genesis. The student was, of course, a Mather—the orphaned grandson of Increase and the nephew of Cotton, Mather Byles, a member of the class of 1725 at Harvard and a contemporary of Benjamin Franklin at the Boston Grammar School. Byles, who had a lifelong felicity with words and achieved a considerable reputation for writing verse, took up his pen with zest on one occasion, in January 1722, and dispatched a letter in stinging rebuke of the *Courant* to the rival *Boston Gazette*: "Every one sees that the main intention of the Vile Courant, is to Vilify and abuse the best Men we have, and especially the Principal Ministers of Religion in the Country."[7] In the next issue of the *Courant*, James Franklin replied with a reference to "a young scribbling Collegian, who has just Learning enough to make a Fool of himself,"[8] little knowing that, in publishing Silence Dogood's letters, he was within months to turn over his lead column on his first page to another sixteen-year-old scribbler.

The *Courant* had a second run-in with Harvard shortly after James Franklin was castigated and cursed by Cotton Mather in the street. Franklin had published some months earlier a pamphlet by a Boston dealer in tobacco and medicinal drugs ("this Poor smoaky Conjurer," Cotton Mather called him[9]) named John Williams, who so brutalized the English language with malapropisms and misspellings that it seemed to many Bostonians that he had constructed a whole new language, which was gleefully called "Mundungian" after Williams' nickname, bestowed when a *Boston Gazette* writer referred to him as "that Crackbrain'd Mundungus [derived from the Spanish word for tripe or offal and applied to bad-smelling tobacco] Williams." Picking up the joke, the Harvard students proposed Williams for a professorship of Mundungian and composed a "Vocabulary of Mundungian," perpetrating some incredible examples of phonetic orthography. When Williams wrote to the *Courant* protesting attacks on his pamphlet and its unorthodox language, James Franklin took the opportunity to furnish a snide introduction to the letter and a glancing blow at Harvard students: "The following Letter I have receiv'd from the Author [i.e., creator] of the *Mundungian* Language; and for the Benefit of those *Sons of Harvard*, who strive in vain or are too lazy

---

[7] *Boston Gazette*, January 15, 1722. Clifford K. Shipton, *Biographical Sketches*, VII, 465n., thought this letter was more likely the work of Samuel Mather, Cotton's son and a member of the class of 1723. But Samuel Mather published an advertisement in the *Courant* of March 21 to March 28, 1722, specifically stating that "I was not concern'd in writing or composing" an earlier communication on the controversy. It was much more in accord with the somewhat less sedate character of Mather Byles to have spontaneously shot off a fairly strong communication to a newspaper, and he is known to have sent another letter, five months later, to the *Courant*, following an attack by Benjamin Franklin on Harvard College. See pp. 618ff., *infra*.

[8] *New-England Courant*, No. 25 (January 15 to January 22, 1722).

[9] Cotton Mather to Dr. James Jurin, May 4, 1723. MS letter in American Antiquarian Society, p. 15. (A copy is in the Royal Society, London, of which Dr. Jurin was secretary.)

to learn the other *learned Tongues*, I will insert it as I receive it, referring
them to the VOCABULARY lately publish'd, for their Assistance in reading and translating it into *English*." In his letter, Williams deplored the
fact that Harvard had nothing better to do than to "find out the fals
Speling in one home you calls *Mondonges* (a pore Eleterate Man)" and
suggested a line of improvement: "How moche in this Country beholden
to Harfet *Coleg* for shoche a gret Gifet [gift] or Arth [art], the which
som old Weman do theche the Children. Bot Sir, ould it not be of equil
Benefet to the Poblecke, if while they are theching the Arth of Lojeche,
they could infuese Onesti in to their Pupels to youse it [i.e., logic]. . . .
Sir, is this the nattral Event of *Harfet Coleg*, to strane at a Nat and swala
a Chamel?"[10] This contribution, published three weeks before Franklin's
Dogood papers began to appear and two months before his Harvard satire,
could very well have inspired the latter. Straining at gnats could very well
have seemed to Franklin a major proportion of the intellectual life at Harvard, just as it was of Puritan theology, and a sampling of the *quaestiones*
disputed by Master of Arts candidates on Commencement Day would
tend to bear out his views. Some of the topics that solicited the interest of
the learned community at Cambridge would have struck Franklin as unworthy of the attention and time of intelligent men ("Were the patri-
archs of the Old Testament thrust down into limbo?"); some as useless
("Were Samson's foxes, as they are commonly called, animals?"); some as
self-evident ("Are charity and mutual tolerance among the professors of
Christianity most conducive to the promotion of true religion?"); some as
capricious ("If Lazarus, by a will made before his death, had given away
his property, could he have legally claimed it after his resurrection?"); and
some as fatuous ("Is agriculture unbecoming a gentleman?").[11]

Despite all this, if the Franklins and the *Courant* equated the Harvard
of 1722 solely with protecting and advancing the interests of an anachronistic ruling class, they were in error and themselves anachronous. By
1722 Harvard had been quite thoroughly liberated from the iron grasps of
the Mathers, Increase having vacated the presidency in 1701 and Cotton
having been replaced as a fellow of the Corporation in 1703 as a result of
nonattendance at meetings out of his pique at being passed by for the
presidency. The Harvard community now consisted of a lay president,
John Leverett, five fellows of the Corporation (three of whom were Boston
and Cambridge ministers), two lay tutors, a librarian, a printer, a steward, a porter, and three sweepers—one for Harvard College Hall, with its
twenty student chambers, an assembly room which also served as a chapel
and the college library, one for Stoughton College Hall, with sixteen
chambers, and the other for the two-year-old Massachusetts Hall, with
thirty-two student chambers. Since Leverett's installation in 1708, the stu-

[10] *New-England Courant*, No. 33 (March 5 to March 12, 1722).
[11] Massachusetts Historical Society, *Proceedings*, XVIII (1881), 119–51.

dent base had broadened considerably, both geographically and as to future occupational interests. As Franklin, in the spring of 1722, took up his pen to satirize the college, the Harvard student body was made up of 168 undergraduates, for whom there were accommodations for only 132 in the Yard, the rest finding lodgings and meals in the town of Cambridge. There were also resident in Cambridge and attached to the college an undeterminable number of graduates—probably about thirty at a given time —who were reading theology to qualify for their master's degrees. (Nontheological candidates, awaiting the passing of the customary three years between baccalaureate and master's degrees, simply returned to Cambridge for the third anniversary of their baccalaureate commencement, prepared to discuss one of the *quaestiones* and take care of one or two other formalities in the space of the single afternoon of Commencement Day.) Of the undergraduates, twenty-three, or a seventh of all four classes, came from outside Massachusetts—not a staggering proportion but impressive enough, since to educate their youth southern New England and New York had Yale, established in 1701, sixty-five years after Harvard, and the colonies to the south had William and Mary, established in 1693, in closer proximity—impressive, too, when compared to the geographic distribution of the "Sons of the Prophets," as pre-Leverett presidents liked to call Harvard students, when Leverett was inaugurated, at which time of a total of fifty-three undergraduates only one, the son of the governor of Rhode Island, was from outside Massachusetts. Of the non-Massachusetts students in 1722, twelve came from New Hampshire, four from Connecticut, three from New York, and one each from England, Ireland, Jamaica, and Rhode Island. Limited as their number was, these students did bring differing heritages and backgrounds to the college; and since all courses were taught to the entire class in single sessions attended by all members of the class, this diversity was of very real significance in widening the awareness of boys from the homogeneous milieu of the Massachusetts meetinghouse and the Boston Latin School.

The seminarian propensity of Harvard was further reduced as the first quarter of the eighteenth century approached its end by the diversity of careers pursued by its graduates. Even though more of the students in 1722—58—were eventually to enter the Congregational ministry than any other single profession, the great majority of the students—110—took up other occupations, including the law, business, medicine, public affairs, teaching, and, in two cases, even the priesthood of the Church of England. This represented an even more significant liberalization of Harvard than the increasing geographic origins of its student body, for of a student body of fifty-three when Leverett's tenure began a majority of twenty-eight became Congregational ministers. In short, under Leverett's enlightened leadership and to the agonized distress of the Mathers, Harvard, far from entrenching itself as a Congregational seminary, was, in fact, becoming more and more a college in the Oxonian and Cantabridgian tradition, educating its students for living rather than for any vocation.

Most of this obviously mattered very little to the young Franklin as he absorbed the inevitable biting comments, about the Harvard connections of the Mathers, from the Couranteers in the printing house during the smallpox controversy and as he looked eagerly for an institutional target for the satirical pen of Silence Dogood. To him any institution out of practical, daily touch with the bustling life of the Boston that he knew, and yet influencing its public affairs more than many of those in the midst of it, was probably a somewhat ludicrous incongruity and therefore a plausible object of attack. Having made his choice and knowing far less about life at Harvard than he did of the street, waterfront, and leather-apron life of Boston, Franklin very prudently chose an allegoric form, allowing all sorts of exaggerations, distortions, and outright fancifications, for his composition rather than the chatty letters he had originally instituted as Silence Dogood's vehicle—the only instance in the whole series where he deliberately chose a literary form that was somewhat unreal and strained for a sensible middle-aged country widow not given by experience or inclination, as Franklin had sketched her self-portrait in the first three papers, to allegoric dreams of Augustan grandeur in their settings and properties. It was a literary form no more natural to a printer's apprentice, particularly one so ungiven to flights of fancy as Benjamin Franklin. And it was, in fact, lifted wholesale from the third *Spectator* paper of James Addison, originally published on March 3, 1711, and readily available in the first volume of the collected *Spectators* in the Franklin printing house library. In Addison's paper, the author, having been concerned with the "Decay of the Publick Credit" during the day, went to sleep that night and dreamed that he was in "the great Hall where the Bank is kept" and "saw toward the upper end of the Hall, a beautiful Virgin seated on a throne of Gold. Her Name as they told me was Publick Credit." The beautiful virgin collapsed and died when the hall was invaded by a dozen phantoms of hideous aspect, bearing such names as "Tyranny and Anarchy" and "Bigotry and Atheism," and the "great Heaps of Gold, on either side of the Throne, now appeared to be only Heaps of Paper." But when some "amiable Phantoms," bearing such names as "Liberty," "Moderation," "Monarchy," and "Religion," appeared, Publick Credit revived and the heaps of paper turned back into pyramids of gold.[12] In Franklin's paper, Silence Dogood, having been concerned with the advisability of sending her son to Harvard College, took an afternoon nap and dreamed that she visited a "large and stately Edifice," and in "the Middle of the great Hall stood a stately and magnificent Throne," on which was seated a female figure called "Learning," "surrounded on every Side with innumerable Volumes in all Languages." Franklin awkwardly broke the spell of his allegory al-

[12] *Spectator*, No. 3 (March 3, 1711), Everyman's Library edition, I, 11–13.

most at the outset by inserting the wholly irrelevant sentence, "She seem'd very busily employ'd in writing something on half a Sheet of Paper, and upon Enquiring, I understood she was preparing a Paper, call'd, *The New-England Courant.*" The intent, of course, was to claim that "Learning" was in league with the *Courant* rather than with "that famous Seminary of Learning in Cambridge," but it came too soon in the satire and was clumsy in a way of which *The Spectator* would never have been capable. However, having made his aside, Franklin got back to his subject—the sad state of learning at Harvard—and kept quite faithful to the form that he had borrowed throughout the rest of the paper.

The attack began with a sweeping derision of the candidates for admission to the college: "Every Peasant, who had wherewithal, was preparing to send one of his Children at least to this famous Place; and in this Case most of them consulted their own Purses instead of their Children's Capacities: So that I observed, a great many, yea, the most part of those who were travelling thither, were little better than Dunces and Blockheads." Franklin may have had it in mind that he led all the students in his class at the Latin School and have considered the body of his contemporaries, therefore, of lesser intelligence—particularly since humility was never one of his limitations. Actually, however, no candidate for admission to Harvard was likely to appear for an oral examination given by the president and tutors every summer unless his schoolmaster or his pastor, who knew the admission requirements, advised him that he was sufficiently qualified for consideration to undertake the journey to Cambridge. From as early as 1642, the "Laws Liberties & Orders of Harvard Colledge confirmed by the Overseers & president of ye Colledge . . . and Published to ye Scholars for ye perpetuall preservation of their welfare & government" set forth the admission requirements in quite specific terms: "When any Schollar is able to Read Tully or such like classicall Latine Author ex tempore, & make and speake true Latin in verse and prose suo (ut aiunt) Marte, and decline perfectly the paradigmes of Nounes and verbes in ye Greeke toungue, then may hee bee admitted into ye Colledge, nor shall any claim admission before such qualifications."[13] Qualifications as to character were further set forth by the overseers at a meeting in 1650: "Whereas by experience wee have found it prejudicial to the p[ro]moting of Learning & good manners in the Colledge to admit such yong Schollars who have been negligent in their studyes & disobedient to their masters in the Schools & so by an evill custome or habit become utterly unfit to improove for their p[ro]fit according to their friends expectation the liberty of students in the Colledge: It is therefore ordered by the President & ffellows of Harvard Colledge that no Schollar whatsoever where these be published shall thenceforth bee admitted from any such Schools unlesse having the Testimony of the Master of the said School of his obedience & submission to

---

[13] Harvard College Records, Pt. I, 24–25.

all Godly School—discipline & his studiousness & diligence at leastwise for our quarter of a year last before his comeing thence, or in case of discontinuance from School then it is expected hee shall bring the testimony of his sober & studious conversation under the hand of a Magistrate, or Elder or two or three competent pious witnesses."[14] In the eighteenth century, the president and fellows, with the consent of the overseers, made the scholarship qualifications for admission even more specific: "Whoever upon Examination by the President, and two at least of the Tutors, Shall be found Able ex tempore to read, construe & parse Tully, Virgil or Such like common Classical Latin Authors; and to write true Latin in Prose, and to be Skill'd in making Latin verse, or at Least in the rules of Prosodia; and to read, construe and parse ordinary Greek, as in the New Testament, Isocrates or such Like, and decline the Paradigms, of Greek Nouns, and Verbs; having withall good Testimony of his past blameless behaviour, shall be Look'd upon as qualified for Admission into Harvard College."[15] Since no candidate was admitted without a personal oral examination in the awesome presence of the president and tutors and the submission of an original Latin thesis read by the president, it is not likely that many "dunces and blockheads" of Franklin's allegory got through. If they had, it is unlikely that they would have survived, since the college rules sternly required that all "Undergraduates shall in their course declaim publickly in the Hall, in one of yᵉ three Learned Languages [i.e., Latin, Greek, or Hebrew], and in no other without leave or direction from the President. . . ."[16]

It is no more likely that Silence Dogood, in her fantasy visit to Harvard, would have encountered on the way a swarm of "peasants" preparing to send their sons to Harvard. Of the 168 undergraduates present when Silence made her strange pilgrimage, 22 were the sons of Harvard graduates. Of the 160 fathers whose occupations are known, 78 were professional men—clergymen, schoolmasters, physicians, judges, public officials—and 25 were prosperous merchants. Of the remaining 57, 40 were tradesmen and craftsmen and 17 were farmers. If Franklin was referring to the two latter categories as "peasant," it could only have been in odd contradiction of the leather-apron coalition with the rural populace whose interests *The New-England Courant* and Silence Dogood were created to reflect. It is most improbable that Franklin had any such intention, and it is obvious that he simply lumped together "peasants," "dunces," and "blockheads" to create a derisive prelude to Silence's adventures once "as a Spectator I gain'd Admittance" to the "Temple of Learning."

Franklin's second indictment of Harvard voiced by Silence Dogood was that only the rich were accepted as students: "The Passage was kept by

[14] Ibid., 29.
[15] Ibid., 134.
[16] Ibid., 138.

two sturdy Porters named *Riches* and *Poverty*, and the latter obstinately refused to give Entrance to any who had not first gain'd the Favour of the former: so that I observed, many who came even to the very Gate, were obliged to travel back again as ignorant as they came, for want of this necessary Qualification." The financial backgrounds of the students who were in the college at the time of Silence Dogood's dream indicate that riches and poverty had little to do with either admitting or rejecting a candidate for admission. A seventh of all students were there on scholarships, and the college waiters, monitors, butlers, and clerks were self-supporting students. Twenty-three of the 168 students were orphans, living in most cases frugally on contributions of relatives, neighbors, or their local church members. Twenty more were the sons of clergymen, whose salaries were almost uniformly fixed at a hundred pounds plus, in most instances, firewood. Fifty-eight were the promising sons of hard-working artisans and farmers, to whom the student's small fees represented a considerable financial sacrifice. Four were the sons of schoolmasters, commonly paid less than the ministers. Only twenty of the entire roster of students are known to have come from families of relative wealth. Tuition, on the other hand, though not easily come by in the case of rural families, who dealt very little in cash, was not high: ten shillings a quarter. This amounted to two pounds a year—about a week's salary for a Congregational minister. Rental of chambers ranged from twelve to twenty shillings for the year, and each student paid his hall sweeper twelve shillings a year. The cost of food varied and was the subject of elaborate formulas based on the cost of provisions to the steward, who sometimes came out ahead and paid some of the surplus to the college and sometimes lost and was indemnified by the college. Judging from complaints about the quality and quantity of the food, it was not expensive. The cost of the entire college education of Middlecott Cooke, of the class of 1723, was met by a note of his Father for £48 4s., and his father, a shady politician and land speculator of the class of 1697, was one of the wealthy parents, who apparently did not have to scrimp. Frequently, college expenses were paid, not in specie, but in products. Nathaniel Huntting, of the class of 1722, paid his bills with quantities of ox tongue from the family farm; his classmate, Matthew Livermore, paid his in beef, cider, and malt, his father being a maltster by trade; and a third classmate, John Smith, paid in sundries from his father's shop in Boston.

If Franklin wanted to make charges about class discrimination at Harvard, he should have based them not on economic grounds but on social distinctions among parents arbitrarily made, often first by the college steward and then usually revised by the faculty and occasionally revised again as graduation approached—in most cases, although no pattern emerges, with scholarly merit receiving at least some attention in the final revision. In any case, socially ranking students on admission and throughout their college careers was patently insipid at best and, at worst, demoralizing in an institution devoted to education, where one would expect intellectual distinction to be the criterion of any system of ranking. The fallaciousness of Harvard's ranking of students is well illustrated by the class of 1724, of which Franklin would have been a member had he gone to Harvard. James Pitts, the son of a rich Boston merchant and property owner whose interests appeared in the college investment portfolio, ranked first in his class on entrance, fell to tenth place in a class of forty-three in the faculty revision, and disappeared altogether in the final ranking at graduation, having left college somewhere in between, distinguished only for paying the largest college bills of his class. He was replaced at the head of the list by Adam Winthrop, great-great-grandson of the first governor of Massachusetts Bay—a plausible enough choice socially but inexplicable on any other ground, since Adam's intellectual capacity was one of the more limited of his class and wholly satisfied by his serving his merchant father as an assistant and the county court as a clerk. At the bottom of the first ranking, a position Franklin might well have occupied, was Israel Chauncy, the son of a country minister, who was moved up to fourth place on the second and third rankings. If ever there was a subject at Harvard appropriate to a biting satirical treatment, it was this muddled ranking of students by confused and confusing social values. No one could possibly defend or even explain it; and yet it persisted until 1749, when the volume of parents' complaints (not at the folly of it but because they resented the particular positions of their sons on the list) put a stop to it. Moreover, the system had a practical effect on students; because the classes were always larger than the college commons could accommodate for meals, as many as half the members of a class had to find eating places in the town: they were always those on the lower half of the ranking list. The absence of any reference to this specious aspect of Harvard student life, in the face of young Franklin's repeated expositions of largely spurious situations at the college, reveals how little knowledge he had of Harvard and how much he depended upon impressions, gathered from overheard comments springing from such isolated and irrelevant episodes as Mather Byles's undertaking from his eminence as a Harvard freshman, the castigating of the *Courant* for its ill-concealed disrespect for his uncle. And yet there were few more useful things that the good and sensible Silence Dogood could have done—and few truer to the character Franklin had given her—than to demolish the social ranking of college students by burlesquing it.

From the point of view of a Boston apprentice, toiling from sunrise to sunset six days a week, with no vacations, for a master with absolute power over him, Benjamin Franklin's charge against Harvard students—that too many of them "idle away" their time—had some merit. To him a six-week summer vacation (though it was reduced to a single week in 1722, because

of time lost in the smallpox epidemic) and leaves of absence of up to
three weeks each academic year must have seemed the epitome of idleness,
though many a Harvard student worked on the farm in the summer and
taught at the village school in the winter. But the student's day, in its long
established program, was not much less full than the artisan's. It began at
sunup, and to Benjamin Franklin, who, for all the menial tasks of the
printing house, was constantly moving around Boston, making deliveries,
hawking pamphlets, and browsing through bookstalls, it would have been
intolerably confining and oppressive. After morning prayers and translating passages from the Old Testament from Hebrew into Greek in the
presence of the class tutor, followed by a substantive analysis of the passages, the day was spent in the study of a single subject, according to the
Ramean method, prescribed at the University of Paris in the sixteenth
century by the French logician Petrus Ramus, who had a considerable if
somewhat belated influence on the thought of the Boston elect well into
the eighteenth century ("That great and famous Martyr of France, *Peter
Ramus*, held forth the light to others,"[17] Increase Mather wrote). The
method called for lectures on the subject of the day in the morning (for
freshmen, logic on Mondays and Tuesdays, Greek on Wednesdays, Hebrew on Thursdays, rhetoric on Fridays, and catechetical divinity on Satur-
days), followed by two hours of individual study of the subject, one hour
of recitations on it, and then two hours of disputation on what they had
been occupying themselves with since breakfast. In the evening, after five
o'clock bread and beer, it was prayer and scripture time again, followed by
study until supper at seven-thirty (preceded by a long blessing and followed by a long thanksgiving) with compulsory bedtime at nine o'clock
for all but seniors. Sunday was, of course, occupied with three sermons, by
the president, by a visiting preacher or one of the clerical fellows of the
Corporation, and at the Cambridge meetinghouse across the road from
the college yard—not much time for prolonged idleness, even though the
Puritan schedule was considerably relaxed in Leverett's time.

Demanding as the routine was, however, no community made up primarily of fifteen-to-nineteen-year-old males was apt to be wholly diligent in
the pursuit of its purposes. Harvard College had achieved no such transcendent excellence. The Honest Wags at the *Courant* knew it, and so
also did the young apprentice overhearing their conversations. The
Franklin circle probably got wind too, of the Board of Overseers' chronic
dissatisfaction with the college and the Leverett administration. The more
knowledgeable of the Couranteers certainly must have known that the
overseers, made up, except for members of the Governor's Council, entirely of Congregational ministers, represented the last dying gasps of the
doctrinal reactionaries' efforts to keep Harvard an orthodox Puritan theo-

[17] In the Preface to James Fitch, *The First Principles of the Doctrine of Christ* (Boston, 1679), quoted in Perry Miller, *The Puritans* (New York, 1938), I, 32.

logical seminary and that, in their attempts to discredit Leverett and the Corporation, they eagerly sowed rumors of the collapse of religion at Harvard, the abandonment of academic discipline, and, according to an overseers' committee's report of a year later which the Board of Overseers itself rejected, the wholesale practice of "stealing, lying, swearing, idleness, picking of locks, and too frequent use of strong drink," the report culminating with the charge that "The Freshman, as well as others, are seen, in great numbers, going into town on Sabbath mornings, to provide breakfasts."

Adding grist to the anti-Harvard mill was the incessant sport of students, in colonial and provincial times, of breaking the college windows, the punishment for which was monetary fines, which sometimes reached incredible accumulative dimensions. Drunkenness was also sufficiently common to evoke no punishment more serious than a fine (five shillings) while profanity, "neglecting analysis of Scripture," or "walking or other diversion on the Sabbath" was adjudged twice as heinous and cost the culprit ten shillings. Blasphemy, fornication, robbery, and forgery were the most serious offenses and resulted in expulsion.[18] No student had been expelled, however, since 1714, when Ebenezer Gray and Joshua Moody, sophomores, were expelled for thievery but, within three months, were readmitted. However, every class had chronic lesser offenders, the most accomplished of whom was Andrew Belcher, of the class of 1714, whose total fines in some terms amounted to as much as his tuition and chamber rent combined. And there were festivities at Commencement which apparently reached such liveliness by 1722 that the Corporation concluded that whereas ". . . a Suitable retrenchm^t of every thing that has the face of Exorbitance or Extravag^e in Expences, especialy at Comcncem^{ts} ought to be endeavrd And Whereas the preparations & p[ro]visions that have bin wont to be made at those times have bin the Occasion of no Small disorders; it is Agreed, and Voted, That henceforc no preparation nor Provision either of Plumb-Cake or rosted, boiled or baked Meats or Pyes of any kind shalbe made by any Comencer, Nor shal any such have any distilled Liquours, or any Composition made therwth. . . ."[19]

It is questionable whether much attention was paid to the order. Commencement Day was the great summer holiday in Massachusetts, occurring on the first Wednesday of July every year since 1684. Everyone converged on Cambridge by foot, on horseback, in carriages, and by ferry from Boston. Alumni, families of graduates, officials and legislators, hawkers, street performers—the whole motley assortment of opportunists and the restless who follow the crowds—and hundreds of eligible young women from all the surrounding towns. The drinking was heavy.

[18] Extracted from the College Laws of 1734 by Morison, *Three Centuries of Harvard*, 112.
[19] Harvard College Records, Pt. II, 470–71.

Significantly, the Corporation's strictures omitted any word about *nondistilled* liquors—beer, hard cider, and wines. Beer was the only beverage served at all meals at Harvard, including breakfast, and individual wine cellars in Stoughton Hall were furnished students for six shillings per annum and to the tutors at no charge. And plum cake was such a strong tradition at Commencement, not because of a passion for plums, but because it was the customary accompaniment of wine when the latter was consumed by the mugful. As early as 1681, the most appropriate way to indulge in some reforms during a period of mourning for the death of President Urian Oakes, six weeks before Commencement that year, seemed to the overseers to order "That no Graduate henceforth shall provide [for themselves and their friends] more than 3 gallons of wine, nor oth^r Students more than one for comencem^t."[20] If this represented a sacrificial gesture, the amount of wine otherwise allowed and consumed was undoubtedly of staggering proportions, so to speak.

Since hundreds of Bostonians visited Cambridge on Commencement Day, in the manner of a country-wide field day, and never saw Harvard College under any other conditions, many of them inevitably went away with the impression that the college population consisted of nothing but time-killing wastrels. Plum cake itself came to be a symbol of high living, and the academic year was imagined to be one long bout of overindulgence. None of those who carried away in their minds this picture of a profligate Harvard had sat through the long days of lectures, study, disputations, prayers, and Scriptures, relieved largely by three sermons on Sundays, which made up the substance of a student life at Harvard that was only punctuated, and not underlined, by window-breaking, occasional rebellions, and at the session's end, the undoubted excesses of Commencement. Certainly, for someone looking to a satirical characterization of the college, nevertheless, there was enough of the exceptional to distort the ordinary, and it is of the whole nature of satire to distort. And so Benjamin Franklin, having ascribed a general atmosphere of idleness to the institution, went gleefully on to further allegations, some more specific but no more solidly based. Silence Dogood had "Learning" seated on her throne surrounded by other figures: "On her Right Hand sat *English*, with a pleasant smiling Countenance, and handsomely attir'd; and on her left were seated several *Antique Figures* with their faces vail'd. I was considerable puzzl'd to guess who they were, until one informed me, (who stood beside me,) that those Figures on her left Hand were *Latin, Greek, Hebrew* &c. and that they were very much reserv'd, and seldom or never unvail'd their Faces here, and then to few or none, tho' most of those who have in this Place acquir'd so much Learning as to distinguish them from *English*, pretended to an intimate Acquaintance with them. I then enquir'd of him, what could be the Reason why they continu'd vail'd, in

20 Ibid., 241.

this Place especially: He pointed to the Foot of the Throne, where I saw *Idleness*, attended with *Ignorance*, and these (he informed me) were they, who first vail'd them, and still kept them so."[21]

The point was, of course, that the "sacred tongues" in the curriculum were an affectation. Actually, Latin was the language of instruction at Harvard, as it was at the universities of Europe; and it wasn't even taught at the college, because all entrants were assumed to have mastered it before they ever went to Cambridge.[22] As to Greek and Hebrew, even the dullest student exposed to them over and over again every day for four years would be bound to absorb much of the two languages from sheer exposure—idle as he might become after he got to Harvard or ignorant as he may have been before he got there. Franklin's real complaint here was somewhat elusive. Though he had had but one year of Latin, he nevertheless used Latin quotations at the head of eight of the Dogood letters and English at the head of only one; and in future years, when considering the place of the classics in a liberal education, he always seemed somewhat ambivalent, half convinced that they constituted the matrix of learning and half convinced that they were really an unessential adornment. Whatever his views, it is unlikely that any student at John Leverett's Harvard either would have survived there without acquiring a working knowledge of the ancient languages or could have avoided it even if he were sentient only half the time.

Returning to the sons of the peasants that she encountered on her way to visit Harvard, Silence Dogood reported, "Now I observ'd, that the whole Tribe who entred into the Temple with me, began to climb the Throne; but the work proving troublesome and difficult to most of them [and here Franklin strayed into a mixed metaphor that was to rise and haunt him], they withdrew their Hands from the Plow, and contented themselves to sit at the Foot, with Madam *Idleness* and her maid *Ignorance*, until those who were assisted by Diligence and a docible Temper, had well nigh got up the first Step: But the Time drawing nigh in which they could no way avoid ascending, they were fain to crave the Assistance of those who had got up before them, and who, for the Reward perhaps of a *Pint of Milk*, or a *Piece of Plumb-Cake*, lent the Lubbers a helping Hand, and sat them in the Eye of the World, upon a Level with themselves." Aside from being the only piece of literature extant that mentions the consumption of milk in connection with eighteenth-century Harvard College, whose records show that it had a college brewery as early as 1674[23] but no evidence that it ever had a tablespoon of milk in the butteries, this phase of Silence Dogood's dream once again reveals Franklin's almost total innocence of Harvard's ways. An essential ingredient of the

---

[21] *Papers*, I, 16.
[22] See Chap. VIII, *supra*.
[23] Harvard College Records, Pt. II, 62.

Harvard teaching method, for better or worse, was that translations, not only from English to Latin but also from Hebrew to Greek and Greek to Latin, were made by the student *ex tempore* when called upon by his tutor in the presence of the entire class. Undoubtedly, there were efforts on the parts of some students to slip translations between the pages of their original texts, but it would have been virtually impossible, without a conspicuous display of excess papers, for anyone so to manage a Bible with slips for three different languages between each page. As to helping a laggard classmate while he was up on his feet under the eye of his tutor and the entire class, the effort would patently have been obvious and impossible of success.

Whatever the process by which the idle and the ignorant managed to extract the baccalaureate degree from Harvard, Silence Dogood was convinced that it all went for nothing anyway. Observing that, as the graduating class left Cambridge, ". . . every Beetle-Scull seem'd well satisfy'd with his own Portion of Learning, tho' perhaps he was *e'en just* as ignorant as ever," Silence wrote that she set out to see what happened to this sorry collection of bachelors of arts. "Some I perceiv'd took to Merchandizing, others to Travelling, some to one Thing, some to another, and some to Nothing; and many of them from henceforth, for want of Patrimony, liv'd as poor as Church Mice, being unable to dig, and asham'd to beg, and to live by their Wits it was impossible." It is doubtful, of course, that Franklin, leading Silence into this avenue of inquiry, had any knowledge at all of what happened to an entire Harvard class in later life, and so Silence reported less with the experienced observations of the old than with the brash assumptions of the young. The class of 1724, Franklin's own theoretical class, had thirty-eight members surviving sufficiently long, out of a total of forty-two who finished college, to undertake careers. Seventeen went immediately into schoolteaching, seven of them continuing as schoolmasters all their lives, ten later entering the ministry, one becoming a physician later, and another leaving teaching to operate the family farm. Seven entered the ministry directly from Harvard. Nine became merchants, largely to run considerable family businesses, but of these two were also in the public service as lieutenant governor and legislator, and a third gave up "merchandizing" to start and conduct a school. Five became physicians, including the one who had been first a teacher. None of the class, from the available evidence, seems to have come to the vacuous end that Silence Dogood reported, though in later life Andrew Belcher, the son of Governor Jonathan Belcher, an alumnus of Harvard, did not achieve his father's political eminence and, through inattention rather than dissipation, managed passively to watch the family fortune drift away. Another, Samuel Coolidge, though an able classical scholar, failed because of personality shortcomings, successively as a teacher, a minister, and librarian of Harvard College, and ultimately, suffering a mental disorder, died a public charge. And Henry Phillips, a bookdealer of charm and wealth, died in exile at twenty-five in France, where he had taken refuge following an indictment for murder as victor in a gambling-debt duel fought with swords on Boston Common. But the overwhelming majority of the class lived useful, able lives, largely in the professions. Contrary to the dire premise of Silence Dogood's fanciful dream, all the classes attending Harvard in 1722 had similar histories. None found themselves, on graduating, in need either of digging or of begging.

It was hard for Harvard men to please Silence in any case. Even those staying in Cambridge to read theology for their master's degrees, preparatory to entering what was still the most honored and most influential profession in the province, aroused her suspicions. "But the most part of the crowd," she wrote of that segment of the graduates, though it was usually only about a quarter of the classes of the 1720s, who went directly into the ministry, "went along a large beaten Path, which led to a Temple at the further End of the Plain, call'd, *The Temple of Theology*. The Business of those who were employ'd in this Temple being laborious and painful, I wonder'd exceedingly to see so many going towards it; but while I was pondering this Matter in my Mind, I spy'd *Pecunia* [i.e., money] behind a Curtain, beckoning to them with her Hand, which Sight immediately satisfy'd me for whose Sake it was, that a great Part of them (I will not say all) travel'd that Road." If any of the class of 1724 entered the ministry for money, he must have been sorely disappointed. Of the ten known competences paid clergymen of the class, there was one of £110, three of £100, one each of £80, £75, and £60, one of £52, and two of £50. Samuel Allis labored in the Enfield parish at a nominal salary of £60 for nineteen years, but the parish could not or would not pay him regularly and dismissed him when he sought some sort of settlement, finally and reluctantly giving him a small farm to work; and Henry Phillips was for sixteen years pastor of the church at Dartmouth without receiving a penny of his promised salary of £50 and whose total compensation was a £10 contribution from the Old South Church in Boston.

Had Franklin wanted to question the motives of those on grounds other than a sense of spiritual mission, he would have been on much sounder ground to have given attention to the use of the ministry as an instrument of power in Puritan life—an extremely timely and germane example of which was occurring at the very time that Franklin was writing. The governance of Harvard College, through the agency of a predominantly clerical Board of Overseers, was launched on a two-year-long conspiracy to distort the liberal terms under which Thomas Hollis, an English dissenter of Baptist persuasion, endowed a professorship of divinity, without regard to any sectarian qualifications on the part of the chair's occupant. Hollis had specified only that the occupant believe "that the Scriptures of the Old and New Testament are the only perfect rule of faith and manners,"[24] but the overseers, without Hollis's knowledge and without even informing him, substituted a requirement that any candidate nominated for the professorship undergo a test of his devotion to the sectarian doctrines of the Massachusetts brand of Calvinism, including infant baptism. As a Baptist, the central premise of whose deviation from Calvinism was that baptism was a rite suitable only to adults capable of making their own profession of faith, Hollis would obviously have little enthusiasm for belief in infant baptism as a test of the Christian faith of a professor of divinity, although he also made it clear that he did not regard it as a disqualification either. Rather than face the issue and either accept or reject the professorship on Hollis's terms, the reverend overseers saw fit to resort to a deception unworthy of their trust and ill attuned to the tone of academic liberalism and religious freedom for which John Leverett had labored so conscientiously. But these matters and such others, deeply significant of the direction that Harvard was to take, as the contest sharpened between Leverett and the overseers over whether Harvard was to be governed by the president and external fellows of the Corporation or by the faculty, were apparently far outside of Benjamin Franklin's awareness and certainly beyond his capacity at the time to subject to satirical treatment—helpful as that may have been in clarifying the issues.

In her castigation of Harvard, however, Silence Dogood concluded with another less subtle allegation against the theology students: "In this Temple I saw nothing worth mentioning, except the ambitious and fraudulent Contrivances of Plagius, who (notwithstanding he had been severely reprehended for such Practices before) was diligently transcribing some eloquent Paragraphs out of Tillotson's *Works*, &c. to embellish his own." Archbishop Tillotson, though an Anglican, was widely read and admired at Harvard under Leverett's liberal regime, and many theological students may well have drawn liberally on the fourteen volumes of his works in the college library. Whatever the merits of the charge of plagiarism, nevertheless, it came with poor grace from the *Courant*, or any other eighteenth-century newspapers, which were far from disciplined in their use, whether outright copying, paraphrasing, or imitating, of materials originated by someone else. Benjamin Franklin himself was heavily dependent on his reading, as a young writer, and very frequently borrowed either the substance or the format of his early output from established English writers. Even when he directly quoted Defoe for twenty-one paragraphs in Silence Dogood's twenty-three paragraphs on widows' relief, he attributed them, in conformity with a somewhat evasive journalistic practice of the time, only to an "ingenius Author."[25] Both the *Courant* and the *Gazette* lifted materials at will from London newspapers, occasionally with vague attributions but seldom—unless to protect themselves—crediting the specific source.

---

[24] Quincy, *History of Harvard University*, I, 263.
[25] *New-England Courant*, No. 54 (August 6 to August 13, 1722).

So chronic was the habit among *Courant* contributors of borrowing freely, without attribution, from other writers that, the week after the Dogood charge of plagiarism at Harvard, James Franklin inserted a notice in his paper about the practice, his conscience possibly pricked by comments on the Dogood letter. The message was obviously less intended as an admonition to contributors, with whom he could readily have discussed the matter, than as a public acknowledgment and apology that plagiarism in his columns had been more than exceptional: "Whereas the Publisher of this Paper is inform'd that some of his Correspondents have borrow'd from other Authors without quoting [i.e., enclosing the passages in quotation marks] the Passages. These are to desire them for the future to mention the Authors from whom such Passages are taken, or distinguish them by commas (") [quotation marks] at the beginning of each Line, otherwise they may expect to have their Writings expos'd by some other of his Correspondents."[26] James Franklin's sensitivity was, however, unusual. The late sixteenth and early seventeenth centuries were generally the most sententious and aphoristic age in history, as Benjamin Franklin discovered and was later to make the most of in packaging maxims gleaned from scores of sources in twenty-five years of publishing *Poor Richard's Almanac.* More than his lapse in the hybrid metaphor of a plow ascending the inner steps of a temple, the pointless and unsupported charge that the *quaestio* declamations of theological students were commonly plagiarized from Archbishop Tillotson furnished convenient ammunition to any Harvard counterattack on Silence Dogood's scolding. Probably gone from his mind was the comment, ironically with its original source fully credited, made by James Franklin, writing as "Timothy Turnstone" in reply to what he regarded as an ill-founded satirical treatment of the *Courant* in the *Boston Gazette,* five months earlier: "Arch Bishop Tillotson . . . very justly observes, That a small *Portion of Wit,* and a *great deal of Ill-Nature* will furnish a Man for Satyr."[27]

All in all, the Harvard College paper of the Dogood series was the most ambitious that Franklin undertook and probably the least successful, as far as the sharpness of perception and the effectiveness of his style went. Not only was it, in its literary quality, heavy, awkward, and unnatural but its contents were, on the whole, a jumble of misinformation, misimpressions, and misjudgments—all because the young Franklin's reach in this instance was beyond his grasp. There is little evidence of the effect, if any, that the paper had upon the Harvard establishment, which was quite accustomed, by 1722, to being berated by the Mathers and their dwindling band of followers, and by Judge Sewall and his fellow overseers, and was not likely to be plunged into anger or despair by the sprightly young paper that had already taken on the Mathers. Leverett was well aware, too, that the college, if it was to take the route he envisioned, would go through a transitional

26 Ibid., No. 42 (May 14 to May 21, 1722).
27 Ibid., No. 20 (December 11 to December 18, 1721).

period of abrupt changes in student values and manners, as an increasing proportion of the student body aspired to other careers than the Congregational ministry. In any case, it was the students who were the target of Silence Dogood, and it was a student who replied to the attack—in all likelihood, though there is no conclusive evidence, Mather Byles.

Of a naturally humorous bend of mind, Byles—possibly still rankled at James Franklin's characterization of him as "a young scribbling Collegian" —sent off to the *Gazette* a good-natured letter, dated in Cambridge May 25, 1772, some ten days after Silence Dogood's attack on Harvard appeared. He leapt with delight on the plagiarism charge's coming from the *Courant*, of all places, and at the mauled metaphor of the plow's ascending the steps to a throne. The letter got directly to the point:

Sir, Pray Desire *Couranto* no more to put upon *Plagius* for fear of hurting himself. I am a Person that have occasion to look into a pretty large number of Books in a Year, which makes me capable of discovering the shameful Thefts of *Couranto* himself, as well as of other less Polite and Inferior Writers. An whole Paper of *Idleness* was taken out of a Book Entitled the *Gentlemans Calling*, written by the Author of the *Whole Duty of Man*; A few weeks ago we had a Paper very nicely differencing the Characters of *the Man of Honour*, and the religious different Principal of each in the same point of vertue: Because, I have used my self these several Years to writing Indexe's, the Reader may find that Discourse in the *Guardian*, Volumn second, page 292. No. 161.——Altho' that Paper cost Mr. *Couranto* but an hour and thirty-three minutes by the Watch (as his Friends offer to depose upon Oath) yet it cost Nestor Ironside [pseudonym of its original author] a-matter of Six Weeks.
As for their Thefts from the Tatlers, Spectators, &c. I omit them; concluding this Story: Dr. [Robert] *South* once having heard at a certain Parish Church a Curate preaching One of the Doctors own Sermons; He very candidly thanked the Minister for his Excellent Discourse; further asking him, Sir, I am sensible that your Avocations from your Studies are frequent, and your Wordly Encumbrances many, pray Sir, how much Time does the studying such a Discourse cost you; to whom the Minister with an Air of Pride and Appreciation replied——I don't know, Sir, perhaps three days,——A Quickster I protest quoth the Doctor, it cost me three Weeks.

I am
Your servant *John Harvard*.
P.S. Is not Couranto a fine Rhetorician, and a correct writer, when he says in his last but One,
   "Now I observed that the whole Tribe, who entred into the Temple
   "with me, began to climb the Throne, but the work
   "proving troublesome and difficult to most of them *they*
   "*withdraw their hands from the Plow*, &c." Friend, who
ever heard of entring a Temple and ascending the Magnificent Steps of a

Throne with a *Plough in his Hand! O rare Allegory!* Well done Rustic Couranto![28]

The Harvard letter of Silence Dogood may well have given Benjamin Franklin more satisfaction from the stir that it created than from any opportunity it afforded him of putting the college in its place. The letter in the *Gazette* would have seemed to him good-tempered and certainly not vindictive or overly grave, but James Franklin, of a more serious bend and full of pride in the integrity of his paper and appropriately sensitive to charges of plagiarism, took a stern view of the *Gazette* letter subscribed "John Harvard," whom he described as "*cunning a Lad as we have at our College.*" James repeated, in no uncertain terms, his absolute disapproval of plagiarism; and there is no reason to believe that he did not mean what he said, once he discovered that some of his contributors had abused the confidence that he had placed in them: ". . . if I have any *Plageries* for my Correspondents, I will not thank them for their Assistance; for as a Lyar is not believ'd when he speaks Truth, so the best pieces in the *Courant* (tho' wrote by some among ourselves) will be thought the Produce of Foreign Wits, if I am at all impos'd upon by those who prey upon other Men's Writings, without doing them the Justice of quoting the Passages."[29] James felt sufficiently concerned about the plagiarism practice and its essential wrongness to devote a long letter, probably also by himself, to the subject in the same issue. In the letter, he seemed to admit that plagiarism may have intruded on his columns but to take the general attitude that such cases were unintentional—except, of course, when they were perpetrated at Harvard, upon which the letter also visited some ironic obiter dicta:

> Whenever we see a Letter in a publick Print dated at *Cambridge*, we are ready to conclude it comes from some Gentleman belonging to the Academy there. And accordingly we expect it to contain the Truth, good Sense, and (at least) civil Language.
> The Author of the late Letter in the *Boston Gazette* (a paper remarkable for Nonsense and Calumny) sign'd by *John Harvard*, and written we suppose by the Instigation of *Plagius*, (a Person of a haughty Temper, and very impatient of Reproof,) is pleas'd to say, that several whole Pieces in the *Courant* were borrow'd from other Authors; which (to say no worse of it) is a very gross Mistake, as will appear to any one who observes that a considerable Part of them had a particular Reference to Persons and Things among our selves.
> It is possible, a Man in writing on any Subject may very nearly conform to Authors he never read, and that both as to Matter and Expression. And when a Man has read Authors on the same Subject a considerable Time before he writes, he may use their Method, and many of their Expressions,

[28] *Boston Gazette*, May 21 to May 28, 1722.
[29] *New-England Courant*, No. 44 (May 28 to June 4, 1722).

and not know that he does so. And what confirms us in this Opinion, is, we are certain the Writers of those Letters in the *Courant*, which Mr. *Harvard* says are all borrow'd never read some of the Books he mentions, and had not seen the others for several years past.

Obviously, James Franklin took the plagiarism charge seriously, and his defense of episodes when it may have occurred was not as disingenuous as it may have appeared. Many experienced writers have been haunted by the dread that some passage that they have written may have been first said by someone whom they had read years earlier. But this would hardly apply to any sustained piece of writing, such as Matthew Adams's verbatim use of the 150-word excerpt from Swift. To such piratings James Franklin still brought genuinely unbending objections:

> To take whole Paragraphs from Books *Verbatim*, and neither mark them nor cite the Author, we condemn as criminal in all who practice it, except the Family of the *Harvards*, some of them being under a Necessity of appearing in *other Men's Cloaths*, or being slighted by the World. The Age we live in is very polite, (as well as censorious,) and their own dull, insipid Productions will never merit Applause. We have known some of the [Harvard] *Family* so free with Authors, as to borrow whole Pages in Folio, and deliver them as their own. A Friend of ours, going to hear a Discourse from a young *Harvard*, and knowing he would preach from the same text the next Sabbath, took with him a Course of Sermons on the same Subject, just brought over the *Atlantick*, and went with him [i.e., followed the student word for word] thro' several Pages. And some Time ago, one of the Family told us, he knew one of his Brethren take a printed Discourse, and (putting a Text at the Head of it) deliver it as his own with all the Assurance imaginable.
>
> But let Mr. *Harvard know*, that the Writers of the *Courant* have Stock enough of their own to live on, and to entertain, inform and edify the Publick.[30]

The extent to which Benjamin Franklin's nescient attack on Harvard evoked the strongest expressions of loyalty to *Courant* writers on the part of James Franklin was reflected in the extraordinary amount of space in the issue of May 28 to June 4, 1722, that he devoted to belittling the Byles letter—two full columns out of a total of four. In his ardor, he added an endorsement, in verse, of Silence Dogood's general indictment of Harvard students, only faintly suggesting that there might have been some "knowing" students among them. The verses were date-lined at Plymouth and signed "Crowdero," but they bore a strong stylistic resemblance to some earlier rhymes in the *Courant* known to have been written by James Franklin. Though they have been attributed to Benjamin,[31] they were

[30] Ibid.
[31] Morison, *Three Centuries of Harvard*, 61. Professor Morison mistakenly quotes the beginning five couplets of the verses as their conclusion.

clearly not his work, having none of the contrived clumsiness of his known verses; nor was it likely that he would have risked Silence Dogood's anonymity by submitting any comments, in verse or prose, on one of her letters. In any case, there was a hopeful note to the verses:

> *Long have the weaker Sons of Harvard strove*
> *To move our Rev'rence and command our Love,*
> *By Means, how sordid, 't is not hard to say,*
> *When all their Merit lies in M. and A.*
> *The knowing Sons of Harvard we revere,*
> *And in their just Defence will still appear;*
> *But every idle Fop who there commences,*
> *Shall never claim Dominion o'er our senses.*
> *We judge not of their Knowledge by their Air,*
> *Nor think the wisest Heads have curled Hair.*
> *May Parents, Ma'am, your Reflections mind,*
> *And be no more to Children's Dulness Blind.*
> *May your sharp Satyrs mend the Lazy Drone,*
> *Who by another's Help ascends the Throne*
> *And not by any Merit of his own.*
> *Then will both Church and State be truly blest*
> *With Men whose Worth will be by both Confest.*[32]

On the whole, the immediate response to Benjamin Franklin's unprecedented public attack on Harvard was far from ugly; it tended, on the contrary, to be almost good-natured. No one took the mutual plagiarism charges particularly seriously, except James Franklin, who had a stubborn, literal honesty about him that rejected any shadings or conditionings. Virtually all the rest of the Boston community with any interest in letters at all were constantly drawing a fuzzy line between imitation and plagiarism. It would be difficult to find, during the 1720s, among productions of the crop of aspiring young men dabbling in writing, a line of verse that was not in imitation of Pope or a line of prose that was not in imitation of Addison; in fact, a short-lived periodical at Harvard, published in manuscript form in 1721, called *The Telltale*, owed not only its manner to Addison's *Spectator* but its very name to his earlier paper, *The Tatler*.

As for Harvard's good name, it was not at an all-time high at the time that Franklin's Dogood fantasy appeared. For the first time in its history, a student had, four years earlier, sued the college for not giving him his master's degree, thus challenging its judgment and testing its authority, when Ebenezer Pierpont, of the class of 1715, brought an action against a tutor of the college, after first filing a complaint with Governor Samuel Shute, who peremptorily dismissed it at a session in his house attended by the Harvard Corporation and Pierpont, referring the matter back to the former, which was not helpful to Pierpont at all since he had already

[32] *New-England Courant*, No. 44 (May 28 to June 4, 1722).

publicly characterized the fellows of the Corporation as "Rogues, Dogs & tygars."[33] The Corporation *Uno Ore* Voted that the s^d Eben^r Pierpont ought not to be admitted to his Second Degree this [Commencement] day."[34] The college records added "The Presid^t and Fellows waited on his Excy [Governor Shute] and the Overseers that were together in the College-Hall, and reported the Opinion of the Corporation as above, Upon wch the Govr said well, there is an End of it, and no more to be s^d. . . ."[35]

Pierpont, abetted by such distinguished enemies of President Leverett as Cotton Mather, former Governor Joseph Dudley's son, Attorney General Paul Dudley, and Chief Justice Sewall, brought suit against one of the fellows in the civil court at Cambridge, which dismissed it on the grounds that only the Harvard Corporation had jurisdiction over the awarding of degrees by the college—a judgment that, in Leverett's words, really "put an end to an affair that was very troublesome, and *that which threatened the dissolution of the College.* . . ."[36] Mather used the fray to denounce Harvard both privately and publicly. Of the Commencement Day that saw Pierpont's repudiation, he wrote, "And this being the Day of the senseless Diversions, which they call, *the Commencement* at *Cambridge,* one of my special Errands unto Heaven, was to ask Blessings for the Colledge, and the Rescue of it from some wretched Circumstances in which it is now languishing,"[37] thus following a custom of boycotting Harvard commencements begun when Harvard rejected him for Leverett as president. Following the Pierpont affair, in which he had no real interest except to use it as an excuse further to harass the president and fellows, Mather embarked on a most mischievous course to the intended detriment of the college. Having already decided that the teaching of "Ethicks" at Harvard constituted "A vile Peece of Paganism"[38] and having fasted and prayed "that our Colledge, which is on many Accounts in a very neglected and unhappy Condition, and has been betray'd by vile Practices, may be restored to better Circumstances . . ."[39] Mather wrote to Governor Shute, urging that he intervene on behalf of "the abused and oppressed Pierpont," asserting authority over "(those unaccountably called) *the Overseers of the College*" and "the pretended President." Mather's craven letter to Shute, in which he flattered the governor unconscionably, would, of course, have wrecked the college as a free and independent institution of learning, and Mather was at his worst, in his curiously tortured and contradictory life, when he begged the governor, in

[33] College Papers in Harvard University Archives, I, 188.
[34] Harvard College Records, II, 441.
[35] Ibid.
[36] Leverett papers, quoted in Quincy, *History of Harvard University*, I, 219.
[37] Mather, *Diary*, II, 544.
[38] Ibid., 357.
[39] Ibid., 473.

the conclusion of his letter to conceal his identity as its author: "And your Excellency's incomparable goodness and wisdom will easily discern and approve the intentions of the freedom used in this letter, and leave it and its writer covered under the darkest concealment."[40] The stratagem failed, and Shute refused to compromise the independence and authority of the Harvard Corporation. Mather consequently took his battle against Harvard overseas and outside the family by urging Elihu Yale in London to support the new college in Saybrook, Connecticut, the last best hope of the New England Puritans, he wrote, as "the seminary from whence they expect the supply of all their synagogues,"[41] suggesting in no uncertain language that his generosity would result in the college's being named for him and later gloating to Governor Gurdon Saltonstall of Connecticut, "I confess, that it was a great and inexcusable presumption in me, to make myself so far the godfather of the beloved infant as to propose a name for it."[42] In 1721, the year before Benjamin Franklin's blast at Harvard, Mather appears to have been a prime if anonymous and ultimately unsuccessful mover in an effort to get Thomas Hollis to divert his philanthropic interest from Harvard to Yale,[43] at the very time that his own son, Samuel Mather, of the class of 1723, was subsisting at Harvard on the bounty provided by a Hollis scholarship, appreciation of which was fulsomely expressed by Mather to Hollis a matter of months before he sought to inspire Hollis to turn his support from Harvard to Yale. "But no person has more cause to celebrate your goodness [to Harvard] and acknowledge the hand of a gracious God inspiring you with it than he who now addresses you," Mather had written Hollis in the late summer of 1720, and he managed to attribute some of the credit for this "prospect of some advantage [to his son] from your beneficence and munificence" to his own virtuous character: ". . . some observers of such things were willing to interpret it as a recompense [remembering that Hollis was a Baptist] of my public appearance to own the church of the godly Baptists in my neighborhood, when some others refused that communion with them."[44]

Despite this long feud of Cotton Mather with Harvard, however, and despite the fact that it was at its peak at the very time that Benjamin Franklin ridiculed the college, the Mathers took an alarmed view of someone outside the family's discrediting the institution. After all, Cotton Mather, for all his contempt for the president, the fellows, and even the

[40] Quincy, *History of Harvard University,* Appendix XXXIV, I, 524.
[41] Ibid., Appendix XXXV, I, 526.
[42] Ibid., Appendix XXVI, I, 527. In the text (I, 226), Quincy misdates the letter as "the 25ᵗ of September"; it was dated "25ᵗʰ d. 6ᵗ month"—i.e., August (old style).
[43] The pleas were put to Hollis in anonymous letters, transmitted by Governor Saltonstall in July 1721; Quincy makes a very good case for Cotton Mather's having been the author of the appeals. Quincy, *History of Harvard University,* I, 227–29, 528.
[44] Silverman, *Letters of Cotton Mather,* 317–18.

more orthodox overseers, did send his son to Harvard and not to Yale. To Mather, there was nothing inconsistent in his behavior in secretly conspiring to embarrass Leverett and the Corporation, even at the price of weakening the college, and at the same time writing the president that he was entrusting his own son "unto your wise, and kind, and paternal tuition . . ." and soliciting "your civilities and benignities toward a child of so much good expectation."[45] The point was that, bitter as he felt about Harvard, Mather thought that, though he could be stinging in his criticism of the college, outsiders had no right to criticize it. And coming on the heels of its criticism of the clergy, the *Courant's* attack on Harvard represented not only an intolerable public nuisance but also an increasing public danger. It was a view shared by the Boston establishment and to be aggravated further by the subsequent journalistic activities of the Franklin brothers.

* * *

Wholly undeterred by the attempts of "John Harvard" to belittle his literary ability, not to mention his originality, Benjamin Franklin, through the person of Silence Dogood, launched within six weeks a much more telling and soundly based attack on the cultural life of Massachusetts—this time on the literary front, with which he was much more familiar, to begin with, than he was with life at Harvard. No less significantly, in this, the seventh Silence Dogood paper, he limited his satirical comment on the quality of the provincial culture to its reflection in the literature of the time, more specifically in the poetry, and even more specifically in the elegiac poetry—though there was little enough of any other kind in the first quarter of the eighteenth century to praise or to condemn. In doing so, however, he inevitably took up the cudgels with the clergy once again, for the principal authors of elegy were the clergy, as they were the principal authors of any verse at all that trickled from Puritan pens.

Franklin, a child of his century, had no deep feeling for poetry, though versification as a literary craft always interested him. When he fell in with James Ralph, a youth who became one of his first friends in Philadelphia and who was enchanted with both the reading and the writing of poetry, he let Ralph know that he thought such time ill spent: "I approv'd the amusing one's self with Poetry now and then, so far as to improve one's Language, but no farther."[46] He appeared to have neglected Shakespeare altogether, though the latter's works were in the *Courant* library; but something of the residue of Puritanism in him shone through in his taste, albeit somewhat controlled, for Milton, whose radiant "Hymn to the Creator" from *Paradise Lost* he quoted at length when he composed his per-

---

[45] Mather to John Leverett, July 31, 1719, ibid., 294.

[46] *Autobiography*, 90. Ralph failed as a poet but became so effective a political pamphleteer that the ministry of Henry Pelham (1743–54) paid him £300 a year *not* to write, since he was against its policies—in his writings, at least.

sonal "Articles of Belief" in 1728.[47] But when he suggested English authors for reading in his "Proposals Relating to the Education of Youth in Pennsylvania," Pope, alone among poets, was named as an exemplar "to be cultivated," though in the same paper Milton, ignored as a poet, was cited as an authority on the need for physical exercise, on the nature of justice, and on the teaching of natural sciences.[48] Even the inclusion of Pope on the reading list seemed to rest less on any poetic substance or point in his work than in his technical ability to be "clear and concise"— an ability not held by Franklin to be so considerable, nevertheless, that he did not devote a page of his autobiography to revising a couplet of an *Essay on Criticism* to make "the Lines stand more justly."[49]

The only poet to whom Franklin seemed really drawn in his life was the competent but second-order James Thomson, whose works apparently touched him, according to his own testimony in 1744, by which time he evidently had abandoned reading any other poet at all. "Whatever Thomson writes," he wrote his publisher friend in London, William Strahan, in his thirty-eighth year, "send me a dozen Copies of. I had read no Poetry for several years, and almost lost the Relish of it, till I met with his *Seasons* [Thomson's major and perhaps sole surviving work, originally published in four separate books, 1726-40]. That charming Poet has brought more Tears of Pleasure into my Eyes than all I ever read before."[50] The word "charming" was right for Thomson—he had a feeling for the real and took a delight in the ordinary that many readers found vastly refreshing in a didactic age, though he hardly qualified for another and more extravagant appraisal by Franklin: one of "the two best English Poets that ever were," the other being Milton.[51]

When Franklin was at work on the Dogood papers, he knew nothing of Thomson, who was then still a divinity student in Edinborough not yet diverted to poetry, and the apprentice's contact with English poetry was probably limited to what came his way in the fragments appearing in the *Spectator* (which also contained a critical analysis of Milton's verse running through several issues of the papers) and in other pamphlets and periodicals that turned up on the *Courant*'s premises. He also kept an eye on contemporary New England poetry. This was limited largely to elegies, for it was a necrophilic age, as the diaries of Cotton Mather, Judge Sewall, and their contemporaries sufficiently document; and its inclination toward the classics led those Puritans who were moved to poetic exercises to turn to the laments, the *elegeia*, of the ancient Greeks for a literary model. Their literary substance, of course, centered on the treatment of death as

[47] *Papers*, I, 101-9.
[48] Ibid., III, 397-421.
[49] *Autobiography*, 66.
[50] *Papers*, III, 13-14.
[51] Ibid., II, 24.

the point of life—not so much by way of intellectual paradox as, for better or worse, its essential spiritual denouement. But while the elegies of early Greece had moved on, by classical times, to celebrate the adventure of war and the glory of love, the elegy transplanted to England during the Renaissance remained by definition a song of lamentation, and it reached the peak of literary distinction there in 1637 with Milton's great but rambling poem "Lycidas," on the drowning of his college classmate, Edward King—a threnody that in mid-stanzas emphasized its lament of the tragic death of a young postulant for holy orders by indicting Church of England bishops who, "for their bellies sake, creep and intrude, and climb into the fold."[52] Cowley, Donne, Dryden, Pope, and a host of lesser talents felt duty-bound to write elegies (but none until 1821, bringing "Adonais," Shelley's renowned dirge for Keats, even approached "Lycidas" in quality). In New England, by the 1700s, elegies were so commonplace as to constitute a familiar form of folk poetry, much as epitaphs did. Through his dipping into English literature, Franklin saw that, despite its sad subject, the elegy did not have to be lachrymose. Matthew Prior's rollicking epitaph for "Saunt'ring Jack and Idle Joan," whose "Beer was strong; their Wine was *Port*;/Their Meal was large; their Grace was short,"[53] was quite possibly known to him; and if he had come across it in his reading, it would probably have confirmed an instinct that reflections on death need not be morbid. Certainly he was familiar with the non-Calvinist defiance in such elegies that found their way into the buoyant pages of *The Spectator* as that on the dowager Countess of Pembroke ("Death, ere thou hast kill'd another,/Fair and learn'd, good as she,/Time shall throw a Dart at thee"[54]) and with the grace of such lines, also in the *Spectator*, as Ambrose Philips's pastoral lament ("Breathe soft ye Winds, ye Waters gently flow,/Shield her ye Trees, ye Flowers around her grow . . ."[55]). Lacking the brooding preoccupation with death as the grim accounting that beset his Boston betters, Franklin saw their stream of elegies as morose to the point of egregiousness. Moreover, after his early efforts at versifying were mercifully brought to a halt by a sensible father, he developed a certain critical condescension toward the very level of rhyming that, undeterred, he may himself have indulged in indefinitely. In the seventh Dogood letter, however, he attempted no formal criticism of bad verse but undertook only to laugh it out of any claim to serious attention. His approach was sardonic: "It has been the Complaint of many Ingenious Foreigners, who have travell'd amongst us, *That good Poetry is not to be expected in New-England*. I am apt to Fancy, the Reason is, not because our Countreymen are altogether void of a Poetical Genius, nor yet because we have not those Advantages of Education which other Countries have,

[52] John Milton, "Lycidas," ll. 114–15.
[53] Matthew Prior, *Poems on Several Occasions* (1718).
[54] *Spectator*, No. 323 (March 11, 1712), Everyman's Library edition, III, 9. The lines were first ascribed to Ben Jonson but later to William Browne (ca. 1591–1645).
[55] Ibid., No. 400, III, 247.

but purely because we do not afford that Praise and Encouragement which is merited, when anything extraordinary of this Kind is produc'd among us. . . ."[56] Franklin knew very well that "Praise and Encouragement" had less to do with paucity of "good Poetry" in New England than did the formulistic, funereal jargon to which the elegy had descended in the hands of the clerical fraternity. The Reverend Nathaniel Pitcher, from his vantage point in Scituate, a harbor town, was absorbed by deaths at sea. He could write:

> What though his Mortal Body Serve as Dishes
> Instead of Feeding Worms, to feed the Fishes . . .

and of another:

> Your Nuptial Knot, the fatal Stroke unty'd,
> By Heavens's Decree, on the Atlantick wide . . .

The Reverend Samuel Wigglesworth, of Ipswich, confused his anatomy on another drowning:

> Add one kind drop unto his watry tomb,
> Weep the relenting Eyes and Ears . . .

and loftily dismissed the muse—"Away fond Muse, I ask no help of thee . . ."—and got none as he poured forth a flood of adjectives:

> He Liv'd and Died Courteous,
> Chearful, Serene, Facetious
> Loving, Belov'd, Officious,
> And Pious too, I do believe.[57]

And the Reverend Edward Holyoke of Marblehead, later president of Harvard, who had mastered doggerel as an almanac-maker while serving as librarian and tutor at Harvard, was probably responsible for:

> Come let us mourn, for we have lost a Wife, a Daughter, and a Sister,
> Who has lately taken Flight, and greatly we have mist her . . .
> *Some little Time* before she yielded up her Breath,
> She said, I ne'er shall hear one Sermon more on Earth.
> She kept her Husband *some little Time* before she expir'd,
> Then leaned her Head the Pillow on, just out of Breath and tir'd.[58]

[56] *New-England Courant*, No. 47 (June 18 to June 25, 1722).

[57] The examples are from Sibley, *Biographical Sketches*, V, 236, 407, 492. An elegy found in 1934 in a facsimile manuscript and now at the University of Pennsylvania was attributed by Carl Van Doren, in *Benjamin Franklin* (New York, 1938), 25, to Franklin; but the only evidence is the subscription "B.F." not in Franklin's handwriting. The editors of the *Papers*, in the absence of stronger, more direct evidence, have constructed (I, 46) a persuasive case against its inclusion in Franklin's works.

[58] *New-England Courant*, No. 47 (June 18 to June 25, 1722). Authorship by Holyoke was suggested by George F. Horner in *Studies in Philology*, XXXVII (1940), 518n.; an examination of the alumni records of Harvard College reveals no other "Doctor H----k," as the *Courant* identified him, in the Boston area.

This last, though some four years old when young Franklin came upon it, was the major object of Silence Dogood's attention in her pointed consideration of the state of the elegy in New England.

The subject of the Holyoke dirge was Mehitabel Browne (Mrs. John) Kittle or Mehitabell Kitel, as Franklin and the *Courant* had it, who was married at Salem in June 1718, died in the adjoining town of Beverly almost exactly three months later, and was elegized presumably by Dr. Holyoke of Marblehead, which also adjoined Salem. Having pointed out that poetry in New England suffered from a lack of sufficient praise and that she proposed, "when I meet with a Good-Piece of New-England Poetry, to give it a suitable encomium," Silence Dogood proceeded to shower praise, all for the wrong reasons, on the worst piece of poetry that she had met with, "in order to encourage the Author to go on, and bless the World with more and more Excellent Productions." The letter praised the Kittle effusion for its "Elegance of Stile" and its "Smoothness of Rhime," both of which it painfully lacked, and then invited a favorable comparison of "the Threefold Appellation in the first Line a Wife, a Daughter, and a Sister" to a "Line in the celebrated [Isaac] Watts, Gunston, the Just, the Generous, and the Young." Silence Dogood, feigning great seriousness, applied an outrageous quantitative test to the poetic merits of the two excerpts: "The latter only mentions three Qualifications of *one* Person who was deceased, which therefore could raise Grief and Compassion but for *One*. Whereas the former, (*our most excellent Poet*) gives his Reader a Sort of the Death of *Three Persons, viz. a Wife, a Daughter, and a Sister,* which is *Three Times* as great a Loss as the Death of *One*, and consequently must raise *Three Times* as much Grief and Compassion in the Reader."

What Franklin was getting after was the tendency of the New England elegy to become a piece of mechanical rhetoric, achieving both the wrong emphasis and the wrong language—in short, the drift toward the empty formula and the ridiculous hyperbole. For indifferent as Franklin was to poetry, he had a craftsman's respect for the art of versification, even to the point of giving it up himself when his father convinced him that he was no good at it. And he was no admirer of innovation or the breaking of established literary principles for its own sake. Of the author of the Kittle elegy, he said sardonically, ". . . the Author had (to his Honour) invented a new Species of Poetry, which wants a Name, and was never before known. . . . Now 'tis Pity that such an Excellent Piece should not be dignify'd with a particular Name; and seeing it cannot justly be called, either *Epic, Sapphic, Lyric,* or *Pindaric*, nor any other Name yet invented, I presume it may, (in Honour and Remembrance of the Dead) be called the KITELIC. Thus much in the Praise of *Kitelic Poetry*."

Franklin was not through with his satirical treatment of the New England elegy, however, and went on to his most devastating point: that the elegy had so degenerated as a literary form under the custodianship of the clerics that one could practically write a recipe for it—in the words of Alexander Pope, whose satirical recipe for an epic may well have inspired Franklin, "Write dull receits how poems may be made."[59] Silence Dogood, in an aside that lay the insipid dilution of the elegy squarely at the door of the clergy, said that she had inherited the "Receipt" from her reverend husband, as though it were just another asset of the estate, much as Franklin himself had referred to the gift of the sermon collection with which his Uncle Benjamin had planned to present him, should he enter the ministry, "as a stock to set up with." The first ingredient prescribed by Franklin's recipe for elegies was the title. He surmised most potential authors had a "ready made" stock of titles; but, if they had not, he cautioned his readers to make certain "not to omit the Words *Aetatus Suae* [year of the deceased's age], which will Beautify it exceedingly." Coming to its subject matter, he got to the heart of the erosion of the elegy, which was, essentially, the reduction to a vulgar indiscriminateness of a literary form of which a heroic discriminateness had once been implicitly the major characteristic: "Take one of your Neighbours who has lately departed this Life; it is no great matter at what Age the Party dy'd, but it will be best if he went away suddenly, being *Kill'd, Drown'd* or *Froze to Death*." Having made his point quickly and sharply as to the subject matter, Franklin went on to the formulist pattern that every elegy in New England was tortured to fit: ". . . take all his [the departed's] Virtues, Excellencies, &c. and if he have not enough, you may borrow some to make up a sufficient Quantity: To these add his last Words, dying Expressions, &c. if they are to be had; mix all these together, and be sure you *strain* them well. Then season all with a Handful or two of Melancholly Expressions, such as, *Dreadful, Deadly, cruel cold Death, unhappy Fate, weeping Eyes*, &c. Have mixed all these Ingredients well, put them into the empty Scull of some *young Harvard*; (but in Case you have ne'er a One at Hand, you may use your own,) there let them Ferment for the Space of a Fortnight, and by that Time they will be incorporated in a Body, which take out, and having prepared a sufficient Quantity of double Rhimes, such as, *Power, Flower; Quiver, Shiver; Grieve us, Leave us; tell you, excel you; Expeditions, Physicians; Fatigue him, Intrigue him*; &c. you must spread all upon Paper, and if you can procure a Scrap of Latin to put at the end, it will garnish it mightily; then having affixed your Name at the Bottom, with a *Maestus Composuit* [composed in sorrow], you will have an Excellent Elegy." Franklin then appended a gratuitous note: "*N.B.* This Receipt will serve when a Female is the Subject of your Elegy, provided you borrow a greater Quantity of Virtues, Excellencies, &c."

[59] Alexander Pope, *An Essay on Criticism*, l. 115. Franklin probably encountered Pope's early verse somewhere; though it was not listed in the *Courant* library, *The Spectator* and the *Guardian* referred to it frequently and it appeared in several miscellanies from 1709 onward.

Amid the company of James Franklin and the Honest Wags the burlesquing of the clerical elegy found a hearty welcome, and the notion was thought good enough to press a bit further. It was obviously discussed by the editor and his circle sufficiently in advance of publication to afford time for one of them to sit down and write a "panegyrick," sixteen decasyllabic couplets, in mock praise of "the Sage and Immortal Doctor H——k on his Incomparable Elegy," ending with the suggestion of a wry reward for him, which were published in the same issue of the *Courant* and appended, with the editor's improbable note that they just happened to arrive at the same time as the Dogood letter. It was an unnecessary embellishment, for it did less successfully in verse, and more heavy-handedly, what young Franklin had already done in prose:

> Thou hast, great Bard, in thy Mysterious Ode,
> Gone in a Path which ne'er before was trod,
> And freed the World from the vexatious Toil,
> Of Numbers, Metaphors, of Wit and Stile,
> Those Childish Ornaments, and gravely chose,
> The middle Way between good Verse and Prose.
>
> . . . . .
>
> For thou with matchless Skill and Judgment fraught,
> Hast Learned Doggerel to Perfection brought.
>
> . . . . .
>
> Then least what is your due should not [now?] be said,
> Write your own Elegy, against you're Dead.[60]

Holyoke, whom, when he was later named president of Harvard, a fellow minister called "as orthodox a Calvinist as any man; though I look upon him too much of a gentleman, and of too catholic a temper, to cram his principles down any man's throat,"[61] left no sign in his long diaries of resenting the *Courant* sallies, if he was their object, and he lived to the good age of eighty, a calm and civilizing influence on both colony and college. But the word "kitelic" to characterize bad elegies entered the vocabulary of the *Courant* and its contributors. In the second succeeding issue of the *Courant* there appeared, from a Rhode Island contributor, some rather melodious idyllic lines, whose author denied "that they should be thought to run Parrallel with the lofty *Kitelic* Strains which flow from those celebrated Bards, that have had the Advantage of breathing a more Sublime Air than we who are confined within these narrow Limits."[62] The Rhode Islander's pastoral inspired another contributor, noting that it fell "far short of either the *Pindaric* or *Kitelic* modes," to compose lines identifying "Thou first deviser of *Kitelic* Verse" as "the mighty Product of *Harvardine* skill,"[63] and almost a year later a versifier in

[60] *New-England Courant*, No. 47 (June 18 to June 25, 1722).
[61] Sibley, *Biographical Sketches*, V, 271.
[62] *New-England Courant*, No. 49 (July 2 to July 9, 1722).
[63] Ibid., No. 53 (July 30 to August 6, 1722).

the *Courant* made reference to the "Kitel" elegiac form: "Or can he half your Praise rehearse/In *Lyrick* or *Kitelick* verse?"[64]

Good-natured as this running *Courant* attack on the elegy that Franklin launched was, it nevertheless hit the Puritan clergy at a doubly vulnerable spot, the role as the final interpreter of the significance of life and death and also as the establisher and conservator of literary standards. The Silence Dogood letter did enough, in a way difficult for the ministerial establishment to answer without being made to appear even more ridiculous than it was made out to be, to cast doubt on the authority and dignity of the clergy in both roles. The attack, however gentle in Benjamin Franklin's youthful and not too deeply disturbed essay, took on bite and severity a few weeks later in the hands of James and his colleagues that could not have avoided causing the clergy the gravest concern, because it attributed to them, with no demonstrated justification, the most sordid of motives in eulogizing the dead: "Funeral Complements are for the most part bestow'd on the Rich & Honourable: not that *they* are the most deserving, for mean obscure People may be, and often are full as pious as they; but the misery is they are not able to bequeath such large Donations to the Orators, to Embalm their Memory, and fix an *Asterism* to their Names. Hence, it comes to pass, that men of sordid selfish Principles, come to be extol'd for publick-Spirited Men and Eminent Saints after their Deccase (for 'till then no one knew of any Good that they ever did, but to themselves,) and many of the precious Sons of *Sion* (whose Death is as sore a Judgment to a Land) are past over in Silence, because they are destitute of Money: by which it plainly appears, that it is Wealth and not Vertue, Gold and not Grace, that will embalm a Man's Memory after he is dead."[65] In Silence Dogood's derision of the "Kitelic" elegy, Benjamin Franklin had launched the *Courant* and its audacious editors on another collision course with the clerical establishment.

* * *

The course was not averted when Silence Dogood turned her attention to an area which the clergy had also staked out as their professional domain: the observation and criticizing of public morals. As early as the fifth Dogood paper, Franklin had specifically made it known that Mrs. Dogood had "left her Seat in the Country . . . to tarry for the Summer Season in Boston, the better to "compleat her Observations of the present reigning Vices of the Town."[66] By the end of the summer, Franklin thought Silence sufficiently qualified to report on two of the town's more conspicuous vices—drunkenness and prostitutes' soliciting on the streets. The reports and accompanying reflections possess not a single aspect of having been written by the middle-aged widow of a country parson. They show no more signs of having been written by an average sixteen-year-old boy.

[64] Ibid., No. 87 (March 25 to April 1, 1723).
[65] Ibid., No. 57 (August 27 to September 3, 1722).
[66] Ibid., No. 43 (May 21 to May 28, 1722).

They sound like the sharp observations, the urbane evaluations, and the witty style of a young man about town, shocked at nothing, amused by everything, and tolerant of most things. Therein lay the certainty of the twelfth and thirteenth Dogood letters' becoming yet another set of thorns in the side of the real custodians of Boston's morals.

On the consuming of alcoholic beverages, Benjamin Franklin and the Mathers were in agreement on three essentials: one, that drinking them was desirable; two, that excessively drinking them was deplorable; and, three, that there was a good deal of excessive drinking going on in the town of Boston. Increase Mather, still at eighty-three in 1722 the ancient patriarchal presence of the Mathers, had declared years earlier, in the second of well over 150 collections of sermons that he published in his lifetime, a volume called Wo to Drunkards, "Drink is in it self a good creature of God, and to be received with thankfulness, but the abuse of drink is from Satan; the wine is from God, but the Drunkard is from the Devil." But in the same publication, Increase Mather allied himself with the cause of public drinking: "I know that in such a town as this there is need of such Houses, and no sober [sic] Minister will speak against the Licencing of them. . . ."[67] And all the Mathers shared in the huge quantities of liquor imbibed at such ceremonial occasions as ordinations and funerals. Moreover, robust drinking was part of the heritage of New England Puritanism. Water was regarded with suspicion from the first planting of the Bible Commonwealth, and the company of the elect not only avoided taking it internally (it was said to be disastrous to the health) but also refrained from applying it externally to their persons (apparently on the same grounds); the most frequent uses to which water was put, according to the formal records, was for transport and for drowning, an event that occurred with such frequency among the coves, creeks, and inlets of the Boston peninsula that it may well have contributed to Bostonians' distaste for water and their distrust of it. In any case, the Puritans fell to the converting of apples into hard cider and apple brandy (applejack), of grain into ale and beer, of grapes into wine, and of sugar imported by sea into rum, and by 1722 excessive drinking was commonplace. The town was full of establishments licensed to dispense liquor to its twelve thousand inhabitants: there were forty-two retailers of liquor, thirty-four inns, four common grocers licensed to sell liquor, and two coffeehouses licensed, like inns, to serve liquor—a total of eighty-two, or one for about every twenty families.[68] "I have seen certain taverns," Cotton Mather lamented, "where the pictures of horrible devourers were hanged out for the signs; and, thought I, 'twere well if such signs were not sometimes too *significant*: alas, men have their estates *devoured*, their names *devoured*, their hours *devoured*, and their very souls *devoured*, when they are so besotted that

---

[67] Increase Mather, Wo to Drunkards (Cambridge, 1673), 4.
[68] New England Historical and Genealogical Register, 1877, 108.

they are not in their element, except they be tipling at such houses."[69] In lower circles of the town, strong drink became a steady adjunct of life, and while drunkenness to the point of stupor was punishable by a session in the stocks and the wearing of a huge "D," for drunkard, it was as often regarded by the wearer and his companions as a merit badge as it was considered by others as a mark of censure. When the town sought further to humiliate drinkers by publicly posting a roster of "Reputed drunkards & comon Tiplers,"[70] it proved as much an honor roll among the incorrigible as it did an *argumentum ad verecundiam* to their judges. On the upper levels of provincial societies, the custom of drinking endless toasts had arisen in the earliest days of the colony and, despite the passing of legislation prohibiting them as early as 1639 as an "abominable practice," continued well into the eighteenth century. Periodical blasts from the clergy were unavailing. "It is too notorious to be denied," Cotton Mather complained, "that it was originally a heathen custom to drink those which were called, 'the cups of health,' in token of respect to the object mentioned in their cups," but his storming against the practice had no more effect than the law, and it is significant that his objection to it consisted less in the nature of the drink consumed than in the rhetorical accompaniment—the toast was "a relique of Paganism."[71]

As drunkenness persisted and yet the taking of strong drink was approved nearly universally, the problem arose as to what constituted the distinction between healthful drinking, endorsed and even practiced by the ministers, and the "excessive" drinking or drunkenness that so distressed them. The Plymouth colony had tried to arrive at definition at the beginning: "And by Drunkennesse is understood a person that either lisps or faulters in his speech by reason of overmuch drink, or that staggers in his going, or that vomitts by reason of excessive drinking, or cannot follow his calling."[72] The Massachusetts Bay Colony was somewhat less specific: "Every person found drunken" was determined to be so because he was "bereaved or disabled in the use of his understanding, appearing in his speech or gesture."[73] Judge Sewall, in a letter rebuking his friend, Major Nathaniel Saltonstall, for having "drunk to excess," was even more inclusive, though in his language more gentle, with his definition: ". . . your head and hand were rendered less usefull than at other times."[74] But it was a time and place of robust drinking, alcoholic beverages in themselves accepted and appreciated as a divine benevolence; and either abstinence or prohibition would have been inconceivable to the Puritan

---

[69] Mather, *Magnalia Christi Americana*, I, 100.
[70] *Report of the Record Commissioners of the City of Boston* (Boston, 1876–1909), XI, 126.
[71] Mather, *Magnalia Christi Americana*, II, 265.
[72] *Plymouth Laws* (Plymouth, 1889), 84.
[73] *General Laws of the Massachusetts Colony* (Boston, 1658), 44.
[74] Sewall, *Diary*, I, 373.

mind. Drunkenness was despised not because drink was inherently evil but because its abuse was irresponsible—a violation of the compact between God who provided it and man who benefited from it. "A Flood of excessive *Drinking*, hath begun to drown very much of *Christianity*, yea, and of *Civility* itself, in many places,"[75] Cotton Mather had declared in some "Articles of Confession" which he appointed himself to compose and promulgate and which were distinguished for, if nothing else, his uncharacteristic lapse in subordinating Christianity to civility.

Young Franklin's indictment of drunkenness in Silence Dogood's letter was inspired not by the sources of distress that rankled Cotton Mather but by the fact that it rendered men aesthetically repellent and socially inefficient. By September 1722, when it was written, he had probably made his way well into the eighth and final volume of *The Spectator* and encountered Addison's essay of July 19, 1714, which also took an aesthetic, social look at the problem—particularly the social phenomenon that accounted drunkenness an offense somewhat glorious and less grievous than humorous. "No Vices are so incurable as those which Men are apt to glory in," Addison wrote. "One would wonder how Drunkenness should have the good Luck to be of this Number." *The Spectator* regarded drunkenness, on the other hand, as a cardinal sin because it diminished, even contradicted, the command of reason—the rule of civility in the Augustan age of Addison: "The sober Man, by the Strength of Reason, may keep under and subdue every Vice or Folly to which he is most inclined; but Wine makes every latent Seed sprout up in the Soul, and shew it self; it gives Fury to the Passions, and Force to those Objects which are apt to produce them. . . . It often turns the Good-natured Man into an Ideot, and the Cholerick into an Assasin." There was something antihumanistic about drunkenness that disturbed the usually imperturbable Addison: "He who jests upon a Man that is drunk, injures the Absent."[76]

Like Addison, Franklin allied himself with the humanistic arguments against excessive drinking, rather than the diabologenic theory of Mather that the devil was behind it all just, in a manner of speaking, for the hell of it. To Franklin, as to Addison, drunkenness contradicted reason and therefore diminished men; and, in diminishing men, it rendered them singularly and abnormally unattractive—"shew them in the most odious Colours," as Addison put it. Oddly enough, however, Franklin at sixteen went more perceptively and more sophisticatedly into the subject than Addison did at forty-two. Franklin, a child of the Puritans and not wholly neglectful of some of their earthier assumptions, began his essay with the merits of alcohol, its beneficial aspects, which Addison ignored but to

[75] Mather, *Diary*, I, 215.
[76] *Spectator*, No. 569 (July 19, 1714), Everyman's Library edition, IV, 291. The axiom is from Publilius Syrus: "*Qui ebrium ludificat laedit absentem*," according to Addison, but the original says "*litigat*"—disputes—rather than "*ludificat*"—derides.

which Franklin devoted over a third of his text. "I doubt not but *moderate Drinking* has been improv'd [i.e., usefully employed] for the Diffusion of Knowledge among the ingenius Part of Mankind, who want the Talent of a ready Utterance, in order to discover the Conceptions of their Minds in an entertaining and intelligible Manner 'Tis true, drinking does not *improve* our Faculties, but it enables us to *use* them; and therefore I conclude, that much Study and Experience, and a little Liquor, are of absolute Necessity for some Tempers, in order to make them accomplish'd Orators. Dic[k] Ponder discovers an excellent Judgment when he is inspir'd with a Glass or two of *Claret*, but he passes for a Fool among those of small Observation, who never saw him the better for Drink." Having made this perspicacious comment, Franklin then allowed Silence Dogood to digress for an unlikely and gratuitous comment on the loquacity of women, borrowed intact from another of Addison *Spectators*, which observed, "It has been said in the Praise of some Men, that they could talk whole Hours together upon any thing; but it must be owned to the Honour of the other Sex, that there are many among them who can talk whole Hours together upon nothing."[77]

Having paid his respects to the more salubrious qualities of strong drink, Franklin condemned its excessive use as a negation of the human responsibility to act within "The *Restraints of* Reason." This is what really went against Franklin's grain with regard to drunkenness. He took a high view of the capacity of human kind to govern its own destiny by rational behavior, which included rational discourse and human relationships based on reason and not on emotion. Significantly, he headed his essay with a Latin proverb, "*Quod est in cordi, est in ore ebrii*"—"What is in the heart [of the sober man] is in the mouth of the drunkard"—reflecting a principle that seemed to have guided Franklin his entire life, for, though expressions of benevolence were characteristic of him until his death, expressions of emotion were notably absent even, in his relations with his wife, for example, to the point of the appearance of insensitivity. Even worse, drunkenness distorted a man, misrepresented him both to himself and to others. "What Pleasure," he asked, "can the Drunkard have in the Reflection, that, while in his Cups, he retain'd only the Shape of a Man, and acted the Part of a Beast; or that from reasonable Discourse a few Minutes before, he descended to Impertinence and Nonsense? . . . 'Tis strange to see Men of a Regular Conversation become rakish and profane when intoxicated with Drink, and yet more surprizing to observe, that some who appear to be the most profligate Wretches when sober, become mightily religious in their Cups, and will then, and at no other Time address their Maker, but when they are destitute of Reason, and actually affronting him. Some shrink in the Wetting [i.e., drinking], and others

[77] Ibid., II, 232. *New-England Courant*, No. 58 (September 3 to 10, 1722).

swell to such an unusual Bulk in their Imaginations, that they can in an Instant understand all Arts and Sciences, by the liberal Education of a little vivifying *Punch,* or a sufficient Quantity of other exhilerating Liquor."

It was a masterly summary of the social effects of drunkenness—clear, concise, strong, neither righteous nor maudlin. Certainly it could not have given offense to the clergy or magistrates. But Franklin, who knew the streets, taverns, and wharves of Boston thoroughly, moved on to enjoy himself with a venture into a lexicography of the vulgar terms relating to drunkenness, none of which would have been remotely within the vocabulary of Silence Dogood and all of which unquestionably impressed the clergy and magistrates as exposing a serious matter of public morals to frivolity and facetiousness. Franklin found his exercise so intriguing and memorable that he repeated it almost verbatim fifteen years later in his *Pennsylvania Gazette,* though without any attendant moral judgment.[78] In any case, it was young Franklin's opinion that semantics were employed by drunkards to disguise their offense—a somewhat feeble case since most of the locutions were applied to the state of drunkenness by other than the indulgers themselves. But, Franklin wrote, "It argues some Shame in the Drunkards themselves, in that they have invented numberless Words and Phrases to cover their Folly, whose proper Significations are harmless, or have no Signification at all. They are seldom known to be *drunk,* tho' they are very often *boozey, cogey, tipsey, fox'd, merry, mellow fuddl'd, groatable, Confoundely cut, See two Moons,* are *Among the Philistines, In a very good Humour, See the Sun,* or, *The Sun has shone upon them;* they *Clip the King's English,* are *Almost froze, Feavourish, In their Altitudes, Pretty well enter'd,* &c. In short, every Day produces some new Word or Phrase which might be added to the Vocabulary of the *Tiplers:* But I have chose to mention these few, because if at any Time a Man of Sobriety and Temperance happens to *cut himself confoundedly,* or is *almost froze,* or *feavourish,* or accidentally *sees the Sun,* &c. he may escape the Imputation of being *drunk,* when his Misfortune comes to be related."

In her next letter, Silence Dogood compounded whatever distress she had caused the establishment by her lighter references to the evil of drunkenness by making even lighter references, and even less compatible with the character and background that he had given Silence Dogood, to the far graver transgression of prostitution. Franklin was undoubtedly acquainted with the *Spectator* essays of January 4 and January 14, 1712, which looked upon prostitution with more critical comment on its patrons, promoters, and social roots than on its practitioners, who were treated with compassion, and, of course, from the point of view of an urbane observer in Queen Anne's London. "To do otherwise than this," Richard Steele wrote, "would be to act like a pedantick Stoick, who thinks

---

[78] *Pennsylvania Gazette,* January 13, 1727.

all Crimes alike, and not like an impartial Spectator, who looks upon
them with all the circumstances that diminish or enhance the Guilt."[79]
Steele took a particularly severe view of aging gentlemen, of opulent
means but reduced potency—"such as can only lay waste and not enjoy
the soil"—whom he charged with commonly furnishing the first introduction of young women to the business of selling sex, and of the madams
("Haggs") who exploited the girls. "With these Preparatives the Haggs
break their Wards by little and little, till they are brought to lose all Apprehensions of what shall befal them in the Possession of younger Men."
With regard to the exploited—"those who offend only against themselves"—*The Spectator* lay their situation "to the uneasy Perplexity under
which they lived under senseless and severe Parents, to the Importunity of
Poverty, to the Violence of a Passion in its Beginning well grounded. . . ."

The social concern characteristically shown by Steele played no part at
all in the observations on streetwalkers in Boston put into the mouth of
Silence Dogood by Benjamin Franklin, however appropriate such concern
would have been to her character and values. Instead, Franklin took a
light, rollicking view far more likely in a robust, somewhat lusty youth
who had broken loose from family and church controls and who had developed a taste for the boisterous life of the waterfront. Of all the letters
of Silence Dogood it was the most improbable, as he had his country
widow wandering at night around the streets of Boston, falling into company with "a Crowd of Tarpolins [sailors] and their Doxies," delighting in
their "eager and amorous Emotions of Body" and in the antics of a pair of
them who, on this late summer night of Silence's rambling, fell rolling to
the ground. But Silence was even more captivated, and rather merrily so,
by "a Company of Females I soon after came up with, who, by throwing
their Heads to the Right and Left, at every one who pass'd by Them, I
concluded came out with no other Design than to revive the Spirit of
Love in Disappointed Batchelors, and expose themselves to Sale to the
first Bidder."

Benignly looking upon these zealous women of the street as public benefactors, Silence Dogood ended her amiable animadversions on a subject,
most disturbing to Puritan moralists, with the utterly preposterous proposition that streetwalkers should be encouraged because they had a stimulating effect both on the sense of well-being of men and on the leather
business by wearing out shoes faster than more sedentary occupations:
"Upon the whole I conclude, That our *Night-Walkers* are a Set of People,
who contribute very much to the Health and Satisfaction of those who
have been fatigu'd with Business or Study, and occasionally observe their
pretty Gestures and Impertinencies. But among Men of Business, the
Shoemakers, and other Dealers in Leather, are doubly oblig'd to them,
inasmuch as they exceedingly promote the Consumption of their Ware:

[79] *Spectator,* No. 274, Everyman's Library edition, II, 317.

and I have heard of a *Shoemaker*, who being ask'd by a noted Rambler, *Whether he could tell how long her Shoes would last*; very prettily answer'd, *That he knew how many Days she might wear them, but not how many Nights; because they were then put to a more violent and irregular Service than when she employ'd her self in the common Affairs of the House.*"[80]

The whole thing was unquestionably the product of youthful exuberance, perhaps with an element of joyous rebellion against a stern society, but certainly not a serious and probably not even a conscious effort to encourage vice. Nevertheless, it seemed to be such in an atmosphere of mounting concern about the essential changes taking place in the New Jerusalem, as the irresistible forces of commerce, of external communications in the form of imported books and periodicals from London, and of the social and cultural ferment generated by new arrivals, not interested in the Bible State as such, overcame the Puritan priests' power to stop them. Destined as he was to see the Boston of his father and his grandfathers swallowed up by all sorts of intrusive elements, Cotton Mather recorded in anguish the existence of "Houses in this Town, where there are young Women of a very debauched Character and extreamly Impudent; unto whom there is a great Resort of young men,"[81] among whom was Cotton's own son, bearing the noble name Increase: ". . . an Harlot big with a Bastard, Accuses my poor Son Cressy, and lays her Belly to him. Oh! Dreadful Case! Oh, Sorrow beyond any that I have mett withal! what shall I do now for the foolish Youth! what for my afflicted and abased Family . . . oh, ye Humiliations!"[82] The tragic odyssey of young Increase Mather made a profound impression on his father as to what was happening to Boston life, for Mather was a deeply emotional man, one who took family relationships and responsibilities very seriously. He had a very genuine, if fumblingly displayed, affection for his children, indeed for all his kinsmen, and was deeply distressed at the introduction of his oldest surviving son, Increase, to the tawdry life surrounding the bawdy houses, and his subsequent downfall and death at sea at twenty-five; and he made agonized efforts to rehabilitate his son. "And what is my Duty in relation to the incorrigible Prodigal,"[83] he wrote, in total bewilderment that, for all his alliance with God, he was wholly unable to manage a situation in his own household, as Increase went from calamity to calamity. For Cotton Mather, the deterioration of morals had become more than a doctrinal matter, had invaded his own family circle, and had left him personally shaken, frustrated, and perplexed. Certainly, the night life of the town that so

[80] *New-England Courant*, No. 60 (September 17 to September 24, 1722).
[81] Mather, *Diary*, II, 129.
[82] Ibid., 484.
[83] Ibid., 611.

beguiled Silence Dogood would have seemed to him and his ministerial colleagues a frightening repudiation of all that they and their forebears had sought as outward and visible signs of an inner godliness. The concern was not limited to the clergy. The selectmen, too, constantly warred with the tendency of taverns to broaden their functions to serve as places of assignation.

James Franklin represented the *Courant* as also disturbed by the repercussions that the commercializing of sex was beginning to develop, and made it clear, as young Increase Mather's antics did, that it was not limited to the lower social levels or to the drifting populace of the waterfront. In the early spring of 1722, he published in the *Courant* the piece, written by Captain Taylor, "to acquaint the Town, that there is an House not an Hundred Doors from the *old South Church*, said to be kept by a very remarkable *British Woman*, who in the Summer Season sometimes makes her publick Appearance in a handsome Jacket, edg'd with a fashionable Gold Lace, wearing a monstrous hoop'd Petticoat and a black Hat with a Gold Edging. This *little Prude of Pleasure* would do well to advertise [i.e., advise] her Nocturnal Gallants (such as Lawyers, Sea-Officers, Journeyman Gentlemen, Merchants Apprentices, and the like) that they do not dance naked any more with young Girls; and to give a very particular Admonition to Two or Three of the chief and most brazen fac'd of them, not to act over their loose Behaviour with herself, at her Window, on the Lord's Day in the Time of Divine Service, in the Hearing if not in the Sight of the Minister."[84] In April another contributor struck a blow against vice in the *Courant*'s columns to "reclaim a young Lady from the abominable Vice of Incontinency," in which she apparently indulged only after holding long and loud conversations with her lovers in the street from her bedroom window: "She first throws open her Chamber Window, and fires a Volley of Oaths and Curses at the impudent Brute that dare to be so bold as to come at that unseasonable Hour to disturb her Rest. . . . And after an Hours Parly of this Nature, down comes *Miss* and lets in her Gallant. . . ."[85] And in the next issue Captain Taylor was back on the front page with a querulous letter about the lawyer who was "cohabiting with a French Tayloress as his Wife without being married according to the laws of this Province," and with plea, in verse, that Bostonians "Hoot *LAWYERS Beaux* and *Harlots* off the Stage:/Restore lost Vertue, and reform the Age."[86]

None of these provocative items in the *Courant*, for reasons quite clear, could impress anyone that its editor and contributors had any real or serious concern about the bawdier side of town life. As a matter of fact, the light anecdotal tone, the admiring attentiveness of Captain Taylor to the

[84] *New-England Courant*, No. 22 (February 26 to March 22, 1722).
[85] Ibid., No. 36 (April 2 to April 9, 1722).
[86] Ibid., No. 37 (April 9 to April 16, 1722).

"British Woman's" garb, the clear delight of the captain in the orgiastic goings-on, taking place within the shadow of the Old South, and his sense of the comedy of the voracious "Miss" and her ultimate admission of her admirers—all these were much more calculated to amuse the readers than to arouse their indignation and much more persuasive that various forms of sexual irregularities were an inevitable part of town life than that they could be stopped either by exhortation or by punishment. In this respect, it put the somber warnings of the clergy in a poor light, diminishing the effectiveness of their homilies on the subject and beclouding the image of their authority.

An anonymous partner of the Couranteers surrounding James Franklin, a sixteen-year-old boy had taken the lead over all of them in putting the Boston establishment on the defensive through the deft use of the pen. Out of the context of its time and place, the satirical exercises of Benjamin Franklin, through the mask of the well-disposed Silence Dogood, brought something wholly new to Boston life—a kind of chronic benevolence, a no-nonsense sort of practicality, an open hostility toward mealymouthedness, an earthy skepticism about the pervasive competence of the clergy to sit in judgment on any matters but the spiritual, and very little enthusiasm about their uniform indefectibility even in regard to the last. It admitted to the counsels of the province the voices of the leather aprons, of the shifting waterfront, of the nondissenting intellectuals, and of the politically conscious—a whole world, at the very doorstep of the Mathers, of Judge Sewall, of Harvard College, and of the rising moneyed class, that had been, if not ignored, at least disregarded by them. And the weapon that the young Franklin wielded was a sharp and pointed one, its slashes and pricks felt and feared—as much for their manner as for their matter— more than any single series of lunges at the establishment had before, even though they undoubtedly more reflected the inevitable than inspired it, so that when the year was ended Cotton Mather could write a friend, paraphrasing Elias, ". . . *woe is me that I sojourn in* Boston, *and that I dwell in the tents of* New England."[87]

[87] Silverman, *Letters of Cotton Mather,* 357.

XV

Denouement
and Departure

Think of three Things, whence you came,
where you are going, and to whom you must
account.

—Benjamin Franklin[1]

During a brief stormy span of ten months, James Franklin's *New-England Courant* had, by June 1722, managed to cast aspersions, some lighthearted and some with a sharper bite, on the orthodox churches, on Harvard College, on the Mathers, and on the values, manners, and mores of the Bible Commonwealth in general. It had, in the inoculation dispute, started—and fanned into a holocaust of fervid rhetoric—a controversy of dimensions never before seen in the American colonies' press. It had given a voice to skeptics, deviationists, and gadflies—not to mention an anonymous apprentice—as well as to serious challengers of the infallibility of the dicta of the Puritan establishment. It had, in its forty-four issues, raised questions, voiced doubts, and made flat contradictions of the civil and ecclesiastical establishment. As a result, the *Courant* was being watched, and it was being scolded. But no move was made against it by the authorities until its forty-fifth issue, when, on June 12, 1722, the day after its appearance, the House of Representatives (which, with the governor and his twenty-eight councilors, who were elected by the House, constituted the Great and General Court) "*Resolved*, that the Sheriff of the County of *Suffolk*, do forthwith commit to the Goal [jail] in *Boston*, the Body of *James Franklin* Printer, for the gross Affront offered to this Government, in his Courant of Monday last, there to remain during this Session."[2]

James Franklin's "gross Affront" consisted, not in any such lofty specific

[1] *Poor Richard Improved*, 1755, in *Papers*, V, 472.
[2] *Journals of the House of Representatives of Massachusetts* (Boston, 1923), IV, 23.

as insulting the clergy or deriding the college, but in publishing a relatively slight news item, on the second page of the *Courant* of June 11, 1722, on the commissioning and fitting out of a vessel to pursue some pirates molesting the coastal shipping lanes. Pirates were a common plague to colonial merchant ships. Having their clandestine bases in the numerous bays and inlets of the islands of the Caribbean, they made frequent forays into northern waters during the spring and summer. There were several years of exceptionally active preying by pirates upon Boston shipping both before and after 1722, and there is no evidence that concern ran unusually high at the time of Franklin's offense. During the early spring of 1722 rather routine reports of acts of piracy to the south appeared in Boston newspapers, including the *Courant*. In March there were reports that two pirate vessels—a three-masted square rigged ship and a slighter schooner, fore-and-aft rigged—blocked the bay at Cape Honduras and burned eight vessels from Boston at anchor there. In April word reached the town that *Weymouth*, a British frigate of fifty guns, was captured by two pirate ships totaling seventy-eight guns and commanded by a good British name, one Captain Roberts, off the coast of Guinea. As May advanced, the pirates came closer to New England waters, which were the original home territory of many of them. Dispatches came from New York that a lone pirate brigantine had taken two London ships off Virginia. And during the first week in June, news was published in the *Courant* of a brutal attack by pirates on a large French transport of four hundred tons carrying over two hundred passengers, all but fifty of whom were killed. The same week the House of Representatives was told officially by John Cushing, one of the governor's councilors, that Governor Samuel Shute had "received Advice from the Government of *Rhode Island*, of a Pirate Brigantine of Two Great Guns, and Four Swivel Guns, and Fifty Men, upon the Coast, and of several Vessels taken by the said Pirate."[3]

Although the brigantine, commanded by a former Bostonian named Low, was not an overwhelming threat as compared to some of the frigates marauding southern waters, it had raided and disabled several small vessels and was a considerable nuisance, largely because of its swift, unpredictable capacity to strike and run. The House consequently concurred in an order of the governor and his Council to appoint a committee of two councilors and three representatives "to consider and Report what may be proper for this Government to do for Defence of the Coast."[4] On the same day the committee reported back to the House, recommending that a vessel to intercept the pirate brigantine be "Equipped and Victualled with all possible Expedition."[5] The next morning, William Clarke, a representative from Boston, reported for the com-

[3] Ibid., IV, 14.
[4] Ibid.
[5] Ibid., 15.

mittee that a ship of Peter Papillion, *Flying-Horse*, had been commissioned to take up the pursuit of the pirates, who were somewhere off Block Island, some 120 miles by sea, around Cape Cod, to the southwest of Boston. Captain Papillion was apparently a gifted negotiator, for not only did he get *Flying-Horse* armed, furnished, and provisioned by the government and wages for his complement of a hundred men totaling over two hundred pounds sterling, but he also arranged for a bounty, which was enacted by the House and concurred in by the Council: "*Voted*, That the Captors shall be Entitled to the Piratical Vessels they shall take, and all the Goods, Wares, and Merchandize whatsoever, that shall be found on Board belonging to the Pirates. . . . And for further Encouragement, that they be paid out of the Public Treasury, the Sum of *Ten Pounds* per Head for every Pirate killed, or that shall be taken by them, convicted of Piracy: And be also Entitled to the Common Wages of the Port. And in case any Man on Board be maimed or wounded in engaging, fighting and repelling the Pirates, he shall be Entitled to a Bounty suitable to the Wounds he or they shall receive, to be Allowed out of the Public Treasury."[6] On the next day, *Flying-Horse's* complement received still another incentive from the House, which "*Resolved*, That the Sum of *One Hundred Pounds* be Allowed and Paid out of the Public Treasury to *Capt. Peter Papillion*, to be by him distributed *Twenty Shillings*, to every able-bodied Man, that shall inlist himself under him for this present Expedition. . . ."[7] On the same day, just twenty-four hours after *Flying-Horse* was commissioned and forty-eight after her expedition was proposed and authorized, she was ready to take on board her guns, provisions, and furnishings, and the crew was being enlisted.

In the tight little port of Boston, where the vessels, including *Flying-Horse*, lay in their berths not a five-minute walk from James Franklin's printing house, the publisher of *The New-England Courant* could not have helped knowing of the speed with which both the government and Captain Papillion had gone about launching a counterattack on the pirates. Not only were the ship and the physical preparations of her for the voyage clearly visible from the streets running along the waterfront but the signing on of seamen for new voyages was the most common subject of conversation among the patrons of the coffeehouses and taverns. Certainly, Franklin knew that the whole project was being organized and activated with exceptional speed for a governmentally inspired and conducted effort. Nevertheless, in the issue of his paper that went to press only two days after the expedition was authorized, he saw fit to insert an item treating the government's undertaking critically, suggesting that it was taking a long time to get under way and offering, by way of odious comparison, a report on the speed with which the people of little Block Is-

[6] Ibid., 16–17.
[7] Ibid., 18.

land had taken action to combat the same piratical menace. In conformity with the general journalistic practice of the time, Franklin incorporated under the date line of his original intelligence additional material originating in Boston. The story was deceptively date-lined "Newport Rhode-Island, June 7"—the date that the General Court authorized the commissioning of a vessel to pursue the pirates but the day before Captain Papillion's ship was specifically named as the pursuing vessel, though the *Courant* reported that fact, too. The whole story, therefore, was obviously written in Boston, based only in part on information received from Rhode Island. "On Monday Morning last [i.e., June 4] His Honour the Governour [Samuel Cranston of Rhode Island] had advice by a Whale-Boat (which came away in the Night) from Block-Island, that there was at that Island a Pirate Briganteer, with two Carriage Guns, and four Swivel Guns, and about 40 or 50 Men on Board, which had taken one Cahoon, belonging to this Island, and another Vessel outward bound from the Westward. Whereupon the Drums were order'd immediately to be beat about Town for Voluntiers to go in quest of the Pirates; and by 3 of Clock the same Day, there were two large Sloops under Sail, Equipt and Man'd; one mounts 10 Guns, and has 80 Men on Board, under the Command of Capt. John Headland, the other has 5 or 6 Guns, and about 50 or 60 Men, under the Command of Capt. John Brown. We hear that the Pirates have said, they are resolved to take a Rhode-Island Sloop for their own Use, the Vessel they are in being a dull Sailor." There then followed the offending sentence that brought James Franklin to the bar of the House: "We are advis'd from Boston, that the Government of the Massachusetts are fitting out a Ship to go after the Pirates, to be commanded by Captain Peter Papillion, and 't is thought he will sail sometime this Month, if Wind and Weather permit."[8] The last two clauses were gratuitous and, under the circumstances, somewhat misleading, since *Flying-Horse* had been commissioned only three days earlier and obviously required some time to man and equip; but the tone of the sentence seemed more a facetious and good-natured teasing than a serious or malicious indictment of the government. Nevertheless, James Franklin was sent for by the Governor's Council on Tuesday, June 12, the day after the *Courant* was delivered to the readers.

The Council was an elite group consisting of the most distinguished residents of the province, who had to be both elected by the House of Representatives and confirmed by the governor. Partaking of the nature somewhat of an upper legislative house, somewhat of an executive cabinet, and somewhat of a judiciary agency, the Council both initiated actions for the General Court as a whole, subject to House concurrence, and gave or withheld assent on actions originated in the House. It was the Council,

[8] *New-England Courant*, No. 45 (June 4 to June 11, 1722).

sitting with the governor (referred to collectively in the formal records of the province as "the Board"), that initiated the action against Franklin. The Board, on Tuesday afternoon, sent to the House three of its most illustrious members, Judge Sewall, Colonel Penn Townsend, and Judge Addington Davenport, to convey the results of its confrontation with James Franklin and its deliberations. They reported, "The Board, having had Consideration of a Paragraph in a Paper call'd The *New-England Courant*, published Monday last, relating to the fitting out a Ship here, to proceed against the Pirates; and having examined *James Franklin* Printer, he acknowledged himself the Publisher thereof: And finding the Paragraph to be grounded on a Letter pretended by him to be received from *Rhode-Island. Resolved*, That the said Paragraph is a high Affront to this Government."[9]

If the facetious paragraph was interpreted as "a high Affront" to the government, James Franklin's behavior before the Council did nothing to ameliorate it. He was cited, in addition to "his Inadvertency & Folly" in publishing his little gibe, for "his Indiscretion & Indecency, when before the Court."[10] The councilors questioned him closely—and to his disadvantage—about his date-lining the critical comment, along with the rest of the story, from Newport, thereby giving the impression that Rhode Islanders thought that the Massachusetts authorities were dragging their heels in dealing with the piracy problem. Franklin really had no defense against the misleading date-line choice, because the story identified Papillion as the captain of the government ship—a fact which it would have been wholly impossible for anyone in Newport to know on the *Courant's* issue date. Franklin, even if he tried to do so, also did not succeed in prevailing upon the Council that date lines were merely a journalistic device not to be taken too literally—as indeed, in the relaxed practices of the times, they were not. In any case James gave the impression that he had little respect for the proceedings of the Council.

Young Benjamin Franklin, as an employee of the *Courant*, who had helped print the offending issue and who had distributed it, was also summoned to the chamber of the Council. Benjamin appears, from his own brief account of the experience, to have gone through what would seem a somewhat awesome adventure—a printer's devil's standing alone before the most august body in the province—with the remarkable sense of self-confidence and ability to handle the situation that characterized his conduct during most of the significant episodes of his life. In recalling James Franklin's censure by the General Court, Benjamin said, "I too was taken up and examin'd before the Council; but tho' I did not give them any Satisfaction, they contented themselves with admonishing me, and dis-

[9] *Journals of the House of Representatives of Massachusetts*, IV, 23.
[10] *General Court Records* (MS volumes in Massachusetts Archives), XI, 319.

miss'd me; considering me perhaps as an Apprentice who was bound to keep his Master's Secrets."[11] By not giving them "any Satisfaction," Benjamin undoubtedly meant that he did not tell them anything, and he had the comfort of knowing that, having put up with the unpleasant aspects of apprenticeship, he had here the opportunity of availing himself of one of its few privileges—keeping his master's secrets.

The Franklin brothers' experience with the authorities was summary at best and, at worst, tyrannical. Benjamin was sent home after a scolding. James was forthwith taken around to the dank stone jail across Queen Street from his printing house and locked up in a cell. Benjamin went back alone to the printing house, where, at sixteen years old, "I had the Management of the Paper."[12]

* * *

The incarceration of James Franklin, without indictment and without trial, on so slight a pretext was an extraordinarily arbitrary act, for which there had been no adequate precedent since newspapers began continuous publication with *The Boston News-Letter* in 1704. The administration of Edmund Andros, who always insisted upon exercising his royal orders to control the press, had—just before the Revolution of 1689 removed both his King, James II, from his throne and him from his office—thrown John Winslow in prison for bringing from England a paper containing reports of the landing of William of Orange at Torbay to rescue England from the Jacobite tyranny. But Joseph Dudley, Andros's successor, rather detachedly watched the press's evolution into an adversary institution, not necessarily as against his rule but also as among contending factors who differed with each other. Dudley's administration extended from 1702 to 1716, and half a generation in Boston had grown up accustomed to the rub of a press, largely pamphleteering, that had some spirit and diversity. Consequently, when Samuel Shute became governor in 1716 and took the gubernatorial "duty" to control the press seriously, he ran into the chronic problem afflicting all those who attempted to reduce the liberties, statutorily explicit or merely assumed, to which Englishmen had been accustomed: resistance and civil disobedience. And Shute's administration, which had effectively suppressed in 1719 John Checkley's effort to print his tract charging that there was no difference, in theological error, between the dissenters running Massachusetts and the deists whom they condemned as atheists, ran headlong into conflict with the House of Representatives over freedom of the press from prior restraint. The issue was the House's authorizing the printing of an answer to the governor's charge, in an official address, that the provincial government had been negligent in some of its duties. Though he jailed no one for violating his orders requiring licensing of everything printed, he threatened Benjamin

[11] *Autobiography*, 69.
[12] Ibid.

Gray, a publisher and bookseller at the "Head of Town-Dock," with imprisonment, in early 1721, if he persisted in selling his pamphlet on the lamentable state of the currency, which contained, according to the Governor's Council, "many Vile, Scandalous, and very Abusive Expressions, which greatly reflect on His Majesty's Government and People of this Province, and tend to disturb the Publick Peace."[13] The grand jury failed to find any bill or make any presentment against Gray, however, and dismissed him.

Consistently jealous of his prerogatives as an appointee of the crown and contentious with the local sources of legislative power, Shute saw the growing freedom of the press, perhaps rightly, as the chief threat to the preservation of the royal authority in the colonies. He frankly did not see how he, so many miles and weeks away from the source of his own authority in London, could govern if his official acts, decisions, and policies were to be questioned, defied, and denounced freely by anyone who had access to a printing press. Thinking at length about this dilemma and of the ineffectiveness of his licensing power if no one paid any attention to it (which fewer and fewer were), Shute, a man to act and not to contemplate, characteristically took action. On March 15, 1721, he put the problem to the House of Representatives, asking for new laws establishing unequivocally his power to censor any book or paper in advance of publication. "I must observe to you that wee have been so unhappy of late as to have many Factious & Scandalous papers printed, & publickly sold at Boston, highly reflecting upon the Government, & tending to disquiet, the minds of his Majestie's Good Subjects, I therefore make no doubt but whoever is a Lover of the priviledges peace and Good order of this province, will be very desirous to have a law made to prevent this pernicious and dangerous practice for the time to Come and more Especially since it is the King my masters positive Commands that no Book or paper, shall be printed without my Licence first obtained. . . ."[14] The House, while deploring "Seditious and Scandalous Papers printed and publicly Sold or Dispersed," flatly refused to pass the legislation recommended by the governor: "Should an Act be made to prevent the Printing any Book or paper, without Licence first obtained from the Governour for the time being, no one can foresee the innumerable inconveniencies and dangerous Circumstances this People might Labour under in a little time."[15] And the House refused to approve a restrictive act passed down to them from the Council.

Yet the House proceeded less out of conviction about the value or even the inevitability of a free press than out of a desire, as a body of native freemen, to keep the royal governor in his place, for the House did not refrain from using its own authority in 1722, barely a week before jailing

[13] *Council Records* (MS volumes in Massachusetts Archives), VII, 236ff.
[14] *General Court Records*, XI, 113.
[15] *Boston News-Letter*, No. 890 (April 3, 1721).

James Franklin, to harass both Philip Musgrave, publisher of the *Gazette*, and John Campbell, publisher of the *News-Letter*. On June 5 it voted, "That the Door-keeper to go to Mr. *Philip Musgrave*, Author of the Boston Gazette, and order him forthwith to appear before this House, to give his Reasons why he printed the Election of Councellors made by the General Court of Assembly on Wednesday last [May 30, 1722], after such a manner, and to demand of him from whom he had the List."[16] In response to this rebuke from one of his rare enterprising moves in journalism—though hardly a brazen or ingenious one, since his printer Samuel Kneeland was also official printer of the House's *Journal*—the unhappy postmaster said he got some of his information from the secretary of the House and that the misinformation that he reported, with regard to the election of the speaker and the clerk of the House, was due entirely to ignorance. He was rebuked and told to print no more actions of the General Court except from officially attested reports. Musgrave had scarcely left the chamber before the House voted to dispatch the doorkeeper to fetch John Campbell, "Author of the Boston News-Letter," to explain some errors that he made regarding the election of councilors. He, too, was rebuked and told to err no more; his printer, Bartholomew Green, was also an official printer to the House. James Franklin, who had no connection with the House, or the Council, or the governor, alone went to jail for his offense.

Three days after his imprisonment, James Franklin, who was not of the hearty constitution of his younger brother, became ill in the bleak dungeon that served as his cell in the Queen Street jail. On June 15 he sent a petition to the House, "acknowledging his Offence, and praying that he may be allowed the Liberty of the Yard . . ."[17] and his petition was accompanied by a medical certificate attesting to his poor condition by Dr. Zabdiel Boylston—the unlikely choice of a physician being due, no doubt, to the fact that any medical evidence by Couranteers Dr. Douglass and Dr. Steward would have been suspect. The House took its time about acting on the petition, and it was not until three more days had passed that it "*Voted*, that Mr. *James Franklin*, now a prisoner in the Stone Goal [jail] have the Liberty of the Prison House and Yard, upon his giving Security for his faithful abiding there."[18] Another two days—a total of a full week after he was so precipitously deposited in his cell—the Council concurred and the governor consented; and "being much Indisposed, & Suffering in his health,"[19] Franklin was released from his cell, though not from the prison.

By the standards of eighteenth-century Britain and its American colonies, the government's conduct was outrageous: A printer, for what was

---

[16] *Journals of the House of Representatives of Massachusetts*, IV, 10.
[17] Ibid., 31.
[18] Ibid., 35.
[19] *General Court Records*, XI, 320.

at worst a very mild teasing of the authorities, was picked up at his shop by an agent of the legislature, required to explain himself, and, not doing so to the satisfaction of his inquisitors, immediately cast into a prison cell. It was the kind of exercise of "parliamentary privilege" that had long been held repugnant to British principles and inconsistent with the restraints imposed by Magna Carta. In the preceding century, a long controversy had occurred between the Stuarts and such giants of legal philosophy as Sir Edward Coke, Thomas Wentworth, and John Pym, who held that there were constitutional limits to parliamentary powers just as there were to sovereign powers. Moreover, the concept of due process, even if not the language, had been implicit in English jurisprudence for five centuries, since 1255, when the thirty-ninth article of Magna Carta declared, "No free man shall be taken or imprisoned or dispossessed, or outlawed, or banished, or in any way destroyed, nor will we go upon him, nor send upon him except by the legal judgment of his peers or by the law of the land," and the language itself became explicit in 1355 during the reign of Edward III: "No man of what state or condition he be, shall be put out of his lands or tenements, nor taken, nor imprisoned, nor disinherited, nor put to death, without he be brought to answer by due process of law."[20] The Massachusetts Body of Liberties, derived from Magna Carta, used even more specific language in 1641 in an attempt to restrain the magistrates in John Winthrop's time: "No mans life shall be taken away, no mans honour or good name shall be stayned, no mans person shall be arested, restrayned, banished, dismembred, nor any wages punished, no man shall be deprived of his wife or children, no man's goods or estaite shall be taken away from him, nor any way indammaged under coulor of law or Countenance of Authorities, unlesse it be by vertue or equitie of some expresse law of the Country warranting the same. . . ."[21]

* * *

Though Benjamin Franklin's dislike and resentment of his brother never abated during the years of his apprenticeship, he was outraged by the General Court's summary treatment of James Franklin, printer. He took on his brother's duties, distributing the type used in the offending issue, assembling the material for the next issue—perhaps aided by some of the Couranteers, perhaps not—setting it up in type and printing it, all of the latter by himself, at least so far as the physical work went, with his brother, during the first week of his imprisonment, held incommunicado in a cell. The issue, the first newspaper ever wholly edited and published by Benjamin Franklin, made no reference to the troubled state into which the *Courant* had fallen or to the plight of its unhappy proprietor. The front page was given over to a lighthearted essay of a somewhat foppish character by a man about town, who prided himself on his conversational

[20] D. Pickering, ed., *Statutes at Large* (Cambridge, 1726–1807), VII, 338.
[21] W. H. Whitmore, ed., *The Colonial Laws of Massachusetts, 1672* (Boston, 1890), 33.

powers with the ladies, and to a well-written letter, signed, in the *Courant* fashion, "Hypercarpus," quarreling with Silence Dogood's thesis in the previous issue that "pride of apparel" gave rise to "pride of heart" (Hypercarpus asserted that it was the other way around); the second page contained some scattered reports from foreign ports, a few domestic shipping notes, two reports of pirate vessels—a sloop near Bermuda and a brigantine off Nantucket—and a deposition by the mate and another mariner regarding the capture of their brigantine by the ubiquitous Boston pirate, Low. It was an undistinguished issue, no better and no worse than some of its predecessors, probably put together hastily and certainly compiled under traumatic circumstances that did not make for thoughtfulness or fine judgment. The second of the three issues that Benjamin edited was occupied almost entirely by his own Dogood paper on elegies and by a few foreign notes. The final issue, that of July 2, 1722, edited by Benjamin contained a message to the readers of the *Courant*, which suggests that Benjamin may have had access to James after the latter had been given the freedom of the prison house and yard, for the message, in its outlook and language, sounded much more like James than like Benjamin. Moreover, James knew that at the end of the week of July 2 the House would be adjourning and, by the terms of its action, he would be freed. The letter took note of the disapproval that the *Courant* had evoked in some quarters, but it was far from obsequious and took a courageous if, under the circumstances understandably, a somewhat righteous view of its mission.

"Hitherto our offerings to the Publick," the letter began, "have met with a general Entertainment and Acceptance. Tho' we do not boast of pleasing all Men, nor do we ever intend to attempt a Task so impossible." The tone was realistic enough, and so was the point. His three weeks in prison, however, seemed to have had little of the humiliating effect upon James Franklin that his sentencers had intended; if anything, the experience was elevating his sense of self-worth and enlarging his sense of moral responsibility. Nor did it put him in fear of his judges and detractors: "There have ever been restless uneasy Spirits in the World; minds that seem peculiarly form'd for Contradiction, and can relish nothing but what is wrought in the Elaboratory of their own Brain." It dealt with the authorities, and such others as the Mathers, who had condemned the *Courant* in direct and uncompromising language: "Nor are we ignorant of the vile abuse and Invidious Calumnies of Licentious Tongues: However, the words *Saucy, Impudent,* (and others too vile for us to mention) in no wise move us; for we can easily soar above the little Vulgar, and look down on those who reproach us, with Pity and Courage." The letter to his readers concluded with James Franklin's declaration of his proposed future course, and reflected nothing but integrity and conviction on the part of a man who had been deprived of his freedom for insisting on going his own way and who, while still under the thumb of his oppressors, refused to change it:

> We are not ashamed the World should know our great Design; it being to promote Virtue and real Goodness: And having lately admitted two of the Fair Sex into our Society [Silence Dogood was still known to James Franklin only as an anonymous woman; the other of the two was probably Madam Staples], we hope we shall be able to prosecute the same with more advantage; reform things that have been amiss, and at once both please and profit others.
>
> The End of moral Precepts, is to form the Soul to Vertue, to excite the Mind in the Pursuit of Great and Worthy Actions; and to Labour by a pure and fervent Emulation, to outvie those who had trod before us in the Paths of Vertue.
>
> A GENEROUS Mind justly Accounts, that one great Part of the Reward of Noble Actions is, *to have done them*: And when by sweet Reflection, he looks back thereon, how does it Exhilarate and revise him, and enable him to Anticipate the expected *Euge* [i.e., "Well done!"] of his Glorious Master! But this is a noble Theme too copious to enter upon at this Time.[22]

Appended to this manifesto was the list of the thirty-eight works and collections of works, ranging from the classics to Cotton Mather, that constituted the *Courant's* impressive library—an asset which James Franklin obviously regarded as a professional credential. Altogether, though there was no cringing before "authority," the statement was a responsible and creditable one. But it immediately aroused the ire of the Governor's Council. The issue containing the statement appeared on Monday, July 2, 1722. On Thursday, July 5, the Council composed and passed a resolution of the most serious implications regarding the conflict between freedom of press and prior restraint in the colonies:

> *Whereas in the Paper call'd the* New England Courant *printed Weekly by* James, Franklin, *many Passages have been published, boldly reflecting on His Majesty's Government and on the Administration of it in this Province, the Ministry, Churches and College: and it very often contains Paragraphs that tend to fill the Readers minds with vanity, to the dishonour of God and disservice of Good Men.*
>
> *Resolved,* That no such Weekly Paper be hereafter Printed or Published without the same be first perused and allowed by the Secretary, as has been usual. And that the said *Franklin* give Security before the Justices of the Superiour Court in the Sum of *l.* 100 to be of the good Behaviour to the end of the next Fall Sessions of this Court.[23]

The House of Representatives, always suspicious of the Council as a tool of the governor, who three years earlier had ordered Boston printers not to

[22] *New-England Courant,* No. 48 (June 25 to July 2, 1722).
[23] *Journals of the House of Representatives of Massachusetts,* IV, 72.

print the "remonstrance" by the House critical of one of his speeches, but historically an inconsistent champion of a free press when its own ox was gored, refused to concur in the Council's resolution. On the next day, July 6, 1722, a motion was made to read the resolution a second time for further consideration. This, too, was rejected. And on the following day, Saturday, July 7, 1722, the second session of 1722 of the Great and General Court was, by command of the governor, prorogued. James Franklin, unindicted and unconvicted of anything, left the prison yard on the July afternoon and went back across the street to resume the management of his printing house and his newspaper, punished but unchastened.

The action of the House, in refusing to concur with the Council in prior restraint of James Franklin, continued, in practical effect, the denial of governmental power to license the press that it had explicitly expressed in 1721.

* * *

"During my Brother's Confinement, which I resented a good deal, notwithstanding our private Differences," Benjamin Franklin was to recall years later, "I had the Management of the Paper, and I made bold to give our Rulers some Rubs in it, which my Brother took very kindly, while others began to consider me in an unfavourable Light, as a young Genius that had a Turn for Libelling and Satyr."[24] There is no question that Benjamin's writings, as Silence Dogood's papers, had become an increasingly sharp irritant to the whole Boston establishment, civil and ecclesiastical, but his recollection chronologically was faulty. During his "Management of the Paper," nothing appeared that could be construed as a gibe or even a criticism of his "Rulers," except the letter to the readers which was clearly the work of James, however it may have made its way across Queen Street from the yard of the stone jail to the printing house, and the satirical treatment of elegies, which was far more annoying to the religious community than to the civil. But Benjamin's first expression of his convictions regarding the government's repressive moves against the *Courant* and his brother, as its publisher, was more thoughtful and perhaps, in a quieter and more sober way, more effective and therefore more irritating to the establishment than his fancied "Rubs" during the specific period of his brother's imprisonment. In the first Dogood paper after his brother's release, Benjamin devoted the entire text to a long excerpt from *The London Journal* of some seventeen months earlier, February 4, 1721. It was an eloquent and perceptive exposition of the indispensability of a free press in a free society—not a defense, but a superbly written and essentially positive exegesis.

The London Journal was a favorite publication of the *Courant* contributors, largely because of the letters of "Cato," a pseudonym for two English pamphleteers, Thomas Gordon and John Trenchard. They were

[24] *Autobiography*, 69.

Whigs, and wrote a spirited political weekly called *The Independent Whig*. Formerly members of the bar, they were well grounded in the law, syllogistic in their arguments, republican in their politics, and Low-Churchmen in their religion. Six times, excerpts from their *London Journal* letters had appeared in the *Courant* during its first year; and among *Courant* contributors both Gardner and Christopher Taylor had quoted them. Incisive advocates of basic freedoms, Gordon and Trenchard were far from being rabble-rousers and addressed their cases to the intellect rather than to the emotions; and they were basically affirmative in their rationales rather than negative and, like good Augustans, fundamentally optimistic and trusting deeply in the power and strength of human reason. Although, like Addison and Steele in the case of *The Spectator* papers, Cato's letters were variously written by Gordon and by Trenchard, they were in substance the joint efforts of both writers, the result of long and closely reasoned discussions.

Their essay on freedom of the press came at a time when the *control* of the press that marked the reigns of the Tudors and the *regulation* of the press that characterized those of the Stuarts had come to an end. By 1721 the Regulation of Printing Act of 1662—formally termed "Act for preventing the frequent Abuses in printing seditious, treasonable and unlicensed Books and Pamphlets, and for regulating of Printing and printing Presses"[25]—was obsolete, having expired in 1694; and William and Mary sought no extension or revival of it, nor did Queen Anne or the first of the Hanovers. But although the crown had abandoned efforts to control or regulate the press, Parliament had not; and it sought to do so, not by regulatory enactments, but through the tax powers. The favorite device was the Stamp Act, first employed in 1712, in response to parliamentary distress at criticism in *The London Daily Courant*, but soon ignored by publishers, who found technical loopholes in it; and newspapers proliferated in the kingdom from one, *The London Gazette*, when the Regulation of Printing Act expired, to nearly a hundred in London and the provinces by 1721. But with the rise to power of Robert Walpole and his brother-in-law, Charles Townshend, noises began to be made about restoring the Stamp Act in a foolproof form, and it was undoubtedly this that stirred Gordon and Trenchard to strike a strong blow for the press's freedom at a time when it had been an effective even if not a theoretic reality in the realm for at least a full generation. In such a context, whatever the legalities of the matter, the idea of a free press was treated, not as innovative or novel, although government control and regulation had begun to decline significantly only within the lifetimes of Gordon and Trenchard, but as a right and, indeed, a necessity of a self-governing people.

As inserted by Benjamin Franklin in the *Courant* during the last week

---

[25] The original act is in 13 and 14 Charles II, Chap. 33, and was renewed in 1664, lapsed in 1679, and was revived in 1685.

of his brother's imprisonment, the letter occupied the entire first page of the paper. Over the subscription, Silence Dogood, the introduction by Benjamin was brief and to the point: "I prefer the following Abstract from the London Journal to any Thing of my own, and therefore shall present it to your Readers this week without any further Preface." With a wisdom surpassing his years, he refrained from any application of the text to the plight of his brother and from any editing of the original or any interpolations, letting the lucid works speak for themselves:

> WITHOUT Freedom of Thought, there can be no such Thing as Wisdom; and no such Thing as publick Liberty, without Freedom of Speech; which is the Right of every Man, as far as by it, he does not hurt or controul the Right of another: And this is the only Check it ought to suffer, and the only Bounds it ought to know.
>
> This sacred Privilege is so essential to free Governments, that the Security of Property, and the Freedom of Speech always go together; and in those wretched Countries where a Man cannot call his Tongue his own, he can scarce call anything else his own. Whoever would overthrow the Liberty of a Nation, must begin by subduing the Freeness of Speech. . . .

Following a truncated recapitulation of the assertion of the royal right to control the press and even public speech by James I and his son, Charles I, the letter got to the heart of the matter:

> That Men ought to speak well of *their Governours* is true, while *their* Governours deserve to be well spoken of; but to do publick Mischief, without hearing of it, is only the Prerogative and Felicity of Tyranny: A free People will be showing that they are *so*, by their Freedom of Speech.
>
> The Administration of Government, is nothing else but the Attendance of the *Trustees of the People* upon the Interest and Affairs of the People: And as it is the Part and Business of the People, for whose Sake all publick Matters are, or ought to be transacted, to see whether they be well or ill transacted; so it is the Interest, and ought to be the Ambition, of all honest Magistrates, to have their Deeds openly examined, and publickly scann'd: Only the wicked Governours of Men dread what is said of them. . . .

The letter then compared the legendary glory of the first Roman Republic of Horatius Cocles, Cincinnatus, and Publius Valerius, when freedom of speech was not only tolerated but encouraged, to the consuming fear and suspicion in the Roman Empire of the gloomy, secretive emperor Tiberius, when the freedom of speech advanced by his stepfather, Augustus, was almost totally suppressed. The Cato letter concluded:

> The best Princes have ever encouraged and promoted Freedom of Speech; they know that upright Measures would defend themselves, and that all upright Men would defend them. *Tacitus*, speaking of the Reign of some of the Princes abovemention'd, says with Extasy, *Rara Temporum*

felicitate, ubi sentire quae velis & quae sentias dicere licet: A blessed Time
when you might think what you would and speak what you Thought. . . .
Misrepresentation of publick Measures is easily overthrown, by representing publick Measures truly; when they are honest, they ought to be publickly known, that they may be publickly commended; but if they are
knavish or pernicious, they ought to be publickly exposed, in order to be
publickly detested.[26]

At the time, Gordon and Trenchard's letter constituted the whole case
that Benjamin Franklin put in defense of the principles that had led his
brother to jail. The rest of the issue was presumably edited by James, who
had only the reverse sheet to fill, and was mild enough; there was a poetry
offering from a Rhode Islander, self-identified as "Rhodian Muse," in response to the "Kitelic" ode letter of Silence Dogood of two weeks earlier.
The only news note, date-lined Boston, was an item, which must have
nettled the authorities a bit, reporting that "Pirates still continue on this
Coast and have taken Captain Mulberry outward bound from this place
[Boston]." The only advertisement was one with which Benjamin might
have felt some sympathy, as he helped set it in type, declaring "Ran away
from his Master Mr. *Josiah Franklin* of *Boston*, Tallow-Chandler, on the
first of this Instant July, an Irish Man Servant, named *William Tinsley*
. . ." and offering a forty-shilling reward to anyone apprehending and returning the runaway.

No sooner was James Franklin back in full command than he not only
challenged his imprisoners, albeit with restraint, but also exploited his
imprisonment. Acknowledging no offense on his part, at least intentional,
he entered no attack upon the government for its treatment of him, however ill deserved he thought it; instead, he commanded the attention of
his audience by giving initial space on the first page of his paper to an attack upon himself in a letter to him—"Thrust into the Grate by an Unknown Hand"—which rejoiced in his troubles, and which, in Franklin's
introductory lines, he compared to "nothing else but the pelting a Criminal with *rotten Eggs*, while he is suffering the Law." The anonymous letter, with its accompanying verses, bore some evidence of Harvard origins—
at least, it expressed particular concern for the learned community.

"The Crimes you have been guilty of are so numerous and heinous, that
we think no Punishment severe enough to inflict upon you.

"The manifest Design of your Paper, is to abuse our Reverend Clergy,
and reproach our learned Youth, to revile the Government, and disaffect
the People to the present Administration, which we are sure *any Man
may*, and *every Man ought* to be easy under."

The author then resorted to the omnipresent couplets to stigmatize
Franklin with a fiery succession of characterizations more worthy of being

[26] The original Cato letter is in *London Journal*, LXXX (February 4, 1720/1); the
Dogood reprint is in *New-England Courant*, No. 49 (July 2 to July 9, 1722).

addressed to a powerful political insurgent than a mildly discordant journalist. Among the vigorously denunciatory rhymes:

> Father of Discord, maker of Division,
> Broacher of Strife, and Sower of Sedition;
> Fomenter of Contention and Debate,
> And Feuds, in Family, in Church and State.
> What! Such a scoundrel Rascal take in Hand,
> To banish Vice, and to reform our Land,
> Boldly to reprimand our Reverend Seers,
> And lug our Ghostly Fathers by the Ears;
> To tax our learned Youth with want of Knowledge,
> And impudently satyrize *our Colledge*,
> To load our pious Judges with Disgrace,
> And fault our Rulers to their very Face?
> Ah scoundrel Wretch! Your vile Courant has spread
> Its Poison far and wide! No matter you were dead,
> And your Courants all burnt, That have such Discord bred.

After some further exercises in Christian forbearance as practiced by the
Bible Commonwealth, the philippic concluded, "We hope to see you on a
Jibbet Dangle,/With all the meddling Crew that love to wrangle."
Franklin put the diatribe in sufficient perspective by observing that "it is a
greater Crime in some Men to discover a Fault, than for others to commit
it."[27]

On the whole, in this issue after the first full week of his freedom,
James Franklin bore himself well. ". . . I know not the Power of a General Assembly in his Majesties Plantations, nor whether an *Englishman*
may have Liberty to answer for himself before the Legislative
Power . . . ." He thus put the question—whether the rights of an Englishman dwindled because he lived in a British colony rather than in the
homeland—that was to dominate the political history of the province
until the day of Concord and Lexington, more than half a century later.

* * *

James Franklin and his contributors very clearly came to the conclusion,
after his release, that they would not be deterred from their purpose of
putting together a sprightly paper that would not be subservient to the establishment but, on the contrary, would keep a critical eye on it and that
would be for the most part in an adversary role. In the issue of July 23,
1722, Benjamin Franklin took direct aim at the Puritan priesthood in the
ninth of his Dogood papers, which addressed itself to hypocrisy, intentionally and determinedly speaking of the rope in the house of a man who
had been hanged. With a proverbial Latin superscription, "*Corruptio op-
timi est pessima*" ("The corruption of the best is the worst"), the paper
represented the first original reflections that Benjamin had had time to

[27] *New-England Courant*, No. 40 (July 9 to July 16, 1722).

allow himself, and to distill and arrange and put into words, since his brother's summary detention. But James, on whom he still lost no love, was now free again, and Benjamin turned his attention less to the injustice of the episode than to the moral fiber of the society that permitted it. The paper, ostensibly questioning "Whether a Commonwealth suffers more by hypocritical Pretenders to Religion, or by the openly Profane," was really directed at the whole mechanism, and behind it the *causa causata*, of the political structure of the Puritan state. Probably the most serious piece of literature that Franklin ever wrote, it was a striking and a biting commentary, incredible in the strength of its conviction and the sharpness of its perception, with its over-all force weakened only by his again turning, unnecessarily in this instance, to Gordon and Trenchard for support, "the better to convince your Readers, that Publick Destruction may be easily carry'd on by hypocritical Pretenders to Religion."

The paper needed no such support. Benjamin answered his own question as to whether the hypocritical or the profane man is the more dangerous—if severely, yet with an extraordinary sense of distinction that eluded far more experienced observers of one of the ugliest dilemmas of the Bible Commonwealth which had driven such good, even saintly, souls as Roger Williams and Anne Hutchinson into the wilderness: ". . . the Hypocrite is the more dangerous Person of the Two, especially if he sustains a Post in the Government, and we consider his Conduct as it regards the Publick. The first Artifice of a *State Hypocrite* is, by a few savoury Expressions which cost him Nothing, to betray the best Men in his Country into an Opinion of his Goodness; and if the Country wherein he lives is noted for the Purity of Religion, he the more easily gains his End, and consequently may more justly be expos'd and detested. A notoriously profane Person in a private Capacity, ruins himself, and perhaps forwards the Destruction of a few of his Equals; but a publick Hypocrite every day deceives his betters, and makes them the Ignorant Trumpeters of his supposed Godliness: They take him for a Saint, and pass him for one, without considering that they are (as it were) the Instruments of publick Mischief out of Conscience, and ruin their Country for God's sake."

The only "Country . . . noted for Purity of Religion" known to Benjamin Franklin or his readers was the Province of Massachusetts Bay. He swiftly moved on to what he was really talking about, the political character of the province and not its religion (about which he really cared very little); and the farther apart church and state were kept, the better off he felt the state would be. "This Political Description of a Hypocrite, may (for ought I know) be taken for a new Doctrine by some of your Readers; but let them consider, that *a little Religion, and a little Honesty, goes a great way in Courts.* 'Tis not inconsistent with Charity to distrust a Religious Man in Power, tho' he may be a good Man; he has many Temptations 'to propagate *publick Destruction* for *Personal Advantages* and Se-

curity': And if his Natural Temper be covetous, and his Actions often contradict his pious Discourse, we may with great Reason conclude, that he
has some other Design in his Religion besides barely getting to Heaven."

Franklin found particularly obnoxious ministers, or those at one time in
their lives committed to the ministry, who left "the Gospel for the sake of
the Law." The specific offenders were not named, though there was no
shortage, and Franklin would have had to look no further for an example
than Judge Sewall, the councilor who moved the imprisonment of James
Franklin, although Sewall could have been in no sense the archhypocrite
he had in mind. "A Man compounded of Law and Gospel," Benjamin asserted, "is able to cheat a whole Country with his Religion, and then destroy them under *Colour of Law*: And here the Clergy are in great Danger
of being deceiv'd, and the People of being deceiv'd by the Clergy, until the
Monster arrives to such Power and Wealth, that he is out of the reach of
both, and can oppress the People without their own blind Assistance. And
it is a sad Observation, that when the People too late see their Error, yet
the Clergy still persist in their Encomiums on the Hypocrite; and when he
happens to die *for the Good of his Country*, without leaving behind him
the Memory of *one good Action*, he shall be sure to have his Funeral Sermon stuff'd with *Pious Expressions* which he dropt at such a Time, and at
such a Place, and on such an Occasion; than which nothing can be more
prejudicial to the Interest of Religion, nor indeed to the Memory of the
Person deceas'd." The elegistic example that Franklin had in mind was
very probably the obsequies in 1720 for the overridingly ambitious Governor Joseph Dudley, who had also studied for the ministry and who was so
bitterly despised as chief justice by his fellow Bostonians that he once had
to be imprisoned to protect him from mob violence and who was given a
funeral so elaborate as to gladden the heart of Judge Sewall ("were very
many people, spectators out of windows, on Fences and Trees, like Pi-
geons"[28]), followed on the next lecture day by a panegyrical sermon by Benjamin Colman. "The Reason for this Blindness in the Clergy is, because
they are honourably supported (as they ought to be) by their People, and
see nor feel nothing of the Oppression which is obvious and burdensome
to every one else."

Franklin, before concluding with the Cato excerpt from *The London
Journal*, made his own feelings, in the person of Silence Dogood, emphatically clear: "But this Subject raises in me an Indignation not to be
born[e]; and if we have had, or are like to have any Instances of this Nature in New England, we cannot better manifest our Love to Religion and
the Country, than by setting the Deceivers in a true Light, and undeceiv-
ing the Deceived, however such Discoveries may be represented by the ignorant or designing Enemies of our Peace and Safety."[29]

[28] Sewall, *Diary*, III, 249.
[29] *New-England Courant*, No. 51 (July 16 to July 23, 1722).

This transparent attack on the establishment, both civil and ecclesiastical, directed to such a central point as the fundamental validity of the Puritan conviction that the state could and should serve the church and that the church should enthrall the state, made James Franklin's jest about the pirate-chaser pale into insignificance. Never had the public prints been so harsh in criticizing the magistrates and the clergy alike, and never did the time seem less propitious for the *Courant* to do so than the fortnight following its publisher's jailing for disrespect to the authorities. In running the ninth Dogood letter, presumably unedited, James Franklin committed himself and his paper to continuing on the course that he had steered it from the beginning.

In the next issue of the *Courant*, over three quarters of the space, including the entire first page, was devoted to a presentation and discussion of the thirty-ninth chapter of Magna Carta, relating to due process, and to Lord Coke's exposition of the latter in his *Institutes,* in which he took the view that Magna Carta's language included the guarantee that "No Man ought to be put from his Livelyhood without Answer"[30]—a transgression that James Franklin felt had been committed against him. Coke had also pressed the view that "by the law of the land" meant due process of the law, and he applied it to just such a situation as the exercise of the parliamentary privilege of summary arrest and imprisonment in James Franklin's case: "As none shall be condemned without a Lawful Tryal by his Peers, so none shall be *taken, imprisoned,* or put out of his Freehold, without *due Process of the Law,* that is by the Indictment or Presentment of good and lawful Men of the Place, in due Manner, or by Writ Original of the Common Law"[31]—none of which procedures had inhibited the General Court in seizing Franklin and depriving him of his liberty. Following "the very words of that Oracle of our Law, the sage and learned Coke," the *Courant* cited the charter granted the province by William and Mary in 1691, a passage of which was construed to reserve as the exclusive power of the judiciary "the Hearing, Trying and Determining of ALL MANNER OF CRIMES, Offences, Pleas, Processes, Plaints, Actions, Matters, Causes and Things whatsoever, arising, or happening within Our said Province. . . ."[32] It was the most serious and most basic appeal, not so much in his own defense as in the reassertion of the liberties and rights of an Englishman, that Franklin put after his arrest, and it could not have helped making a sober impression on the thoughtful reader.

In his *Courant* of four weeks later, after dropping in the interval even remote allusions to tyrannical governments, during which time Benjamin Franklin's pieces were concerned with widows' being insured against los-

---

[30] Edward Coke, *The Second Part of the Institutes of the Laws of England* (London, 1642); 47.
[31] The exact language does not appear in Coke, but appears to be a summary of Coke (ibid., 46), who used the phrase, "by the course and process of law."
[32] *New-England Courant,* No. 52 (July 23 to July 30, 1722).

ing their husbands and spinsters against not having any in the first place, James Franklin inserted in his paper a long tribute, as from the city of Athens, to Demosthenes for "his Wise and Just Government in State Affairs, wherein he carried himself much better than any in his Time, as well as in the Preservation of the Liberties of the People, as in his Good Will towards them . . ."—the clear impression being conveyed that the government of Massachusetts could well use Demosthenes for a model. He also inserted a bill of particulars, again as from the city of Athens, against Demades, including "obstructing the *due Course of the Law* . . . Endeavouring totally to subvert the Laws . . . crafty and unjust Management in State Affairs . . . as well in the Incroaching on the Liberties of the People"—clearly a caution to any arrogant figures that might have achieved authority in Massachusetts, who were reminded that, in the end, "Demades *hath nothing left but his Paunch and his Tongue.*"[33] The exercise was not calculated to persuade the General Court that it had taught James Franklin a lesson.

In his next issue, James Franklin allotted the major part of the *Courant* to yet another attack on deceitful funeral orations, and the clergy who usually delivered them, as indulgence in "little Arts and Contrivances wherein mean and sordid *Flattery* discovers it self [which] do never appear with a more hateful Aspect than when they are practis'd by Men of a *religious character;* whose Lips ought to preserve Justice, Impartiality and Truth, as well as Knowledge. . . ."[34] In committing such offenses, the *Courant* charged, the clergy were guilty not merely of concessions to vanity but to greed. To a society in which the dispatching of the dead to their eternal fate had long been a major preoccupation(more funeral sermons were published than any other form of pulpit literature, which itself exceeded in volume any other form of native literature for over a century), this rebuke of the clergy was a most shocking matter. Once again James Franklin had "abused our Reverend Clergy," and once more the *Courant* was headed toward trouble with the establishment.

By September 17, 1722, James Franklin's imprisonment was sufficiently far behind him that he could take a lighter, though no less concerned, view of the vulnerable state into which the legislature had plunged the press. Reverting to his old love of narrative verse, he accounted in facetious couplets for the rise of a government that would suppress the spread of knowledge of its activities.

> Thro' various Forms of Government
> They pass'd, till many Years were spent;
> But always us'd (to blind the People)
> To join the *State* unto the *Steeple;*
> And those who left the *State* i' th' Lurch,

[33] Ibid., No. 56 (August 20 to August 27, 1722).
[34] Ibid., No. 57 (August 27 to September 3, 1722).

Wou'd cry, *The Danger of the Church!*
Till some o' th' Clergy and the College,
Declar'd against the Sin of *Knowledge*:
And truly 'tis a fatal Omen,
When Knowledge, which belongs to no Men
But to the Clergy and the Judges,
Gets in the Heads of common Drudges.[35]

This was the real "rub" that both the Franklins, as "leather aprons,"
had against the Massachusetts establishment: that there should be any restraints on knowledge or information that belonged to the lowliest as well
as to the loftiest. And the alliance between "State and Steeple" to control information and its free flow constituted, in their minds, an indefensible conspiracy between magistrates and ministers. The uneasiness of
both the latter at the *Courant*'s lightheartedly dispensing such views was
exacerbated by the fact that the rollicking but deadly seriously intentioned
poem was the dominant feature of an issue sandwiched between two
others which featured Benjamin's somewhat flippant Dogood pieces on
drunkenness and streetwalkers.

In his final Dogood letter, which appeared in the *Courant* of October 8,
1722, Benjamin lectured the clergy on the perils of intemperate religious
zeal. The ministers of Boston did not welcome the intrusion of blanket lay
criticism into matters that they thought best left in their hands. This was
particularly true in times of spiritual crisis, and the president of Yale,
Timothy Cutler, and some of his academic and ministerial colleagues had
precipitated a shocking crisis in the autumn of 1722 by repudiating Puritan doctrine and practice, by embracing those of the Church of England,
and by expressing their skepticism about the validity of non-episcopal ordination or, in the case of most of the converts, by flatly denying it. Never
of a fanatical bend, Benjamin borrowed a line from Cicero, urging that
the cause of each side in the resultant dispute be weighed; and in the letter, Silence Dogood, making her last appearance, criticized the Yale
ministers, not for their conversion to the Church of England, which
Franklin had Silence refer to as "the Establish'd Religion of our Nation,"
but for the absolutist attitude some of the converted ministers adopted
in the process, especially toward ordination. With his disinterest in theological disputes, Franklin turned the Yale dons around to confront them
with the irrationality of their position: ". . . since they have deny'd the
Validity of *Ordination* by the Hands of *Presbyters*, and consequently
their Power of Administring the *Sacraments*, &c. we may justly expect a
suitable Manifestation of their Repentance for invading the *Priests* Office,
and living so long in a Corah-like Rebellion. All I would endeavour to
shew is, That an indiscreet Zeal for spreading an Opinion, hurts the cause
of the Zealot. There are too many blind Zealots among every Denomina-

[35] *Ibid.*, No. 59 (September 10 to September 17, 1722).

tion of Christians; and he that propagates the Gospel among *Rakes* and *Beans* without reforming them in their Morals, is every whit as ridiculous and impolitick as a Statesman who makes Tools of Ideots and Tale-Bearers."[36]

The letter was restrained. If it could be construed at all as favoring one side over another, it was on the side of the Puritan ministers, who both were ordained by presbyters and were themselves participants in the presbyterial ordination of others. Nevertheless, the Dogood paper charged, with some incisiveness, that the clergy were capable of excessive, unreasoned zeal. In a society where the clergy was supposed also to constitute the intellectual leadership, it was a very grave and dangerous imputation. The ministers of Boston were troubled enough by Timothy Cutler's appalling work at Yale without having an obstreperous newspaper fanning the flames with its talk of clerical weaknesses. It was remembered all too painfully that it was one of their number, Cotton Mather, who not five years earlier, during one of his fits of pique at Harvard, had written Elihu Yale urging him to give his money and his name to "the infant College at Connecticut."[37] It was remembered, too—at least by the Mathers—that Yale was supposed to have been the second line of defense of Puritan orthodoxy after Harvard as a first line failed with its repudiation of the Mathers and its deliverance into the hands of the liberal layman John Leverett. Orthodoxy in Massachusetts was in trouble. The valedictory letter of Silence Dogood, never to be heard from again, helped, in a small way, to speed it on its way.

* * *

Silence Dogood slipped into extinction as mysteriously as she had surfaced from oblivion. Benjamin Franklin simply let her disappear, as her letters peremptorily ceased, recalling later that "my small Fund of Sense for such Performances was pretty well exhausted."[38] It was eight weeks before there was even a mention, in the *Courant's* columns, of Silence Dogood, whose fourteen letters had appeared over a period of six months. The omission was probably intentional on James Franklin's part. He had been tricked into giving his apprentice the place of honor and highest visibility in his paper—a fact which he discovered only when Benjamin, having no more compositions whose publishing prospects might be endangered, disclosed, in all likelihood with some swagger, his identity as Silence Dogood after the publication of the last letter. The other contributors immediately started taking notice of the apprentice, including him in their discussions and paying attention to his views. It was a heady experience for a sixteen-year-old boy, and his natural inclination toward a pert self-confidence may have been sufficiently increased to make him something of

[36] Ibid., No. 62 (October 1 to October 8, 1722).
[37] Cotton Mather to Elihu Yale, January 14, 1718, in Quincy, *History of Harvard University*, I, 526.
[38] *Autobiography*, 68.

a problem to his brother and master. ". . . I began to be considered a little more by my Brother's Acquaintance, and in a manner that did not quite please him, as he thought, probably with reason, that it tended to make me too vain."[39] James's irritation probably accounted for the fact that his paper completely ignored Silence's unexplained absence for so long, despite what must have been considerable curiosity on the part of readers who had become accustomed to her fortnightly visits. In December, however, when Benjamin's ego had possibly subsided, James could once again bear the sight of the name of Silence Dogood in the columns of the *Courant*. In the seventieth issue of the paper, a letter appeared, with the subscription "Hugo-Grim," enclosing another letter that the writer asked the *Courant* to forward to the now long absent Mrs. Dogood, so that "if she be in the Land of the Living we may know the Occasion of her *Silence*." The author of the letter was obviously a reader familiar with the Dogood series, who took some good-natured pains to remind Mrs. Dogood of her mauled metaphor of the Harvard student's climbing the stairs to a throne with his hand on the plough: "Why have you so soon *withdrawn your Hand from the Plough* (with which you tax'd some of the Scholars) and grown weary of *Doing Good?*" And the letter writer came close to the mark in suspecting the cause of Mrs. Dogood's retirement: "Is your Common-Place Wit all Exhausted, your stock of matter all spent? We thought that you were well stor'd with that by your striking your first blow at the *College*. You say (in your No. 2) that you *have an Excellent Faculty at observing and reproving the Faults of others*, and are the Vices of the Times all mended? Is there not Whoring, Drinking, Swearing, Lying, Gaming, Cheating and Oppression, and many other Sins prevailing in the Land? Can you *observe* no fault in others (or your self) to *reprove?* Or are you married and remov'd to some distant Clime, that we hear nothing from you? Are you (as the Prophet supposed *Baal* that sottish Deity) *asleep*, or *on a Journey*, and cannot write? Or has the Sleep of *inexorable unrelenting Death* procur'd your *Silence?* and if so you ought to have told us of it, and appointed your Successor. But if you are still in Being, and design to amuse the Publick any more, proceed in your usual Course; or if not let us know it, that some other hand may take up your Pen."

The letter aroused in James Franklin sufficient awareness of the value of Mrs. Dogood—despite the annoying author of her being—to keep the myth alive. Immediately after the letter of Hugo-Grim, he inserted an "Advertisement: If any Person or Persons will give us a true Account of Mrs. Silence Dogood, whether Dead or alive, Married or unmarried, in Town or Country, that so, (if living) she may be spoke with, or Letters convey'd to her, they shall have Thanks for their Pains."[40] There was, of

---

[39] Ibid.
[40] *New-England Courant*, No. 70 (November 27 to December 2, 1722).

course, no answer—and that was the last of Silence Dogood. It was also
the last of Benjamin Franklin as a contributor to *The New-England
Courant*, until once again his brother was the victim of an enforced absence at the hands of the authorities.

Throughout the autumn and early winter of 1722, the *Courant* continued to fly in the face of the establishment, both ecclesiastical and civil.
With the majority of its steadiest contributors Low Church Anglicans, the
paper would not let the Yale conversions lapse into history, and there was
nothing that alarmed the Boston ministers more than the prospects of
widespread attention to Cutler and his associates resulting in widening the
breach in the wall of orthodoxy. So feverently had the Mathers pressed for
the advancement of Yale as the new citadel of New England Congregationalism (Cutler, as a matter of fact, was originally sent from Charlestown, Massachusetts, to Stratford, Connecticut, in 1709, by a synod of
ministers from both colonies, to stem a tide of Anglicanism at Stratford,
and from his ministry there he went on to become rector of Yale in 1719)
that the defection of practically its entire leadership, including, in addition to the rector, its two tutors, and the four ministers most prominently
associated with the college, was a very disturbing source of embarrassment
to the disgruntled clergy among Harvard alumni—a fact not lost on the
Couranteers. Nor was the anguish visited upon the elect lost on them:
". . . how our fountain," wrote two Harvard graduates, residents in Connecticut, Stephen Buckingham and John Davenport, to Cotton Mather,
"hoped to have been and continued the repository of truth, and the
reserve of pure and sound principles, doctrine and education, in case of a
change in our mother Harvard, shews itself in so little time corrupt. How is
the gold become dim! and the silver become dross! and the wine mixt
with water."[41] The resentment, among the orthodox, of the *Courant's* fanning the flames of schism was deepened by the common suspicion, erroneous as it was, that John Checkley was still calling the tune in the
paper's editorial councils. It was no less commonly suspected that it was
John Checkley who had originally planted the seeds of Anglicanism in the
mind of Timothy Cutler as early as 1714, when Checkley visited Stratford
—a notion later bolstered when Checkley accompanied Cutler on a triumphant journey from New Haven, through five towns with Anglican
churches, to Boston. Cutler and his two tutors had further irked the elect
of Boston by repudiating an opportunity offered them with the four erring
Connecticut ministers, on October 16, 1722, to recant their schismatic
views. The occasion was a debate arranged by Governor Gurdon Saltonstall of Connecticut, an orthodox Harvard man, between the Yale apos-
tates and some devout Calvinists; the four ministers all returned to Congregationalism, but Cutler and his tutors persisted in their headstrong course,

[41] "Episcopacy in Connecticut," in Massachusetts Historical Society, *Collections*, 2nd
Ser., IV, 297ff.

eventually going to England to enter holy orders in the Church of England. From the day after the Saltonstall-inspired debate, when Cutler was formally dismissed from Yale, until November 5, 1722, when he sailed with his tutors for England, the great Yale apostasy preoccupied Boston, with the *Courant* devoting a major part of every issue to the subject, beginning with the Dogood letter on intemperate religious zeal. In the following four issues, the subject was treated with both maturity and balance. This may well have been due to the moderating influence of the Reverend Henry Harris of King's Chapel, the contributor to an earlier *Courant*, who felt that the brand of Anglicanism embraced by Cutler and Checkley smacked too much of Jacobinism and of disloyalty to the reigning monarch, George I, and that it also had a quality of belligerence, in a community still overwhelmingly dissenting in its religious disposition, that was impolitic as well as un-Christian.

Whether due to Henry Harris's influence or to James Franklin's essentially temperate mind, the *Courant*, in the issue following the last of the Dogood papers, published a long piece by "a true Son of the Church" (i.e., of England) with the appropriate pseudonym "Harry Concord" (probably Henry Harris), which was far from incendiary. Indeed, if the Puritan priests were as concerned with reconciliation as they were haunted by heresy, they would have welcomed it; but the very tolerance of the letter was anathema to Puritan doctrine, as was also its insistence that the division of the church between conformists and nonconformists was bound to be antithetical to true reformation. The language of the piece was eloquent, persuasive, and, in its tone and purpose, imbued with genuine Christian altruism. Through it also was a strong current of common sense. "I have often thought with Astonishment, how strange it is, that there should be such bloody Bickerings and Jars between *Conformists* and *Nonconformists*, about Trifles and Circumstantials, when they all agree in the Fundamental Articles of the Christian Religion. And it is by no Means reasonable to suppose, that either Side can be free from Blame, while one [the Church of England] are too rashly charg'd with *Idolatry, False Worship,* and *symbolizing with Papists,* and the other [Congregationalists] stigmatiz'd with the invidious Names of *Puritans, Fanaticks, Schismaticks, Conventiclers,* and the like; and all this attended with Fulminations, Thunders and Anathemas. . . . The Church of *England* is doubtless a true and excellent Church; but (tho' I am of that Communion) I dare not say, as some do, that it is *The true Church,* exclusive of all others . . . for Christ's Church is not limited to any Sect or Party whatsoever."[42] The letter, published on October 15, 1722, carried the convictions of Henry Harris, who seemed—alone among Boston's Church of England following —to have been less than swept off his feet by the conversion of the rector of Yale back to the faith of his fathers, and he wrote to the perplexed

[42] *New-England Courant,* No. 63 (October 8 to October 15, 1722).

Bishop of London, the aging John Robinson, to whose see the colonial churches were entrusted, that Cutler had been led by Checkley "to declare for the Church of England upon Jacobite principles namely, the invalidity or nullity of the Baptism & other ordinances administered by the Dissenters."[43] Though the total disinterest of Harris's utterances may have been qualified by the fact that Dr. Cutler, and not he to his regret, had been called to the rectorship of the new Church of England parish (Christ Church) at Boston's "North End," the letter was a powerful document, unanswerable in its argument, with regard to the mounting Anglican-Congregational wrangling, that ". . . while this fatal and *scandalous Division* lasts, it . . . will not only be dangerous to the State, but breed Animosities, Strife and bitterness in the different Parties." In response to it, there was an unaccustomed silence from the Puritan preceptors.

In the same issue of the *Courant*, there was a letter, signed "Ireaneus, Junior" (after the second-century Bishop of Lyons, who labored to reconcile the quarrelsome sects of early Christendom), which cited, *inter alios*, Richard Bancroft, seventy-fifth Archbishop of Canterbury (from 1604 to 1610) a stern opponent of the Puritan movement from its earliest days, who nevertheless decreed that Scotch presbyters could be consecrated bishops, without first being reordained in the Anglican communion, and that Carolinian archfoe of Puritanism, Archbishop William Laud, who was willing to concede that the reformed churches, overseas at least, were of "the true Religion, and the same which we profess and honour at Home."[44] But the complaint of the Puritan priests was not that the Church of England had adherents that questioned the validity of their ordinations but that they, including *Courant* correspondents, did *not* question the validity of episcopal ordination with its connotation of an apostolic succession. To them the *Courant* was impudent in defense of something that needed no defense—presbyterial ordination—and citing archbishops did not improve their case.

The *Courant* kept it up in the next issue. "Irenaeus, Junior" wrote another longer letter, occupying most of the first page and pressing his argument that the great minds of the Church of England accepted the validity of presbyterial ordination. The grounds that he introduced in support of his view were less impressive than those in his first letter. They were not much more than a semantical claim that the word "apostolic," as prized by the Anglican Church, had nothing to do with an episcopal succession but referred only to the acceptance by the church of the faith and doctrine of the apostles—a reduction of the "Apostolic Church" of the Nicene Creed to an empty phrase in the minds of most churchmen and

[43] *Papers Relating to the History of the [Protestant Episcopal] Church in Massachusetts* (Boston, 1873), 175.

[44] *New-England Courant*, No. 63 (October 8 to October 15, 1722).

most dissenters. Not much more impressive was an anonymous communication, occupying the rest of the first page, which disputed the thesis, advanced by an Anglican critic, of the Yale converts to the effect that their change in religious convictions was governed by their material interests—a charge of some merit in the case of Timothy Cutler, who frankly stated that he kept his conversion to himself "until a favorable opportunity offered" (i.e., the call to the rectorship of Christ Church).[45] The letter also suggested that the critic should question no one's conversion since his own wife had been a convert. The quality of the *Courant's* treatment of the controversy deteriorated notably in that issue of October 20, 1722. It contributed nothing to either an understanding of the principles involved or a diminishing of the heat generated.

In the next issue, the *Courant* continued to fan the flames. Significantly, however, it reverted to the light, satirical tone that had first won it distinction in the grim literature of the Bible Commonwealth. The lead article poked fun at the grave sense of concern with which the Yale conversions had been taken in Boston. In doing so, the paper necessarily treated lightly some matters most sacred to the Puritan sensibilities. It suggested that husbands and wives should love each other all the more in order to avoid the possibility of separation that might follow the news that the ordinations of the ministers who married them were invalid. The real offensiveness, however, came with a further suggestion that mocked baptism—the very cornerstone of the Puritan faith: ". . . what shall those Persons do who have been *christened*, alias *couzened*, in plain English, *cheated* by their Ministry, who had no Commission to baptize? It is thought many of them will turn *Anabaptists*, and be dipt . . . it is well worthy of Enquiry, If the Administrators be wrong, the Mode or Manner of Baptizing wrong, and the Subjects (to wit, Infants) wrong, whether they be not all wrong."[46] This implication of a curse on both your houses was, of course, tantamount to dismissing all the doctrinal advocacy and insistences of the Puritan teachers as just so much jargon and doctrinal straining at gnats. Never before had a publication, even though it was on the side of episcopacy or of adult baptism, suggested that *all* such dogma was perhaps in error. It was explicable, though not congenial and usually not tolerable, to the Puritan mind to have differences in doctrine; but to have no doctrine at all, or to question the validity of all, was totally beyond comprehension. James Franklin was steering a hazardous course.

On Monday, November 5, 1722, Timothy Cutler, and his two tutors from Yale, Samuel Johnson and Daniel Browne, set sail from Boston for England—much to the relief of the Puritans, though they would be back —and the great crisis, with a new rector and new tutors installed at Yale,

---

[45] Cutler to Thomas Hollis, as reported by the latter in a letter to Benjamin Colman, January 14, 1723, cited in Quincy, *History of Harvard University*, I, 365.
[46] *New-England Courant*, No. 65 (October 22 to October 29, 1722).

seemed at its end. The *Courant*, however, took yet another step to keep it alive by publishing an answer to a declaration, published by John Campbell in his *News-Letter*, by Yale College to the effect that the conversion of its ex-rector and his colleagues to the Church of England amounted, for all practical purposes, to their embracing the Roman Church and Popery. The response to this charge was written by the two Yale tutors and by James Wetmore, a Yale graduate and minister of the Congregational parish at North Haven, who resigned his charge in 1722 to join Cutler in seeking ordination in the Anglican Church in England, from which he returned to become rector of the Church of England parish in Rye, New York. The gist of the Yale declaration was that Cutler had maintained that there was no salvation outside of the Church of England and that other churches having no diocesan bishops were not true churches. Cutler's three defenders said, in the *Courant*, "that he said and (as we are firmly perswaded) intended no such thing." The letter, a moderate one that occupied the lead position in the paper, stated that Cutler had simply joined the church "which could best make out its Claim to the Appelation of the true Church, with Relation to the Regularity of those Offices and Powers, which relate to its Constitution as a Society. . . ."[47] This was substantially true, since what Cutler really couldn't stand was the chaos and disorder of Congregationalism as a sect; but his manner was more abrasive than his defenders conceded, and the *Courant* offended once more the Puritans by publishing this defense of Cutler.

* * *

Throughout the remainder of November, through December and into January, James Franklin and his *Courant* continued to nip at the heels of the establishment, here snapping at the civil and there at the ecclesiastical authorities. The *Courant* resumed the battle, started by Silence Dogood six months earlier, against elaborate and insincere funeral elegies and the impoverished verse in which they were couched. The attack was, of course, directed at the ministers, the chief practitioners of the art, and at the students in Harvard College, their heirs apparent. "It is very much to be desir'd that the Reverend and Learned President and Fellows of our College," the *Courant* concluded, "would exert their Authority and Influence to refrain young Students from publishing in Print those things, which, (tho' they might be tolerable if they were compos'd by *Tom Law*, Father *French*, or any other Honest Plough-man, yet) are a Disgrace to the Academy and a Scandal to the whole Country." The piece castigated the elegies not only for the false witness that they bore to the dead but also for their dreadful literary craftsmanship and their woeful bankruptcy of expression in slavish capitulation to their rhyme schemes: "He wrote what he did never think,/Meerly to make the Verse cry, *Clink*:/ And

[47] Ibid., No. 66 (October 29 to November 5, 1722).

rather than offend the Metre,/Black should be White, or *Paul* be *Peter.*"[48]

Early in December, James Franklin added fuel to the fires he had set by publishing a strong article on the disastrous effect that flatterers had upon those appointed to govern. Though it spoke of "Princes and Rulers," the message was lost on no one that the "pernicious consequence" of such flattery also afflicted governors of less regal status. The *Courant* found the flatterers equally guilty with the flattered, and to make its point clear, singled out a particularly repugnant class of flatterer. It was, of course, the clergy. And once again the ministers of Boston were convinced that the *Courant* and its publisher were bent on destroying their authority and, therefore, their effectiveness. As a matter of fact, the language of the *Courant* left them little grounds to doubt it. After quoting Psalm 12, "The wicked walk on every side, when the Vilest Men are exalted," the article hit hard at the ministers and in such a manner as to make the Mathers, fully aware of their political meddling, especially squirmish: "Nor is the Matter much mended, when *Clergymen* turn Flatterers, and take upon them to prescribe and dictate to a Prince [Increase Mather had hand-picked Sir William Phips as royal governor], or the Consequence like to be more pernicious to a People. I would hope the Clergy *in general* are good Men; but it is notorious, that many of them are but *Tygers* and *Wolves* in Sheps Clothing, and that the World has suffered extreamly by their blind and furious Conduct. It is a true Observation which some have made, That of all Men living they are the worst [i.e., the most opportunistic] Politicians."[49]

Such assertions, made with no accompanying evidence or specific examples, left the ministers frustrated and angered, for none of them could come forward and say that it was not he about whom the *Courant* was talking without raising the question in the readers' minds as to what made him think that he was; the ministers were put by the paper in a damned-if-they-do-and-damned-if-they-don't position. The next week the *Courant* took a stand against the driving of hackney coaches to churches on Sunday as an infringement of the command to keep the Sabbath holy, on the grounds that it both created a racket in the streets and required the coachmen to labor—a view which the ministers might have regarded as a creditable one. But the article, in the form of a dialogue, seemed to go out of its way to take a gibe at the clergy. The query was put, "But if this be so great an Evil, why have we not been told of it from the Pulpit? Our Ministers are very faithful to warn us of our Sin and Danger." A derogatory answer was given: "I am of Opinion that if the Common People had followed this Practice, the Pulpit had rung with [i.e., condemned] it long ago, And besides, the Clergy are not Lords over our Consciences; nor are

[48] Ibid., No. 68 (November 5 to November 12, 1722).
[49] Ibid., No. 71 (December 3 to December 10, 1722).

we (blessed be GOD) reduc'd to such Servitude and Ignorance, as not to know what is Sin, and what is Duty without them."[50] The comment was gratuitous; it is not likely that James Franklin and the Couranteers were greatly disturbed by coaches on the streets on Sundays. It was another, a homely, way, apt to be popular with the leather aprons, of again striking out at the establishment—the rich who could afford hackney coaches and the toadying who condoned their use.

On Christmas Eve, 1722, the *Courant* injected itself into yet another theological dispute—the celebration of Christmas. For almost a century it had been totally forbidden, but with the coming of the royal governors and the founding of parishes of the Church of England, local laws and customs could no longer prevent traditional observations of the Feast of the Nativity by those not under the discipline of the dissenting churches. The *Courant* published two long poems, in the inevitable couplets, the first declaring, "In Heart and Voice we'll our Affections raise,/Whilst the glad Organ labours in its Praise," while the second took the opposite view, with the complaint less that Christmas was celebrated than that it was celebrated on the wrong date—December 25, "the *Popish* Christmas"—instead of September 11, basing its argument on the strained notion that Palestine's climate was like New England's and there could be no shepherds "watching their flocks by night" in December. Franklin preceded the rhymed dialogue with a note that he was "neither *Conformist* nor *Nonconformist.*"[51] but the Puritan ministers would have regarded his views as suspect, at the outset of his introduction of the discussion, in his reference to "the Festival of *Christmas* drawing nigh," since to the orthodox it was neither a festival nor Christmas but an anti-Christian pagan rite. A sensible letter appeared in the next issue of the *Courant*, doubting whether anyone could prove the exact date of the Nativity and suggesting that the best manner of celebrating Christ's birth, in any case, was not, in Archbishop Tillotson's words, "to run into all Manner of Excess for Twelve Days together, in Honour of our Saviour."[52] The saintly tone was a bit out of character for the *Courant*. It was also short-lived. In the same issue, leading the local news items was a report and sardonic comment on the secret departure of Governor Shute for London. It was the beginning of another contretemps between the *Courant* and the authorities.

* * *

By December of 1722, after six years of uneasy rule over the province, Samuel Shute had apparently concluded that Massachusetts was ungovernable. From the beginning, the House of Representatives, always distrustful of royal governors on the grounds that they served the crown rather than the colony, had quarreled with Shute, a soldier who was used

---

[50] Ibid., No. 72 (December 10 to December 17, 1722).
[51] Ibid., No. 73 (December 17 to December 24, 1722).
[52] Ibid., No. 74 (December 24 to December 31, 1722).

to commanding. He was opposed by the House on currency reform, on the extent of his power to adjourn the legislature and to confirm the speaker of the House, and on his conduct of the Indian wars of the early 1720s. The House also humiliated him by cutting his salary in the face of a badly depreciated currency, and they sprinkled their proceedings with petty rudenesses and rebukes. The members of the House, the popular repository of power in the province, set an example of contempt for the governor and his office eagerly seized upon by the populace. "It was known to his friends," said a successor, Thomas Hutchinson, "that as he sat in one of the chambers of his house, the window and door of a closet being open, a bullet entered, through the window and door passages, and passed very near him."[53] During the legislative session of December 1722, the House of Representatives was in open defiance of the governor, making its disdain for him clear in the process, over an inquiry into the conduct of the war; and the representatives challenged his authority over theirs to command the military and to appoint officers. On Wednesday, December 19, the House sent a committee on the war to demand that the governor order Colonel Shadrach Walton, in command of the forces on the eastern frontier, to present himself in the House for questioning. Shute refused, saying that ". . . if his Officers are to answer for any thing, it should be before the General Court [i.e., the governor and the Council, as well as the House of Representatives]."[54] Walton appeared before the House anyhow, in response to a summons, but refused to answer any questions without the permission of the governor, who refused such permission unless the governor and councilors were present; but the House refused to question the colonel in the presence of the governor and Council.

Weary of the stalemate, Shute took Judge Sewall "aside to the Southeast Window of the Council Chamber, to speak to me about adjourning the Gen¹ Court to Monday next because of Christmas."[55] This was, of course, a sensitive matter to bring up with so strictly orthodox a Puritan as Judge Sewall—all the more sensitive since Shute, to add to his political difficulties, was regarded as a religious renegade, having been the grandson of a nonconformist minister and a pupil of Charles Morton (minister of the dissenting church at Charlestown and a fellow of Harvard) when Morton was the leading nonconformist teacher in England, with such children of the Puritan revolution as Daniel Defoe and Samuel Wesley among his students; and now Shute was occupying a special pew in King's Chapel with his arms adorning it, was heading its vestry, and was the principal subscriber to its building fund. Sewall told Shute that he would have to think it over and then invited Cotton Mather to dinner to see what *he* thought. Confident that it would be roundly defeated, they agreed that

---

[53] Thomas Hutchinson, *The History of Massachusetts*, 3rd ed. (Boston, 1795), II, 260.
[54] *Journals of the House of Representatives of Massachusetts*, IV, 156.
[55] Sewall, *Diary*, III, 314.

Shute should put the proposal to a vote of the whole General Court. On Friday, December 28, the governor discussed the matter with the Council. "I spake against it," Sewall recorded, seeing it as a threat by the Church of England to cram its practices down dissenting throats, ". . . The Dissenters came a great way for their Liberties and now the Church had theirs, yet they could not be contented, except they might Tread all others down."[56] Perhaps as a final act of defiance of a body that had constantly defied him, Shute, shortly before noon on Saturday, without bringing it up for a vote either of the Council or the General Court as a whole, adjourned the session until the Wednesday after Christmas. Meanwhile, he had an even greater surprise for his archfoe, the House. Having secretly gotten permission from Whitehall to go back to London for consultation, he made only one more appearance before the Council, on Wednesday, December 26, when he dined with the members. On Friday, to the astonishment of the entire province, the lieutenant governor, William Dummer, read a letter from Shute saying that he was on board *Seahorse*, a frigate of the Royal Navy at Nantasket, and was about to sail for England, where he intended to stay almost a year. Sewall was appalled by this event and Shute's failure to "salute the Council" before his departure. The House was no less distressed (". . . a very great surprise . . .") for fear Shute intended to prefer charges against its members for repeated insurrection against his authority "in attempting to encroach upon the Royal Prerogative, or coming into things they had not a Right to. . . ."[57]

All this culmination of the six-year feud between the province's administrative and legislative authorities occurred on Friday, December 28, 1722. James Franklin had no reason to support either faction, since one has sought to silence him and the other had jailed him. But on the following Monday he managed to offend both, less by any specific statement than by once again chipping away at the authority and the sense of responsibility of the civil establishment. The news content of the offending item was accurate enough and seemed to be based on access to members of the General Court, since it did no more than say that the governor had left a letter with the lieutenant governor revealing his boarding *Seahorse* with the intent of being absent until the fall. But the *Courant* added a comment that could be taken only as disrespectful of the governor, if meant sardonically, and disrespectful of the House, if meant seriously: "The Reasons of his Excellency's sudden Departure (at this Juncture) are variously guess'd at; but it being our Business to relate Matters of Fact, we shall purposely omit mentioning the different Surmises of People. However, it is certain that he has hereby depriv'd the Town of an Opportunity of showing those publick Marks of Respect, which are undoubtedly due to him for his WISE and JUST Administration among us."[58]

[56] Ibid.
[57] *Journals of the House of Representatives of Massachusetts*, IV, 173.
[58] *New-England Courant*, No. 74 (December 24 to December 31, 1722).

Not satisfied with its ambivalent comment on the chaotic civil estab-lishment, the *Courant* shortly cut a broad, jagged swath through the religious character of the Bible Commonwealth. All the first and part of the second page of the *Courant's* second issue of 1723 was devoted to a hard-worded essay, in the characteristic form of an anonymous letter, on the nature of hypocrisy. It was fundamentally an attack upon any religiocentric society, its thesis being that hypocrisy was inevitably implicit in a society that would have all its institutions and all its motivations depend for their justification upon a firmly established religious order—further that the hypocrisy was apt to develop in direct proportion to the degree of religious pretensions. "For my own part," the author concluded, in his most scathing paragraph, "whenever I find a man full of religious Cant and Pellaver, I presently suspect him of being a Knave: Religion, is indeed the *principal Thing*; but too much of it, is worse than none at all. The World abounds with Knaves and Villains, but of all Knaves, the *Re-ligious Knave* is the worst; and Villanies acted under the Cloak of Religion are the most Execrable. Moral Honesty, tho' it will not of it self carry a Man to Heaven, yet, I am sure there is no going thither *without it*: And however such men, of whom I have been speaking may palliate their wick-edness, they will find, that *Publicans* & Harlots will enter the Kingdom of Heaven before themselves." The essay caused such a furor that Christo-pher Taylor, who was rumored to have been its author, felt called upon to write, in the next week's edition of *The Boston News-Letter,* a denial that he had written it or another letter, in the same *Courant,* accusing the peo-ple, obviously through the agency of the House, of goading a "good spirited Governour to such an *inflexible Resolution* as that (*when he re-turns*) he will make you *know he is your Governour.*"[59] Taylor failed, however, to deny authorship of another letter, in the same issue, which ad-vised the dispatching of "two Persons born among us" to London to coun-tervene Shute's probable efforts to discredit the province in Whitehall; in the *Courant* of January 28, 1723, an advertisement pointing this out ap-peared, obviously with Taylor's knowledge and permission. Shute never did return, but the House was badly bitten by the warning that he might do so with a vengeance backed by Whitehall directives to keep the legisla-ture in its place.

Though the House had repudiated Shute's efforts, only six months earlier, to impose prior restraints upon James Franklin and his *Courant* by requiring the latter's contents to be cleared with the provincial secretary, the representatives now sensed a danger to themselves as well as to the ad-ministration in the *Courant's* insolence. Accordingly, when the councilors took action on the morning of January 14, 1723, to institute repressive measures against the *Courant,* the House found itself in agreement—partly reassured, no doubt, by the fact that Shute was gone and no longer dominating the Council. The vote of the Council, reported to the House

[59] Ibid., No. 76 (January 7 to January 14, 1723).

in the afternoon, was to the point: "Whereas the paper called the *New-England Courant,* of this days date contains many passages in which the Holy Scriptures are perverted, and the Civil Government, Ministers and People of the Province highly reflected on. Ordered, that *William Tailer, Samuel Sewall,* and *Penn Townsend* Esqrs; with such as the Honourable House shall joyn, be a Committee to consider and report what is proper for this Court to do thereon."[60] On concurring, the House named Francis Fulham, of Weston, Jonathan Remington, of Cambridge, Ebenezer Stone, of Newton, and Nathaniel Knowlton, of Ipswich, as its members of the committee.

The joint committee went to work almost immediately and dealt with the subject with precipitousness, for it had agreed upon its report on Tuesday, January 15, 1723, the day after it was appointed. That the committee would be of one mind was almost implicit in its make-up. Of the three councilors, Judge Sewall and Colonel Townsend had already passed judgment on James Franklin and found him wanting. Judge Sewall, who had by then achieved the rank and title of Chief Justice of the Province, was seventy-one and not likely to change his mind on the *Courant*'s constituting "a high Affront to this Government"—as he had reported the previous July. Penn Townsend was a colonel of militia and an investor in various small enterprises and had held public office of one sort or another for forty years. He was a contemporary and close friend of Sewall, with whom he shared an enthusiasm for funerals and who mentioned him as a fellow bearer on well over a hundred occasions. William Taylor was also a veteran officeholder of fifty years' service, a colonel in the militia, and a contemporary of Sewall, who was, of course, one of the bearers at Taylor's wife's funeral. Of the four members of the committee from the House, none came from Boston, whereas all three of the councilors did. Like the Councilors, however, all of them were active members of the Congregational Church. All of them had served in the House for at least eight years, except for Stone, who had served four. Fulham and Stone, like Townsend and Taylor, were officers in the militia. Fulham, Remington, and Knowlton were friends and dining companions of Sewall, and Remington was a judge of the Court of Common Pleas and often served as a kind of junior emissary of Sewall in the latter's efforts to keep Harvard College on the track of orthodoxy. Altogether it was a group of highly orthodox figures, long active as part of the civil establishment and unswerving in their devotion to the ecclesiastical establishment. James Franklin could expect no deliverance from them.

On the afternoon of Tuesday, January 15, 1723, Colonel Taylor, on behalf of the committee of seven from the Council and the House, submitted its report to the upper house:

The Committee appointed to Consider the Paper Called the New England Courant published Monday the 14[t] Curr[t]: are humbly of opinion,

[60] *Journals of the House of Representatives of Massachusetts,* IV, 205.

That the Tendency of the Said paper is to Mock Religion, & bring it into Contempt, That the Holy Scriptures are therein prophanely abused, that the Revr^d and faithfull Ministers of the Gospell are Injuriously Reflected upon, his Majesties Government affronted, and the peace & Good Order of his Majesties Subjects of this Province disturbed by the Said Courant, and for prevention of the like offense, for the future,—The Committee Humbly propose that James Franklyn the Printer & Publisher thereof be Strictly forbidden, by this Court to print, or publish the New England Courant, or any Pamphlet or paper of the like Nature, Except it be first Supervised, by the Secretary of this Province, And the Justices of his Majesties Sessions of the peace for the County of Suffolk, at their next adjournm^t be directed to take Sufficient Bond of the Said Franklyn for his Good Behavior for Twelve Months.[61]

The report was an extraordinarily severe one, clearly in the nature of a bill of attainder. For all practical purposes, it would reinstitute a licensing system that it had flatly denied Governor Shute the power to establish and that the British Parliament had repealed, by refusing to renew it, as early as 1694, nearly thirty years earlier. The sweeping character of the restriction of the *Courant*, as expressed in the phrase "or any Pamphlet or paper of the like Nature," was of tyrannical dimensions. But the committee's report was more. Without any trial at all, it would deprive Franklin of his means of livelihood, commandeer his property by requiring him to post "Sufficient Bond," and harass him by ordering him to submit everything that he printed to the secretary of the province, who could not only censor his copy, or that of anyone else he printed or published, but also delay clearing it until it was so dated or irrelevant as to be useless.

On Wednesday, January 16, 1723, the day after it adopted the Draconian report, the Council sent Edward Bromfield, one of its oldest and most influential members, to convey the report to the House. Bromfield was one of the wealthiest merchants in the colonies, a member of the Old South, an intimate crony of Judge Sewall and a patron and benefactor of Cotton Mather. The House dutifully listened to the reading of the report and concurred without dispute or amendment. James Franklin was now explicitly ordered no longer to print his *Courant*, or any other paper or pamphlet, unless it was cleared in advance, and moreover he was to post bond to be forfeited if he should do otherwise.

The order was so extreme and so anachronistic that Franklin refused to take it as an act seriously intended to be executed. He ignored and defied it. On the following Monday, January 21, 1723, *The New-England Courant* came out as usual—not in some bland version to test the will of the General Court but in a spirited edition to try its patience. The first page was devoted to two carefully selected psalms of David, as translated by Isaac Watts. The first was Psalm 50, which, as rendered by Watts into rhymed verse some five years earlier, seemed designed for the use of one less in the predicament of the intrepid King of Israel than in that of the

[61] *General Court Records*, XI, 493.

obstinate printer of Boston. Most of the stanzas could not avoid construction, in the context of the preceding week's events, as an expression of open contempt of the Great and General Court:

> The Sons of Violence and Lies
>   Join to devour me, Lord;
> But as my hourly Dangers rise
>   My refuge is thy Word . . .
>
> They wrest my Words to Mischief still,
>   Charge me with unknown Faults;
> Mischief doth all their Counsels fill,
>   And Malice all their Thoughts.
>
> Shall they escape without thy Frown?
>   Must their Devices stand?
> O cast the haughty Sinner down,
>   And let him know thy Hand![62]

It was the first time that the members of the Council and House were publicly equated in the Bible Commonwealth with the "Sons of Violence" and "haughty Sinners" that had plagued David when, an outlaw from the vengeful Saul, he sought survival on the steppes of Judah. The second selection, Psalm 58, historically identified in the King James Version as "Reproof of Wicked Judges," thundered even more directly to Judges Sewall and Remington and their colleagues:

> Judges, who rule the World by Laws,
> Will ye despise the righteous Cause,
>   When th' injured poor before you stands?
> Dare ye condemn the righteous Poor,
> And let rich Sinners 'scape secure,
>   While Gold & Greatness bribe your Hands?
>
> Have ye forgot or never knew
> That God will judge the Judges, too?
>   High in the Heavens his Justice reigns;
> Yet you invade the Rights of God,
> And send your bold Decrees abroad
>   To bind the Conscience in your Chains.[63]

Lest any reader mistake the judges to whom the *Courant* was applying the verses, the issue brazenly printed both the order of the Council creating the committee to pass judgment on it and the report of the committee ordering James Franklin to cease its publication. "The Courant comes out very impudently,"[64] Judge Sewall fumed. Before the issue appeared, the House had been prorogued until March, but the Council was in session and on Thursday, January 24, 1723, "Voted that it be recommended to

---

[62] *New-England Courant*, No. 77 (January 14 to January 21, 1723).
[63] Ibid.
[64] Sewall, *Diary*, III.

Penn Townsend, Edward Bromfield & Josiah Willard [son of Judge Sewall's old pastor and friend, Samuel, and the secretary of the province, who would have been the official censor of the *Courant* had Franklin followed the General Court's order] Esq^rs to issue out their Warrant for apprehending James Franklyn of Boston Printer, & that they bind him over to answer, at the next Assizes to be held for the County of Suffolk, for his high contempt of ye order of the Genl Assembly at their last Session referring to his Paper called the New England Courant."[65] Meanwhile, James Franklin was preparing the copy for his next issue, to be published four days later on Monday, January 28, 1723, but which would be set up in type by sundown on Saturday, January 26, by James and Benjamin, working intensely to have the job finished during the brief hours of the January daylight.

The issue appeared on schedule. It was given over for the most part to a bitingly satirical letter of advice, obviously written by James Franklin and using phrasing that he had used in previous writings, as to how to publish a newspaper "without ministering just occasion of Offence to any, especially to the polite and *pious* People, of whom there is considerable numbers in this Land." Ten rules were advanced to insure acceptability, all of them aimed, like so many arrows, at the heart of the rationale used by the General Court to suppress the *Courant*: "Whatever you do, be very tender of the *Religion of the Country*, which you were brought up in and Profess. . . . Take great care that you do not cast injurious Reflections on the *Reverend and Faithful Ministers of the Gospel* . . . when you abuse the Clergy you do not consult your own Interest, for you may be sure they will improve their influence to the uttermost, to suppress your Paper . . . you ought to take great care that you are not *too general* in your reflections. . . . By no means cast any Reflections on the *Civil Government*, under the Care and Protection of which you live . . . avoid Quotations from prophane and scandalous Authors. . . . On the other hand, we think it very unsuitable to bring in Texts of *Sacred Scripture* into your Paper, (unless on extraordinary Occasions) for hereby Men lose that Reverence & Veneration which is due to the Divine Oracles [i.e., the clergy] . . . avoid the Form and Method of Sermons, for that is vile and impious in such a Paper as yours. . . . Be very general in your Writings, and when you condemn any Vice, do not point out any particular Persons. . . . BEWARE of casting dirty Reflections on that worthy Society of *Gentlemen*, scoffingly called THE CANVASS CLUB . . . some of them are Men of Power and Influence, and (if you offend them) may contribute not a little to the crushing of your Paper."[66] The point of all this contradictory advice, of course, was that no paper worth its salt could be published if the editor worried about pleasing everybody and offending nobody.

[65] *Council Records*, VII, 452–53.
[66] *New-England Courant*, No. 78 (January 21 to January 28, 1723).

On the day that the issue appeared, the sheriff and undersheriff of Suffolk County were ordered by that county's Court of General Sessions "in His Majesties Name to attach the body of James Franklin of Boston . . . and bring him before the Court of General Sessions. . . ." The undersheriff, John Darrell, "made Diligent Search and I cannot find him in my precinct," he reported in his endorsement on the warrant.[67]

James Franklin, printer, had gone into hiding, it would seem, rather than either stopping publication of his paper or yielding to censorship.[68] *The New-England Courant*, the press that printed it, the contributors who wrote for it, and the apprentice, Benjamin, were still to be found in Queen Street. But neither the order of the General Court nor the warrant of the Court of General Sessions was directed at them collectively or as individuals, nor were they—due no doubt to legal carelessness—enjoined from publishing the *Courant* or "any Pamphlet or paper of like Nature." The order applied only to James Franklin. And so they went ahead.

* * *

The last issue of *The New-England Courant* to appear over the imprint "*James Franklin,* at his Printing-House in Queen Street, near the Prison," appeared, with the editor-publisher in absentia, on Monday, February 4, 1723. It is not unlikely that the Couranteers, his family, and Benjamin knew where he was (Undersheriff Darrell did not persist very vigorously in his "Diligent Search," which could have lasted no more than one afternoon), and that he was consulted and had a voice as to what went into the paper and the editorial tone that it would take toward an establishment that had a warrant out for his arrest. Whatever James Franklin's clandestine role, the *Courant* did not back down but pressed the matter, and its tone remained far from conciliatory. The lead piece concerned the practice of good King Alfred, the lawgiver, in the ninth century, of treating judges as guilty of heinous crimes if they punished men "*against Law* or where there was *no Law* provided," and it related instances of where Alfred ordered the hanging of judges for rash judgments imposed without indictment and without appeal "lest it should be made a Precedent afterwards for condemning Men *without Law*."[69]

A second longer piece was addressed to an unnamed ringleader, unquestionably Judge Sewall, in the Council's prosecution of Franklin. It was an extremely strong, direct, and valiant attack on the legislative arrest of a man who had broken no law, rooted in a sound awareness of the principles of British jurisprudence and expressed with forthrightness and dignity—

---

[67] Suffolk Court Files, 16480.

[68] James Franklin's marriage date to Ann Smith is given in the carefully constructed genealogy in *The Papers of Benjamin Franklin*, I, lix, as February 4, 1723, which would have occurred midway between his fleeing the sheriff's warrant on January 28 and his return on February 12, 1723. The date of the marriage record is obviously old style, or 1724 new style. The date in the warrant is also old style, 1722, or 1723 new style.

[69] *New-England Courant*, No. 79 (January 28 to February 4, 1723).

the work of an unknown but sure hand, very possibly that of Mr. Gardner. To the judge, whose religious devotion the *Courant* so sorely tried that he forgot legal probity, his anonymous remonstrator wrote:

I am inform'd that your Honour was a leading Man in the late Extraordinary procedure against F[rankli]n the Printer: And inasmuch as it cannot be long before you must appear at *Christ's* enlightened Tribunal, where every Man's work shall by tryed, I humbly beseech you, in the Fear of God, to consider & Examine, whether that Procedure be according to *the first Rules of Justice and Enquiry?* It is manifest, that this Man had broke no *Law*; and you know, Sir, that where there is no Law, there can be no Transgression: And, Sir, methinks you cannot but know, that it is highly *unjust* to punish a Man by a Law, to which the Fact committed is *Antecedent.* The *Law* ever looks *forward*, but never *backward*; but if once we come to punish Men, by vertue of Laws *Ex post Facto,* Farewel *Magna Charta,* and *English Liberties,* for no Man can ever be *Safe,* but may be punished for every Action he does by Laws made afterwards. This, in my humble Opinion, both the Light of Nature and Laws of Justice abhor, and what ought to be detested by all Good men. . . .

The end of Humane Law is to fix the boundaries within which Men ought to keep themselves; But if any are so hardy and presumptuous as to break through them, doubtless they deserve punishment. Now, if this *Printer* had transgress'd any Law, he ought to have been presented by a Grand Jury, and a fair Tryal brought on.

I would further observe to Your Honour the danger of ill Precedents, and that this Precedent *will not sleep*; And, Sir, can you bear to think that Posterity will have Reason to Curse you on the Account hereof; By this our Religion may suffer extreamly hereafter; for, whatever those Ministers (if any such there were) who have push'd on this matter, may think of it, they have made a Rod for themselves in times to come. Blessed be God, we have a good King at present; but if it should please him for our Sins to punish us with a bad one, we may have a S[ecretar]y that will *Supervise* our Ministers Sermons, as to suffer them to print none at all.

I would also humbly remind your Honour, that you were formerly led into an Error, which you afterwards Publickly and Solemnly (and I doubt not, Sincerely) Confess'd and repented of; and Sir, ought not this to make you the more Cautious & Circumspect in your Actions which relate to the publick all your Days.[70]

The reference in the last paragraph was to Judge Sewall's standing at the mourners' bench at meeting in the South Church twenty-six years earlier and listening with bowed head as the Reverend Samuel Willard read that the judge, as a participant in the Salem witchcraft trials, "Desires to take the Blame and shame of it, Asking pardon of men, And especially desiring prayers that God, who has an Unlimited Authority, would pardon that sin. . . ."[71] The reminder was not a cruel personal

[70] Ibid.
[71] Sewall, *Diary*, I, 445 (p 113–34, *supra*).

thrust at the judge for a long-ago act of contrition but a just and convincing example of how the best intentioned of men can err, and later realize it, in the administration of justice. The *Courant* article was entreating the judge to be guided by experience in a strongly relevant case.

The *Courant* apparently knew, too, that the judge represented the last gasps of an old order that had had its day and that suppression of the press was not a particularly popular measure. The undersheriff had obviously given no more than perfunctory response to his orders. And the same issue of the *Courant* that admonished Judge Sewall, a brief but significant item—buried between a report of the funeral of a Narragansett Indian king, who had died "by drinking too largely of that Princely Liquor vulgarly called Rhum, of which he is said to have drank two Gallons at a Sitting," and the shipping news—carried the information that the adoption of the report of the Council citing Franklin was passed in the House by a single vote.

Nevertheless, the warrant was still out for Franklin's arrest; and, the memory of his stay in the prison still fresh in his mind and the minds of his friends, they all knew that he could and probably would be immediately slapped into a wintry cell and left there until he stopped printing his paper or posted security that he did not have for his future good behavior. At some time between February 4 and February 11, the decision was made—and James Franklin, according to Benjamin's recollection, participated in it—that the *Courant* would continue to be printed. This may have been against the spirit of the legislative action on the *Courant's* future, but it was strictly in accord with the letter, for the General Court's order, of course, forbid only James Franklin to publish the paper but did not forbid it to be published by anyone else. "There was a Consultation held in our Printing House among his Friends what he should do in this Case," Benjamin Franklin remembered. "Some propos'd to evade the Order by changing the Name of the Paper; but my Brother seeing Inconveniences [among them was the order's prohibiting his printing not only the *Courant* but "any Pamphlet or paper of the like Nature"], it was finally concluded on as a better Way, to let it be printed for the future under the Name of *Benjamin Franklin*."[72] And at seventeen, Benjamin Franklin became a publisher and editor—an activity that he did not wholly abandon until, an old man in his eightieth year, he left France in 1785 and closed the private press he had set up at his country house at Passy to publish the little light essays—"Bagatelles," he called them, baubles or trifles—for distribution to his friends.[73]

Significantly, in view of James Franklin's plight as a fugitive, there was a

[72] *Autobiography*, 69.
[73] The most authoritative source on the *Bagatelles* is Luther S. Livingston, *Franklin and his Press at Passy* (New York, 1914), but Claude-Anne Lopez, *Mon Cher Papa: Franklin and the Ladies of Paris* (New Haven, 1966), illumines, with scholarship, delight, and insight, the context of their composition. See also pp. 205–6 *supra*.

conspicuous change, in the imprint in addition to that of the publisher's name. The last issue over James Franklin's name bore the imprint, "BOSTON: Printed and Sold by *James Franklin*, at his Printing-House in Queen-Street, near the Prison, where Advertisements and Letters are taken in. . . ." The issues printed over Benjamin's name omitted "near the Prison."

* * *

The New-England Courant's eightieth issue, the first of Benjamin Franklin's long line of publications, appeared on Monday, February 11, 1723. With James Franklin absent, the paper was edited, printed, delivered, and, in considerable part, written by the apprentice. It was not a distinguished achievement. It carried, at the head of the first column, a somewhat dissembling note regarding the change of publishers: "The late [i.e., former] Publisher of this Paper, finding so many Inconveniences would arise by his carrying the Manuscripts and publick News to be supervis'd by the Secretary, as to render his carrying it on unprofitable, has intirely dropt the Undertaking, the Present Publisher having receiv'd the following Piece, desires the Readers to accept of it as a Preface to what they may hereafter meet with in this Paper." James Franklin, of course, had not "intirely dropt the Undertaking" at all; he simply took advantage of the technicality arising from the order that specified James Franklin rather than the *Courant*, or its publisher whoever he was, in its interdiction. But Benjamin Franklin followed it with a long piece, evidently of his own composition, that sounded so wholly unlike James that it could have left no doubt in the minds of the reader that there was a new editorial voice calling the tune, even if not for long.

After a somewhat jumbled and telescoped excerpt from Ovid's *Tristia* relating to separating the satirical from the poisonous, Benjamin began by saying that the press had too long been guilty of "bringing forth an hateful but numerous Brood of Party Pamphlets, malicious Scribbles, and Billingsgate Ribaldry." By this reference, he had to mean primarily the *Courant* itself, since its competitors were usually innocuous to the point of agonizing dullness; but he went on to promise a paper of "Diversion and Merriment . . . Pleasancy and Mirth. . . ." The names of the editor and contributors were to be kept secret, though the former, referred to as "a Doctor in the Chair," was called Janus, whose principal qualification as an "observator" was "being a Man of such remarkable *Opticks*, as to look two ways at once." He then described himself—"a chearly Christian . . . A Man of good Temper, courteous Deportment, sound Judgment, a mortal Hater of Nonsense, Foppery, Formality, and endless Ceremony."[74] This facetious, somewhat sophomoric piece, well below the level of the Dogood series, was followed, clearly as a long space filler, by a reprint of a four-month-old parliamentary address by George I that had already been

[74] *New-England Courant*, No 80 (February 4 to February 11, 1723).

printed and circulated in Boston. Possibly in order to annoy the General Court, the issue also carried an advertisement (repeated in the next two issues) that the *Courant* was selling so many more copies than ever before, and that the two other Boston papers, that advertisers would get a bargain by using its columns. The paper obviously was profiting more than it was suffering from the condemnation visited upon it by the General Court.

Meanwhile, James Franklin's ruse of simply changing the first name of the publisher from James to Benjamin to accommodate a court order that was fully intended to stop the paper altogether, or subject it to prior restraints on its contents, worked. The day after the first issue over Benjamin's name appeared, James Franklin reappeared in Queen Street, still a fugitive from the sheriff's order to appear before the Court of General Sessions but no longer in contempt of the General Court's order to cease printing his paper. He enlisted his fellow printer and *Courant* contributor, Thomas Fleet, and a young baker named James Davenport, to post, in equal parts, the one hundred pounds' surety for his "Good Behavior towards His Majesty and all his Liege People for the space of Twelve Months"[75]—any such sum being far beyond his own resources. He was arrested, however, for the contempt he had shown for the cease and desist order of the General Court when he published three issues of the *Courant* in spite of its order. But the grand jury refused to indict him. It still went against the grain of the people to restrict freedom of speech and the press. The instinct against such restriction was not limited to Boston or to New England. As far away as Philadelphia, the Anglican Andrew Bradford's *American Weekly Mercury*, the only newspaper in Pennsylvania and thus far the first and only in the colonies outside of Boston, rallied forcefully to James Franklin's defense:

My Lord *Coke* observes, that to *punish first and then enquire*, the Law abhors, but here Mr. *Franklin* has a severe sentence pass'd upon him even to the taking away Part of his Livelihood, without being called to make Answer. An Indifferent [i.e., disinterested] Person would judge by this vote against *Couranto*, that the Assembly of the Province of the *Massachusetts Bay* are made up of Oppressors and Bigots who make Religion only the Engine of Destruction to the People; and the rather, because the first Letter in the Courant of the 14th of *January* (which the Assembly Censures) so naturally represents and exposes the *Hypocritical Pretenders to Religion*. Indeed, the most famous Politicians in that Government (as the infamous Gov. D[udley] and his Family) have ever been remarkable for Hypocrisy; and it is the general Opinion that some of their Rulers are rais'd up and continued as a Scourge in the Hands of the Almighty for the Sins of the People. Thus much we could not forbear saying, out of Compassion to the distressed People of the Province, who must now resign all Pretences to Sense and Reason, and submit to the Tyranny of Priestcraft, and Hypocrisy. P.S. By private Letters from Boston we are informed, That the

75 *Records of General Sessions of the Peace [Suffolk County] 1719–1725,* 186.

Bakers there are under great Apprehensions of being forbid baking any more Bread, unless they will submit to the Secretary as Supervisor General and Weigher of the Dough, before it is baked into Bread, and offered to Sale.[76]

Bradford's words reflected accurately the misgivings of the leather aprons about a controlled press, his parallel of the bakers' being regulated as to their recipes perhaps influencing James Davenport's decision to post surety for James Franklin. And so the grand jurors in Boston flatly refused to indict Franklin on the charges of contempt brought by the General Court and, in due time, ". . . the said James Francklyn was Discharged by Proclamation from his said Recognisance."[77] And James Davenport, baker, and Thomas Fleet, printer, got their hundred pounds back.

In the first issue of the *Courant* after his brother's return, Benjamin wrote the only feature piece (the rest of the contents consisted almost entirely of overseas news from the previous October)—a pungent, sprightly essay, equal to the best of the Dogood papers, on the folly of titles of honor. It was in part, too, a brilliant satire of *No Cross, No Crown*, the eloquent plea for universal tolerance and social reform and against economic injustice, luxurious living, and the waste of time, written as William Penn, its author, lingered, a twenty-three-year-old prisoner, in the Tower of London for refusing to take his hat off in court while being tried for unlawful preaching in the street. Franklin had probably been well acquainted with the book; and he certainly shared many of Penn's views, though little of his religious devotion. In any case, he cast into the form of *No Cross, No Crown* his reflections on the emptiness of titles: "In old Time it was no disrespect for Men and Women to be call'd by their own Names: Adam was never called *Master* Adam; we never read of Noah *Esquire*, Lot *Knight* and Baronet, nor the *Right Honourable* Abraham, *Viscount* Mesopotamia, *Baron* of Carran; no, no, they were plain Men, honest Country Grasiers, that took Care of their Families and Flocks. Mosen was a great Prophet, and Aaron a Priest of the Lord, but we never read of the *Reverend Moses*, nor the *Right Reverend Father in God*, Aaron, by Divine Providence, *Lord Arch-Bishop of Israel*: Thou never sawest Madam Rebecca in the Bible, my *Lady* Rachel, nor Mary, tho' a Princess of the Blood after the Death of Joseph, call'd the *Princess Dowager of Nazareth*; no, plain Rebecca, Rachel, Mary, or the *Widow* Mary, or the like: It was no incivility then to mention their naked Names as they were expressed." It was the last of Benjamin's known writings for the *Courant*, though he may have made a few further contributions of less distinctive qualities, and it was the knowing, confident young writer at his best.

* * *

But the great day of the *Courant* was past. Though James Franklin continued the paper, over Benjamin's name, for three more years, he seemed

[76] *American Weekly Mercury*, February 26, 1723.
[77] *Records of Superior Court of Judicature* [Suffolk] 1721–1725, 119.

to have lost the spark and spirit that animated its pages before his latest brush with the legislature and courts. He was probably acutely aware, too, that his friends Baker and Fleet were liable to a financial loss of considerable dimensions for artisans for the three months between his arrest in February and his release from the surety in May. At twenty-six he was tiring of his bachelorhood and was within the year to take an extremely able young woman, Ann Smith, as his wife. And he was also tiring of his bright young apprentice, whom events, as well as the boy's own emerging genius, kept elevating above his master. Already well and admiringly known among the Couranteers as a gifted and witty writer, Benjamin was now becoming well known also throughout the town—not with total admiration. James seemed inclined to steer the *Courant* into less turbulent channels, though it remained the most spirited paper not only in Boston but in all the colonies and continued to publish, albeit less consistently, humorous and pointed essays.

The apprenticeship of Benjamin Franklin was entering its sixth year—and the seventh, eighth, and ninth years stretched out interminably before him. An apt and eager student, he had learned all of the craft that there was to know in the little shop and all that his brother and master had to teach. He felt the heady triumph of seeing his own words in print, of seeing them impress those of his elders whose approval he prized, the Couranteers, and of jolting those who, he thought, were standing in the way of reason or of social progress. He had twice had the satisfaction and experience, however briefly, of the management of the paper and of the printing shop. And he had come to know Boston thoroughly from the taverns and bordellos of the waterfront to the study of Cotton Mather and the chambers of the Governor's Council. He had read widely and wisely; he had developed disciplined habits of thought and inquiry; and he had learned, sometimes painfully, the need and nature of personal diplomacy. Always self-confident, occasionally to a fault, and never either dejected or apprehensive, he felt ready to be on his own, to make his own way, and to govern his own life.

There were others who would also like the cocky young printer to be on his way. Boston was a tightly knit community, for geographic reasons if nothing else, and everyone knew everyone else. Benjamin Franklin was beginning to be known as a pernicious young know-it-all, disrespectful, mischievous, and irreligious. There was genuine feeling in high clerical places that his deistic views, which he had kept no secret, could be a corrupting influence on his own and future generations. His steadfast and articulate defense of his brother's cause had made him no less suspect as a source of future trouble to the civil authorities.

Benjamin Franklin was fully aware of all this: ". . . I reflected that I had already made myself a little obnoxious to the governing Party; and from the arbitrary Proceedings of the Assembly in my Brother's Case it was likely I might if I stay'd soon bring myself into Scrapes; and farther that my indiscrete Disputations about Religion began to make me pointed at with Horror by good People, as in Infidel or Atheist."[78]

The relationship between the brothers was deteriorating, too. Differences between them, which had mangled their association from its beginning, got worse, with James insisting upon the deference from Benjamin due a master, despite the fraternal bond, and Benjamin expecting more indulgence, despite the apprentice articles. "Our Disputes were often brought before our Father," Benjamin recalled, "and I fancy I was either generally in the right, or else a better Pleader, because the Judgment was generally in my favour: But my Brother was passionate and had often beaten me, which I took extremely amiss; and thinking my Apprenticeship very tedious, I was continually wishing for some Opportunity of shortening it. . . ."[79]

The opportunity was of James's, not of Benjamin's, making. In order to make possible the use of Benjamin's name as publisher of the *Courant*, James had to terminate legally the apprentice agreement, for otherwise he could be charged with continuing publication through using an apprentice wholly in his command. Accordingly, he returned the indenture papers to Benjamin, endorsing them with a full discharge. A new agreement was signed secretly, but it would, of course, have had little weight, legally or otherwise, in the context of its execution. Benjamin Franklin was, for all practical purposes, a free being as long as he had in his possession that endorsement on the original agreement, and he was shrewd enough to know it and opportunistic enough to use it. Confident as always, Benjamin did not steal away but informed his brother that he intended to leave, abrogating the secret agreement. Quickly, James Franklin spread the word among the other printers in town about his apprentice's unauthorized departure, and none of them would give him work. His father, too, saw that Benjamin was taking unfair advantage of his master, and sided with James. Benjamin could work on his trade only by leaving Boston and seeking his way in a strange town where he was wholly unknown. With characteristic self-reliance, he made arrangements for a furtive departure from Boston lest his brother or his father take steps to deter him, as, for example, by alerting shipmasters against accepting him as a passenger.

On a September day in 1723, Benjamin went among the Boston booksellers whose wares he had come to know so well, and he sold some of his precious books to them to raise money for passage to New York, where Andrew Bradford's father ran a printing house. He gave the money to his friend, John Collins, with whom he had debated the theses of the books they had both read, to buy him a place on a sloop bound for New York. Collins told the sloop's captain a typical Franklinian story, since all ship-

78 *Autobiography*, 71.
79 Ibid., 68–69.

masters were leery of runaway apprentices, to abet whose escapes was a criminal offense. Collins told the captain that Franklin had to board the ship furtively because he had gotten a girl pregnant and that if he were seen boarding the vessel he would probably be hauled off by her friends and forced to marry her.

Benjamin Franklin, at seventeen, sailed out of Boston Harbor just forty years after his father, Josiah, at twenty-six, had sailed into the port. With him sailed into a larger, more exultant, less somber world most of the pragmatic and none of the dogmatic content of Puritanism. In the eyes of the boy, shining perhaps with wonder at the unknown that lay ahead, was also the radiant assurance of the man, confident, knowing his own strengths and aware of the world's weaknesses. He was sailing, on that soft September night with its benevolent winds (". . . as we had a fair Wind in three Days I found my self in New York near 300 Miles from home . . ."),[80] not only from place to place, staying only a day in New York and then going on to Philadelphia, but also from one age to another. Wholly a product of Cotton Mather's Boston, with its contradictory reliance on curiosity and the intellect and its stubborn insistence upon the orthodoxy of the faith, he was a joyous voyager between the short, stern, resolute tradition of the Puritans and the simmering awareness, in the New World, of liberty as a condition of human society and of reason as an arbiter of human behavior. The child of the Boston tallow chandler was on his way to becoming an emissary of the Enlightenment.

At home, the last words in the last column of the last page, in September 1723, of *The New-England Courant*, of which Benjamin Franklin was still the nominal publisher, was a succinct advertisement that did not waste a word: "James Franklin, Printer in Queen Street, wants a likely lad for an Apprentice."[81]

[80] Ibid., 71.
[81] *New-England Courant*, No. 113 (September 23 to September 30, 1723).

Epilogue

Before his death in 1790 at eighty-four, Benjamin Franklin returned to Boston, with almost decennial regularity: in the spring of 1724, when he had an uneasy reunion with James Franklin and his friends in the printing house and obtained his parents' blessing on his Philadelphia ventures; in 1733, as the successful publisher of *The Pennsylvania Gazette* and of *Poor Richard: an Almanack*, to visit his family again; in 1743, when a meeting with a Scottish experimental philosopher, Archibald Spencer, first turned his interest to electricity; in 1753, when Harvard College gave him his first honorary degree, Master of Arts, in recognition of his advancement of man's knowledge of electricity; in 1754, when he tried unsuccessfully to persuade Governor William Shirley of the merits of his prescient "Albany Plan" for a union of the colonies; in 1763, after a five years' absence as Pennsylvania's agent in England and honorary doctorates from St. Andrew's and Oxford; and, finally, in 1775, when the British Army occupied the town, after the battles of Lexington and Concord, and Franklin could look upon its spires and chimney tops only from across the Charles. In 1789 he wrote a codicil to his will, providing a thousand pounds to the town of Boston to establish a revolving fund for loans to help young artificers launch their careers—the last and lasting gesture of an old man recalling the beginning of a great and varied life.

By then, all of his family, except his youngest sister, Jane Mecum, who survived him by four years, had died—Josiah, his father, at the good age of eighty-eight, in 1745, and Abiah, his mother, at eighty-five in 1752. James Franklin died young, in 1735, at thirty-eight. Three years after Benjamin abrogated his apprentice agreement, James had closed a struggling, dispirited *Courant* and moved his printing house to Newport, where Benjamin visited him during his fatal illness and, in expiation for his desertion of his apprenticeship, undertook to send James's son to school and to train and set him up in the printing trade.

Of Benjamin's three known classmates during his single year at the Boston Latin School, Mather Byles became the liberal minister of the Hollis Street Church in Boston, a Loyalist during the Revolution, and died in 1788, at eighty-two; Samuel Freeman, the brewer's son, prospered briefly in business but died at twenty-two and left his money to help Anglican students at Harvard and the Anglican Church in Boston; and Jeremiah Gridley became an able Tory lawyer, who died a decade before the Revolution began. The postschool companion of Franklin, the "bookish lad" with whom he used to discuss his reading, John Collins, joined Franklin in Philadelphia in 1724, became addicted to alcohol and gambling and, after living on loans from Franklin, had a falling out with him and disappeared on a voyage to Barbados.

The contributors to the *Courant* gradually scattered. The first of them, John Checkley, became rector of King's Church, the first Anglican parish in Providence, but only after he had been indicted and fined in Boston, before his ordination, for publishing a treatise in defense of episcopacy that was judged "a false and scandalous libel," presumably of dissenters. Dr. William Douglass, belatedly convinced of the value of smallpox inoculation, became one of the first epidemiologists in America, attained wide recognition for his work on scarlet fever, and wrote expertly in economics, particularly on the application of Gresham's law to the economy of the colonies. His fellow physician-contributors, George Steward and John Gibbins, practiced medicine in Boston until the 1740s and the 1760s respectively, and both remained active officials of King's Chapel until their deaths. The Reverend Henry Harris, the young associate rector of King's Chapel, continued in that post until, in 1729, he died, sad and disappointed that the Bishop of London had never seen fit to advance him to the rectorship. John Eyre, the wealthy young Harvard graduate who had written the "Peter Hakins" letter that so aroused the Mathers, encountered financial difficulties very early in his career and left Boston to re-establish, successfully, the fortunes of his young family in New Hampshire and to distinguish himself as a soldier at the siege of Louisburg. The rebellious mariner, Captain Christopher Taylor, never married, but, dying in 1734, he left most of his estate to his uxorial servant, Anne Bell, and to Charles Taylor, their natural son. Matthew Adams, the good man who loved literature and who made his library freely available to the boy Franklin, spent much of his time and resources as an executor of the literary estate and a publisher of his favorite nephew, the poet, John Adams. The transplanted Shropshire printer, Thomas Fleet, who posted bond for James Franklin during the latter's interdiction by the General Court, was himself charged with publishing a newspaper that was a "sink of sedition, error and heresy," in 1741, and a year later, "a scandalous and libelous reflection upon His Majesty's Administration"; but the prosecutions failed, and Fleet continued to publish his paper, *The Boston Evening-Post*, until his death in 1758; and his sons continued it after him until the outbreak of Anglo-American hostilities at Lexington in 1775. The other Couranteers—the mysterious and gifted Mr. Gardner, Thomas Lane, Madam Staples, and John Williams—were not heard of further and presumably lived out their lives without unduly alarming church or state.

But it was the Boston of the Mathers that had particularly molded the values and the resistances of the young Franklin, as he sought to absorb all learning that he could reconcile with reason, increasingly doubted what he found uncongenial with it, and deepened his suspicions of the certainty of absolutes and the prudence of extremes. As Benjamin was setting forth, at seventeen, from Boston to Philadelphia and thence into the flowering of the eighteenth century, the body of old Increase Mather, a lingering apostle of the seventeenth, was borne by three of his fellow ministers and by the acting governor, William Dummer, the president of Harvard, John Leverett, and by that doughty defender of the faith, Judge Sewall, "round the North-Meeting House, and so up by Captain [Thomas] Hutchinson's and along by his own House and up Hull Street, into the Tomb in the North burying place, and laid by his first wife," his long life, beginning in 1639, having spanned all but three years of the resolute Puritan experiment of carving out a corner of the wilderness surrounding the Shawmut peninsula as an earthly version of the Heavenly City. But Increase's tortured and gifted son, Cotton, was still alive, and Franklin visited him when he returned to Boston in 1724. "He received me in his library, and on my taking leave, showed me a shorter way out of the house, through a narrow passage, which was crossed by a beam overhead. We were still talking as I withdrew, he accompanying behind, and I, turning partly toward him, when he said hastily, *Stoop, stoop!* I did not understand him till I felt my head hit against the beam. He was a man that never missed any occasion of giving instruction, and upon this he said to me, 'You are young, and have the world before you; STOOP as you go through it, and you will miss many hard thumps.'" This advice, thus "beat into my head," Franklin recalled sixty years later, "has frequently been of use to me; and I often think of it when I see pride mortified, and misfortunes brought upon people by their carrying their heads too high." It was the last that Franklin saw of the Mathers, though he corresponded with Cotton's son, Samuel, and his nephew, Mather Byles, in his last years. Three years after Benjamin's visit to him, Cotton Mather was dead, leaving behind only two of his fifteen children and a long-deranged widow, his third wife. Though not one of the architects of the Bible Commonwealth and, in some sad respects, an unreal parody of it, he was, in a significant way, a magnificent fruition of it and, for future generations, its principal advocate. Aside from Josiah Franklin, his father, and James, his brother, Cotton Mather was perhaps the most lasting single influence of the Boston years on the young Franklin's development, both for his contributions to the boy's thinking and for his articulations of dogma and authority that the boy found sufficiently suspect or repellent to devote much of his long life to resisting and countervening.

Two years later, Judge Sewall, chronicler of the Boston of the Mathers and the Franklins, died and was carried to his family's tomb where he had spent so many hours in happy contemplation of his dead kinsmen, with no one left to record the names of his bearers, the number of scarves and rings distributed, or the size of the assemblage of mourners, as he had done so fondly and faithfully for others for half a century. Perhaps the death of the old judge— "A strong, gentle and great man," in Moses Coit Tyler's words, ". . . a man built, every way, after a large pattern," who stood astride the Bible Commonwealth's civil and ecclesiastical forces, which were at first in league with one another and then contentious, who was among the first to befriend the uprooted young dyer, Josiah Franklin, in 1683, when he arrived with a wife and three small children in a strange land, and who was among the swiftest to chasten Josiah's sons, forty years later, when they rebelled at "authority"—perhaps the death of this sturdy man in 1729 marked, as much as any single event could, the end of the Puritan Boston that planted in the young Benjamin Franklin the seeds of his character, his mind, and his achievement.

Bibliographical Note

For general bibliographies of works by and about Benjamin Franklin, readers are referred to Paul Leicester, *Franklin Bibliography, A List of Books Written by, or Relating to Benjamin Franklin* (Brooklyn, 1889), and, for later works, Charles E. Jorgenson and Frank Luther Mott, *Benjamin Franklin, Representative Selections*, rev. ed. (New York, 1962), pp. cli–clxxxix.

The edition of Benjamin Franklin's writings used in this work is Leonard W. Labaree, ed., Vol I–XIV, and William B. Willcox, ed., Vol. XV– , *The Papers of Benjamin Franklin* (New Haven, 1959–). For Franklin's writings after 1770, not, as of this writing, yet reached in the *Papers*, the edition used is Albert Henry Smyth, ed., *The Writings of Benjamin Franklin* (New York, 1905–7). Sources for excerpts from Franklin's writings not in either of the foregoing are specified in the footnotes.

The most extensive treatment of Franklin's youth among the many Franklin biographies is still James Parton, *Life and Times of Benjamin Franklin* (New York, 1864), I, 18–96, though Parton did not have the advantage of some later sources regarding Franklin's Boston years. There is a reliable, concise selective genealogy in *Papers*, I, xlix–lxxvii, with helpful charts. Genealogical data of considerable value for Josiah Franklin's immediate family, by Benjamin Franklin the Elder, are in manuscript at the libraries of Yale University and Dartmouth College. There is additional information in the manuscript glebe book of the Franklin parish church, St. Mary Magdalen, in Ecton, Northamptonshire, which is in the collection of the Massachusetts Historical Society and a copy of which the present author has given the Ecton parish. John Cole, *The History and Antiquities of Ecton* (London, 1825), has useful supplementary material but is not wholly reliable for dates. Manuscript records in the Northamptonshire Record Office in Delapre Abbey, Northampton; in the Oxfordshire County Record Office, County Hall, Oxford; and, for the Folger family, in the Norfolk and Norwich Record Office, Central Library, Norwich, are helpful in reconstructing the movements of the English antecedents of Franklin.

The best edition of Franklin's *Autobiography* is Leonard W. Labaree, ed. (New Haven, 1964), which has useful notes and introductory matter.

The file of *The New-England Courant* marked by Franklin as to the authorship of the contents of the first forty-three issues is in the British Museum.

Such essential archival sources as the records of the town of Boston, Suffolk and Middlesex counties, the colony and province of Massachusetts Bay, and Harvard College and such documentary sources as the collections of the American Antiquarian Society, the Colonial Society of Massachusetts, and the Massachusetts Historical Society are identified for specific materials in the footnotes, as are all secondary references.

Index

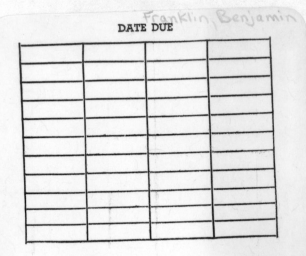

Franklin, Benjamin

DATE DUE

The TOWN of BOSTON

IN

New England

by
Cap.t *John Bonner*

1722

Ætatis Suæ 60.

Engraved from a copy in the possession of W.m Taylor Esq.
and published by
GEORGE G. SMITH, ENGRAVER
Corner of Washington and Franklin Streets Boston.
1835.

I have examined this plan and find it a
copy of the original
Boston July 2.d 1835 —
Stephe

West Hill

Fox Hill

Beacon Hill

Garden

Powder House
Watch House

Roxbury Flatts

COMMON

School Sf

Marlbro

Newbury

Orange Str

Pond

Coals Garden

Summer Str

From Town H.
One Mile

Orange Str

Beech Str

Rainford L

Pond Str

Gallows

Fortification

Marlines Pass

Shorts

Hills Wharfe

Cow L

South

Scale of ¼ a Mile.

Wind Mill Point

Dartys W

Bulls W

Adams L

Sea Str

Townss L

Pikes

Engraven and Printed